THE PRICE SYSTEM AND RESOURCE ALLOCATION

TENTH EDITION

THE PRICE SYSTEM AND RESOURCE ALLOCATION

TENTH EDITION

ROSS D. ECKERT
Claremont McKenna College

RICHARD H. LEFTWICH
Leftwich Associates

The Dryden Press
Chicago   New York   San Francisco
Philadelphia   Montreal   Toronto
London   Sydney   Tokyo

Acquisitions Editor: Elizabeth Widdicombe
Developmental Editor: Deborah Acker
Project Editor: Holly Crawford
Design Director: Alan Wendt
Production Manager: Barb Bahnsen
Permissions Editor: Cindy Lombardo
Director of Editing, Design, and Production: Jane Perkins

Text Designer: Hunter Graphics
Copy Editor: JoAnn Learman
Compositor: Waldman Graphics
Text Type: 10/12 Times Roman

Library of Congress Cataloging-in-Publication Data

Eckert, Ross D.
   The price system and resource allocation.

   Leftwich's name appears first on the previous ed.
   Includes bibliographies and index.
   1. Microeconomics. I. Leftwich, Richard H.
II. Title.
HB172.L45 1988   338.5'2   87-5068
ISBN 0-03-012533-2

Printed in the United States of America
789-016-987654321
Copyright © 1988, 1985, 1982, 1979, 1976, 1973, 1970, 1966,
1960, 1955 by The Dryden Press, a division of Holt, Rinehart and
Winston, Inc.

Address orders:
111 Fifth Avenue
New York, NY 10003

Address editorial correspondence:
One Salt Creek Lane
Hinsdale, IL 60521

The Dryden Press
Holt, Rinehart and Winston
Saunders College Publishing

To Enid F. Eckert and Maxine D. Leftwich

THE DRYDEN PRESS SERIES IN ECONOMICS

PREFACE

Intermediate price theory is one of the most important courses economics and business students take. Since its subject matter is critical to an understanding of how a market economy operates, anyone else desiring a solid liberal arts undergraduate program is also well advised to take it. The course is usually offered at the third-year undergraduate level, following an introductory principles of economics course and prior to advanced courses in the discipline. *The Price System and Resource Allocation*, classroom tested by almost a million students, is written primarily for such a course.

The book can also be used at other points in business and economics curricula. Since graduate programs in business often attract students with other undergraduate degrees, it can be used to provide a part of the necessary economics background for them. Although an introduction to economics and training in elementary calculus are helpful, any good student can use the book to cut his or her economic teeth.

FEATURES OF THE BOOK

A textbook should be judged by its success in helping students learn. *The Price System and Resource Allocation* meets this test in several ways.

Our book is written for students. We consciously and deliberately aim at a level of difficulty that will challenge, but not confuse, upper division students. Although many economists tell us that *The Price System* was a key part of their review for Ph.D. examinations, it is not a graduate-level book. We try to walk the fine line between the simplicity of exposition required in lower division courses and the complexities of graduate training.

The content of the book has been carefully selected. It contains all the major facets of price theory necessary for analysis and evaluation of most economic aspects of a market system, and it lays a solid foundation for graduate study in microeconomic theory. It is not, however, an all-inclusive "encyclopedia." Undergraduate students should not be expected to learn every aspect of price theory.

Recalling some of our own frustrations as neophytes in price theory, we have tried to avoid gaps in our exposition. We use a careful step-by-step process in building each set of microeconomic principles. Then we tie them together into a complete and integrated whole.

We want the book to be useful to students in their understanding of the world in which they live. Toward this end we include an unusually broad set of applications of theory to real world events. We are not content with small, short, boxed items. The last part of each chapter contains in-depth analyses of economic issues, called **applications**, for which the theory of the chapter is especially suited. They may be selected on a cafeteria basis. All of the applications are based on real-world events, giving the book a ''hands-on'' applicability to events in students' lives. Many of them are business examples, which makes the text particularly appropriate for a business school microeconomics course.

An *Instructor's Manual and Test Bank* is also available. It includes chapter outlines, suggestions for teaching, true-false and multiple-choice questions, solutions to all of the end-of-chapter problems, and additional problems for testing purposes or classroom discussion. A *Computerized Test Bank* for the IBM® PC will contain the objective test questions from the *Instructor's Manual*.

For the first time, a *Workbook* will be available with the text. The *Workbook* will include a rich selection of applications, as well as multiple choice questions. It is written by Rodney Fort and Thomas Lowinger, both of Washington State University.

CHANGES IN THIS EDITION

Few texts run ten editions, and even fewer reach this milestone without room for further improvement. Several significant changes make this tenth edition superior to the ninth.

1. Graphs. We redrew all the figures, using a two-color treatment where appropriate to highlight specific areas of discussion. We added a detailed caption to each to encapsulate its essential points for students.

2. End-of-Chapter Problems. We almost doubled the number of end-of-chapter problems. New problems link theory with the applications and extend the end-of-chapter applications to new subjects. These problems are indicated by an asterisk. Solutions to the odd-numbered problems (including appropriate figures) appear at the end of the book.

3. Math Footnotes. We revised the mathematical footnotes and presented them in a tighter format.

4. Annotated Readings. We expanded the end-of-chapter list of ''Suggested Readings'' and indicated each entry's relevance or degree of difficulty.

5. Property Rights. We added new material on the economics of property rights to Chapter 2.

6. Imperfect Competition. We developed a new chapter (Chapter 13) on imperfect competition to include materials on oligopoly and monopolistic competition that previously appeared in separate chapters.

7. Resource Markets. We developed a new chapter (Chapter 14) on the theory of resource pricing and employment to include materials on competitive and noncompetitive resource markets that previously appeared in separate chapters. It is followed by a chapter containing a variety of resource-market applications. (This chapter, like Chapter 4 in Part One, contains applications only.)

8. Applications. We developed new applications on the economics of "free" medical care (Chapter 1); property rights in "lost" goods and natural resources and the economics of organ transplants (Chapter 2); the use of "play money" to ration student registrations in the most popular M.B.A. courses at a major university (Chapter 4); and the effects of agricultural marketing cartels in Canada and the United States (Chapter 13).

We updated all other applications and revised some of the most topical to reflect such recent events as the change in the flavor of Coke, the sale and scalping of tickets at the 1984 Olympic Games, the bankruptcy crisis in American farming, strikes by professional baseball players, and OPEC's 1986 price war. As noted above, there are two full chapters of applications: Chapter 4, on the competitive market, and new Chapter 15, on resource markets.

ORGANIZATION

Assembled with students in mind, *The Price System* is logically organized, starting with a small basic foundation, then enlarging and building on that foundation. Part One, consisting of the first four chapters, is a review of key principles that should have (but often have not) been learned in the introductory course. It can be omitted in those classes in which the students have uniformly good backgrounds. Much can be gained, however, from devoting one or two class meetings to review, even for the best of students.

Our intermediate-level exposition of microeconomics begins with Chapter 5. There is no better place to start than with individual consumers, since the whole thrust of economic activity in predominantly private enterprise economies is toward satisfying human wants as fully as resources and technology will allow. It seems to us that the theory of consumer choice should emphasize the indifference curve approach. Consequently, we place the special case of utility analysis in a chapter of its own, Chapter 7, *after* the general case, where it can be omitted by those desiring to do so without loss of continuity.

In some instances, it may not be important to develop some topics in the theory of consumer choice. Likely candidates for omission are the constant real income demand curve, consumer's surplus, corner solutions, and Giffen goods. All of these can be dropped without loss of continuity.

Since production theory lays the foundation for the theory of costs, it logically precedes the theory of the firm. It also fills a large gap left by those texts that jump immediately into the markets for goods and services, leaving students high and dry regarding the bases for the shapes and positions of cost curves. In Chapter 9, the section on the three stages for capital is not essential to continuity and can be omitted. We do recommend that it be used, however, on the basis of the many favorable comments about it from users.

The building blocks are now in place for the theory of pricing and outputs of goods and services. It makes sense to us to begin with the "frictionless" case of pure (or perfect) competition (Chapter 11), to follow with the polar extreme of pure monopoly (Chapter 12), and then to examine imperfectly competitive markets (Chapter 13). However, each of these three chapters is complete in itself, and a reordering can be accomplished easily enough. In Chapter 11, on competitive markets, the section on producers' surplus can be omitted without breaking continuity. This is also the case for any or all of the price discrimination discussion in Chapter 12. Chapter 13 combines oligopoly and monopolistic competition into a single chapter on imperfect competition, enabling us to present the common elements of both in a more efficient manner.

The theory of resource pricing and employment in Chapter 14 requires as background the theories of consumer choice and demand, the theories of production and costs, and the theory of pricing and outputs of goods and services if it is to be well understood by students. It leans strongly on the theory of production and sets the stage for remaining materials: Chapter 15, devoted exclusively to applications of the theory of resource pricing; Chapter 16, on resource allocation; and Chapter 17, on income distribution.

Chapter 18 is a summary chapter. It breaks little new ground. Its main function is to pull together the most important concepts of the book, putting them into an integrated framework of analysis and into proper perspective relative to one another.

We place our applications section after the theory section in each chapter for two reasons. First, we do not want to break the continuity of the theory exposition. Second, we want students to have all of the theory necessary to tackle the applications.

We have provided the mathematics of intermediate microeconomics in footnote form. Since we want our book to be understandable to students who do not have a calculus background, we do not use it in the text itself. But we want it to be readily available to those students who do have such a background. We think footnotes are the best method for supplying the mathematics because they allow it to be juxtaposed with the verbal and geometric discussions of the text.

PEDAGOGY

Numerous pedagogical features serve to assist the learning process. Each part of *The Price System* begins with a brief *overview* of its chapters and topics. The opening *chapter outline* presents the sequence of topics to be covered.

A *running glossary* defines key terms in the margins of the pages where they are introduced. Terms in the running glossary are printed in boldface type in the text. A complete *alphabetical glossary* of terms also appears at the end of the book.

At the end of each chapter, a list of *suggested readings* provides further references, and a set of *problems and questions for discussion* allows students to test their grasp of the material. *Solutions to the odd-numbered problems* at the end of the book allow students to check their work.

ACKNOWLEDGMENTS

We extend our thanks to many who have contributed to this and past editions of *The Price System*. Professor Shirley Yu of Texas Tech University provided the mathematical footnotes initially and revised them for this edition. We have benefited greatly from suggestions of reviewers of both the previous edition and the manuscript of the present edition. These include Professors Louis DeAlessi, University of Miami; George W. Hilton, University of California, Los Angeles; Richard K. Vedder, Ohio University; Jonathan Cave, University of Illinois; Alvin Cohen, Lehigh University; Donald Holley, Boise State University; Thomas McCullough, University of California, Berkeley; Robert Pennington, George Mason University; Bruce Seaman, Georgia State University; Sharon Levine, University of Missouri, St. Louis; William M. Wadman, University of North Carolina; Jack E. Adams, University of Arkansas, Little Rock; Thomas E. Borcherding, Claremont Graduate School; Thomas D. Willett, Claremont Graduate School; William Craig Stubblebine, Claremont McKenna College; Colin Wright, Claremont McKenna College; Michael A. Leeds, Temple University; Beth Allen, University of Pennsylvania; Aurelius Morgner, University of Southern California; Larry DeBrock, University of Illinois; Timothy J. Gronberg, Texas A&M University; Kenneth O. Alexander, Michigan Technological University; H. Brian Moehring, California State University, Northridge; Blair C. Currie, Hobart and William Smith Colleges; W. David Eberly, Boise State University; Steven A. Morrison, Northeastern University; Bassam Harik, Western Michigan University; Thomas R. Ireland, University of Missouri, St. Louis; Bill Rickman, Fort Hays State University; and DeVon L. Yoho, Ball State University. We are also grateful for comments and suggestions made by innumerable students and professors who have used the book in the past.

Since we are responsible for mistakes, feel free to pass along to us any that you find. Even more important, let us know what you would like to see in the next edition.

Ross D. Eckert
Richard H. Leftwich
September 1987

ABOUT THE AUTHORS

Ross D. Eckert, Ph.D. (U.C.L.A.), is Professor of Economics at Claremont McKenna College and the Claremont Graduate School. He is a member of the American Economic Association, the Western Economic Association, and the Public Choice Society. He is the author of numerous articles in economics journals and law reviews as well as several monographs, including *The Enclosure of Ocean Resources: Economics and the Law of the Sea* (Hoover Press, 1979). He has been a consultant to private organizations and governmental agencies, including the Executive Offices of the President and the Treasury, and is also an Adjunct Scholar of the American Enterprise Institute for Public Policy Research in Washington, D.C. He is a member of the editorial board of *Economic Inquiry*. He currently teaches undergraduate and graduate courses in microeconomic analysis, industrial organization and transportation, and the economic analysis of law.

Richard H. Leftwich, Ph.D. (The University of Chicago), former Regents Professor of Economics, Oklahoma State University, is an independent economic consultant. He has served as Senior Economist, University of Chicago Project, Santiago, Chile; Distinguished Visiting Professor, American University of Cairo, Cairo, Egypt; and as Distinguished Visiting Professor, Tunghai University, Taichung, Taiwan. He is a member and past president of the Southern Economic Association, the Midwest Economics Association, the Southwestern Economics Association, and the Western Social Science Association. He is also a member of the American Economic Association. He is the author of *An Introduction to Economic Thinking* (Holt, Rinehart & Winston, Inc., 1969), *A Basic Framework for Economics* (Business Publications, Inc., 1980, 3d. ed., 1987), and coauthor of *Economics of Social Issues* (Business Publications, Inc., 1974, 6th. ed., 1984). He has contributed articles to several economics journals. He has received a Ford Foundation Faculty Research Fellowship, an Amoco Foundation Outstanding Teaching Award, and a Leavy Award for Excellence in Teaching Private Enterprise from the Freedoms Foundation. He has been a Beta Gamma Sigma Distinguished Scholar and a Mid-America State Universities Association Honor Lecturer, and is listed in *Who's Who in America* and *Who's Who in Economics*. He has worked as a frequent consultant to private industry on antitrust and pricing problems.

CONTENTS

THE PRICE SYSTEM AND RESOURCE ALLOCATION
TENTH EDITION

A REVIEW OF BASIC ECONOMIC ANALYSIS

THE level of economic sophistication that students bring to the intermediate microeconomics course varies greatly from one university to another and from student to student. The first four chapters, which compose Part One, provide a review of the nature and purpose of microeconomic analysis. They also review the fundamentals of demand, supply, and price determination. In some institutions in which students have been uniformly well trained in principles courses, Part One may be omitted at no great cost to the students. But in most universities it will reinforce the foundations on which microeconomic analysis is built.

Chapter 1

ECONOMIC ACTIVITY AND ECONOMIC THEORY

Chapter Outline

Application

Most of us want our economy to produce the largest possible value of goods and services and to distribute the proceeds with some degree of equity. Economies of the world come up short on both counts—and some come up much shorter than others. There is much debate as to the type of system that will best facilitate efficiency and equity. Capitalistic or private enterprise systems have been severely criticized on both counts. Some of the criticism pinpoints weaknesses, and some of it reveals much ignorance on the part of critics about the nature and performance of such systems.

This book provides background for the debate. It spells out the conditions that any economic system must meet if it is to be efficient and shows how a price system can move the economy toward those conditions. Equity, because of its subjective nature, is much more slippery to treat than efficiency. But we can at least look at the objective determinants of income distribution and the means of modifying that distribution to whatever degree is thought desirable. Although there are many ways of organizing economic activity, including command-and-control techniques, we will be concerned primarily with the price mechanism.

In this introductory chapter we review the nature of economic activity, the basic methodology of economics, and the relationship of price theory to the general body of economic theory. The next three chapters complete the background for the detailed exposition of price theory that begins in Chapter 5.

ECONOMIC ACTIVITY

economic activity
The interaction among economic units involved in the production, exchange, and consumption of goods and services.

Economics is concerned with humanity's well-being or welfare. It encompasses the social organization and the relationships involved in using scarce resources and available technology to satisfy seemingly unlimited human wants and in allocating those resources among diverse alternative wants. The key elements of **economic activity** are (1) human wants, (2) resources, and (3) technology.

Human Wants

wants
The varied and insatiable desires of human beings that provide the driving force of economic activity.

Economic activity is directed toward the satisfaction of human **wants.** Their fulfillment is generally thought of as the end or goal of economic activity. The wants important in any economic system may be those of the general public, powerful special interest groups, or government leaders, to name a few. Different societies are likely to attach different relative weights as to whose wants are the most important.

Wants have two characteristics—they are varied in kind and, in the aggregate, over time seem to be insatiable. Insatiability does not imply that any one individual's desire for a particular commodity is unlimited. The quantity of a good—say, pizzas—consumed each week that contributes to one's well-being may well be finite. It is commodities in the aggregate for which wants are unlimited, partly because of the great variety of wants that individuals can conjure up.

Origins of Wants The insatiability of wants becomes evident when we consider a few of the ways in which they arise. Some come into being because the human organism must have them in order to continue functioning. The need for food is the most obvious case in point. At least two other desires arise from necessity—for shelter and for clothing. One or the other or both must be fulfilled to some degree if humans are to survive the rigors of freezing temperatures or the extreme heat of the tropics.

Wants arise too from the influence of the culture in which we live, for every society has its requisites for "the good life"—certain standards of housing and food consumption; patronizing of the arts; and possession and consumption of such items as automobiles, computers, television sets, and stereo systems. The status of individuals in society depends to some extent upon their levels of consumption.

The satisfying of biological and cultural needs requires a wide variety of goods. Individual tastes vary. Some people like roast beef, some prefer ham, and others enjoy mutton. Over time individuals seek to satisfy their hunger with different foods. Health concerns have increased the popularity of fish and chicken relative to beef and pork in recent years. Tastes in clothing differ, and various social occasions call for different modes of dress. Differences in age, climate, social position, education, and the like give rise to variety in the goods desired by society in general.

Finally, new wants are generated in the process of satisfying existing ones. No better illustration can be found than that of a student pursuing higher education. Attending a college or university opens up new vistas of potential desires—intellectual and cultural—that heretofore the student may not have known existed. The generation of new wants in the process of endeavoring to satisfy old ones plays an important role in multiplying human desires.

These sources are not an exhaustive classification but merely illustrate the infinite expansion of wants over time and the impossibility of an economy's ever satiating all the wants of all its people.

Want Satisfaction and Levels of Living The level of want satisfaction, or **living standard,** achieved in a given economic society is ordinarily measured by per capita income—sometimes gross and sometimes net, depending on the availability of data. There may be a great dispersion around the average, and the average income figure may be misleading because of distribution problems. Nevertheless, per capita income appears to be one of the best measures available.

Sometimes people judge the performance of an economy by whether per capita incomes are at a "satisfactory" level. The implication is that everyone is entitled to a satisfactory level of living. Judgments of this kind are not very valuable from the point of view of economic analysis.

In the first place, the level of living satisfactory to a society is entirely relative to the historical time under consideration. A living standard that most people in the United States would have accepted 50 years ago would not be satisfactory today. What is satisfactory today will probably not be satisfactory 50 years from now. As the economy's capacity to produce increases, the concept

living standard
The level of well-being or welfare that an economic system provides for the members of a society, usually measured by per capita income.

of what constitutes a satisfactory level of living shifts upward. The insatiability of human wants, which for some includes the accumulation of wealth for its own sake, together with increases over time in productive capacity, leads to an ever-changing concept of what constitutes a satisfactory level.

In the second place, the concept of what constitutes a satisfactory level varies among different geographic areas. A level of living high enough to make most Southeast Asians content for the present may not be high enough for most Europeans or Americans. People become accustomed to certain living levels, and a satisfactory one for them becomes one just a little higher than what they currently have.

For most purposes it is not even relevant to judge the performance of an economy simply on the basis of whether it provides a satisfactory level of living. It is more to the point to ask whether it provides the highest level of living that its resources and techniques will permit at a given time, making due allowance for some part of current production to be set aside to augment future productive capacity. One can ask no more of an economy. It should not be expected to provide much less.

Resources

The level of want satisfaction that an economy can achieve at a given point in time is limited, a major restriction being the quantities and qualities of its known resources. **Resources** are the means or ingredients available for producing the goods and services that are used to satisfy wants. Hundreds of different kinds of resources exist in an economy. Among these are all kinds of labor, raw materials, land, machinery, buildings, semifinished materials, fuel, power, transportation, and the like.

resources
The means or ingredients, consisting of labor resources and capital resources, available for the production of goods and services used to satisfy human wants.

Classification of Resources   Resources can be classified conveniently into two categories: (1) labor, or human, resources and (2) capital, or nonhuman, resources. **Labor** resources consist of labor power or the capacity for human effort, both of mind and of muscle, used in producing goods. The term **capital** can be misleading, since it is used in several different ways by both economists and laypersons. We use the term to include all nonhuman resources that can contribute toward placing goods in the hands of the ultimate consumer. Specific examples are buildings, machinery, land, available mineral resources, raw materials, semifinished materials, business inventories, and any other nonhuman tangible items used in the productive process.[1] We need to guard against confusing capital and money particularly. Money is not capital as the term is used in this book. Money as such produces nothing. It is an exchange technology[2]

labor
The capacity for human effort of both mind and muscle available for use in producing goods and services, ranging from unskilled, undifferentiated to highly skilled, specialized labor power.

capital
The nonhuman ingredients that contribute to the production of goods and services, including land, raw and semifinished materials, tools, buildings, machinery, and inventories.

---

[1]In a basic sense inventories of goods in the hands of ultimate consumers also constitute capital, since it is the satisfaction yielded by goods rather than the goods themselves that consumers desire. Thus, such goods are still means of satisfying ultimate ends or desires of consumers; that is, they have yet to produce the want satisfaction they are supposed to produce. We shall not cut it this fine in our discussions. Goods in the hands of the ultimate consumer will be called consumer goods rather than capital, and this will avoid some complexities.

[2]See p. 8.

facilitating the exchange of goods and services and resources. By and large, the use of money enables us to obtain higher satisfaction levels than we can reach with barter techniques because it makes exchange of goods and services more efficient.

The significance of this classification of resources should not be overstated. It is more descriptive than analytical. Within each category there are many different kinds of resources, and the differences between two kinds falling within the same classification may be more important analytically than the differences between two kinds in separate classifications. Consider, for example, a human ditchdigger and an accountant. Both fall under the descriptive classification of labor. However, from an analytical point of view, the human ditchdigger is more closely related to a mechanical ditchdigger, which comes under the descriptive classification of capital, than to the accountant.

Characteristics of Resources   Resources have three important characteristics: (1) most are limited in quantity, (2) they are versatile, and (3) they can be combined in varying proportions to produce any given commodity. These will be considered in turn.

Most resources are *scarce* in the sense that when fully employed they are not producing quantities of goods and services as large as people would desire. These are called *economic resources*. Some resources, such as the air used in internal combustion engines, are so abundant that they can be had for the asking. These are called *free resources,* since they cannot command a price. If all resources were free, there would be no limitation on the extent to which wants could be satisfied, and no economic problem would exist. We are interested in scarce economic resources because it is their scarcity that generates the economic problem.

The population of an economy sets an upper limit on the quantities of labor resources available. Various factors—education, custom, state of public health, age distribution—determine the actual proportion of the population that can be considered the labor force. Over a short period of time—say, one year—the total labor force cannot expand very much, but over a longer period it may be variable as population has time to change and as changes occur in the factors determining the quantity and the quality of the actual labor force.

Generally, the total capital equipment of the economy expands over time, but this expansion occurs slowly. The amount that an economy can add to its total stock of capital equipment in a year, without reducing current consumption, is a fairly small proportion of its existing capital. Therefore, over a short period of time the quantity of capital available to produce goods is limited.

The *versatility* of resources refers to their capacity to be put to different uses. Almost any kind of resource can be used in the production of a wide variety of goods. Common labor can be used in making almost every conceivable good. The more highly skilled or specialized a resource becomes, however, the more limited are its uses. There are fewer job opportunities for skilled machinists than for common laborers; there are still fewer for the brain surgeon, the ballet dancer, or the professional athlete. Even with a high degree of resource specialization, supplies of one kind of specialized resource can be developed over time only at the expense of other kinds. Individuals can be trained as physicians rather than as dentists; more bricklayers can be trained at the expense of carpenters; more tractors but fewer combines can be produced. The resources of the economy are quite fluid with respect to the forms they can take and the kinds of goods they can produce. The longer the period of time under consideration, the greater their fluidity or versatility.

Possibilities of combining resources in *different proportions* to produce a given good usually exist. Few, if any, goods require rigid proportions of resources. Generally, it is possible to substitute some kinds of labor for capital, or for other kinds of labor, and vice versa. This characteristic of resources is closely related to the characteristic of versatility. Substitution possibilities and versatility generate the potential for an economy to switch productive capacity from one line of production to another; they enable an economy to adjust output to the changing character of human wants. Resources can be transferred into industries producing goods for which wants are expanding and out of those turning out items for which wants are diminishing.

Technology

technology
The state of the arts available for combining and transforming resources into goods and services.

Technology, together with quantities and qualities of resources in existence, sets limits on the level of want satisfaction that an economy can achieve. **Technology** refers to the state of the arts available for transforming resources into want-satisfying forms. Its development is generally considered to lie in the province of engineering. However, the simultaneous choices of goods to be produced, quantities to be produced, and the technology to be used all fall within the scope of economics.

METHODOLOGY _____

To make a useful, systematic study of economic activity, one must use economic theory. But what is economic theory? Like the theory of any other science, it consists of sets of principles or causal relationships among the important "facts" or variables that surround and permeate economic activity. We look first at the construction of and functions of sets of economic principles; then we turn to the place of price theory within the overall framework of the economics discipline.

The Construction of Economic Theory

theory
A set of related principles providing insight into the operation of some phenomenon.

Any set of principles, or **theory,** must have bedrock starting points consisting of propositions or conditions that are taken as given—that is, as being so without further investigation. These we call the **premises** or **postulates** upon which the theory is erected. In aerodynamics the forces of gravity, the operation of centrifugal force, and air resistance may be among the postulates of a theory involving lift, thrust, and drag. In economics we may build a theory of consumer behavior on the postulate of consumer rationality, defined as the general desire of consumers to secure as much satisfaction as they can in spending their in-

premises (postulates)
Bedrock starting points for the construction of a theory, consisting of propositions or conditions that are taken as given or as being so without further investigation.

comes. The first step, then, in the construction of a theory is the specification and definition of its postulates.

The second step is the observation of "facts" concerning the activity about which we want to theorize. For example, if the activity in question is the exchange of groceries between supermarkets and consumers, the activity should be looked into as thoroughly as possible. As facts emerge from continued and repeated observation, it will become apparent that some are irrelevant and can be discarded while others are obviously significant. In the grocery exchange case, the hair color of consumers is not likely to matter, but the weekly amounts of money that consumers have to spend, the number of supermarkets available to them, and the weekly quantities of groceries available to be purchased will most certainly be important.

The third step—and this one will frequently be taken concurrently with the second—is the application of the rules of logic to the observed facts in an attempt to establish causal relationships among them and to eliminate as many irrelevant and insignificant facts as possible. *Deductive* chains of logic may lead us to believe that certain effects follow certain causes in a regular manner. We may reason that because consumers with larger incomes are willing to pay higher prices for specific goods, an increase in consumer incomes is likely to lead to higher prices. Or, on the other hand, we may reason *inductively*. Repeated observations may indicate that increases in consumer incomes and increases in prices occur simultaneously. So, putting two and two together, we reach the tentative conclusion that higher incomes cause prices to rise. Such tentative statements of cause-and-effect relationships are called **hypotheses.**

hypotheses
Tentative statements of cause-and-effect relationships among variables.

The fourth step in the process of establishing a set of principles is a crucial one. Once hypotheses have been formulated, they must be thoroughly tested to determine the extent to which they are valid, that is, the extent to which they yield good explanations and predictions. The tools of statistics and econometrics are of particular value in this respect. Some hypotheses will not withstand the rigors of repeated testing and, consequently, must be rejected. Others may look promising with modifications; then, the modified hypotheses must be tested. Still other hypotheses may be found to hold up most of the time in most of the circumstances to which they are relevant. These we usually refer to as **principles.**

principles
Statements of cause-and-effect relationships that have undergone and survived thorough testing.

It would be foolish to regard a set of principles or a theory as absolute truth. The testing process in economics and in other sciences never ends. At any given point in time we think of principles as the best available statements of causal relationships; however, additional data and better testing techniques may enable us to improve on them over time. Economic theory is not a once-and-for-all set of principles. It is continually evolving and growing.

The Functions of Economic Theory

The principal functions of economic theory fall into two categories: (1) to explain the nature of economic activity and (2) to predict what will happen to the economy as facts change. The explanation of the nature of economic activity enables us to understand the economic environment in which we live—how one part relates to others and what causes what. We would also like to be able to predict with some degree of accuracy what is likely to happen to the key variables that affect our well-being and to be able to do something about them if we dislike the predicted consequences.

Economists differentiate between positive economics and normative economics on the basis of whether the users of theory are concerned with causal relationships only or whether they intend some kind of intervention in economic activity to alter the course of that activity. **Positive economics** is supposed to be completely objective, limited to the cause-and-effect relationships of economic activity; it is concerned with the way economic relationships *are*. By way of contrast, **normative economics** is concerned with what *ought* to be. Value judgments must necessarily be made; that is, possible objectives to be achieved must be ranked, and choices must be made among those objectives. Economic policymaking—conscious intervention in economic activity with the intent of altering the course that it will take—is essentially normative in character. But if economic policymaking is to be effective in improving economic well-being, it must obviously be rooted in sound positive economic analysis. Policymakers should be cognizant of the full range of consequences of the policies they recommend.

positive economics
Study of the cause-and-effect relationships that exist in economics, involving no value judgments.

normative economics
Study of the way that economic relationships ought to be, in which value judgments play an integral part in the ranking and choosing of possible objectives.

PRICE THEORY AND ECONOMIC THEORY ————

Price theory (microeconomic theory) and the theory of the economy as a whole (macroeconomic theory) constitute the basic analytical tool kit of the discipline of economics. The principles of both are applied to special subject areas such as monetary economics, international trade and finance, public finance, manpower economics, agricultural economics, regional economics, and so on. Both parts of the kit are essential to a thorough understanding of economic activity.

Microeconomics is concerned primarily with the market activities of individual economic units such as consumers, resource owners, and business firms. It is concerned with the flow of goods and services from business firms to consumers, the composition of the flow, and the process for establishing the relative prices of the component parts of the flow. It is concerned too with the flow of resources (or their services) from resource owners to business firms, with their evaluation, and with their allocation among alternative uses.

Macroeconomics treats the economic system as a whole rather than treating the individual economic units of which it is composed. The particular goods and services making up the flow from business firms to consumers are not integral parts of the analysis, nor are the individual resources or services moving from resource owners to business firms. The value of the overall flow of goods (net national product) and the value of the overall flow of resources (national income) receive the focus of attention.

Price index numbers or general price level concepts in macroeconomics replace the relative-price concepts for individual goods used in microeconomics. Macroeconomics concentrates on the causes of change in aggregate money flows, the aggregate movement of goods and services, and the general employ-

microeconomics
The economics of interacting subunits of the economic system, such as individual consumers and groups of consumers, resource owners, firms, industries, individual government agencies, and the like.

macroeconomics
The economics of the economy as a whole, including the forces causing recession, depression, and inflation together with the forces resulting in economic growth.

ment level of resources. Prescription of cures for economic fluctuations and for unemployment of resources follows logically from the determination of their causes. Macroeconomics has much to say about the nature of economic growth and the conditions necessary for the expansion of productive capacity and national income over time.

Price theory is somewhat abstract. It does not give a complete description of the real world. It will not tell us why a price differential of $.05 per gallon for gasoline exists between Oklahoma City and Cleveland on any given date. But it helps us understand the real world. It shows us, in general, how the prices of gasoline are established and the role that those prices play in the overall operation of the economy. It helps us understand how the rewards they reap and the costs they bear affect the actions of economic units in the marketplace. It also helps us understand better the consequences of government economic activities, thereby making us better informed voters.

Price theory is abstract because it does not and cannot encompass all the economic data of the real world. To take all of the factors that influence economic decisions of consumers, resource owners, and business firms into consideration would require minute descriptions and analyses of every economic unit in existence—an impossible task. The function of theory is to single out what appear to be the most relevant data and to build an overall conceptual framework of the price system in operation from these. We concentrate on the data and principles that seem to be most important in motivating most economic units. In eliminating less important data and in building up a logical theoretical structure, we lose some contact with reality. However, we gain in our understanding of the overall operation of the economy, because we reduce the factors to be considered to manageable proportions. We may lose sight of some individual trees, but we gain more understanding and a better view of the forest. The end-of-chapter applications in this book show how this process works.

The sets of principles comprising price theory should show the directions in which economic units tend to move and should explain the more important reasons why they move in those directions. They should be sets of logically consistent approximations of how the economy operates. The abstraction and precision of theory are essential to clear thinking and to policymaking in the real world, but we should guard against the notion that it provides an unqualified description of reality. Theory should be the tool, not the master. Our ultimate goal is not the theory itself but a better understanding of the economic society in which we live, along with the ability to use and apply the theory in a policymaking context to push it toward what we want it to be.

WELFARE

welfare
The level of economic well-being or satisfaction attained by individuals and groups of individuals in a society.

Economic **welfare** is defined as the level of economic well-being of those who live in the society. The welfare, or well-being, of individuals presents no great conceptual difficulties. The simplest case is one in which individuals (or family units) are thought to be the best judges of what does or does not contribute to their own well-being. An individual's welfare is increased or decreased according to the individual's evaluation of the impact of events that affect her or him. As outside observers, we simply ask how events affect individuals and accept their answers at face value.

The welfare of a group is much more difficult to handle. As a starting point we can say that events that increase the well-being of every individual in the group increase that of the group as a whole. But very often an event that increases the well-being of one person decreases that of another. When such is the case, the gain in the welfare of the first must be compared with the loss in the welfare of the second if any conclusions are to be drawn about the welfare of the group as a whole. Comparisons of this sort raise serious problems. How can changes in the well-being of different persons be compared? In some specific cases we can make rough subjective judgments. Taking a Rembrandt away from a connoisseur of art and giving it to a person who does not understand or value art would surely reduce group welfare. But in general, we have no objective means of measuring and comparing the gain of one person or group of persons with the loss suffered by another individual or group when an event causes both.

Pareto optimum
A situation in which no event can increase the well-being of one person without decreasing the well-being of another.

We are left with a group welfare concept known as a **Pareto optimum.**[3] A Pareto optimal situation exists when no event can increase the well-being of one person without decreasing the well-being of someone else. To consider the matter another way, a situation is not Pareto optimal if one or more persons can be made better off without making anyone else worse off. If a situation is not Pareto optimal, a movement toward it—making at least one person better off without making anyone else worse off—increases group welfare.

There is no unique Pareto optimal situation in an economy. Suppose that all production and all exchanges that bestow advantage on anyone without disadvantaging anyone else have taken place. If any redistribution of purchasing power now occurs—for example, the imposition of income taxes on the rich and the granting of cash subsidies to the poor—the conditions of the original Pareto optimum are violated. But a new Pareto optimum, given the new distribution of income, is possible. In fact, there will be a different set of Pareto optimal conditions for every pattern of purchasing power distribution. If the economy moves from one Pareto optimum to another in this fashion can we say that the welfare of the group has increased or decreased? There are no objective measures that will provide the answer. We can discuss objectively, using positive economics, the conditions that lead to Pareto optimality given the distribution of income, but if we want to discuss the impact of income redistribution on welfare, we fall back on subjective value judgments and normative economics to support whatever stand we take.

SUMMARY

Economic activity revolves around three key elements: (1) human wants that are varied and insatiable; (2) resources that are limited, versatile, and capable

---

[3]Originated by the early twentieth-century Italian economist Vilfredo Pareto.

of being combined in varying proportions to produce a given commodity; and (3) the technology for utilizing resources to produce goods and services that satisfy wants. The achievement of a level of want satisfaction (standard of living) as high as the economy can provide is a primary goal of economic activity in most societies. To approach this end, resources and technology are not used merely to produce goods and services that satisfy wants; they must also be used to produce the items that contribute most to aggregate want satisfaction. The best possible technology must be used; resources must be fully employed and properly allocated or distributed among the alternative wants of consumers.

The methodology of economics is like that of other sciences. Sets of principles are developed through the formulation and testing of hypotheses. These, in turn, are outgrowths of logic applied to basic premises and observations of facts.

At the outset the relationship of price theory both to the overall discipline of economics and to the real world should be understood. Price theory is an essential part of the economist's tool kit and is used, together with national income theory, in the special subject areas of economics. Rather than explaining in detail the activities of economic units in the real world, it establishes general principles concerning activities on the basis of what appear to be the most important economic data. Activities of economic units in the real world approximate or tend toward those of theory. But this loss in the way of detailed contact with the real world means gain in the understanding of the main forces at work.

This book is concerned with welfare in the Pareto optimum sense; that is, it will have much to say about the conditions of economic efficiency for any given income distribution, but it will not have much to say about whether one income distribution is more efficient than another.

APPLICATION

How Would You Like Some "Free" Medical Care?

Human wants, as we noted, are unlimited and differ among individuals. In the case of medical care, some people are health conscious while others deliberately take health risks. Almost everyone wants *competent* medical care in emergencies, however, and many increasingly view regular, competent health care as an important part of "the good life."

Although wants are unlimited, the resources to satisfy them are not. Whether medical care is priced or not, it costs something to society to provide it. Many consumers will seek more care when it is provided "free" (at zero price), such as by a government agency or as an employee fringe benefit, than when it is sold at some positive price. Many also will tend to accept care from the zero-price provider rather than engage in extensive "comparison shopping" among providers through the price system. In buying a car, for example, a shopper will make fewer quality comparisons between Fords and Chevrolets if her employer will provide Chevrolets at a 25 percent discount.

How this distortion of incentives can have serious consequences in choosing among providers of medical care is shown in the following article from the *Los Angeles Times*. Sometimes it pays to keep a copy of the *Physicians' Desk Reference* around the house.

PRESCRIBING CAPITOL PHYSICIAN ALSO TREATED SEN. EAST REHNQUIST '81 DRUG DEPENDENCY DETAILED

From the Washington Post

WASHINGTON—Dr. Freeman H. Cary, the Capitol physician who recently retired after questions were raised about his treatment of the late Republican Sen. John P. East of North Carolina, prescribed the drug for Supreme Court Justice William H. Rehnquist that led to his 1981 problems with drug dependency, according to informed sources.

Cary prescribed the powerful hypnotic Placidyl over a nine-year period in doses that exceeded the recommended limits, the sources said. Placidyl is recommended for use for no more than two weeks at a time, according to pharmacologists.

Cary, 59, who saw Rehnquist in the office of the attending physician on the first floor of the Capitol, retired three weeks ago at the suggestion of Republican senators, a Senate source said. The senators were concerned about Cary's role in Rehnquist's and East's medical care, according to a Senate source.

East committed suicide in June, saying in a note that Cary "failed to diagnose my hypothyroidism," according to five persons who read the note.

Cary prescribed Placidyl for Rehnquist from 1972 through 1981 to help Rehnquist sleep while he was suffering from chronic and severe back pain, according to sources familiar with Rehnquist's medical records. Rehnquist, now awaiting Senate confirmation as chief justice, underwent surgery for a "slipped disk" in 1971.

Rehnquist's dependency on Placidyl became public in December, 1981, when he was weaned off the drug during a 10-day stay at George Washington University Hospital. Lawyers and reporters had noticed earlier that while speaking from the bench Rehnquist's words were slurred, a possible symptom of drug dependency, according to physicians.

While Rehnquist was withdrawing from the drug at the hospital, he experienced "disturbances in mental clarity" and "distorted" perceptions of reality, a hospital spokesman said at the time.

Until now it was not publicly known that Cary, a Capitol physician since 1972, had prescribed the drug for Rehnquist or that Rehnquist had taken the drug over a period of at least nine years. It is unclear whether Cary was the first or only physician who prescribed Placidyl for Rehnquist, and whether Rehnquist alternated periods of not taking the drug with periods of taking it.

The usual adult dose of Placidyl is 500 milligrams, taken orally at bedtime, according to Physicians' Desk Reference and medical experts familiar with the drug. Originally, in 1972, Rehnquist was prescribed 200 milligrams daily, according to one Senate source, but he was prescribed 1,500 milligrams a day during 1981.

Sources familiar with Rehnquist's medical records refused to divulge the length of time Rehnquist took the drug continuously during the nine years, although one senator said Rehnquist took it on a daily basis during 1981.

Members of the Senate Judiciary Committee have agreed not to question Rehnquist about his health during the confirmation process. But that agreement is subject to change once the committee has reviewed an evaluation of Rehnquist's health by an independent physician.

Cary, a cardiologist, joined the Office of the Attending Physician in 1972 and became head of the office in 1973. The office, established in 1928, treats members of Congress, their families, staffs, pages and Capitol police, and provides emergency treatment for tourists. Supreme Court justices also are entitled to free medical care at the office.

Source: "Prescribing Capitol Physician Also Treated Sen. East—Rehnquist '81 Drug Dependency Detailed," *Los Angeles Times*, August 12, 1986. © *The Washington Post*. Reprinted with permission of *The Washington Post*.

Suggested Readings

For a further analysis of the basic problems that every economy must solve, see

Knight, Frank H. *The Economic Organization*, 3–36. New York: Harper and Row, 1965.

The scientific method that applies to natural and social sciences alike is explained in

Hempel, Carl G. *The Philosophy of Natural Science,* Chaps. 1–4. Foundations of Philosophy Series. Englewood Cliffs, N.J.: Prentice-Hall, 1966.

Problems and Questions for Discussion

1. Explain the effects on the per capita income of an economy of each of the following:
   a. A 10 percent increase in the population
   b. Restrictions on the importation of automobiles
   c. Development of a substantially improved process for recovery of shale oil deposits
   d. Large gifts of food to foreign populations experiencing serious nutrition problems

2. Evaluate the following statement: "The most important test of a set of economic principles is whether or not it describes realistically the economic activity to which it is applied."

3. Which, if any, of the following issues are amenable to economic analysis?
   a. Why designer clothing is popular
   b. Why Van Gogh cut off his ear
   c. Why others on your street may follow the lead of one who fails to maintain the front yard
   d. Why Hitler was a vegetarian

4. Which type of reasoning—deduction or induction—do you think is more common in science generally and in economics in particular? As a starting point, do you think that economists have generated a theory of monopoly by interviewing monopolists and asking whether or not they charge higher-than-competitive prices?

5. Read *The New York Times* or *The Wall Street Journal* and collect statements from four persons in each of the following categories: entrepreneurs; science experts; university professors; attorneys; editorial writers; government officials; and politicians. Now analyze each statement for its positive or normative content. Are there groups with statements that are mainly positive? Normative? If you find patterns, do they coincide with your previous thinking about what to expect from each group?

Chapter 2

THE ORGANIZATION OF AN ECONOMIC SYSTEM

economic system
The institutional framework within which a society carries on its economic activities.

private enterprise system
An economic system characterized by private property rights, voluntary private production, and exchange of goods and services and of resources.

socialistic system
An economic system in which the government owns and/or controls resources and goods and services, carries on production, and specifies terms and conditions under which exchange may take place.

Any given society or country develops an institutional framework within which its economic activity is carried on. Such a framework is called an **economic system**. Economic systems of the modern world fall somewhere along a continuum between pure private enterprise at the one extreme and pure socialism at the other. The pure **private enterprise system** is characterized by private ownership of resources as well as goods and services. Private individuals, business enterprises, and associations of various kinds can engage in whatever voluntary production and exchange activities they desire. In the pure **socialistic system** there is no private property. Resources, goods, and services are owned and/or controlled by the government. Production takes place in government enterprises, and the government specifies the conditions under which exchanges can occur. Whereas the private enterprise system is decentralized, the socialistic system is highly centralized.

Present-day economies are a mixture of socialism and private enterprise. Some part of an economy's output will be produced by the profit-oriented *private sector* of the economy. Another part will be produced in a socialistic manner by the *public sector*. In addition, many economies have a *not-for-profit sector*—hospitals, schools, and the like—that is neither fish nor fowl. However, it should be taken into account for any complete analysis of an economic system.

Our primary interest in this book is the operation of a price system in organizing economic activity, that is, in the profit-oriented private sector of a predominantly private enterprise economy. In this chapter we present an overview of such an economy that enables us to fit details, as we come to them throughout the book, into their proper places and to put them in proper perspective. We discuss the functions of an economic system, with special reference to prices as the mechanism for performing those functions. But much of what we have to say is relevant to socialistic systems, to the not-for-profit sector, to situations where resource ownership is not strictly private, and to the public sector of mixed systems. The chapter closes with brief illustrations of the important roles that different forms of ownership rights play in determining how scarce resources are used in an economic system.

THE FUNCTIONS OF AN ECONOMIC SYSTEM

Every economic system, whatever its form, must somehow perform five closely related functions. It must determine (1) what is to be produced, (2) how production is to be organized, (3) how the output is to be distributed, (4) how goods are to be rationed over very short-run periods during which their supplies are fixed, and (5) how the productive capacity of the economy is to be maintained and expanded over time.

Determination of What to Produce

The determination of *what* is to be produced in an economy is a question of determining what wants in the aggregate are most important and to what degree they are to be satisfied. Should the amount of steel currently available be used for the production of automobiles or tanks or refrigerators or for the erection of sports arenas? Or, should it be used to provide some of each? Since the resources of the economy are scarce, all wants cannot be fully satisfied. The problem is one of picking and choosing from the unlimited scope of wants those that are most important for the society as a whole. The economy must provide some method of placing values on different goods and services that reflects the relative desires of the group for the goods and services it can produce.

The value of an item to society is measured by its price in a private enterprise private property economy, and the valuation process is accomplished by buyers as they spend their incomes. Consumers are confronted with a wide range of choices in the goods they can buy. The dollar values they place on the various items depend on how urgently they desire each relative to other goods, their willingness and ability to back up desire with dollars, and the supplies of the things available. The more urgently certain goods are desired and the more willing consumers are to back up desire with dollars, the higher their prices. The less strong the desire for certain goods, the lower their prices. The greater the available supply of any particular good, the lower its price. Any one unit of the good will be of less importance to the consumer when the supply is great than when the supply is small. The more bread available to eat per week, the smaller the value each loaf will have to consumers. Conversely, the smaller the supply of any particular commodity, the higher consumers will value any one unit of it. Thus, the ways in which consumers spend their incomes establish a price structure in the economy that reflects the comparative values of different goods and services to the consuming public as a whole.

Changes in tastes and preferences modify the patterns of consumer spending. These changes in spending patterns change the structure of prices in turn. The relative prices of goods that consumers now want more urgently go up, while the relative prices of those becoming less desirable decline. The price structure of goods and services changes to reflect such shifts in consumers' tastes and preferences.

This analysis is positive in nature, telling us how goods are actually valued by means of a system of prices. It does not tell us how goods *ought* to be valued; that problem is normative. A consumer with a larger income will exert more influence on the price structure than a consumer with a lower income. Conceivably, biscuits for rich people's dogs may be placed higher in the scale of values than milk for poor people's children, provided there are enough rich people casting their dollar votes in this direction and not enough poor people able to spend dollars for milk. The price system, though working perfectly in this case, may lead to social consequences the public considers undesirable and which it may then attempt to modify through political processes. Income redistribution, price fixing, and progressive income taxes are examples of policies effected through political processes.

Organization of Production

Concurrent with the determination of what is to be produced, an economic system must determine *how* its resources are to be organized to turn out the desired goods in the proper quantities. The organization of production involves (1) drawing resources from industries producing goods that consumers value less and channeling them into industries producing goods that consumers value more and (2) efficient use of resources by individual firms.

The price system in a private enterprise economy organizes production. Firms producing goods and services that consumers want most urgently receive higher prices relative to costs and will be more profitable than those producing goods and services that consumers want less urgently. The more profitable firms can, and do, offer higher prices for resources in order to expand. Those making less profit or incurring losses are unwilling to pay as much for resources. Resource owners, in the interest of increasing their incomes, want to sell their resources to firms offering the higher prices. There is a constant channeling of resources away from firms producing goods and services that consumers want least toward firms producing goods and services that consumers want most. Resources are moving constantly from lower-paying to higher-paying uses, or out of less important into more important uses.

The use of the term *efficiency* in economics differs slightly from the use of the term in physics or mechanics, although in both contexts it involves the ratio of an output to an input. With regard to mechanical efficiency, we know that a steam engine is inefficient because it fails to transform a large part of the heat energy of its fuel into power. Mechanically, an internal combustion engine is more efficient. However, if fuel for steam engines is cheap and fuel for internal combustion engines is expensive, cheaper power may be obtained from the steam engine.

economic efficiency
The ratio of the value of outputs obtained from an economic process to the value of inputs necessary to produce them. The higher the value of output per dollar's worth of resource input, the greater the efficiency of the process.

The **economic efficiency** of a particular production process is the ratio of useful product output to useful resources input. The usefulness of product output, or its value to society, is measured in dollars. Similarly, the usefulness or value of resource input is measured in dollars. Thus, the steam engine, while less efficient mechanically, will be more efficient economically than an internal combustion engine if it furnishes *cheaper* power for a particular production process.

The quest for profits provides the primary incentive for efficient production. The more efficient a firm's operation given the price of the product, the greater its profits will be. To rephrase the definition of efficiency, it is the value of product output per unit input of resource value. The greater the dollar value of product output per dollar's worth of resource input, the greater is economic efficiency. Likewise, the less the dollar value of resource input needed per dollar's worth of product output, the greater is economic efficiency. Measurement of economic efficiency requires that values be placed on resources of different types and on the same type of resource in different uses. Resources tend to be valued in the market according to their contributions to the production of goods and services.

Economic efficiency within a firm requires that the firm make choices among the different combinations of resources and technology that can be used in the production process. The choice of techniques to use will depend on relative resource prices and the quantity of product to be produced. The aim of the profit-oriented firm is to produce its output as cheaply (efficiently) as it can.

Thus, if labor is relatively expensive and capital relatively cheap, the firm will want to use technology making use of much capital and little labor. If capital is relatively expensive and labor relatively cheap, the most efficient technology will be that using little capital and much labor. The technology to use for most efficient operation will also differ at differing levels of output. Mass production methods and complicated machines cannot be used efficiently for small outputs, but for large outputs they can be very efficient.

Output Distribution

Distribution of output in a private enterprise economy, or *for whom* the output is produced, is determined by the price system simultaneously with the determination of what is to be produced and the organization of production. Product distribution depends on personal income distribution. Those with larger incomes obtain larger shares of the economy's output than do those with smaller incomes.

The income of an individual depends on two things: (1) the quantities of different resources that he or she can put into the production process and (2) the prices received for them. If labor power is the only resource an individual owns, that person's monthly income is determined by the number of hours worked per month multiplied by the hourly wage rate received. If, in addition, the individual owns and rents land to others, the amount of land so rented, multiplied by the monthly rental per acre, will be income from the land. Income from labor added to income from land is total monthly income. The example can be expanded to as many different resources as the individual owns.

Income distribution thus depends on the distribution of resource ownership in the economy and whether or not individuals place their resources in employments producing goods that consumers want most—that is, where the highest prices are offered for resources. Low individual incomes result from small quantities of resources being owned and/or the placing of resources owned in employments contributing little to consumer satisfaction. High individual incomes result from large quantities of resources being owned and/or the placing of resources owned in employments where they contribute much to consumer satisfaction. Thus, income differences result from channeling resources into low-value production processes by some individuals and from differences in resource ownership among individuals.

Income differences that arise from inefficient channeling of certain resources into the production process tend to be self-correcting. Suppose that a number of individuals are capable of doing the same amount of labor per week in a certain skill category and that two groups are employed in the making of two different products. Let the value of the product added to GNP by a worker in the first group be much higher than that added by a worker in the second. Since society values the contribution of any one worker in the first group more highly than that of any one worker in the second, the first group of workers receives greater individual incomes. When workers in the second group perceive the income differential, some move to the higher-paying employment. The increased supply of the first commodity lowers consumers' valuation of it, while the decreased supply of the second commodity has the opposite effect. This, in turn, lowers the incomes of the first (but now larger) group of workers and raises the incomes of the second (but now smaller) group of workers. When the income differential between workers in the two groups disappears, movement of workers from the second to the first group ceases. The self-correcting mechanism requires time to operate and may, in some cases, be side-tracked by ignorance on the part of the workers of the second group or by institutional barriers that prevent them from moving. In such cases the income differentials tend to become chronic.

A large part of the income differentials arising from differences in resource ownership will not be self-correcting. The major sources of differences in resource ownership are discussed in Chapter 17. They can be classified under differences in labor power owned and differences in kinds and quantities of capital owned. Differences in labor power owned by different individuals stem from differences in physical and mental inheritance and in opportunities to acquire specific types of training. Differences in kinds and quantities of capital owned come from many sources. These include initial differences in labor resources owned, differences in material inheritance, fortuitous circumstances, and propensities to accumulate.

If society believes that income differences should be smaller, modifications can be imposed on the private enterprise economy without materially affecting the operation of the price system. Society, through the government, may levy income taxes on and pay subsidies to persons for redistribution purposes. Such a redistribution of income will, however, affect the wants to be satisfied by economic activity by changing the effective pattern of social desires for goods and services. Reduction of high incomes through taxation makes the individuals who are taxed less influential in the marketplace, while augmentation of low incomes with subsidies makes those who are helped more influential. The price system will reorganize production to conform with the new pattern of effective desires for goods and services.

Rationing in the Very Short Run

very short run (market period)
A time period with respect to a given good or service so short that the quantity of it placed on the market cannot be changed.

An economic system must make some provision for rationing commodities over the time period during which the supplies of these cannot be changed. This time period is called the **very short run** by some and the **market period** by others. Suppose that wheat is harvested throughout the country in the same month each year. From one year to the next the supply of wheat available for consumption is fixed, assuming there is no carry-over from one year to the next. The very short run for wheat in such a case is one year. The economy must ration the fixed supply in two ways: (1) it must allocate the fixed supply among the different consumers in the economy and (2) it must stretch the given supply over the time period from one harvest to the next.

In a private enterprise economy, *price* is the device that allocates the fixed supply among different consumers. Shortages will cause the price to rise, decreasing the amount that each consumer is willing to buy. The price will continue to increase until all consumers together are just willing to take the fixed supply. Surpluses will cause the price to fall, raising the amount consumers are willing to buy until they take the entire supply off the market.

Price also is the device for rationing the good over time. If the entire supply were to be dumped in consumers' hands immediately after harvest, price would be driven low. At the low price, consumption would proceed at a rapid pace. As the next harvest approached, the disappearance of most of the commodity in the first part of the period would leave very small supplies for the latter part. Consequently, price would be high in the latter part of the very short-run period.

Speculation plays an important role in smoothing out the consumption of the good over time. Knowing that the price will tend to be low early in the period and high late in the period, speculators will buy up a large part of the supply early on, expecting to sell it later at higher prices and thus realize a net gain on their investment in the product. Their purchases will raise the price in the early part of the period above what it would otherwise be, thus slowing the rate at which the product is consumed at that time. Their sales in the later part of the period will reduce price below what it would otherwise be, thus providing greater quantities of the product for consumption at that time. The actions of speculators modify the price rise that would take place over the very-short-run period and bring about a more even flow of the product to consumers over time.

Economic Maintenance and Growth

Every economy is expected to maintain and expand its productive capacity. *Maintenance* refers to keeping the productive power of the economic machine intact through provision for depreciation. *Expansion* refers to continuous increase in the kinds and quantities of the economy's resources together with continuous improvement in technology.

Labor power can be increased through population increases and through the development and improvement of skills by means of training and education. Development and improvement of skills in a private enterprise economy are motivated largely through the price mechanism—the prospects of higher pay for more highly skilled and more productive work. The extent to which skills can be developed and improved is conditioned by training and educational opportunities together with physical and mental abilities.

Capital accumulation depends on a variety of complex economic motives, and much debate centers around their relative importance. For capital accumulation to occur, some resources must be diverted from the production of current consumer goods and put to work producing capital goods in excess of the amount needed to offset depreciation.

Improvements in technology make possible greater outputs with given quantities of resources. The motives behind the search for and the discovery of inventions and improvements are not always easy to determine. The inventor may invent because that type of activity is interesting. Frequently, improvements in technology are the by-products of scholarship intended primarily to advance knowledge. However, a large part of the improvements in technology is a direct result of the quest for profits, as is well illustrated by the increasing flow of fruitful results coming from the growing research and development departments of large corporations.

The role of the price mechanism and its degree of importance in providing for economic maintenance and growth are not clear. Certainly prices and profit prospects are important elements in determining whether or not maintenance and growth occur. But the area of economic maintenance and growth is virtually an applied subject area in itself. Consequently, we shall be concerned mainly with the first four functions as they are performed by the price system in a private enterprise economy.

OWNERSHIP RIGHTS AND RESOURCE ALLOCATION _____

How resources are used depends on the legal rights owners have. For example, the owner of a car has the right to drive it or lend it, but not without liability insurance in some states. A few states do not allow a vehicle to be sold unless its air pollution equipment passes a test. A car is more than a bundle of physical characteristics—with it come certain rights and responsibilities that influence its use.

Compare the way individuals typically drive their own cars versus rented cars. The full costs of poor maintenance or sloppy driving are borne by owners in lower resale prices. Individual renters do not bear directly the full costs of carelessness when fees are based on mileage alone. Car rental firms do require that customers buy insurance against accidents, or self-insure, but it is difficult to take into account individual drivers who have a "heavy braking foot" or who may knock the front end out of alignment by careless parking. The costs of repairs and resale prices clearly are influenced by the nature of the resource rights: vehicles that are owned generally will require fewer repairs than those that are leased. And so it is with other resources.

property rights
The rights and duties of ownership that are established by our legislatures and courts.

Property rights also affect how authors and publishers allocate their resources. Owners of copies of *The Price System,* under the laws of the United States, unambiguously have the right to keep, discard, give away, or sell them. But they may not make or sell additional copies.

That right belongs to our publisher *exclusively*. Neither we nor our publisher has the exclusive rights to the economic theory this book contains, however much we might wish it so. Price theory is part of humankind's stock of knowledge that is available for use by anyone who can master it. But the language we have used to express these ideas is protected under the U.S. Copyright Act. Not even the U.S. government can copy and sell this book without our publisher's permission. Anyone seeking such permission should expect to pay a fee. Notice at the bottom of each article we reprint that we had to obtain permission from owners of copyrights to those works, most of whom charged us a fee.

We wrote this book in part because we wanted to give our students a better understanding of how easily price theory can be used in everyday life. Like most authors, however, we also did it for profit. We invested time and effort in writing successive editions of this book. Our publisher invested its capital to manufacture a finished product that is advertised, distributed, and sold around the world. Pirates who attempt to take a "free ride" on these investments without bothering to write their own books will have to cope with the excellent attorneys that our publisher has retained. The laws of most countries overwhelmingly favor authors and publishers, so the costs of *enforcing* their exclusive rights are low.

The copyright law was not written in our favor because some members of Congress were authors or were chummy with publishers. The purpose was to create an economical structure of incentives. Exclusivity means that we and our publisher get 100 percent of the returns of our effort. If our book is in demand, we do well; if we flub it, the losses are strictly ours. This leads us to compare price-cost margins in producing this book versus alternative uses of our resources and to allocate our resources to the highest-valued uses. We would have less incentive to act in this socially productive way if our profits or losses were shared with others.

Exclusive rights, inexpensively enforced, are what most economists mean by *private property*. The hypothetical goods we use to explain price theory in the discussion and diagrams of following chapters are usually of the private property kind. The importance of exclusive and enforceable property rights is pervasive. Would families redecorate their homes if they could not exclude transients from camping out indefinitely in the living room? Would Holiday Inn build hotels if it could not capture the room rents? In some countries, building owners may not evict squatters who refuse to leave or pay rent. Owners' incentives to maintain such buildings are weak, their sale prices are low, and so fewer new buildings are constructed.

By establishing exclusive copyrights, Congress decided that the value obtained by producers *and* consumers from more (and probably better) books exceeds the gains of pirates and their customers from more copies of fewer books. Casual evidence suggests that this structure of property rights has affected the allocation of resources in socially productive ways. The modern novel emerged in Victorian England after courts enforced rights for authors and publishers. And in our own time, many new books are published and sold in the United States each year, and bookstores dot most towns and shopping malls.

THE NOT-FOR-PROFIT SECTOR

The economic system discussed thus far is composed on the producing side of business firms owned as private property by proprietors or shareholders seeking to earn returns on their investments. These firms create products as diverse as furniture, aspirin, automobiles, plumbing, lettuce, and clothing. But we have conceptualized the economy too narrowly. Many economies contain a large and growing sector of not-for-profit organizations—firms, foundations, government units, and related organizations—that are not "owned" in the conventional private property sense; that is, ownership rights are not in the form of shares that are bought or sold in public securities markets such as the New York Stock Exchange. Private colleges and many hospitals, for example, are owned by their trustees in the technical or legal sense of ownership, but these people cannot sell out their "shares" for gain because such shares, if they exist, are not legally salable. Moreover, many of these organizations have rules against distribution of earnings to such people so that the organizations may maintain a highly valued tax-exempt status (sums that they may have left over at the end of their fiscal years are rarely called "profits" in their financial statements for this very reason). The same situation exists for governmental units which, although technically owned by all of their citizens, are *effectively* owned by none of them, since they have no right to sell their "shares" except by moving to different governmental jurisdictions. It is small wonder, then, that market criteria—prices, costs, and profits—play a relatively small role in determining resource allocation among and within these organizations.[1]

If prices and profits do not guide and direct such organizations, what does? Economists who specialize in the study of these institutions have yet to answer the question fully, but research to date supports two inferences.

First, competition for dollars among these organizations is less important than it is in the for-profit sector. In not-for-profit organizations resources are less likely to be used in ways that would capture earnings, because "owners" cannot take such earnings home the way ordinary owners can. For this reason, some not-for-profit organizations are less responsive to consumer demands than are ordinary firms that can capture earnings by being responsive. (Have you been as successful with the Postal Service or your county government in persuading them to provide quicker deliveries or better service as you have been with your local department store or filling station?)

Second, the forms of competition that replace "dollar votes" among not-for-profit organizations tend to be unpredictable in the usual economic sense. They cover a wide range of possibilities that depend on the particular institutional situations, and sometimes even the individual personalities, involved. For example, in not-for-profit organizations there is less likelihood that employees will be hired for their productivity (which is very important in a for-profit organization) and a greater chance that they will be hired for their personal characteristics—their likability, ethnic characteristics, "connections" with existing managers, and so on. We should emphasize that we are not expounding an all-or-nothing hypothesis: it is unlikely that all for-profit firms operate strictly by

---

[1] For more reading on this point, see Armen A. Alchian and Reuben A. Kessel, "Competition, Monopoly, and the Pursuit of Pecuniary Gain," in *Aspects of Labor Economics,* A Conference of the Universities-National Bureau Committee for Economic Research, A Report of the National Bureau of Economic Research, New York, Special Conference Series (Princeton, N.J.: Princeton University Press, 1962), 14:156–183.

market criteria (prices and profits) or that all not-for-profit organizations operate according to the foregoing standards. Each type of organization will probably display some of each kind of conduct. But we would expect relatively more emphasis on the market criteria among for-profit firms than among not-for-profits, because the former group of owners can take home the earnings that efficiency brings.

SUMMARY

The purpose of this chapter has been to obtain a picture of the economic system as a whole and to gain some appreciation of how the price mechanism guides and directs a private enterprise economy. We listed five basic functions of an economic system and discussed the ways in which a private enterprise economy performs those functions. A system of prices is the main organizing force. Prices determine what is to be produced. They organize production and play a major role in the distribution of the product. They serve to ration a particular good over its very short-run period during which the supply of the good is fixed. They are also an element in providing for economic maintenance and growth.

How the price system allocates resources is affected by the resource ownership rights that society establishes. Incentives to make new or maintain old investments are weaker when property rights are not exclusive. An entire field of economics is now devoted to studying the effects of different ownership structures on resource-use outcomes.

Modern mixed economies have a public sector as well as the private one discussed in the chapter. A not-for-profit sector cutting across the public sector and the profit-oriented private sector can also be identified. Ordinarily, in the not-for-profit sector prices and profits are not given free reign to guide and direct economic activities. Decision makers typically give other—usually personal—criteria greater weight.

APPLICATIONS

As one reads and listens to the news media innumerable illustrations of the points made in this chapter appear. Many are obvious examples of the price system at work. Others, showing shortcomings and limitations of the price system, are somewhat more obscure, so we prefer to concentrate on them. First we examine situations where property rights must be established to goods that are unowned. Then we study cases where externalities intrude. Finally we look at real-world not-for-profit problems.

FINDERS, KEEPERS

Earlier we emphasized how property rights can affect resource use. We illustrate it here by examining how society establishes rights to things that are lost and found.

In most states, the law requires that lost goods be returned by finders to rightful owners—if they can be identified. This is a sensible legal rule. It enforces the initial owner's exclusive rights without encouraging excessive measures by owners to protect their property. It discourages legal controversies over ownership or wasteful attempts to establish frivolous claims.

Lost goods normally may be kept by finders, however, if the rightful owner cannot be identified or located. This is also an economically sensible rule. It encourages owners of valuables to take economical safeguards in proportion to their value. As a result, most of the things lost are of relatively low value. By encouraging finders, the rule readily returns lost valuables to the stream of commerce, making them available for use and enjoyment by others.[2]

This legal rule can often be seen in operation at resort beaches. Around sunset, when the tourists are back in their hotels, beachwalkers with metal detectors attempt to find valuables lost in the sand. They must turn up gold watches or rings often enough to make such work worth the time involved and the expense of the equipment. The items they find are sold or pawned and thereby put back in circulation.

The following story from the *Los Angeles Times* shows how exclusive rights were established to $6 million worth of cash and precious metals found in an abandoned car in an airport parking lot. Several individuals appear to have found the goods simultaneously and therefore to have made rival claims. The stakes were large, so claims were also entered by California and the U.S. government. This made a lawsuit inevitable.

The federal judge ruled that the goods were the property of the U.S. government. The evidence was ambiguous, but some decision had to be made. The

---

[2]RobertJohn Ranucci, "A Glance at the Economics of: The Law of Finds and the Law of Salvage" (Claremont, Calif.: Claremont McKenna College, 1985); and Walter M. Kelly, "Recent Decisions: Personal Property—Rights of Finders," *Baylor Law Review* 7 (Summer 1955): 330–334.

U.S. AWARDED LOOT FOUND IN RENTAL CAR

SAN FRANCISCO (AP)—Nearly $6 million in cash, platinum and gold found in the trunk of a rented car at San Francisco International Airport was awarded to the federal government Monday by a judge who said there was reason to believe that the money was drug-related.

The amount of cash, the presence of cocaine residue and a federal agent's statement about a man who had come from Miami and rented the car all were indications that the money was involved in the buying or selling of illegal drugs, U.S. District Judge Samuel Conti said.

The $5.64 million in cash, 450 Canadian gold coins worth $157,500 and 500 platinum bars worth $162,500 were found last October in the locked trunk of a car that had been parked in the airport's long-term lot for three weeks.

The federal government claimed the money under a federal law pro-

viding for forfeiture of money or property seized as the profits or the purchase price of illegal drugs.

Claims also were made by Budget Rent-A-Car, which had rented the 1984 Ford; by three of its employees and a security guard, all of whom said they found the money, and by the state, which sought to tax the money and also claimed the entire amount as "unclaimed property."

But Conti said a sworn affidavit submitted to the court by Michael Fiorentino, an agent of the U.S. Drug Enforcement Administration, established that the money probably was drug-related.

The judge said Fiorentino's affidavit, which Conti had sealed until Monday, stated that a man using a fraudulent Florida driver's license had rented the car from Budget about Aug. 9, and left it in the parking lot on Oct. 1.

After Budget employees opened

the trunk and turned over the luggage to authorities, a drug-sniffing dog detected narcotics in the suitcases, and a search found 15 milligrams of cocaine, Conti said, quoting from Fiorentino's report.

The judge also quoted the affidavit as saying the unidentified man who rented the car had come from Miami, "the major source city for cocaine in the United States," and had used the address of an unidentified Marin County motel "known for drug transactions."

These and other statements in the report established probable cause that the money in the car was related to drugs, Conti said.

He also said the other claimants were not entitled to question Fiorentino about his statement because they did not even allege that the results of their questioning would refute the agent's conclusions about the origin of the money.

Source: "U.S. Awarded Loot Found in Rental Car," *Los Angeles Times*, April 23, 1985. Reprinted with permission of the Associated Press.

federal law that the judge enforced reduces the federal deficit a tiny bit, but it does not implement society's goal to establish economically sensible incentives for resource allocation. Why should people find and report abandoned goods if they may not keep at least some of the loot?

THE LAW OF CAPTURE

Property rights to mobile natural resources, such as fish and game, are often established by the law of capture—what you can catch, you can keep. But the rule generates practical problems for resource allocation that are often difficult to correct.

Each fisherman faces a dilemma: he could benefit by postponing a catch in the expectation of catching a bigger and more valuable fish later, but whatever fish he fails to take today is likely to be caught by another fisherman in the interim. Throwing the little ones back makes it likelier that each fish will reproduce before it is caught again. But abstinence by one fisherman is a gift to rivals unless all act accordingly.

Enforceable agreements to limit catches would benefit everyone. But usually they are costly to reach because so many fishermen are involved and costly to police because each has an incentive to catch more than allowed. Competition leads to accelerating catches and investing in better gear. Unless fishermen and their intensity of effort are limited, reproduction and catches will decline and the species may eventually be wiped out.

The key problem with communal ownership, which economists also refer to as the *common pool* problem, is that no one has property rights to *uncaught* fish. The problem arises not because people are self-interested, but because communal property rights do not channel self-interest in socially productive ways. Every fisherman has a right to fish, but no one has the right to exclude others.

One way to establish a right to exclude is to combine public ownership with regulation. In many states, fish and game departments require fishing licenses and set limits on catches, seasons, or the kinds of boats and gear that may be used. Fishing in some lakes or streams is prohibited until stocks recuperate. Overfishing and restocking are never really eliminated, however, because fishermen tend to shift to unrestricted areas. But regulation may be better than nothing if policing costs are low.

Government regulation is less effective for large coastal areas where policing costs are higher. Rising fish values, however, have made it economical for coastal nations to claim and enforce exclusive zones out to 200 miles from shore rather than adhere to the 3-mile limit that applied for centuries. In the United States' zone, the U.S. Coast Guard boards foreign ships and seizes catches that exceed limits. (American boats are lightly regulated because of domestic politics, so overfishing continues in some areas.)

Regulation of deep-sea fishing is usually ineffective because fishermen of several nations have communal rights by tradition. Preventing overfishing requires force or a treaty, and treaties are more difficult to negotiate and police the more nations involved. Not surprisingly, fish and animals that migrate long distances and are hunted by several countries may become endangered species. Whales and fur seals are periodically threatened, and catches of tuna and salmon fluctuate widely. Similar problems hobble protection of migratory birds and fur animals when their ranges cross borders.[3]

Another solution to the common pool problem is to establish exclusive ownership to uncaught animals. This is difficult to do for coastal or deep-sea fisheries but is feasible for lake and land animals. Private lakes and hunting ranches are common in the United States, Canada, Western Europe, and some parts of Africa. Owners police against poaching and may charge users a fee based on the number and kinds of animals killed. Seasons and hunts are limited according to species populations and environmental conditions. Creating property rights to unkilled animals is not impossible: North American Indian tribes

---

[3]Ross D. Eckert, *The Enclosure of Ocean Resources: Economics and the Law of the Sea* (Stanford, Calif.: Hoover Press, 1979), Chap. 5.

prevented overkilling of fur animals three centuries ago, as Eskimos and Aleuts do today.[4]

EXTERNAL EFFECTS IN SOLAR ENERGY AND DUTCH TOADS

A private enterprise economy uses the price mechanism to guide resources into the production of goods most urgently desired by consumers. But some goods present problems. These generate spillover effects, or *externalities*—sometimes called neighborhood effects—when they are produced or consumed, and the price system may not allocate resources to them correctly. If one's German shepherd barks at night, keeping neighbors awake, external costs are imposed on those neighbors over and above what it costs the owner to obtain and maintain the dog. If barking dogs impose costs on their neighbors all over the country, the price system will induce an overabundance of dog ownership. The newspapers have recently treated this problem in stories on the property rights of solar access and on the threatened extinction of Dutch toads.

Rights of Solar Access

The accompanying article from the *Los Angeles Times* illustrates spillover problems from solar energy. Vegetation and multistory buildings on one piece of property may impose short-run costs on adjacent property owners who use solar collectors by blocking their access to sunlight. In the long run, they retard others from making similar solar investments. However, if cities assign sunlight rights to owners of solar collectors, they impose costs on the owners of neighboring land by reducing shade and raising air conditioning and building construction costs.

The key question is whether the owners of trees and buildings will be permitted to reduce the values of solar collectors or the owners of solar collectors will be permitted to reduce the values of adjacent trees and buildings. Elimination of economic harm in this situation is impossible. Owners of solar collectors cannot be helped without harming owners of neighboring land with conflicting uses, and vice versa. The problem is caused by both parties. If society's goal is to allocate scarce land and allied resources efficiently to maximize the consumer-determined value of production, then it should select the higher valued of the two conflicting uses. This avoids the greater economic harm.[5]

The price system does a better job of resolving externality problems when bargaining, contracting, and enforcement costs are relatively low. The owner

---

[4]Harold Demsetz, "Toward a Theory of Property Rights," *American Economic Review, Papers and Proceedings* 57 (1967):347–359; George Laylock and Les Line, "The Legacy of Gerasim Pribilof," *Audubon* 88 (January 1986): 93–103.

[5]This analysis is developed in a landmark article by R. H. Coase, "The Problem of Social Cost," *Journal of Law and Economics* 3 (1960): 1–14.

'RIGHT TO LIGHT': ISSUE IN SOLAR ERA
by Joan Sweeney, *Los Angeles Times*

Three months after Brian Hunter began installing a $14,000 solar energy system at his Victorian home in San Jose, he learned that a 17-story, 310-unit condominium project was to be built in the next block.

The high-rise project would have shaded his solar collectors during some winter hours, he said, robbing his system of 30% of its capability.

Hunter and his neighbors, who live in an area near downtown San Jose where the city is encouraging high-rise building, fought the project. Eventually the City Council ordered the project scaled down so that it would no longer shade Hunter's collector.

Protecting the "right to light" of property owners like Hunter is becoming more important as more and more people install solar water and space heaters.

Direct Sunlight Needed   Solar collectors need direct sunlight, but because of the sun's angle, its rays hit a site diagonally. So at times, depending on the time of day and year, neighboring buildings and vegetation can shade collectors.

But as Brian Hunter's situation demonstrated, protecting one person's right to sunlight may restrict another's right to develop his property as he wants. This clash of conflicting rights is a knotty problem for government officials who want to promote solar energy use.

Happily for Hunter, he was able to resolve his problem through political pressure because, as some owners of solar systems have unhappily discovered, very little in American law guarantees their place in the sun.

Most courts follow a landmark 1957 case, Fontainbleau Hotel vs. Forty-Five Twenty-Five Inc., involving a Miami Beach hotel's decision to build a 14-story addition that would shade the swimming pool area of another hotel.

Despite evidence of potential economic loss to the hotel with the shaded pool, the Florida District Court of Appeals ruled, "a landowner has no legal right to the free flow of light and air across the adjoining land of his neighbor."

More recent court decisions have also been unfavorable.

Unfavorable Ruling   Glenn Prah of Muskego, Wis., found his solar collector would be partially shaded by a house to be built on a vacant lot next door by Richard D. Maretti. Maretti agreed to move his house 10 feet farther away from Prah's lot, but when Prah wanted it moved an additional five feet, Maretti declined. Prah sued him and lost. The case is now being appealed.

The right to light has been a legal issue since ancient times. In Pompeii, the local government had to buy the right to block the sunlight reaching the Temple of Apollo. The Justinian Digest of Roman civil law compiled in the early 6th Century devoted a section to the right to light.

In English common law, the doctrine of ancient lights held that a landowner had a right to unobstructed light and air across adjoining land after he had used it for many years.

The Fontainbleau ruling rejected this doctrine, saying that U.S. public policy favored full development of land.

In recent years in the United States at least 16 states, including California, and a number of municipalities have tackled the problem of solar access with legislation.

A state Energy Commission survey last year found that 10 California counties or cities had implemented some kind of solar access protection. Fifty others were considering it.

Legislative approaches have generally fallen into the categories of private agreements, land use controls, nuisance laws, vesting by public permit and designation of solar access as a property right.

California's legislation embraced a combination of approaches. The Solar Rights Act of 1978 is enabling legislation providing for creation of private solar easements and authorizing local governments to require, as a condition of subdivision approval, the dedication of easements to protect solar access.

Under a second law, the Solar Shade Control Act, trees and other vegetation, planted or grown after a neighbor installs a solar collector,

of the solar device could protect access to sunlight by moving the device away from trees, installing mirrors to reflect light, and perhaps moving his or her residence or business to another location. If vegetation is the problem, the adjacent neighbor could protect the solar device by planting trees elsewhere as opposed to paying higher air conditioning costs. If new construction is the issue, the neighbor could design a stairstep building that would block less light but can be declared a public nuisance if they shade 10% or more of the collector between 10 a.m. and 2 p.m.

However, the act offers no protection from structures, only from vegetation, and municipalities may vote to exempt themselves from the act. State and local officials could cite no case where the law had been invoked.

The legislative approach favored by most states has been to sanction voluntary private agreements—easements and covenants. At least 11 states in addition to California have taken this approach, even though critics note such laws are unnecessary because private easements can be granted without them.

Problems with Easements   But, while state legislatures find it easy and politically uncontroversial to give their blessing to private easements, property owners often find it difficult or complicated or too expensive to secure them.

Neighbors understandably are reluctant to give or sell an easement that restricts in perpetuity how their property can be developed. Such a burden on the title could reduce the property's value when they want to sell it.

As a result, in densely populated urban areas, easements could be prohibitively expensive and might be required from several neighboring property owners for adequate protection. As in Brian Hunter's case, a high-rise a block or more away can shade collectors.

One state in which easements have been used is Colorado, where some lending institutions require them as a condition of making a loan for a solar system.

Double-Edged Sword   The other type of private agreement, restrictive covenant, ironically has been a double-edged sword for solar access. It has sometimes been used by homeowners associations to veto installation of collectors on aesthetic grounds.

But now some state legislatures, including California's, have not only prohibited using restrictive covenants to unreasonably prevent solar installation, but have also provided that developers can insert covenants protecting solar access that are binding on all lot purchasers.

The land-use control approach is most easily imposed in new subdivisions where local governments can require the developer to protect solar access in placing the structures or to dedicate solar easements or covenants.

In already built up areas, a few local governments have experimented with bulk plane zoning.

Solar Envelope Concept   The most talked about concept in this area is the solar envelope, developed by two architecture professors at USC, Ralph L. Knowles and Richard D. Berry.

The envelope is the largest "tent" over a specific lot in which a building can be constructed without impinging on its neighbors' solar access during crucial midday hours.

The "roof" of this abstract tent may have, depending on the site, several angles. As a result, particularly in denser urban areas, the buildings designed to fit in the envelope frequently are irregularly shaped and rise in stairstep fashion.

The city of Los Angeles studied the possibility of using the solar envelope concept, and the Energy L.A. plan recommended experimenting with it, according to Mark Braly, Mayor Tom Bradley's energy coordinator.

Simpler Zoning Plan   Since 1977, on a limited basis, Albuquerque, N.M., has been using a simpler form of bulk plane zoning that protects a 45-degree plane projected from the north side of a property. It is expanding it to all residential areas.

Several local governments are using or considering a permit system to protect solar access.

In Minneapolis if a solar access permit is issued for a system, the city cannot issue a building permit for a structure that would encroach on the permittee's solar access.

In Claremont, Calif., once a solar collector has been installed, neighbors cannot construct buildings or plant vegetation that will shade it.

Source: " 'Right to Light': Issue in Solar Era," Joan Sweeney, May 27, 1981, *Los Angeles Times*. Reprinted by permission.

would also offer less floorspace to rent or use. Each option is expensive, but the two parties have incentives to select the *least-cost* adjustment and perhaps to share the costs. If few parties are involved and *the cost of the adjustment is less than the gain*, then they have incentives to reach a bargain to resolve the problem via the price system.

In our newspaper article, bargaining apparently occurred in the initial stages of the Wisconsin dispute, whereby Mr. Prah induced Mr. Maretti to locate his new house away from the property line. When Prah decided he wanted even more sunlight, however, it apparently was cheaper to bring a lawsuit than to pay Maretti for the extra inconvenience of situating the new house an additional five feet from the property line. In such cases judges replace the price system in determining resource allocation by ruling for either cheaper energy or cheaper buildings according to current legal theories. Property rights evolve and change through this judicial case-by-case, common-law approach, as well as through statutes that legislatures enact.

Environmental disputes may move into legislative bodies when many parties are involved and bargaining costs are therefore high. One function that legislatures serve in such cases is to define the property right unambiguously so that it is clear in conflicting-use situations who must purchase rights from whom. Usually this reduces negotiating costs and avoids the uncertainty that comes from the absence of clear ownership. According to the article, legislation under consideration in Los Angeles may lead to clever new forms of property rights such as the "solar envelope." This concept grants each landowner access to a certain quantity of sunlight, which may then be sold to a person for whom the value of more trees or higher buildings exceeds the value of the extra sunlight to the original landowner.

Other cities, however, may define property rights in ways that discourage bargaining. Apparently Albuquerque, N.M., rigidly applied the same regulations to *any* new buildings constructed on adjacent land regardless of the amount and value of obstructed light. This would eliminate the problems and costs of bargaining, but it would impose the flat and perhaps erroneous judgment that the value of solar uses will always exceed the value of conflicting uses on adjacent land. Economic theory suggests that property rights should be designed, if possible, to make private exchanges a practical alternative by keeping bargaining costs relatively low. This gives the price system a chance to resolve conflicting-use disputes and pushes them into courts only after bargaining fails.

Bargaining is often impractical for big environmental problems such as urban air pollution because of the number of persons involved who would have to reach agreements to curtail them. These problems usually require legislative solutions. It may be relatively inexpensive to create exchangeable pollution rights that firms can buy and sell like land titles (an example of this is given in Chapter 16). In many cases arrangements analogous to the price system will reduce an external cost. Setting tolls for freeway use on hot summer mornings to reduce automobile emissions is another price-system-oriented approach, but politicians shy away from the difficulties of explaining to voters why they will have to pay for using scarce highway space that they formerly received "free."

Dutch Toads

Perhaps the most intractable externalities occur when human activities threaten other species. The accompanying article from the *Los Angeles Times* shows that it is expensive but not impossible to protect toads in Holland that migrate across

EUROPEANS MOVE TO KEEP TOADS HOPPING
by Vera Frankl

Frogs and toads throughout Western Europe are breathing a sigh of relief and looking forward to a carefree summer. For the most grueling experience on the amphibian calendar—migration—is all but over.

Migration is a hazardous business. The trek from winter habitats to breeding sites in lakes and ponds can mean a 114-mile journey, often across busy roads. And until recently as many as 50% of grass frogs and 80% of common toads (or *Bufo bufo,* to give them their proper title) used to fall victim to passing vehicles.

Over the last decade, however, a growing army of volunteers, backed by local and even national governments in Western Europe, have marched to the rescue. Enormous amounts of time, effort, money, and ingenuity have been invested in what has become an annual spring rite to preserve the wandering amphibians. The casualty rate has been dramatically reduced.

To the uninitiated, the interest generated by these little creatures is, to say the least, bewildering. As a British nature lover points out, frogs and toads have long suffered from "a bad public image." But that is changing and changing fast.

So these days, when the word goes out across Europe that frogs and toads are on the march, volunteers from Scandinavia to the Netherlands and Switzerland to West Germany reach for their gum boots and prepare to mount "toad patrols" along known migration routes.

Aided by Press and Radio   The local press and radio muster extra recruits. In parts of Holland, activists even resort to telephone campaigns, and a Dutch national "toad-saving day of action" was organized last year.

The volunteers settle down at the roadside with Thermos flasks for a two- to three-week vigil during which they will spend five or six hours each evening trapping thousands of the migrants in plastic buckets sunk into the ground. Then they ferry them to safety across the road.

Plastic buckets are all very well (a conservation group near Zurich saved about 8,000 frogs by this method last year), but gradually, more sophisticated techniques are being introduced. West Germany currently leads the way in toad safety, with Holland and Switzerland close behind.

Delegates from these countries attend international "toad-crossing" symposiums each year to help them keep abreast of the latest developments. In many rural areas of West Germany the federal government has installed official traffic signs—a green triangle with a frog in the middle—which warns motorists: "Beware toads crossing."

Conservation groups in Holland and Switzerland have painted and set up their own warning signs, to the dismay of officialdom. But Swiss and Dutch police are proving very amenable. They help carry toad-laden buckets—and even close roads on heavy migration routes between dusk and dawn, bringing traffic to a grinding halt.

But the most technologically advanced projects, already introduced in Switzerland and West Germany, involve building "toad tunnels" under roads and highways. Both the Swiss and West German authorities now budget for these when drawing up plans for the construction of new *autobahns*. In Switzerland, ecologists advise the federal and cantonal governments on the best spots for "toad tunnels" before road construction begins.

The most complex of these systems is at Cossonay in Switzerland, where two parallel tunnels about 40 feet long have been built side by side. Why two? To provide for two-way traffic, of course: one for outward, the other for inward migration. But, as Kurt Grossenbacher of Bern's Natural History Museum, explains:

"Tunnels are not proving very popular with toads; they like to see the horizon when migrating and have trouble adapting to new situations. We find that many of them tend to turn back."

So, if the toads won't go to the ponds, the ponds must go to the toads—and it is already happening. Fine-mesh fences are strung out along the roadside to deter toads and frogs from trying to return to the pond they have in mind, while conservationists create an identical, artificial pond on the side that the creatures are coming from. Experts say it is too soon to tell how many will fall for it. But in Switzerland, according to the locals, plenty of them already have. There are currently six toad- and frog-filled artificial ponds near Bern alone.

There is a serious aspect to all this. Industry, urbanization, drainage projects, intensive farming, and new roads have done a lot of damage to European wildlife since World War II. The natural habitats of many frogs and toads have been polluted or destroyed and, said Keith Corbett of the British Herpetological Society, their numbers have declined considerably.

By cutting road casualties, conservationists have helped halt the decline—and helped focus attention on other amphibian species, such as the great crested newt, which are in serious danger of becoming extinct.

Source: "Europeans Move to Keep Toads Hopping," Vera Frankl, British journalist and broadcaster. © Vera Frankl. Originally appeared in the *Los Angeles Times*, Friday, May 27, 1983. Reprinted with permission.

land used for roads. As with solar energy, the situation involves competing harms. Traffic-as-usual imposes costs on society in the form of a reduced stock of toads. Protection of toads raises the costs of driving by requiring circuitous routes, road closings, and expenditures for "toad tunnels."

What society should do to allocate scarce resources efficiently in this case is unclear. It is easier for economists to compare the costs of cheaper energy versus cheaper buildings than to compare the costs of less driving versus a smaller population of earthly species. The value of the toads in Holland's eco-system is unknown, and it cannot be estimated by consumers' demands through the price system as can the values of energy and buildings. The toads cannot bargain, so their fate must be settled through political processes in which each person votes according to individual judgments about the value of conservation. Here the role of economists is to explain that eliminating harm altogether would be impossible and that the mix of outputs and environments we get depends on the patterns of resource rights that society establishes.

SUPPRESSING MARKETS IN ORGAN TRANSPLANTS

Which of many terminally ill patients get the organs available for transplant each year is determined in this country strictly by not-for-profit organizations.

Transplants of hearts, kidneys, or livers used to be experimental. The body's normal process of rejecting foreign material meant, until recently, that new organs would last only a year or two. Now cyclosporine—a miraculous drug that suppresses the rejection mechanism—enables many to last longer. Increasingly, transplant procedures are reimbursable under federal, state, and private insurance—up to $110,000 for a heart transplant and $238,000 for a liver transplant. Thus, demand has risen sharply.[6]

The supply of organs has increased slowly. The law requires that donors be "brain dead"—otherwise healthy people who are kept alive mechanically following a stroke or accident until a recipient of the right blood and tissue type is located. Teenagers riding motorcycles without protective headgear make ideal donors. Only 10 to 15 percent of families will donate organs, however. About 7,000 kidneys were transplanted in 1985; probably that many more patients were on dialysis awaiting organs. Desperate patients grow hopeful around Christmas and New Year's Day, because they know auto accidents will increase. In 1985, only 600 livers were transplanted; probably 5,000 persons died from liver failure since no mechanism existed for extending their lives until a suitable transplant was found. Infant hearts are so scarce (few babies die in auto acci-

---

[6]Alan L. Otten, "Rising Success in Organ Transplants Strains Hospitals and Governments," *The Wall Street Journal*, September 25, 1985, and "Federal Support for Organ Transplant Programs Grows Amid Mounting Pressure from Congress," *The Wall Street Journal*, June 24, 1986.

dents) that one California surgeon in 1986 attempted to transplant a baboon's heart into an infant.[7]

Why organs are not rationed by price in the short run, like the wheat we described earlier in this chapter, is partly explained by Fern Schumer Chapman in the following article from *The Wall Street Journal*. Many people object on ethical grounds to dying patients' bidding against one another for a few scarce organs even if it would cause more organs to be supplied. But some of those who object on ethical grounds also benefit by suppressing prices and competition. In the third paragraph she refers parenthetically to nonprofit "regional organizations" that match donors with patients. In 1984, Medicare or insurers paid such organizations between $5,000 and $12,000 to find, store, and ship a kidney. Annual fees were expected to increase from $70 million to between $200 and $400 million by 1990. The nonprofit American Red Cross, looking for new opportunities because its "lucrative blood-banking program" may have peaked owing to the AIDS crisis, quietly prepared to enter the transplant organ procurement business. Entry by a financially strong, nationwide organization threatened the 110 other programs that provided similar services, each a monopolist in its own region.[8]

It was easier for regional transplant monopolies to suppress competition from for-profit organizations. Senator Gore's bill was enacted after a Virginia physician in 1983 began the International Kidney Exchange, Ltd., and suggested that a kidney could fetch $10,000.[9] This threatened the existing network of surgeons and transplant professionals who allocated available organs. They objected to selling kidneys on the grounds that removing a person's second healthy kidney was risky, which was only partly true. In most healthy donors the remaining kidney will enlarge to provide up to 70 percent of original kidney function. Some people live with only one kidney owing to disease, and transplants between live siblings are common. Some well-informed donors might give up their "spare" kidney to break out of poverty or finance a college education. "Kidneys for sale" were advertised before the Gore bill imposed penalties.[10]

At least some of the $70 million that went in 1984 to regional bureaucracies to distribute relatively few organs could have gone to donors or their families and stimulated organ supply. More transplants would also have reduced somewhat the $2 billion that the federal government spent in 1984 for dialysis. But

---

[7]Fern Schumer Chapman, "The Life-and-Death Question of an Organ Market," *Fortune,* June 11, 1984, 108–118; Paul Recer, "Kidney Disease Brutal to Young Patients," *Los Angeles Times,* October 9, 1983; and Robert Steinbrook, "Organ Transplant Networks Face Ethics, Supply Problems," *Los Angeles Times,* June 16, 1986.

[8]"Getting Donors Key to Organ Transplants," *Los Angeles Times,* April 17, 1983; and Michael Waldholz, "Red Cross's Plan to Procure Organs Could Hurt Smaller Organizations," *The Wall Street Journal,* August 8, 1984.

[9]"Plan to Sell Kidneys for Transplants Draws Fire," *Los Angeles Times,* September 24, 1984; Arthur Kaplan, " 'Cash Market' Is No Place for Trade in Vital Organs," *Los Angeles Times,* September 21, 1983.

[10]Chapman, "The Life-and-Death Question," 110–114.

COUNTING ON PEOPLE TO DONATE ORGANS ISN'T ENOUGH
By Fern Schumer Chapman

In February, doctors in Tucson, Ariz., and Pittsburgh performed the 15th and 16th implants of the Jarvik 7 artificial heart. These implants, which were intended to keep the patients alive until human donors were found, underscore an important lesson—artificial hearts seem to work best as a transitional device, sustaining life until a human organ becomes available. Of the 16 artificial heart implants, 12 were bridges to human transplants and only four were permanent implants. Recipients of permanent implants have done poorly, with strokes and other complications. No mechanical device, not even a kidney dialysis machine, works as well as a human organ. Given this reality, the same old stubborn problem remains—America has a vital-organ shortage.

Unfortunately, people simply don't donate enough organs to meet the demand. There's a simple solution to the shortage—a commercial market in cadaver organs, which would give an incentive to both doctors and relatives to supply organs. This option, however, has been foreclosed by a recent federal law that explicitly bans the buying and selling of live or cadaver organs and carries a $50,000 fine or a prison term as long as five years. "Things are bought and sold; people are not, and parts of people should not," declares the law's author, Sen. Albert Gore Jr. (D., Tenn.).

That same federal law created the Organ Transplantation Task Force, a 25-member body of doctors, surgeons, lawyers, ethicists and experts in insurance and organ procurement that is to advise the secretary of health and human services on what to do about the current organ-transplant system. (The system is now run by some local hospitals and overlapping regional organizations.) The task force's report will be debated at a public meeting Monday and released in mid-May; however, sources say that the report offers little of substance.

The report will, for example, endorse state enactment of legislation requiring hospitals, where nearly 80% of Americans die, to ask relatives of all suitable patients to donate organs. Already, eight states have adopted this legislation and similar bills are pending in 26 states. The task force is also recommending that Medicare and Medicaid pay for coverage of heart and liver transplants. In addition, it will suggest that the Health Care Finance Administration develop a process to designate specific medical centers as the sites for certain types of transplants in the interests of efficiency. All this may help, but there is an underlying problem—the shortage of vital organs. The task force's recommendations rely entirely on good will, offering no incentive to donate organs beyond some selfless impulse.

Each year, organs are taken from only 13% of the nation's 20,000 potential donors (otherwise healthy the nascent market was cut off before anyone could determine how many dollars and lives it would have saved.

The thorniest problem for nonprofit transplant monopolies is how to allocate an organ when two patients have compatible blood and tissue types and about the same prospects for recovery. In the 1960s, hospitals rationed time on scarce kidney dialysis machines among competing patients by favoring those who were young, male, employed, and "congenial" or "likable."[11] "Need"—the code word for subjectivity—becomes important when price is suppressed.

Occasionally the waiting list for transplants is bypassed through dramatic television appeals, as the article described. In 1986, arrangements between families and doctors in California and Michigan for an infant's heart were aided by newspapers and the Phil Donahue television program. A transplant official

---

[11]George Getze, "Factors in Choice of Kidney Machine Patients Surveyed," *Los Angeles Times*, March 10, 1969.

people who suffer brain death in a hospital). Most physicians shy away from asking the next of kin for donations immediately after informing them that their loved ones are beyond hope. And relatives have no reason, beyond altruism, to offer a loved one's organs.

The choice is simple—an organ and a price, or no organ and no price. Society doesn't expect people to work for free. So why does it expect people to give organs for nothing? In a cadaver market, donors could contract with a firm to sell their usable body parts upon their death, with a fee to be paid to their estates. Or a health-insurance agency could pay the closest living relative for his dead relative's organs.

A cadaver market also skirts the unappetizing implications of a living-organ market, where poor people might grow desperate enough to sell organs they could live without. Most people would feel uncomfortable with the idea of a Beverly Hills resi-dent bribing someone from the ghetto out of his kidney. And a live-organ market does nothing for people who need livers or hearts.

A market is more palatable than some of the alternatives, such as European-style "presumed consent" laws. Here, the state assumes that it can harvest the organs of anyone who dies in a hospital, unless the patient stipulates otherwise. Americans, understandably, are sure to resist the notion that they automatically become state property when they breathe their last.

Under the capricious existing system, what often determines who lives and who dies is how deftly someone manipulates the media. Few have forgotten Charles Fiske, who two years ago pleaded on national television for a liver donation for his nine-month-old daughter, Jamie. After reciting the lyrics to one of her favorite songs, "You Are My Sunshine," he said, "She is my sunshine and I love her very much." Mr. Fiske's affecting speech saved his daughter's life. But others aren't so lucky.

This year death will claim thousands of Americans whose lives could have been prolonged by organ transplants. The long-term solution for the shortage may lie in the use of artificial organs. But until they are perfected, a cadaver market seems to be the only reasonable solution to increase the number of human organs available for transplantation.

It is naive to think that medicine operates on some high plane, beyond the considerations of profit and price. It is a market like any other and functions by the same principles as, say, the oil market. Oil men need incentives to drill and when they don't have them, a shortage develops. Likewise for potential organ donors. But here, the stakes are incomparably higher: life or death for thousands. Organ donations are too important to be entrusted to altruism.

Source: "Counting on People to Donate Organs Isn't Enough," *The Wall Street Journal,* April 24, 1986. Reprinted with permission of Fern Schumer Chapman, a writer based in Evanston, IL.

groused that it was "totally inappropriate" to "use the media" for "bypassing the procurement program that is functioning at their hospital."[12]

[12]Harry Nelson and Louis Sahagun, "Baby Jesse Case Angers Organ Donor Officials," *Los Angeles Times,* June 13, 1986.

Suggested Readings

For more on the incentives of decision makers in organizations of different kinds, see

Clarkson, Kenneth W., and Donald L. Martin, eds. "The Economics of Nonproprietary Organizations." In *Research in Law and Economics: A Research Annual,* suppl. 1, edited by Richard O. Zerbe. Greenwich, Conn.: JAI Press, 1980.

How resource pricing can prevent environmental pollution is described in

Elliott, Ward. "The Los Angeles Affliction: Suggestions for a Cure," *The Public Interest* 38 (Winter): 119–128.

Resource rights of different types are described in

De Alessi, Louis. "The Economics of Property Rights: A Survey of the Evidence." In *Research in Law and Economics: A Research Annual,* edited by Richard O. Zerbe, 2:1–47. Greenwich, Conn.: JAI Press, 1980.

Problems and Questions for Discussion

1. Consider one of the world's lesser-developed countries—say, Ethiopia—in which quantities of capital are small and of unskilled labor large. What kinds of technology would you expect to find in agriculture? In industry?

2. What effects would you expect improved access to educational opportunities to have on the incomes of minority groups? Why?

3. In a private enterprise economic system is profit making an evil or a beneficial kind of behavior? Explain your answer carefully.

4. California lets litigants in civil cases avoid court delays of up to two years by "renting judges"—usually retired jurists. Such judges often have special expertise in the problems at hand, and their decisions, once filed with the court, have the same force of law as those of regular judges. "Rent-a-judge" alternatives have been used by major entertainment figures, large corporations, and some governmental agencies wanting quicker trials or less publicity. The system is criticized on the grounds of allowing wealthier persons access to justice not available to poorer people. Does "rent-a-judge" benefit the general public or only the litigants involved? What do you see as its economic consequences? Would you vote to support it? (G. Christian Hill, "California Is Allowing Its Wealthy Litigants to Hire Private Jurists," *The Wall Street Journal,* August 6, 1980.)

5. The California Legislature has 120 members. During a 30-month period from 1977 to 1979, over half were involved in 100 accidents causing damages to the cars they were driving. Apparently most were hit-and-run cases in which the cars were parked and unoccupied. One legislator had four accidents in a four-month period, two involving his two teenage sons; the next year he had two more. Another had two accidents within two months. Another was hit while driving by a falling tree limb. Still another hit a big dog. Some accidents involved spouses and office staff. (George Frank, "Legislator Car Damage Claims Common; 100 Incidents Involving Leased Autos Reported in 30 Months," *Los Angeles Times,* August 10, 1979.) Consider the following explanations:

   a. Does it seem likely that this rate of accidents is normal or random? (Legislators drive more than the average Californian, who in the same period had a collision claim every 10.4 years.)

    b. Do you think it is possible that legislators worry more about their jobs than do other professionals and therefore are more accident-prone?

    c. Can you think of an economic explanation that makes careless driving by legislators *rational* given the structure of incentives that they face? Explain.

6. The British National Health Service owns most of the nation's hospitals. Since it is financed by taxation, it makes only nominal charges to patients. At a Liverpool women's hospital in 1980, nine patients arrived on schedule for nonemergency surgeries and were told the hospital had only four available beds that day. How would you expect the four beds to be rationed? Would you expect shortages more often at public or at private hospitals? Why? (Stanley Goldsmith, "Women Draw Lots for Hospital Beds," *The Daily Telegraph,* London, October 16, 1980.)

*__7.__ In 1971, in one of the first airline hijackings, the highjacker, D. B. Cooper, forced the plane to take off and parachuted with his $200,000 ransom over Washington State. In 1980, a 14-year-old Oklahoma boy found $6,000 in tattered, water-soaked $20 bills buried in a river bed that bore the serial numbers of the ransomed cash. The FBI, after holding the money as evidence until 1986, released it for division between the boy and the insurance company. The insurance company planned to sell the $20 bills to collectors in the hope of earning more than it would get by redeeming the money for new bills at the U.S. Treasury. The boy planned to use his share of the reward for his college education. ("Newsmakers: Thanks, D.B., Wherever You Are," *Los Angeles Times,* June 12, 1986.) Why do you think the U.S. government tried to claim the drug-related cash discussed earlier in the text but not the $6,000 here?

*__8.__ Antarctica is larger than the United States and Mexico combined but has only 4,000 inhabitants (mostly explorers in research stations). Twelve countries dropped claims to portions of Antarctica in a 1961 treaty and agreed to keep it demilitarized and to govern it by committee. Until recently, its only resources of commercial value have been fish and krill, a miniature shrimp vital to the food chain. Now scientists have found possible evidence of gigantic subterranean oil fields and of gold and diamonds. Third World nations are making their claims to Antarctica, and the treaty is up for review in 1991. (Bryan Burrough, "If Antarctic Oil Search Is a Success, Pollution, Discord May Follow," *The Wall Street Journal,* December 9, 1985.) What kinds of issues will affect the treaty's renegotiation and the property rights it establishes?

*__9.__ Shooting grouse, a delectable game bird, is popular in Britain, especially among the well-to-do. The bird, indigenous to the northern moors, will not

_____

*Denotes an application-oriented problem.

breed in captivity. Estate owners nurture the heather where the birds thrive and keep out foxes and other predators. The season does not begin until the chicks are grown and ends when the weather gets foul. Seasons are curtailed or suspended when nasty winters limit reproduction. In 1980, some estates charged shooters $700 per day plus room and board. Each shooter gets to keep only one pair of dead birds per day; the moor owner keeps the rest to sell to restaurants. (Alan L. Otten, ''Talk May be Cheap, but Grousing Isn't, at Least in Britain,'' *The Wall Street Journal,* August 11, 1980.)

a.   Does an estate owner have incentives to allow so many birds to be shot that grouse become an endangered species?

b.   Compare the cost of establishing and enforcing property rights to grouse as opposed to migrating whales.

*10. Presumably to reduce crime, the City of San Diego considered installing 17,000 high-pressure sodium streetlights that use less electricity and produce brighter light than those currently in use. But the brighter night sky would have reduced the effectiveness of Caltech's famous Mt. Palomar Observatory, 60 miles away, in the process of expanding our knowledge about the universe. Astronomers preferred low-pressure sodium lamps that may use even less electricity, but these have a yellowish cast that distorts color and that some people find depressing. They also argued that the 200-inch telescope at the Observatory would be extremely expensive to move. The city made the point that later in the decade telescopes on satellites would make observatories less important. Do you see any possibilities of solving this dispute with the price system? What criteria would you use to choose among the alternatives? (Lee Dembart and Lanie Jones, ''Palomar Wants a Dark Future,'' *Los Angeles Times,* August 14, 1983; ''Astronomers Win Street Light Battle,'' ibid., February 7, 1984.)

*11. It was reported in 1985 that a Pittsburgh hospital had given priority for kidney transplants to a member of the Saudi Arabian royal family, a physician, and the child of a physician over other Americans on the waiting list. (American Association of Blood Banks, *Blood Bank Week,* May 31, 1985, p. 7.) A U.S. Department of Health and Human Services study in 1986 found that foreigners tend to get kidneys more quickly than Americans, and that in some cities 25 percent of kidneys were transplanted into or shipped to foreigners even though many Americans were waiting. (''The Nation,'' *Los Angeles Times,* August 12, 1986.) The hospitals involved were not-for-profit institutions. How would you explain their rationing of scarce kidneys?

Chapter 3

THE PURELY COMPETITIVE MARKET MODEL

The concepts of *demand, supply, markets,* and *the degree of competitiveness in markets* are basic to a working knowledge of how a price system guides and directs the economic activity of a private enterprise economy. Most people have come in contact with these terms and often use them loosely, but for sound economic analysis they must be precisely defined and used. In this chapter we discuss demand, supply, and markets within the context of the purely competitive model, in which they can be most clearly defined and most easily used. The other types of markets with respect to competitiveness—pure monopoly and imperfect competition—are introduced in Chapter 8. For now, we discuss first the concept of competition and then turn to the concepts of demand and supply. Next, we analyze the essence of the market model—how prices are determined when the demand and the supply for a particular item are brought together. Finally, we examine the concept of price elasticity of demand.

PURE COMPETITION

pure competition
A market situation in which (1) individual buyers or sellers of an item are too small relative to the market as a whole to be able to influence its price, (2) units of the item are homogeneous, (3) the price of the item is free to move up or down, and (4) units of the item can be sold by any potential seller to any potential buyer.

The term *competition* is ambiguous not only in ordinary conversation but in economic literature as well. Its common meaning is rivalry, but in economics, when used along with the word *pure,* it carries a different meaning. We begin by examining the conditions necessary for the existence of **pure competition** and then consider its role in economic analysis.

The Necessary Conditions for Pure Competition

There are essentially four conditions that set purely competitive markets apart from other market structures. Perfectly competitive markets impose a fifth requirement.

Homogeneity of the Product   For pure competition to exist in a market, all sellers of the product being exchanged sell homogeneous units of the product—or at least the buyers of that product believe this is so. Buyers think, for example, that the bushels of No. 1 hard winter wheat sold by Farmer Brown are identical to those sold by Farmer Smith. Thus they have no reason for preferring the output of Farmer Brown to that of Farmer Smith or any other seller of No. 1 hard winter wheat.

Smallness of Each Buyer or Seller Relative to the Market   Each buyer and each seller of the product under consideration is too small in relation to the entire market to influence significantly its price. On the selling side, the individual seller supplies such a small proportion of the total supply that if the vendor drops out of the market altogether total supply will not be decreased enough to cause any rise in price. Or, if the individual marketer sells the maximum amount that it can supply, the total supply will not be increased enough to cause price to fall. The individual sellers of most farm products are in this position. On the buying side, any single buyer takes such a small proportion of the total amount placed on the market that he or she is unable to influence its price. As consumers, we are in this position with respect to most of the items that we buy. Individually we have no impact on the price of bread, meat, milk, safety pins, and so on. The influence in a purely competitive market of any one individual buyer or seller of a product is virtually nonexistent.

Absence of Artificial Restraints   Another condition necessary for the existence of pure competition is that there be no artificial restrictions on the demands for, the supplies of, and the prices of whatever is being exchanged. Prices are free to move wherever they will in response to changing conditions of demand and supply. There is no governmental price fixing or any institutional setting or administering of price by producers' associations, labor unions, or other private agencies. There is no supply restriction enforced by the government or by organized producer groups. Control of demand through governmental rationing is nonexistent.

mobility
The capability of a seller to sell to any of various alternative buyers or of a buyer to buy from any of various alternative sellers.

Mobility   An additional requirement for pure competition is that there be **mobility** of goods and services and of resources in the economy. New firms are free to enter any desired industry, and resources are free to move among alternative uses to those where they desire employment. Sellers are able to dispose of their goods and services wherever the price is highest. Resources are able to secure employment in their highest-paid uses.

"Pure" and "Perfect" Competition

Economists sometimes distinguish between "pure" and "perfect" competition. The distinction is one of degree. The four conditions just discussed are usually considered necessary for the existence of pure competition, whereas **perfect competition** requires that one more condition be met—that all economic units possess complete knowledge of the economy.

perfect competition
Pure competition plus the additional condition of perfect knowledge of the economy on the part of buyers and sellers enabling them to make instantaneous adjustments to disturbances.

In perfect competition, all discrepancies in prices quoted by sellers will be known immediately, and buyers will buy at the lowest prices. This forces sellers charging higher prices to lower their prices at once. If different purchasers offer different prices for whatever they are buying, sellers will know it immediately and will sell to the highest bidders. The low bidders must, of necessity, raise their price offers. In the market for any particular product or resource, a single price will prevail. Examples of perfect competition are very rare, but stock transactions on the New York Stock Exchange may approximate these conditions. The terms of stock transactions are flashed on the Exchange Board as they are concluded. The information is distributed immediately to interested parties all over the country. Under conditions of perfect competition, adjustments of the economy to disturbances in the conditions of demand and supply will be instantaneous. Under conditions of pure competition, it will take some time for adjustments to occur because of incomplete knowledge on the part of individual economic units.

Pure Competition in Economic Analysis

In economics competition is impersonal in nature. There is no reason for enmity to develop between two wheat farmers over the effect that either one has on the market, since neither has any effect whatsoever. Each one simply does as well as possible with what is available. Farmer Brown is not out to get or defeat Farmer Smith. By way of contrast, intense rivalry may exist between two automobile agencies or between two filling stations in the same city. One seller's actions influence the market of the other. In these cases there is rivalry but not competition in the economic sense of the term.

No economist insists that pure competition characterizes any economy, nor does anyone claim that it ever has. The question arises, then, as to why one should study the principles of pure competition at all. Three important answers may be given. First, the principles of pure competition furnish a simple and logical starting point for economic analysis. Second, a large measure of competition does exist in the United States today, although perhaps not in pure form. Third, the theory of pure competition provides a sort of norm against which the actual performance of the economy can be checked or evaluated.

With regard to the first answer, we can draw an analogy to the study of mechanics. No one questions the procedure of starting a study of mechanics with a frictionless world. This is unrealistic, of course, since friction inevitably occurs in the real world, but the temporary postponement of its consideration allows a clear statement of mechanical principles. Competitive economic theory principles occupy about the same role in economic analysis as do frictionless principles in the study of mechanics. Once we understand how the frictionless (competitive) economy works, we can observe the effects of friction (imperfect competition and restraints of various sorts) and take them into account. To study the theory of pure competition does not mean that one must believe the real world is one of pure competition, nor does it preclude the very legitimate study of imperfect competition—in fact, it brings out fundamental cause-and-effect relationships that are also important in imperfect competition. It is simply a logical place to start if one is to understand the principles of imperfect competition and their applications as well as those of pure competition.

With regard to the second answer, studies indicate that there is substantial competition in the United States economy.[1] Enough competition exists and enough economic units buy or sell under conditions approaching pure competition to give us valid answers to a great many economic problems.

In answer to the third question, in the theory of a market economy pure competition tends to lead toward the set of conditions defining maximum economic welfare or well-being given the distribution of income. The actual performance of the economy can then be appraised against its potential "best" performance. Imperfectly competitive or monopolistic forces are important in

---

[1]F.M. Scherer, *Industrial Market Structure and Economic Performance*, 2d ed. (Chicago: Rand McNally, 1980), Chap. 3; and G. Warren Nutter and Henry A. Einhorn, *Enterprise Monopoly in the United States, 1899–1958* (New York: Columbia University Press, 1969).

preventing the attainment of the ''best'' allocation and use of economic resources. Thus, the purely competitive model frequently is used as the basis for public regulation of imperfectly competitive situations. Presumably it underlies the philosophy and enforcement of the amended Sherman Antitrust Act of 1890, government regulation of public utilities, and many other public policy measures.

DEMAND

demand
The various quantities per unit of time of an item that a buyer (buyers) is (are) willing to buy at all alternative prices, other things being equal; represented in table form as a demand schedule or graphically as a demand curve.

Turning now to the development of a market model, we define **demand** for a good as the various quantities of it per unit of time that consumers will take off the market at all possible alternative prices, other things being equal or constant. The quantity that consumers will take will be affected by a number of variables including (1) the price of the good; (2) consumers' tastes and preferences; (3) the number of consumers under consideration; (4) consumers' income; (5) the prices of related goods; (6) the range or number of goods available to consumers; and (7) consumers' expectations regarding future prices of the product.[2] Additional variables could be listed, but these seem to be the most important ones.

Demand Schedules and Demand Curves

The definition of demand singles out the relationship between alternative prices of the good and the quantities of it that consumers will take. Variables (2) through (7) are held constant in defining a given state of demand. Usually we think of quantity taken as varying inversely with price. The higher the price of the good, the smaller the quantity that consumers will take; and the lower the price of the good, the greater the quantity that consumers will take—other things being equal or constant. Exceptions may occur in which quantity taken varies directly with price, but these must be few.

Note that the term *demand* is used to refer to an entire demand schedule or demand curve.[3] A demand schedule lists the different quantities of the product

---

[2]In functional form we can represent the demand relationship as $x = f(p_x, T, C, I, p_n, R, E)$, in which

x is the quantity of good or service X
p_x is the price of X
T represents consumers' tastes and preferences
C is the number of consumers under consideration

I represents total consumers' income and its distribution
p_n represents the prices of related goods
R represents the range of goods and services available to consumers
E represents consumers' expectations.

[3]The equation of the demand curve for X can be written as $x = f(p_x)$, in which the other variables listed in Footnote 2 are parameters. Or, we can reverse the dependency relationship and write $p_x = g(x)$, thus expressing the demand equation in the form in which it is usually shown graphically.

Although the demand equations and curves are represented in this section as being linear, this need not be the case. Linear demand curves are simply easier to draw and explain than are curvilinear ones. The equation for a linear demand curve takes the form $p_x = a - bx$.

Figure 3.1   Demand for Product X

(a) Demand Schedule

Price	Quantity per Unit of Time (hundreds)
$10.00	0
9.25	1
8.50	2
7.75	3
7.00	4
6.25	5
5.50	6
4.75	7
4.00	8
3.25	9
2.50	10
1.75	11
1.00	12
0.25	13

(b) Demand Curve

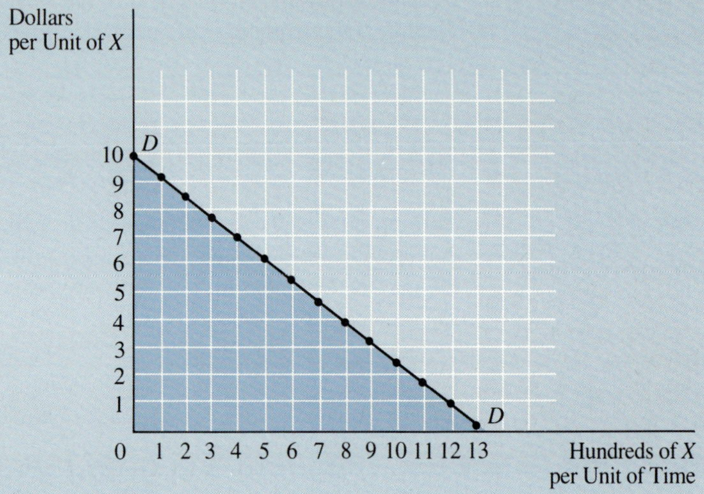

Demand for a product refers to an entire schedule or curve showing the quantities per unit of time consumers will take at alternative prices, other things being equal. *DD* is the demand curve for product *X* and is plotted from the demand schedule of panel (a).

that consumers will take opposite its alternative prices. A hypothetical demand schedule is shown in Figure 3.1(a). A demand curve is a demand schedule plotted on an ordinary graph. Such a curve is shown in Figure 3.1(b). The vertical axis of the graph measures price per unit, and the horizontal axis measures quantity of the good per unit of time. The almost universal inverse relationship between the price and the quantity demanded makes most demand curves slope downward to the right.

The quantities referred to in Figure 3.1 have no consistent meaning unless they are put in terms of *flows* per time period. They may be stated in terms of a week, month, or year, or whatever time period seems appropriate. It means nothing to say, "At a price of $4 per unit, eight units of product will be taken by consumers." The statement becomes meaningful when we say, "At a price of $4 per unit, eight units of product per week (or month, or whatever the time period happens to be) will be taken by consumers." We are not dealing with quantities as *stocks* but with flows per unit of time. They are rates of purchase, such as 500,000 cars per month or 60 million bushels of wheat per month.

The demand curve in Figure 3.1 separates the purchases that consumers are willing to make from those they are not willing to make. It shows the maximum prices that consumers can be induced to pay for the various quantities indicated on the scale of the horizontal axis, that is, the maximum price at which each of

**Figure 3.2
Movement Along a
Demand Curve**

At a lower price p_1
buyers will demand a
larger quantity X_1 than
they will demand at a
higher price p. The
increase in quantity
demanded as a result of
such a price change is
not a change in demand.
It is a movement along a
demand curve, *given the
state of demand*.

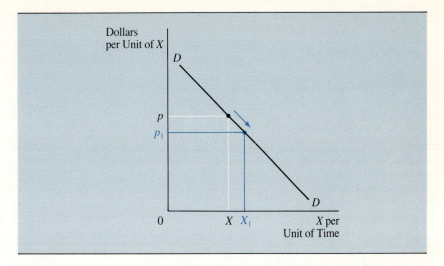

those total quantities can be sold. Or, it can be viewed as showing the maximum
quantities that consumers can be induced to take at the price levels indicated on
the vertical scale. Any quantity and price shown by a point on or to the left of
and below the demand curve is a possible or feasible price-quantity combination
to consumers. No point to the right of and above the demand curve is a possible
or feasible combination.

A Movement Along a Given Demand Curve versus a Change in Demand

A clear distinction must be drawn between a *movement along* a given demand
curve and a *change* in demand. A movement along a given demand curve
represents a change in quantity taken resulting from a change in price of the
good itself when all the other circumstances influencing the quantity taken remain unchanged. In Figure 3.2 a decrease in price from p to p_1 increases the
quantity taken from X to X_1. This is not called a change in demand, since it
occurs on a single demand curve and the term *demand* refers to that entire
demand curve. In defining demand we assume that the underlying demand circumstances remain constant while we change the price of the commodity and
observe what happens to the quantity demanded.[4]

When any of the circumstances held constant in defining a given state of
demand change, the demand curve itself will change. Thus, in Figure 3.3 an
increase in consumer incomes will shift the demand curve to the right from *DD*
to D_1D_1. With higher incomes, consumers are usually willing to increase their

---

[4]In the equation $p_x = a - bx$, the coordinates of p_x and x trace out a unique demand curve as long
as the parameters a and b remain constant. A change in the value of p_x results in a movement along
the curve to the corresponding value of x.

**Figure 3.3
Changes in Demand**

A change in demand for a product results from a change in one of the "other things being equal." For example, an increase in consumers' incomes will increase the quantities demanded at each price, shifting the demand curve from *DD* to *D₁D₁*. A decrease in the price of substitutes will shift the demand curve from *DD* to *D₂D₂*.

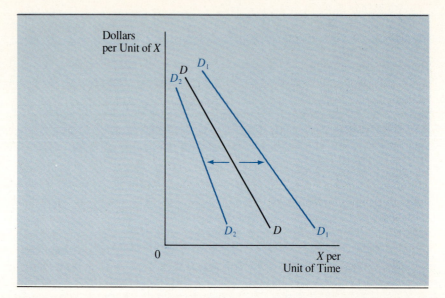

rates of purchase at each alternative price. A shift in consumers' tastes and preferences toward commodity *X* will have the same results; so too will an increase in the number of consumers in the market. An increase in the range of goods available to consumers may cause them to allocate less of their incomes to commodity *X*, thus shifting the demand curve to the left to position *D₂D₂* in Figure 3.3.[5]

The effects on the demand for *X* of changes in the prices of goods related to *X* define the nature of the relationships. A related good is a *substitute good* if an increase in its price causes the demand curve for *X* to shift to the right. The shift results from consumers turning away from the now relatively higher-priced substitute to *X*. Suppose, for example, that *X* is beef and that the price of pork rises. Consumers shift away from pork toward beef, thus increasing the demand for beef.

A related good is a *complementary good* if an increase in its price causes a shift to the left in the demand curve for *X*. The higher price of the related good induces consumers to take less of it. If in taking less of it they have less desire for *X*, there is an indication of complementarity. In this case, suppose that *X* is milk and that the price of cereal rises enough to curtail cereal consumption. The smaller quantity of cereal consumed reduces the desire for milk— the demand curve for milk shifts to the left.

---

[5]In the equation $p_x = a - bx$, a change in a will shift the price axis intercept of the curve and a change in b will alter its slope.

Figure 3.4   Supply of Product X

(a) Supply Schedule

Price	Quantity per Unit of Time (hundreds)
$4.00	0
4.25	1
4.50	2
4.75	3
5.00	4
5.25	5
5.50	6
5.75	7
6.00	8
6.25	9
6.50	10
6.75	11
7.00	12
7.25	13

(b) Supply Curve

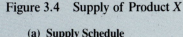

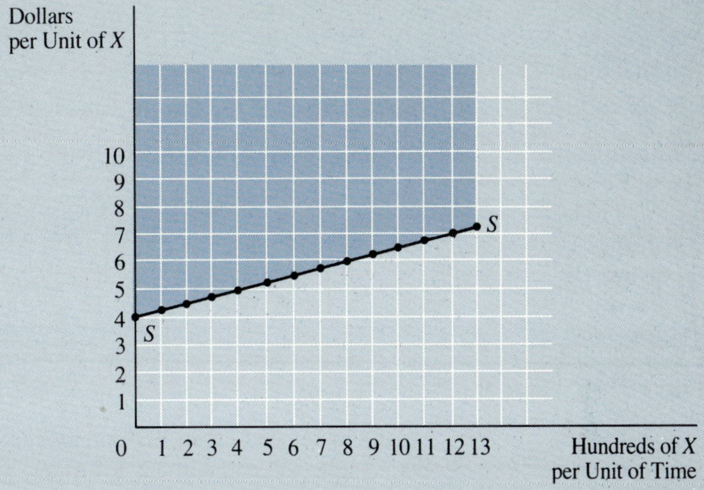

Supply of a good means the quantities per unit of time sellers will place on the market at alternative prices, other things being equal. It refers to the entire schedule or curve. The supply curve SS plots the supply schedule of panel (a).

SUPPLY

supply
The various quantities per unit of time of an item that a seller (sellers) is (are) willing to sell at all alternative prices, other things being equal; represented in table form as a supply schedule or graphically as a supply curve.

The **supply** of a good is defined as the various quantities of it that sellers will place on the market at all possible alternative prices, other things being equal. It is the relationship between prices and quantities per unit of time that sellers are willing to sell. The same distinction is made between a supply schedule and a supply curve that is made between a demand schedule and a demand curve. A supply curve is a supply schedule plotted on a graph. Usually it will be upward sloping to the right, since a higher price will induce sellers to place more of the good on the market and may induce additional sellers to come into the field. A hypothetical supply schedule and the corresponding supply curve are shown in Figure 3.4.

The "other things" that are held constant in defining a given supply curve are basically (1) the set of prices of the resources used to produce the product and (2) technology.[6]

_____

[6]The supply function can be written as $x = s(p_x, p_r, K)$, in which
x is the quantity of good or service X
p_x is the price of X
p_r is the set of prices of resources used in producing X
K is the technology available.
For a short-run supply function we would add M to the list of independent variables, with M representing the number of firms supplying X.

**Figure 3.5
A Change in Supply
versus a Movement
Along a Supply
Curve**

As with demand, an
increase in the quantity
supplied because of an
increase in price from p_1
to p_2 is not called an
increase in supply.
Rather it is a movement
along a given supply
curve. An increase in
supply is a shift in the
entire curve resulting
from a change in one of
the ''other things being
equal.''

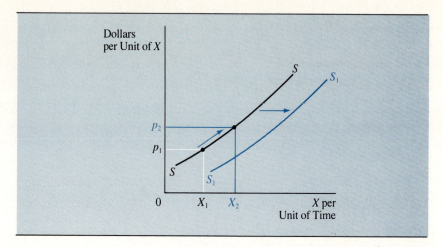

Like the demand curve, the supply curve is a boundary line between what economic units will and will not do. At any given price, sellers would be willing to supply less than the quantity shown by the supply curve at that price, but they cannot be induced to supply more. To be induced to supply any given quantity sellers must receive at least the price shown by the supply curve at that quantity. They would supply that quantity for a higher price per unit, but they would not supply it for less. Any point on or above and to the left of the supply curve represents a possible or feasible quantity supplied at the indicated price. Any point below and to the right of it is not possible or feasible.[7]

For consistency and accuracy in definitions, it is necessary to distinguish between a movement along a given supply curve and a change in supply. In Figure 3.5 a change in the price of X from p_1 to p_2 increases the quantity supplied from X_1 to X_2. This represents a movement along a supply curve—not a change in supply. A change in supply is defined as a shift in the supply curve (for example, from SS to S_1S_1) and results from a change in one of the ''other things.''[8]

---

[7]We can express the supply equation as $x = h(p_x)$, or, alternatively, as $p_x = s(x)$, treating the other independent variables of Footnote 6 as parameters. Movements along the supply curve are movements from one set of coordinates to another, with the parameters of the equation remaining constant. A change in supply means a change in the supply equation parameters. Again, when we use linear functions it is because of their simplicity, not because they are more representative of actual supply conditions. The equation for a linear supply function is $p_x = c + dx$.

[8]In the equation $p_x = c + dx$, the coordinates of p_x and x trace out a unique supply curve as long as the parameters c and d are constant. A change in c shifts the price axis intercept of the curve, while a change in d alters its slope.

MARKET PRICE

Placing the demand curve and the supply curve for any given good or service on a single diagram highlights the forces determining its market price. The demand curve indicates what consumers are willing to do, while the supply curve shows what sellers are willing to do. Consumer demand is assumed to be independent of the activities of sellers. Similarly, the supply curve is assumed to be in no way dependent on consumers' activities. Consumers are assumed to operate independently of one another, and so are sellers.

Market Price Determination

In Figure 3.6 market price determination is illustrated. At price level p_1, consumers are willing to take quantity X_1 per unit of time. However, suppliers will bring quantity X'_1 per unit of time to the market; thus, **surpluses,** or excess supplies, of $X_1 X'_1$ per unit of time accumulate. Any seller with a surplus believes that by undercutting other vendors a little surpluses can be disposed of. Thus, an incentive exists for individual sellers to lower their prices and cut back the quantity supplied. The price will be driven down by the sellers; quantities supplied will decrease; and quantities demanded will increase. Eventually, when the price has dropped to p, consumers will be willing to take exactly the amount that sellers want to place on the market at that price.

Suppose, alternatively, that sellers initially establish the price at p_2. At this price level consumers want quantity X_2 per unit of time, but sellers will place only X'_2 per unit of time on the market. Therefore, **shortages,** or excess demand, equal to the difference between X_2 and X'_2 per time period occur. Faced by the shortages, consumers bid against one another for the available supply and will

surplus
A situation, caused by a price being above the equilibrium level, in which sellers want to sell larger quantities than buyers want to buy.

shortage
A situation, caused by a price being below the equilibrium level, in which buyers want to buy larger quantities than sellers are willing to sell.

**Figure 3.6
Equilibrium Price
Determination**

A price such as p_1 generates a surplus, inducing sellers to reduce the prices they are asking. Price p_2 results in a shortage, causing buyers to offer higher prices. At the equilibrium price p, buyers are willing to take all that sellers will place on the market.

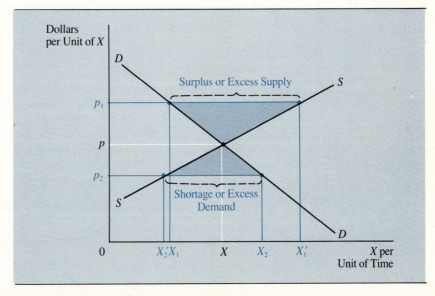

continue to do so as long as shortages exist. When the price has been driven up to p by consumers, the shortages will have disappeared and buyers will be taking the quantity that sellers want to sell.

equilibrium price
That price at which the quantity per unit of time that buyers want to buy is just equal to the quantity that sellers want to sell; it generates neither a surplus nor a shortage, and there is no incentive for buyers or sellers to change it.

Price p is called the **equilibrium price.** Given the conditions of demand and supply for commodity X, it is the price that, if attained, will be maintained. If the price deviates from p, forces are set in motion to bring it back to that level. A price above the equilibrium price brings about surpluses that induce sellers to undercut one another, driving the price back down to the equilibrium level. A price below the equilibrium level results in shortages that cause consumers to bid the price back up to equilibrium. At a price level of p_1, so much of the good is placed on the market that the value consumers place on any one unit of it is less than the supply price. At price p_2, the quantity placed on the market is so small that the value of one unit of it to consumers is greater than the supply price. At the equilibrium price, p, the quantity that suppliers place on the market is such that the supply price and consumers' valuation of a unit of the good are the same.[9]

Changes in Demand and Supply

What happens to the equilibrium price and the quantity exchanged of a good when the demand for it changes? Suppose that DD and SS in Figure 3.7 represent the demand for and supply of apartment units in a given community. Now a private college is established in the community, and its enrollment expands rapidly. The influx of apartment consumers brings about an increase in demand to D_1D_1. At the original price or rental rate p, there will be a shortage equal to XX' apartments, and consumers will bid up the price to p_1. The quantity placed on the market and rented out will increase to X_1 as the higher rental rate induces some property owners and builders in the community to construct apartments. After the increase in demand, the new equilibrium price and quantity demanded are thus p_1 and X_1, respectively.

The same diagram can be used to illustrate the effects of a decrease in demand on the price and the quantity exchanged of a product. Let D_1D_1 be the initial demand curve for apartments, while SS is the supply curve. Now suppose that the state university, located in a city 30 miles away, cuts its tuition rates substantially, drawing students away from the private college community. Demand for apartments in the community drops to DD, and at the initial equilibrium price p_1 there is a surplus of $X_1'X_1$. Rental rates will decrease, and fewer apartments will be rented out as property owners find it less worthwhile to make

_____

[9]The equilibrium price and quantity are determined mathematically by solving the demand and supply equations simultaneously. If these are, respectively, $p_x = g(x)$ and $p_x = s(x)$, we have two equations, two unknowns, and a determinate solution.

More specifically, representing demand and supply as lines or curves, let the demand and supply equations be

$p_x = 10 - \frac{3}{4}x$ (Demand)

$p_x = 4 + \frac{1}{4}x$ (Supply).

Solving these simultaneously, we find that $x = 6$ and $p_x = 5.50$.

**Figure 3.7
Effects of a Change
in Demand**

An increase in the
demand for apartments
causes a shortage at the
initial equilibrium price
p. The resulting shortage
causes those seeking
apartments to offer higher
prices, increasing the
quantities placed on the
market. The new
equilibrium price is p_1.

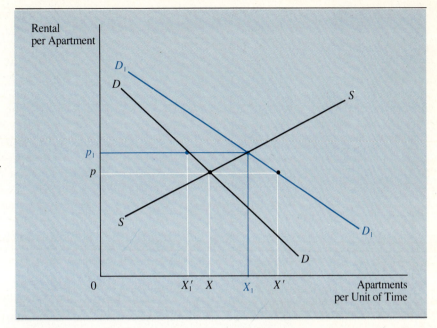

available and maintain some of their apartments. The new equilibrium price and
quantity demanded will be p and X, respectively.

Similarly, changes in supply, given the demand curve for a good, will bring
about changes in the equilibrium price and quantity exchanged. In Figure 3.8,
let DD and SS represent the initial demand curve and initial supply curve for
bales of cotton. Suppose that growing conditions become much better than was
initially expected, causing supply to increase to S_1S_1. At the initial equilibrium
price p, there will be a surplus of XX', causing the price to fall to p_1 and the
quantity exchanged to increase to X_1. On the other hand, if S_1S_1 were the initial
supply curve and a drought reduced the supply of cotton to SS, a shortage
amounting to $X_1'X_1$ bales per unit of time would occur at the equilibrium price,
p_1. The price would rise to p, and the quantity exchanged would fall to X.

PRICE ELASTICITY OF DEMAND _look at notes_

**price elasticity
of demand**
The responsiveness of the
quantity taken of an item
to a small change in its
price, given the demand
curve; its coefficient or
measure is computed as
the percentage change in
quantity divided by the
percentage change in
price.

The concept of *elasticity* is very useful in economic analysis. **Price elasticity
of demand** measures the responsiveness of the quantity that will be demanded
to changes in the price of a good or service, given the demand curve for it. If
the quantity taken is highly responsive to a small price change, a price increase
will cause the total expenditures on the good to decrease and a price decrease
will cause them to rise. If the quantity demanded is not very responsive to price
changes, an increase in the price will increase total expenditures on the good,
whereas a price decrease will cause them to fall. These points are of such
importance that we develop them at some length here. First, however, we examine the technical aspects of elasticity measurement.

Figure 3.8
Effects of a Change in Supply

An increase in the supply of cotton causes a surplus at the initial equilibrium price p. Sellers undercut each other's prices until at the new equilibrium price p_1 buyers will take the quantities placed on the market.

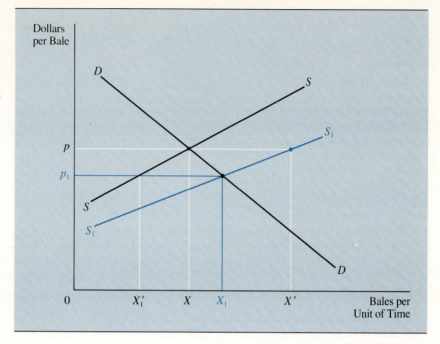

Measurement of Price Elasticity

Intuitively, it appears that the slope of a demand curve is a sufficient measure of the responsiveness of quantity taken to price changes. The slope of a small segment of such a curve can be obtained by observing how much quantity taken changes when the price goes up or down by a certain amount. For example, if a decrease of 10¢ in the price of potatoes causes a 100-bushel increase in quantity taken, the slope of that portion of the curve is $-10/100$, or $-1/10$. However, if we redraw the demand curve measuring the price in dollars instead of cents, the slope of the same segment of the demand curve becomes $(-1/10)/100$, or $-1/1,000$. The shift from cents to dollars in measuring the price causes a drastic decrease in the measurement of the downward slope of the demand curve, even though there has been no real change in the demand curve itself. If we draw the demand curve again, measuring the price in dollars and the quantity taken in pecks, the slope of the same segment of the curve becomes $(-1/10)/400$, or $-1/4,000$. Obviously, the slope of the demand curve is a very unreliable indicator of how responsive quantity taken is to changes in price.

The comparative slopes of demand curves for different goods are also useless as measures of the comparative responsiveness of quantities taken to changes in prices. In comparing the demand curve for wheat with the demand curve for automobiles, suppose that we want to know in which case quantity taken is more responsive to a change in price. The comparative slopes of the two demand curves tell us nothing. A $1 drop in the price of wheat may increase quantity

Figure 3.9
Measurement of Arc Elasticity

The computation of arc elasticity from A to B on demand curve DD is not the same as that from B to A because of the differences in the prices and quantities used to compute the requisite percentage changes. Use of the lower price p_1 and the lower quantity x as divisors in computing the percentage changes provides a simple, useful average measurement.

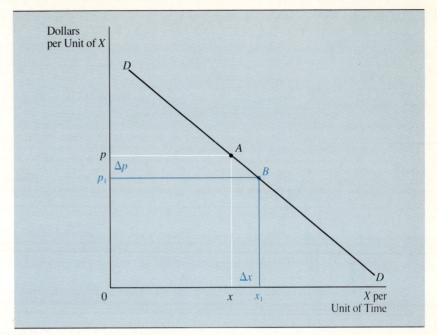

taken by 20 million bushels per month. A $1 decrease in the price of automobiles may increase quantity taken by five automobiles per month. This situation, however, does not mean that the quantity taken of wheat is more responsive to changes in its price than is the quantity taken of automobiles to changes in the automobile price. A $1 change in the price of wheat is a very large relative change. A $1 change in the price of automobiles is of little relative consequence. Further, a unit of wheat and a unit of automobile are completely different concepts, and there is no basis for comparing a unit of one with a unit of the other.

The great British economist Alfred Marshall, in response to this difficulty, defined the price elasticity of demand as the percentage change in quantity demanded divided by the percentage change in price *when the price change is small*.[10] In terms of algebra, the basic definition becomes

$$\epsilon = \frac{\Delta x/x}{\Delta p/p}.$$

arc elasticity of demand
The coefficient of price elasticity measured between two distinct points on a demand curve.

Consider the movement from A to B in Figure 3.9. The change in quantity from x to x_1 is Δx; the change in price from p to p_1 is Δp. The number or coefficient denoting elasticity is obtained by dividing a percentage by a percentage; it is a pure number independent of such units of measurement as bushels, pecks, or

---

[10]Alfred Marshall, *Principles of Economics,* 8th ed. (London: Macmillan, 1920), Bk. III, Chap. IV.

**point elasticity
of demand**
The coefficient of price
elasticity measured at a
single point on a demand
curve.

dollars. Elasticity will be the same between two given points on a demand curve
for wheat regardless of whether the price is measured in dollars or cents and of
whether the quantity is measured in bushels or pecks. The elasticity computed
between two separate points on the demand curve is called **arc elasticity of
demand.** The elasticity computed at a single point on the curve for an infinitesimal change in price is called **point elasticity of demand.** We discuss the
two concepts in turn.

Arc Elasticity

Suppose that we want to compute the elasticity of demand between A and B in
Figure 3.9, and the coordinates of the two points are as follows:

	p (cents)	x (bushels)
At point A	100	1,000,000
At point B	90	1,200,000

If we move from point A to point B, substituting the appropriate numbers in the
elasticity formula, we find that

$$(3.1) \qquad \epsilon = \frac{\dfrac{200,000}{1,000,000}}{\dfrac{-10}{100}} = \frac{200,000}{1,000,000} \times \frac{100}{-10} = -2.$$

However, if we move in the opposite direction from point B to point A, then

$$(3.2) \qquad \epsilon = \frac{\dfrac{-200,000}{1,200,000}}{\dfrac{10}{90}} = \frac{-200,000}{1,200,000} \times \frac{90}{10} = -1.5.$$

The percentage changes in quantity and price are different, depending on the
price and quantity from which we start. The differences in the starting points
lead us to different values of the elasticity coefficient.

These computations show that arc elasticity between any two points on a
demand curve must be an approximation. The farther apart the points between
which arc elasticity is calculated, the greater will be the discrepancy between
the two coefficients obtained, and the less reliable either will be. If arc elasticity
is to be meaningful, it must be computed between points on the demand curve
that are close together.

To avoid these discrepancies, a modification of the basic elasticity formula
can be used. With reference to Figure 3.9, suppose that elasticity is calculated
as

$$(3.3) \qquad \epsilon = \frac{\Delta x/x}{\Delta p/p_1},$$

where p_1 is the lower of the two prices and x is the lower of the two quantities. Using this to compute elasticity between A and B, we find that

(3.4)
$$\epsilon = \frac{200{,}000}{1{,}000{,}000} \div -\frac{10}{90} = \frac{200{,}000}{1{,}000{,}000} \times -\frac{90}{10} = -1.8.$$

The modified formula provides a very usable average between the two coefficients obtained with the basic formula.[11]

The demand elasticity coefficient shows the approximate percentage change in quantity demanded for a 1 percent change in price and will be negative in sign since the price and the quantity change in opposite directions. However, when economists speak of the magnitude of elasticity, they mean the absolute value of the coefficient, ignoring the minus sign. Thus, they say that an elasticity of minus one is greater than an elasticity of minus one-half, and an elasticity of minus two is greater than an elasticity of minus one.

Point Elasticity

The point elasticity concept is more precise than that of arc elasticity. If the two points between which arc elasticity is measured are moved closer and closer together, arc elasticity becomes point elasticity as the distance between the points approaches zero.

Elasticity at a point can be measured by a simple geometric method. Figure 3.10 shows a straight line (linear) demand curve. To measure elasticity at point P, we start with the basic formula:

(3.5)
$$\epsilon = \frac{\Delta x/x}{\Delta p/p} = \frac{\Delta x}{x} \times \frac{p}{\Delta p}.$$

This can be rearranged to read[12]

(3.6)
$$\epsilon = \frac{\Delta x}{\Delta p} \times \frac{p}{x}.$$

On the demand curve, $\Delta p/\Delta x$ is the algebraic expression of the slope of the curve for small price changes from point P. Geometrically, the slope of the demand curve is MP/MT. Therefore, $\Delta p/\Delta x = MP/MT$, or, inverting both fractions, $\Delta x/\Delta p = MT/MP$. Price at point P is MP, and quantity at that point

---

[11]Another arc elasticity formula frequently used is: $\epsilon = \dfrac{x - x_1}{x + x_1} \div \dfrac{p - p_1}{p + p_1}$.

Elasticity computed with this formula between points A and B in Figure 3.9 is -1.7. This formula, too, strikes an average between the coefficients arrived at by means of the basic formula when we work first from A to B and then in reverse from B to A. See George J. Stigler, *The Theory of Price*, 3d ed. (New York: Crowell-Collier and Macmillan, 1966), 331–333.

[12]In terms of calculus: $\epsilon = \lim\limits_{\Delta p \to 0} \dfrac{\Delta x}{\Delta p} \times \dfrac{p}{x} = \dfrac{dx}{dp} \times \dfrac{p}{x}$.

**Figure 3.10
Measurement of
Point Elasticity**

The algebraic formula for
elasticity is $\Delta x/\Delta p \times$
p/x. Geometrically, on
the linear demand curve
DD $\Delta x/\Delta p$ is measured
by MT/MP, while
$MP/0M$ is the same as
p/x. Therefore the
geometric measure of
elasticity at P is MT/MP
$\times MP/0M$. The MPs
cancel each other,
leaving the measure as
$MT/0M$.

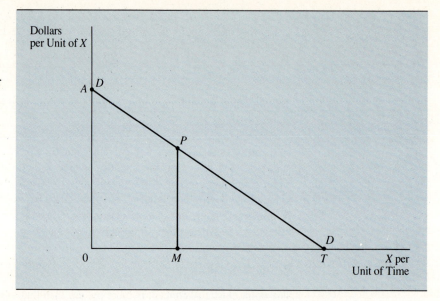

is $0M$. Thus, at point P

$$(3.7) \qquad \epsilon = \frac{MT}{MP} \times \frac{MP}{0M} = \frac{MT}{0M}.$$

Price elasticity coefficients are separated into three absolute value classifications.
When they are greater than one, demand is said to be **elastic.** When they equal
one, it is said to be of **unitary elasticity.** When they are less than one, demand
is said to be **inelastic.** These classifications are illustrated on the linear demand
curve in Figure 3.11. Point P is located so that $0M = MT$. Since elasticity of
demand at point P equals $MT/0M$, it is unitary at that point. Consider any point
farther up the demand curve—point P_1, for example. Since M_1T is greater than
$0M_1$, elasticity at point P_1 is greater than one. The farther up the demand curve
we move, the greater elasticity becomes until, as we approach point A, elasticity
approaches infinity (∞). Moving down the demand curve to the right from point
P, elasticity is less than one and becomes progressively smaller the farther we
move. As we approach point T, elasticity approaches zero.[13]

This technique for measuring point elasticity can also be used on a nonlinear curve. Suppose that elasticity is to be measured at point P on the demand
curve in Figure 3.12. First, draw a tangent to the demand curve at point P and

elastic demand
A situation in which the
absolute value of the
price elasticity coefficient
is greater than one.

**unitary elasticity
of demand**
A situation in which the
absolute value of the
price elasticity coefficient
is equal to one.

inelastic demand
A situation in which the
absolute value of the
price elasticity coefficient
is less than one.

_____

[13]Mathematically, consider that $\epsilon = \dfrac{dx}{dp} \times \dfrac{p}{x}$. For the linear demand curve of Figure 3.11, the
dx/dp term of the elasticity coefficient is constant. As $x \to 0$, then the term $p/x \to \infty$ and $\epsilon \to \infty$.
As $p \to 0$, then $p/x \to 0$ and $\epsilon \to 0$.

**Figure 3.11
Elasticity
Measurement
on a Linear
Demand Curve**

At point P, where $0M = MT$, price elasticity of demand = 1. At a point such as P_1, where $0M_1 < M_1T$, $\epsilon > 1$. At a point such as P_2, $0M_2 > M_2T$ and $\epsilon < 1$. It follows that as point A on the demand curve is approached, $\epsilon \rightarrow \infty$, and as point T is approached, $\epsilon \rightarrow 0$.

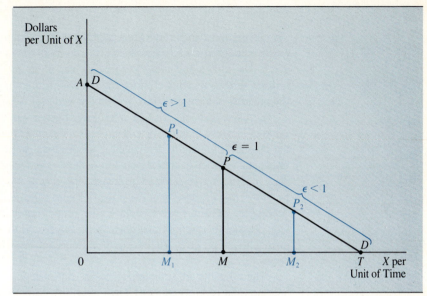

**Figure 3.12
Elasticity
Measurement
on a Nonlinear
Demand Curve**

On the nonlinear demand curve DD elasticity can be measured by drawing a straight line tangent to the curve at the point where measurement is desired. At such a point P, where the curves coincide, measure the elasticity $MT/0M$ of the straight line. This is also the elasticity of the curved line at point P.

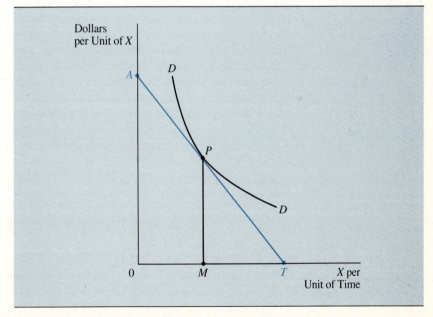

extend it so that it cuts the quantity axis at point T. At point P, the demand curve and the tangent coincide and have the same slopes; therefore, their elasticities must be the same at that point. Measurement of elasticity can proceed as before. Drop a perpendicular from P to $0T$ and call its intersection with the quantity axis point M. Elasticity of demand at point P is equal to $MT/0M$.

Elasticity and Total Money Outlays

One of the most important aspects of demand elasticity is the relationship that exists among price changes, elasticity, and total amount of money spent for the good. The total amount spent can be viewed either as total buyers' outlay (*TO*) or total sellers' receipts (*TR*) for the item. This amount is found by multiplying the quantity sold by the price per unit at which it is sold.

Suppose that for a certain small price decrease demand is elastic—the percentage increase in quantity sold exceeds the percentage decrease in price. Since the increase in quantity demanded is proportionally greater than the decrease in price, such a price decrease increases sellers' total receipts. Similarly, if demand were inelastic for such a price decrease, the increase in quantity demanded would be proportionally less than the price decrease, and sellers' total receipts would decline. If elasticity were unitary, the proportional increase in quantity sold would equal the proportional decrease in price, and total receipts would remain unchanged. For price increases, the effects on total receipts will be just the opposite.[14]

These results are summarized on the linear demand curve of Figure 3.13(a) and the total receipts curve of Figure 3.13(b). Moving down the demand curve from *A* toward *J*, the elasticity of demand is decreasing but exceeds one; *TR* will be increasing. For example, at price *B* and quantity *S*, *TR* is equal to the area of rectangle *0BGS* in panel (a) and the vertical distance *SN* in panel (b). At price *C* and quantity *M*, *TR* is the area of rectangle *0CJM* in panel (a) and the vertical distance *MQ* in panel (b).

By inspection it is apparent that *0CJM* is larger in area than *0BGS*. As we move down the demand curve from *J* toward *T*, elasticity continues to decrease, becoming less than one, and *TR* decreases. At price *F* and quantity *V*, *TR* is the area of rectangle *0FRV* in panel (a) and the vertical distance *VW* in panel (b). It is evident that this area is smaller than that of *0CJM*. It follows that at point *J*, where elasticity is unitary, *TR* is maximum.

---

[14]The total receipts equation is $TR = p \times x$. Differentiating with respect to x,

$$\frac{dTR}{dx} = p + x\frac{dp}{dx} = p + p\left(\frac{x}{p} \times \frac{dp}{dx}\right) \qquad \left[\text{Multiplication of } x\frac{dp}{dx} \text{ by } \frac{p}{p}\right]$$

$$= p + \frac{p}{\dfrac{p}{x} \times \dfrac{dx}{dp}} \qquad \left[\text{Since } \frac{x}{p} \times \frac{dp}{dx} = \frac{1}{\dfrac{p}{x} \times \dfrac{dx}{dp}}\right]$$

$$= p + \frac{p}{\epsilon}. \qquad \left[\text{Since } \epsilon = \frac{p}{x} \times \frac{dx}{dp}\right]$$

The sign of ϵ is negative, since dx/dp is negative; however, in terms of the absolute value of ϵ, $\frac{dTR}{dx} = p - \frac{p}{|\epsilon|}$. Therefore, for any increase in x, if

1. $|\epsilon| > 1$, then $dTR/dx > 0$ and TR increases.
2. $|\epsilon| = 1$, then $dTR/dx = 0$ and TR is unchanged.
3. $|\epsilon| < 1$, then $dTR/dx < 0$ and TR decreases.

**Figure 3.13
Elasticity, Price
Changes, and *TR***

Changes in the total
revenue of sellers for
price changes in the
product sold depend on
the elasticity of demand.
In panel (a) price
decreases where demand
is elastic result in the
rising *TR* curve of panel
(b). Price decreases
where demand is inelastic
cause *TR* to fall. *TR* is
maximum at the sales
level where demand
elasticity is one.

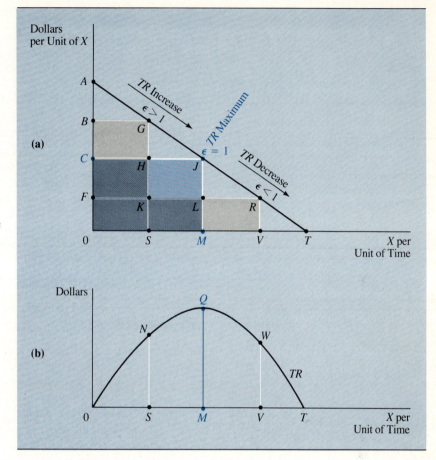

When a demand curve is a rectangular hyperbola, the elasticity of demand
at all points on it is unitary. Such a curve is illustrated in Figure 3.14. Its basic
characteristic is that the price multiplied by the quantity demanded yields the
same total receipts, regardless of what price is charged and whether price increases or decreases; that is, $x \times p = x_1 \times p_1 = \cdots = x_n \times p_n$.[15]

A seller of a good, contemplating a change in price, needs to know the
elasticity of demand for the price change. If demand is inelastic, a price increase
is advisable, but a price decrease is not. The former would increase the seller's
total receipts, but at the same time it would cut sales; the latter would increase
the seller's sales but would cut total receipts.

---

[15]If the demand curve is a rectangular hyperbola, then $x \times p = TR = k$, in which k is a constant.
Therefore, $x = \dfrac{k}{p}$. Differentiating with respect to p, $\dfrac{dx}{dp} = -\dfrac{k}{p^2}$; thus, $\epsilon = -\dfrac{p}{x} \times \dfrac{dx}{dp} = \dfrac{p}{x} \times$
$\left(-\dfrac{k}{p^2}\right) = \dfrac{k}{xp} = -1$ for all values of x and p.

Figure 3.14
Unitary Elasticity,
Price Changes,
and *TR*

If the elasticity of
demand for all price
changes is unitary, all
percentage changes in
price are just offset by
opposite percentage
changes in quantity taken
and no changes occur in
sellers' *TR*. The demand
curve that would yield
such results is a
rectangular hyperbola.

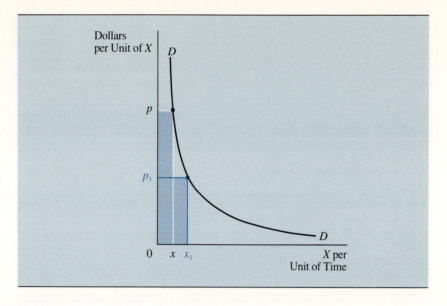

Factors Influencing Price Elasticity

The major factors influencing elasticity are (1) the availability of good substitutes
for the item under consideration, (2) the number of uses to which that item can
be put, (3) its price relative to buyers' purchasing power, and (4) whether the
price established is toward the upper end of the demand curve or the lower end.
These should be thought of as points to look for in trying to determine whether
demand will be more or less elastic in the neighborhood of the ruling price.

The availability of substitutes is the most important of the factors listed. If
good substitutes are available, demand for a given product or resource will tend
to be elastic. If the price of whole wheat bread is decreased while the prices of
other kinds remain constant, consumers will shift rapidly from the other kinds
to whole wheat bread. Conversely, increases in the price of whole wheat bread
while the prices of other kinds remain constant will cause consumers to shift
rapidly away from it to the now relatively lower-priced substitutes.

The wider the range of uses for a product or resource, the more elastic
demand for it will tend to be. The greater the number of uses, the greater the
possibility for variation in quantity taken as its price varies. Suppose that aluminum can be used only in the making of airframes for aircraft. Not much
possibility exists for variation in quantity taken as its price varies, and demand
for it would likely be inelastic. Actually, aluminum can be put to hundreds of
uses requiring a lightweight metal. The possible variation in quantity taken is
quite large. Increases in its price subtract from and decreases in its price add to
the list of its economically desirable uses. These possibilities tend to make
demand for aluminum more elastic.

Demand for goods that take a large amount of buyers' budgets is more
likely to be elastic than demand for goods that are relatively unimportant in this

**Figure 3.15
Dependency of
Elasticity on
Comparative
Percentage Changes**

The absolute price
movements between pp_1
and p_2p_3 are the same.
So are the absolute
quantity changes xx_1 and
x_2x_3. But for the price
change pp_1, the
percentage change in
price is small and the
percentage change in
quantity taken is large,
resulting in elastic
demand. For the price
change p_2p_3, the
magnitudes of the
percentage changes are
just the opposite, and
demand is inelastic.

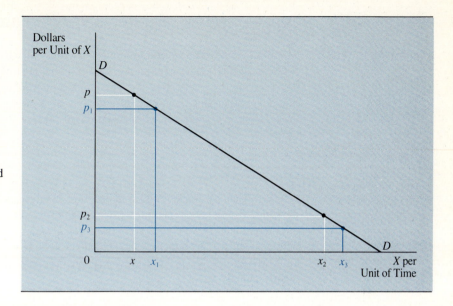

respect. Goods such as deep freezers, which require large monetary outlays,
make consumers price conscious and substitute conscious. An increase in the
price of deep freezers causes shifts toward the use of commercial lockers. Quantity demanded, therefore, is likely to vary considerably in response to price
changes. For goods such as salt or spices, which take a negligible part of
consumers' incomes, changes in price are likely to have little effect on the
quantity taken, and consumers are likely to be much less substitute conscious.

If the ruling price is toward the upper end of the demand curve, demand is
more likely to be elastic than if it were toward the lower end. This is a mathematical determinant of elasticity, and its validity depends on the shape of the
curve. It rests on a different footing from that of the other three determinants.
Figure 3.15 shows a linear demand curve.[16] If the original price is p and changes
to p_1 and the original quantity demanded is x and changes to x_1, the percentage
change in quantity is large, because the original quantity is small compared with
the quantity change, while the percentage change in price is small, because the
original price is large compared with the change in price. A large percentage
change in quantity demanded, divided by a small percentage change in price,
means that demand is elastic.

If the original price is p_2 and changes to p_3 and the original quantity is x_2
and changes to x_3, the reverse is the case. The percentage change in quantity
demanded is small because the original quantity is large, while the reverse is
true for the percentage change in price. A small percentage change in quantity

---

[16]The following argument does not apply to a demand curve that is a rectangular hyperbola or to
one that has greater convexity to the origin than has a rectangular hyperbola. It applies only to those
with less convexity.

demanded, divided by a large percentage change in price, means that demand is inelastic.

With the possible exception of the availability of substitutes, the factors just listed are not infallible criteria of elasticity of demand; they simply express the nature of the forces affecting it. In addition, they need not all work in the same direction at the same time. One or more may be working against the others, and the magnitude of elasticity will depend on the relative strengths of the opposing forces.

cross elasticity of demand
The responsiveness of the quantity taken of one item to a small change in the price of another; its coefficient or measure is computed as the percentage change in the quantity of one divided by the percentage change in the price of the other.

Cross Elasticity

Another elasticity concept useful in economic analysis is the **cross elasticity of demand.** It provides a measure of the extent to which commodities are related to one another. If we consider commodities X and Y, the cross elasticity of X with respect to Y is defined as the percentage change in the quantity demanded of X divided by the percentage change in the price of Y. This is expressed mathematically by[17]

(3.8)
$$\Theta_{xy} = \frac{\Delta x/x}{\Delta p_y/p_y}.$$

Goods and services—or resources for that matter—may be related as substitutes or as complements.

When two goods are substitutes for each other, the sign of the cross elasticity coefficient between them will be positive. For example, an increase in the price of frankfurters will increase hamburger consumption. Changes in the price of frankfurters and in the consumption of hamburger are in the same direction, whether price moves up or down; the cross elasticity is positive.

Goods that are complementary have negative cross elasticity coefficients. For example, an increase in the price of notebook paper cuts paper consumption and, consequently, the consumption of pencils; a decrease in the price of paper will increase its consumption and also the consumption of pencils. The change in the price of notebook paper is accompanied by a change in the consumption of pencils in the opposite direction. Therefore, the cross elasticity coefficient will be negative.

Cross elasticity of demand is frequently used in attempts to define the boundaries of an industry; however, its use for this purpose has certain complications. High cross elasticities indicate close relationships or goods in the same industry; low cross elasticities indicate remote relationships or goods in different industries. A commodity whose cross elasticity is low with respect to all other commodities is sometimes considered to be in an industry by itself. A commodity group with high cross elasticities within the group but with low cross

---

[17]Or, in terms of calculus, $\Theta_{xy} = \lim\limits_{\Delta p_y \to 0} \frac{\Delta x}{\Delta p_y} \times \frac{p_y}{x} = \frac{\partial x}{\partial p_y} \times \frac{p_y}{x}.$

elasticities vis-à-vis other commodities is often said to constitute an industry. Various kinds of women's shoes will have high cross elasticities among one another but low cross elasticities with regard to other articles of women's clothing. Thus, we have a basis for separating out a women's shoe industry.

One difficulty with cross elasticity as a means of determining industry boundaries is that of establishing how high the coefficients among commodities must be if they are to be considered in the same industry. Cross elasticities among some foods are quite high—those among frozen peas, frozen green beans, frozen asparagus spears, and the like. Others, such as those between frozen vegetables and frozen meat, are likely to be quite low. Is there a frozen food industry? Answers cannot be given unequivocally. Some general economic problems can best be solved by considering all frozen foods to be in the same industry. Narrower or more specific economic problems will require narrower industry groupings—a frozen vegetable industry or, perhaps, even a frozen pea industry. Cross elasticities furnish a guide to, but not a hard and fast determination of, industry boundaries.

Another complication is that of chains of cross relationships. Cross elasticities may be high between passenger cars and station wagons, and between station wagons and pickup trucks. But passenger cars and pickup trucks may have low cross elasticities. Are they in separate industries or in the same industry? Again, the nature of the problem to be attacked must be the guide to the proper definition of industry boundaries.

SUMMARY

The nature of pure competition and its role in economic analysis should be clearly understood. Pure competition is essentially the ideas of (1) smallness of the individual economic unit in relation to the markets in which it operates, (2) freedom of prices to move in response to changes in demand and supply, and (3) a considerable degree of mobility for both goods and resources in the economy.

The concept of pure competition does not provide an accurate description of the real world, but its usefulness is not thereby negated. It supplies the logical starting point for economic analysis. Enough competition does exist to give us valid answers to many economic problems. Additionally, competition provides norms for evaluating the actual performance of the economy.

Demand shows the quantities per unit of time that consumers will take of a commodity at alternative prices, other things being equal. It can be represented as a demand schedule or a demand curve. We must distinguish carefully between changes in demand and movements along a given demand curve. Changes in demand result from changes in one or more of the "other things." Movements along a given demand curve assume that the "other things" do not change.

Supply shows the different quantities of a commodity per unit of time that sellers will place on the market at all possible prices, other things being equal, and, together with demand, determines the equilibrium price of the commodity.

The equilibrium price of a commodity is that price which, if attained, will be maintained. Actions of sellers attempting to dispose of surpluses will push a higher-than-equilibrium price toward the equilibrium level. Actions of buyers attempting to buy short supplies will drive a lower-than-equilibrium price toward equilibrium. An increase in demand, given the supply, ordinarily causes an increase in both the price and the quantity exchanged of a good, while a decrease in demand has the opposite effect. An increase in supply, given the demand for a good, ordinarily decreases the price and increases the quantity exchanged; a decrease in supply usually increases the price and decreases the quantity exchanged.

Price elasticity of demand measures the responsiveness of quantity taken of a commodity to changes in its price. Price elasticity of demand is defined as the percentage change in quantity divided by the percentage change in price when the price change is small. Arc elasticity is an approximate measure of elasticity between two separate points. Point elasticity measures elasticity at one single point on the demand curve. Price elasticity of demand is the key element in determining what happens to total business receipts for a commodity when its price, given demand, changes. When demand is inelastic, increases in price increase total receipts, while decreases in price decrease total receipts. When demand is elastic, the opposite results occur when price is increased or decreased. The degree of demand elasticity for a certain good depends on the availability of substitutes, the number of uses for the good, the importance of the good in consumers' budgets, and the region of the demand curve within which price moves.

The cross elasticity of demand among products is also an important micro-concept. High positive cross elasticities indicate a high degree of substitutability between products and are frequently used to mark off the boundaries of particular industries. High negative cross elasticities indicate a high degree of complementarity between products.

APPLICATIONS

In assessing the impact of an economic happening on the price and quantity exchanged of a product, it is useful to start with its effects on demand and supply. As the first three illustrations indicate, clear analysis requires that the concepts be carefully defined. Later in this section we turn to the 1984 Olympics for a case of price fixing and ticket scalping.

DEMAND VERSUS QUANTITY DEMANDED

Failure to make a clear distinction between changes in demand for a product and changes in quantities demanded leads at worst to serious errors of economic analysis and at best to confusion. The accompanying article from *The Wall Street Journal* demonstrates the point. Can you spot analytical problems in the article?

Consider first the title. The first part confuses a *movement along the demand curve for pork* with an *increase in demand*. Either of two editing changes—one in the first clause or one in the second—could make it conform with sound economic analysis. The next part compounds the problem by saying that the movement along the curve *is* an increase in demand attributable to a permanent change in consumer preferences! The article then plays back and forth between these two different demand concepts, using them interchangeably and making it impossible for the reader to come to any sound conclusions.

We can read economic sense into some of the statements made in the article. There is an indication that the quantity demanded of pork (even though it is confused with the demand for pork) depends on consumer preferences, the prices of substitutes such as beef, and expectations regarding future pork prices. Some correct statements regarding the effects of changes in supply on prices are made, but these also tend to be confused with movements along supply curves. The critical and most sensible part of the article is the recognition that the *demand* (curve?) for pork depends heavily on the price of *beef*.

AN EMPIRICAL SUPPLY CURVE FOR BLOOD

College students are often asked for their blood (literally) in either of two ways. First, they are asked to donate freely and altruistically to the American National Red Cross. The blood is used mostly for lifesaving purposes and surgeries. Second, some students at urban universities can sell their blood to commercial blood banks for a price. This blood is used to make serums, clotting agents, and other commercial products. The question that arises is whether the tools developed in this chapter can be used to conceptualize the supply of human blood—a ''commodity'' about which many people have strong altruistic feelings

STRONG PORK DEMAND, DUE TO LOW PRICES, MAY INDICATE PERMANENT SHIFT FROM BEEF
by Steve Weiner, *The Wall Street Journal*

Beef remains America's favorite meat, but surprisingly strong demand for pork this fall is intriguing the meat industry.

At least some analysts think pork may increase its share of the nation's meat menu. ''Beef is still the preferred item, because that's the way we were born and raised,'' says Chuck Levitt, livestock analyst for Shearson Loeb Rhoades Inc. in Chicago.

''But in the long run, you may get a change in consumption habits,'' he adds. ''The new generation is getting a heavy dose of pork.''

Robin Fuller, livestock analyst for Dean Witter Reynolds Inc. in Chicago, agrees: ''The price of pork has become favorable to the price of beef at other times, but never for this prolonged period of time. There may be some permanent switch in consumption patterns after all this is over.''

Pork's price has been its big lure, of course. The Agriculture Department says the average retail price of pork this year was $1.44 a pound, about the same as last year. But beef's average retail price rose nearly 20%, to $2.26 a pound. Next year, pork is expected to fall to $1.40, while beef climbs to $2.46.

More than Meets the Pocketbook
Apart from the price gap, some officials think there is more to pork's popularity than meets the pocketbook. Millions of hogs were slaughtered this fall, they note, and if everything had happened according to plan, the meat market would have been glutted with pork and prices would have plummeted.

Instead, after a modest slump in November, key pork prices are about the same as they were in late September. The brisk demand that caused prices to hold up so well surprised nearly everyone in the industry. Currently, some hog specialists are predicting big things for pork.

Mark W. Thomas, executive secretary of the National Livestock and Meat Board's pork industry group, says it is realistic to think that in five to eight years per-capita pork consumption may reach a steady 100 pounds a year, up from about 65 pounds this year. Beef consumption this year is estimated at 78 pounds a person, measured by retail weight.

Pork Consumption to Grow
Orville Sweet, executive vice president of the National Pork Producers Council, believes pork consumption will grow to over 70 pounds a person next year.

Mr. Sweet says that ''whenever we start eating as much as 80 pounds of pork per person or more, we'll have people who have never eaten pork before. I think pork is destined to have a larger share of the red-meat market.''

Prices for hogs and pork in the fourth quarter have tended to bolster such producer optimism. As of Sept. 1, the government estimated the number of hogs and pigs in 14 top-producing states at 57 million head, up 16% from last year. And, going into the usual autumn liquidation period, slaughter was correspondingly high, up 15%. The expectation was that hog producers, fearing a price crash caused by 1979's overproduction, would swamp the market by reducing herds—thus reducing prices even further.

Confirming the Theory
The number of animals offered for slaughter seemed to be confirming the theory. Daily slaughters early in the year ran from 310,000 to 335,000 head regularly. But in November, daily slaughters began to approach 400,000 head, a high figure even taking into account seasonal factors.

Prices did slip as a consequence, but they didn't collapse, as had been feared. Supermarkets featured pork specials, and booming demand kept retail prices relatively high. With good retail profits to be made, supermarkets sought more pork from packers, who suddenly found profit margins restored as they bought inexpensive animals and sold the meat for good prices.

Prospects are for better prices for producers next year. Greater production also is expected next year. The Agriculture Department says 1980 pork production should reach 16.5 billion pounds, up 9% from this year. Analysts think a quarterly hog and pig report, to be issued today, will show a 10% to 13% higher animal inventory. But they believe it also will show signs that the hog herd's size will level off or be reduced in 1980.

The beef industry isn't showing signs of worry about pork's growth, though. The National Cattlemen's Association says it is confident beef will regain its solid following when supplies grow. And Dennis Schmidt, director of meat merchandising for Super Valu Stores Inc., a big wholesaler, says he doubts pork will maintain its gains. ''After all, when you want to have a nice dinner, what do you have? Pork chops?'' says Mr. Schmidt.

BLOOD AND AMERICAN SOCIAL ATTITUDES

Social institutions can have strange effects on the normal economic forces of supply and demand. A test conducted by one of the authors gives some insight into the way this social attitude to giving and selling blood affects its supply curve. A mass lecture class of principles of economics students, 213 in attendance, were asked to indicate whether or not they would give or sell one pint of blood at various prices. The instructor specified that the question related to giving blood safely, which can be done once each six-week period, and that only one pint could be given or sold at each price by each individual.

The results are listed in Table 3.1.

There is, of course, an important difference between hypothetical supply curves and individual supply behavior. (A 'bloodmobile' visited the campus two weeks after the experiment and only 7 students, in a check, indicated that they had given blood at a zero price!) What is significant, however, is that 18 individuals listed themselves as willing to give blood at a zero price, but not at a price of $1. Independently from their later action, their responses to the questionnaire indicated an institutional difference between a commercial and a partially philanthropic motivation.

Further, some of the students chose to use the questionnaire to air their complaint that the professor's whole discussion of the possibility of buying blood was immoral. Thus, while the actual values might not represent points along the supply curve for the class, the general shape of the supply curve is probably indicative of society as a whole (Figure 3.16). The characteristics of this supply curve are that there is a sharp reduction in the quantity supplied when the offer price is raised from zero to the first positive price.

**Table 3.1
Giving and
Selling Attitudes
Demonstrated**

Dollars/Pint	Number of Individuals Saying They Would Give One Pint	Dollars/Pint	Number of Individuals Saying They Would Give One Pint
$ 0.00	59	30.00	163
1.00	41	35.00	163
5.00	65	40.00	165
10.00	109	45.00	165
15.00	132	50.00	170
20.00	145	55.00	170
25.00	161	60.00	170

**Figure 3.16
A Supply Curve
for Blood**

The supply curve for blood seems to have one peculiar characteristic. A movement from a zero to a small positive price may decrease the quantity placed on the market because some donors at a zero price refuse for idealistic reasons to participate when a price is paid. Once these have dropped out, the curve assumes the expected upward slope.

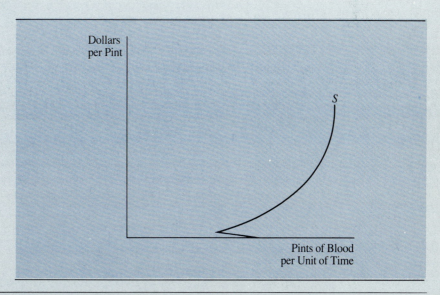

Source: Thomas R. Ireland and James V. Koch, ''Blood and American Social Attitudes,'' in *The Economics of Charity* (London: The Institute of Economic Affairs, 1973), 152–153. © I.E.A., London, England. Reprinted with permission.

and which is supplied through donations in most countries. Curiously, the Soviet Union, Sweden, and most Eastern European countries have a strong tradition of selling blood for cash rather than donating it. The accompanying excerpt from an article on the supply of blood illustrates one actual attempt by two economists to construct a supply-of-blood curve and the rather interesting twist to the results that their sample of college students revealed.

TICKET SHORTAGES AND SCALPING AT THE 1984 OLYMPICS

Prologue

The 23rd Olympiad, held in Los Angeles in August 1984, included 350 events for which some 4.9 million of the 7 million tickets available were sold to the general public. About 30 percent were set aside for the media, the official Olympic "family," sales abroad, and corporate sponsors who early on had bought tickets and paid promotional fees for advertising rights to help finance the games. The average price was $14 per ticket, but the range was from $3 to $7 for such "nonpremium" events as soccer, volleyball, and track and field and from $50 to $200 for such "premium" events as boxing, basketball, gymnastics, and the opening and closing ceremonies. Season tickets for all events of one type (limited to 10 percent of all tickets) were $100 for soccer, $210 for fencing, $400 to $950 for track, $850 to $2,200 for boxing, and $900 to $2,000 for gymnastics.[18]

Tickets went on sale in June 1983. However, the higher prices charged for premium events were not set high enough to eliminate shortages. This was intentional. Moreover, the difference between the actual ticket prices and the equilibrium prices—that is, the difference between p_2 and p in Figure 3.6— was greater than had been initially expected for many of the premium events. The Los Angeles Olympic Organizing Committee, the not-for-profit organization in charge of the games, claimed that it expected oversubscription of tickets to only about 10 percent of the premium events—but in fact, it was between 20 and 30 percent. The committee further perpetrated shortages through attempts to prevent scalping by firms that buy blocks of tickets for the express purpose of reselling them at higher prices.

Ordering tickets for the Olympics was not like buying a shirt at one's favorite neighborhood department store or other commercial transactions in the for-profit sector of the economy. The committee distributed 7 million brochures describing how tickets could be purchased. The rules were rigid and the outcomes uncertain.

---

[18]Kenneth Reich, "Early Rush for Olympic Tickets Reported, Costliest Events Drawing Best," *Los Angeles Times,* September 15, 1983; John Kendall and Kenneth Reich, "Ticket Order Forms for Olympics Available Today," *Los Angeles Times,* June 14, 1983; and John Kendall, "Olympics Tickets Post Brisk Sales," *Los Angeles Times,* August 4, 1983.

The general public could order tickets only by mail, specifying the date of attendance, price, and number of tickets up to a maximum but without knowledge of seat locations or seating charts. Buyers could choose price, but the committee did not disclose what fraction of tickets for each event would be in higher- versus lower-priced categories. Computers matched buyers with available seats approximately six weeks after orders were submitted. Seats for oversubscribed events were rationed by lottery, and each order was limited to two tickets for 30 premium events and four tickets for 45 semipremium events. (By contrast, does your department store or automobile dealer usually limit the number of items you can buy?) Orders not submitted by the six-week deadline were accepted on the basis of seat availability up to the date of the event, and an unspecified portion of tickets was sold at general admission at each event. Orders had to be accompanied by full payment plus a nonrefundable service charge of $1 per ticket; losers in the lottery were given refunds without interest after three months, and winners were notified after six months.

Prospective scalpers could see profit possibilities in eliminating the shortages for premium events that the committee created. The committee, however, planned to mail tickets only about a month before the games began in order to discourage scalpers from making deals far in advance, as the following article from the *Los Angeles Times* describes. The usual argument against scalping is that commercial ticket agencies buy blocks of tickets all at once and thus get better seats than can individuals. The argument in favor of scalping is that exchange benefits all parties concerned. Agencies require a higher resale price to cover the costs of buying, holding, and selling the tickets. However, they perform valuable services for persons who enter the market late because their incomes have gone up, their interest in the Olympics has increased, they have lost in the lottery, or they prefer to pay higher money prices rather than deal with the time-consuming and bureaucratic procedures just described. Scalpers also benefit ticketholders who cannot attend the event by purchasing their tickets from them. To most economists, scalping tickets is as innocuous as exchanging secondhand cars, houses, or shares of stock, all of which may involve brokers or agents.

The committee's rules for ticket distribution made scalping through agencies more expensive, causing less of it to occur. The higher cost of exchanging tickets made late buyers worse off and also hurt those foreigners and travel agents who sought to book package tours of airlines and hotels as well as Olympics ticket reservations. These rules also worsened the position of those foreign Olympics officials who did not plan to attend the 1984 games. It became more difficult for them to scalp tickets they had earned for providing ''volunteer'' services.

Analyzing who gains from such rules provides insight into why tickets to the best events were underpriced. The bureaucratic rules favor all buyers who can plan their activities well in advance. But they also favor members of the Olympics committee who would attend the games, along with the friends, associates, or clients to whom they give tickets (they are not supposed to sell them), perhaps in exchange for other favors.[19] The rules discouraging scalping make these tickets more valuable. They also favor employees and customers of influential sponsors of the games and others who are sufficiently well connected to get tickets.

The committee claimed in the article that it underpriced some events to ensure that lots of people would attend the games, and this may have been a factor in its decisions. But it does not explain why the underpricing was mostly for the *best* events. These tickets could have been sold at higher prices while still filling the stadia. It is always possible, of course, that the committee simply misjudged its market. But not-for-profit organizations appear to have systematic incentives to underprice the better events (or the better seats at better events), since their leaders do not take home as personal income the extra amounts that come from charging market-clearing equilibrium prices. Underpricing also occurs for tickets to nonprofit university football games, particularly the popular postseason bowl games.[20] (If you attend a college or university that has a prominent football or basketball team, discreetly ask one of the players about the number of tickets given players at a zero price. Are there effective rules against reselling the tickets at market equilibrium prices?)

Since we went to press before the Olympics were held, we cannot report on whether the committee's rules against scalping were effective. It is unlikely that scalping fell to zero, although the committee's rules surely made it more expensive. For example, an agency in New York began taking orders soon after the committee's announcement, expecting they would be able to get tickets. One broker was ''. . . making a list of foreign dignitaries, people with Olympic corporate sponsors, and others who have told him they will receive good tickets and sell them at a markup . . . He is also counting on average folks to sell him some of the pairs of good seats they win in the Olympic Committee's lottery.''[21] By late 1983, some Los Angeles residents who had received confirmations from the committee that they would get prime tickets were attempting to sell them to local ticket agencies. Some agencies were quoting resale prices generally five times higher than the prices set by the committee.

One reason why ticket sales were so brisk is that some general public buyers may have ordered extra tickets to scalp, anticipating that the committee's rules would cut scalping by agencies. In the summer of 1983, the Olympics had become a hot topic around Los Angeles, but not as much for the purpose of attending the games as for making forward contracts with travel agents and housing brokers to rent their homes for the three-week games at premium prices.

---

[19]This argument was made for Rose Bowl tickets by Armen A. Alchian and William R. Allen, *University Economics: Elements of Inquiry,* 2d ed. (Belmont, Calif.: Wadsworth Publishing Company, 1972), 145–146.

[20]Ibid.

[21]Roy J. Harris, Jr., ''Group Planning 1984 Los Angeles Olympics Tries to Keep Influence Out of Ticket Sales,'' *The Wall Street Journal,* June 6, 1983; Peter H. King, ''Ticket Brokers Gearing Up for Brisk Olympics Trade,'' *Los Angeles Times,* December 29, 1983.

Apparently the nonprofit Olympics offered all sorts of opportunities for transactions mutually profitable to buyers and sellers.

We should add that the committee did set very high prices on certain ticket packages. It established 2,000 special passes of two high-quality tickets per day for persons who qualified as Olympic patrons by shelling out $25,000 each. These payments were tax deductible, because they included some sponsorship of the games for the benefit of underprivileged youth, the aged, and the handicapped.[22] Published reports suggested the special passes were selling briskly in late 1983 to qualify for a 1983 tax deduction.[23]

Epilogue

We did not alter the preceding section about the Olympics that appeared in the previous edition of *The Price System*. We want students to see whether our predictions came true. We were right that people would attempt to speculate and that the best tickets would sell fastest. But in the end, to our surprise, the speculators were outfoxed.

By spring 1984, advertisements of tickets for sale began to appear in Los Angeles Sunday newspapers. But demanders were not buying at the prices asked. Demand had declined owing to worldwide newspaper stories saying that Los Angeles in August would be smoggy, crowded, and beset with security risks. Hotel and car rental bookings declined, and airlines began to discount flights they had expected to sell out. The committee's refusal to sell blocks of tickets hurt the group-tour business badly.

On the supply side, it became clear by April that getting some tickets, although not necessarily first choices, was easier than expected. The boycott by the Soviet bloc countries meant that even more tickets would be sold to the public. Tickets to some events were increased because more bleachers were added. The committee did not sell many season tickets with face values of $2,000 at the asking price of $4,000, and it sold only 700 of the patron packages at $25,000. These tickets also were offered to the general public. People on the waiting list from the first round of computer-matched orders were informed that more tickets were available. Seventy percent of all orders were filled. Over 2

---

[22]Peter H. King, "Games Patron Ticket Program Is Taking Off," *Los Angeles Times,* December 30, 1983.

[23]Underpricing the *best* seats often occurs in such for-profit businesses as movie houses, professional sports events, and theatres, although for different reasons. If the superior seats are not priced to sell out, people who purchase inferior seats tend to move to the better seats during intermissions. To prevent this, additional ushers must be hired and patrons occasionally asked to show their ticket stubs—which may distress purchasers of the better seats. Thus the manager of the event has incentives to underprice the better seats a bit to ensure that they are sold out. Those who buy superior seats restrain the undesirable behavior of those who buy inferior seats, saving policing costs. Steven N. S. Cheung, "Why Are Better Seats 'Underpriced'?" *Economic Inquiry,* 15 (October 1977): 513–522; and "Rose Bowl vs. Hong Kong: The Economics of Seat Pricing," in *Research in Law and Economics: A Research Annual,* ed. Richard O. Zerbe (Greenwich, Conn.: JAI Press, 1980), Suppl. 1, 27–49.

INTRICATE PLANS MADE TO CUT OLYMPICS TICKET SCALPING
by Kenneth Reich, *Times Staff Writer*

The Los Angeles Olympic Organizing Committee will sell all of its public tickets in the United States through a mail order and voucher system, backed by extensive computer checks and auditing to minimize scalping opportunities, according to a developing plan.

Olympics President Peter V. Ueberroth, while stressing that elements of the plan are subject to change, sketched out this scenario for ticket sales for the 1984 games:

—In the spring and summer of 1983, selected major retailers and banks will distribute mail-order forms to the public.

—Once mail orders are received, Olympic committee staff members will check in ways Ueberroth prefers not to specify as to their legitimacy.

—If a prospective buyer tries to order tickets only for premium events, such as opening and closing ceremonies and basketball finals, the committee will communicate with him, probably to propose a ticket package including some lesser events. Such communications will be an integral part of the process.

—When an order is in acceptable form, a voucher will be issued for the agreed-upon tickets. But the actual tickets will not be delivered until just before the games, reducing the pos-sibility that they can be resold to ticket agencies.

"An important goal is that we are able to sell our tickets directly to sports fans, particularly in Southern California, so they can buy them at our rates, which we think will be attractive," Ueberroth said.

"Our intent is to make available in Southern California a greater number of tickets than have been available in any prior Olympic Games," Ueberroth said.

He noted that, including preliminary events and events in sports of lesser relative popularity, no recent Olympics has had more than 68% of its tickets actually used.

Questions Increasing   The Olympic president spoke about ticket planning at a time of increasing questions about obtaining tickets to see the 1984 games. Olympic officials and staff members, commercial sponsors and others affiliated with the games in any way have all found the subject frequently broached by family, friends and associates.

At the same time, ticket agency owners who handle an estimated one million tickets here annually at above face-value prices have quietly been looking into the Olympic ticket situ-ation. Two of four principal operators, interviewed on the understanding that they would not be quoted by name, said this week that they either have or will approach foreign Olympic committees that will be allocated tickets to see about buying them for resale in Los Angeles at premium prices.

Ueberroth has considerable background knowledge about what the agencies might do. As chairman and chief executive officer of First Travel Corp., operator of the Ask Mr. Foster travel agencies, before becoming Olympics president, he dealt with some of them in connection with arranging tours.

Ueberroth, discussing the foreign ticket situation, acknowledged that about 30% of all Olympic tickets, perhaps 2 million, are nominally allocated to foreign interests under Olympic procedures. But, he noted, traditionally two-thirds of these tickets have not been used.

In 1984, breaking with past policies of other host cities, the Los Angeles committee intends to require payment before delivering any tickets abroad, Ueberroth disclosed. Unlike the domestic dealings with individuals, the committee will deal only with authorized Olympic ticket receivers in foreign countries.

million tickets were sold at ticket offices in the last few weeks rather than the 1.5 million originally planned.[24]

By June, the greater-than-expected future supply of tickets became widely known and was reflected in current offer prices. Telephone calls to agencies

[24]Roy J. Harris, Jr., "Summer Olympics Failing to Yield Anticipated Bonanza for Businesses," *The Wall Street Journal*, March 27, 1984; and the following articles from the *Los Angeles Times:* Kenneth Reich, "Eight Sports Sold Out for Games," April 18, 1984; Cathleen Decker, "Three Million Olympic Tickets Will Be Mailed in June," May 24, 1984, and "Speculators Went for the Gold in Olympic Tickets, Washed Out," June 11, 1984; Eric Malnic, "Choice Olympic Tickets to Be Sold by Invitation," July 17, 1984.

Olympic officials are willing to acknowledge privately that some of these tickets may work their way back to the United States to be scalped here. Although they prefer to say little about it publicly, they think some scalping is inevitable. But they hope to minimize it through such stratagems as their U.S. distribution system and their cash-for-tickets foreign system.

Revenue Estimated   Ueberroth said that if the Olympic committee were to sell all its tickets, it would receive estimated revenues of $85 million to $95 million.

The committee is not apt to realize its maximum potential revenue from tickets, because it is not likely to sell all its tickets, Ueberroth said. This was an apparent reference to such sports as team handball, field hockey and fencing, which have not traditionally had great crowd appeal.

Ueberroth said the Los Angeles Olympic committee will organize its own strong internal security and auditing systems to prevent the kind of internal under-the-table sales that have allowed scalping to run rampant at certain past Los Angeles rock concerts and other events.

He said the committee has "no plans at this time" to deal with any

of the Los Angeles area ticket agencies that sell tickets to the public at above face value. No contacts, incidentally, have been made from the other side, he said.

However, most agents are apparently going ahead with plans to try to obtain Olympic tickets that can be remarketed to the public at a substantial markup.

Checks with four leading agents on Ueberroth's plans found that, on a not-for-attribution basis, they were willing to give him and other committee planners high marks for trying to avoid scalping but were predicting that there will be ways to break the system.

"I'm sure we'll have tickets," one broker said. "I can put together a list of 200 names, send in, get tickets back and resell them."

But this same agent said it was "a smart thing" for the committee to sell the tickets in packages and to sell foreign tickets only for cash as a means of keeping scalping under some control.

Plan Criticized   The agent was most critical of the expressed hope to sell prime unused seats the day of the events, which he predicted would be unworkable, and he said any attempt

to mail out tickets as the games approached would risk "ripoffs" such as mailbox raids and the like, particularly if the ticket envelopes were readily identifiable.

Another agent predicted that an important leak in the system would be tickets allotted to commercial sponsors of the Olympics, ostensibly for their employees or business customers. Already, this broker said, he has heard reports of commercial sponsors agreeing to resell their tickets to travel agencies which have traditionally packaged tours and resold tickets for vastly inflated prices.

The agents agreed that private sales of tickets between individuals will be widespread and predicted that outside entrepreneurs may well come to Los Angeles for the period of the games.

But Ueberroth said the Olympic committee remains confident that the situation will evolve satisfactorily. The whole matter has been studied intensively and changes will continue to be made in plans to outwit scalpers, even in the last 60 days before the games, he predicted.

"I don't want to provide too much detail," he said. "The more detail, the easier it would be to break the system."

Source: Kenneth Reich, "Intricate Plans Made to Cut Olympics Ticket Scalping," *Los Angeles Times,* July 22, 1982. Copyright 1982 *Los Angeles Times.* Reprinted by permission.

from persons wanting to sell tickets outnumbered calls from persons wanting to purchase by 200 to 1. Tickets for the opening ceremonies were selling at only twice their face value. By July, tour companies that had obtained tickets but were disappointed by the low demand for them dumped some at half price. The Sunday before the games began, 750 advertisements to sell tickets appeared in the city's major newspaper, some at face value. Season passes purchased for $4,000 were going for their $2,000 face values. It was an open and competitive market.[25]

---

[25]Anne C. Roark, "Market for Olympics Tickets in Sharp Dive," *Los Angeles Times,* July 19, 1984; Eric Malnic, "Ticket Gripes Turn to Grins," *Los Angeles Times,* July 28, 1984.

The last surprise occurred in the final two days before the games began. The relay runners who carried the symbolic Olympic torch throughout the sprawling communities of Southern California ignited tremendous enthusiasm among observers along the route and among the media. Newspapers showed maps of the route, and television covered the event daily. Suddenly, almost as if it had been orchestrated, the demand for tickets surged. Prices for the opening ceremonies shot up to five times face value, and for other popular events, three to four times. The speculators who bailed out a month earlier acted too soon. And, yes, some pregame, illegal scalping outside the stadiums did occur.[26]

As Mr. Ueberroth and his colleagues predicted, however, the games went off without a mishap, without a cash commitment from Los Angeles taxpayers, and without a deficit. Attendance was 5.5 million persons, compared with 5.2 million in Moscow and 3.2 million in Montreal. The committee netted $150 million—ten times what was anticipated. Ticket sales—expected to be $98 million—were $151 million, partly because the Soviet bloc boycott allowed the committee to sell even more tickets.[27] But think how much more money the committee could have made if it had not underpriced the best seats!

---

[26]Robert Welkos, "Relay Sparks Late Surge of Ticket Buying," *Los Angeles Times,* July 29, 1984; Marita Hernandez and Tim Waters, "Ticket Demand Soars as Olympic Fever Rises," *Los Angeles Times,* July 30, 1984.

[27]"Attendance at Olympics Was a Record 5.5 Million," *The Wall Street Journal,* August 14, 1984; Kenneth Reich, "Olympic Surplus a Huge $150 Million," *Los Angeles Times,* September 12, 1984.

Suggested Readings

A terse, modern, and more mathematical statement regarding the demand curve and the price elasticity of demand is contained in

Baumol, William J. *Economic Theory and Operations Analysis*, 4th ed., 179–190. Englewood Cliffs, N.J.: Prentice-Hall, 1977.

The philosophic underpinnings of demand, supply, and market price (and more) are well presented in Chapter III of the classic

Knight, Frank H. *Risk, Uncertainty, and Profit.* Boston: Houghton Mifflin, 1921.

For the classical pioneer work on elasticity of demand and on markets and market equilibrium see

Marshall, Alfred. *Principles of Economics.* 8th ed., Bk. III, Chap. IV; Bk. V, Chaps. I–III. London: Macmillan, 1920.

Problems and Questions for Discussion

1. What would be the direction of change in the demand for beef as a result of each of the following changes that occurred in the markets for either chicken or beef in 1985:

    a. Rising consumption of chicken over a 20-year period

    b. Declining costs of production for chicken producers

    c. Declining costs of production for beef producers

    d. Bankruptcies of beef producers

    e. New medical research finding that chicken and fish are healthier than beef and pork

    f. Development of precooked, prepackaged steaks, roasts, and beef sandwiches that are ready for microwave ovens. (Marj Charlier, ''Beef's Drop in Appeal Pushes Some Packers to Try New Products,'' *The Wall Street Journal,* August 28, 1985.)

2. In each of the following situations find the errors, if any, in economic analysis (Jeffrey H. Birnbaum, ''Pricing of Products Is Still an Art, Often Having Little Link to Costs,'' *The Wall Street Journal,* November 25, 1981):

    a. A firm selling a nationally advertised brand of liquor raised its price about $1 per bottle over a two-year period and concluded that the number of bottles sold increased. Says the article, ''Only the price—and the bottle, belatedly—was changed to attract liquor-store patrons. The bottle has a new and apparently more salable oblong shape.''

    b. A marketing manager for a national brand of designer jeans was asked why they were priced at $9.86 per pair rather than $9.99. He replied, ''When people see $9.99 they say, 'That's $10.' But $9.86 isn't $10. It's just psychological.''

    c. A major producer of household products questioned 800 shopping mall patrons about the price of air fresheners. Says the article, ''Only 28% quoted figures within 15% of actual prices; 39% quoted figures that were off by more than that; and 33% had no idea at all what they paid.'' The firm concluded that ''many shoppers appear to pay little attention to price.''

    d. A New York City retailer attempted to build volume in its lagging sterling silver department by offering ''a five-piece silver coffee set for only $60, just above the store's cost. Thousands of sets sold at that price, but no more sold than also sold after the store raised the price to $70 a set.'' The store apparently concluded that price wasn't important.

3. Explain how each of the following would affect supply:

    a. A change in technology

    b. Implementation of environmental controls on a producer

    c. Imposition of an excise tax

4. Correct each of the following for errors in economic analysis:

    a. From *The Wall Street Journal,* September 18, 1980: ''University of Chicago Press offers a 'Year of Economists' engagement calendar. Each week features a picture of an economist and an excerpt from his writings. Everyone from Adam Smith to Gustav von Schmoller gets his say. But will demand equal supply when the price is $6.95 a copy?''

    b. From *The Washington Post,* October 8, 1976: ''Supply of Lettuce Dwindles as Price Soars Here.''

    c. From *The Wall Street Journal,* February 24, 1983: ''Energy Outlook: Oil Price Cuts Appear Unlikely to Bring Back Old Levels of Demand.''

    d. From *The Wall Street Journal,* September 16, 1981: ''Commodities: Medium-Term Uranium Price Rise Seen as Supply, Demand Start to Come in Line.''

5. Draw hypothetical demand and supply curves for beef.

    a. Show and explain the equilibrium quantity and price. Show and explain the effects of (1) a support price and (2) a price ceiling.

    b. What would be the effects on price and quantity exchanged of an epidemic of hoof-and-mouth disease?

    c. Show and explain the effects of a consumer boycott on the price and quantity exchanged.

    d. How would a prohibition of beef imports affect demand, supply, price, and quantity exchanged?

6. Suppose that the carpenters in a large city are unorganized and that there are many employers of carpenters' labor.

    a. Under what circumstances would unionization and an increase in wage rates result in an increase in total wages paid to carpenters?

    b. Would all carpenters who want to work be able to find employment? Explain.

    c. Will a wage rate increase always raise the total wage bill of the carpenters?

*7. Beginning with the 1985 spring semester, the nine 2-year junior colleges in the Los Angeles area imposed a $50-per-semester fee for a full load of courses. Previously, there was no tuition charge. Enrollment declined 18 percent relative to that of the previous year. Another fee of $20 was imposed on students who dropped more than one course after the first month of classes. Classes had begun the previous fall semester two weeks earlier than normal—in mid-August rather than early September—on the ''early semester'' system designed to allow students to complete the fall semester before the Christmas recess, so the spring semester also began about two weeks early. (David G. Savage, ''Junior Colleges in L.A. Bracing for New Drop in Rolls,'' *Los Angeles Times,* January 9, 1985; ''L.A. Community College Enrollment Falls 18%,'' *Los Angeles Times,* March 7, 1985.)

    Assume that the colleges hire you as an economist to make a ''quick and dirty'' estimate of elasticity based on Equation 3.3. Explain the complexities of this seemingly simple assignment and why an estimate cannot be made with the available data.

_____

8. An article in *The Wall Street Journal,* March 16, 1981, states: "And the rule of thumb in the pork business is that a 10% cut in production leads to a 30% rise in prices. Because of labor and transportation costs and retail price markups, that translates into a rise in the retail price of about 12%." What information does this give you about the price elasticity of demand for pork at retail in 1981?

"Wholesale" ← [handwritten annotation pointing to "30% rise in prices"]

*9. Would you predict that the distribution of tickets and the rules to prevent scalping would have differed if the Olympics committee had contracted with a large merchandising organization such as Sears to sell its tickets? Consider rigidity of the rules, presale information regarding ticket prices and seat locations, and the average price of tickets.

*10. Under the "package deal" rules for tickets that the Olympics committee established, tickets to the lesser-demanded, lower-priced events could be bought without purchasing tickets to the premiere, higher-priced events. But tickets to the higher-priced events could not be bought without purchasing tickets to the cheaper events.
    a. Did this system increase the price of the cheaper tickets or the best tickets? Explain.
    b. Which demand would you predict was less elastic: tickets for the higher-priced events or for the cheaper events?

Chapter 4

POLICY APPLICATIONS OF THE MODEL

Chapter Outline

Agricultural Price Supports

Oil and Gasoline Price Ceilings
    Consequences of Price Ceilings
    Consequences of Price Decontrol

Economic Effects of an Excise Tax

"Pricing" M.B.A. Classes

We conclude the Part One review of basic economic concepts and principles with some important current applications of those fundamentals. The competitive market model is applicable to a variety of public policies and everyday economic events. This chapter, unlike other chapters, is comprised entirely of applications. Here we focus on such current applications as (1) agricultural price supports, (2) oil and gasoline price ceilings, (3) the economic effects of an excise tax, and (4) a system for pricing seats in university classes. Many public policies are devised and promulgated with the express aim of correcting inequities in income distribution. However, when we use the model as an analytical tool, we find that the results of these measures are not always what they are expected to be.

AGRICULTURAL PRICE SUPPORTS

price floor
An administered level below which the price of an item is not allowed to fall.

The outstanding example of **price floors,** or minimum price policies, imposed by government is the agricultural price support program developed by the federal government during and since the Great Depression of the 1930s. Prices of farm products sold are thought by proponents of support programs to be too low relative to the prices of products that farmers buy; that is, they are considered to be inequitable. These relatively low farm prices are deemed an important factor in causing per capita farm income to be lower than the average per capita income in the United States. Consequently, price supports on a wide range of agricultural products have been authorized by Congress to be used as a partial answer to the farm income problem.

The most important support program historically—the storage and loan program—is illustrated in Figure 4.1 with respect to wheat. In an uncontrolled market, with the price free to move, the equilibrium price level is p per bushel, and the quantity exchanged is X bushels per year when demand and supply are DD and SS, respectively. Suppose that price p is thought to be relatively too low, and a support price is set at p_1. The government supports the price effectively by purchasing the wheat that farmers cannot sell at price p_1.[1] In Figure 4.1 consumers will buy X_1 bushels per year, leaving a surplus of X_1X_1' for the government to acquire.

In recent years Congress has added a per-bushel subsidy to the storage and loan program, guaranteeing farmers a higher price than the loan price. This target price is shown in Figure 4.1 as p_2, and farmers are paid a cash sum of

---

[1]Under the various Agricultural Adjustment Acts, the support price has been maintained by means of a storage and loan program. A farmer, instead of selling wheat in the market at price p, can obtain a loan on the wheat from the government at price p_1 per bushel, provided the farmer puts the wheat in storage in government-approved facilities. When the loan is due, the farmer can either sell the wheat and repay it or turn it over to the government as repayment in full. What would be done if the market price of wheat were above p_1 when repayment was due? What would the farmer do if it were below p_1? In effect, the government is guaranteeing that the price will not fall below p_1. Farmers sell what they can in the market at that price, and, in essence, the government buys the surplus.

**Figure 4.1
Effects of
Agricultural Price
Supports**

If the price of wheat is supported at p_1 by means of a storage and loan program, a surplus of X_1X_1' bushels per year is generated and acquired by the government. A target price of p_2, superimposed on the storage and loan price and paid as a direct subsidy to farmers, induces them to increase output to X_2, increasing the surplus to X_1X_2 bushels per year.

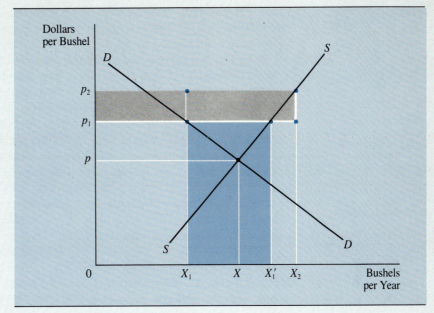

p_1p_2 per bushel over and above the loan price. This induces them to increase their output level to X_2, augmenting the surpluses and increasing the amounts put in storage.

A support price will be effective only if it is above the equilibrium level; and if it is effective, surpluses will occur. If it were below p, shortages would induce buyers to bid the price up to the equilibrium level so that the support price would not be effective. Thus, it will be effective only at price levels above p. Yet members of Congress, government officials, farmers, and most of the general public profess amazement that surpluses accumulate from a price-support program and deduce from the existence of surpluses that something about the program is not being handled properly.

The government has tried to handle surplus problems partly through supply restrictions. Acreage reductions by individual farmers have been required as a condition of eligibility for the loan program and for target price subsidies. The most extensive acreage restriction in history occurred in 1983 under the Payment In Kind (PIK) program. Farmers were paid in government-owned wheat to add to their acreage reductions, with the amount paid per acre depending upon the farmer's average wheat yield. Farmers compensate partially for acreage reductions by setting aside the least productive acres and fertilizing the used acres more heavily. Although it was supposed to save the taxpayer money, PIK wound up costing six times what was expected.

Costs to the taxpayer also rose owing to the schedule of loan prices that was established by law in 1981 for the next five years. Commodity prices had increased in the 1970s because of world crop failures and inflation, and the "experts" expected this trend to continue. Instead, world commodity prices plunged in the 1980s, so farmers let the government keep the crops rather than repay their "loans." The government bought more wheat than planned, and paid more for it than it was worth.

The government attempts to reduce surpluses by subsidizing school lunches, food stamps, and food exports. But these programs make only a dent in the surpluses. In 1986, the U.S. had enough wheat stored to make 27 loaves of bread for each of the world's 4.9 billion inhabitants, and enough milk, cheese, and butter to give about nine pounds' worth to every American.[2] The government wants to give away part of the dairy surplus to low-income families. But dairy farmers fear that donations will reduce commercial sales, and in response to their concerns Congress in 1986 ordered the U.S. Department of Agriculture to study the matter. The department found that every 100 pounds of cheese donated reduced commercial sales by 40 pounds, and every 100 pounds of margarine donated reduced retail sales by about 80 pounds.[3] One need not wonder why surpluses stay high.

In 1985, the Reagan Administration attempted to phase out target prices gradually and replace them with the price system. The following column from *The Wall Street Journal* shows why Congress resisted. By mid-1986, just six months after the new law was adopted, experts estimated that it would cost taxpayers 20 percent more than had been expected.

The farm problem in the daily headlines and on the network news in 1986 was not surpluses but bankruptcies. Creditors auctioned off family farms, and some owners became renters. The source of this problem was the rising crop prices of the 1970s, which increased the value of farmland. Land values rose so much that some farmers succumbed to the temptation to use their land as collateral for bigger mortgages. They expected rising crop prices to generate enough income to pay the interest and more inflation to reduce the value of their debts. Their gambles on continued inflation were like others' speculation in gold, real estate, and collectibles throughout the 1970s.

It was a mistaken gamble. Food prices plummeted in the 1980s, and the stronger dollar in terms of foreign currencies made U.S. food more expensive to foreign countries (until 1985 when the dollar's value started to decline). Thus, values of farmland declined from their 1980 levels. Not all farmers were in dire straits—just the 20 percent or so who literally "bet the farm" on continued inflation instead of anticipating disinflation.

The real farm problem is that our economy allocates too much of its resources to this purpose. The U.S. farm population declined from over 30 million in the 1930s to about 5.5 million in the early 1980s. Further reductions must occur for surpluses to shrink. Subsidies perpetuate the real farm problem by encouraging farmers to either keep land idle or allocate it to growing what the

---

[2]Ford S. Worth, "Getting Uncle Sam Off the Farm," *Fortune,* March 18, 1985, 128–132; and Wendy L. Wall and Charles F. McCoy, "New Farm Law Raises Federal Costs and Fails to Solve Big Problem," *The Wall Street Journal,* June 17, 1986.

[3]"Free Food Hurts Sales, Study Says," *Daily Oklahoman,* July 23, 1986.

price system says should not be grown. The demand for food is not strong because families are smaller, and the nature of food demand has changed sharply. For example, too many farmers continue to produce grain to feed cattle that are redundant now that the demand for beef has declined. Reallocations will occur rapidly when changes in subsidies change farming incentives.[4]

In the meantime, some agricultural entrepreneurs facing high debt and falling prices for traditional crops have decided to make money by growing what consumers want rather than what they don't want. In suburban New England, small farms sell branded vegetables, fruit, poultry, eggs, and milk at farmers' markets. Roadside stands are found in suburban California, Ohio, Michigan, New York, and along the eastern seaboard. Around Los Angeles they sell strawberries and vegetables grown on adjacent land, citrus fruit from nearby orchards, and watermelons from Texas. The stands reappear each year, so they must be profitable.

Innovative farmers have also adjusted to new food demands. Some grow organic crops without pesticides or chemicals for health- and diet-conscious consumers. Others make up to $10,000 per acre by growing such high-value novelties as kiwi fruit or such exotics as white tomatoes and red pears. They are demanded by gourmet cooks, specialty food brokers, expensive restaurants, and upscale grocers. As one observer commented, ''Steak and potatoes are giving way to sushi and tofu.'' Supermarket produce departments, formerly ho-hum affairs, are now big attractions.[5] Unlike the wheat farmers, these entrepreneurs follow the price system rather than fight it.

OIL AND GASOLINE PRICE CEILINGS

For more than 25 years the United States followed energy policies that temporarily improved the current position of certain groups in society but had adverse long-run effects for the economy as a whole. In the late 1950s and the 1960s, the dominant policy was an ''oil import quota'' program, created under pressures from the lobbies of the domestic oil industry. It set quotas, or limits, on the amount of foreign oil that could be imported into the United States each year. This policy raised domestic oil prices somewhat by protecting American producers from foreign competition. However, the amounts by which prices were increased must have been relatively small, since gasoline was only about 30 cents per gallon during that period. The irony of the policy, however, was that it tended to induce an overly rapid rate of recovery from domestic reserves and thus contributed to an increased reliance on foreign supplies during the so-called

---

[4]Bruce Gardner, ''The Farm Problem and the Taxpayers' Problem,'' *AEI Economist* (June 1985): 1–4; Lindley H. Clark, Jr., ''Many Farmers Have It Rough but the Economy Will Survive,'' *The Wall Street Journal*, March 25, 1986.

[5]Bruce Keppel, ''Taste Goes Exotic—So Do Growers,'' *Los Angeles Times*, August 29, 1986; Robert Rodale, ''Finding Self-Reliance in the Market,'' *Rodale's Organic Gardening*, May 1986, 110–111; Jeff Cox, ''New Haute Cuisine,'' *Rodale's*, 68–75.

NEW FARM LAW RAISES FEDERAL COSTS AND FAILS TO SOLVE BIG PROBLEMS
by Wendy L. Wall and Charles F. McCoy, Staff Reporters of *The Wall Street Journal*

Jimmie White, a debt-swamped Iowa farmer cut adrift by his lenders, is using government payments to plant hundreds of acres of corn and soybeans this spring. Come harvest, he expects to unload his crop on Uncle Sam.

The government will have paid Mr. White to plant unneeded crops that it may well end up buying; those crops will add to already-mountainous grain surpluses, depressing prices and driving up government costs. And Mr. White? In bankruptcy court for the second time in three years and hounded by creditors trying to sell off his land, he sees a good chance that he will be out of farming within two years anyway. Much of his more than $400,000 in federally backed debt would probably go unpaid.

This wasn't what policy makers had in mind when they patched together a new five-year farm bill last December. The program slashes the levels at which the government props up prices of most major crops, a nervy gamble that falling prices will spur farm exports and shrink surpluses. In theory, crop prices will rebound once the gluts dwindle. Meanwhile, the law reaches deep into taxpayers' pockets to blunt the battering that further price drops will inflict on farmers.

Scars of Its Birth

But the bill emerged only after months of deal-cutting between Reagan-administration free-marketeers and farm-state congressmen. Critics say the program bears the scars of its birth. Some provisions of the program are contradictory, and it is at odds with other government policies, spending billions of dollars to do things for farmers that other programs spend billions to undo. It will give more federal money than ever to well-off farmers who don't need it to survive. And it won't make much of

a dent in the root causes of farm distress: too much crop, too many cows, too much debt.

Admittedly, the new program will do some good. It probably will increase U.S. farm exports moderately, and a new conservation reserve could take some 45 million acres of poor land out of production for years. The law also forestalls a collapse in farm-land prices that would further ravage troubled farm lenders. And the federal payments will allow some farmers to survive long enough to benefit from falling fuel and fertilizer prices.

Major Embarrassment

But even so, critics say, the new law is an ill-conceived patchwork that will waste billions of taxpayer dollars. "When we look back in a year or two, it will be a major embarrassment," says John Schnittker, a Washington consultant and former under-secretary of agriculture.

Mushrooming costs could prompt legislators to scrap much of the program earlier than originally intended. The Agriculture Department estimates farm-program outlays for the full five years at $80 billion, before any cuts required by the Gramm-Rudman deficit-reduction act. But cost overruns are almost inevitable. The department puts the cost for the first three years alone at $54 billion, but the Congressional Budget Office estimates $64 billion, and many economists guess perhaps $70 billion or more. The previous farm bill, budgeted at $11 billion, eventually cost nearly six times that over four years.

Where does all this money go? Huge chunks go to people who farm for fun or tax breaks, to foreign investors and to big time farmers with the financial muscle to survive on their own. In 1984, 15% of all federal handouts went to farmers with net worth exceeding $1 million,

according to the department; under the new farm program, they will get even more.

Varied Beneficiaries

Frederick Joseph, the chief executive of Drexel Burnham Lambert Inc., retreats every weekend from the big Wall Street firm to his 160-acre dairy farm in upstate New York. He says he is "troubled" by the economic impact of dairy price supports. But they will make the million pounds or so of milk that his farm will produce this year a lot more valuable.

Mohammed Aslam Khan grows rice in Butte City, Calif. He is a U.S. citizen, but four relatives, passive investors in the farm, aren't. They live in Faisalabad, Pakistan. Uncle Sam paid the four $152,010 for Mr. Khan's 1984 crop. Like other big rice, cotton, wheat and corn growers, the Khans will probably get even more this year. The new farm law exempts large portions of crop payments from limits on how much an individual can receive.

In Vincennes, Ind., Dennis Carnahan's family has pushed corn-production costs so low that they could probably turn a profit if the farm program were abolished. But the 33-year-old farmer figures that the program is "the best ball game in town." The Carnahans expect to collect $81,180 from the government for the corn grown on their 3,800-acre farm this year.

"Farmers are farming the government as well as the land," says John Baize, a soybean lobbyist.

Ironically, the new program is actually driving some big operators into the government fold. The policy sharply raises the stakes by slashing price supports—and thus market prices—for major crops, while increasing direct federal handouts to farmers who agree to idle some land.

Salyer American, a Corcoran,

Calif., corporation that runs one of the nation's largest cotton farms, hasn't participated in a farm program since the early 1970s. But this year, the company, anticipating steep declines in cotton prices, is signing on. It expects to glean more than $1 million from Uncle Sam, while diverting much of its "idled" land to other crops.

Two Time Bombs

Nevertheless, the two biggest time bombs now menacing agriculture, debt and overproduction, won't be defused.

The nation's farmers owe about $199 billion. About 75% of that is concentrated in the books of half of them, mostly operating the medium-sized family farms that policy makers aim to help.

But under the new farm law, only about 17 cents out of every federal dollar being spent goes to full-time farmers in desperate straits, says Frank Naylor, the newly appointed head of the Farm Credit Administration and a former undersecretary of agriculture. That is largely because federal payments are based on how much a farmer grows.

Many debt-soaked farmers will get just enough to put in one more crop but not enough to survive. Paul Harbaugh, a Kiowa, Kan., wheat grower, will use his record federal payments to pay for planting this year's crop. But he doesn't expect to be able to trim his $600,000 debt enough to stay in farming. All the farm law is going to do is "prolong the agony," the 36-year-old farmer says.

Huge Losses Likely

Failure to deal with the debt problem is likely to cause huge federal losses on top of the farm-bill expenditures themselves. Uncle Sam holds or backs nearly half of all farm debt,

including the shakiest part of it. That puts taxpayers in triple jeopardy.

Timothy Hartsock, an insolvent Ohio grain farmer, says the Farmers Home Administration recently wrote off a $200,000 loan that it backed for him in 1984. But, cut off by his lenders, he used fat federal payments to sow thousands of acres of corn and soybeans this spring. When the crop is reaped, he expects to get more money for shoveling it into storage bins.

Those bins are already bursting. Last fall, mountains of excess corn literally buried Main Street in some Midwestern towns. Surplus cotton stuffs Southern warehouses. And as the winter wheat harvest began last month, the U.S. already had enough wheat to make 27 loaves of bread for each of the world's 4.9 billion inhabitants.

Export Problems

The mammoth gluts guarantee that prices will stay low while government costs soar. And exports won't rise enough to substantially shrink the stockpiles anytime soon, economists say. Although lower price supports should make the U.S. more competitive abroad, rivals such as Argentina and the European Community are expected to cut their prices to hang onto markets. Even one-time importing nations have begun to export food.

Meanwhile, the program encourages U.S. farmers to plant. Government subsidies are based on the amount farmers produce. With federal payments guaranteed, many farmers plant every permissible patch, regardless of economics.

In Indiana, Mr. Carnahan says his leased river-bottom land probably "would have grown weeds this summer" were it not for the program; otherwise, the land, costly to farm, wouldn't be profitable.

Dairy Policy

Dairy policy similarly chases its tail. The Agriculture Department is spending $1.8 billion to get some dairymen to kill their cows and quit the business; that program is supposed to slash milk-product surpluses that the government is forced to buy. But other farm-bill provisions will make milk production more profitable and encourage the remaining farmers to expand their herds. Meanwhile, pressured by cattlemen, Uncle Sam is buying up meat to ease a glut caused by slaughtering dairy cows.

The farm law is at odds with other government policies, too. The program will dish out $1 billion in subsidies to help spur U.S. farm exports. But the Reagan administration has barred one of farmers' biggest potential customers, the Soviet Union, from the export-subsidy program; irritated by this move, the Soviets have steered clear of U.S. wheat markets.

The bill seeks to recapture markets lost to cheap farm exports from Third World debtors such as Argentina and Brazil; but the Treasury Department opposes anything that might cut into those exports and crimp debt payments to the banks. Federal water programs pour out billions of dollars so that farmers can produce heaps of cotton and other surplus crops where only cactus would otherwise grow.

The new farm legislation treats some problems with heavier doses of old medicines that have never proved a cure. For instance, farmers have to idle more land than in the past to get subsidies. But Don Sutter, a heavily indebted Iowa farmer, says that won't stop him from reaping a near-record corn crop. "I'll idle the wet spots, the patches, the rocky ground that don't grow anything anyway," he says. "You just do whatever you can to outsmart them. It's not hard."

energy crisis of the 1970s. (Would it have made more sense to have imported larger quantities of foreign oil when it was relatively cheaper, leaving larger domestic reserves for the era when foreign oil would become relatively more expensive?)

The import quota policy, which supported oil prices when energy was relatively abundant, was followed by price ceilings when supplies became relatively scarce in the 1970s. Growing affluence (rising incomes) in the United States caused the demand for oil to increase over time. Supply, too, was increasing, but not as fast as demand. Under these circumstances the price per barrel would be expected to rise. Gasoline, the most important petroleum product, was subjected to some degree of price controls from August 1971 through March 1974. Before the autumn of 1973 there had been some spot shortages, but with the Middle East embargo on crude oil shipments to the United States in the fall and winter of 1973–74 shortages of gasoline suddenly became acute. These triggered great public and congressional pressure on the Federal Energy Office (later, the Department of Energy) to hold the line on the price of gasoline so that the poor as well as the rich could have access to available supplies.

Consequences of Price Ceilings

price ceiling
An administered level above which the price of an item is not allowed to rise.

Effective **price ceilings** ensure that shortages will persist so long as the controlled price is below the equilibrium market price. In Figure 4.2, DD and SS represent the demand and supply curves for gasoline in July 1971, with p as the equilibrium price. Suppose that by October 1973 demand had increased to D_1D_1 and supply to S_1S_1. If the price was controlled at p cents per gallon, a monthly shortage of X_2X_1 gallons occurred. Suppose that an embargo on, or curtailment of, shipments of crude oil to the United States shifted the supply curve of gasoline back to SS. The shortage then became XX_1 gallons per month.

When the available supplies of a commodity fall short of the quantities that demanders want, a rationing problem emerges. If the price of gasoline had been permitted to rise to p_3, the quantity available per month would have been X_3. At that price consumers would have limited themselves *voluntarily* to that amount, and no rationing problem would have been evident. An equilibrium market price induces consumers to limit themselves to the supplies available. With the price controlled at p, however, the price of gasoline could no longer perform its rationing function.

Having created the shortages with price controls, the federal government was faced with the task of rationing available supplies by nonprice means. A number of devices were employed at different times. One of the first was a ban on Sunday sales of gasoline. Later, retailers were given broad discretionary powers as to which buyers could get gasoline, and how much, at the controlled price. This led to much arbitrary conduct—restricted hours of selling that created long and wasteful gas lines at the pump, purchase limits of five gallons that increased wasteful driving to and from filling stations, and preferential treatment to long-standing customers. These practices produced considerable discontent among customers, and in some cases violence became the nonprice method by

Figure 4.2
Effects of Price Controls on Gasoline

Let an increase in demand for gasoline from *DD* to D_1D_1 exceed an increase in supply from *SS* to S_1S_1. A price ceiling fixed at *p* brings about a shortage of X_2X_1 per month. If an embargo on oil imports is now imposed, shifting the supply curve to the left to *SS*, the shortage is increased to XX_1.

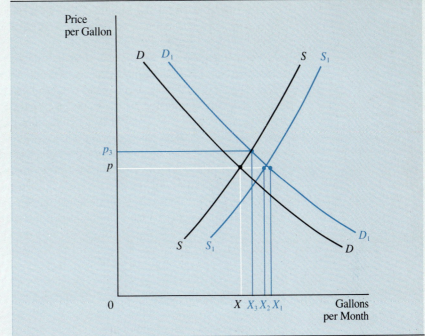

which scarce supplies were rationed. There were fistfights between anxious buyers, "fender-bender" accidents as drivers vied for better places in the gas queue, and occasional quarrels between customers and station personnel when gas lines were arbitrarily terminated. Some states adopted an "odd-even" method of rationing, in which cars with license plates ending in an odd-numbered digit could gas up only on odd-numbered days of the month. But this plan had mixed results. Although intended to shorten gas lines on any given day, it induced motorists to fill up their tanks on every possible day that they could do so. Many more tanks were "topped off" than would have been otherwise, and much gas still was wasted in queuing.

Did the controls help people obtain gasoline at "reasonable" prices? The answer turned upon the costs of queuing that each customer faced—for example, the cost of having to wake up extraordinarily early in order to get gas before going to work. People accustomed to getting up early may have obtained gasoline at relatively lower costs with price controls than they would have without them, since on the average they lost less valuable time in lines. But others, forced to take time off from work or to adopt other costly behavior in order to be at the station during its restricted operating hours, could have been net losers from price controls, depending upon the value of the time that they gave up. For example, if the controlled price of gas was $.75 per gallon and the average purchase 10 gallons, the total sale amounted to $7.50. But if the buyer's time was worth $7.50 per hour and it was necessary to wait in line an hour to make the purchase, the total cost to the consumer became $15 rather than $7.50, and the effective price per gallon was $1.50 rather than $.75. Under these circumstances the advantages of price controls were illusory, and many customers would have been better off without them.

Even though the general price controls established on August 15, 1971, were lifted in 1974, gasoline prices continued to be controlled. During the 1974–79 period, market gasoline prices remained generally below the controlled levels. But the suspension of crude oil sales by Iran in early 1979 and the consequent dramatic rise in OPEC crude oil prices caused the market prices of gasoline to rise sharply. Shortages and long gas lines reappeared wherever the equilibrium price was superceded by the controlled price. The situation was made worse in 1979 by Department of Energy rules that required refiners to produce more heating oil relative to gasoline than they would have preferred and by a regional "allocation" formula that funneled more gasoline to areas of lower population density than to more densely populated areas.

Consequences of Price Decontrol

The occasional acute shortages of gasoline and chronic shortages of domestically produced crude oil created by controls rekindled a national debate over decontrol of crude oil and petroleum product prices. Favoring decontrol were many economists concerned with economic wastes from nonprice rationing, some officials in the Department of Energy who saw the difficulties in trying to manage the production and distribution of crude oil and petroleum products by regulation rather than by market forces, domestic oil companies who saw the possibility of greater net earnings if prices were decontrolled, and members of Congress from oil-producing states. Opposing decontrol were certain consumer groups who did not believe higher petroleum product prices would yield much of an increase in oil production and members of Congress from non-oil-producing states who thought their constituents could get gasoline and fuel oil at lower prices with price controls with little or no diminution in quantities supplied.

Much of the debate over decontrol of domestic crude oil and gasoline prices turned implicitly on the issue of elasticities of demand and supply. Proponents of decontrol argued as though demand elasticities for gasoline and for crude oil were relatively high, that is, the price increases engendered by decontrol would curtail consumption substantially. Many also stated that decontrol of domestic crude oil prices would increase the quantities supplied and curtail American dependence on foreign oil. Opponents of decontrol took a different stance. They argued as though demands for petroleum products and for crude oil were highly inelastic and that decontrol of prices would have little effect on consumption. They also claimed that most of the potential supplies of petroleum in the United States had already been discovered. Thus they maintained that decontrol would not result in any substantial reduction in our dependence on foreign oil—it would result only in "windfall" profits for oil companies. Government action emerging from the debate was a compromise, resulting in a three-year, three-step decontrol process coupled with a $225 billion excise tax levied on oil producers.

Decontrol of oil prices brought about to a large degree the results its proponents predicted. Higher energy prices caused people to drive less, buy smaller cars, weatherize their houses, and use less fuel. Domestic oil production increased and oil imports decreased. OPEC's success spawned new discoveries and more production by countries outside OPEC, such as Britain, Mexico, Norway, and the Soviet Union. Also, OPEC could not control the typical forces within cartels that lead to overproduction, which we will discuss in detail in Chapter 13. Oil prices began to collapse in November 1985, falling from $31 per barrel to under $10 by mid-1986. World inventories were so high that oil entrepreneurs cut staffs, reduced exploration, and sold some refineries. Their prospects, once so rosy, became debatable.

It is not yet clear whether politicians have learned how dysfunctional it is to prevent the price system from allocating oil. In 1986, Vice President George Bush, embarking on a trip to Saudi Arabia, announced that falling oil prices would cause domestic problems in the United States and implied that the Reagan administration might have to abandon its support for free-market oil prices, which the administration subsequently said it would never do.[6] If a price-support or oil import–quota program is brought back, however, then U.S. energy policy will have come full circle—from the price controls of the 1970s and early 1980s to the import restrictions and price supports of the late 1950s and the 1960s. Many of the economic misallocations we have described in this chapter, and the social divisiveness that accompanies them, will reoccur.

ECONOMIC EFFECTS OF AN EXCISE TAX

excise tax
A per unit tax on an item, which may be a specific tax based on the physical unit of the item or an *ad valorem* tax based on its price.

A classic application of the competitive market model is its use in analyzing the incidence of an excise tax placed on a good or service. An **excise tax** may be a given amount per unit of product, such as a state gasoline tax, or it may be a percentage of the selling price of the product, such as a state sales tax. The former is called a *specific tax;* the latter is termed an *ad valorem* tax. The analysis is essentially the same for either type, but since the specific tax is a little easier to manipulate graphically, we shall focus our discussion on it.

One of the 1980 presidential candidates advocated a federal gasoline tax of $.50 per gallon to induce petroleum conservation. Figure 4.3 illustrates the mechanics of such a proposal and suggests why it was not popular among voters. Suppose there are no price controls on gasoline. The equilibrium price is p per gallon, and the equilibrium quantity is X gallons per week. Now let t represent a specific tax placed on gasoline.

tax incidence
The distribution of a tax among economic units.

How much of the tax is passed on to buyers? How much of it must be paid by sellers? Does the **tax incidence** depend on from whom the tax is collected? Many people think so.

Consider first the case in which the tax is collected from sellers. In Figure 4.3(a) the supply curve SS shows the amounts per gallon that sellers as a group

_____

[6]Robert W. Merry and Michael Siconolfi, ''Reagan Aides Dispute Bush and Affirm Free-Market Oil Policy; Prices Up Again,'' *The Wall Street Journal,* April 8, 1986.

Figure 4.3   The Incidence of an Excise Tax on Gasoline

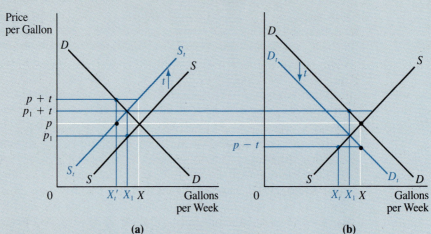

(a)   (b)

The incidence of an excise tax does not depend on whether it is collected from sellers or buyers. In panel (a) the tax is collected from sellers and has the effect of shifting the supply curve upward by the amount of the tax. The difference between $p_1 + t$ and p represents the amount of the tax passed on to buyers, while $p_1 p$ is the amount paid by sellers. As panel (b) shows, collecting the tax from buyers shifts the demand curve downward by the amount of the tax. The incidence on buyers and on sellers is the same as in panel (a).

must receive to induce them to place on the market the various quantities that comprise the horizontal axis of the diagram. Thus, imposition of tax t simply shifts the supply curve upward by the amount of the tax, to $S_t S_t$. If sellers are to be induced to place X gallons per week on the market, they must receive amount p per gallon for themselves; that makes it necessary for them to collect $p + t$ from buyers. However, buyers will not take X gallons per week at a price, including tax, of $p + t$ per gallon. At this level of expenditure per gallon the demand curve shows that they will take X_t' only, leaving a surplus of $X_t' X$ per week on sellers' hands. Undercutting by individual sellers will move the price plus tax down to level $p_1 + t$, at which buyers will take the entire quantity X_1 that sellers will offer at a price, not including the tax, of p_1. The difference between p and $p_1 + t$ shows the amount of the tax that is passed along to buyers. The difference between p_1 and p shows the amount of the tax that must be borne by sellers.

The incidence will be exactly the same if the tax is collected from buyers instead of from sellers. The demand and supply curves, DD and SS, in Figure 4.3(b) are identical to those of Figure 4.3(a). Consider next that DD represents the outlays per gallon that consumers are willing to pay for each of the various quantities per week, measured along the horizontal axis. The demand curve from the consumers' viewpoint is not affected by the imposition of tax t, but from the sellers' viewpoint the tax shifts the demand curve they face downward by the amount of the tax to D_tD_t. Consumers will buy X gallons per week, only, if they are required to pay p per gallon. After the imposition of the tax, only $p - t$ per gallon would be left for sellers; consequently, sellers' offerings would be reduced to X_t, leaving a shortage of X_tX. Bidding for the short supply by buyers will increase the price received by sellers to p_1. Quantity exchanged will be X_1, and buyers will be paying a total of $p_1 + t$ per gallon. The incidence of the tax is the same as in the previous case. Buyers now pay $(p_1 + t) - p$ per gallon more than they did before tax; sellers receive $p - p_1$ less.

Who bears the greatest tax incidence—sellers or buyers? It depends on the elasticities of demand and supply. Figure 4.3 shows that the tax is borne partly by buyers in the form of a higher price *including the tax* and partly by sellers in the form of a lower price *net of the tax*. If the demand curve were perfectly elastic, or if the supply curve were perfectly inelastic, the incidence would be entirely on sellers. On the other hand, if the demand curve were perfectly inelastic, or if the supply curve were perfectly elastic, the incidence would be entirely on buyers. (Draw these diagrams for yourself to test your understanding of elasticity concepts.) Generally, then, buyers bear a greater proportion of the tax the less elastic the demand curve is and/or the more elastic the supply curve is in the neighborhood of the price change. Similarly, sellers bear a greater proportion of the tax the more elastic the demand curve and/or the less elastic the supply in the neighborhood of the price change.

Would an excise tax on gasoline be a useful measure to increase the well-being of the general public? It would indeed cause consumers to reduce consumption from X to X_1 gallons per week. But the tax also imposes extra costs on producers, reducing both their outputs and their earnings. Consumers would get less gasoline at higher prices. Producers would place less gasoline on the market and would have lower earnings. Do these results imply higher levels of well-being for the public?

"PRICING" M.B.A. CLASSES

Take a quick mental survey of the goods and services that your university or college rations by price as opposed to queuing or some other method of nonprice competition. The price-rationed group probably includes meals at student restaurants, items at the student bookstore, and tickets for movies or athletic events. The nonprice-rationed group probably includes the courses that you want to take, seats in classes of popular instructors when more than one person teaches the subject, certain widely used books that your library has in short supply, interviews for job-searching seniors with popular companies, and better rooms in the most popular student residence halls. If this list is correct, some of the most important activities of college life are rationed without prices.

Consider a student's problem of getting the courses or instructors wanted most when registration is determined by one of the traditional nonprice meth-

MBA STUDENTS LEARN THE COST OF EDUCATION
by John Curley, Staff Reporter of *The Wall Street Journal*

Summer-session students registering at the University of Chicago business school today won't have to line up at dawn or take their chances in a lottery to get the classes they want. They'll *buy* their courses.

Starting today, students are bidding for the courses they want with points handed out by the dean's office. How much will it take to get into a popular professor's class? "The market will decide the price," says Stephen T. Schreiber, associate dean of students.

Going Rate for Courses

Point Cost*	Professor	Course
11,000	Merton H. Miller	Corporate Finance
8,000	James H. Lorie	Topics in Investment
4,000	Edward T. Lazear	Micro-economics
2,000	Hillel J. Einhorn	Cognitive Models of Judgement
1,500	Robert Blattberg	Marketing
1,000	Jonathan E. Ingersoll	Investment

Prices as of last fall

Classes won't be the only commodities getting the capitalist treatment. Students will also bid for computer time and interviews with potential employers.

Campus Trend

The innovation is typical of those that many business schools are trying in response to student pressure for fairer means of allocation. Stanford business school has heeded students' request for a ranking system that tries to match each student with seven companies he or she wants to talk to. Northwestern's school of manage-ment, meanwhile, has melded the Chicago and Stanford systems: It gives students 100 points every two weeks to bid for interviews, plus five "priority points" that all but assure a student at least a few important interviews.

Chicago doesn't believe in that kind of safety net. It prefers a free-market system that "really forces students to choose their priorities and allocate their resources," as Mr. Schreiber puts it.

At registration, students get 8,000 points plus 1,000 for each course they have completed. Then they submit four possible course schedules, telling how much they're bidding for each. If a class will hold, say, 100 students, the 100 highest bidders will get in. However, in a slight softening of the harsh rules in the real world, students won't be charged as much as they bid but only as much as the 100th-place bidder offered.

The system was tried out last March in the school's night program in downtown Chicago. Of the 1,000 students involved, only 34 didn't get any of their choices. The school says that was a marked improvement from the old system, under which students who had completed the most courses got to sign up first, but had to go in alphabetical order.

Free to Choose

"I really think it's the way to do things," says Michael VonderPorten, a first-year student. "It gives you more control over your life."

It also provides the faculty a handy way to practice what it preaches. Richard J. Thain, dean for career development and counseling, says that "all of us have been so tickled, because it's such a good ex-ample of putting the market philosophy to work." Besides, it helps him know which companies interest students most. And other faculty members say the bidding makes it easier to allocate classroom space.

There still are problems to be ironed out. New students may be confused and unable to estimate the market price for classes or job interviews. That happened at the night-school trial run, when some students bid only 50 points for courses that were selling for 200 or 300 points. (The highest bid, by the way, was 40,000 points for Merton Miller's corporation-finance class; but 11,000 was enough to win a place.)

Dean Schreiber concedes the problems. "Students don't understand all the details, which is logical, since *we* don't understand all the details," he says. The administration is thinking about scheduling classes on how to bid for classes.

To bid for job interviews, students are given a basic ration of 350 points. They get an added 221 points each fall and 371 more in the spring, when more companies come to campus. Two weeks before an interview, students punch their bids into a computer.

Dean Thain says recruiters like the system because it assures them that the people they're talking to are truly interested. It also helps them know how they're doing; noticing unusually low bids for a large indus-trial company two years ago, Mr. Thain advised its recruiters to change the job description from "foreman" to "production assistant," increase the salary and raise the concern's campus profile through beer parties and talks by executives. The next year the company hired three Chicago MBAs.

Source: "MBA Students Learn the Cost of Education," John Curley, *The Wall Street Journal,* May 18, 1981. Reprinted by permission of *The Wall Street Journal,* © Dow Jones & Company, Inc., 1981. All Rights Reserved.

Figure 4.4
Rationing Seats in a
University Class

Price p just fills the class
with students who value
each available seat at p
or more. If the fee per
seat in the class is less
than p, say p_1, a shortage
occurs—some students
for whom a seat is worth
less than p are induced to
take the class, and
queuing or some other
arbitrary method of
rationing must be used.

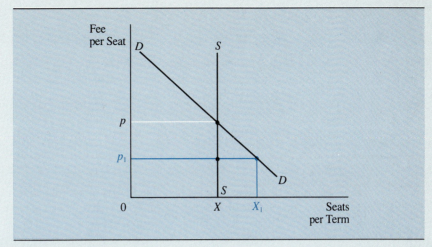

ods—by using the alphabet, by rewarding whoever is willing to stand longest
in line, or by having students hurry around campus to get instructor approval.
In Figure 4.4, assume that X is the fixed quantity of seats available in a popular
class scheduled for the coming semester. With the tuition or fee held at p_1,
below the market-clearing level p, the shortage at the beginning of registration
is the difference between X and X_1. Some seats are filled by students who would
have been willing to pay less than p if price had been the rationing device, while
queuing costs lead some students who would have been willing to pay p to take
other courses instead.

The following clipping from *The Wall Street Journal* suggests that students
have strong preferences for certain classes and instructors in the Master of
Business Administration degree program at the University of Chicago's School
of Business. Chicago removed price controls for classes by creating markets
through which students bid for them with points. Each semester, the school
offered a supply schedule of courses and class times, and students submitted
their demand schedules. The resulting allocation of courses and instructors
among students differed from what occurred when traditional nonprice rationing
methods were used. The market-clearing prices for different courses and instructors varied by as much as eleven to one. It was easier for students with intensely
strong preferences for certain classes and professors to get them by bidding than
by wasting time standing in lines.

Chicago allocated bigger point budgets to students who had completed more
classes. This was an equity adjustment in favor of senior students who had fewer
courses to complete and were likely to have relatively low elasticities of demand
for them. It parallels the practice of many universities and colleges that allow
seniors to register first under traditional methods of rationing.

Chicago considered establishing a class on how to bid for courses so that
entering students would not be at a disadvantage. In markets for most goods
and services in our economy, this information is acquired by trial and error

through repeat purchases. But the university, as the sole supplier of its courses, could provide this information more efficiently than if students attempted to research the subject individually.

Apparently Chicago's idea is popular among its students and is catching on at other institutions. The business schools at Stanford and Northwestern adopted point systems to allocate company interviews, and Princeton is using a similar system for all of its graduating seniors.[7]

_____ ## SUMMARY _____

The competitive market model provides useful insights into the effects of certain economic policymaking by both government and private firms. It shows that effective agricultural price supports of the storage and loan type will result in the accumulation of surpluses of the supported products. It also demonstrates that effective price ceilings create shortages that are exasperating to consumers and, in certain cases, politically divisive.

Application of the model to the problem of excise tax incidence shows that there is no difference if the tax is levied on buyers or on sellers but that the incidence of the tax on each group depends upon the relevant elasticities of supply or demand.

The University of Chicago's conversion from rationing seats in popular M.B.A. classes by queuing to "pricing" on the basis of points allocated to each student shows how sensitive resource allocation is to the method of rationing used.

Suggested Readings

Two useful surveys of U.S. agriculture are

Suits, Daniel B. "Agriculture." In *The Structure of American Industry,* 6th ed., edited by Walter Adams. New York: Macmillan, 1982.

Weiss, Leonard W. *Case Studies in American Industry.* 3d ed., Chap. 2. New York: John Wiley & Sons, 1980.

For another example of the misallocations caused by failure to charge market-clearing prices, see

Eckert, Ross D. *Airports and Congestion: A Problem of Misplaced Subsidies.* Washington, D.C.: American Enterprise Institute for Public Policy Research, 1972.

Problems and Questions for Discussion

1. If you owned a firm that produced fertilizers or farm equipment, would you favor (1) an acreage-reduction program in which wheat farmers are paid cash to idle acres, as under the scheme enacted in 1985; or (2) a program in which farmers are compensated with wheat from government inventories, as under the former PIK scheme? Explain.

_____

[7]Monci Jo Williams, "The Baby Bust Hits the Job Market," *Fortune,* May 27, 1985, 125.

2. Will the surpluses caused by the price support programs for wheat depicted in Figure 4.1 grow or decline if the demand curve is more elastic? Diagram and explain your results.

3. Suppose that a ceiling price of $2 per thousand cubic feet is placed on natural gas by the government and that the equilibrium price is above that level. Who is helped and who is hurt by the price ceiling? Would you advocate continuing the ceiling over time? Why or why not?

4. Usury laws limit the interest rate lenders may charge on installment loans. The purpose is to protect borrowers from ''gouging.'' During the 1970s, inflation drove equilibrium market interest rates above the 10 percent ceilings that many states imposed. (Eileen Alt Powell, ''Move to Ban Usury Ceilings Starts Fight over Federal Role, Gouging,'' *The Wall Street Journal,* January 7, 1982.)
   a. Over 40 states raised or abolished their usury ceilings. Why was this more common among states with lower ceilings?
   b. Are usury ceilings necessary to prevent gouging (i.e., charging a noncompetitive rate) on, say, new car loans? Make a list of local lenders. Would you judge that the local car loan market is competitive?

5. In the United States jurors are ''conscripted'' from the rolls of eligible voters, paid nominal wage rates for their time, and given less than full reimbursement for their expenses. Persons in some occupations, with travel plans, or with illnesses may be excused from duty.
   a. What effects would you expect the low pay to have on
      i. The willingness of people to serve as jurors?
      ii. The willingness of women as compared with men to be jurors this year? As compared with 1950?
      iii. The willingness of higher- as compared with lower-income persons to serve?
      iv. Diversity in jury composition?
   b. Those in jury pools often remark that much time is wasted waiting for lawyers and judges to act and because of the duplicate juries set up for certain trials. Do you think higher pay for jurors would affect the amount of person-hours wasted? Explain.
   c. Since the 1970s some firms have reimbursed employees serving as jurors up to maximums of 75 to 100 percent of wages lost from jury service. Why do you think firms take on this cost? Who do you think ultimately pays for it? Would you expect ''reimbursable'' wages on the average to be in wage categories as high as ''nonreimbursable'' wages? Compare your answers to those of Donald L. Martin in ''The Economics of Jury Conscription,'' *Journal of Political Economy* 80 (July 1972): 680–702.

6. During the inflation of the late 1970s, Los Angeles adopted rent controls to protect tenants from rents that seemed to escalate each time a rental building changed hands. The measure applied only to apartments and, to

avoid a reduction in the housing supply, exempted those apartment houses constructed after the controls took effect. What effects would you expect the controls to have on

a. Surpluses or shortages of apartments?

b. Conversion of apartments to condominiums?

c. Replacement of older but serviceable apartment houses by new ones?

d. Pressure from the community for increases in government-financed or subsidized housing?

e. The average cost of housing units in Los Angeles.

7. Santa Monica, Calif., where 80 percent of the residents rent apartments, has the nation's strongest rent control law. An elected Rent Control Board holds rent increases to about two-thirds of the rise in the Consumer Price Index. Owners may not evict tenants, convert apartments to condominiums, demolish buildings, or go out of business. The Ellis Act, a new California law, permits owners to idle buildings but not to allocate them to another use without the board's permission. Because of high maintenance and damage costs, some owners plan to idle buildings even though mortgage and property tax payments would continue. (Dave Larsen, "The Ellis Act: Going-Out-of-Business Bill for Santa Monica Landlords?", *Los Angeles Times,* June 22, 1986.)

a. Diagram and explain how the Ellis Act will affect the apartment shortage in Santa Monica.

b. Show in apartment demand-and-supply diagrams what will happen in nearby cities without rent control. With rent control.

c. Would you predict that Senator James Ellis represents one of the 18 California cities with rent control?

d. How would you expect the city of Santa Monica to discourage buildings from being idled under the new law?

8. Consider the payroll tax levied on both employers and employees to pay Social Security benefits. What would be the effect on a typical employee's take-home pay if the tax were collected entirely from employers? Entirely from employees?

9. What has the legalization of abortion done to the demand for and supply, price, quantity, and quality of that service?

10. In 1980, a study of gasoline demand in the United States, Canada, Japan, Britain, France, Italy, and West Germany by the International Monetary Fund estimated the average long-run price elasticity in the range of 0.7 to 1.4. ("How Low Gasoline Taxes Invite OPEC Increases," *Business Week,* May 26, 1980.)

a. All the European countries had higher excise tax rates on higher prices per gallon than the United States, and the revolution toward smaller cars already had occurred in Europe. Would you estimate that the long-run elasticity in the United States would have been at the upper or lower end of this range? Explain.

    b. Would the answer you gave to (a) support or undermine the arguments for energy price decontrol in the United States? Based on this information, would you have favored energy price decontrol at the time?

11. Based on the experience of pricing M.B.A. classes at the University of Chicago,
    a. Would you favor this approach at your college? Why?
    b. What would you guess the political support for such a change at your campus might be among (i) students, taking into account the different interests of freshmen and seniors; (ii) the faculty; and (iii) the registrar?
    c. Would you expect to find innovations like Chicago's more frequently at small colleges, large private universities, or large public universities? Explain.

THE UNDERPINNINGS OF DEMAND

Tʜᴇ demand curves for goods and services that were used in Chapters 3 and 4 are rooted in choices made by individuals or households. The more we know about how those choices are made and what affects them, the better we can understand the nuances of demand. In Part Two we develop the theory of choice and demand. In Chapters 5, 6, and 7 the analysis is focused on the individual consumer unit, but to complete the demand picture we look at it from the point of view of the individual business concern in Chapter 8.

The modern theory of demand is presented in Chapters 5 and 6. The indifference curve analysis, which forms the core of the modern theory, evolved from the utility approach to demand developed in the latter part of the nineteenth century; however, it is not dependent on the utility approach. Many economists shun the utility approach, or at least relegate it to a secondary position. Because we believe that it contains much of interest and importance we have developed it in detail in Chapter 7. But those who eschew its usefulness can omit it without loss of continuity.

Chapter 5

THE MODERN THEORY OF CONSUMER CHOICE

The theory of consumer choice provides a logical starting point for the systematic development of microeconomic principles. In this chapter we focus on indifference curve analysis, the general theory of consumer choice. Although indifference curve techniques date from the 1880s, they were not integrated into the main body of economic thought until the 1930s. A British economist, Francis Y. Edgeworth, introduced the concept in 1881.[1] Edgeworth's techniques, with some modification, were adopted by an Italian economist, Vilfredo Pareto, in 1906.[2] It remained for two British economists, John R. Hicks and R. G. D. Allen, to popularize and extend the use of indifference curve analysis in the 1930s,[3] and it has since become the central core of choice and demand theory.

THE CONSUMER'S PREFERENCES

We begin the study of an individual consumer's behavior by examining preferences.[4] These are summed up in graphic form as the consumer's *indifference map*. We then examine the main characteristics of the *indifference curves* that make up the indifference map.

The Consumer's Indifference Map

In the modern world, a consumer has available a large number of goods and services among which to express preferences. The number of possible combinations of goods confronting a consumer approaches infinity. What can be said in an analytical way about how the consumer views this wide range of possibilities?

In order to set up a formal analysis, it is necessary to specify the postulates underlying consumer behavior. We assume that

1. *The consumer is able to set up a preference ranking of the combinations available.* The person can determine which combinations are preferable to others and among which combinations he or she is indifferent.

2. *The consumer's preference ranking is consistent or transitive.* If combination *A* is preferred to combination *B* and combination *B* is preferred to combination *C*, then combination *A* must be preferred to combination *C*. Similarly, if combination *D* is equivalent to combination *E* and combination *E* is equivalent to combination *F*, then combination *D* must be equivalent to combination *F*.

---

[1]Francis Y. Edgeworth, *Mathematical Psychics* (London: C. K. Paul, 1881).

[2]Vilfredo Pareto, *Manuel d'économie politique* (Paris: V. Giard & E. Briere, 1909). The work was first published in Italian in 1906.

[3]John R. Hicks and R. G. D. Allen, ''A Reconsideration of the Theory of Value,'' *Economica,* New Series, No. 1 (February, May 1934): 52–76, 196–219.

[4]The basic consuming unit in an economy is more often a family than a single individual. The term *individual consumer* is used broadly to cover both families and unattached individuals.

3. *The consumer prefers more of any good or service to less of it;* that is, the consumer is not satiated with any one good.[5]

These postulates enable us to construct an individual consumer's indifference map. To simplify matters, we shall act as though the world contains only two goods—bread (*B*) and wine (*W*). The consumer is asked to rank the many possible available combinations, showing those preferred over others as well as those among which he or she is indifferent.

indifference curve or schedule
A curve or schedule showing the different combinations of two items among which a consumer is indifferent.

A set of combinations among which the consumer is indifferent forms an **indifference schedule** or **indifference curve.** If, for example, the consumer considers all the combinations listed in Figure 5.1(a) as equivalent to one another, these constitute an indifference schedule. Plotting these combinations (and all those intermediate to the ones in the schedule) in Figure 5.1(b), we have indifference curve U_1.

Although Figure 5.1(b) contains only two indifference curves, an infinite number can be drawn. The commodity space enclosed by the *B* and *W* axes contains all possible combinations of the two goods. A combination such as *G*, containing 5 loaves of *B* and 5 liters of *W*, will be preferred to combination *C* containing 4 loaves of *B* and 4 liters of *W*. (Remember postulate 3.) Other combinations equivalent to *G* can be located, and these trace out indifference curve U_2. In this manner we can draw as many indifference curves as we wish. All combinations on higher indifference curves—those farther from the origin—are preferable to those lying on lower indifference curves. The whole set of indifference curves constitutes the **indifference map** of the consumer.[6]

indifference map
A family of indifference curves showing the complete set of a consumer's tastes and preferences—the individual's preference rankings of different combinations and sets of combinations—for two items.

Indifference Curve Characteristics

A set of indifference curves exhibits three basic characteristics: (1) *the individual curves slope downward to the right;* (2) *they are nonintersecting;* and (3) *they are convex to the origin of the diagram.* These features will be considered in turn.

Downward slope to the right of indifference curves is ensured by the postulate that a consumer prefers more of a good to less of it. If an indifference

---

[5]Satiation with any one good is not impossible. We have all seen it occur temporarily with food, liquor, and other items. As we shall see, however, rational economic behavior usually rules out satiation with items that are not abundant enough to be had for the asking.

Also, there are items in the economy, like polluted water and garbage, of which the consumer desires less rather than more. These items are sometimes referred to as "bads" rather than "goods." Controls over them, such as purification and disposal services, become goods and services which we can assume the consumer prefers in greater rather than lesser amounts, up to their saturation levels.

[6]The consumer's preference function or indifference map for two goods, *X* and *Y*, can be represented by $U = f(x, y)$, in which *U* represents levels of preference expressed in ordinal terms only. The equation for one indifference curve is $U_1 = f(x, y)$, in which U_1 is a constant, that is, it represents a given level of preference. Other values assigned to *U* define other indifference curves, all of which make up the consumer's indifference map. These assigned values show the order of preference magnitudes, not absolute (measurable) magnitudes.

Figure 5.1   The Indifference Concept

(a) An Indifference Schedule

B (loaves)	W (liters)	Combination
3	7	A
4	4	C
5	2	D
6	1	E
7	½	F

(b) Indifference Curves

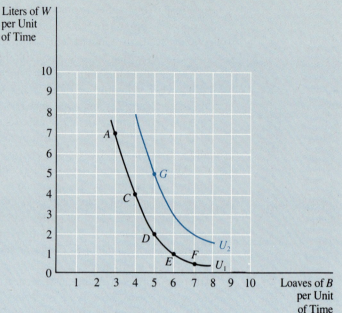

Panel (a) shows a schedule of combinations of B and W about which a consumer is indifferent. These are plotted in panel (b) to form indifference curve U_1. Indifference curve U_2 shows a preferred set of combinations, with the consumer indifferent to its various elements.

curve were horizontal, this would mean that the consumer is indifferent between two combinations both of which contain the same amount of one good, Y, but one of which contains a greater amount of another good, X. A curve could be horizontal only if the consumer were receiving enough X to be saturated with it; that is, additional units of X alone would add nothing to the person's total satisfaction. Similarly, if an indifference curve were vertical, this would mean that the two combinations of X and Y, both with the same amount of X but with one containing more Y than the other, yield equivalent satisfaction to the consumer. Again, this would be the case only if the consumer had reached a saturation point for Y. For the consumer to remain indifferent among combinations after giving up units of one commodity, the loss must be compensated for with additional units of another commodity. The result, shown graphically, is a curve that is downward sloping to the right.

Indifference curves are nonintersecting if the transitivity postulate holds. In Figure 5.2 we see the logical contradiction of intersecting curves. Combination C is preferred to combination A, and combination A is equivalent to combination

**Figure 5.2
Consequences of
Indifference Curve
Intersection**

A consumer who prefers
more to less will prefer
combination *C* to
combination *A*. But if U_1
and U_2 intersect, *A* is
equivalent to *B* and *C* is
equivalent to *B*, thus
violating the transitivity
postulate.

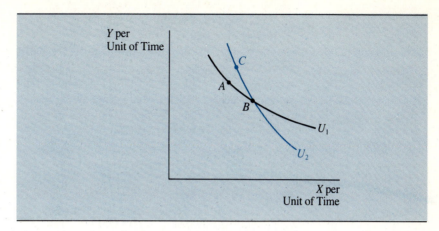

**marginal rate of
substitution**
The amount of one good
or service that a con-
sumer is just willing to
give up to obtain an ad-
ditional unit of another,
measured for any combi-
nation of goods and serv-
ices by the slope of the
indifference curve
through the point repre-
senting that combination.

B. But combination *C* is also equivalent to combination *B*. According to the transitivity postulate, *C* should be *preferred* to *B*. Thus, the intersection of indifference curves violates the transitivity postulate. To say that indifference curves are nonintersecting is not to say that they are parallel or that they are equidistant from each other. They may run farther apart at some points and closer together at others. The only restriction placed on them here is that they do not intersect.

We cannot prove conclusively at this point that indifference curves are convex to the origin, but we can show that they are likely to be so. To get at the issue, we introduce the **marginal rate of substitution** concept.

The marginal rate of substitution of one product for another, say of *X* for *Y*, is abbreviated as MRS_{xy} and is defined as the maximum amount of *Y* the consumer is willing to give up to get an additional unit of *X*—the trade-off between bundles of goods among which he or she is indifferent. For example, suppose that in Figure 5.1 the consumer is taking initially 7 liters of *W* and 3 loaves of *B*. To move to a consumption rate of 4 loaves of *B*, he or she would be just willing to give up the consumption of 3 liters of *W* per unit of time. The marginal rate of substitution for this move, or the MRS_{bw}, would be 3.

The more of one good and the less of another a consumer has, the more important units of the second become relative to units of the first. In Figure 5.3, the *X* axis is marked off in equal quantity units between *A* and *B*. At point *A*, the consumer would be willing to give up a relatively large amount of *Y* to get an additional unit of *X*. At point *B*, at which there is much more *X* and much less *Y* than at *A*, a unit of *Y* would be more important as compared with a unit of *X* than it was at point *A*, and the consumer would be willing to give up less *Y* to get an additional unit of *X*. At point *A* the indifference curve shows the consumer just willing to give up *CD* units of *Y* to get an additional unit of *X*. With more and more *X* and less and less *Y* per unit of time, the importance of a unit of *Y* becomes progressively greater as compared with that of a unit of *X*. The amounts of *Y* the consumer is just willing to give up to get additional units of X become progressively smaller; that is, the marginal rate of substitution of X for Y is decreasing.[7]

If the marginal rate of substitution of X for Y is decreasing, the indifference curve must be convex toward the origin. If it were constant, the amounts of Y the consumer would give up to get additional units of X would be constant instead of decreasing; the indifference curve would be a straight line sloping downward to the right. If the marginal rate of substitution were increasing, the indifference curve would be concave to the origin.[8]

Complementary and Substitute Relationships[9]

Indifference curve techniques allow us to examine complementary and substitute relationships in more depth than we did in Chapter 3. Suppose the consumer is no longer confined to a two-commodity world but has choices among X, Y, and a host of other goods and services. Let the quantities of the other goods and services be measured in money terms and X and Y be measured in physical terms such as bushels and pints. In Figure 5.4, monetary units M are measured on the vertical axis while the axes of the horizontal plane show units of Y and X. The consumer now has the options of substituting X for M, Y for M, and X for Y. If the consumption level of Y is zero, indifference curve AB represents combinations of M and X that yield to the consumer a given level of satisfaction. If the consumption level of X is zero, indifference curve BC shows combinations of M and Y that yield the *same* level of satisfaction as do those on AB. If the consumption level of Y is y_1, indifference curve A_1B_1 shows combinations of M and X that, together with y_1 of Y, yield the *same* level of satisfaction as do those on AB and BC. A family of curves, such as A_1B_1, one for each level of consumption of Y, can be drawn to trace out an *indifference surface* bounded by ABC that is convex toward the origin of the diagram.

---

[7]It may be helpful to work out the MRS_{bw} arithmetically between different points on indifference curve U_1 of Figure 5.1 before proceeding to the more abstract geometric representation of it in Figure 5.3.

[8]The total differential of the preference function of Footnote 6 is $dU = f_x dx + f_y dy$. For a given indifference curve $dU = 0$, so $0 = f_x dx + f_y dy$ and

$$-\frac{dy}{dx} = \frac{f_x}{f_y} = MRS_{xy}. \qquad \left[\frac{dy}{dx} \text{ is the slope of an indifference curve and must be negative.}\right]$$

To determine the curvature of an indifference curve, we look at the derivative of the MRS_{xy} with respect to x. Since $MRS_{xy} = -\frac{dy}{dx}$, then $\frac{d}{dx}(MRS_{xy}) = \frac{d}{dx}\left(-\frac{dy}{dx}\right) = -\frac{d^2y}{dx^2}$.

If $\frac{d^2y}{dx^2} > 0$, then $-\frac{d^2y}{dx^2} < 0$, or $\frac{d}{dx}(MRS_{xy}) < 0$, and the indifference curve is convex to the origin.

If $\frac{d^2y}{dx^2} < 0$, then $-\frac{d^2y}{dx^2} > 0$, or $\frac{d}{dx}(MRS_{xy}) > 0$, and the indifference curve is concave to the

origin. If $\frac{d^2y}{dx^2} = 0$, then $-\frac{d^2y}{dx^2} = 0$, or $\frac{d}{dx}(MRS_{xy}) = 0$, and the indifference curve

is linear.

[9]This subsection can be omitted without loss of continuity by anyone preferring the less precise and simpler definition of complements and substitutes contained in Chapter 3.

Figure 5.3
Diminishing Marginal Rate of Substitution

Since combination A contains relatively more Y and relatively less X than does combination B, a unit of Y is relatively less important and a unit of X is relatively more important to the consumer at A than at B. Consequently, the consumer would be willing to give up more Y to obtain an additional unit of X at A than at B.

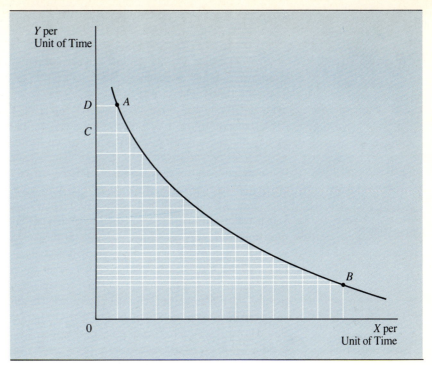

Figure 5.4
Substitutes and Complements

At a zero consumption level for Y, the consumer's MRS_{xm} at x_1 of X is measured by the slope of tangent ab. At a y_1 consumption level for Y, the consumer's MRS_{xm} at x_1 is measured by the slope of a_1b_1. The decrease in the MRS_{xm} at x_1 as the quantity of Y consumed increases indicates that the goods are substitutes—the consumer is willing to give up less and less money to obtain an additional unit of X; a unit of X is becoming less and less important.

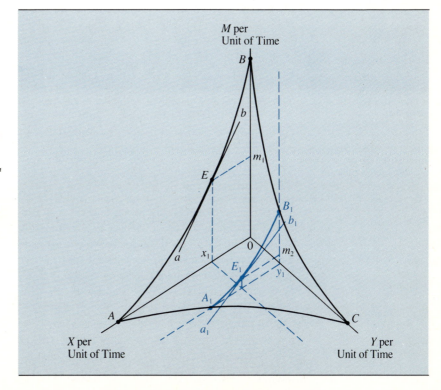

complementary goods
Goods related in such a way that an increase in the consumption of one, holding the consumer's satisfaction level and quantity consumed of the other constant, increases the marginal rate of substitution of the other for money.

substitute (competitive) goods
Goods related in such a way that an increase in the consumption of one, holding the consumer's satisfaction level and quantity consumed of the other constant, decreases the marginal rate of substitution of the other for money.

To determine whether X and Y are **complementary goods** or **substitute goods** we hold the consumer's satisfaction level constant; that is, we stay on a given indifference surface such as ABC. Suppose that initially the consumer is using no Y and has a combination of x_1 units of X and m_1 units of M. The MRS_{xm} at point E as measured by the slope of line ab shows the amount of money the consumer is just willing to give up for a unit of X at that point; that is, it shows the *money value* to the consumer of a unit of X. Now, holding the consumption level of X and the consumer's satisfaction level constant, we increase the amount of Y consumed to y_1. To compensate for the increased consumption of Y, the amount of money in the new combination is reduced to m_2. Has the increase in the consumption of Y increased or reduced the money value of a unit of X? The MRS_{xm} at point E_1 as measured by the slope of line a_1b_1 provides the answer. The MRS_{xm} at E_1 is less than the MRS_{xm} at E, meaning that the increase in the consumption of Y, with the consumption level of X and the consumer's satisfaction level held constant, has caused a decrease in the money value of a unit of X to the consumer. Therefore, good Y is a *substitute* for good X. If the MRS_{xm} at E_1 had been greater than the MRS_{xm} at E (and this will be the case for many goods), then good Y would be a *complement* to good X.

Examples of complementary and substitute goods abound in the world around us. Tennis rackets and tennis balls, bread and jelly, coffee and doughnuts, and automobiles and gasoline are among the many sets of complementary goods. Sets of substitute goods include ham and steak, automobile travel and airplane travel, electric razors and safety razors, and many others.

CONSTRAINTS ON THE CONSUMER

budget line or constraint
All combinations of goods and services available to the consumer when all of the consumer's income (purchasing power) is being utilized, given that income and the prices of the goods and services.

What the consumer is able to do has thus far been left aside; we have presented a picture of tastes and preferences only. The constraints on the individual's consumption activities are shown by **budget lines or constraints,** sometimes called *lines of attainable combinations*.

The Budget Line

The consumer's purchasing power and the prices of what the consumer wants to buy determine his or her budget line. Purchasing power is usually referred to as income. The term is not limited to current earnings but is used broadly to include any supplements to, or deletions from, whatever those earnings may be. We think of the consumer's income defined in this way as a weekly, monthly, or yearly average. The prices faced by the consumer are the market prices of the items he or she purchases.

To show how the budget line is established, we again limit the consumer to a two-good world. Suppose that in Figure 5.5 Mary Smith has an income of $400 per week and prices of X and Y are $8 and $4, respectively. If she were

Figure 5.5
The Budget Line

Suppose the consumer's income level is $400 per week and the prices of X and Y are $8 and $4, respectively. The consumer can purchase 50 units of X if no Y is taken or 100 units of Y if no X is taken. The budget line is BA and the triangle 0BA shows all combinations of X and Y the consumer can purchase.

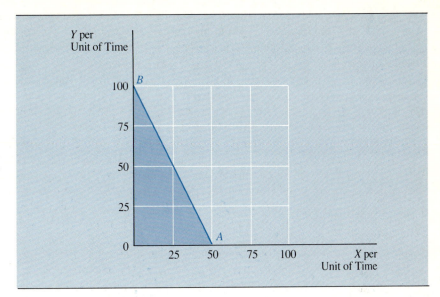

to spend her entire income on X, she could consume 50 units per week—she would be at point A. On the other hand, if she were to buy Y and no X, she could consume 100 units of Y and would be at point B. If she is at point B and desires to include X in her consumption pattern, she must decrease her consumption of Y to do so. A decrease of 2 units in her consumption of Y releases $8 that can be used to purchase a unit of X. Every 1-unit increase in the quantity of X consumed requires a 2-unit decrease in her consumption of Y, so long as p_y remains at $4 and p_x is $8. Thus, her budget line is a straight line joining points B and A.

The slope of the budget line is determined by the ratio of p_x to p_y. Suppose that in Figure 5.6 Thomas Green's income is I_1, the price of X is p_{x1}, and the price of Y is p_{y1}. If he should spend all of his income on Y, then I_1/p_{y1} would show the total number of units of Y that he could purchase. If he were to spend all of his income on X, then I_1/p_{x1} would show the number of units of X that he could purchase. The budget line B_1A_1 joins the two extreme points.[10]

The slope of the budget line in Figure 5.6 is

$$-\frac{I_1/p_{y1}}{I_1/p_{x1}} = -\frac{I_1}{p_{y1}} \times \frac{p_{x1}}{I_1} = -\frac{p_{x1}}{p_{y1}}.$$

---

[10]The budget line equation for the two-commodity example of the text is $xp_x + yp_y = I$. Solving for y, we obtain $y = \frac{I}{p_y} - \frac{p_x}{p_y} \times x$, indicating that the Y axis intercept is I/p_y and that the slope of the line is $-p_x/p_y$.

**Figure 5.6
Changes in the
Budget Line**

The slope of the
consumer's budget line
B_1A_1 is p_{x1}/p_{y1}. An
increase in the price of X
to p_{x2} shifts the budget
line to B_1A_1'. An increase
in income to I_2 with the
prices of X and Y
constant at p_{x1} and p_{y1}
shifts the budget line to
B_2A_2.

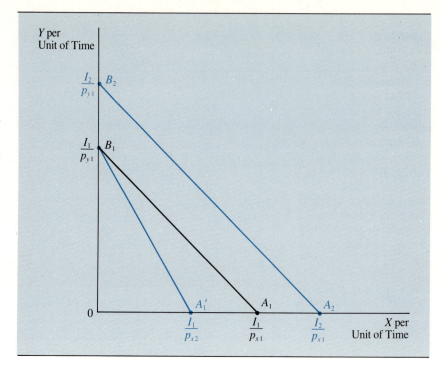

In more general terms, the slope of any budget line is

(5.1)
$$-\frac{I/p_y}{I/p_x} = -\frac{I}{p_y} \times \frac{p_x}{I} = -\frac{p_x}{p_y}.$$

It measures the amount of Y the consumer would be required to give up in the
market to obtain an additional unit of X. Note that the consumer can obtain any
combination of goods within or on the boundaries of the triangle $B_1 0 A_1$ in Figure
5.6. All of these constitute his set of *feasible* combinations. The budget line
B_1A_1 separates the feasible combinations—what the consumer is able to purchase—from those combinations beyond his financial reach.

Shifts in the Budget Line

Changes in a consumer's income and changes in the prices of the goods and
services available will shift that individual's budget line. Referring back to
Figure 5.6, suppose that Thomas Green's income is now I_1 initially, that the
prices of X and Y are still p_{x1} and p_{y1}, respectively, and that his initial budget
line is still B_1A_1. If the price of X now increases to p_{x2} while his income and
the price of Y remain constant, the budget line becomes B_1A_1'. There is no change
in the amount of Y that his income will purchase if it is all spent on Y; however,
the higher price of X reduces from $0A_1$ to $0A_1'$ the amount of X that he could

**Figure 5.7
The Consumer's
Satisfaction-
Maximizing
Combination**

Given the budget
constraint determined by
I_1, p_{y1}, and p_{x1},
indifference curve U_3
represents the highest
level of satisfaction the
consumer can reach. It
can be reached only with
combination C,
containing x_1 of X and y_1
of Y.

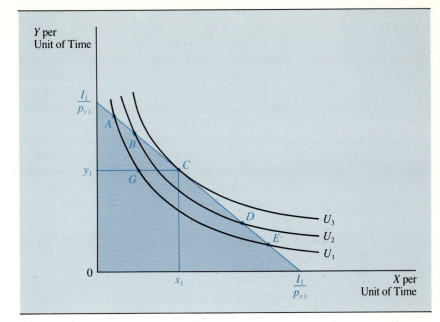

purchase if his money were all spent on X. The new budget line therefore joins
B_1 and A_1'.

Suppose now that from an initial budget line B_1A_1 Green's income rises
from I_1 to I_2 while the prices of X and Y remain constant. The budget line shifts
to the right parallel to itself to B_2A_2. The larger income enables him to purchase
greater amounts of X if X alone is purchased or greater amounts of Y if Y alone
is purchased, so that A_2 lies to the right of A_1 and B_2 lies above B_1. Since the
prices of X and Y have not changed, both budget lines have a slope of $-p_{x1}/p_{y1}$
and are therefore parallel.[11]

MAXIMIZATION OF CONSUMER SATISFACTION

The theory of consumer behavior is built on the premise that an individual
consumer, given a budget constraint, seeks to *maximize satisfaction*. To show
the conditions under which a consumer can attain this goal, his or her preference
factors (the indifference map) and restraining factors (the budget line) are
brought together in Figure 5.7. Any combination, such as A, B, C, D, or E, on
the budget line is available; so is any combination, such as G, lying to the left

---

[11]Note that in Footnote 10 changes in p_x change the slope of the budget line but not its Y axis
intercept. Changes in I shift the budget line up or down without changing its slope.

of or below it. Because of the budget constraint, combinations lying to the right of or above it are not available.

The combination chosen must lie on the budget line. A consumer who takes combination G violates the postulate that more of a good is preferred to less. By moving from G to C, the consumer obtains more X without sacrificing any Y and consequently gets on a higher indifference curve. This sort of move is always possible for a combination below the budget line. Of the combinations on the budget line, the consumer is expected to choose the one on the highest indifference curve touched by that line; this will be combination C. (Combinations A, B, D, and E all lie on lower indifference curves.) Combination C is on the highest indifference curve that the consumer can reach and, further, is the only combination available on that indifference curve. Thus, the satisfaction-maximizing combination is that at which the person's budget line is tangent to an indifference curve. But note that in order for this to be so, indifference curves must be convex to the origin. In Figure 5.7 that combination contains x_1 of X and y_1 of Y.

Tangency of the budget line to an indifference curve means that the rate at which the consumer is *willing* to give up Y to obtain X is equal to the rate at which he or she would be *required* by the market to give up Y to obtain X. The slope of an indifference curve at any point on it is the consumer's MRS_{xy} at that point. The slope of a budget line at any point on it is p_x/p_y. At the point of tangency—point C—the slopes of the two curves are necessarily the same; that is,

(5.2)
$$MRS_{xy} = \frac{p_x}{p_y}.^{12}$$

Consider point A in Figure 5.7. The slope of indifference curve U_1 is greater than the slope of the line of attainable combinations. In other words, the amount of Y that the consumer is *willing* to give up to get an additional unit of X is greater than the amount of Y that he or she *would have* to give up to get that additional unit (that is, $MRS_{xy} > p_x/p_y$). The consumer would give up units of Y for additional units of X because by doing so it is possible to move to a preferred position. The same would be the case at point B. At point D, the slope of indifference curve U_2 is less than the slope of the line of attainable combinations, meaning that the amount of Y that the consumer is willing to give up to get an additional unit of X is less than the amount that he or she would have to give up (that is, $MRS_{xy} < p_x/p_y$). Therefore, the consumer would not move beyond point C to such a point as D, for such a movement is toward a less preferred position. The consumer is maximizing satisfaction at point C, where

---

[12]Since the indifference curves and the budget lines both have negative slopes, we shall disregard the minus signs of the slope measurements and consider the absolute values only. This practice is conventional and avoids problems arising from mathematical semantics.

the marginal rate of substitution of X for Y is equal to the ratio of their respective prices, and the consumer is disposing of his or her entire income.[13]

In Figure 5.7 let Y be milk and X be honey. Assume that the price of milk, p_y, is \$1 per pint, while that for honey, p_x, is \$2 per pound. At point A, $MRS_{xy} > p_x/p_y$; assume that it is 4. Thus, the MRS_{xy} tells us the consumer is just willing to give up 4 pints of milk for an additional pound of honey. The slope of the budget line, p_x/p_y, tells us that if the consumer gives up only 2 pints of milk the market will let him or her purchase an additional pound of honey. So the consumer clearly reaches a higher satisfaction level by giving up 2 pints of milk and acquiring 1 pound of honey in the market. The satisfaction increase is that yielded by the additional 2 pints of milk the consumer would have been willing to sacrifice for the additional pound of honey.

PRICE INDEX NUMBERS

The inflation that has been occurring over the last two decades has brought to the foreground two questions on which indifference curve analysis can shed light. First, how is the rate of inflation measured? Second, what impact does inflation have on the welfare of a consumer? The Laspeyres price index and the Paasche price index are commonly used to provide partial answers.

---

[13]To solve the consumer's maximization problem mathematically, let his or her preference function be

(1) $U = f(x, y)$.

The budget constraint is $xp_x + yp_y = I$, or

(2) $xp_x + yp_y - I = 0$.

To maximize (1) subject to (2), we use the Lagrange multiplier method, forming a new function in which V is a function of x, y, and λ such that

(3) $V = g(x, y, \lambda) = f(x, y) - \lambda(xp_x + yp_y - I)$.

For maximization of V, the necessary conditions are the simultaneous equations:

(4) $\dfrac{\partial V}{\partial x} = f_x - \lambda p_x = 0$, or: $f_x = \lambda p_x$;

(5) $\dfrac{\partial V}{\partial y} = f_y - \lambda p_y = 0$, or: $f_y = \lambda p_y$;

(6) $\dfrac{\partial V}{\partial \lambda} = xp_x + yp_y - I = 0$, or: $xp_x + yp_y = I$.

Dividing (4) by (5) and letting (6) stand as is, the necessary conditions for maximum satisfaction become $f_x/f_y = p_x/p_y$; that is,

(7) $MRS_{xy} = \dfrac{p_x}{p_y}$,

with

(8) $xp_x + yp_y = I$.

The Laspeyres Price Index

Laspeyres price index
An index that measures
the relative change in the
cost of purchasing a year
0 bundle of goods be-
tween year 0 and year 1;
provides the *maximum*
estimate of the cost-of-
living increase during
that time period.

The **Laspeyres price index** is illustrated in Figure 5.8. The diagram is for one
individual and covers a two-year time series composed of year 0 and year 1.

Suppose that in year 0 the individual exercises free choice in the spending
of income. Let the income level be I_0^L and the prices of X and Y be p_{x0} and p_{y0},
respectively. The most preferred position is combination B_0 containing x_0 of X
and y_0 of Y. Total expenditures on this bundle of goods are described by

$$(5.3) \qquad I_0^L = x_0 p_{x0} + y_0 p_{y0}.$$

Next, consider how much money bundle B_0 would cost in year 1. If the prices
of X and Y in that year are p_{x1} and p_{y1}, respectively, and we let I_1^L be the cost
of the bundle, then

$$(5.4) \qquad I_1^L = x_0 p_{x1} + y_0 p_{y1}.$$

The Laspeyres price index (L) is, in turn,

$$(5.5) \qquad L = \frac{I_1^L}{I_0^L} \times 100 = \frac{x_0 p_{x1} + y_0 p_{y1}}{x_0 p_{x0} + y_0 p_{y0}} \times 100.$$

Figure 5.8
**The Laspeyres Price
Index**

The Laspeyres price
index is the ratio of
income I_1^L to income I_0^L in
which I_1^L is the income it
would take in year 1 to
purchase the same bundle
of goods B_0 that income
I_0^L purchased in year 0.
Actually it overstates any
increase in the cost to a
consumer of maintaining
a given level of
satisfaction U_0, since the
consumer in year 1 with
income I_1^L and year 1
prices would not continue
to take combination B_0
but would move to
combination B_1 and a
higher level of
satisfaction U_1.

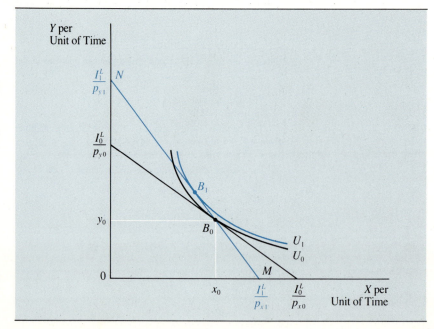

It measures the expenditure that the consumer must make in year 1 as a percentage of the expenditure in year 0 in order to obtain in year 1 the same bundle of goods that maximized satisfaction in year 0.

The Laspeyres index is the *maximum* estimate of the increase in the individual's cost of living, since it erroneously presumes that with expenditure I_1^L the consumer would be at the same level of satisfaction—with bundle B_0 on indifference curve U_0—in year 1 as in year 0. It is a maximum because in actuality, with an expenditure level of I_1^L in year 1 at prices p_{x1} and p_{y1}, the consumer would not want to stay at bundle B_0. By giving up some of the now relatively higher-priced X for some of the now relatively lower-priced Y, he or she can move to bundle B_1 and to the higher preference level shown by indifference curve U_1. Thus, the change in the expenditure level that must occur to enable the consumer to continue to purchase in year 1 the same combination that was purchased in year 0 *overstates the increase* in the cost of maintaining a given level of consumer welfare—unless it should happen that the prices of X and Y increase in the same direction and in the same proportion. In such a case B_1 will coincide with B_0, and the index will measure accurately the change in the cost of living.

What happens to the consumer's welfare from year 0 to year 1? Note that while I_0^L is the actual year 0 expenditure, I_1^L is *not* the actual expenditure in year 1. Rather, I_1^L is the *hypothetical* expenditure that would be necessary in that year to purchase the year 0 satisfaction-maximizing bundle of goods. Let the consumer's *actual* expenditure in year 1 be I_a^L.

We can be sure that the consumer's welfare is greater in year 1 than in year 0 if

$$(5.6) \qquad \frac{I_a^L}{I_0^L} > \frac{I_1^L}{I_0^L}.$$

This means that the percentage increase in the consumer's income exceeds the maximum estimate of the percentage increase in the cost of living. In Figure 5.8 the *actual* budget line for year 1 would lie to the right of *NM* and be parallel to it. It would thus be tangent to an indifference curve even higher than U_1. However, if

$$(5.7) \qquad \frac{I_a^L}{I_0^L} \leq \frac{I_1^L}{I_0^L},$$

we cannot be certain that the consumer's welfare is the same as or less than it was in year 0—it may be greater. In that case, the *actual* budget line for year 1 would lie to the left of *NM* and be parallel to it. If it is tangent to an indifference curve *between* U_0 and U_1, the consumer is better off in year 1 than in year 0. If it is tangent to indifference curve U_0, there is no change in the consumer's welfare. If it lies far enough to the left of *NM* to be tangent to an indifference curve below U_0, the consumer is worse off in year 1. The fly in the ointment is, of course, the fact that the real increase in the cost of living may be less than I_1^L/I_0^L.

The Paasche Price Index

Paasche price index
An index that measures the relative change in the cost of purchasing a year 1 bundle of goods between year 0 and year 1; provides the *minimum* estimate of the cost-of-living increase during that time period.

A different estimate of changes in the cost of living over time is provided by the **Paasche price index.** Whereas the Laspeyres index shows the relative change in the cost of purchasing a *year 0* bundle of goods between year 0 and year 1, the Paasche index shows the relative change in purchasing a *year 1* bundle of goods between year 0 and year 1.

Suppose the consumer exercises free choice in spending year 1 income. In Figure 5.9, with an income level of I_1^P and at prices p_{x1} and p_{y1} for goods X and Y, respectively, combination B_1 is the preferred set of purchases. Combination B_1 contains x_1 of X and y_1 of Y, and the consumer's total expenditures are described by

$$(5.8) \qquad I_1^P = x_1 p_{x1} + y_1 p_{y1}.$$

The same bundle of goods in year 0 at year 0 prices p_{x0} and p_{y0} would have cost

$$(5.9) \qquad I_0^P = x_1 p_{x0} + y_1 p_{y0}.$$

The Paasche price index (P), then, is

$$(5.10) \qquad P = \frac{I_1^P}{I_0^P} \times 100 = \frac{x_1 p_{x1} + y_1 p_{y1}}{x_1 p_{x0} + y_1 p_{y0}} \times 100.$$

Figure 5.9
The Paasche Price Index

The Paasche price index is the ratio of income I_1^P to income I_0^P in which I_0^P is the income it would have taken in year 0 to purchase the same bundle of goods B_1 that I_1^P purchases in year 1. It understates any increase in the cost to a consumer of maintaining a given level of satisfaction U_1, since in year 0 at year 0 prices the consumer would not have purchased bundle B_1 with I_0^P but would have obtained a higher level of satisfaction U_0 by purchasing bundle B_0.

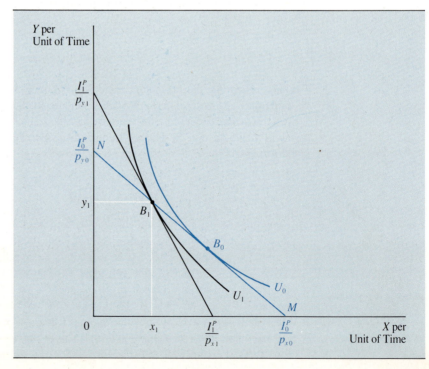

The Paasche index represents the *minimum* estimate of the increase in the cost of living from year 0 to year 1. It reflects the increase from I_0^P to I_1^P in the cost of combination B_1. However, with an expenditure level of I_0^P, the consumer would have purchased combination B_0 in year 0 and would have been on indifference curve U_0 in that year. The expenditure level of I_1^P in year 1 yields a lower level of satisfaction than did I_0^P in year 0. The actual increase in the cost of living thus exceeds $I_1^P - I_0^P$ by whatever money value the consumer attaches to the reduction in satisfaction represented by the movement from indifference curve U_0 to indifference curve U_1. However, if p_x and p_y change by the same proportional amount and in the same direction between year 0 and year 1, then B_0 and B_1 coincide and the index correctly measures the change in the cost of living.

Consider again the change in a consumer's welfare between year 0 and year 1. Let the actual income in year 0 be I_a^P. If

$$(5.11) \qquad \frac{I_1^P}{I_a^P} \leq \frac{I_1^P}{I_0^P}$$

we can be sure that his or her welfare has decreased between year 0 and year 1, because the increase in actual income is less than the minimum estimate of the increase in the cost of living. In Figure 5.9, the budget line for *actual* income in year 0 would lie on or to the right of NM and be parallel to it. It would be tangent either to indifference curve U_0 at B_0 or to a higher indifference curve. Thus, the welfare loss to the consumer from year 0 to year 1 would be that involved in dropping back from indifference curve U_0 or a higher indifference curve to indifference curve U_1. If

$$(5.12) \qquad \frac{I_1^P}{I_a^P} > \frac{I_1^P}{I_0^P}$$

we cannot be certain whether or not the consumer's welfare has decreased, increased, or remained constant. The budget line for *actual* income in year 0 will lie to the left of NM and be parallel to it. If it is tangent to an indifference curve *between* U_1 and U_0, and the consumer's welfare decreases between year 0 and year 1, since he or she must drop back from that indifference curve to combination B_1 on indifference curve U_1. If the year 0 actual budget line is tangent to indifference curve U_1, there is no change in the consumer's welfare between year 0 and year 1, although there will be a change in the combination of goods purchased (a movement up and around indifference curve U_1). If the actual budget line of year 0 is tangent to an indifference curve lower than U_1, then the consumer's welfare does indeed increase between year 0 and year 1.

SUMMARY

The indifference curve apparatus provides a useful framework for the theory of consumer choice and exchange. The consumer's tastes and preferences are represented by his or her indifference map. The consumer's opportunity factors—

income and the prices of goods or services purchased—are represented by his or her budget line. The point at which the budget line is tangent to an indifference curve represents the combination of goods that the consumer prefers of those available.

By using indifference curve analysis, the construction of price index numbers can be examined and evaluated. A Laspeyres price index provides a maximum estimate of increases in the cost of living over time, while a Paasche price index provides a minimum estimate of such increases.

APPLICATIONS

The theory of consumer choice can be used in many ways to raise questions about what goes on in the world around us. It can help us evaluate and come to sound decisions on the economic policy issues of the day. In this section we present a broad range of examples of how the theory can be used.

INDEX NUMBERS IN PRACTICE[14]

The Consumer Price Index (CPI) came into being in 1919, based on 145 commodities in 32 cities. Its calculation now requires 1.5 million quotations of prices, rents, and taxes for 400 commodities in 85 areas. It was originally designed for the limited purpose of settling shipbuilding wage disputes during World War I. But it is now used as a broadly based cost-of-living escalator for 40 government programs amounting to one-third of the federal budget. In 1985,

_____

[14]This section is based on Phillip Cagan and Geoffrey H. Moore, *The Consumer Price Index: Issues and Alternatives* (Washington, D. C.: The American Enterprise Institute for Public Policy Research, 1981).

each rise of one percentage point in the index increased the federal deficit by $4.6 billion.

Its calculation affects the incomes of 60 million people, including 32 million recipients of Social Security benefits, 2.4 million retired military and federal workers and their survivors, the retired employees of 21 state governments, 20 million food stamp recipients, and 25 million children who receive paid school lunches. In 1980, this calculation also changed the wages of 58 percent of the workers covered by collective bargaining agreements. It affects the federal and state income tax calculations of many businesses and corporations that use the last-in, first-out system for valuing inventories, as well as the rental, child support, and other payments in myriad private contracts. It is no exaggeration to say that its calculation is one of the most important functions of the U.S. government.

Perhaps the most important conclusion about price indexes is that they are, as the name implies, measures of changes in the average prices of particular consumer goods and services rather than changes in the cost of living. The CPI is a Laspeyres index based on a fixed "market basket" of goods and services established in six surveys since 1919, most recently in 1972–73. It does not allow consumption substitutions when relative prices change, and, as shown in Figure 5.8, overstates the actual cost of achieving a given level of satisfaction.

Over time the CPI's fixed basket becomes very out of date, and its periodic revision does not always reduce the weights of those goods rising the most in price. Revisions since the 1930s have decreased the weight of food and apparel, which subsequently declined in price, and increased the weights of housing and transportation, which subsequently increased in price. The resulting overstatement is especially great during a period of rapid inflation, such as the late 1970s, in which many people changed their buying habits, purchasing fewer of those goods that had become relatively more expensive (for example, fuels). However, some groups benefit from this exaggeration. One such group is retired military and federal officials, whose living expenditures apparently went up by less than those of the urban consumers to whose behavior their pensions were indexed by the CPI. One retiree's view of this dilemma is found in the accompanying article from *Business Week*.

To include all consumer goods in the CPI is not feasible, but the following omissions and problems make it a dubious measure of living costs:

1. The CPI excludes savings and all taxes that are not reflected in the prices of goods. Ironically, an income tax cut that was exactly offset by higher excise taxes would raise the CPI.

2. The CPI excludes the value of goods and services produced by the public sector. Environmental restrictions that raise goods prices will increase the CPI even though they may increase living standards on net. This is because the CPI is an index of prices, not of living standards.

3. The CPI excludes personal income taxes, which in 1980 were the fastest-rising component of total living costs. During 1967–79, personal income

tax collections increased 222.9 percent—more than food (145.9), medical care (146.9), transportation (113.9), housing (108.7), and clothing (67.2). In New York City, federal, state, and local personal income taxes combined increased by 311 percent, or more than twice that of food (148).[15]

4. The CPI ignores many price discounts, such as grocery coupons and airline rebates, because it is too expensive to keep track of them or to know how much consumers indirectly may have paid for them.

5. The CPI incorporates quality changes awkwardly at best. An attempt is made to hold quality ''constant'' by including price changes only of items that have not changed in quality. Otherwise, a new item of the same type is substituted for the old without changing the index. If possible, the index makers attempt to subtract manufacturers' production costs of such changes from prices, as for example the cost of adding catalytic converters to new automobiles. But the CPI cannot reflect improvements in *living* due to such new goods as computers, CAT scanners, quartz watches, or Boeing 747s.

6. The CPIs for different eras are not comparable. It is the government's policy never to revise the CPI for a given period once published, no matter how much out of date its market basket has become. Thus, marked changes in the weights of the ''fixed'' basket, such as those that were made in 1972–73, make the later index incomparable with the earlier index. Failure to revise the CPI makes it less useful for economists, but removing the extra uncertainty of retroactive adjustments makes it more useful for indexing various private contracts.

It is easier to improve the CPI's accuracy by tinkering with what it includes rather than with what it leaves out. For example, increases in imported oil prices raise the CPI and, ironically, incomes chained to the CPI, while at the same time such increases reduce national wealth. This led Denmark in 1980 to delete oil prices from its CPI counterpart. The United States did not follow suit.

A more serious overstatement of the CPI stems from its treatment of housing. The CPI includes such usual cost-of-living expenses as insurance, property taxes, and repairs. But it also includes as a current expense 100 percent of the mortgage interest committed to be paid on a typical 30-year loan, even though the interest may be paid within the first 15 years of the debt or even if the family sells the home after 5 or so years. The index uses data on *current* housing prices and *current* interest rates for new loans to account for everyone's housing costs, even though few people buy or borrow each year. Moreover, no account is taken of the fact that mortgage interest expenses are deductible from federal and many state income tax calculations; nor does it recognize that land does not depreciate. These are reason enough to exclude the portion of the housing price, tax, and mortgage interest that is attributable to land. The CPI treats houses strictly as

---

[15]William G. Flanagan, ''Your Money Matters: Figuring Out Your Personal Rate of Inflation: Surprise! Taxes Are Your Fastest-Rising Costs,'' *The Wall Street Journal,* July 7, 1980.

Table 5.1
Inflation Rates
According to the
CPI and the PCE
Deflator, 1968–1980

Year	CPI	PCE
1968	4.2	4.0
1969	5.4	4.5
1970	5.9	4.6
1971	5.9	4.3
1972	3.3	3.6
1973	6.2	5.7
1974	11.0	10.1
1975	9.1	7.6
1976	5.8	5.2
1977	6.5	6.0
1978	7.7	6.8
1979	11.3	8.9
1980	13.5	10.2

Source: Phillip Cagan and Geoffrey H. Moore, *The Consumer Price Index: Issues and Alternatives* (Washington, D.C.: The American Enterprise Institute for Public Policy Research, 1981): 48.

consumption goods and ignores the fact that they last 40 or more years, are treated by many families as investment goods or inflation hedges, and often are substantially taxed at time of sale.

In 1979 the weight given to housing in the CPI's "basket" was 24.9 percent, compared to only 5.3 percent for rents, a ratio of five to one. Eliminating land from housing prices and property taxes would have reduced housing's weight by 28 percent. Using the mortgage interest actually paid rather than the interest commitment implied in a 30-year loan would have reduced the 1979 rise from 13.3 to 11.7 percent. Ignoring the inflation in housing prices during 1979–80 would have eliminated 3 of the 14 percentage points increase for the year ending June 1980 and one-third of the total rise between 1979 and 1981.[16]

The contrast between a Laspeyres index and a Paasche index is shown in Table 5.1, which compares changes from 1968 to 1980 in the CPI and the Personal Consumption Expenditures (PCE) Deflator. In most years the Laspeyres price increase exceeds the Paasche, which measures the cost of a current basket of goods with its "constant-dollar" cost in some base period year. The CPI is calculated by the Bureau of Labor Statistics of the U.S. Department of Labor and the PCE Deflator by the Bureau of Economic Analysis of the U.S. Department of Commerce as part of the national income and product accounts that are usually studied in macroeconomics courses. The CPI has always been calculated monthly, which is another reason for its popularity, and until recently the PCE Deflator has been calculated quarterly.

---

[16]Cagan and Moore, *The Consumer Price Index*, 5–6 and 32–43; and Eileen Alt Powell, "Indicator Infighting: Substituting Rent for Homeowners' Costs in the Consumer Price Index Stirs Debate," *The Wall Street Journal*, May 18, 1982.

The two indexes have three important differences:

1. The CPI is based on purchases of urban consumers, or about 80 percent of U.S. population, whereas the PCE Deflator includes fewer urban but more rural transactions.

2. The national income accounts include residential housing as an investment rather than a consumption good, so the PCE Deflator does not include mortgage interest or any other interest rates. It does, however, include rents.

3. The PCE Deflator is not a pure index of prices, since the weights of its market basket are continually revised to reflect changes over time in the current distribution of consumers' expenditures. Since the PCE Deflator has no "base period" market basket, it is an index of quantities as well as prices. Table 5.2 shows the different weights each index used during 1972–79 and that the weights for the fixed-basket CPI were constant while those of the PCE Deflator were adjusted. This accounts for much of the CPI's overstatement of inflation relative to the PCE.

The CPI is a useful index of consumer prices, but it would be a more realistic escalator for wages and other contracts if it were modified in the three ways just discussed. In January 1983, it was revised to reflect more rents relative to home ownership and to reduce its "shelter" component from 22.8 percent to 15.0 percent. The 1970s' housing boom was over by 1981 even though *nominal* sales prices continued to rise. To get those higher prices, however, sellers had to give buyers "concessionary" financing at lower rates than institutional lenders would offer. This meant that *real* sales prices were perhaps 15 or 20 percent lower than nominal prices. The CPI, of course, reflected only nominal prices and only the higher interest rates that institutional lenders charged (even if few people were borrowing at those rates). Thus, the CPI continued to inflate after 1981 by an extra one to two percentage points even though real sales prices were falling.[17] But the Labor Department's timing in switching from houses to rents was wrong: The revised CPI in early 1983 was rising faster than it would have with the old weights, because rents were rising and the nominal prices that houses were selling at were finally falling.[18]

In 1986, the Labor Department was preparing a new "fixed basket" for the CPI, scheduled to be introduced in February 1987. The 1972–73 basket no longer reflected typical consumption patterns. For example, Americans in 1986 were buying smaller cars, smaller houses, more insulation, and many other energy-saving substitutions that were uncommon 13 years earlier. The 1972–73 basket gave so much weight to energy use that the decline in oil prices that

[17]William J. Eaton, "Inflation Hits Double-Digit Levels Again," *Los Angeles Times,* August 26, 1981; and the editorial "CPI: Confusing Price Index," *The Wall Street Journal,* September 30, 1981.

[18]Eileen Alt Powell, "Consumer Prices Seen Rising Faster in '83 After '82's 3.9% Pace, Slowest in 10 Years," *The Wall Street Journal,* January 24, 1983.

Table 5.2
Comparison of
Selected Categories
of CPI and PCE
Weights, 1972–1979

	CPI	PCE Deflator[b]			
	1972–73	1972	1977	1978	1979
Food	19.2%	20.5%	19.2%	18.6%	18.2%
Shelter	29.8	15.3	16.3	16.7	17.3
Mortgage Cost	9.7	0.0	0.0	0.0	0.0
Apparel[a]	4.8	7.5	7.8	8.1	8.3
Energy	8.5	6.8	6.4	6.3	6.0
Gasoline	4.2	3.4	3.1	3.1	2.9

[a]In the PCE Deflator this category includes clothing and shoes.

[b]PCE Deflator weight equals 1972 dollar outlays on component divided by total 1972 dollar consumer expenditures.

Source: Business News and Trends, Pittsburgh National Bank, May 8, 1980, 3.

began in November 1985 caused the entire CPI to drop by 0.4 percent in February 1986—its first monthly drop since December 1982.[19] We will not know what distortions the new index will introduce for at least a decade, however.

THE HAZARDS OF ARTIFICIAL SWEETENERS

One of the most fruitful ways of using economic analysis is in perusing the daily newspaper. We use such analysis to seek information on the major issues of the day, about which we will have to make judgments in the course of everyday life. As consumers, we have to decide which goods to buy, whether they be houses, shares of stock, or prescription medicines. As producers, we have to decide what careers to pursue or businesses to establish. As voters, we face at times a bewildering array of candidates, referenda, or initiatives on the ballots. Newspaper reporters are in the business of informing their readers about major events and issues, but the comparative advantage reporters enjoy lies more in description than analysis. This is especially so for economic issues, subjects in which relatively few journalists are trained. The analysis and diagrams presented in this chapter will, when applied to the factual situations that the newspapers recount, enable you to conceptualize better what is *really* going on in your economic world. Economics in many instances can reveal useful angles, nuances, and implications about the story that the reporter who wrote it did not fully understand.

Consider, for example, the controversy in the late 1970s over the use of artificial sweeteners, such as saccharin—a so-called *hazardous product*—in the production of diet soft drinks and other products calling for sugar substitutes. The basic problem is one of trade-offs, so typical of situations that we encounter in daily living. Artificial sweeteners enable diabetics and people who are con-

[19]Irwin Ross, "Economic Statistics: Why They Often Lie," *Fortune,* April 28, 1986, 58–60.

THE INDEX THAT FEEDS INFLATION

On Jan. 31, 1980, William D. Howard, a retired federal employee, wrote a letter to Mrs. Janet Norwood, Commissioner of Labor Statistics. Business Week *has obtained his permission to reprint it. The editors consider it an interesting and informative study of the inflationary impact that results when cost-of-living adjustments in wages or pensions are based on the consumer price index compiled by the Bureau of Labor Statistics.*

Dear Mrs. Norwood:

According to the Jan. 2, 1980, issue of *The Wall Street Journal*, you spoke to the National Association of Government Labor Officials and defended the BLS consumer price index against claims that it exaggerates the inflation rate. . . . I submit to you that an honest analysis of my own personal financial status reveals more about the impact of the BLS's actions than can be derived from opinions of economists.

Let's start with my 43rd birthday,

July 1, 1968, when as a middle-management federal accountant, Grade 15, Step 8, I was earning $22,000. Federal workers then became subject to the "Comparability Pay" law. My salary would have changed little had the "average" pay of the private sector surveyed been used, but it wasn't. The BLS used special weighting curves and other refinements they felt necessary to achieve "comparability," and instead of my pay increasing 22% in the next 4½ years, it spurted 54% to $34,971 by January 1973, without any promotions. It would be $50,112 a year today if I had not retired on my 50th birthday, July 1, 1975.

During the 4½ years since my retirement from federal employment, my Civil Service annuity (#1 810 115), which started at $1,922 a month, will reach $3,075 based on the CPI-W (the index that applies to wage earners and clerical workers) of 230.0 at December, 1979. Thus, I now receive 63% more retired than I did working in mid-1968, primarily

due to the impact of the BLS's determination of "comparability pay" and calculation of CPI-based cost-of-living allowances.

In your speech, which I referred to at the outset, you stated:

"We have one official consumer price index, and we will continue to have one official consumer price index."

"The CPI is the best measure of purchasing power we have."

"The purpose of CPI cost-of-living adjustment has been to permit people to purchase in today's prices the bundle of goods and services they purchased in the base period, thereby leaving them at least as well off as they were then."

This means that I do not have to switch to pork, chicken, or even pasta, as others do, because the cost of beef and veal has gone up more in the last eight years than meat substitutes. I am entitled, according to you, to eat the same quantity and quality of beef and veal as I did in 1972–73, when it was cheap.

cerned about their weight to enjoy foods that would otherwise not be suitable for them, but the chemicals used in them may carry other risks. Initially there was some evidence linking large doses of these substances to bladder cancer in laboratory rats. The U.S. government wrestled with this problem for about a decade. The accompanying column from *The Wall Street Journal* describes the uncertainties and the bureaucratic wrangling that surrounded this issue.

The Effects of Information and Warnings

A consumer's choices between diet drinks and sugared drinks is represented by the black line indifference map of Figure 5.10. Since these products are ordinarily substitutes for each other, the indifference curves for them exhibit the usual convex-to-the-origin shape, reflecting a diminishing MRS_{sd} at any given level of satisfaction as more diet (D) and fewer sugared (S) drinks are consumed. Given an annual soft drink budget of I dollars, a price per unit of p_s for sugared

I still get to drive gas-guzzling big cars at 6 to 8 mi. a gal., just like people did when the CPI was "based" and gasoline cost 41¢ instead of the $1.20 now. When the government urges conservation, it is at variance with your contention that we (CPI-based COLA recipients) should be left at least as well off as before. Heating oil was 19¢ a gal. at the CPI base, plentiful too. I can ignore the government's urging that I insulate my home, roll back the thermostat, etc., and heat with the same amount of oil as before at today's prices.

As to my home, I live in a new house acquired just before I retired in 1975, and although the value has doubled and I can take $100,000 tax-free profit, and the monthly payments are not a bit more, the housing components of my CPI increases of more than 50% have handsomely increased my income. Is it true that the CPI assumes that I can only sell my house for the equity I have paid into it and assumes that I repurchase and refinance a portion of my house every year?

My radial tires for my cars get 40,000 mi. these days, but my cost-of-living allowances based on the CPI assume that I still get only 15,000 because quality improvements (except for new automobiles) are ignored.

Medical care costs have risen dramatically in the last eight years, and my CPI-based income has been raised accordingly, yet my former employer continues to pay a large portion of my health insurance, and my costs are about the same.

I know that I am very fortunate to have your CPI income protection, as are 50 million other people who are similar beneficiaries. But don't you think, honestly, that it is unjust enrichment? Frankly, it scares me to contemplate what this transfer of payments from one group of citizens to another means. For myself, I am busily engaged in a second career in the private sector but not everyone is—due to the influence on incentives.

For example: A local fellow who used to work for the same governmental bureau I did retired 1½ years ago. I called him last week about a job opening similar to the one I got after retirement. He is a CPA and figured that from the $24,000 salary to start, on top of his CPI-based federal annuity, federal, state, city, and FICA taxes, and commuting expenses would leave him only $9,000 for working, and he therefore was not interested. Why should he support the system?

I understand the BLS's *Monthly Labor Review* welcomes communications that are factual and analytical, not polemical in tone. Although this one is a bit embarrassing to me personally, it is a story that needs to be told, even if it ultimately results in less unjust enrichment to CPI cost-of-living benefit recipients.

Sincerely,

William D. Howard

drinks, and a price per unit of p_d for diet drinks, the soft drink budget line is established. The consumer maximizes satisfaction with combination C, consuming s cans per year of sugared drink and d cans per year of diet drink.

How does the consumer react to the revelation that there may be a link between diet drink consumption and bladder cancer? There are at least two significant results.

First, combination C no longer maximizes satisfaction, even though it remains obtainable to the consumer. At that combination—or any other combination, for that matter—a can of diet drink now yields less satisfaction to the consumer than it did before relative to the satisfaction yielded by a can of sugared drink. In technical terms, the information increases the MRS_{sd} for each and every combination shown on the indifference map. At any combination, such as C, the consumer is now willing to give up *more* cans of diet drink to obtain an additional can of sugared drink than before. The slope of an indifference curve through point C, or any other point on the map, increases. The indifference

Figure 5.10
The Effects on Consumer Behavior of Information and Warnings

In the absence of health warnings on diet drinks a consumer's indifference encompasses the black curves, and the consumer with a given budget line takes combination C. Warnings that diet drinks are hazardous increase the MRS_{sd} for every possible combination, resulting in a new indifference map that contains the blue curves U_1' and U_2'. The consumer now maximizes satisfaction with combination C_1, containing less of the diet drink.

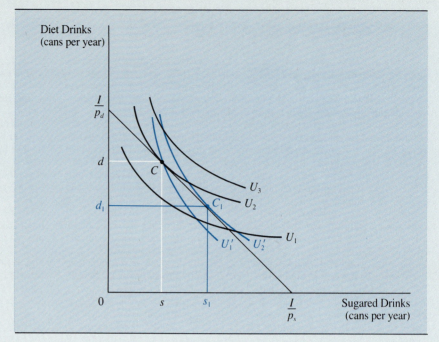

map showing the consumer's new preference pattern is the set of blue curves. To maximize satisfaction the consumer moves down the budget line from combination C to combination C_1, giving up cans of diet drink and purchasing more cans of sugared drink.

Second, combination C now represents a lower level of satisfaction than it did before the consumer received the information on the threat of cancer. Quantity d of diet drink now yields less satisfaction because of that threat; quantity s of sugared drink yields neither more nor less satisfaction than before. Consequently, the total satisfaction level of the consumer at combination C is decreased by the new information. Another way to say this is that the satisfaction level now yielded by indifference curve U_1' is less than that formerly yielded by indifference curve U_2.

The government at various times considered issuing a permanent, official warning about the possible hazards associated with artificial sweeteners (although this possibility is not mentioned in the accompanying newspaper story). An official warning can be interpreted in the same fashion as for the situation where information is released without the warning. The official warning would tend to occasion an even greater reduction in the rate of diet drink consumption relative to the consumption of sugared drinks—indeed, this is about what happened following the Surgeon General's admonitions about smoking cigarettes. The official nature of the warning led more smokers to take the dangers of smoking more seriously and, over time, led to reductions in the rate of smoking—although some users of cigarettes merely shifted to increased rates of consumption of other "bad" habits, such as eating more food.

The Effects of Prohibition

The Wall Street Journal article also raises the possibility that Congress would have allowed the FDA to ban artificial sweeteners, enforcing the ban with fines and other penalties on producers or consumers, or both. Two questions arise on which the theory of choice can shed light. First, how large would the fines have had to be in order to reduce an individual's consumption level of diet drinks to zero? Second, what would have been the effects on consumer well-being of prohibiting the product as compared with providing consumers with full information on its possible health hazards?

With regard to the first question, it makes sense to suppose that along with making consumption of diet drinks illegal consumers are given information as to why this is done. A consumer's preferences are altered by the information, as in the previous case. In Figure 5.11, the consumer's indifference map, originally the black lines, becomes the set of blue lines. A consumer who purchases illegal diet drinks faces the probability of paying a fine. If we convert the probable fine to a per unit basis so that f is the probable penalty per can, the price of the illegal diet drinks to the consumer becomes $p_d + f$. The higher the fine the closer to the origin the upper left end of the budget line will rest. The size of the fine needed to reduce consumption to zero is that which will just

Figure 5.11
The Effects on Consumer Behavior of Prohibitions

Suppose that in addition to the warnings that change the consumer's indifference map to the blue curves, diet drinks are prohibited by the government by means of a fine f per can. The effective price of a can to a consumer becomes $p_d + f$. The size of the fine that will just induce the consumer not to consume diet drinks is that which will make the consumer's budget line tangent to an indifference curve where it intersects the sugared drinks axis. This curve is labeled U'_1.

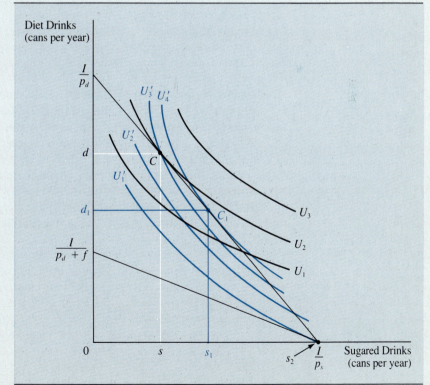

make the budget line tangent to indifference curve U_1' at consumption level s_2 for sugared drinks. Now the consumer would maximize satisfaction with s_2 of sugared drinks and no diet drinks.

What about the satisfaction level of the consumer when the fine is such that the consumption level of the diet drink is zero? As we have previously determined, if the consumer has information on the health hazards of diet drinks and there is no fine, combination C_1 will be purchased. The consumer's satisfaction level index is that of indifference curve U_4'. The imposition of a fine sufficient to cause the consumer to reduce his or her consumption level of diet drinks to zero clearly pulls the consumer down to indifference curve U_1'.

Prohibition of a potentially hazardous product, enforced by means of fines and other penalties, thus means that government functionaries place a higher value than do individual consumers on the risks involved in consuming it—even when all have the same information concerning the risks. Who is the best judge of what you and I should consume?

Using the theory of consumer choice to analyze the diet drink problem reveals, as we earlier suggested that it might, issues that would not otherwise be apparent. The greater the constraints that confront consumers, other things being equal, the lower their satisfaction level will be. In this case, the satisfaction level of a typical consumer is lower when an outright prohibition is imposed than when only an official warning is given. Satisfaction declines when people are prohibited from engaging in some activity altogether, even when the activity carries a certain degree of risk. People tend to prefer (that is, gain more satisfaction by) *reducing* the rate at which they engage in hazardous activities rather than *eliminating* such activities. This is a principle well understood by students and professors of economics, whether or not it is well articulated by newspaper reporters.

It is also a principle well understood by politicians, not only those aspiring to office but those attempting to keep the offices they hold. Perhaps this explains the reticence on Congress' part to give the FDA the full authority to institute an outright ban on artificial sweeteners. Government agencies have attempted to ban saccharin since 1911—it was discovered in 1879—but Congress always stopped them. The ban moratorium on the FDA, which still claims that saccharin is hazardous, comes up for renewal in 1987. But public discussion and warnings about saccharin stigmatized it and led to the invention of new sweeteners that the FDA approved. Makers of soft drinks using aspartame advertise the absence of saccharin.

Congress has not stopped the FDA from banning other chemicals. In 1986 the FDA banned sulfites used to preserve fresh fruits and vegetables in supermarkets and restaurant salad bars. In 1969 it banned cyclamate, a precursor of saccharin, but in 1985 it was evaluating new evidence suggesting that cyclamate may not be a carcinogen after all.[20]

---

[20]Michael Shodell, "Risky Business," *Science 85*, October 1985, 43–47; Marlene Cimons, "Cyclamate Fails to Win Clearance in Cancer Issue," *Los Angeles Times*, June 11, 1985; Laralyn Sasaki, "FDA Bans Use of Sulfites on Some Foods," *Los Angeles Times*, July 10, 1986.

HAZARDS OF ARTIFICIAL SWEETENERS EXIST, BUT NOT TO EXTENT SUSPECTED, REPORT FINDS

Artificial sweeteners aren't as hazardous as previously suspected but do pose some risks, especially among heavy users and cigaret smokers, according to a federal study.

"There isn't any epidemic going on of saccharin causing bladder cancer in the country," observed Robert Hoover, who directed the $1.5 million study for the National Cancer Institute. Nevertheless, the study concluded, both saccharin and cyclamate, another artificial sweetener, "should be regarded as potential risk factors for human bladder cancer." An earlier Canadian study suggested that men who consume small amounts of saccharin daily have a 60% increased risk of bladder cancer.

The cancer institute also found that individuals who consume 16 ounces or more of dietetic beverages a day as well as six or more servings of sugar substitute have a 60% greater chance of developing bladder cancer than nonusers. The cancer risk also was higher among heavy smokers, although investigators couldn't determine the specific magnitude of the risk. There also were indications that women who used artificial sweeteners were more prone to developing the disease.

Interviews with 9,000   The investigation involved interviews with 9,000 persons, 3,000 of them bladder-cancer patients. It was conducted in five states and five metropolitan areas.

Congress requested the cancer institute study in 1977, after placing an 18-month moratorium on the Food and Drug Administration's plan to ban the use of saccharin as a food additive. The FDA proposal grew out of findings that the sweetener could cause bladder tumors in laboratory rats.

The moratorium has expired, but the FDA hasn't renewed the proposed ban. The Senate is considering legislation to extend the moratorium through June 1981; the House passed such a bill in July.

Jere Goyan, FDA commissioner, said the agency "will evaluate these new National Cancer Institute data." He reiterated his concern about young people consuming large amounts of saccharin. "We may have to wait 20 or 30 years to assess the possible effects on our young people of consuming large amounts of a weak carcinogen," or cancer-causing agent, he said.

Source: "Hazards of Artificial Sweeteners Exist, But Not to Extent Suspected, Report Finds," *The Wall Street Journal,* December 21, 1979, p. 10. Reprinted by permission of *The Wall Street Journal,* © Dow Jones & Company, Inc., 1979. All Rights Reserved.

INCOME IN KIND VERSUS INCOME IN CASH

The total income package of many individuals contains income in kind as well as income in cash. Employers, for example, may provide *fringe benefits* such as medical insurance, payments into retirement funds, access to company recreational facilities, and the like. Governmental units may make available food stamps, low-cost housing, "free" education, and similar items. The question we consider here is whether individuals who receive such payments would be better off if they were received in cash rather than in kind. We will assume initially that there are no tax advantages to payments in kind.

Suppose that an individual's initial income, with no fringe benefits, is $0I_1$ dollars, measured along the vertical axis of Figure 5.12(a). Units of medical insurance are measured along the horizontal axis, and the amount that the person's total income will purchase at price p_{m1} per unit is $0D$. With the indifference map shown and budget line I_1D, the individual spends I_1C_1 of income for $0M_1$ units of medical insurance.

The employer decides to give the individual a pay increase in the form of "free" medical insurance amounting to $0M_1'$ units per month. The fringe benefit

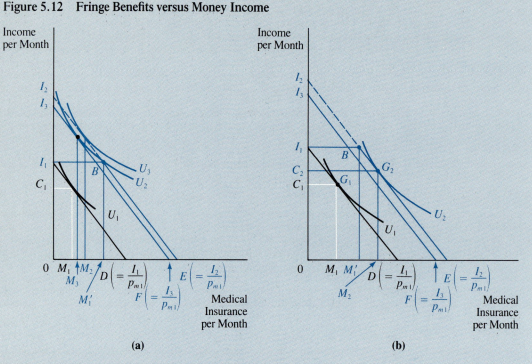

Figure 5.12   Fringe Benefits versus Money Income

Panel (a) shows circumstances in which an increase in pay in cash I_1I_2 will yield a higher satisfaction level U_3 than would a fringe benefit in kind of equal value. The latter would yield a satisfaction level of U_2. Panel (b) shows circumstances in which the form of the increase makes no difference—either yields a satisfaction level U_2. Taxes on a cash increase, reducing income from I_2 to I_3, may make an untaxed fringe benefit in kind yield more satisfaction.

obviously increases the welfare of the individual—but if the pay increase were given in the form of money rather than in the specific form of a good or service, would the individual's welfare be increased by more, by less, or by the same amount?

Figure 5.12(a) illustrates a case in which welfare is increased less by the fringe benefit than it would be by an equivalent amount of money paid to the individual. Free medical insurance of $0M_1'$, combined with a money income of $0I_1$, shifts the budget line to I_1BE. The I_1B segment is determined by the money income $0I_1$ (which has not been increased) and the $0M_1'$ (which equals I_1B) units of medical insurance that can now be obtained *without using any of the money income available to the individual*.

If, however, more than $0M_1'$ units of medical insurance per month were consumed, the individual would be required to pay p_{m1} for each unit in excess of $0M_1'$. These circumstances are shown by the BE segment of the budget line.

Note that BE is parallel to I_1D. The slope of both curves is equal to p_{m1}, since the market price of medical insurance is not changed by the increase in fringe benefits. Note also that $DE = 0M_1'$. The new budget line is "kinked," or has a corner in it at B. Indifference curve U_2 is the highest that the individual can reach, so that in this case the entire amount of free medical insurance is consumed, leaving $0I_1$ dollars to spend on other goods and services.

If the individual receives the pay increase in additional money equal to the value of the fringe benefit medical insurance, the budget line becomes I_2E. The increase in money income, I_1I_2, is equal to $0M_1' \times p_{m1}$, that is, what the value of the fringe benefit medical insurance would be in the market. The BE segment of the budget line is the same as in the fringe benefit case, since the individual would, if at point B, be spending I_1I_2 dollars for $0M_1'$ of medical insurance, leaving $0I_1$ dollars to be spent as desired. The segment of I_2E above point B is the significant one. It represents opportunities open to the consumer that were not available under the fringe benefit arrangement. The consumption of medical insurance can be reduced below $0M_1'$ units, and for each unit that it is so reduced the consumer will have p_{m1} more dollars to spend on other things. Given the indifference map of 5.12(a), the individual would indeed reduce consumption of medical insurance to $0M_2$ per month—where indifference curve U_3 is tangent to the I_2E segment of the budget line (which was not available under the fringe benefit arrangement). In this case the individual's welfare would be greater if the pay increase were in the form of money rather than "free" medical insurance.

If an individual's preferences are such that after a pay increase more medical insurance per month is desired than the pay increase would buy or provide, the person's welfare will not be affected by the form of the increase. This situation is illustrated in Figure 5.12(b). Prior to the pay increase the individual has an income of $0I_1$ and maximizes satisfaction at G_1, taking $0M_1$ units of medical insurance per month. Suppose that a pay increase in the form of medical insurance amounting to $0M_1'$ is given, changing the employee's budget line to I_1BE. The new satisfaction-maximizing position is G_2, and in addition to the $0M_1'$ of "free" medical insurance the individual purchases $M_1'M_2$ at the market price of p_{m1} per unit.

If the pay increase were in the form of money equivalent to the value of the fringe benefit medical insurance, the employee's new satisfaction-maximizing position would also be G_2: The budget line becomes I_2E rather than I_1BE, but since the tangency to an indifference curve occurs in the BE segment common to both budget lines, the results are the same either way.

If an equivalent cash payment to an individual is subject to an income tax while a fringe benefit or payment in kind is not, a person may very well be better off receiving the fringe benefit or the payment in kind. The crux of the matter is again illustrated in Figure 5.12. Suppose in each panel that the individual receives a cash payment that brings before-tax income to I_2 and that an income tax on the payment results in after-tax income of I_3. Let the income tax be just sufficient to put the person on indifference curve U_2 in panel (a), taking M_3 of medical insurance. In this case it makes no difference in the individual's welfare whether the payment is in cash or in the form of an untaxed fringe benefit. But if the income tax is greater, pulling after-tax income below I_3, the untaxed fringe benefit will be the better alternative. If the person's indifference map is that shown in panel (b), any tax at all on the equivalent cash payment would result in lower welfare than would the untaxed fringe benefit.

Suggested Readings

The classic treatment of the theory of indifference curves is
Hicks, John R. *Value and Capital,* 2d ed., Chaps. 1, 2. Oxford: The Clarendon Press, 1946.

For more advanced treatments of consumer choice, see
Friedman, Milton. *Price Theory,* Chap. 2. Chicago: Aldine Publishing Co., 1976.
Vickrey, William S. *Microstatics,* Chap. 2. New York: Harcourt, Brace & World, Inc., 1964.

A major recent contribution to the economic theory of the household is
Becker, Gary S. *A Treatise on the Family.* Cambridge: Harvard University Press, 1981.

Problems and Questions for Discussion

1. Draw a consumer's indifference map for pounds of pork and pounds of fish.
   a. What can you say about all combinations on a given indifference curve?
   b. Select two indifference curves and make whatever inferences of a comparative nature you can about them.
   *c. Suppose that a research report, carefully done and widely distributed,

_____

*Denotes an application-oriented problem.

clearly demonstrates that pork consumption results in higher cholesterol levels in humans than had previously been thought. Show and explain what happens to the consumer's indifference map.

2. A consumer purchases and consumes two goods, food and clothing.
   a.   Under what circumstances does this consumer maximize satisfaction?
   b.   Move up the budget line to the left, and at some selected point explain the incentives that influence the person.

3. Draw indifference curves for an individual between food and garbage.
   a.   Explain the shapes of the curves.
   b.   What do higher indifference curves mean compared to lower curves?

4. Using separate diagrams for each of two individuals, plot cans of cola Brand A per unit of time on the horizontal axis and cans of cola Brand B per unit of time on the vertical. Draw each person's preference map in the following situations:
   a.   One individual likes the third unit per day of Brand B relative to Brand A more than the other does.
   b.   One individual will drink only Brand A and the other will drink only Brand B whatever the relative prices may be.

*5. *The Wall Street Journal* reported on January 16, 1985, that Norway is facing its first decline in population. A hundred years ago the average family had four or five children; twenty years ago it was three; now it is two. Treat a "typical" couple as having one preference map, with children per lifetime plotted on the horizontal axis and all other goods along the vertical.
   a.   How would a change in preferences for children versus other things, without a change in the slope or position of the budget line, reduce the birth rate? What changes in modern society could cause preferences to change in this way?
   b.   How would a rise in the cost of raising children, without a change in preferences between children versus other things, change the birth rate? What changes in modern society could cause the cost of raising children to rise?

6. In 1985, Republicans in the U.S. Senate were persuaded to accept cuts in defense spending of $1.3 billion after Democrats in the U.S. House of Representatives threatened to oppose a provision in the same bill that would allow senators to accept an additional $7,510 each year in honoraria for speeches. (Sara Fritz and Bob Secter, "Conferences OK Fiscal Year Funds," *Los Angeles Times,* December 19, 1985.)

   Draw an indifference diagram for the typical Republican senator who agreed to this trade-off, placing speech income per year on the horizontal axis and defense spending on the vertical axis. What shape would you expect the indifference curves to have?

7. Assume you are a passenger in a friend's car that stops for gasoline. The friend has $10 but spends only $5, filling half the 10-gallon tank. When

you ask why the tank was not filled up, the friend responds that "Five dollars was all I could afford." Draw the indifference map and budget line that appear to be consistent with the friend's choice. Explain what the friend may have meant by "all I could afford."

*8. We explained in Chapter 2, pp. 25-27, why it was cheaper for managers in not-for-profit firms to shift resources from profit-making activities to the purchase of emoluments—for example, the hiring of employees on the basis of their likability, bigger life insurance or pension benefits for managers, and larger offices with fancier furnishings.

a. Assume that profits per unit of time and emoluments per unit of time are substitutes. Draw an individual manager's indifference map, plotting emoluments on the horizontal axis and profits on the vertical. Now draw a budget line for the manager of a for-profit firm where devoting more resources to emoluments means lower profits and vice versa, and where any choice along the budget line is feasible. The budget line's slope shows the relative prices between the two goods. Show where the manager maximizes satisfaction and the quantities of profits P_1 and emoluments E_1 purchased each period.

b. Now assume that the government limits by law the profits this firm is allowed to earn to P_0, which is less than P_1. Draw the new budget line and explain how and why it has changed. Indicate and explain the manager's new satisfaction-maximizing choice between profits and emoluments.

*9. The U.S. Food Stamp Program provides enough extra food for families below a certain income level to achieve a nutritionally adequate diet. The recipient purchases stamps for less than their market value when exchanged for food at grocery stores. The program places a maximum allotment on the number of stamps a recipient can obtain and therefore the income that can be spent on stamps, but assume that the recipient can buy any number of stamps up to the maximum. The stamps are supposed to be used by the recipient, not resold. (Kenneth W. Clarkson, "Welfare Benefits of the Food Stamp Program," *Southern Economic Journal* 43 [July 1976]: 864–878.)

a. Draw a recipient's preference map between food items per unit of time and nonfood items per unit of time. Then draw the budget line assuming that the restriction against resale is enforced. Explain how the recipient maximizes satisfaction.

b. For the same recipient, draw the budget constraint on the presumption that the food obtained at a discount will be resold at market value. How much extra satisfaction does the recipient gain in this situation relative to (a)? Explain.

c. How do your answers to (a) and (b) change if the recipient has a strong preference for food relative to income? Diagram and explain.

*10. In the *Business Week* item reproduced in this chapter, Mr. Howard claimed ". . . an honest analysis of my own personal financial status reveals more about the impact of the BLS's actions than can be derived from opinions of economists." Do you agree with him on the impact of the BLS's actions on his own financial status? Do you agree with his criticisms of economists? Explain carefully in each case.

Chapter 6

ENGEL CURVES, DEMAND CURVES, AND EXCHANGE

The indifference curve tools and techniques developed in Chapter 5 underlie Engel curves, demand curves, and exchange. In this chapter we again focus on individual consumers. Initially we explain Engel curves; next, we show how demand curves are generated; finally, we examine the incentives for exchange of goods and services among individuals.

ENGEL CURVES

Engel curve
A curve showing the various quantities of a good or service that a consumer (consumers) will take at all possible income levels, other things being equal.

An **Engel curve**[1] shows the quantities of an item per unit of time that a consumer will take at various levels of income, other things being equal. These curves are of particular importance in an expanding economy and in one in which the inflation rate is greater than consumers think it will be. They help us predict what will happen to the consumption rate of different goods and services as consumers' money incomes rise—for which ones the consumption rate will more rapidly rise or fall. We will see the significance of Engel curves more clearly if we jump immediately into their construction.

From Indifference Analysis to Engel Curves

Consider the consumer's indifference map depicted in Figure 6.1. Let the vertical axis measure pounds of steak per month and the horizontal axis show units of housing. To keep the analysis manageable, we limit the consumer to a two-commodity world. Assume that the consumer's tastes and preferences, along with the price of steak p_{s1} and the price of housing p_{h1}, are held constant while income I is allowed to vary.

income consumption curve
A curve showing the various combinations of goods and services that a consumer will take at all possible income levels, given the prices of the goods and services.

In panel (a) an increase in income from I_1 to I_2 shifts the consumer's budget line to the right, parallel to the original one. The points of tangency of the budget lines with the indifference curves of the consumer show the combinations of housing and steak that will be taken at various income levels. These combinations trace out the consumer's **income consumption curve.** Together with the corresponding income levels, they provide the data for the construction of the consumer's Engel curves. At an income level of I_1, the consumer will take quantity h_1 of housing; this choice is plotted as point A in panel (c). At income level I_2, quantity h_2 will be taken; this choice is plotted as point B. If budget lines corresponding to other levels of income were shown in panel (a), corresponding quantities of housing could be determined and plotted against those income levels in panel (c) giving us the Engel curve $e_h e_h$.[2]

---

[1] Engel curves are named after Ernst Engel, a German pioneer of the last half of the 1800s in the field of budget studies. See George J. Stigler, "The Early History of Empirical Studies of Consumer Behavior," *Journal of Political Economy* 62 (April 1954): 98–100.

[2] In Footnote 13 of Chapter 5, the solutions of equations (4), (5), and (6) yield values for x, y, and λ in terms of p_x, p_y, and I. Thus, for good X, $x = x(p_x, p_y, I)$. If p_x and p_y are held constant, the Engel curve equation for good X becomes $x = E(I)$. The Engel curve for Y is obtained in the same way.

Figure 6.1
The Consumer's
Engel Curves for
Two Goods

As a consumer's income
changes, with the prices
of goods purchased held
constant, tangencies of
the resulting budget lines
with indifference curves
trace out the consumer's
income consumption
curve of panel (a). Data
from this diagram,
quantities of each good
purchased at different
income levels, can be
plotted to form the
consumer's Engel curves
for the goods in panels
(b) and (c).

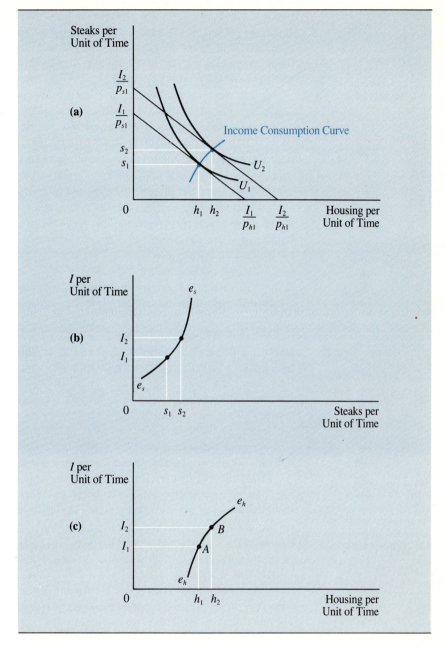

superior goods
Goods whose consump-
tion increases as con-
sumers' incomes in-
crease, individually
or in the aggregate.

Goods and services are sometimes classified as superior or inferior, depending upon how their consumption varies as income changes. A **superior
good** is one for which the consumption level increases as consumer income
increases. The Engel curves of panels (b) and (c) in Figure 6.1 indicate that
housing and steak are superior. The distinguishing characteristic of **inferior**

inferior goods
Goods whose consumption decreases as consumers' income increases, individually or in the aggregate.

goods is that as the consumer's income increases the consumption level of these goods decreases. Hamburger is a case in point, since at high income levels consumers tend to substitute more expensive meat cuts—prime rib and steak—for it. A graphic picture of the income consumption curve and of the Engel curve for such a good is presented in panels (a) and (b) of Figure 6.2.

At income level I_1, panel (a) of Figure 6.2 shows that the consumer takes x_1 pounds of hamburger (X) in his or her most preferred position. This is plotted as point A on the Engel curve in panel (b). Similarly, at income level I_2 the consumer takes x_2 pounds, and point B on that Engel curve is located. Note that both the income consumption curve with respect to hamburger and the Engel curve slope upward to the *left*.

Examples abound of both superior and inferior goods. Among the former are stereo equipment, college educations, housing, better cuts of meat and, until recently, automobiles. A recent study by the U.S. Department of Agriculture found that while consumers' after-tax incomes increased by 8 percent, outlays for housing during the period 1960–79 rose by 8.5 percent, health expenditures by 11 percent, and recreation expenditures by 9.5 percent. Food expenditures during the same period fell by an average of 7 percent, suggesting that food as a category tends to be an inferior good. According to a second USDA study, the income elasticity for food in 1979 was 0.36, indicating that a 10 percent increase in consumer after-tax income boosted expenditures on food by only 3.6 percent.[3] Within each of these categories there will be exceptions. Although housing as a broad category may be superior, slum housing will be inferior. Recreation as a whole is a superior good, but black-and-white television sets are not. Food may be inferior as a category, but liquor and gourmet items are superior goods. Salt, cheap hamburger, cheap wines, and discount airline tickets for "red-eye" flights in the wee hours of the morning are all probably inferior. Another clear example of an inferior good is travel between American cities by railroad, which we consider in more detail later in the chapter.

Engel curves provide valuable information regarding consumption patterns for different commodities and for different individuals. For certain basic commodities, such as food, as the consumer's income increases from very low levels consumption may climb considerably at first; then, as income continues to rise, the increases in consumption may become smaller and smaller relative to those in income. A pattern of this type is illustrated in Figure 6.1(c). One of the Department of Agriculture studies just referred to estimated in 1980 that families in the lowest income group spent 34 percent of their pretax income on food, over three times the 10 percent that families in the highest income group spent. For other items such as housing, as the consumer's income goes up the quantity purchased per unit of time may increase in greater proportion than income. Figure 6.1(b) reflects a situation of this type. It is also quite possible that an

---

[3]Bill Abrams, "People Spend Less of Their Income on Food Even Though Its Price Keeps Rising Sharply," *The Wall Street Journal,* August 16, 1979.

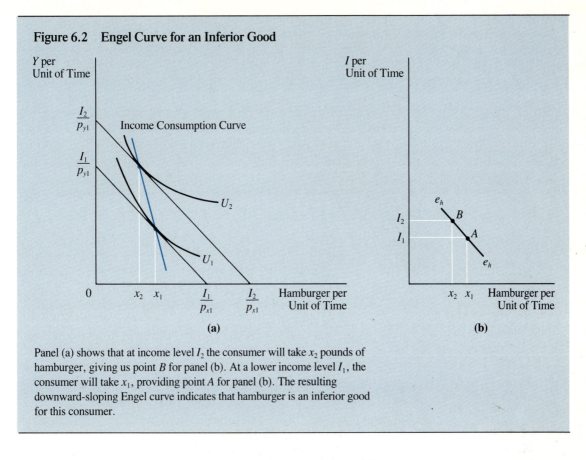

Figure 6.2   Engel Curve for an Inferior Good

Panel (a) shows that at income level I_2 the consumer will take x_2 pounds of hamburger, giving us point B for panel (b). At a lower income level I_1, the consumer will take x_1, providing point A for panel (b). The resulting downward-sloping Engel curve indicates that hamburger is an inferior good for this consumer.

income elasticity of demand
The responsiveness of quantity taken of a good or service to small changes in income, other things being equal, computed as the percentage change in quantity divided by the percentage change in income when the change in income is small.

item is a superior good at low income levels and becomes inferior at high income levels.

Income Elasticity of Demand

The responsiveness of the quantity taken of an item to income changes is called the **income elasticity of demand** for that item. The elasticity concept is not a new one at this point, so we need only to spell it out in this particular context. It is defined as

$$(6.1) \qquad \Theta = \frac{\Delta x/x}{\Delta I/I}$$

that is, the percentage change in quantity divided by the percentage change in the level of income when the change in the level of income is small.[4] For an

_____

[4]In terms of calculus, this becomes $\Theta = \lim\limits_{\Delta I \to 0} \dfrac{\Delta x/x}{\Delta I/I} = \dfrac{dx/x}{dI/I} = \dfrac{dx}{dI} \times \dfrac{I}{x}$.

Figure 6.3   Income Elasticity of Demand

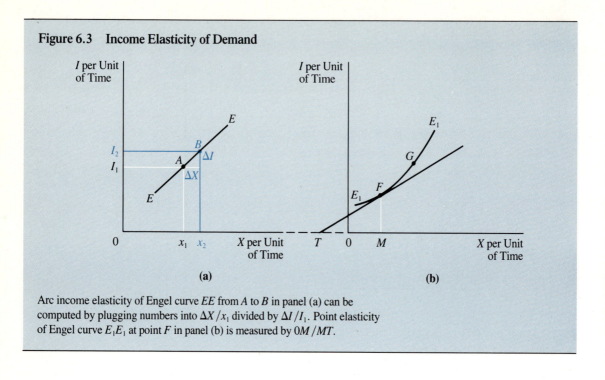

Arc income elasticity of Engel curve *EE* from *A* to *B* in panel (a) can be computed by plugging numbers into $\Delta X / x_1$ divided by $\Delta I / I_1$. Point elasticity of Engel curve E_1E_1 at point *F* in panel (b) is measured by $0M / MT$.

arc such as *AB* in Figure 6.3(a), the appropriate data can be fed into the elasticity formula to determine the magnitude of elasticity. In Figure 6.3(b), income elasticity at point *F* will be $MT/0M$ and be greater than one. The derivation of the point income elasticity measurement is exactly the same as it is for a point price elasticity measurement. At point *G* would the income elasticity of E_1E_1 be greater than or less than one? What would an Engel curve with an income elasticity of one at all points look like?

DEMAND CURVES

individual consumer demand curve
A curve that shows the quantities of a good or service that a consumer will take per unit of time at alternative prices, other things being equal.

An **individual consumer demand curve** for a good or service shows the quantities that the consumer will take per unit of time at alternative prices, other things being equal. The most important "other things" are (1) the consumer's tastes and preferences, represented by a set of indifference curves; (2) the consumer's income; and (3) the prices of other goods and services. We shall consider in turn the generation of a demand curve, the nature of "corner" solutions, and the price elasticity of demand.

From Indifference Analysis to Demand Curves

To obtain a consumer's demand curve for one good, we vary the price of the good and observe the quantity the consumer will take when maximizing satisfaction at each price. In Figure 6.4(a) gallons of gasoline are measured on the

Figure 6.4   The Consumer's Demand Curve for One Good

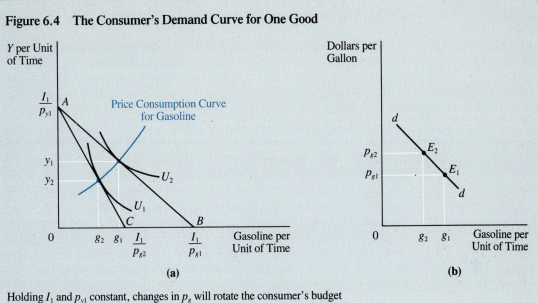

Holding I_1 and p_{y1} constant, changes in p_g will rotate the consumer's budget line with A as its focal point. Points of tangency of the budget lines with the consumer's indifference curves trace out the consumer's price consumption curve for gasoline. At each price of gasoline, the consumer takes the quantity that will maximize satisfaction. These combinations locate points such as E_2 and E_1, forming the consumer's demand curve for gasoline.

horizontal axis. Let Y be all other goods and services measured in terms of identical baskets of them. The consumer's income is I_1, the price of gasoline is p_{g1}, and the price per basket of other goods and services is p_{y1}. We hold I_1 and p_{y1} constant throughout the following analysis. The budget line is AB, so we note that at price p_{g1} the consumer takes g_1 gallons per unit of time when maximizing satisfaction.

An increase in the price of gasoline to p_{g2} shifts the budget line from AB to AC. Given the consumer's income of I_1, a higher price per gallon for gasoline means that if the entire income were spent for gasoline the total amount the consumer could purchase would be smaller. Budget line AC lies below AB and has a steeper slope.[5]

Line AC is necessarily tangent to a lower indifference curve than was line AB, and the new combination of gasoline and other goods and services preferred by the consumer will differ from the original one. Initially, the consumer preferred the combination g_1 of gasoline and y_1 of Y. The new preferred combination will be g_2 of gasoline and y_2 of Y. Different prices of gasoline cause the budget line to assume different positions, with its focal point always remaining at A.

---

[5] The slope of AB is $-p_{g1}/p_{y1}$; the slope of AC is $-p_{g2}/p_{y1}$. Since $p_{g2} > p_{g1}$, then $p_{g2}/p_{y1} > p_{g1}/p_{y1}$.

**price consumption
curve**
A curve showing the var-
ious combinations of
goods and services that a
consumer will take at all
possible prices of one,
given the prices of the
others and the consum-
er's income.

Higher prices rotate it clockwise, making it tangent to lower indifference curves;
lower prices rotate it counterclockwise, making it tangent to higher indifference
curves.

The line joining satisfaction-maximizing combinations of goods at the various prices of gasoline is called the **price consumption curve** for gasoline and
is illustrated in Figure 6.4(a). Note that in reality it shows no prices. It is traced
out by preferred combinations of gasoline and Y when the consumer's tastes
and preferences, income, and the prices of other goods and services are held
constant while the price of gasoline is varied.

The necessary information for establishing the consumer's demand schedule
and demand curve for gasoline is obtained from Figure 6.4(a). When the price
of gasoline is p_{g1}, the consumer will take quantity g_1 of it. This choice establishes
one point on the demand schedule or demand curve. At the higher price p_{g2},
the consumer will take the smaller quantity g_2, establishing a second point on
the demand schedule or demand curve for gasoline. These points are plotted as
E_1 and E_2 in Figure 6.4(b). Additional price-quantity points can be found in a
similar manner and plotted on a conventional demand diagram in the usual way.
Most such demand schedules or demand curves show an inverse relationship
between price and quantity—the higher the price of a good, the lower the quantity taken, and vice versa.[6]

Corner Solutions

Among the wide array of goods and services from which a consumer can choose
there will be items that he or she does not buy. The consumer's tastes and
preferences may be such that some of these are not desired under any circumstances, even if their prices are zero; as such they simply do not enter into an
analysis of that consumer's choices. But other commodities may or may not be
purchased, depending upon their prices.

Consider an item such as champagne. In Figure 6.5 quantities per unit of
time are measured along the horizontal axis. The vertical axis shows quantities,
say, identical baskets, of a composite of all other goods and services (Y) that
enter into the consumer's field of choice. Let the price of each basket of the
composite be p_{y1}, and let the consumer's income be I_1. Representative difference curves are shown by U_1, U_2, U_3, and U_4. Price p_{c3} for champagne is the
price at which the consumer's budget line is just tangent to indifference curve
U_2 at point A. At any champagne price below p_{c3}, champagne enters the consumer's budget. If the price is p_{c2}, the quantity taken is c_2. If the price is still
lower, say p_{c1}, the quantity taken increases to c_1. But if the price is p_{c3} or
higher, champagne is ruled out of the consumer's purchases; the quantity taken
becomes zero. The consumer will be on the highest possible indifference curve—
indifference curve U_2—with combination A, which contains no champagne.

---

[6]From Footnote 2, $x = x(p_x, p_y, I)$. Treating p_y and I as given parameters, the demand equation
can be expressed as $x = D(p_x)$. The demand curve for Y can be derived similarly.

Figure 6.5
A Corner Solution

Given I_1 and p_{y1}, the consumer will have an indifference curve U_2 that passes through point A. At champagne price p_{c3}, the consumer's budget line is tangent to U_2 at point A. At this or any higher price the consumer will not buy the product. At any lower price the budget line will have a lesser slope, inducing the consumer to make purchases of the good.

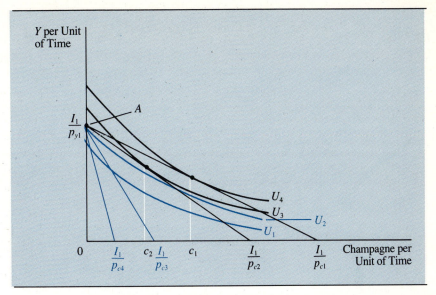

Combination A is called a *corner solution* to the consumer's maximization problem.

A corner solution occurs only if $MRS_{cy} \leq p_c/p_y$ at a point such as A, where the consumer's budget line intersects the Y axis. At such a point, if $MRS_{cy} > p_c/p_y$, the consumer is willing to give up more Y to obtain a unit of champagne than the market requires and will thus maximize satisfaction by moving down the budget line; this would be the case if the price of champagne were p_{c2} or p_{c3}. Translating prices and corresponding quantities of champagne into terms of a demand curve, p_{c3} is the price at which the consumer's demand curve for champagne intersects the price axis.

Price Elasticity of Demand and the Price Consumption Curve

If the X axis represents units of any good X and the Y axis represents purchasing power not spent on X,[7] the slope of the price consumption curve indicates whether price elasticity of demand for the good is unitary, greater than one, or less than one.

In Figure 6.6(a), the indifference curves are such that the price consumption curve PCC is parallel to the X axis, or has a slope of zero. As the price of X rises from p_{x1} to p_{x2} the portion of the consumer's income *not* spent on X remains constant at $0y_1$; thus, the amount spent on X must remain constant also. If a rise

---

[7]A given indifference curve thus shows combinations of purchasing power and X among which the consumer is indifferent. The budget line is drawn in the usual way. The price of purchasing power, or p_{y1}, in dollars is $1 a unit. Hence, I_1/p_{y1} is the consumer's income. Since the slope of the budget line is p_{x1}/p_{y1} and p_{y1} equals $1, that slope is p_{x1}.

Figure 6.6 Price Consumption Curves and Elasticity of Demand

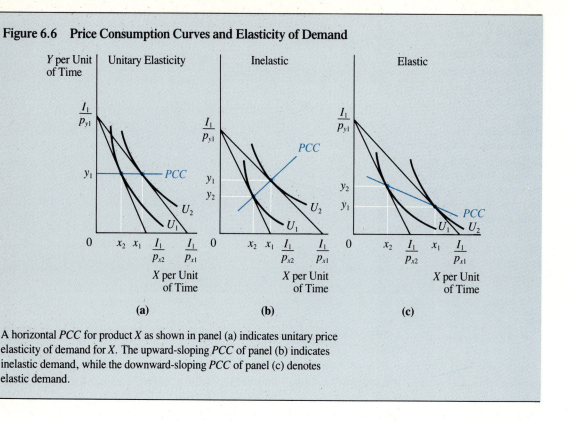

A horizontal *PCC* for product *X* as shown in panel (a) indicates unitary price elasticity of demand for *X*. The upward-sloping *PCC* of panel (b) indicates inelastic demand, while the downward-sloping *PCC* of panel (c) denotes elastic demand.

in the price of *X* causes no change in the consumer's spending on *X*, then the consumer's demand for *X* must have unitary elasticity for the price increase.

The upward slope of the price consumption curve in Figure 6.6(b) means that demand for *X* is inelastic. A rise in the price of *X* from p_{x1} to p_{x2} brings about a decrease in the portion of income not spent on *X* from $0y_1$ to $0y_2$. In other words, more income is spent on *X* at the higher price. An increase in expenditures on *X* as the price of *X* rises can result only when demand for *X* is inelastic for the price increases.

Figure 6.6(c) shows a downward-sloping price consumption curve, meaning that demand for *X* is elastic. The rise in the price of *X* increases the portion of income not spent on *X* from $0y_1$ to $0y_2$; therefore, less is spent on *X*. An increase in the price of *X* that decreases total expenditure on *X* results from an elastic demand curve for *X* between two prices.

Income Effects and Substitution Effects ·

The inverse relationship that most demand curves show between the price of an item and the quantity of it per unit of time that a consumer will take is the combined result of a **substitution effect of a price change** and an **income effect of a price change.** When the price of an item rises and consumers turn away

---

substitution effect of a price change
That part of a change in quantity taken of a good or service in response to a price change resulting solely from the change in its price after eliminating the effects of the price change on the consumer's real income.

income effect of a price change
That part of a change in quantity taken of a good or service in response to a price change resulting solely from the change in the consumer's real income occasioned by the price change.

**Figure 6.7
Income and
Substitution Effects
of a Price Change**

An increase in the price of X induces the consumer to move from combination A to combination B of X and Y. The decrease in the quantity of X taken is composed of a substitution effect and an income effect. An increase in income from I_1 to I' would just compensate for the consumer's loss in satisfaction, returning the consumer to indifference curve U_2. However, the consumer, now at point C, takes x' of X rather than the original x_1. This reduction in consumption is the substitution effect. Removing the compensating variation in income shows the income effect—a further reduction in consumption from x' to x_2.

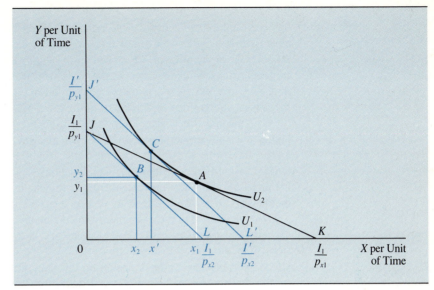

from it toward now relatively lower-priced substitutes, a decrease in quantity taken occurs. In addition, the rise in the price of the item lowers the consumer's real income, or purchasing power, causing the consumer to reduce purchases of all superior goods. To the extent that the reduction in real income affects that individual's consumption of the item under consideration, we have an income effect.

The separation of income and substitution effects is illustrated in Figure 6.7. The consumer's income is I_1 and the prices of X and Y are p_{x1} and p_{y1}, respectively. The budget line is JK. Combination A, containing x_1 of X and y_1 of Y, is the consumer's preferred combination. Suppose that the price of X now rises to p_{x2}, rotating the budget line clockwise with I_1/p_{y1}, or J, as its focal point until it cuts the X axis at I_1/p_{x2}, or L. Note that because of the increase in the price of X the slope of the new budget line (p_{x2}/p_{y1}) is greater than that of the old one, p_{x1}/p_{y1}. Combination B, containing x_2 of X and y_2 of Y, is the consumer's preferred combination after the rise in the price of X.

That the consumer's real income has been decreased by the increase in the price of X is illustrated graphically by the fact that combination B lies on a lower indifference curve than does combination A. The movement from A to B, with the reduction in the quantity of X taken from x_1 to x_2, shows the combined income and substitution effects of the price change.

To isolate the substitution effect and determine its magnitude, we increase the consumer's money income enough to compensate for the loss in purchasing power. The additional purchasing power, or the *compensating increase in income,* will move budget line JL to the right, parallel to itself. When just enough has been given the consumer to offset the loss in real income, it will lie at $J'L'$, tangent to indifference curve U_2 at point C. Combination C is at the same level of preference for the consumer as is combination A; but because of the now higher price of X, combination A is not available to that individual. He or she has been induced to substitute the relatively cheaper Y for the relatively more expensive X in order to avoid a less preferred position. The income effect of the increase in the price of X has been eliminated by the compensating variation in the consumer's income; hence, the movement from A to C, or the decrease in X taken from x_1 to x', is the pure substitution effect. It results solely from the change in the price of X relative to the price of Y.

The income effect, apart from the substitution effect, can be determined by taking the compensating variation in income away from the consumer. The budget line shifts to the left, and the highest indifference curve to which it is tangent is indifference curve U_1. Combination B, y_2 of Y and x_2 of X, is the preferred position. The movement from C to B is the income effect; it reduces the quantity of X taken from x' to x_2.

The movement of the consumer from combination A to combination B, with the increase in the price of X from p_{x1} to p_{x2}, is thus broken down into two steps, one showing the substitution effect and the other showing the income effect.[8] Usually these effects operate in the same direction. If X is an inferior good, however, the income effect will work in the opposite direction from the substitution effect. In such a case, the increase in the price of X causes a tendency

---

[8]To show the separation of substitution effects and income effects for good X mathematically, we return to equations (4), (5), and (6) of Footnote 13 in Chapter 5. The total differentials of these equations are, respectively, shown in Footnote 8 Equations on page 110.

(9) $$f_{xx}dx + f_{xy}dy - \lambda dp_x - p_x d\lambda = 0$$

(10) $$f_{yx}dx + f_{yy}dy - \lambda dp_y - p_y d\lambda = 0$$

(11) $$dI - x dp_x - p_x dx - y dp_y - p_y dy = 0,$$

or

(9) $$f_{xx}dx + f_{xy}dy - p_x d\lambda = \lambda dp_x$$

(10) $$f_{yx}dx + f_{yy}dy - p_y d\lambda = \lambda dp_y$$

(11) $$-p_x dx - p_y dy \qquad = -dI + x dp_x + y dp_y.$$

Regarding the right-hand terms as constants, we obtain the determinant

(12) $$D = \begin{vmatrix} f_{xx} & f_{xy} & -p_x \\ f_{yx} & f_{yy} & -p_y \\ -p_x & -p_y & 0 \end{vmatrix},$$

in which D_{ij} represents the cofactor of the element in the ith row and the jth column. Then Cramer's rule is used to solve for dx, dy, and $d\lambda$. With respect to good X:

(13) $$dx = \frac{\lambda D_{11}dp_x + \lambda D_{21}dp_y + D_{31}(-dI + x dp_x + y dp_y)}{D}.$$

Now, from equation (13), assuming that p_y and I remain constant (i.e., $dp_y = dI = 0$) and dividing through by dp_x, we obtain the total response in the quantity taken of X to a change in its price:

(14) $$\frac{dx}{dp_x} = \frac{\lambda D_{11}}{D} + x \frac{D_{31}}{D}.$$

If in equation (13) p_x and p_y are held constant, (i.e., $dp_x = dp_y = 0$) then

(15) $$\frac{dx}{dI}\bigg|_{dpx=dpy=0} = -\frac{D_{31}}{D}.$$

If a change in the price of good X is compensated for by an income change such that the consumer remains on the same indifference curve when the price of X changes—that is, $dU = 0$—then on the part of the consumer to substitute relatively lower-priced goods—but at the same time, the lower real income of the consumer induces an increase in the consumption of X.

The substitution effect is usually much stronger than the income effect. A consumer who purchases a great many goods will not ordinarily experience a large drop in real income when the price of one of the goods rises. There may be a large substitution effect, however, when good substitutes are available for the commodity in question.

Constant Real Income Demand Curves

constant real income demand curve
A demand curve in which the consumer's real income is held constant based on the initial price level; shows money income rising (falling) as price increases (decreases) to keep the initial real income level unchanged, reflecting only the substitution effects of price changes.

constant money income demand curve
A demand curve in which the consumer's money income is held constant regardless of the price level; shows real income rising (falling) as price decreases (increases), reflecting both the substitution and income effects of price changes.

The separation of the income effects and the substitution effects of price changes for a good enables us to develop a consumer's **constant real income demand curve** for that good. The demand curve that we have worked with thus far and that we obtained from the consumer's indifference map in Figure 6.4 is a **constant money income demand curve,** based on the assumption that the consumer's money income remains fixed as the demand curve is established. Although for the most part the demand curves we use are constant money income demand curves, for some purposes constant real income demand curves provide better analytical results.

In Figure 6.8 both the constant money income demand curve and the constant real income demand curve of a consumer for a normal good are derived from the indifference map of panel (a). Consider first that the consumer's money income is I_1, and that the prices of Y and X are p_{y1} and p_{x1}, respectively. The consumer is maximizing satisfaction on indifference curve U_1 at point A in panel (a); point a of the consumer's demand curve is established in panel (b). The consumer is taking quantity x_1; since this is the initial observation, the consumer's money income and real income are taken to be the same. Now let the price of X fall to p_{x2}. If the consumer's money income remains constant, the new satisfaction-maximizing amounts of X and Y are at combination B in panel (a). Quantity x_2 results from the combined substitution and income effects of the

---

$f_x dx + f_y dy = 0$ (see Chapter 5, Footnote 8). Since, for the consumer to be in equilibrium,

$$\frac{f_x}{f_y} = \frac{p_x}{p_y},$$

then $p_x dx + p_y dy = 0$. This expression is the left-hand side of equation (11); therefore, that equation becomes $0 = -dI + x dp_x + y dp_y$, and from equation (13),

(16)
$$\left. \frac{\partial x}{\partial p_x} \right|_{dU=0} = \frac{\lambda D_{11}}{D}$$

Substituting the equalities of equations (15) and (16) in equation (14), we obtain

(17)
$$\frac{dx}{dp_x} = \left. \frac{\partial x}{\partial p_x} \right|_{dU=0} - x \times \left. \frac{\partial x}{\partial I} \right|_{dp_x = dp_y = 0},$$

or
$$\begin{array}{c} \text{Total effect} \\ \text{of a change} \\ \text{in } p_x \end{array} = \begin{array}{c} \text{Substitution} \\ \text{effect} \end{array} - \begin{array}{c} \text{Income} \\ \text{effect} \end{array}.$$

Figure 6.8
The Consumer's
Constant Real
Income and Money
Income Demand
Curves

Panel (a) provides the
information for the
constant money income
and the constant real
income demand curves of
panel (b). A decrease in
the price of X from p_{x1} to
p_{x2} induces the consumer
to increase consumption
of X from x_1 to x_2,
locating points a and b
of the constant money
income demand curve
$d_m d_m$. A compensating
decrease in income to I_2
reduces the consumption
of X to x_3, locating point
c, which with point a is
on the consumer's real
income demand curve
$d_r d_r$.

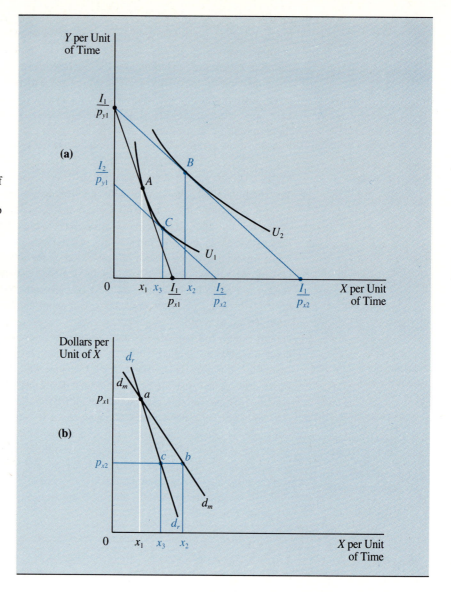

price decrease; in panel (b) point b is established, and points such as a and b
trace out the constant money income demand curve, $d_m d_m$.

But suppose the increase in real income brought about by the decrease in
the price of X is removed by taking away a compensating variation in money
income sufficient to bring the consumer back to indifference curve U_1. Combination C in panel (a), containing x_3 of X, maximizes the consumer's satisfaction after the money income decrease. Points a and c in panel (b) trace out the

consumer's constant real income demand curve, $d_r d_r$. This curve is less elastic for the price decrease, because it takes into account only the substitution effects of the price change.[9] It is often called a *compensated* demand curve, since money income is adjusted for each price change to remove the effects of that change on the consumer's real income.

Consumer's Surplus

consumer's surplus
The amount that a person would be willing to pay for any given quantity of an item purchased minus the amount the market requires the person to pay.

In general, a consumer is willing to pay more for a given quantity of a product than it is necessary to pay. The difference between the total expenditure that must be made to obtain that quantity and what the consumer would be willing to pay rather than go without it is called **consumer's surplus.** It is ordinarily, but not quite correctly, measured as the total area under the demand curve up to the designated quantity minus what the consumer must actually pay for that quantity.

In panel (a) of Figure 6.9 we construct a stairstep curve for dining out by asking Susan Brown how many additional dinners per year she would be willing to eat away from home at each successively lower price. Suppose she would take none at any price above $20, preferring to eat at home, but at $20 she would eat out 10 times. If the price were decreased to $18 she would eat out an additional 10 times, at $16 she would eat out 10 more times, and so on. Let the market price of dinners be $10. Ms. Brown would take 60 dinners per year, paying $600 for the entire amount. But she would have been willing to pay $200 + $180 + $160 + $140 + $120 + $100 = $900. Her consumer's surplus is $300.

---

[9]The demand equation of Footnote 6 is the consumer's constant money income demand curve for good X. To obtain a constant real income demand curve we start with the following budget constraint and the preference function of the consumer:

(1) $x \cdot p_x + y \cdot p_y = I$

(2) $U = f(x,y)$

The mathematical problem is that of finding the minimum income required to maintain each of various levels of satisfaction; i.e., to minimize (1) subject to the constraint imposed by (2).

From (1) and (2) we form the Lagrangian function:

(3) $V = v(x,y,\lambda) = x \cdot p_x + y \cdot p_y - \lambda[f(x,y) - U]$

To minimize V it is necessary that:

(4) $\dfrac{\partial V}{\partial x} = p_x - \lambda f_x = 0$

(5) $\dfrac{\partial V}{\partial y} = p_y - \lambda f_y = 0$

(6) $\dfrac{\partial V}{\partial \lambda} = f(x,y) - U = 0$

Equations (4), (5), and (6) are then solved to find values of x, y, and λ in terms of p_x, p_y, and U. For good X

(7) $x = x(p_x, p_y, U)$

Assigning fixed values to p_y and U the constant real income demand equation for good X can be expressed as:

(8) $x = r(p_x)$.

Figure 6.9   Measurement of Consumer's Surplus

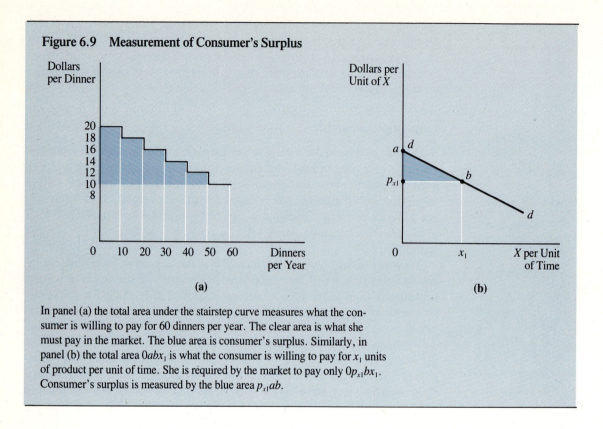

In panel (a) the total area under the stairstep curve measures what the consumer is willing to pay for 60 dinners per year. The clear area is what she must pay in the market. The blue area is consumer's surplus. Similarly, in panel (b) the total area $0abx_1$ is what the consumer is willing to pay for x_1 units of product per unit of time. She is required by the market to pay only $0p_{x1}bx_1$. Consumer's surplus is measured by the blue area $p_{x1}ab$.

Employing the same reasoning, Ms. Brown's consumer's surplus in panel (b) is easily measured at any given price level. At price p_{x1}, she takes x_1 units per unit of time. She would have been willing to pay the amount represented by $0abx_1$, but she is required by the market to pay only $0p_{x1}bx_1$. Consumer's surplus at that price is measured by area $p_{x1}ab$.

But we must stop for a minute. In panel (b) dd may not be the constant money income demand curve with which we have been working. We have not taken the income effects of the price decreases into account in constructing the curves. We have used substitution effects only, discovering at each price level the consumer's MRS_{x1}—that is, how many dollars the consumer would just be willing to give up for a one-unit addition to the level of consumption.

In terms of indifference curve analysis, a demand curve like that of panel (b) in Figure 6.9 could have been derived in either of two ways. These are illustrated in Figures 6.10 and 6.11.

First, in Figure 6.10, we derive both a constant real income demand curve and a constant money income demand curve, assuming that X is a superior good. In panel (a), let I_1 be the consumer's purchasing power when no X is consumed. Now let the price of X be p_{x2}, the price that makes the budget line tangent to indifference curve U_1 at the vertical axis. Successively lowering the price to p_{x1}

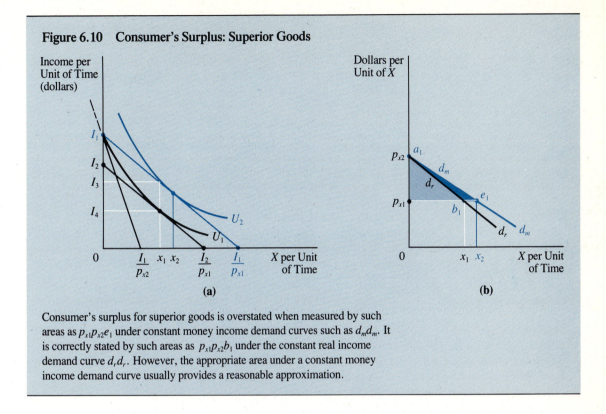

Figure 6.10 Consumer's Surplus: Superior Goods

Consumer's surplus for superior goods is overstated when measured by such areas as $p_{x1}p_{x2}e_1$ under constant money income demand curves such as d_md_m. It is correctly stated by such areas as $p_{x1}p_{x2}b_1$ under the constant real income demand curve d_rd_r. However, the appropriate area under a constant money income demand curve usually provides a reasonable approximation.

and at each lower price taking away a compensating variation in income sufficient to leave the consumer on curve U_1, let the consumer move to quantity x_1. The sum of the compensating variations in income measures consumer's surplus and is equal to I_2I_1, which is the same as I_4I_3. A constant real income demand curve, d_rd_r in panel (b), is generated. This is the type of demand curve that we constructed in Figure 6.9. The ordinary constant money income demand curve is, of course, d_md_m.

For superior goods, the constant money income demand curve overstates consumer's surplus. In panel (b) of Figure 6.10, at a price of p_{x1} dollars consumer's surplus is measured by area $p_{x1}p_{x2}b_1$, the area under the constant real income demand curve, d_rd_r. The constant money income demand curve, d_md_m, measures it by area $p_{x1}p_{x2}e_1$, overstating it by the area $b_1a_1e_1$.

Second, suppose that the consumer's indifference map is made up of *vertically parallel* indifference curves. In Figure 6.11(a) this means that indifference curve U_2 has the same slope as indifference curve U_1 for each consumption level of X. When in panel (b) we derive both a constant real income demand curve and a constant money income demand curve, we find that they are identical. There are no income effects, since the income consumption curve through R and S in panel (a) is vertical; changes in income cause no changes in the

Figure 6.11   Consumer's Surplus: Neutral Goods

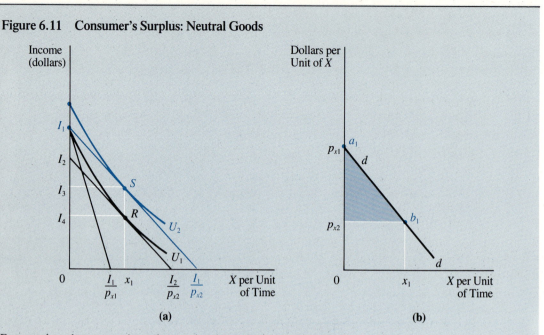

For neutral goods, consumer's surplus at a given level of consumption such as x_1 in panel (b) is correctly stated by the blue area $p_{x2}p_{x1}b_1$ under the constant money income demand curve dd. Changes in the price of such a good do not cause income effects; they cause substitution effects only. Consequently, the consumer's constant money income demand curve coincides with the constant real income demand curve. For this to occur, the consumer's indifference curves must be vertically parallel like those of panel (a).

quantity of X consumed; the good in question is appropriately called a *neutral good*, as distinguished from a superior or an inferior good. Thus there can be no problem of overstatement or understatement of consumer's surplus.[10] But an indifference map with vertically parallel indifference curves must be a rather rare occurrence.

    The bottom line is that consumer's surplus, measured as the area under an ordinary demand curve, is an approximation, not an exact measurement. The smaller the income effects of a price change relative to the substitution effects, the more accurate the measurement will be. Most economists believe that for most goods the measurement is accurate enough to be a useful tool of analysis.

---

[10]Equation (8) of Footnote 9 can be rewritten as $p_x = \phi(x)$. If at some given price p_{x1} the consumer takes quantity x_1, then $\int_0^{x_1} \phi(x)dx - p_{x1} \cdot x_1 = S_1$ or consumer's surplus at quantity x_1.

The Giffen Paradox

A price change for an inferior good may conceivably generate an income effect that more than counteracts the substitution effect, leading to a demand curve that slopes upward to the right for the price change. This unusual case is called the Giffen Paradox.

The Giffen case is illustrated in Figure 6.12. Let the consumer's income be I_1 and the initial prices of X and Y be p_{x1} and p_{y1}, respectively. In panel (a) the consumer maximizes satisfaction with combination A, taking x_1 of X per unit of time at price p_{x1}. Point A' in panel (b) is thus determined on the consumer's demand curve for X. Now let the price of X rise to p_{x2}, at the same time giving the consumer a compensating increase in income to offset the loss in real income—that is, sufficient to bring the consumer back to indifference curve U_3. The consumer would maximize satisfaction at combination B with the substitution effect working in the usual way, reducing consumption of X from x_1 to x'. When we remove the compensating increase in income, combination C maximizes the consumer's satisfaction. Since X is an inferior good, the reduction in the consumer's income from I_1' to I_1 *increases* consumption of X from x' to x_2. A second point, C', on the consumer's demand curve for X in panel (b) is determined. For the price increase from p_{x1} to p_{x2}, we show the income effect not only *working in the opposite direction* from the substitution effect, but also *outweighing* the substitution effect. When this happens we have the Giffen Paradox, in which an increase (decrease) in the price of a good brings about an increase (decrease) in the quantity per unit of time that will be consumed. Goods for which price changes yield income effects in the opposite direction from and smaller than the substitution effects are inferior goods, but they are not Giffen goods. All Giffen goods are inferior goods, but not all inferior goods are Giffen goods.

The range of prices over which a Giffen effect would operate must be small. In Figure 6.12 we show it occurring for the rise in the price of X from p_{x1} to p_{x2}. For the further price increase from p_{x2} to p_{x3}, we show no Giffen effect—the substitution effect is dominant.

The actual number of Giffen goods in the real world is probably small, if any exist at all, since they must exhibit relatively large negative income effects on quantities taken. Some economists have thought that potatoes in nineteenth-century Ireland were an example, arguing that they were an inferior good. Consequently, with a decline in price and the subsequent increase in the real income of consumers, most of which had been devoted to this commodity, consumers became able and willing to shift consumption away from potatoes to superior forms of food they could now afford. This argument has been challenged by recent research into the matter.[11]

---

[11]Gerald P. Dwyer, Jr., and Cotton M. Lindsay, "Robert Giffen and the Irish Potato," *American Economic Review* (March 1984): 88–91.

Figure 6.12
The Giffen Paradox

For a Giffen good, the consumer's indifference map must be such that the income effects and the substitution effects of price changes work in opposite directions, with the income effects outweighing the substitution effects. In panel (a) an increase in the price of X to p_{x2} results in a substitution effect of $x_1 x'$. The income effect is $x' x_2$ and more than offsets the substitution effect. The result is the upward-sloping section of dd in panel (b).

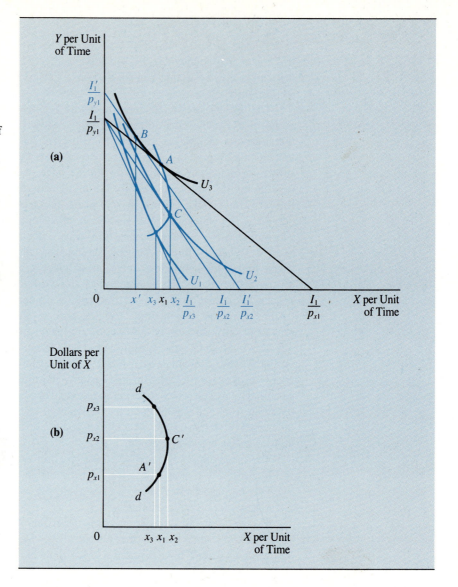

Market Demand Curves

market demand curve A demand curve that shows the quantities of a good or service that all consumers together will take per unit of time at alternative prices, other things being equal; it is the horizontal summation of the individual consumer demand curves for that item.

The **market demand curve** for a good is built up from the individual consumer's demand curves for it. We defined the demand curve of an individual consumer in much the same way as we defined a market demand curve. It shows the different quantities that the consumer will take at all possible prices, other things being equal. Thus, by summing the quantities that all consumers in the market will take at each possible price, we arrive at the market demand curve.

The process of summing individual consumer demand curves to obtain the market demand curve is illustrated in Figure 6.13. Suppose that there are two

Figure 6.13   Construction of a Market Demand Curve

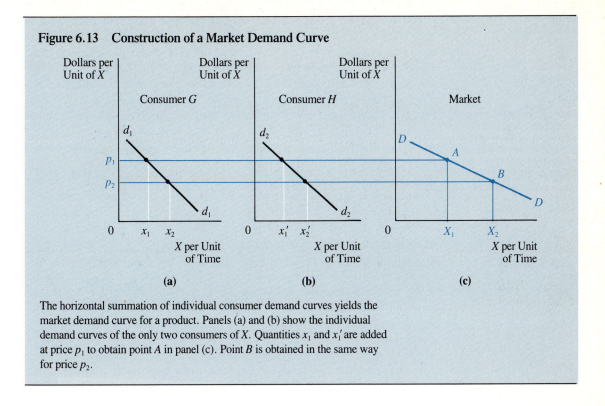

The horizontal summation of individual consumer demand curves yields the market demand curve for a product. Panels (a) and (b) show the individual demand curves of the only two consumers of X. Quantities x_1 and x_1' are added at price p_1 to obtain point A in panel (c). Point B is obtained in the same way for price p_2.

consumers only—G and H—who buy commodity X; their individual demand curves are d_1d_1 and d_2d_2, respectively. At a price of p_1, consumer G will be willing to take x_1 per unit of time while consumer H will be willing to take x_1'. Together, in panel (c), they will be willing to take quantity X_1 ($=x_1 + x_1'$) at that price, and A is located as a point on the market demand curve. Likewise, at price p_2 consumer G will be willing to take x_2 units per unit of time while consumer H will be willing to take x_2'. Together they will be willing to take X_2 ($=x_2 + x_2'$) at that price, and B is located as a point on the market demand curve. Additional points can be located similarly, and the market demand curve DD is drawn through them. The market demand curve for a commodity, then, is the horizontal summation of the individual consumer demand curves for that commodity.

EXCHANGE AND WELFARE

The forces giving rise to voluntary exchange of items among individuals and the impact of voluntary exchange on welfare can be readily explained in terms of indifference curve analysis. Suppose that we consider two consumers, A and B, each of whom receives two commodities, X and Y.

Individual A's tastes and preferences for X and Y are shown on the conventional part of Figure 6.14. The indifference map of B is rotated 180 degrees and is superimposed on that of A so that the axes of the two diagrams form what is called an **Edgeworth box.** The diagram for B can be placed so that 0_aM represents the entire amount of Y received by the two individuals and 0_aN represents the entire amount of X received. The indifference curves of A are convex to 0_a, while those of B are convex to 0_b. Any point on or in the rectangle represents a possible distribution of the goods between the two individuals.

The initial distribution of X and Y can be represented by any point, such as F, lying within the rectangle formed by the two sets of axes. Individual A gets 0_ay_1 of Y per unit of time, and B gets y_1M. The amount of X received per unit of time by A is 0_ax_1 and that by B is x_1N. Individual A is on indifference curve U_1, and individual B is on indifference curve U_1'. For A, the marginal rate of substitution of X for Y at point F is greater than it is for B. Individual A would be willing to give up more Y to get an additional unit of X than B would require to induce him or her to part with a unit of X. Thus, the stage is set for exchange.

Whenever the initial distribution of the two commodities is such that the MRS_{xy} for one party is not equal to the MRS_{xy} for the other party, either or both may gain from exchange. If F is the initial distribution of X and Y, exchanges of Y by individual A to individual B for X could take place in such a way that indifference curve U_1 would be followed downward to the right. Individual A would be made no worse off, and individual B would be made progressively better off until the distribution of goods between the two became that represented by point G, at which indifference curve U_1 is tangent to indifference curve U_3'. No further exchange could occur without making one or both parties worse off than they are at G. Similarly, individual A could exchange Y to individual B for X in such a way that indifference curve U_1' would be followed downward to the right. Such exchanges would leave B no worse off than before but would place A on successively higher indifference curves, or in more preferred positions, until the distribution of goods became that represented by point H, at which indifference curve U_1' is tangent to indifference curve U_3. Any further exchanges would result in a decrease in well-being for one or both parties.

Again, starting at F, both parties could gain from exchanges that followed a path from F to J, falling somewhere within the lens-shaped area bounded by FGK, and FHK. Both parties would reach higher preference levels until some point, J, at which an indifference curve of individual A is tangent to an indifference curve of individual B, was reached. Further exchanges would result in one or both parties being made worse off.

Exchanges that alter the distribution of goods from a distribution at which an indifference curve of one consumer intersects an indifference curve of another consumer toward a distribution within the lens-shaped area bounded by the two indifference curves and within which tangency occurs lead toward a *Pareto optimum,* or an *efficient* distribution of goods.

In Chapter 1 we defined a Pareto optimum condition as one in which no one can be made better off without making someone else worse off. It is this condition that occurs at G or J or H in Figure 6.14 or at any other point at

Figure 6.14
The Basis of
Exchange

At an initial distribution
F of goods X and Y,
MRS_{xy} for individual A
is greater than that for
individual B; thus either
or both can gain (can get
on higher indifference
curves) by exchange.
Exchanges that benefit A,
leaving B at the same
level of satisfaction,
move the distribution
along U'_1 to H. Similarly,
exchanges along U_1 to G
benefit B without
harming A. Exchanges
moving from F to J put
both on higher
indifference curves.
Points such as G, H, and
J, at which the $MRS^A_{xy} =
MRS^B_{xy}$, comprise the
contract curve.

contract curve
A curve generated in an
Edgeworth box showing
Pareto optimal distribu-
tions of products (re-
sources) between two
consumers (producers).
(See Chapter 9 for the
use of a contract curve
in production theory.)

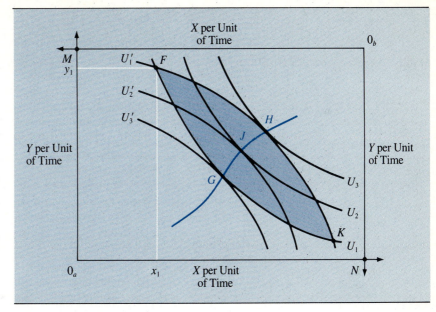

which an indifference curve of consumer A is tangent to an indifference curve
of consumer B. A line joining all of these tangency points, GJH as extended in
Figure 6.14, is called a **contract curve.**

For an efficient distribution of goods between the two parties to exist, or
for a Pareto optimum in distribution to exist, the MRS_{xy} for one must be equal
to the MRS_{xy} for the other—that is, if the maximum amount of Y that individual
A is willing to give up to get an additional unit of X is equal to the minimum
amount of Y that B would accept in exchange for a unit of X, then no gain from
such an exchange would occur for either party. This condition is fulfilled at
every point along the contract curve. At each such point, an indifference curve
of A is tangent to an indifference curve of B; that is, individual A's indifference
curve has the same slope as does individual B's—or MRS_{xy} is the same for A
as it is for B.

Although this analysis shows that some redistributions of goods (income)
among consumers will increase the welfare of a community, we are left in the
dark with respect to other redistributions. From an initial distribution F in Figure
6.14, a redistribution that moves to any distribution from G to H inclusive
increases community welfare. But once a contract curve distribution is achieved,
redistributions along it increase the satisfaction level of one consumer and decrease that of the other. We have no way of making interpersonal comparisons
of satisfaction—we cannot determine objectively whether the gain in satisfaction
by one consumer is greater than, equal to, or less than the loss experienced by
the other. Every distribution that is shown by the contract curve is a Pareto
optimal distribution, given the total quantities of goods and services per unit of
time available to the consumers.

_____ ## SUMMARY _____

The indifference maps of consumers are the foundations on which various choice and demand patterns of analysis are constructed. From them, Engel curves and demand curves can be derived and, among other things, such maps can illustrate clearly the benefits to a society of voluntary exchange.

Engel curves for commodities are derived by varying the consumer's income, holding tastes and preferences and the prices of all other goods constant. The points of consumer equilibrium form the income consumption curve. The indifference curve diagram furnishes the necessary data for setting up Engel curves.

The consumer's demand curve for one good is obtained by varying the price of the good while holding constant tastes and preferences, income, and prices of other goods. The resulting points of consumer equilibrium trace out the price consumption curve for the commodity. Information for the demand curve can be taken from the indifference curve diagram.

The slope of the price consumption curve for a commodity indicates the elasticity of demand when the commodity under consideration is measured on the X axis and money is measured on the Y axis. A horizontal price consumption curve means that demand has unitary elasticity. When the price consumption curve slopes upward to the right, demand is inelastic; when it slopes downward to the right, demand is elastic.

The change in quantity taken as a result of a price change, as shown by the demand curve for an item, is the combined result of two forces—an income effect and a substitution effect. For normal goods, these work in the same direction to produce a decrease in quantity for an increase in price, or an increase in quantity for a decrease in price. For inferior goods, the two effects work in opposite directions, but the substitution effect is usually the much stronger of the two.

By means of an Edgeworth box, the condition for an efficient, or Pareto optimal, distribution of goods among consumers can be established. This is that the MRS_{xy} of one consumer for any two goods, X and Y, be the same as the MRS_{xy} of any other consumer for the same two goods. Distributions of goods satisfying this condition form the contract curve. For any distribution of goods not on the contract curve, a redistribution toward the contract curve can increase community welfare. No conclusions regarding community welfare can be drawn from redistributions that occur along the contract curve.

APPLICATIONS

There are many possible examples of demand principles. One of the more interesting is that of the demand for railroad passenger services, an area in which nostalgia often competes with hard economic analysis. So we consider the case of Amtrak in some detail. Next we turn to a piece of recent research, illustrating the law of demand, in the mundane, everyday activity of garbage collection. Finally, we look at the "bandwagon" effects on demand for designer jeans and the "snob" effects on the demand for Rolls-Royces.

THE CASE OF AMTRAK[12]

The long-term decline of railroad passenger service in the United States well illustrates the market for an inferior product and its negatively sloped Engel curve. Demand probably peaked in the mid-1890s, when railroads are thought to have provided about 95 percent of intercity trips. More recent data, for 1920–1970, are shown in Table 6.1. Electric street railways and interurbans grew rapidly around the turn of the century and, together with cars and trucks after

---

[12]This discussion is drawn from George W. Hilton, *Amtrak: The National Railroad Passenger Corporation* (Washington, D.C.: American Enterprise Institute for Public Policy Research, 1980). © 1980, American Enterprise Institute for Public Policy Research. Reprinted with permission.

**Table 6.1
Output and Financial Performance of American Railroad Passenger Service, 1920–1970**

Year	Passengers (millions)	Passenger-Miles (millions)	Net Revenue (thousands of dollars)	Passenger Deficit as Percentage of Freight Net Revenue
1920	1,270	47,370	N.A.	N.A.
1925	902	36,167	N.A.	N.A.
1930	708	26,876	N.A.	N.A.
1935	448	18,509	N.A.	N.A.
1940	456	23,816	$ − 262,058	27.8%
1945	897	91,826	230,060	18.5
1950	488	31,790	− 508,508	32.9
1955	433	28,546	− 636,693	36.1
1960	327	21,284	− 466,289	32.9
1965	306	17,162	− 398,029	21.6
1970	289	10,786	− 449,579	26.2

N.A. means not available.

Source: George W. Hilton, *Amtrak: The National Railroad Passenger Corporation* (Washington, D.C.: American Enterprise Institute for Public Policy Research, 1980), 3–4. © 1980, American Enterprise Institute for Public Policy Research. Reprinted with permission.

1910, provided substitutes for passenger trains. Within a decade after World War I, the automobile became dominant for short-haul passenger trips. By 1930 railroads were losing money even on long-haul trains, and by 1940 their passenger level amounted to less than half that of 1920. There was a resurgence of railroad passenger traffic during World War II because of restraints on the use of gasoline and commercial aviation, but the downward trend reappeared soon thereafter. Railroads dieselized their fleets during 1947–1952 and made strong attempts to upgrade passenger services. But the growth of airline service accelerated the decline, especially after the introduction in the late 1950s of such commercial jet transports as the Boeing 707.

Most economists of the period explained the decline in terms of the industry's demand conditions. By 1960 the fare differential between Chicago and Los Angeles by air relative to train was only about $20, but the time differential was some 40 hours. Most of the people who could afford to spend extra time to save a few dollars were those like the unemployed, the very poor, or the retired elderly—all of whom placed a relatively low value upon the opportunity costs of their time. A few were railroad enthusiasts who rode trains as a form of recreation. Business and vacation travelers, who placed a relatively high opportunity cost on their time, preferred airplane or auto travel to trains, depending on travel distances, and they deserted trains in droves. In 1955 economists estimated that the income elasticity of rail travel was -0.6; that is, for every additional 1 percent increase in income, quantity demanded declined by 0.6 percent, yielding a backward-bending Engel curve like that of Figure 6.2. This elasticity estimate would probably have been even smaller had it been made in the 1960s after the introduction of jet transports. Estimates of the income elasticities for the rivals to intercity trains during the 1960s were $+1.2$ for automobiles and $+2.5$ for airlines.

During this period an alternative hypothesis for the decline in rail passenger services was put forward. This hypothesis was that railroads were withdrawing the luxury services (such as sleeping and dining cars), which were complements to unadorned passenger travel, as a deliberate discouragement to passenger travel. This view was particularly supported by rail enthusiasts and the affluent elderly, many of whom feared flying, although it was never clear why railroad managements would discourage passengers if the service were profitable. Some of the debate over this issue centered on whether railroads' losses from passenger services were fact or fiction. These advocates of passenger service formed the National Association of Railroad Passengers to lobby for a nationalized railroad passenger corporation that would give managers explicit incentives to revitalize luxury services. So Congress created the Amtrak system in 1970.

The experience under Amtrak has been more consistent with the demand hypothesis than the discouragement hypothesis. In its early years ridership increased owing to increases in routes served, rising world crude oil prices, domestic gasoline price controls, and subsidies. Table 6.2 shows that Amtrak ridership peaked in 1979–1980. Table 6.3 shows that by 1983 Amtrak had not reversed the decline in its share of intercity passenger miles in spite of huge subsidies. It is not likely to, barring another self-inflicted energy "crisis."

Table 6.2
Amtrak Ridership
and Subsidy per
Passenger, 1972–1983

Year	Millions of Passengers	Subsidy per Passenger
1972	16.2	$14
1973	17.1	3
1974	17.9	25
1975	17.3	39
1976	18.2	36
1977	19.2	42
1978	18.9	58
1979	21.4	58
1980	21.2	59
1981	20.6	67
1982	19.0	68
1983	19.0	60

Source: John Semmens, *Time to Take Amtrak Subsidies Off the Rails* (Washington, D.C.: The Heritage Foundation, Backgrounder No. 424, April 15, 1985), 3.

Table 6.3
Estimated Market
Shares of Intercity
Passenger Miles
by Mode

	1970	1980	1983
Auto	88.3 %	84.4 %	84.2 %
Air	9.0	13.4	13.9
Bus	2.2	1.8	1.6
Rail	.53	.43	.33

Source: John Semmens, *Time to Take Amtrak Subsidies Off the Rails* (Washington, D.C.: The Heritage Foundation, Backgrounder No. 424, April 15, 1985), 4.

Amtrak has estimated its own *price elasticity* of demand at about -2.2 for one-way trips, reflecting the abundance of competitive travel modes that it faces as well as the fact that most of its customers travel for recreation or novelty as opposed to more compelling business reasons. Regionally, Amtrak's lowest estimated price elasticity is -0.67 for the northeast, where business trips are numerous and relatively short and where time lost in riding trains is small. Its estimate of cross elasticity against air travel in the northeast is 0.6 (that is, a 1 percent rise in rail fares will raise air travel by 0.6 percent), but the cross elasticity between rail and bus is 1.29. Thus, Amtrak is much more competitive with bus than with air travel even in the region where business travel by rail is relatively important. Amtrak management appears to take these estimates of elasticity seriously, having held fare increases to two-thirds of the rise in the Consumer Price Index over the period of its operation.

Amtrak has not yet compiled a statistically significant estimate of its *income* elasticity, but for internal working purposes it appears to use a number slightly greater than zero. At first glance this number seems high when compared with the historic decline in rail travel demand, but it is probably a reasonable estimate given Amtrak's current routes and demand conditions. The population of elderly persons will grow over time, but if more of them work past age 65, they will find rail travel relatively unattractive because of its time intensiveness. The portion of elderly persons who fear flying is likely to decline absolutely and eventually be replaced by a generation accustomed to air travel throughout their lives. The number of rail enthusiasts is probably static and, in any case, is unlikely to grow enough from its present base (no more than 200,000) to make a dent one way or another in Amtrak's utilization. Moreover, if Amtrak continues to decline, so will the number of train buffs. Thus, Amtrak's demand conditions viewed demographically are not at all favorable.

What keeps Amtrak running is congressional largesse: $684 million in 1985. Fares are about 60 percent of costs. In 1981, the per-ticket subsidy was $137 on the Washington-Cincinnati run, and in 1985 it would have been cheaper to buy every passenger on the New York-Boston, Chicago-New York, and Portland-Seattle trains a full-price bus or plane ticket. Amtrak trains are no more energy efficient than automobiles, and they pollute more than airplanes. But governmental agencies are tough to kill off, as Presidents Ford, Carter, and Reagan learned after taking on Amtrak. Well-orchestrated letter-writing campaigns to members of Congress from a coalition of cities and towns that liked train service managed to keep Amtrak alive, if not well.[13]

THE DEMAND FOR REFUSE COLLECTION

Market demand curves are obtained by summing the quantities that individuals in the market want to purchase at alternative prices. The quantity that each individual demands at each alternative price is in turn dependent upon the individual's preference map and budget line. This chain of reasoning and behavior—from preferences to individual demand curves to market demand curves—applies not only to such commodities as eggs, furniture, and automobiles, which are produced in the private sector, but also to certain goods and services produced in the public sector. However, it is much more difficult for economists (or even political scientists) to assess the demand for governmentally provided goods and services, owing to the way in which these preferences are registered. In some elections we vote more for candidates than for particular issues, and in voting for specific candidates we in effect approve the whole bundle of positions the politicians take during the course of their campaigns. In other elections—for example, certain school board elections—there is an all-important issue on which the candidates are divided, and in such cases electing the person is tantamount to a community decision on the critical issue.

---

[13]Albert R. Karr, "As Congress Comes to Rescue, Amtrak Envisions the Best Passenger-Train Service in Its History," *The Wall Street Journal,* June 25, 1981; Christopher Conte and Daniel Machalaba, "Amtrak May Have to Drop Some Weight to Survive," *The Wall Street Journal,* May 8, 1985; Ronald D. Utt, "Fiscal Befuddlement and the Federal Budget," *Economic Outlook,* March 1985, 6.

Opinion polls are another commonly used surrogate for detecting trends in electoral opinion, but these devices work imperfectly. Assume that a national polling organization surveys 1,500 persons on whether or not they want more national defense. The answers of respondents usually will not reveal actual demands unless they understand what the implications of their answers might be. Individuals are left with their own thoughts about whether their vote for more defense implies cuts in other programs that they might desire more urgently than extra defense spending. Here a more meaningful polling question might be: "Would you prefer that the federal government spend an additional billion dollars in tax revenues on more missiles or on more medical care for poor children?" The typical polling question does not inform the respondent as to what tax price the answer carries. Again, a more meaningful polling question might be: "Would you prefer X additional long-range missiles if it is certain to cost you an additional Y dollars in taxes next year?"

Questions of the last type, while relatively expensive for polling organizations to use for nationwide surveys, are feasible for detecting the demands for certain goods and services provided by local governments. A small college town of 25,000 is renowned in its region for the attention it gives to aesthetic considerations. It is the town's policy for its municipal refuse collectors to pick up garbage, trash, and refuse directly from the backyard of each home rather than from containers placed at curbside by each resident. This policy is more convenient for most householders, but primarily it is designed to avoid unsightly rubbish cans and refuse piles along the street on trash day and to prevent the mess that can be caused when animals tip over the cans. However, the policy of backyard pickup is much more expensive than curbside pickup. In addition to the large truck and two or three persons that curbside pickup requires, backyard service requires four or five small, gasoline-powered vehicles (much like golf carts) to carry trash cans from the backyard to the large truck as it moves down the street. Each of the small carts requires its own driver. The cost of the service has become an important consideration in this town, since in 1978 a statewide law cut property taxes by one-third—and the property tax is a major source of the town's revenue.

Recently a study was made of the demand for backyard versus curbside trash pickups by surveying the residents directly.[14] The survey avoided the relatively meaningless questions described earlier in favor of the *specific price-*

---

[14]The following discussion is based on Ronald K. Teeples, "Preference Intensities for Private and Collective Goods: The Case of Refuse Services," Claremont Working Papers in Economics, Business and Public Policy, No. 22 (Claremont, California: The Claremont Colleges, 1980).

Table 6.4
Relative Price
Combinations for
Refuse Collection
from a Town Survey

Price Combination	Curbside Service Price	Backyard Service Price	Absolute Price Difference	Percentage Premium for Backyard Service
1	$5.50	$5.50	$0.00	0 %
2	4.50	6.50	2.00	30.8
3	4.00	7.00	3.00	42.9
4	4.00	7.50	3.50	46.7
5	3.50	7.50	4.00	53.3
6	3.00	7.50	4.50	60.0
7	3.50	8.50	5.00	58.9

Source: Ronald K. Teeples, ''Preference Intensities for Private and Collective Goods: The Case of Refuse Services,'' Claremont Working Papers in Economics, Business and Public Policy, No. 22 (Claremont, Calif.: The Claremont Colleges, 1980).

quantity alternatives shown in Table 6.4. The demand questions in the survey took the following form: ''Would you prefer (1) service X at a price of P_x per month or (2) service Y at a price of P_y per month?'' The researchers queried a random sample of 500 households throughout the city and obtained 275 usable replies, a large enough number to give their sample statistical meaning.

The first question was whether or not the resident favored a price-related choice between backyard versus curbside pickups. Almost 73 percent of the sample respondents wanted such a choice, although about 67 percent expressed concern over the aesthetic effects of curbside service. This finding was in sharp contrast to a discussion that had occurred at a city council meeting a year earlier, when the possibility of curbside pickups was first discussed. At that time a few highly vocal residents denounced curbside service, leading the city council to reject the possibility on the mistaken presumption that these views were representative.

The results of the demand survey, listed in Table 6.5, show clearly that the type of service residents prefer is a function of the price differential involved. The survey revealed no significant statistical difference in the preferences between backyard versus curbside service of households attributable to such non-price variables as having families of different sizes, different ages, or different home values, or differences in the average number of trash cans that the family filled per week. Table 6.5 thus shows a clear inverse relationship between price and quantity demanded. A price premium of only 35 percent for backyard service would cause a majority of the community to prefer the cheaper curbside pickups. The table also reveals that some people are highly concerned with aesthetic considerations. This group is the 18.2 percent of the sample who are willing to pay a premium of at least 58.9 percent for backyard over curbside service.

Table 6.5
Preference for Refuse Collection Based on the Various Price Combinations in Table 6.4

Price Combination	Absolute Price Difference	Percentage Favoring Curbside Service	Percentage Favoring Backyard Service
1	$0.00	9.6%	90.4%
2	2.00	49.5	50.5
3	3.00	66.2	33.8
4	3.50	74.4	25.6
5	4.00	74.5	25.4
6	4.50	74.4	25.6
7	5.00	81.8	18.2

Source: Ronald K. Teeples, ''Preference Intensities for Private and Collective Goods: The Case of Refuse Services,'' Claremont Working Papers in Economics, Business and Public Policy, No. 22 (Claremont, Calif.: The Claremont Colleges, 1980).

A ROLLS-ROYCE DEMAND CURVE IS ALSO DOWNWARD SLOPING[15]

Our students occasionally attempt to counter our emphasis on the pervasiveness of downward-sloping demand curves by searching for realistic Giffen-type goods. A frequent example is the Rolls-Royce, for which a snob's demand presumably decreases the more of it others buy. This reaction is similar to, but is the opposite of, the bandwagon effect for a fashionable good for which a person's demand increases the more of it others buy. However, Rolls-Royce demand is not really a counter-example to the law of demand. The notion that it is contains one of the most common errors in economics: the confusion of a movement along a given demand curve with a shift in the curve itself. The problem can be illustrated by constructing the market demand curves for designer jeans, another fashionable good, and for Rolls-Royce automobiles.

In the designer jeans market of Figure 6.15, suppose a survey of consumers is made obtaining the demand curve for each when the total quantity taken is assumed to be R. The resulting individual consumer demand curves are summed horizontally to obtain Σd_a, and for that quantity the demand price is p_1. However, the greater the assumed total quantity purchased, the further to the right each individual's demand curve will be, and summations for the market will generate Σd_b, Σd_c, Σd_d, and Σd_n. For each market quantity greater than R—say, T—a demand price such as p_2 exists. The actual market demand curve, DD, consists of points like E_a and E_c.

Why would the market demand curve be expected to slope downward to the right—that is, why would p_2 be less than p_1? Only if every consumer's

[15]Harvey Leibenstein, ''Bandwagon, Snob, and Veblen Effects in the Theory of Consumers' Demand,'' *The Quarterly Journal of Economics* 64 (May 1950): 183–207.

**Figure 6.15
A ''Bandwagon''
Demand Curve for
Designer Jeans**

Summing individual
consumer demand curves
for jeans yields curve
Σd_a when the total
quantity expected to be
placed on the market is
$0R$. For quantities greater
than $0R$, bandwagon
effects shift individual
consumer demand curves
and the Σd curves to the
right; thus DD represents
the total that can be sold
at each possible price
taking bandwagon effects
into account.

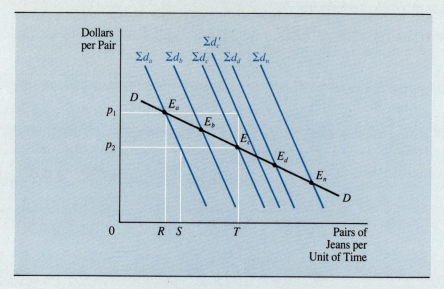

reaction to expected increases in purchases by others increases in the same proportion for his or her own purchases could an increase in quantity from R to T be sold at price p_1. If this were indeed the case, market quantity T would require that the horizontal summation of individual consumer demand curves be $\Sigma d_c'$. But for any one consumer the bandwagon reaction to an increase in the quantity that other consumers buy is unlikely to be a demand increase in the same proportion—certainly it will not be for all consumers. For one thing, regardless of the external stimulus to a consumer to buy a bandwagon good, his or her indifference curves will undoubtedly display a diminishing marginal rate of substitution between that good and any other good. Second, each consumer faces a budget constraint that limits what he or she can do to keep up with the proverbial Joneses. Either or both of these factors tend to ensure that the market demand curve will follow the usual downward-to-the-right path.

The Σd curves are not true market demand curves even though the curves from which they are constructed may be true individual consumer demand curves. The individual consumer can do nothing about the amounts of bandwagon goods that others buy but can only anticipate what those amounts will be and adjust quantities taken at various possible price levels accordingly. The individual consumer's demand curve cannot and does not include bandwagon effects experienced by other consumers; only the market demand curve, DD, can and does take into account the bandwagon effects exhibited by all consumers.

The market demand curve is more elastic than the individual consumer demand curves and the family of Σd curves. If the price of jeans declines from p_1 to p_2, the effect on quantity taken can be divided into two parts. First, we have the usual substitution and income effects that increase quantity from R to S. Second, bandwagon effects increase quantity from S to T. The combined or total effect is an increase in quantity from R to T. The Σd curves include the substitution and income effects only.

For a snob good like Rolls-Royces, just as in the case of a bandwagon good, individual consumer demand curves exist for each total quantity placed on the market. In Figure 6.16, Σd_a is the horizontal summation of those curves when the market quantity is expected to be L. But for a snob good an increase in the total market quantity will shift each individual consumer demand curve, and consequently the Σd curve, to the left. This will be the case because the buyers seek exclusiveness through purchases of a good that sets them apart from their fellows. For each larger market quantity there will be a Σd curve lying farther to the left, like Σd_b, Σd_c, Σd_d, and Σd_n. When the market quantity is L, the Σd curve is Σd_a and the demand price is p_1. Repeating the process at market quantity M generates Σd_b and demand price p_2, establishing point E_b on the market demand curve. Other points tracing out the market demand curve, DD, can be obtained in a similar fashion.

The snob good market demand curve is less elastic than any one of the Σd curves, but it is not vertical or upward sloping to the right unless we have a true Giffen good—one for which income effects work in the opposite direction from and outweigh substitution effects. A price decline from p_1 to p_2 sets in motion substitution and income effects that would change quantity taken from L to N for Rolls-Royces, but the snob effect decreases the quantity from N to M. The net increase in quantity is thus LM.

The snob effect can never exceed the combined income and substitution effects of a price change for a non-Giffen good like Rolls-Royces. For such a good the Σd curves must slope downward to the right. Curve Σd_a exists when the market quantity is L; if a decrease in price were to cause quantity demanded

**Figure 6.16
A "Snob" Demand
Curve for Rolls-
Royces**

When quantity L is expected to be placed on the market, Σd_a is the horizontal summation of individual consumer demand curves for Rolls-Royces. For a snob good, the more that is placed on the market the smaller will be each consumer's demand and the farther to the left the Σd_a curve will lie. Thus DD represents the total number that can be sold at each price.

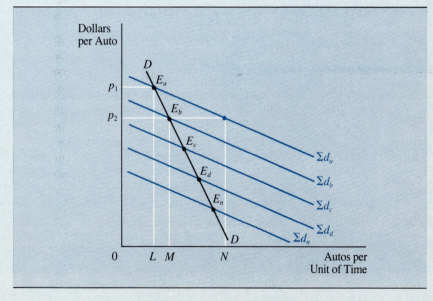

ROLLS-ROYCE DEALER IN ST. LOUIS CERTAINLY IS NOT SINGING BLUES
by Robert Johnson, *The Wall Street Journal*

In the dawn mist of a recent Sunday, Charles D. Schmitt wheels a new white Bentley to a stop beside a twin-engine Gulfstream private jet. The plane's owner, an Arab business-man, has paused briefly in his search for U.S. farmland for investment to do some car-shopping.

Mr. Schmitt, the St. Louis repre-sentative of Rolls-Royce Motors, the British maker of Rolls-Royce and Bentley automobiles, is only too happy to be of service. When the Arab rejects the white Bentley, Mr. Schmitt offers other possibilities. Fi-nally, the Arab settles on a $150,000 Rolls-Royce Corniche in peacock blue to match the color of his jet, dashes off a down-payment check of $25,000 and is once again airborne. The deal is closed before 7 a.m.

In the early hours of this tradi-tional day of rest, the 69 other U.S. Rolls-Royce dealers may well be resting comfortably at home in en-claves of the wealthy like Newport Beach and Beverly Hills, Calif., Las Vegas, Dallas and Houston. But any

time is the right time to peddle cars for St. Louis's Mr. Schmitt, who has used unorthodox tactics like this early morning call to become the na-tion's leading dealer in the world's most expensive production car in an unlikely place at an unlikely time.

Staggering Industry   Last year wasn't a cheery time for the stagger-ing auto industry, and the luxury Rolls was no exception; U.S. sales of Rolls-Royce Motors declined 22%. All of the U.S. Rolls dealers sur-vived, but Mr. Schmitt flourished. He sold 87 Rollses and Bentleys (the least expensive of which lists for $93,000), about 10% of the U.S. to-tal and 22 more than his nearest com-petition. Added to the 900 used Roll-ses, Jaguars, Mercedes-Benzes and Cadillacs he peddled, sales for the year came to $27 million.

The 47-year-old Mr. Schmitt's tactics haven't made him popular among his peers. For one thing, he sharply discounts new Rolls-Royces;

it is a tactic, other dealers argue, that cheapens the car's luxury image. The cars are overpriced, Mr. Schmitt re-torts. He has knocked as much as $7,000 off the price tag of certain models.

Mr. Schmitt also advertises his discounted cars nation-wide, spend-ing about $800,000 annually to lure out-of-state customers. About 20% of his sales are to Californians, which irks Beverly Hills dealer Tony Thompson no end. "Our job is to cultivate our own yard instead of somebody else's garden," says Mr. Thompson, the nation's second-ranked Rolls dealer last year.

Over the past few years, Mr. Schmitt turned down all-expenses-paid vacations to Greece, China and Egypt that he and a half-dozen other dealers won in national Rolls-Royce sales contests. "Other dealers say Mr. Schmitt didn't cruise the Greek Islands because he knows he'd be shoved off the boat," one competitor says. Replies Mr. Schmitt: "You know when people don't like you."

to drop below *L*, it would necessarily be because of a sufficiently large shift to the *left* of that curve. But any quantity smaller than *L* results in a Σd curve that lies to the *right* of Σd_a because of the snob effect—that is, snobs enter rather than leave the market as the market quantity declines. Therefore, a shift to the left of the Σd curves because of a price decrease is ruled out.

Those who still think that Rolls-Royces may be Giffen goods in addition to snob goods should read the accompanying article from *The Wall Street Journal* about Mr. Schmitt, the entrepreneurial Rolls dealer in St. Louis who ad-vertised nationally and catered to the rich of Beverly Hills and Saudi Arabia by giving them price discounts of some 5 percent. Apparently snobs also liked price cuts—or some 20 percent of this dealer's sales would have been made by other dealers who catered to them less competitively than he did.

Mr. Schmitt's claim that he would be selling Rollses in St. Louis for some time was in doubt in 1985. The 61 other Rolls dealers in the United States were

Larry Wolff, an Elizabeth, N.J., beauty-aids wholesaler lured to the St. Louis dealership by a newspaper advertisement, purchased three cars, after Eastern dealers wouldn't match Mr. Schmitt's price. "They say Charlie's prices are ridiculous," he says.

Leo Quello, a San Antonio heart surgeon who raises Arabian horses (including the equine star of the film "The Black Stallion"), haggled unsuccessfully with Rolls-Royce dealers in Dallas, Houston and Reno, Nev. But he got a Rolls for $5,000 under the listed price after a telephone conversation with Mr. Schmitt.

Dial-a-Car   About 20% of Mr. Schmitt's sales are completed on the telephone; he has a 24-hour answering service and keeps a beeper with him everywhere.

Mr. Schmitt's luxury surroundings extend to his home. He and his wife, Stephanie, live in an eight-bedroom mansion furnished largely with antiques, many of which were taken as part of the price of a car. His general manager, Ray Hummel, is a former pawnshop owner who evaluates the merchandise. "We occasionally take jewels, antiques and collector firearms," Mr. Hummel says.

Basic business sense made Mr. Schmitt a winner, says David V. McCay, the president of Boatmen's Bank of Concord Village, Mr. Schmitt's primary banking source. "Charles owns his own house, an entire city block for his business, and he doesn't owe a penny on his inventory," Mr. McCay says. Mr. Schmitt has a secured line of credit of $1 million, the banker adds, "but anything he borrows he pays back in a month."

But it hasn't all been caviar and crankcases for the dealer. In 1974, when gasoline shortages scared away many big-car buyers, Mr. Schmitt's former bank called in nearly $2 million of demand loans, forcing him to sell about 100 cars at fire-sale prices and unload a used-car lot he had just opened in Beverly Hills. Some say the California operation was his downfall. He "went Hollywood" after he opened the lot and spent more time hobnobbing with film actors than selling cars, a friend says.

Tribute from a Friend   But one of his film-world friends (and a customer), Polly Bergen, believes Mr. Schmitt showed "real character" in handling the crisis. "When he had to close in Beverly Hills," she says, "instead of putting his tail between his legs, he worked harder than ever in St. Louis."

Mr. Schmitt plans to be selling cars at this spot for some time. "I'll never retire," he insists. "I'll do this until they have to carry me out of here."

When that time comes, he has instructed that it be done in a Rolls.

furious over his making sales in territories that Rolls-Royce had assigned to them, and perhaps also over that article about him in *The Wall Street Journal.* Rolls-Royce cancelled Mr. Schmitt's dealership, and each filed a lawsuit against the other.[16] The company said that Mr. Schmitt's practice of selling cars for only $300 over wholesale was contrary to its marketing strategy of emphasizing the prestige of its cars. Our analysis of snob goods suggests that the company's claim is not illogical.

---

[16]Robert Johnson, "Former Top Dealer, Rolls-Royce Motors Are Slugging It Out," *The Wall Street Journal,* September 9, 1985.

Suggested Readings

For advanced treatments of the difference between money-income constant and real-income constant demand curves, see

Friedman, Milton. "The Marshallian Demand Curve." *Journal of Political Economy* 57 (December 1949): 463–474.

Machlup, Fritz. "Professor Hicks' Revision of Demand Theory." *American Economic Review* 47 (March 1957): 119–135.

Vickrey, William S. *Microstatics,* Chap. 2. New York: Harcourt, Brace & World, Inc., 1964.

An analysis of the snob demand curve is developed by

Leibenstein, Harvey. "Bandwagon, Snob, and Veblen Effects in the Theory of Consumers' Demand." *Quarterly Journal of Economics* 64 (May 1950): 183–207.

Problems and Questions for Discussion

1. Suppose that Ms. Smythe purchases three goods only: food (F), clothing (C), and housing (H). At any given level of her income, what can you say about the *average* of the income elasticities of the three goods? Explain.

2. Refer to Problem 5 in Chapter 5 concerning declining birth rates in Norway. From the theory presented in Chapter 6, what additional explanation could you give, in terms of preference maps and budget lines, for why Norway's birthrate declined?

3. Assume that the Norwegian government hires you as an economic consultant to analyze the likely effect of each of the following measures on the Norwegian birthrate:
   i. subsidies for extended paid maternity leaves
   ii. state-provided full nursery school coverage
   iii. state-provided recreational centers to allow longer school days for 7- to 9-year-olds
   iv. a larger per-family subsidy, regardless of the number of children or their ages
   v. a reduction in income taxes.
   a. Use indifference curves and budget lines to show the expected direction of change (if any) in fertility.
   b. Assume your analysis is challenged by newspaper critics for relying on economics only, when most families will make a decision about more children additionally or primarily on noneconomic factors. How would you respond to this criticism and what kinds of evidence would you marshal to support your conclusions?

*4. Review the application in Chapter 4 about M.B.A. classes at the University of Chicago. Students who bid more than the market-clearing value of budgeted points were "charged" only the market-clearing amount.
   a. What term would you use to describe this differential?

_____

*Denotes an application-oriented problem.

    b. Draw an indifference diagram and a demand diagram for an individual student showing this differential between the bid price and the price charged.

5. Draw a set of indifference curves that are concave to the origin. Now draw a budget line. Show and explain the satisfaction-maximizing combination of the two goods. Is it possible to induce a change in the combination through a change in the relative prices of the two goods? Explain. Is there anything peculiar about your solutions?

6. For each of the following cases draw an indifference curve diagram showing the maximum dollar amounts that would pay for the right to purchase the optimum quantity of cigarettes that the consumer would choose at market prices when the alternative is to do without them entirely.
    a. A "light" smoker
    b. A "heavy" smoker.

7. Show with an indifference curve diagram that even an inferior good generates consumer's surplus.

8. Why must a Giffen good always be an inferior good while an inferior good need not be a Giffen good? Support your answer with a diagram.

9. Consider the following model:
    i. There are two consumers, Mr. A and B.
    ii. They consume two products—gasoline (G) and other goods (O)—and the total supplies available of these are fixed.
    iii. Mr. A is much richer than Mr. B.
    iv. The greater the amount of G consumed by Mr. A given the amount of O that he consumes, the smaller is his MRS_{go}.
    v. The greater the amount of G consumed by Mr. B given the amount of O he consumes, the smaller is his MRS_{go}.
    Show with a diagram and explain an equilibrium distribution of the goods between the two consumers. Can you say anything about p_g and p_o? Label this equilibrium distribution as point S.

10. For the model in Problem 9, suppose that:
    i. The supply of gasoline available to A and B is reduced but all of the reduction is initially borne by Mr. A—Mr. B's consumption bundle remains fixed.
    ii. Show diagrammatically and explain the impact on welfare (a) when price controls are imposed, preventing p_g and p_o from rising; (b) when these price controls are removed.

*11. Some shoppers purchase "designer" clothing or accessories that prominently display the manufacturer's brand label. Why do some prefer to pay higher prices and advertise the manufacturer's goods when similar goods by less famous manufacturers without the labels often are less expensive?

Chapter 7 _____

THE UTILITY APPROACH TO CONSUMER CHOICE AND DEMAND—A SPECIAL CASE _____

The general theory of consumer choice and demand discussed in Chapter 6 evolved from an older utility approach that has subsequently come to be recognized as a special case of the general theory. The general theory—indifference curve analysis—is self-contained; it does not depend on the utility analysis from which it grew. Consequently, it may be omitted without loss of continuity by anyone who desires to do so. We include it in reasonably complete form even though there is much that is repetitive as one compares this chapter with the preceding one. There is much in the utility approach that provides additional insight into consumer behavior. Also, the literature on consumer demand makes constant reference to it.

Utility theory, or subjective value theory, came on the scene in the 1870s with the almost simultaneous publication of its basic aspects by three economists working independently—William Stanley Jevons of Great Britain, Karl Menger of Austria, and Léon Walras of France. Present-day utility theory owes much to all three.

THE UTILITY CONCEPT

utility
The satisfaction that a consumer obtains from the goods and services that he or she consumes.

The term **utility** refers to the satisfaction that a consumer receives from the goods and services that he or she consumes. We consider first the cardinal versus the ordinal aspects of measurement. Then we distinguish between total utility concepts and marginal utility concepts under those circumstances in which goods are not related to one another and under those in which they are related.

Cardinal versus Ordinal Measurement

cardinal measurement
A system of measurement that indicates rankings among items in objectively measurable unit gradations; for utility, it indicates measurement of intensity as well as order of preferences.

Cardinal measurement of an item implies objectively measurable quantities of it. Examples are abundant: water can be measured in gallons; distance can be measured in feet or light-years; temperature can be measured in degrees—either Celsius or Fahrenheit. The most important characteristic of a cardinal measurement is that *differences* in the measurement scale can be observed and will have the same meaning regardless of where or to what the scale is applied. A difference of 10 degrees in temperature is the same in New York as it is in San Francisco; 10 gallons of water in a bathtub is the same as 10 gallons of water in the Pacific Ocean. The starting point, or zero point, of the scale is immaterial; it doesn't matter whether or not the bathtub is half full or the ocean completely full when the measurements are made.

ordinal measurement
A system of measurement that indicates rankings among items without constancy or regularity in unit gradation; for utility, it indicates only order and not measurement of intensity of preferences.

Ordinal measurement requires no such constancy in quantity differences—it is subjective in nature. The purpose of ordinal measurement is to provide a ranking among items in terms of more, less, or the same; this ranking is not transferable among different kinds of things. We find ordinal rankings all around us. Street numbers are assigned to indicate which houses are at the upper as compared with the lower end of the block, but the numerical differences between the numbers of adjacent houses are meaningless except for conveying order. League standings among baseball teams, hierarchies in government or business firms, and even grades in an economics class convey orderings without measuring the differences between adjacent positions within any given ranking. Intensities of such feelings as love, hate, pain, or pleasure are usually thought of as being susceptible to ordinal ranking but not to cardinal measurement.

Nonrelated Goods and Services

Different kinds of items are unrelated insofar as their consumption is concerned if the utility or satisfaction obtained from one is in no way dependent upon that obtained from the others. It is unlikely, for example, that the utility obtained from consuming nails has any significant bearing on that obtained from consuming gasoline.

total utility
The entire amount of satisfaction a consumer obtains from consuming an item at different possible rates.

Total Utility   The **total utility** obtained from a commodity refers to the entire amount of satisfaction a consumer receives from consuming it at various rates. Suppose for the present that it is cardinally measurable.[1] The more of an item a consumer consumes per unit of time, the greater will be the total utility or satisfaction received from it—up to a point. At some rate of consumption, total utility reaches a maximum. It yields no greater satisfaction even though more of it is thrust upon the consumer. This state is called the *saturation point* for that commodity.[2]

A hypothetical total utility curve showing these properties is drawn in panel (a) of Figure 7.1. In plotting the curve we assume that utility can be quantified objectively and measured and that different quantities of utility to the consumer can be added to arrive at a meaningful total. The saturation point is reached at a consumption level of 6 units of X per unit of time. Up to that level, total utility increases as consumption increases; beyond that level, total utility decreases.[3]

marginal utility
The change in the total utility to a consumer that results from a one-unit change in the consumption level of an item.

Marginal Utility   The change in total utility resulting from a 1-unit change in consumption per unit of time is the **marginal utility** of a good. In panel (a) of Figure 7.1, if the consumer were consuming 2 units per unit of time and increased the consumption level to 3, the individual's total utility would increase from 18 to 24 units and the marginal utility would be 6.

The slope of the total utility curve between points A and B shows the increase in utility resulting from the increase in consumption from 2 to 3 units

---

[1]The theory presented here does not really require cardinal measurability but requires only that the consumer be able to distinguish between greater and lesser amounts of utility. For expositional purposes, cardinal measurement is useful.

[2]Conceivably, still more units of the good forced upon the consumer can cause total utility to decrease if for no other reason than storage problems. However, the possibility of decreases in total utility beyond the saturation point is of no importance for our purposes.

[3]In Figure 7.1(a), the rate of consumption is increased by discrete units. Total utility is maximum at 5, as well as at 6, units of X per unit of time. However, there are pedagogical advantages to considering the maximum as occurring at 6 units.

Figure 7.1
Total and Marginal
Utility

Larger quantities of a
good consumed per unit
of time will add to the
consumer's total utility
up to the quantity at
which the consumer is
satiated. The total utility
curve of panel (a) shows
this characteristic for
quantities up to 6. The
marginal utility curve of
panel (b) shows the
increase in total utility
for each 1-unit increase
in the consumer's rate of
consumption.

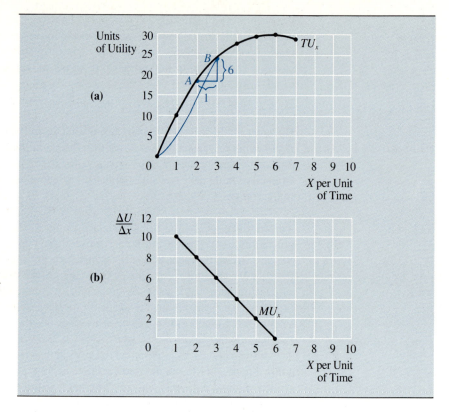

of X and is equal to $6/1$ if that segment of the curve is considered to be a straight line. The total utility curve is not necessarily a straight line between A and B, but the error involved in considering it linear is not significant; it becomes progressively less the smaller the distance between points. If the distance on the X axis that measures 1 unit of X is infinitesimal, marginal utility at any given level of consumption is measured by the slope of the total utility curve at that point.[4]

Marginal utility is reflected in the shape of the total utility curve as the rate of consumption is increased or decreased. In panel (a), marginal utility decreases as consumption per unit of time increases between 0 and 6. This statement can be rephrased by saying that each additional unit of consumption per unit of time adds less and less to total utility, until finally the sixth unit adds nothing at all. Note also that as consumption per unit of time increases, the average slope of the total utility curve between any two consecutive consumption levels becomes

---

[4]In terms of differential calculus, if the total utility curve were $U = \cdot f(x) = 12x - x^2$, then $MU = \dfrac{dU}{dx} = f'(x) = 12 - 2x$. Marginal utility at 2 units of X is 8 units of utility; at 3 units of X, it is 6 units of utility.

smaller and smaller until, between 5 and 6 units of X, it becomes 0. The concept of diminishing marginal utility and the concavity of the total utility curve, when viewed from below, are the same thing.

Diminishing marginal utility need not be the case for all levels of consumption between 0 and 6 units of X. The blue curve in panel (a) could conceivably be the total utility curve between 0 and 3. Suppose, for example, that a single television set in a home with several children causes so much friction over program selection that it adds little to the satisfaction of the family. Two sets—one for the parents and one for the children—may yield more than twice the satisfaction of one. But the successive increases in total utility yielded by three, four, and five sets will surely be successively smaller. Thus, through some range of consumption levels, marginal utility may increase as the rate of consumption increases, and the total utility curve would be convex downward for that range. But if a saturation point for a commodity exists for a given consumer, as his or her consumption level approaches that point marginal utility must be decreasing even though it may have been increasing at lower levels.

The marginal utility curve of panel (b) is constructed from the total utility curve of panel (a). In (b) the utility axis is stretched so that the vertical distance measuring 1 unit is greater than it is in (a). The X axis is the same for the two diagrams. Marginal utility is plotted as a vertical distance above the X axis at each level of consumption. At a consumption level of 6 in panel (a), the increase in the total utility curve between 5 and 6 is 0. Hence, marginal utility is 0; in panel (b) the marginal utility curve intersects the X axis at that consumption level. In (b) the line MU_x joining the plotted marginal utilities at each level of consumption is the marginal utility curve for X.

A set of a consumer's marginal utility curves for the different commodities consumed provides a graphic picture of the consumer's tastes and preferences at any given time. For those commodities with which the individual is easily satiated, the marginal utility curves will slope off very rapidly, reaching zero at relatively low levels of consumption. For those products with which the consumer is not easily satiated, the marginal utility curves will slope off gradually and will reach zero at relatively high levels of consumption.[5] Changes in the consumer's tastes and preferences will change the shapes and positions of the marginal utility curves for different goods.

Related Goods and Services

A great many of the goods and services that an individual consumes are related to one another in some way—that is, the quantity that the person takes of one affects the utility that is obtained from others. These may be complementary relationships, or they may be substitute relationships. In general, goods that are

---

[5]As a practical matter, no consumer will reach the saturation point for any good that commands a price, except by accident. The reason for this statement will become apparent in the next section of the chapter.

consumed together, such as bread and butter or tennis rackets and tennis balls, are complementary goods, while those that compete with each other in the consumer's scale of preferences, such as beef and pork, are substitute goods.

The nature of relatedness is illustrated in the three-dimensional diagram in panel (a) of Figure 7.2. The X and Y axes define a horizontal plane, and total

**Figure 7.2
The Utility Surface**

In panel (a) total utilities for different combinations of X and Y consumed are shown as distances above the XY plane. The TU curves show total utility for quantities of X consumed with each of three different quantities of Y. These curves are shown in a conventional two-dimensional diagram in panel (b) and the marginal utility curves derived from each of them are shown in panel (c).

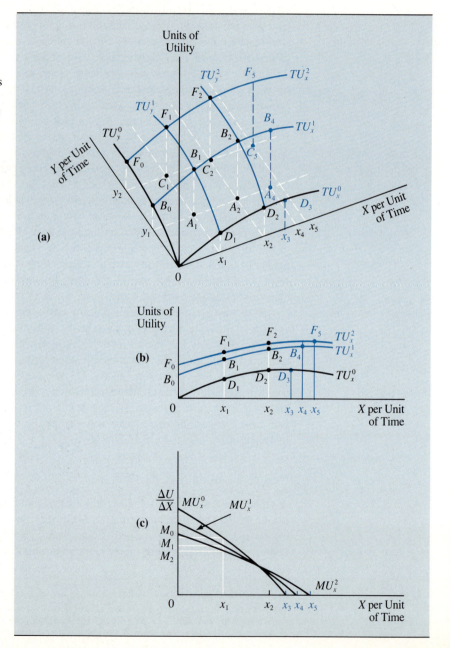

utility is measured as a vertical distance above it. For example, if the individual consumes combination A_1 per week, containing x_1 units of X and y_1 units of Y, the total utility for that consumer from both will be A_1B_1. Points such as B_1, B_2, B_4, F_1, F_2, and F_5—showing total utility for different combinations of X and Y—trace out a total *utility surface* lying above the XY plane.

The utility surface pictured in panel (a) shows not only the total utility obtained by the consumer from the consumption of X and Y in various combinations but also how total utility changes as the rate of consumption of one good is changed given the rate of consumption of the other.

Consider, for example, variations in the consumption of X at each of three different levels of consumption of Y. If no Y is consumed, the total utility of the consumer, as shown in panel (a), is TU_x^0 for different rates of consumption of X. The same curve is also pictured in the two-dimensional diagram of panel (b). If the amount of Y consumed per week is y_1, total utility is y_1B_0 if no X is taken. Changes in quantity of X, with the consumption level of Y held constant at y_1, trace out the total utility curve TU_x^1. We can visualize the consumer in panel (a) as starting from point B_0 on the utility surface and moving up over the surface directly above the dashed line $y_1A_1A_2A_4$. Again, the resulting TU_x^1 curve is plotted in two dimensions in panel (b). The meaning of the third total utility curve for X, labeled TU_x^2, is now obvious. In panel (a), if no X is consumed, total utility from y_2 of Y alone is y_2F_0. If Y is held constant at y_2, increasing levels of consumption of X will yield the total utility curve TU_x^2 on the utility surface and in the two-dimensional diagram of panel (b). The curves TU_y^0, TU_y^1, and TU_y^2 are derived in a similar fashion.[6]

Taking the interrelatedness of goods X and Y into account undoubtedly makes utility theory more realistic, but it makes it more complex, too. For one thing, there are innumerable possible total utility curves for each product. There is a different total utility curve for X associated with each different quantity of Y that the individual might consume. Similarly, there is a different total utility curve for Y for each different level of consumption of X. There are also innumerable marginal utility curves for each product. Since the total utility curves for X differ at each different level of consumption of Y, so do the corresponding marginal utility curves for X. For example, in panel (c) MU_x^0, MU_x^1, and MU_x^2 are derived from TU_x^0, TU_x^1, and TU_x^2, respectively. Here we see that at a consumption level of x_1 of X the marginal utility of X depends on the amount of Y consumed as well as on the quantity x_1 of X. If no Y is consumed, it is M_0, or the slope of TU_x^0 at point D_1 in panel (b). If y_1 of Y is consumed, it is M_1, or the slope of TU_x^1 at B_1 in panel (b). If y_2 of Y is consumed, it is M_2, or the slope of TU_x^2 at F_1 in panel (b). Similar reasoning applies to Y. If diminishing marginal utility occurs with any increase in the consumption of either X or Y, the utility surface will have the inverted bowl shape exhibited in panel (a); that is, any total utility curve drawn for either X or Y will be convex upward.

---

[6]If all goods consumed are related, the consumer's utility function is of the general form $U = f(x, y, \ldots, n)$. If all goods consumed are independent of one another, it takes the form $U = f(x) + g(y) + \cdots + \Psi(n)$.

INDIFFERENCE CURVES

We take a side trip at this point to show how indifference curve analysis evolved from utility theory. However, utility theory itself was a self-contained theory of consumer choice and demand—albeit a special case. In the next section we get back on the main utility theory road (which depends in no way on this section).

In panel (a) of Figure 7.3, suppose that a consumer initially consumes good Y only and that he or she consumes it at a rate of y_1 per unit of time. Total utility is y_1A_1 or $0U_1$. Is it not possible that by giving up the consumption of a small amount of Y and by increasing the consumption of X in some amount the consumer can keep the level of utility constant? Reducing consumption of Y and increasing consumption of X in the manner described, the consumer moves around the indifference surface at a constant distance about the XY plane, tracing out the curve A_1B_2. Projected vertically downward on the XY plane, the A_1B_2 curve becomes the dashed line y_1x_2. This curve is redrawn with respect only to the XY plane in panel (b).

The curve y_1x_2 shows all combinations of X and Y that yield levels of utility equal to $0U_1$ or y_1A_1. For example, at point E in panel (a), the consumer is taking y_0 of Y and x_1 of X; this combination yields a total utility of EF ($=y_1A_1$). Similarly, if he or she consumes X alone at level x_2, total utility is x_2B_2 ($=y_1A_1$). Curve y_1x_2 is in every sense an indifference curve like those of Chapter 6. Since all combinations of X and Y shown by this curve yield the same total utility, the consumer is indifferent as to which of them he or she consumes.

Higher levels of utility are shown by contour lines higher up on the surface, while lower contour lines show lower levels of utility. Projected on the XY plane, the indifference curves corresponding to higher contour lines lie further from the origin—for example, y_2x_3 as compared with y_1x_2 in panel (b). The projections of lower contour lines lie closer to the origin. These observations are based on the assumption that the utility surface tapers toward a summit as we move upward. It is usually thought of as having an inverted bowl shape, although this restriction is not really necessary for the foregoing observations to hold.

The marginal rate of substitution of X for Y is measured by the *ratio* of the marginal utility of X to the marginal utility of Y, that is, $MRS_{xy} = MU_x/MU_y$. In Figure 7.3(b), suppose that the consumer is originally consuming combination A. If he or she were to move from combination A to combination B, the consumer would give up Δy of Y and acquire Δx of X with *no change* in his or her total utility level. The loss in utility from giving up Y is $\Delta y \times MU_y$; the gain from acquiring X is $\Delta x \times MU_x$. Therefore,

(7.1)
$$\Delta y \times MU_y = \Delta x = MU_x;$$

or,

(7.2)
$$\frac{\Delta y}{\Delta x} = \frac{MU_x}{MU_y} = MRS_{xy}.$$

**Figure 7.3
Indifference Curves
from a Utility
Surface**

A consumer in panel (a)
at point A_1 on the utility
surface consumes y_1 of Y
and no X. Proceeding
around the surface in
such a way as to keep
utility constant traces out
line A_1B_2. Line y_1x_2 is
the projection of A_1B_2 to
the XY plane and is an
indifference curve
showing the combinations
of X and Y that yield a
constant level of utility.
Indifference curve y_2x_3,
showing a higher level of
utility, is derived in the
same way. Both are
shown in panel (b) in the
usual form.

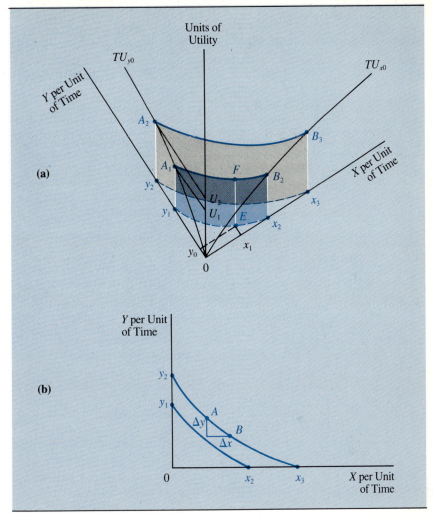

In this discussion we have continued to assume that utility is measurable. For
example, in Figure 7.3(a) the distance $0U_1$ is a definite measurable magnitude,
say, 8 units of utility, while $0U_2$ is 10 units of utility. Accordingly, in Figure
7.3(b) we would attach the number 8 to the y_1x_2 indifference curve and 10 to
the y_2x_3 curve. However, is it essential that we attach absolute utility *magnitudes*
to each indifference curve? Would it not be possible, once we have an indifference map, to attach a utility *ranking* to each curve instead?

   If we did so, the 8 and the 10 would have no significance as absolute
measures. They would show only the order of utility magnitudes—that is, that

10 is greater than 8. We could accomplish the same thing by attaching the number 1 to y_1x_2 and the number 2 to y_2x_3.[7]

If the order, but not the absolute measure, of utility magnitudes is all that is required, we can forget about how high the utility surface rises above the XY plane; only its general shape is important. Suppose that we think of it as being collapsible from the top down in such a way that contour lines from bottom to top retain their original shapes. If we do so, we are free of the assumption that utility is measurable. The indifference map is the same in all essential respects as those developed earlier in Chapter 5.

CONSUMER CHOICE

Returning now to the main road, the utility concepts provide a basis for determining how a consumer will allocate income among the various goods and services that confront the individual. They are more awkward to use than the more general indifference curve analysis. To keep the discussion as simple as possible, we assume that (1) the goods and services contemplated by the consumer are nonrelated; (2) utility is cardinal; and (3) the marginal utility of each item consumed is diminishing.[8] None of these do any violence to the conclusions reached, but they do much to smooth the path toward them.

Objectives and Constraints

The objective usually postulated for a rational consumer is the maximization of satisfaction or utility. The consumer's preferences are described by utility curves for the various goods and services available. The choice problem is to select from these the kinds and amounts that will yield the greatest total amount of utility.

The consumer is constrained by income (the dollars per unit of time available to spend) and prices of goods and services. Typically, income per unit of time is a more or less fixed amount, as are the prices faced (since the consumer is a pure competitor in the purchase of most things). Subject to these constraints, the consumer chooses the utility-maximizing combination of goods and services.

---

[7] If the consumer's utility function is represented by $U = f(x, y)$, then the equation for one indifference curve is $U_1 = f(x, y)$, in which U_1 is a constant. Other values assigned to U define other indifference curves, all of these making up the consumer's indifference map. It is necessary only that the assigned values show the order of utility magnitudes; it is not necessary that they show absolute (measurable) utility magnitudes.

[8] Actually, all that we need to assume is that the marginal utility of one good decreases relative to the marginal utilities of other goods as consumption of the one is increased in proportion to the consumption of the others. The marginal utility of X could be increasing. However, if the additional consumption of X raises the marginal utilities of other goods, that of X has decreased *relative* to those of the other goods.

**Table 7.1
Marginal Utility
Schedules**

(a)

Product X		Product Y	
Quantity (dollars' worth)	MU_x (units of utility)	Quantity (dollars' worth)	MU_y (units of utility)
1	40	1	30
2	36	2	29
3	32	3	28
4	28	4	27
5	24	5	26
6	20	6	25
7	12	7	24
8	4	8	20

(b)

Product X		Product Y	
Quantity (bushels)	MU_x (units of utility)	Quantity (pints)	MU_y (units of utility)
1	50	1	30
2	44	2	28
3	38	3	26
4	32	4	24
5	26	5	22
6	20	6	20
7	12	7	16
8	4	8	10

Maximization of Utility

To avoid unnecessary complexity, we limit the consumer to two goods, X and Y, priced at p_x and p_y, respectively. If p_x and p_y are given and constant, we can measure quantities of the goods in terms of dollars' worths. For example, if a bushel of X costs $2, we can record that physical quantity as $2 worth; a half bushel is equivalent to $1 worth. Table 7.1(a) records a consumer's hypothetical marginal utility schedules for X and Y, measuring quantities in dollars' worths and assuming independence between the two goods.[9]

 If the consumer has an income of $12 per unit of time, what is the allocation of it between X and Y that will maximize utility? Suppose that only $1 per unit of time is spent. On Y, it will yield only 30 units of satisfaction, whereas spent on X, it will yield 40. Thus, the dollar will be allocated to X. If the expenditure

[9]Assuming that the marginal utility schedule of each commodity is independent of the level of consumption of the other commodity, we can go directly to the conditions necessary for maximization of satisfaction. If X and Y were substitutes, the more of X consumed, the lower the marginal utility of Y would be at various consumption levels of Y. If they were complements, the more of X consumed, the higher the marginal utility of Y would be at various consumption levels of Y. These possibilities do not change the conditions necessary for maximization of satisfaction, but they make numerical exposition of these conditions virtually impossible.

level is increased to $2, where should the second dollar go? Spent on X, it will increase the consumer's total utility by 36 (the marginal utility of a second dollar's worth of X), but spent on Y, it will add only 30 units. The second dollar will be spent on X, and so will the third dollar. The situation changes when the total expenditure increases from $3 to $4. A fourth dollar spent on X will increase the total utility by 28 units, but if it is spent on the first dollar's worth of Y, the increase will be 30 units and the fourth dollar will go for Y. As expenditure per unit of time is increased dollar by dollar, the fifth should go for Y; the sixth and seventh, one each for X and Y; the eighth, ninth, and tenth for Y; and the eleventh and twelfth, one each for X and Y. The consumer is now taking $5 worth of X and $7 worth of Y. The marginal utility per dollar's worth of X is equal to that of a dollar's worth of Y—both are 24 units of utility.

We know that the consumer's utility for the $12 expenditure is maximum, because it was placed dollar by dollar where each dollar made its greatest contribution to total utility.

Generalizing, we can say that a consumer *maximizes utility* by allocating income among the goods and services (including savings) available in such a way that (1) the marginal utility per dollar's worth of any one is equal to the marginal utility per dollar's worth of any other and (2) all of the income is spent. Savings, which may appear to pose a problem, is simply treated as any other good. Since a consumer obtains utility from savings, the marginal utility of savings, like that of other goods and services, presumably diminishes as the quantity of savings is increased.

Suppose we look at the problem again with data arranged a little differently. Consider another consumer whose marginal utility schedules are based on bushels and pints like those of Table 7.1(b). The price of X is $2 per bushel, and that of Y is $1 per pint. This consumer's income is $15 per unit of time. How should it be allocated between X and Y?

Since the marginal utility schedules are in physical measurements of X and Y rather than in dollars' worths, we need a means of converting the information that they contain into marginal utilities per dollar's worth. To do this, consider the fourth bushel of X. If the consumer takes 4 bushels of X, the fourth bushel has a marginal utility of 32 units. The fourth bushel (like any other bushel) costs $2. At this consumption level the marginal utility per bushel of X divided by the price of X, or MU_x/p_x, is the marginal utility per dollar's worth of X. Thus the marginal utility per dollar's worth of X is 16 units at this point. Likewise, the marginal utility per pint of Y at any consumption level divided by the price of Y, or MU_y/p_y, can be read as the marginal utility per dollar's worth of Y at that level. The first condition for maximizing satisfaction becomes

(7.3)
$$\frac{MU_x}{p_x} = \frac{MU_y}{p_y} = \frac{MU_z}{p_z} = \cdots$$

The requirement that the consumer be spending all of his or her income—no more and no less—is expressed as

(7.4)
$$x \times p_x + y \times p_y + z \times p_z + \cdots = I.$$

The total expenditure on X is the price of X times the amount of X purchased. The same holds for the expenditure on each other good or service, including savings. The total of these must equal the income, I.

Since the price of X is $2 per bushel and the price of Y is $1 per pint, we must find some combination of X and Y at which the marginal utility per bushel of X is twice the marginal utility per pint of Y. In Table 7.1(b), this combination occurs at 6 bushels of X and 8 pints of Y. However, the total amount spent on X would be $12, and the total amount spent on Y would be $8—the consumer is exceeding his or her income. Thus the second condition for maximization of total utility is not met, although the first one is satisfied. Another possible combination is the one containing 4 bushels of X and 7 pints of Y. The first condition is met, since $32/\$2 = 16/\$1$. The second condition is fulfilled also, since 4 bushels $\times$ \$2 + 7 pints $\times$ \$1 = \$15. Thus the consumer should take 4 bushels of X and 7 pints of Y to maximize his or her total utility.

To demonstrate that utility is maximized, transfer $1 from X to Y. Giving up a dollar's worth of X, or half of the fourth bushel, reduces total utility by 16 units, while spending the dollar for an eighth pint of Y increases total utility by 10—creating a net loss of 6 units. If the dollar were transferred in the opposite direction, there would also be a net loss of utility—3 units in this case.[10]

The data confronting the consumer may not yield the neat solution of this example. Suppose the consumer's income were $14 per unit of time instead of $15. How should it be allocated? The consumer could give up either a half bushel of X or a pint of Y; in either case total utility would be decreased by 16 units. If the consumer's income were $16 instead of $15, he or she could take half of the fifth bushel of X, increasing total utility by 13 units, whereas by taking the eighth pint of Y, total utility would increase by only 10 units. Thus, the consumer seeking maximum satisfaction should allocate income among various goods so as to approach as nearly as possible the condition that the marginal utility of a dollar's worth of one good equal the marginal utility of a dollar's worth of any other good purchased.

How would the theory work for a typical family? Suppose that the family budget is composed of the following items: food, clothing, housing, automobile, medical care, recreation, and education. Over a short period of time, expenditures in some of the classifications are more or less fixed in amount. The mortgage payments, for example, are a fixed monthly amount. The grocery bill and medical expenditures are sometimes dictated by necessity rather than choice.

---

[10]The mathematical problem is that of maximizing the consumer's utility function subject to the budget constraint. Using the symbols of the text, the utility function is $U = f(x, y)$, and the budget constraint is

$$xp_x + yp_y = I, \quad \text{or} \quad xp_x + yp_y - I = 0.$$

The maximization problem is identical to that shown in Footnote 13 of Chapter 5, in which

$$f_x = MU_x = \lambda p_x \quad \text{and} \quad f_y = MU_y = \lambda p_y.$$

Therefore,

$$\frac{MU_x}{MU_y} = \frac{\lambda p_x}{\lambda p_y}, \quad \text{or} \quad \frac{MU_x}{p_x} = \frac{MU_y}{p_y} = \lambda.$$

Note that λ measures the marginal utility of money.

The other categories are likely to be more variable, but habit may be influential in determining them in the short run.

Over a longer period of time, however, expenditures on any or all of the budgeted items are subject to change. The family seeking to get the greatest possible satisfaction from its limited income will periodically reappraise its budget. For example, the family car begins to rattle more, and at the same time it appears desirable to add a new bedroom to the house for Junior. It is out of the question to purchase both a new car and a new room, and a choice must be made regarding the direction of expenditure. Further, if either is to be purchased, it may be necessary to cut down on educational expenses for the older daughter, who has been attending a private university. Should she be transferred to the state university where expenses are less? Changes in food and clothing budgeting may also be required to make the new car or the new room possible. Likewise, the family may need to economize on recreation and even on medical expenses—when Junior has a minor illness, he may have to get over it without a visit to the doctor. A whole chain of decisions will have to be made on the basis of marginal utility principles if maximum satisfaction for the family is to be attained.

The family subjectively estimates the marginal utilities of dollars spent in each of the various directions. Transfers of expenditures from the items where marginal utility per dollar's worth is less toward items where marginal utility per dollar's worth is greater serve to increase total satisfaction.

DEMAND CURVES

The utility approach to consumer choice can be extended to explain individual consumer demand curves for goods and services. Again, we limit the consumer to a two-commodity world in which X and Y are independent goods. Throughout the following analysis, the consumer's utility curves are given and remain constant, and the marginal utility of each good is assumed to be diminishing for increases in its consumption.

The Demand Curve for X[11]

To establish the consumer's demand curve for X, suppose that initially the price of X is p_{x1} and the price of Y is p_{y1}. We shall assume that at all times the

---

[11]The analysis presented here is essentially that of Léon Walras. See his *Abrégé des eléments d'économie politique pure* (Paris: R. Pichon et R. Durand-Auzias, 1938), 131–133. The transition from the theory of consumer behavior to demand curves set out in the text differs from the usual Marshallian treatment, which considers the marginal utility of money constant and simply converts the marginal utility curve for a commodity into the demand curve for it. See Kenneth E. Boulding, *Economic Analysis*, 4th ed., Vol. 1 (New York: Harper & Row, 1966), 520–527.

The Marshallian approach ignores the income effects of price changes. The approach used in the text includes income effects as well as substitution effects. This approach in turn makes the utility analysis of this chapter more nearly parallel to the indifference curve analysis of Chapter 6.

Figure 7.4   Determination of Quantities Demanded

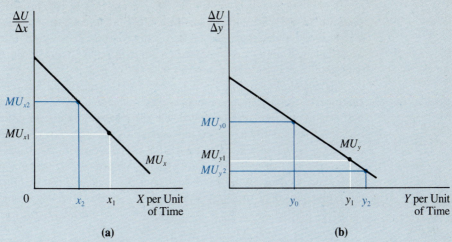

Let p_{x1} and p_{y1} be the initial prices of X and Y with p_{x1} twice as high as p_{y1}. The consumer would take quantities x_1 and y_1 such that MU_{x1} would be twice MU_{y1}. A rise in the price of X to p_{x2} would induce the consumer to shift dollars from X to Y, reducing the quantity of X and increasing the quantity of Y taken to levels, designated x_2 and y_2, that will again make $MU_x/p_x = MU_y/p_y$ for the consumer.

consumer is operating at the limit of the income restraint. The consumer will maximize satisfaction, or be in equilibrium, when taking that quantity of X and Y at which

(7.5)
$$\frac{MU_{x1}}{p_{x1}} = \frac{MU_{y1}}{p_{y1}}.$$

Thus, at price p_{x1} the consumer is taking a definite quantity of X—that quantity which makes the marginal utility of a dollar's worth of X equal to the marginal utility of a dollar's worth of Y. We shall call this quantity x_1.[12]

The consumer's initial position of equilibrium is shown graphically in Figure 7.4. Assuming that p_{x1} is twice p_{y1}, the consumer takes quantity x_1 of X and y_1 of Y in panels (a) and (b), respectively. These quantities are such that MU_{x1} is twice MU_{y1}.[13] One point on the consumer's demand schedule or de-

---

[12]The consumer will also be taking some definite quantity, y_1, of Y; however, we are primarily concerned with the quantity of X that is taken.

[13]For any given ratio of p_x and p_y, quantities of X and Y taken must be such that $p_x/p_y = MU_x/MU_y$, or $MU_x/p_x = MU_y/p_y$.

mand curve for X has now been established: at price p_{x1} the consumer will take quantity x_1.

The problem is to establish the quantities of X that will be taken at other prices of X when the consumer is in equilibrium at each of those prices, with the price of Y remaining constant at p_{y1}, the consumer's marginal utility curves or tastes and preferences remaining constant, and income also remaining constant.

Suppose in Figure 7.4 that the price of X rises to p_{x2} and that the consumer continues to take the same amount of X as before. The marginal utility per bushel of X will remain unchanged, but the marginal utility per dollar's worth of X, MU_{x1}/p_{x2}, will be less. At the higher price p_{x2}, the consumer spends more income on X than before, leaving less to be spent on Y. Since p_{y1} is the given price of Y, the consumer necessarily cuts purchases of Y to some quantity such as y_0. The decrease in the number of pints of Y consumed raises the marginal utility per pint of Y to MU_{y0}. The marginal utility per dollar's worth of Y is increased to MU_{y0}/p_{y1}, and

(7.6)
$$\frac{MU_{x1}}{p_{x2}} < \frac{MU_{y0}}{p_{y1}},$$

that is, the marginal utility of a dollar's worth of X is now less than the marginal utility of a dollar's worth of Y. The consumer is not maximizing satisfaction.

The consumer clearly will not continue to take quantity x_1 of X after the price has gone up to p_{x2}. Satisfaction can be increased by transferring dollars from X to Y. The loss from taking a dollar away from X is the marginal utility of a dollar's worth of X; the gain from buying an additional dollar's worth of Y is the marginal utility of a dollar's worth of Y. Since $MU_{x1}/p_{x2} < MU_{y0}/p_{y1}$, such a transfer will yield a net gain in total utility.

The transfer of dollars from X to Y will continue so long as the marginal utility of a dollar's worth of X is less than the marginal utility of a dollar's worth of Y. However, as the consumer gives up units of X the marginal utility per bushel of X increases, causing the marginal utility per dollar's worth of X to increase, since its price remains at p_{x2}. As the consumer buys additional units of Y, the marginal utility per pint of Y declines, as does the marginal utility per dollar's worth of Y. The transferring will stop when the consumer has again equalized the marginal utility per dollar's worth of X with the marginal utility per dollar's worth of Y and is thus maximizing satisfaction. The quantity of Y taken will have increased from y_0 to some quantity such as y_2. The quantity of X taken will have decreased from x_1 to x_2. Quantities x_2 and y_2 must be such that

(7.7)
$$\frac{MU_{x2}}{p_{x2}} = \frac{MU_{y2}}{p_{y1}}.$$

The quantities of X and Y that bring MU_x and MU_y into the proper relationship are shown in Figure 7.4 as x_2 and y_2. We now have another point on the consumer's demand curve for X; at price p_{x2} the consumer takes x_2 of X. The analysis has shown that an increase in the price of X causes a decrease in the quantity taken.

Using $MU_{x2}/p_{x2} = MU_{y2}/p_{y1}$ as a new starting point, we can change the price of X again and repeat this process. In the resulting new equilibrium position, the quantity of X taken at the new price is established. Through continued repetition of the process, we can determine a series of price-quantity combinations that represents the demand schedule and that can be plotted as the demand curve. Such a curve is shown in Figure 7.5.

Quantities Taken of Other Goods

As a corollary to this analysis, it may be instructive to take a closer view of what happens to the quantity of Y taken. When the price of X increases to p_{x2}, is the quantity of Y at the new equilibrium position greater than the original quantity? The answer is "not necessarily," even though we show it to be greater in Figure 7.4. The crucial factor is the elasticity of demand for X. If demand for X is elastic, the increase in the price of X must decrease total spending on X, leaving more of the consumer's income to spend on Y. In this case, quantity y_2 would indeed be greater than quantity y_1, as we depict it to be in Figure 7.4. However, if elasticity of demand for X is unitary, total spending on X and total spending on Y will each remain constant, and there will be no change in the quantity of Y taken. If demand for X is inelastic, the price increase for X will increase total spending on X and decrease total spending on Y; the new equilibrium quantity of Y taken will be smaller than y_1.

Figure 7.5
Individual Consumer Demand Curve

At each price level for X, given the consumer's income and utility curves and the price of Y, the consumer will take a quantity of X (and Y) that will maximize utility. These quantities of X, together with the corresponding prices of X, locate the consumer's demand curve for X.

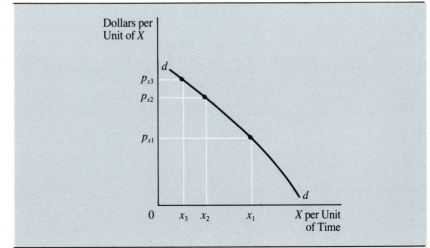

EXCHANGE AND WELFARE

In any voluntary exchange of goods among individuals, all parties to the exchange expect to increase their satisfaction or welfare. It is this prospect of gain that causes voluntary exchange to occur. This point can be illustrated clearly by means of utility analysis. We limit ourselves to two consumers, A and B, each of whom receives constant quantities per unit of time of two goods, X and Y. Marginal utility schedules for the two goods for each consumer are shown in Table 7.2.

Comparative marginal utilities of the goods indicate their comparative worths or values to a consumer. Suppose consumer A has 5 bushels of X and 6 pints of Y. A bushel of X at this point contributes 10 units of utility to A's total satisfaction, and a pint of Y contributes 5 units. If A were to lose a bushel of X, the loss in satisfaction would be 10 units of utility; or, if A were to lose a pint of Y, the loss would be 5 units. Thus a bushel of X to A is worth 2 pints of Y. Alternatively, we can say that a pint of Y is worth half a bushel of X.

Suppose that total supplies of goods X and Y are fixed at 12 bushels of X and 12 pints of Y per week and that these are initially distributed between the two consumers so that A has 9 bushels of X and 3 pints of Y while B has 3 bushels of X and 9 pints of Y. Since for A the marginal utility of a bushel of X is 6 units of utility and a pint of Y is 8 units of utility, a pint of Y is worth $1\frac{1}{3}$ bushels of X to A. For B the marginal utility of a bushel of X is 18 units of utility and that of a pint of Y is 4 units; thus, for consumer B a pint of Y is worth only $\frac{2}{9}$ of a bushel of X.

Under these circumstances both parties will gladly do some exchanging, and exchange will increase community welfare. Individual A will be willing to trade a bushel of X to individual B for a pint of Y, and individual B will be willing to trade a pint of Y for a bushel of X. For individual A, the pint of Y

Table 7.2   The Basis of Exchange

	Individual A				Individual B		
Product X		Product Y		Product X		Product Y	
Quantity (bushels)	MU_x (units of utility)	Quantity (pints)	MU_y (units of utility)	Quantity (bushels)	MU_x (units of utility)	Quantity (pints)	MU_y (units of utility)
1	14	1	10	1	20	1	18
2	13	2	9	2	19	2	17
3	12	3	8	3	18	3	16
4	11	4	7	4	17	4	14
5	10	5	6	5	16	5	12
6	9	6	5	6	15	6	10
7	8	7	4	7	14	7	8
8	7	8	3	8	13	8	6
9	6	9	2	9	12	9	4
10	5	10	1	10	10	10	2

gained will be worth $1\frac{1}{3}$ times the bushel of X given up; for individual B the pint of Y given up will be worth only $\frac{2}{9}$ of the bushel of X gained. To put it another way: In trading a bushel of X for a pint of Y, individual A will give up 6 units of utility in exchange for 7 units, experiencing a net gain of 1 unit of utility; individual B will give up 4 units of utility in exchange for 17 units, experiencing a net gain of 13 units of utility.[14] The welfare of both is increased by the exchange, and no one's welfare is decreased.

Once this exchange has been consummated, an additional exchange can result in a further gain for both parties. Individual A, with 8 bushels of X and 4 pints of Y, will no longer be willing to exchange on a bushel-for-pint basis, since the loss from such a transaction would be greater than the gain. However, individual B can still gain from trading pints of Y for bushels of X. Since trade is no longer attractive to A on a bushel-for-pint basis, B will alter the terms of the trade. If B, who now has 4 bushels of X and 8 pints of Y, gives up 2 pints of Y for a bushel of X, then B will give up 14 units of utility, gain 16 units, and still experience a 2-unit net gain in utility. Individual A will find this offer attractive, for 11 units of utility would be received in exchange for 7.

Once the second exchange has occurred, no further gains will be available from trade between the two parties; a Pareto optimum will have been reached, and exchange will cease. Individual A will have 7 bushels of X and 6 pints of Y, with marginal utilities of 8 and 5 units of utility, respectively. Individual B will have 5 bushels of X and 6 pints of Y, with marginal utilities of 16 and 10 units of utility, respectively. For A the unit of X will be worth $1\frac{3}{5}$ units of Y. Individual B's relative valuations of X and Y will be exactly the same; hence, neither will gain from further exchange.

The general principle underlying this discussion is that for exchange to occur two or more individuals must place different relative valuations on the goods involved. Relative valuations of goods by a single party depend on relative marginal utilities of the goods. Thus for all consumers to be in simultaneous equilibrium—that is, for there to be no incentives to exchange—each individual's holdings of goods must be such that the ratio of the marginal utilities of the goods for him or her is the same as it is for everyone else. In our simple example, for A and B to be in equilibrium MU_x/MU_y for A must equal MU_x/MU_y for B. When these conditions do not hold, it becomes worthwhile for the parties to engage in exchange until they do.

SUMMARY

The indifference curve approach of the two previous chapters has replaced the older marginal utility analysis in much formal economic analysis for at least two reasons. First, it avoids the whole issue of whether utility is measurable in

---

[14]The one-for-one exchange ratio used here is not the only one at which the initial exchange can occur. Both parties can gain from any exchange ratio at which the amount of X that A is willing to give up to get a pint of Y exceeds the amount of X that B would require to give up a pint of Y.

a cardinal sense or in an ordinal sense only; that is, it is based on a simpler set of assumptions. Second, it is easier to manipulate and apply. Nevertheless, almost every treatment of consumer behavior in professional economic literature makes reference to or uses utility concepts in some form or other. We believe we would be remiss in our obligations to students if we omitted a systematic treatment of the utility approach.

The utility approach to the theory of individual consumer choice and demand is a special case of the indifference curve approach. It can be used to explain, among other things, the consumer's allocation of income among the goods that he or she buys, the consumer's demand curve for any given product, and the exchange of goods among individuals. The conclusions reached depend on the principle of *relatively* diminishing marginal utility of any one good or service as the consumption of it is increased relative to that of other goods and services.

A consumer seeks to maximize the satisfaction derived from the goods and services obtainable with his or her given income. Maximization requires that the individual allocate income in such a way that when spending the entire income the marginal utility per dollar's worth of one good is equal to the marginal utility per dollar's worth of every other good or service.

To establish the consumer's demand curve for any one commodity we vary its price, holding constant the prices of other goods, the consumer's income, and tastes and preferences as shown by that individual's utility schedule or curves. At each price the consumer maximizes satisfaction, thus determining the quantity that will be taken at that price. The resulting price-quantity combinations form the consumer's demand schedule and can be plotted as that person's demand curve.

Voluntary exchange of goods among individuals increases the welfare of both parties to the exchange. Incentives for voluntary exchange occur wherever the ratios of the marginal utilities of goods for one consumer differ from the corresponding ratios for another. The condition for simultaneous equilibrium for all consumers is that the ratios of marginal utilities of all goods be the same for all.

APPLICATIONS

Utility analysis has a variety of applications. It can be used in many instances to illustrate points in theory, to distinguish sound from unsound economic policies, and to explain certain behavior patterns of individuals. Examples of such applications follow.

VALUE IN USE AND VALUE IN EXCHANGE

The development of a utility theory of choice and exchange enabled economists to explain what the early classical economists of the late eighteenth and early nineteenth centuries called the diamond-water paradox. The paradox was that some goods, like diamonds, have a limited total *value in use* to any one person, yet in markets they have a very high *value in exchange*. Other goods, like water, have a very great total use value to any one person but a very low exchange value in markets. Early economists were unable to provide a satisfactory explanation of this phenomenon.

The subjective value, or marginal utility, economists of the late nineteenth century used a device like Table 7.3 to provide the answer. Measuring water in 100-gallon units and diamonds in 5-carat units, suppose that when consumer Hughes is maximizing satisfaction 900 gallons of water and two 5-carat units of diamonds are purchased per year. The total utility of water to Hughes is 196 units of utility. But what is the value of any one of the 100-unit increments of the total supply? The definition of marginal utility informs us that at the 900-gallon consumption level, 100 gallons contribute 12 units of utility to Hughes's satisfaction level. He would be willing to trade 100 gallons of water for units of any other good that provided a marginal utility of 12 or more utility units.

Table 7.3 The Diamond-Water Paradox	Water			Diamonds		
	Gallons per year	MU per 100 Gallons	TU	Units per Year	MU per Unit	TU
	100	30	30	1	40	40
	200	28	58	2	36	76
	300	26	84	3	24	100
	400	24	108	4	10	110
	500	22	130	5	0	110
	600	20	150			
	700	18	168			
	800	16	184			
	900	12	196			
	1,000	8	204			

Diamonds, on the other hand, provide a total of 76 units of utility at the 2-unit level of consumption. But the marginal utility of a unit of diamonds is 36 units. Hughes would not be willing to trade a unit of diamonds for units of any other good unless the marginal utility of such a good were 36 utility units or more.

The water, which has great use value to Hughes, has a low exchange value, because to him its supply is large and its marginal utility is low. The diamonds, which have a much lower use value to Hughes, have a high exchange value, because their supply to him is small and their marginal utility is high. Exchange value of a good, then, is really determined by the use value to the consumer of the marginal unit—that is, by the marginal utility of a unit of the good at the current rate of consumption.

CHARITABLE GIVING[15] _____

Although most microeconomic theory is oriented toward organized markets like those for gasoline, automobiles, housing, food, and clothing, it can be used advantageously to analyze a much wider range of phenomena. Recently economists have begun to apply it to such utility-enhancing occurrences as friendship, love, marriage, divorce, church attendance, and aesthetics. It is being drawn increasingly into the analysis of crime and punishment, as well as the study of other aspects of the legal system.

Despite much public opinion to the contrary, economists are human beings too and generally recognize that people receive satisfaction from nonmarket as well as from market activities. In addition, they understand that most people in making their choices consider to some degree the interests of other members of society. Economic theory does not require that all of us be uniformly selfish. Such a view would contradict much human behavior, like giving aid to others— sometimes even to complete strangers—through blood donations, gifts of food in times of catastrophe, and contributions to health organizations. People sometimes make valiant efforts to save the lives of strangers, even at the risk of their own.

Charitable activities constitute a major nonmarket source of satisfaction, or utility, to many people. Charity is the intentional transfer of resources or command over resources at below-market prices, or even zero prices, with the aim of making the recipient better off. Charity may begin at home, but it is regularly extended to those outside the family. In one or another form, it is as old as civilization itself. Organized charities received sizable boosts from such undertakings as the efforts of Florence Nightingale during the Crimean War of 1854–56, the relief work of American women during the Civil War, and the founding

---

[15]This discussion is drawn from Louis De Alessi, ''The Utility of Disasters,'' *Kyklos* 21 (1968): 525–532; and ''A Utility Analysis of Post-disaster Cooperation,'' *Papers on Non-Market Decision Making* 3 (Fall 1967): 85–90.

of the International Red Cross by the Swiss banker Jean Henri Dunant in 1858. Much present-day charity is involuntary—carried on by government units and funded by tax receipts. But the following discussion is concerned with private charity.

Charitable activity usually increases after disasters that strike large numbers of people, such as earthquakes, floods, tornadoes, famines, and war. There is substantial evidence that following such events nonaffected persons tend to provide victims with more shelter, food, medical supplies, and other articles at below-market prices than they were willing to provide before the events occurred. Why does charity increase after such events?

People may obtain additional utility not only when their own income increases but also when the well-being of others is enhanced.[16] For this reason, many people give away part of their own incomes. For most of us the marginal utility of charitable giving tends to be diminishing as the giving per unit of time increases. Thus in panel (a) of Figure 7.6, A's total utility curve TU_1^A reflects the utility A obtains from charitable giving (G) to B when B's base income is I_1^B. The curve TU_2^A shows A's total utility from giving to B when B's base income is at a higher level, I_2^B. Both increase at decreasing rates, reflecting A's diminishing marginal utility from giving. The corresponding marginal utility curves are shown in panel (b).

In panel (a) we show TU_1^A peaking at a higher level of giving than TU_2^A. This pattern says that the worse off B is, the more contributions A would be willing to make before becoming satiated with giving. As such, this seems reasonable and in conformity with everyday observations. Further, if TU_1^A peaks at a higher level of donations than does TU_2^A, as well as lies above TU_2^A, then the increments on TU_1^A per \$1 increment must exceed, on the average, the increments on TU_2^A per \$1 increment up to the g_1 level of giving. Another way of saying the same thing is that for any level of annual giving below g_1, the marginal utility per dollar given, shown in panel (b), is greater the worse off B is—that is, MU_1^A lies above MU_2^A.

Consider now A's situation when the base income of B is I_2^B. To maximize satisfaction, A allocates income among goods and services, *including charitable giving,* so that

$$\frac{MU_x}{p_x} = \frac{MU_y}{p_y} = \frac{MU_g}{p_g} = \cdots = \frac{MU_n}{p_n},$$

in which p_g is \$1.

Suppose that in Figure 7.6 the satisfaction-maximizing level of giving is g_2, yielding a total unit utility level from giving of T_1 and a marginal utility of M_1.

Now suppose that a disaster strikes, reducing B's base income to I_1^B— possibly a zero level. At the g_2 level of giving, A's total utility from giving to

---

[16]With reference to Footnote 10, the utility function for A, who contemplates giving a portion of his or her income to B, thus augmenting B's income, I^B, takes the form $U^A = f^A(x, y, I^B)$.

Figure 7.6
The Dependence of
***A*'s Utility on *B*'s**
Income Level

A's utility curves for
dollars of giving to *B*
when *B*'s income level is
I_2^B are TU_2^A and MU_2^A.
Suppose that when
allocating income so as
to maximize satisfaction
A's gifts are g_2. Now a
disaster strikes that
reduces *B*'s income to I_1^B.
A's utility curves shift to
TU_1^A and MU_1^A. The
marginal utility of *A*'s
giving rises from M_1 to
M_2, inducing him to
reallocate his income in
such a way that giving is
increased to some greater
amount g_3 dollars.

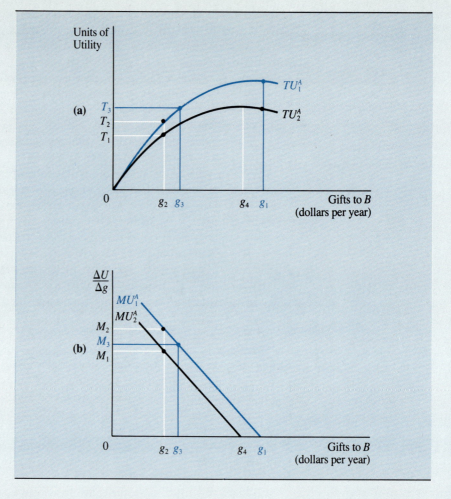

B increases from T_1 to T_2 and the marginal utility of giving rises from M_1 to
M_2. *A* now finds that

$$\frac{MU_x}{p_x} = \frac{MU_y}{p_y} < \frac{MU_g}{p_g} > \cdots \frac{MU_n}{p_n}.$$

To maximize satisfaction *A* increases the level of giving, transferring dollars
from other lines of expenditure. Marginal utilities per dollar's worth of other
goods and services increase, while utility per dollar's worth of giving decreases.
At some level of giving, say, g_3, marginal utilities per dollar's worth will again
be the same for all goods and services, including giving. The total utility of
giving for *A* will be T_3, and the marginal utility of giving will be M_3.

The foregoing analysis explains why charitable giving tends to increase
following some disastrous event. Donors and potential donors perceive the reductions in income of those affected by it. Giving becomes more meaningful to

donors, because it will provide assistance that is now more ''needed.'' The possibility of its being channeled to worthy recipients is increased, and, in widespread catastrophes, there is even a possibility of friends or relatives of the donor becoming recipients. For all these reasons, the total utility and the marginal utility curves shift upward for any individual donor, thus inducing him or her to engage in a higher level of charitable giving.

Suggested Readings

The history of utility theory is surveyed in

Stigler, George J. ''The Development of Utility Theory. I'' *Journal of Political Economy* 58 (August 1950): 307–324.

The classic treatment of the subject is

Marshall, Alfred. *Principles of Economics.* 8th ed., Bk. 3, Chaps. 5 and 6. London: Macmillan, 1920.

For a modern statement of utility theory and its limitations, see

Alchian, Armen A. ''The Meaning of Utility Measurement.'' *American Economic Review* 43 (March 1953): 26–50.

Problems and Questions for Discussion

1. Tom Jones has an income of $50 per day, which he spends on food and clothing. His total utility schedules for each are listed in the following table.

The price of food is $2 per pound, and the price of clothing is $4 per yard.

Food		Clothing	
Pounds	TU_f	Yards	TU_c
1	50	1	120
2	95	2	230
3	135	3	330
4	170	4	420
5	200	5	500
6	225	6	570
7	245	7	630
8	260	8	680
9	270	9	720
10	275	10	750

a. How much of each good should he purchase to maximize utility? Why?
b. What will happen to his utility level if he transfers a dollar from food to clothing?
c. If a dollar is added to his income, on which item should he spend it? Why?
d. If the price of food rises to $3 and his income remains at $50, how should he allocate it between food and clothing?

2. If the marginal utility of a person's income decreases as his or her income increases, would you expect that the individual would be willing to make a bet in which the chance of winning $100 is exactly the same as the chance of losing $100? Why or why not?

3. Suppose a consumer can allocate income among any number of goods and services. Does it make sense for that consumer to purchase that quantity of any one good that will maximize his or her total utility for that good?

4. Evaluate this quotation: "The observation that the marginal rate of substitution between any two goods is ordinarily decreasing for a consumer rests on the older observation that the marginal utilities of the goods to the consumer are decreasing."

5. A 1913 Liberty nickel sells for over $50,000, while a nickel of recent mintage is worth only $.05. Only five such 1913 nickels were minted.
a. Explain the difference in price.
b. What can you say about the total utility of 1913 nickels as compared with that of nickels currently in circulation?
c. What about the comparative marginal utilities?

*6. The diamond-water paradox discussed in this chapter makes it clear that the relatively high value in exchange of a unit of diamond comes from the good's relative scarcity. Suppose you discover that diamonds are really more plentiful; that diamond mines are found in only a few countries; and

_____

*Denotes an application-oriented problem.

that these countries keep the supply placed on the market relatively low. What effects does the fact that the scarcity is artificial have on the nature of the paradox?

*7. The De Beers Central Selling Organisation in London is the worldwide wholesale diamond cartel. Combining the supplies from its own mines and those in Australia and the Soviet Union, De Beers controls about 80 percent of world sales (the rest is attributed to smuggling). The world's largest inventory of diamonds, of course, is contained in the jewelry of millions of families. What would be the effect on the diamond-water paradox if a large portion of this supply was suddenly put on the market? (Why this is not likely to happen is explained in Edward Jay Epstein, "Have You Ever Tried to Sell a Diamond?", *The Atlantic Monthly,* February 1982, 23–34.)

*8. On April 7, 1986, *The Wall Street Journal* reported that the chairman of the board of IBM would retire owning 48,429 shares worth $7.2 million based on that day's closing share price. He also owned rights to acquire another 193,868 shares. The founder and chairman of a relatively small firm that supplies computer software to IBM sold 80,000 of his shares when his company went public, from which he realized a gain of about $1.7 million. His remaining stake of 11,142,000 shares was valued at $309.2 million based on that day's closing share price.

These data illustrate two important lessons of economics. First, it can be more lucrative to be an entrepreneur than to rise to the top of a gigantic firm. Second, estimates of the values of stock holdings hinge on a crucial assumption. What is that assumption?

9. One of the authors has two backyard bird feeders that are refilled with seed regularly. The ground under each is littered mainly with cracked husks but also with some seed that the birds spill accidentally. The finches do not sort the seed from the husks until both feeders are empty, and after a day or so of sorting on the ground they forage elsewhere until the feeders are refilled. Which behavioral principle(s) set forth in this chapter do the finches appear to be following? Explain.

*10. Show the theory of charitable giving with indifference curves. Let your own income be I_y, measured on the vertical axis of an indifference diagram. The object of your donations is person X, who has a lower income level I_x in the absence of donations from you. Measure X's income on the horizontal axis of the diagram. Let the cost of transferring income to X through some charitable organization be p_x.
   a. Draw the appropriate budget line.
   b. Draw your indifference map showing your trade-off desires between your income and that of X. How are your indifference curves shaped? How much will you donate? Why?
   c. If a disaster strikes that reduces X's income to I_x'' but does not change your income, draw the resulting new budget line. How much will you donate to X now? Is this amount greater or less than the amount you donated in part (b)? Explain.

Chapter 8

MARKET CLASSIFICATIONS AND DEMAND AS VIEWED BY THE SELLER

demand curve faced by the firm
A curve that shows the quantities of a good or service that a single firm can sell per unit of time at alternative prices, other things being equal.

There are three demand concepts that are important in microeconomics. Two of these—the *individual consumer's demand curve* and the *market demand curve* for a product—have been treated in detail in Chapters 5 through 7. The third one, how demand looks to an individual seller of a product, or the **demand curve faced by the firm,** is examined in this chapter. Explicit discussion of the third demand concept at this point not only rounds out the theory of demand but lays the market-structure groundwork for Part Four of this book.

No special definition of a firm is necessary at this point. It is an individual business concern; it may be a single proprietorship, a partnership, or a corporation. To simplify exposition, we shall assume that it sells one product only.

The demand curve facing the firm for its product shows *the amounts that it can sell at different possible prices, other things being equal;* thus it could appropriately be called a sales curve. Its nature depends on the type of market in which the firm sells. Selling markets are usually classified into three types based on (1) the importance of individual firms in relation to the entire market in which they sell and (2) whether or not the products sold in a particular market are homogeneous. The market types are (1) pure competition, (2) pure monopoly, and (3) imperfect competition. Markets of the real world do not always fall neatly into one classification or another; they may be a mixture of two or more. However, it is useful to analyze the demand curve faced by the firm in each of the theoretical or pure classifications. A detailed analysis of pricing and output under each follows in Part Four.

PURE COMPETITION

The conditions necessary for pure competition to exist in a market were outlined in Chapter 3. The essence of *pure competition* in selling is that there are many firms selling the identical product with no one of them large enough relative to the entire market to influence the market price. If one firm drops out of the market, supply will not be decreased enough to cause the price to increase perceptibly. Neither is it feasible for one firm to expand output enough to cause any perceptible decrease in market price. No single seller believes that it affects or is affected by other sellers in the market. No rivalries arise. There will be no reactions of other firms to actions taken by any one firm. Relationships among firms are impersonal.

The Demand Curve

In a purely competitive market, the demand curve facing the firm is virtually horizontal at the prevailing market or equilibrium price—at any price above that level it can sell nothing. Since all firms in the market sell the identical product, consumers will turn to firms charging the market price if one of them raises its selling price above that level. The proportion of the total market filled by one seller is so small that the firm can dispose of its entire output at the prevailing market price; hence, there is no necessity for lowering the price below that of the other sellers. Any firm attempting to do so will find itself swamped with buyers who will promptly bid the price back to the equilibrium level.

A firm selling potatoes faces this sort of demand curve. When it hauls its potatoes to market, it receives the going market price. If it asks for more than the market price and sticks to its request, it will undoubtedly haul the potatoes home again. On the other hand, no amount of potatoes that it alone can bring to market will drive the price down; it can dispose of all it desires to sell at the going market price.

In reality the demand curve faced by the firm is an infinitesimal segment of the market demand curve in Figure 8.1 in the neighborhood of quantity X stretched out over the firm diagram. Any one firm can be thought of as supplying the last small portion of quantity X. Stretching this small segment out over the firm diagram makes the demand curve faced by the firm appear to be horizontal.

The nature of the demand curve faced by the firm is illustrated by dd in panel (a) of Figure 8.1. In panel (b), the market demand curve and the market supply curve are DD and SS, respectively. The market price is p; it determines the horizontal *infinitely elastic* demand curve faced by the firm. The price axes of the two panels are identical; however, quantity measurements of the market panel are compressed considerably as compared with those of the firm panel. For example, if x_0 measures 10 units of X for the firm, let X_0 measure 10,000 units of X for the total market.

Figure 8.1 The Demand Curve Facing the Firm: Pure Competition

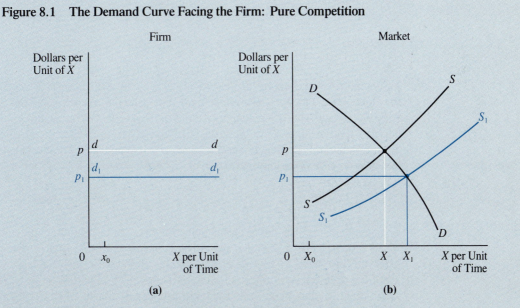

Since the individual firm is too small relative to the market to influence price, the demand curve facing the firm is horizontal at the going market price.
Where p is the equilibrium price, the demand curve facing the firm is dd.
At equilibrium price p_1 it becomes $d_1 d_1$.

Influence of the Firm on Demand, Price, and Output

Any forces that change market demand or market supply will change the market price of the product and, consequently, the demand curve faced by the firm. The firm by itself can do nothing about either the demand curve it faces or the market price; it must accept both as given data. In Figure 8.1, if market supply increases to S_1S_1, the market price decreases to p_1, and the demand curve faced by the firm shifts downward to d_1d_1. Any such change is beyond the control of the individual firm. It can adjust only its output, and it will gear that output to the prevailing market price.

PURE MONOPOLY

pure monopoly
A market situation in which a single seller sells a product for which there are no good substitutes.

A market situation in which a single firm sells a product for which there are no good substitutes is called **pure monopoly.** The firm has the market for the product all to itself. There are no similar products whose price or sales will perceptibly influence the monopolist's price or sales, and vice versa. Cross elasticity of demand between the monopolist's product and other products will either be zero or be small enough to be ignored by all firms in the economy. The monopolistic firm does not believe that its actions will evoke retaliation of any kind from firms in other industries. Similarly, it does not consider actions taken by firms in other industries to be of sufficient importance to warrant taking them into account. The monopolist *is* the market from the selling point of view. A case in point is the supplier of telephone service to a particular community.

The Demand Curve

The market demand curve for the product is also the demand curve faced by the monopolist. Figure 8.2 shows the market demand curve for the product that is produced and sold by a monopolist. It shows the different quantities that buyers will take off the market at all possible prices. Since the monopolist is the only seller of the product, it can sell at all possible prices exactly the amounts that buyers will take at those prices.

Influence of the Firm on Demand, Price, and Output

The monopolist is able to exert some influence on the price, output, and demand for its product. The market demand curve delineates the limits of the monopolist's market. Faced by a given demand curve, the firm can increase sales if it is willing to lower its price, or it can raise its price if it is willing to restrict its sales volume. Additionally, over time, the firm may be able to affect the position of the demand curve itself through various sales promotion activities. The firm may be able to induce more people to want its product, thus increasing demand; it may also be able to make demand less elastic if it can convince enough people that they cannot afford to be without the product. It follows that if the monopolist

Figure 8.2
The Demand Curve
Facing the Firm:
Pure Monopoly

The pure monopolist is
the market from the
selling side.
Consequently, the firm
faces the market demand
curve *DD*.

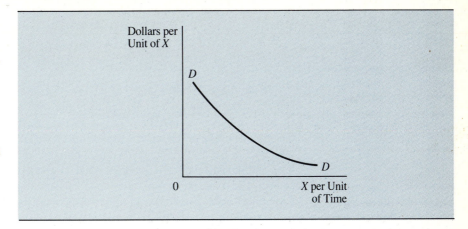

is able to increase demand, it can increase sales to some extent without lowering
the price or, alternatively, it can increase the price to some extent without
restricting its sales volume.

IMPERFECT COMPETITION

Between the extremes of pure competition on the one hand and pure monopoly
on the other are market structures of *imperfect competition*. These are subclassified into markets of *monopolistic competition* and markets of *oligopoly*. Imperfectly competitive markets usually exhibit one or more of four characteristics.
First, product differentiation may occur. Second, individual sellers may be able
to influence the product market. Third, government intervention in the market
may exist. Fourth, private groups of sellers may be able to influence the pricing
and distribution of the product. The first two characteristics require elaboration.

product differentiation
A situation in which sellers sell essentially the
same product but each
seller's product has, at
least in the minds of consumers, certain characteristics that distinguish it
from that of other sellers.

Product differentiation exists when each seller of a product markets what
consumers think is a slightly different version of it. Actually the differences
may be real or fancied. They may consist of real differences in quality and
design, as in the automobile market, or they may consist only of imagined
differences—for example, in brand names—as tends to be the case in aspirin
markets. The products of all firms in such a market are good substitutes for one
another—they have high cross elasticities of demand—but consumers believe
that each has some unique features.

monopolistic
competition
A market situation in
which there are many
sellers with no one of
them important enough to
be able to influence any
other seller and with each
seller's product differentiated from those of the
others.

The distinction between pure competition and monopolistic competition
turns on product differentiation. In **monopolistic competition,** as in pure competition, there are many sellers of a product. Each is so small relative to the
market as a whole that its activities have no effect on the market or on other
sellers. Relationships among firms are impersonal. Each firm operates as though
it were independent of other firms in the market. The product differentiation

oligopoly
A market situation in which the number of sellers is small enough for the activities of one to affect the others and for the activities of any or all of the others to affect the first.

differentiated oligopoly
An oligopolistic market situation in which the sellers sell differentiated products.

pure oligopoly
An oligopolistic market situation in which the sellers sell homogeneous or identical products.

that sets monopolistic competition apart from pure competition takes such forms as brand names, trademarks, quality differences, or differences in conveniences or services offered to consumers. Examples of markets approaching monopolistic competition include women's hosiery, various textile products, and service trades in large cities.

In an **oligopoly,** the number of sellers is small enough so that one or more can affect the market as a whole and therefore what other sellers are able to do. Changes in the output and the price charged by one firm will affect the amounts that other sellers can sell and the prices that they can charge. Hence, other firms will react in one way or another to price-output changes on the part of a single firm. Individual sellers are *interdependent,* not independent as they are in pure competition, pure monopoly, and monopolistic competition. Product differentiation may or may not occur in oligopolistic markets. Where it does occur, we call the market one of **differentiated oligopoly.** If there is no differentiation—for example, among producers of basic steel, cement, and aluminum—it is referred to as **pure oligopoly.**

The Demand Curve

The shape of the demand curve faced by the firm under monopolistic competition depends entirely on product differentiation. To see the effects of product differentiation, we first assume its absence. This assumption leaves us with the case of pure competition and a horizontal demand curve such as d_1d_1 in Figure 8.3. Now we introduce the concept of product differentiation and observe how d_1d_1 is affected. When products are differentiated, consumers become more or less attached to particular brand names. At any given price for commodity X,

Figure 8.3
The Demand Curve Facing the Firm: Monopolistic Competition

Product differentiation attaches customers to one firm's product with varying degrees of tightness. The monopolistic competitor at price p_1 and quantity x will attract competitors' marginal customers by lowering the price and will lose marginal customers to competitors by raising the price. Thus, the firm faces demand curve dd instead of the horizontal curve d_1d_1.

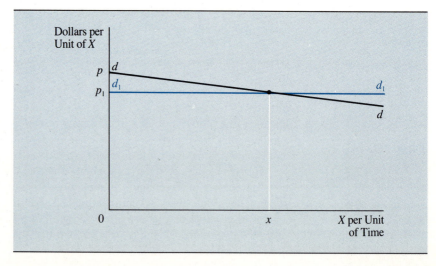

some consumers will be on the margin of switching to other brands, while others will be attached to X at that price with varying degrees of tightness.

Suppose that for the monopolistic competitor quantity x is taken initially at price p_1. If the firm raises the price, those consumers who were on the verge of switching to other brands will make the switch, since the other brands are now relatively lower in price. The higher the firm raises its price, the more customers it will lose to relatively lower-priced brands. Since other brands are good substitutes for that of the seller under consideration, the rise in price necessary for it to lose all its customers (p_1p) will not bc large. For price increases above p_1, the demand curve faced by the firm will be the black line in the diagram. Similarly, if the firm lowers the price below p_1, it will pick up marginal customers of other sellers, since its price will now be relatively lower as compared with other firms' prices. It will not have to lower price by much to pick up all the additional customers it can handle. Thus, for decreases in price below p_1, the black line in the diagram shows the demand curve faced by the one firm. The demand curve faced by the monopolistic competitor is one such as dd.

It may appear that price reductions by one firm that attract customers away from the other firms in the industry would evoke some kind of retaliatory action on the part of the other firms. This is not the case, however, because there are many firms in a monopolistically competitive market. The one that reduces its price will attract so few customers from each of the others that they will not notice or feel the loss. Nevertheless, for that one firm the total increase in customers will be relatively large.

Likewise, it may seem that the price increases by one firm that drive customers away would increase demand for the products of the other firms. The customers shifting to other firms, however, will be widely scattered among those firms. Not enough will go to any other single firm to cause any perceptible increase in demand for its product, even though the loss of customers to the price-raising firm will be relatively large.

There is no typical demand situation facing an oligopolistic firm. The interdependence of sellers in an oligopolistic market makes the location of the single seller's demand curve imprecise. In some situations the demand curve faced by the firm is indeterminate; in others it can be located with some degree of accuracy.

The oligopolistic seller's demand curve will be indeterminate when the firm cannot predict what the reactions of its rivals will be to price and output changes on its part. The output that this firm can sell if it changes its price depends on the manner in which other firms react to that price change.

The range of possible reactions is broad. Rivals may just meet the price change, change price in the same direction but by less than the change of the original seller, exceed the price change, improve the quality of their products, engage in extensive advertising campaigns, or react in other ways. Inability of the individual seller to predict which reactions will occur and to what degree amounts to inability to determine the demand curve faced by that seller.

**Figure 8.4
The Demand Curve
Facing the Firm:
Oligopoly**

The demand curve facing
the oligopolistic firm
depends on how rivals
react to its price changes.
If other firms match its
price changes the firm
can expect only to hold
its market share for price
decreases and faces a
demand curve such as
dd. If at prices below *p*
rivals more than match
price decreases, the
firm's market share
decreases also, and the
demand curve faced is
one such as *d'* .

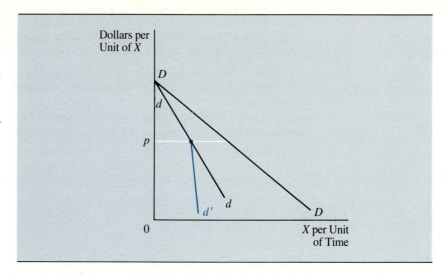

When the single seller knows with some accuracy how its rivals will react
to price changes on its part, the demand curve facing it becomes correspondingly
more certain. If reliable judgments with regard to the probable effect on rivals'
reactions to its own sales can be formed, the firm can take these into account.
However, each different reaction by each individual rival will result in differing
quantities that the single seller can market. Consequently, ascertaining the effects of rivals' reactions to the quantities that can be sold at different prices is
at best a complex process for the individual firm. A few examples should improve our grasp of the problems involved.

Suppose in Figure 8.4 that there are two producers in a given market and
that price changes by either will be just matched by the other. Suppose also that
the producers are of approximately equal size and prestige and turn out virtually
identical items. The market demand curve is *DD*. If each firm knows that the
other will just match its price changes, at any given price each will expect to
get approximately half the market and will face a fairly determinate demand
curve, *dd*, for its output. Such a demand curve will lie about halfway between
DD and the price axis.

Next, suppose that one producer does not behave in the way just described—
when firm *A* cuts the price from an initial price of *p*, firm *B* cuts the price still
further. Firm *B* will take some of firm *A*'s customers away. The demand curve
faced by *A* will then not follow *dd* but will follow some path such as the blue
line *d'*. Since its rival reacts by cutting its price still more, *A* loses a part of its
share of the market when it cuts its price. It may undercut *B*'s price again, and
the situation may develop into a price war—an indeterminate situation.

Suppose that the producers in a given oligopolistic market form a cartel.
Under the cartel arrangement the firms act as a single unit, each having some
voice in the setting of price, output, and other market policies. When all firms
act as a unit, the amount that one firm can sell at different possible prices

becomes irrelevant as long as the cartel can prevent each firm from dealing secretly with favored clients at prices and terms more favorable than the cartel's. The cartel is concerned with how much the market as a whole can sell at different possible prices. Thus, the cartel is in much the same position as is a pure monopolist, and it is the cartel that faces the market demand curve. The demand curve faced by a single firm is of no consequence.

These examples provide a small sample of the possible demand situations faced by an oligopolistic seller. Additional illustrations will be presented in Chapter 13. Our objective at this point is to show that the demand curve's position and its shape will depend on what the reactions of rivals will be to price changes on the part of the single firm.

Influence of the Firm on Demand, Price, and Output

The individual firm in a monopolistically competitive market may be able to influence demand for its own product to some perceptible degree through advertising. However, the existence of many good substitutes will preclude much success in this direction.

The firm is subjected to highly competitive forces, yet it is to a small extent a sort of monopolist, since it has some discretion in setting price and output. But if the firm raises price by very much it loses all its customers—and it does not have to lower price very far to secure all the customers it can serve. Within that limited price range the firm has price-setting discretion; outside that price range it is subject to competitive forces. The demand curve faced by a firm under monopolistic competition will be highly elastic throughout its relevant range. The cause is not hard to find. The products of all firms in the market, even though differentiated, are very good substitutes for one another.

In general, the oligopolistic firm is able to influence to some degree the demand curve faced by it, its price, and its output. Through sales promotion efforts the firm may be able to shift the demand curve for what it sells to the right—partly by increasing consumer demand for this type of product but mostly by inducing consumers to desert its rivals and buy its brand. The firm may be able to accomplish this through advertising or through design and quality changes, provided such changes give its brand more customer appeal. Rivals will not be sitting idly by in such cases and may retaliate with vigorous campaigns of their own. The firms with the most effective campaigns, of course, succeed in increasing demand for their brands.

Whether the firm does or does not face a determinate demand curve, it knows that in general its demand curve slopes downward to the right. To increase sales it must usually lower price, unless the sales increase is made possible by a shift to the right of the demand curve. Higher prices can be obtained at the expense of sales, unless they are obtained through or in conjunction with increases in demand. The demand curve faced by an individual oligopolist is likely to be fairly elastic because of the existence of good substitutes produced by other firms in the market. However, elasticity of demand, as well as the position of the demand curve, will depend on rivals' reactions to the price and output changes of the single seller.

SUMMARY

Analysis of the demand situation facing the individual business firm is organized around three market classifications. The conditions of demand facing the individual firm differ from one classification to another, the differences stemming from two sources: (1) the importance of the individual firm in the market in which it sells and (2) product differentiation or product homogeneity.

Pure competition stands at one extreme of the classification system and pure monopoly at the other. Purely competitive firms sell homogeneous products, and each is so small relative to the entire market that it cannot by itself influence market price. Hence, the demand curve faced by the firm is horizontal at the equilibrium market price. A monopolist firm is a single seller of a product not closely related to any other product. It faces the market demand curve for its product.

Imperfect competition fills the gap between these two extremes. Monopolistic competition differs from pure competition in one respect only: products of different sellers are differentiated. This fact gives the monopolistic competitor a small amount of control over its price; however, each firm is so small relative to the entire market that it cannot by itself affect other firms in the industry. It faces a downward-sloping, highly elastic demand curve.

With regard to the number of firms in the industry, oligopoly lies between the extremes of pure competition and monopolistic competition on the one hand and pure monopoly on the other. Its primary characteristic is that there are few enough firms in the industry for the activities of one to have repercussions on the prices and sales of the others. Hence, rivalries develop under oligopoly. The demand curve faced by a single oligopolistic seller depends on the reactions of rivals to market activities on its part. If the reactions of rivals cannot be predicted, the demand curve faced by that firm cannot be determined.

APPLICATIONS

MARKET STRUCTURE IN THE UNITED STATES: A BROAD TABLEAU

How do the markets of the U.S. economy fit into the classification scheme that we have described in this chapter? Some fit nicely, while others cut across classification boundaries. However, most economists find the classification scheme a useful starting point for clear thinking about microeconomic problems. We use it in this section to present a broad working picture of market structure in the United States.

Pure Competition

Markets that approach pure competition, at least in numbers of sellers of a given product, include most of agriculture—growers of grain, produce, and flowers, as well as all kinds of livestock. They include too most labor markets, in the absence of unions. Each seller in these markets provides an item that is essentially identical to that of competitors, and none supplies a sufficiently large share of the market to affect the price or to make advertising worthwhile. Each seller faces an infinitely elastic or horizontal demand curve. Most of us are pure competitors in the stock market with the few hundred shares that we buy or sell at any one time, although institutional dealings in thousands of shares at a time may belong in the oligopoly classification.

Government actions make some ordinarily competitive markets less competitive. Taxicabs and buses in many cities tend to be competitive since their products are relatively homogeneous and costs of entry are low enough for many operators to offer demand-responsive services. However, most city governments limit entry and fix rates to protect existing operators. In many cases they prohibit private buses in order to protect city-owned monopoly bus lines, which we discuss in Chapter 11.

The federal government intervenes extensively in agricultural markets that would otherwise be purely competitive. As we noted in Chapter 4, it limits acreage, sets price floors, imposes tariffs or quotas on imports, and sometimes places embargoes on exports to certain countries. One or more of these restrictions applies to barley, corn, sugar, tobacco, and wheat. In 1983 marketing orders issued by the Department of Agriculture, which we analyze in Chapter 13, applied to $5.2 billion worth of 34 commodities, including beans, cherries, citrus fruits, hops, nuts, and raisins.[1] These items are sold by producer cartels

---

[1]Leonard W. Weiss, *Case Studies in American Industry*, 3d ed., Chap. 2 (New York: John Wiley & Sons, 1980); and Jeffrey H. Birnbaum, ''Farm, Budget Officials Clash on Supply Curbs by Marketing Boards,'' *The Wall Street Journal*, December 7, 1982.

called "cooperatives" under such trade names as "Sunkist" oranges, "Diamond" almonds, and "Calavo" avocados. Producer cartels reduce supplies marketed in order to jack up prices. The excess grown over what is sold fresh is destroyed, sold overseas, sold at lower prices for livestock feed, or used to make less profitable frozen juice concentrates. Some cooperatives operate under "closed shop" rules that limit entry by new growers. Higher-than-competitive prices in these markets provide incentives for many producers to sell too much product, leading to surpluses.

In the absence of union activities, most labor markets would approach pure competition. Airline pilots, auto workers, carpenters and other construction industry workers, clerical workers, dock workers, machinists, municipal employees, plumbers, and steelworkers are relatively homogeneous groups, and individual workers face infinitely elastic demand curves. Union activities tend to raise wage rates above competitive levels and to restrict the number of workers employed in any given market.

Pure Monopoly

The essence of pure monopoly is zero cross elasticity of demand between the product being sold by a firm and other products. The monopolist has no rivals or competitors and faces the market demand curve for the product. Sometimes the sellers of a product get together in the form of an association or cartel to control production and marketing of the entire group, effectively setting up a monopoly position for the group.

In the United States some monopolies come under the heading "natural monopoly," as we explain in Chapter 12. Local telephone companies, for example, require so much investment in switching stations and lines that only one firm can efficiently service the city or region. A second firm of efficient size entering the same market area would cause both to incur losses in the long run. The same situation exists for local electric power, gas, and water companies with equally complex networks of distribution lines to individual homes and businesses. Most cities or states grant each of these public utilities a monopoly franchise and regulate the rates and services offered.

Monopoly-like cartels are sometimes created by governments. Until 1978, airlines in the United States could not fly between given pairs of cities without permission of the Civil Aeronautics Board. For years a single airline flew between Los Angeles and Minneapolis—and not because of an absence of demand or because its pilots were the only ones who knew the correct compass heading. In many large air travel markets all but two or three airlines were excluded. In the trucking industry, the Interstate Commerce Commission has limited entry and in some cases granted monopoly rights to individual trucking companies. It has now relaxed some of those restrictions. The Food and Drug Administration serves to protect monopoly and near-monopoly positions in the production and sale of certain pharmaceutical products through procedures that slow the testing and approval of new drugs.

In some instances strong, vigorous firms achieve monopoly or near-monopoly positions for a time. Such organizations as Campbell's Soup, Eastman Kodak, General Electric, IBM, Polaroid, and Xerox have had very strong market positions that have come about through aggressive independent behavior rather than through collusive practices.

Imperfect Competition

Markets of imperfection run the gamut from pure competition to pure monopoly. We illustrate monopolistic competition first and then turn to examples of oligopoly.

Monopolistic Competition   The presence of many sellers in the market and product differentiation among those sellers' outputs characterize monopolistic competition. The types and ranges of product differentiation are wide. Professional people such as physicians, dentists, attorneys, and accountants differ in their skills, and we usually select them on the basis of their reputations, not by lottery or by scanning the Yellow Pages. Location and convenience also vary within a profession. All of these factors create important differences for buyers of their services.

Locational differences, quality differences, brand name differences, and the like all create in our minds differentiation among the various purveyors of many goods and services. Included in this classification are apartment houses, appliance repair shops, beauticians, barbers, department stores, drugstores, gas stations, hotels, restaurants, supermarkets, and many specialty stores. These goods and services may also differ in terms of prices, credit terms, home delivery and other amenities, and even courtesy, all of which affect our choices of where and when to buy. Most such markets fall into the monopolistic competition classification.[2]

Retail markets in general show relatively low concentration, even though they are predominantly local in character. Table 8.1 lists local four-firm concentration ratios for a group of retail and service industries in six states and the District of Columbia. (Compare these with the oligopolistic industries that dominate Table 8.3). Table 8.2 suggests further that on a nationwide basis concentration in retailing is quite low.

Oligopoly   The wide range in the number of sellers in oligopolistic markets and the variety of arrangements they may make mean that no one situation is typical. In Table 8.3 we show 1982 concentration ratios and numbers of firms in a sample of U.S. industries, many of which appear to be oligopolistic. The concentration ratios measure the fraction of sales accounted for by the four largest and eight largest firms in each industry. The top line of the table shows

---

[2]Weiss, *Case Studies*, Chap. 5.

Table 8.1
Four-Firm
Concentration Ratios
among 18 Retail and
Service Industries in
Six States* and the
District of Columbia,
1963

Industry Description	Four-Firm Concentration Ratio
Hardware stores	25
Department stores	34
Food stores	38
Automobile dealers	2
Gasoline dealers	10
Tire and battery stores	33
Apparel and accessory stores	10
Furniture stores	25
Eating and drinking establishments	8
Drugstores	39
Jewelry stores	25
Hotels	8
Laundries	13
Photography stores and studios	19
Barber shops	4
Automobile service establishments	12
Movie theaters	40
Amusements	4

Source: Kenneth D. Boyer, ''Informative and Goodwill Advertising,'' *Review of Economics and Statistics* 54 (November 1974): 541–548.

*Colorado, Delaware, Hawaii, Oregon, Rhode Island, and Utah. They were chosen because each one is dominated by a single Standard Metropolitan Statistical Area, simplifying the problem of estimating sales in each.

that the most concentrated of the group was the household refrigerator and freezer industry, with the four largest producers accounting for 94 percent of sales in the United States. The bottom line shows that the women's and misses' dresses industry is highly competitive, with 5,489 producers of which the four largest have only 6 percent of U.S. sales.

Table 8.3 shows a sample of only 35 out of about 475 industries for which census data are collected periodically by the U.S. Bureau of the Census. About

Table 8.2
Four-Firm National
Concentration Ratios
in Various Lines of
Retailing, 1972

Industry Description	Four-Firm Concentration Ratio
Variety stores	51.1
Department stores	38.8
Grocery stores	11.4
Women's ready-to-wear	11.2
Liquor stores	11.0
Furniture stores	4.4
Gas stations	3.7

Source: U.S. Bureau of the Census, *Census of Retail Trade* 1 (1972): 1–3. Reprinted from Leonard W. Weiss, *Case Studies in American Industry,* 3d ed. (New York: John Wiley & Sons, 1980), 241.

Table 8.3
Concentration Ratios
for 35 Industries,
1982

Industry	Four-Firm Ratio	Eight-Firm Ratio	Number of Firms
Household refrigerators and freezers	94	98	39
Motor vehicles and car bodies	92	97	284
Electric lamps	91	96	113
Cereal breakfast foods	86	N.A.*	32
Malt beverages	77	94	67
Tires and inner tubes	66	86	108
Aircraft	64	81	139
Primary aluminum	64	88	15
Soap and detergents	60	73	642
Storage batteries	56	79	129
Electron tubes, all types	55	78	86
Farm machinery and equipment	53	62	1,787
Watches, clocks, and watchcases	51	62	227
Metal cans	50	68	168
Glass containers	50	73	41
Radio and TV receiving sets	49	70	432
Blast furnaces and steel mills	42	64	211
Cotton-weaving mills	41	65	209
Flour and other grain mill products	40	60	251
Motors and generators	36	50	349
Bread, cake, and related products	34	47	1,869
Cement, hydraulic	31	52	119
Nitrogenous fertilizers	28	73	109
Petroleum refining	28	48	282
Men's footwear, except athletic	28	45	129
Pharmaceutical preparations	26	42	584
Paints and allied products	24	36	1,170
Folding paperboard boxes	22	35	457
Newspapers	22	34	7,520
Upholstered household furniture	17	25	1,129
Sawmills and planing mills	17	23	5,810
Fluid milk	16	27	853
Bottled and canned soft drinks	14	23	1,236
Ready-mixed concrete	6	9	4,161
Women's and misses' dresses	6	10	5,489

Source: U.S. Bureau of the Census, *1982 Census of Manufactures; Concentration Ratios in Manufacturing,* MC82-S-7 Subject Series (Washington, D.C.: Government Printing Office, April 1986).

*not available

half of the industries have four-firm concentration ratios of at least 40, and about two-thirds have ratios of at least 30. Although these numbers suggest that oligopoly is common in manufacturing industries, they can be misleading. We can improve our understanding of U.S. market structures by looking at several conceptual and technical measurement problems of concentration ratio data.[3]

---

[3]For a more detailed discussion, see F. M. Scherer, *Industrial Market Structure and Economic Performance,* 2d ed. (Chicago: Rand McNally College Publishing Company, 1980), 56–74.

First, the selection of four- and eight-firm ratios is purely arbitrary and is for convenience only. Nothing in economic theory suggests that the cutoff points should be four and eight instead of three and six.

Second, the ratios do not tell us much about how effective competition is among the largest four firms or between them and the rest of the industry. The ratios conceal such information as whether the first four or eight firms are of similar size or are dominated by a single seller, how frequently the membership in the largest four turns over, and how the remaining market is distributed among the smaller firms. An industry with a four-firm concentration ratio of 50, consisting of eight firms of equal size, each with 12.5 percent of market sales, will no doubt behave differently from one that has a four-firm concentration ratio of 50 but consists of 54 firms, the largest with 47 percent and the rest with 1 percent each of the market. This is clouded over by the identical concentration ratios.

Third, the Bureau of the Census defines industries according to production characteristics rather than by markets in which products are sold. This makes it impossible to calculate cross elasticities of demand among products sold in any one market area. Economists use the Census classification of industries, however, because it is the best data available, and they understand that actual categorization of industries based on cross elasticities within markets may be broader or narrower than the classification indicates.

The U.S. automobile industry, for example, is defined too narrowly by the Bureau of the Census, because it excludes imports and exports. In 1972, one out of every seven cars sold in the United States was made abroad; in 1983 Japan alone had 20 percent of the U.S. market. The four-firm concentration ratio thus greatly understates the amount of competition in the U.S. market for autos. Imports are also important in the markets for jewelry, shoes, computers, stereos, television sets, and watches.

Other examples of industries defined too narrowly include containers and aluminum. Glass containers are classified separately from metal containers, even though they are good substitutes for each other. In the aluminum industry, competition from the sizable scrap market is ignored.

A number of industries are defined too broadly. One problem is that a national industry may be identified when it is really composed of a great number of local markets. Fluid milk is a case in point. There are many producers nationwide, but most are not in competition with one another—in fact, in certain areas the producers often form local cartels. Additionally, the cost of transporting milk is so large relative to its value that most milk markets are local in scope. Similar situations exist for beer, bricks, cement, construction materials, oil refinery products, and soft drinks. Newspapers too sell in largely local markets.

Although we cannot take the data of Table 8.3 at complete face value, they provide a convenient starting point for obtaining a grasp of the extent of oligopoly in the United States. Some understanding of the pitfalls in the defining of industries and the measurement of concentration ratios helps us to go beyond the ratios to find out where the markets for products really are.

Suggested Readings

For useful surveys of selected industries and their competitiveness, see

Adams, Walter. *The Structure of American Industry*. 6th ed. New York: Macmillan Publishing Co., Inc., 1982.

Brozen, Yale. *The Competitive Economy: Selected Readings*. Morristown, N.J.: General Learning Press, 1975.

Weiss, Leonard W. *Case Studies in American Industry*. 3d ed. New York: John Wiley & Sons, 1980.

Problems and Questions for Discussion

1. Draw and explain the demand curve facing an oligopolistic firm if other firms in the market will match any price decreases but will not follow any price increases by that firm. Is this a plausible situation? Why or why not?

2. Evaluate the following statement: "For an industry to be one of monopolistic competition, it is not important that there be *actual differences* in the items sold by the various sellers; it is only necessary that consumers *think* that differences exist."

3. Some popular writers argue that large firms are almost all-powerful in the sense that they can get the public to buy almost all they produce at whatever price they want to charge. Draw and explain the implied demand curve(s). Evaluate the argument.

4. In which of the market classifications would you expect firms to advertise their products? Why? Do you think such advertising is in the best interests of consumers? Explain.

5. How would you classify the General Store in Dodge City in 1900? How would your answer be affected by widespread dissemination in the area of the Sears & Roebuck mail-order catalog?

6. How would you classify firms that sell each of the following: aspirin, haircuts, wheat, gasoline at retail, automobiles at wholesale to dealers, automobiles at retail to consumers, steel, pantyhose, contract construction, restaurant food, and laundry services?

*7. The four-firm concentration ratio does not provide a full description of an industry's competitive characteristics. What key issues does it leave out?

*8. The United States has only a few domestic aircraft producers, such as Boeing, Lockheed, and McDonnell-Douglas. In spite of the relatively high four-firm concentration ratio of 64 in Table 8.3, competition among them to sell aircraft to airlines around the world is intense. What could account for this?

*9. Explain which of the following markets are likely to have high national concentration ratios relative to local or regional ratios: cement production, petroleum refining, passenger airlines, soft-drink bottling, railroads, and perishable farm products such as eggs and milk.

*10. Some states have branch-banking laws permitting commercial banks to operate branch offices throughout the state. Other states allow branching but limit it to one or more adjacent counties. A third group prohibits branching, confining each commercial bank's operations to its head office.

    a.   Comparing the fraction of total banking deposits accounted for by the two largest banking organizations in cities of similar size, in which of the three groups of states would you predict two-firm concentration ratios would be lowest? (See ''Recent Changes in the Structure of Commercial Banking,'' *Federal Reserve Bulletin* 45 (March 1970): 201, 207; and Douglas F. Greer, *Industrial Organization and Public Policy* [New York: Macmillan, 1980], 126, 133.)

    b.   Some states are relaxing the restrictions regarding operation within their borders of banks licensed by other states. How will interstate banking affect local concentration ratios? National ratios?

*11. What would you expect the effects of inexpensive personal computers and word processing to have been on the number of new textbooks published in a given subject? Would you expect it to have increased competition among publishers? Among authors?

THE FOUNDATIONS OF COSTS AND SUPPLY

WE do for costs of production in Part Three what we did for demand in Part Two. We examine the individual firm—its production possibilities, its motivations, and its behavior—to see what determines its costs of producing goods and services. These costs in turn form the basis of supply.

The type of selling market in which the firm operates is not important in Part Three. The principles of production and the cost curves of the firm do not depend on the type of market in which it sells its product. However, market structure becomes an important consideration again in Part Four.

Chapter 9

THE PRINCIPLES OF PRODUCTION

Chapter Outline

Applications

To understand costs and supply one must first understand the principles of production. But in microeconomic theory these principles extend beyond costs and supply: they also provide the foundations for the analyses of resource pricing and employment, resource allocation, and product distribution that are presented in Part Five.

In this chapter we first draw a comparison between the theory of producer choice and the theory of consumer choice. Second, we explain the concept of a firm's production function. Third, we look at the nature of the law of diminishing returns. Fourth, we analyze key resource product curves and the comparative efficiencies of different resource combinations. Finally, we develop the production possibilities curve for an economy as a whole.

PRODUCER CHOICE AND CONSUMER CHOICE: A COMPARISON

As we proceed through the principles of production it will become apparent that there are a number of parallels between the theory of producer choice and the theory of consumer choice. The following tabulation matches the points of similarity and explains their subtle differences—but there is also much analysis that is new and different.

Consumer Choice	Producer Choice
1. The consumer purchases *goods* to generate *satisfaction* or *utility*.	The producer purchases *resources* to produce *goods*.
2. The consumer's *satisfaction "output"* depends upon the quantities and the mix of *"inputs"* of goods: $S = f_s(x, y)$.	The producer's *product output* depends upon the quantities and the mix of *inputs of resources*: $x = f_x(a, b)$.
3. The consumer is constrained by *income* and the *prices of the goods* purchased: $I = xp_x + yp_y$.	The producer is constrained by *total cost outlay* and the *prices of the resources* purchased: $C = ap_a + bp_b$.
4. The consumer maximizes *satisfaction* subject to the *income constraint.* The satisfaction level is *not measurable cardinally*, but is ordinal, only.	The producer maximizes *output* subject to the *cost constraint* (minimizes cost for a given output). The output level is *measurable cardinally*.
5. The consumer's *income* is *not readily variable* but is taken to be constant, except in the case of Engel curves, in which it is taken to increase or decrease over time.	The producer's *cost outlay* is *variable*, depending upon the output desired.
6. The consumer's *demand curves* and *Engel curves,* along with *exchange*, are the immediate end results of the theory.	The producer's *cost curves*, along with *resource exchanges* and *production possibilities* for the economy, are the immediate end results of the theory.

THE PRODUCTION FUNCTION

What do we mean by the term "production function?" We look first at the concept and then at its graphic representations.

The Concept

The term **production function** refers to the physical relationships between a firm's inputs of resources and its output of goods or services per unit of time, leaving prices aside. It can be expressed in general mathematical terms as

$$x = f(a, b, c).$$

(9.1)

production function
The technical physical relationship between the quantities of a firm's resource inputs and the quantities of its output of goods or services per unit of time.

The firm's output level is represented by x, and its input quantities are represented by a, b, and c. The equation can be expanded readily to include as many different resources as are used in the production of any given item. It furnishes a convenient way of relating product output to resource inputs.

Firms can usually vary the proportions in which they combine resources in production processes. This flexibility brings about several possible types of relationships among inputs, among inputs and outputs, and among outputs. Where inputs can be substituted for one another in the production of a commodity, there will be a number of alternative sets of input quantities that will produce a given level of product output, and the firm must make choices among them. By increasing or decreasing the quantities of all resource inputs used, the firm can increase or decrease its output level. It can also increase or decrease output within limits by increasing or decreasing the quantity used of one or more resource inputs, holding the quantities of other resource inputs constant. And, given the bundle of resources available to it, a firm that produces more than one product can increase its output level of one product by reducing its output level of another, transferring the resources thus released to the production of the first.

The input-input, input-output, and output-output relationships that characterize a firm's production function depend on the production technology used. Of the range of technologies available we assume that the firm will use those that are most efficient—that is, those that will provide the greatest value of output for a given value of input. Generally speaking, an improvement in technology will increase the output possible from given quantities of resources.

The Production Surface

In many ways a firm's production function is analogous to the preference function or the utility function of an individual consumer, although one must be careful not to confuse the two. A firm uses resource inputs to generate product or service outputs. Usually these quantities have cardinal properties—the product output can be measured, added, and, in most cases, seen. An individual consumer purchases and uses products and services to generate a much more nebulous kind of output—satisfaction—that cannot be measured, added, or seen. It therefore has ordinal properties but not cardinal properties.

Suppose, then, that a firm uses two resource inputs, A and B, to obtain outputs of product X. In the three-dimensional diagram of Figure 9.1(a), the coordinates in the horizontal AB plane show input combinations. Product output associated with each input combination is measured vertically above the plane. If no resource A is used, total product curve TP_b^0 is generated on the XB plane

Figure 9.1
A Production Surface and Its Isoquants

In panel (a) E_3F_3 is a contour line around the production surface; therefore, $b_3E_3 = MN = a_3F_3$. Projected down to the AB plane the contour line becomes isoquant b_3a_3, showing all combinations of A and B that produce output level $0x_3$. Isoquant b_1G is similarly formed. These isoquants are shown in conventional form in panel (b).

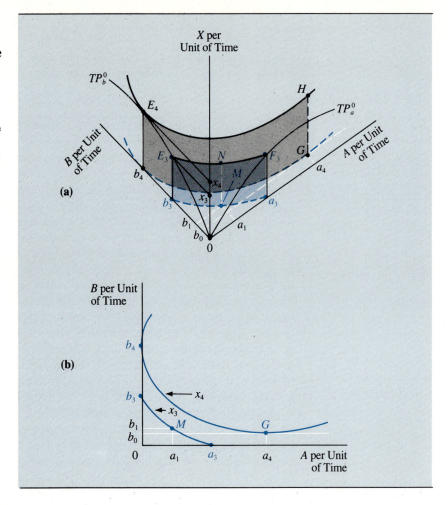

by varying the quantity of resource B used; an output of $b_3E_3(=0x_3)$ is produced with b_3 of B alone. Similarly, if no resource B is used, TP_a^0 is generated on the XA plane by varying the quantity of resource A used; with a_3 of A, the output level is $a_3F_3(=0x_3)$. A combination of b_1 of B and a_1 of A yields an output level of $MN = 0x_3$. The whole range of input combinations generates an inverted, sort of bowl-shaped *production surface* that shows the output associated with every possible input combination.

isoquant curve
A curve showing the combinations of resources required by a firm to produce a given level of product output.

Isoquants   Contour lines can be drawn around the production surface of Figure 9.1(a) at each possible level of output. All points on a given contour line are equidistant from the AB plane—that is, any one contour line represents a constant or given level of production. These contour lines can be projected downward onto the AB plane, forming a set of **isoquants,** or product indifference

isoquant map
The family of isoquant curves of a firm describing the resource combinations required to produce all possible levels of output.

curves. Any one isoquant—for example, any combination of inputs making up isoquant b_3a_3—generates a constant level of product output—in this case, x_3. If the production surface has an inverted bowl shape, higher contour lines like E_4H, when projected to the AB plane, become isoquants like b_4G, lying farther from the origin of the diagram. A complete set of isoquants for the firm is called its **isoquant map.**[1]

Isoquant Characteristics   The general characteristics of isoquants are the same as those of indifference curves. First, they slope downward to the right for those combinations of resources that firms will want to use. They may slope upward to the right for some resource combinations, as do x_3, x_5, and x_6 in panel (a) of Figure 9.2 (but as we shall see later it would not be in the firm's best interests to use such combinations). Second, the isoquants do not intersect. Third, they are convex to the origin of the diagram.

Isoquants slope downward to the right for resources that can be substituted for one another in the production process. For example, usually there are possibilities of substitutions between capital resources and labor resources used. If less of one is used, more of the other must be applied to compensate for the decrease in the first if the level of output is to remain constant. Exceptions may occur when resources cannot be substituted for one another at all, or when fixed proportions of resources may be required.

An intersection of isoquants is not logical. An intersection point would mean that a single combination of resources produced two different maximum outputs, thereby implying that an increase in the level of output could be accomplished with no increase in the amount of any resource used. To the right of the intersection point, the implication would be that by decreasing the quantities of all resources used product output could be increased. Thus isoquant intersections are economic nonsense.

Convexity to the origin reflects the fact that different resources are not ordinarily perfect substitutes. Consider the labor and capital used in digging a ditch of a given length, width, and depth. Within limits they can be substituted for each other. But the more labor and the less capital used to dig the ditch, the more difficult it will become to substitute additional labor for capital. Additional units of labor will just compensate for smaller and smaller amounts of capital given up. The same reasoning applies to other resources.

marginal rate of technical substitution
The amount of one resource that a firm is just able to give up in return for an additional unit of another resource with no loss in output. For any given resource combination it is measured by the slope of the isoquant through the point representing that combination.

The more of resource A and the less of resource B the firm uses to produce a constant amount of product X, the more difficult it becomes to substitute additional units of A for B—that is, additional units of A will just compensate for smaller and smaller amounts of B given up. This is called the principle of diminishing **marginal rate of technical substitution** of A for B ($MRTS_{ab}$). The

[1]Let the production function be $x = f(a, b)$, in which x is the quantity produced of the good or service and a and b are quantities of resource inputs. An isoquant is the locus of all combinations of resources A and B that yield a given output level; that is, $x_3 = f(a, b)$ defines an isoquant. A family of isoquants, or an isoquant map, is described by treating x as a parameter and assigning different values to it.

**Figure 9.2
From Isoquants to
Total Product for
One Resource**

In panel (a) larger
quantities of resource *A*
used with b_1 of *B* move
the firm across its
isoquant map along path
b_1J, showing us the
amounts of product
produced with b_1 of *B*
and the various quantities
of *A*. These product
amounts, plotted against
the corresponding
quantities of *A*, generate
the TP_a of panel (b).

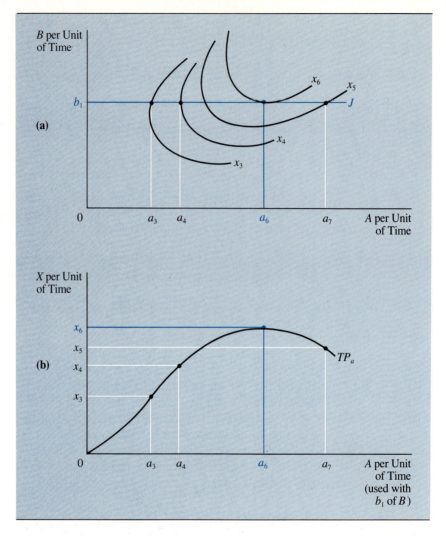

$MRTS_{ab}$ is measured at any point on an isoquant by the slope of the isoquant at
that point. It is defined as the amount of *B* that can just offset an additional unit
of *A* with no change in the product output level.

Product Curves

Product schedules and product curves for either resource *A* or resource *B* can
be derived from the firm's system of isoquants. With reference to panel (a) in
Figure 9.2, suppose that the firm considers the employment of alternative quantities of *A* per unit of time with a fixed amount b_1 of *B*. A movement to the
right along the line b_1J measures the use of larger quantities of *A*. Each isoquant
intersected by line b_1J shows the output level obtained with each quantity of *A*.

Thus, when a_4 of A is used with b_1 of B, total product will be x_4. The greater the amount of A used, the greater will be the total output up to a_6 units of the resource. With still greater quantities of A, line b_1J intersects lower and lower isoquants, showing that the total product decreases. Thus the firm would never use more than a_6 of A with b_1 of B, even if A were free; that is, the firm would never want to use a resource combination lying on the upward-sloping portion of an isoquant. The total product curve for larger and larger quantities of A used with the fixed amount of B increases, reaches a maximum at a_6 units of A, and then decreases. The resulting curve, TP_a, is in panel (b) of Figure 9.2.

The average product and marginal physical product schedules or curves of a resource are derived from the total product schedule or curve for that resource. Suppose a firm conducts a series of experiments to determine the total product output it can get from various quantities of labor per unit of time used with a unit of capital. Let the results be those listed in column (3) of Table 9.1 as the *total product* of labor. Increases in the amount of labor used up to 7 units increases output. At 7 and 8 units of labor the maximum total product that a unit of capital will produce is obtained.

The *average product* of labor, computed from columns (2) and (3), is the total product of labor at each level of employment divided by that quantity of labor. Note that in column (4) average product rises as the quantity of labor is increased, reaches a maximum at 3 and 4 units of labor per unit of capital, and then decreases as the employment of labor is increased further.

The change in total product per unit change in the quantity of labor employed, holding the quantity of capital constant, is called the **marginal physical product** of labor. In Table 9.1, an increase in the employment of labor from zero to 1 unit increases total product from zero to 3; thus in column (5) the marginal physical product of labor at the 1-unit level of employment is 3 units of product. Two units of labor employed increase total product to 7 units; the marginal physical product of labor at the 2-unit level of employment is 4 units of product. The rest of column (5) is computed in a similar fashion.

marginal physical product of a resource The change in total output of a firm resulting from a one-unit change in the employment level of the resource, holding the quantities of other resources constant.

Table 9.1
Product Schedules for Labor

(1) Capital	(2) Labor	(3) Total Product (labor)	(4) Average Product (labor)	(5) Marginal Physical Product (labor)	
1	1	3	3	3	
1	2	7	3½	4	Stage I
1	3	12	4	5	
1	4	16	4	4	
1	5	19	3⅘	3	Stage II
1	6	21	3½	2	
1	7	22	3⅐	1	
1	8	22	2¾	0	
1	9	21	2⅓	−1	Stage III
1	10	15	1½	−6	

**Figure 9.3
Product Curves
for Labor**

In panel (b) the AP_l curve is generated by dividing each product output shown on the TP_l of panel (a) by the corresponding amount of labor and by plotting the results; i.e., $l'a'$ in panel (b) is determined by $l'A'/0l'$ in panel (a). The numerical values of the slope of TP_l at different quantities of l are plotted as MPP_l in panel (b). The range of labor-capital ratios for which AP_l is rising is called Stage I for labor. The range for which AP_l is falling but TP_l is still rising is designated Stage II. That for which both AP_l and TP_l are falling is Stage III.

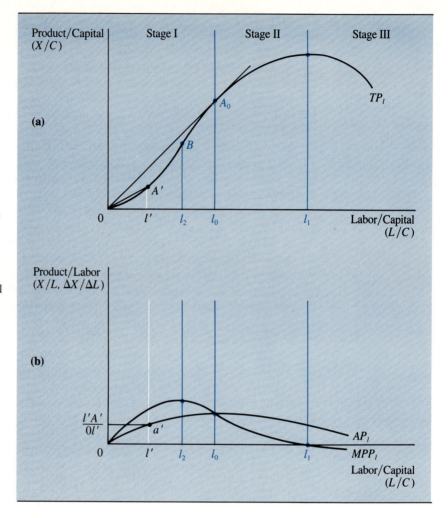

The total, average, and marginal physical product concepts are shown graphically in Figure 9.3. The vertical axis of panel (a) measures product produced per unit of capital (Product/Capital), and the horizontal axis measures labor used per unit of capital (Labor/Capital). The total product curve for labor (TP_l) is in all essential respects like that of Figure 9.2(b).[2] When l_1 units of

---

[2]The total product curve of Figure 9.3(a) begins at the origin of the diagram, but it is not necessary that it do so. For some resources not absolutely essential in the production of the product, it may begin above the origin—cottonseed meal fed to cows to increase milk production is a case in point. In other cases, no product may be obtained until several units of the variable resource have been applied to the fixed complex of other resources. For example, one worker in a steel mill will produce nothing, and two workers will do no better. A certain minimum complement of labor is necessary before any production can be obtained. In this case, the total product curve of labor begins to the right of the origin.

labor are used on the unit of capital, total product reaches a maximum. Additional units of labor per unit of capital cause total product to decrease.

The average product curve for labor (AP_l) in panel (b) is derived from the total product curve (TP_l) of panel (a). The vertical axis of panel (b) measures product per unit of labor (Product/Labor); the horizontal axis is the same as that of panel (a). Since average product is total product divided by the number of units of labor used, average product in panel (a) at l' units of labor is $l'A'/0l'$, which measures the slope of the line $0A'$—this ratio is plotted in panel (b). As the quantity of labor is increased from zero to l_0 in panel (a), the slopes of the corresponding $0A$ lines increase—that is, the average product of labor increases. At l_0 units of labor the slope of line $0A_0$ is greater than that of any other $0A$ line drawn from the origin to the total product curve; thus the average product of labor is maximum at this point. Beyond l_0 units of labor the average product decreases, but it remains positive so long as total product is positive. The slopes of the $0A$ lines corresponding to the various quantities of labor in panel (a) are plotted at the AP_l curve in panel (b).

The slope of the total product curve at any given quantity of labor measures the marginal physical product of labor at that point. Both the slope of TP_l and the marginal physical product of labor (MPP_l) are defined as the change in total product per unit change in the quantity of labor ($\Delta X/\Delta L$) used. Marginal physical product reaches a maximum at point B, where the total product curve turns from concave upward to concave downward. At quantity l_1 of labor, the total product is maximum; hence marginal physical product is zero. Beyond l_1, additional units of labor cause the total product to decrease, meaning that the marginal physical product is negative.[3] The slopes of TP_l at the various quantities of labor in panel (a) are plotted as MPP_l in panel (b).

An additional guide to the proper location of the marginal physical product curve is its relationship to the average product curve. When average product is increasing, marginal physical product is greater than average product. When average product is maximum, marginal physical product equals average product. When average product is decreasing, marginal physical product is less than average product.[4] These relationships are verified by columns (4) and (5) of Table 9.1.

---

[3]Let the production function be $x = g(k, l)$. Total product of labor can be expressed as $TP_l = x = g(\bar{k}, l) = f(l)$, in which $\bar{k}$ represents a fixed amount of capital. The average product of labor becomes

$$AP_l = \frac{TP_l}{l} = \frac{f(l)}{l}, \quad \text{and} \quad MPP_l = \frac{dTP_l}{dl} = f'(l).$$

[4]To illustrate these relationships, consider a succession of persons entering a room, each taller than the preceding one. As each enters, the average height of those in the room increases; however, except for the first one, average height will be less than that of the one currently entering. The height of each person at the time of entry is marginal height and is analogous to marginal physical product, while average height is analogous to average product. Thus for average product (height) to be increasing, marginal physical product (height) must exceed the average.

Suppose that additional persons enter, each successively shorter than the preceding one and

(*continued on page 236*)

THE LAW OF DIMINISHING RETURNS

law of diminishing returns
The principle stating that if the input of one resource is increased by equal increments per unit of time while the quantities of other inputs are held constant there will be some point beyond which the marginal physical product of the variable resource will decrease.

The product schedules of Table 9.1 and the product curves of Figure 9.3 illustrate the celebrated **law of diminishing returns,** which describes the direction and the rate of change that the firm's output takes when the input of only one resource is varied. It states that *if the input of one resource is increased by equal increments per unit of time while the inputs of other resources are held constant, total product output will increase; but beyond some point, the resulting output increases will become smaller and smaller.*[5] If the increases in the variable resource are carried far enough, total product will reach a maximum and may then decrease. This law is consistent with observations that there are limits to the output that can be obtained by increasing the quantity of a single resource applied to constant quantities of other resources.

Diminishing returns may or may not occur for the first few one-unit increases in the variable resource used with the fixed quantities of other resources. It is possible for diminishing returns or diminishing increases in total product to occur for all such increments. This is frequently the case with the application of fertilizer to given complexes of seed, land, labor, and machinery.

But a stage of increasing returns may also characterize the initial increases in the variable resource before diminishing returns begin. An example of this situation is the amount of labor used to operate a factory of a given size. Smaller quantities of labor than that for which the factory is designed tend to operate inefficiently because of the multiplicity of jobs to be performed by each individual and because of time lost in changing from one task to another. Equal increments in labor used bring about successively greater increments in total product, up to some point. In Table 9.1, through 3 units of labor, and in Figure 9.3, through l_2 units of labor, we show increasing returns.[6] Beyond these points, increases in the quantity of labor used lead to diminishing returns.

(continued from page 235)

all shorter than the average height before they entered. Average height will decrease but will not be as low as marginal height.

When average height is maximum, the height of the last person who entered must have been equal to average height, since it caused neither an increase nor a decrease in average height. Mathematically, if AP_l is increasing, then

$$\frac{d(AP_l)}{dl} = \frac{d\left(\frac{f(l)}{l}\right)}{dl} > 0, \quad \text{so} \quad \frac{l \times f'(l) - f(l)}{l^2} > 0, \quad \text{or} \quad f'(l) - \frac{f(l)}{l} > 0.$$

Therefore, $f'(l) > \dfrac{f(l)}{l}$,

that is, $MPP_l > AP_l$. Similarly, it can be shown that if AP_l is constant or maximum, $MPP_l = AP_l$, and if AP_l is decreasing, $MPP_l < AP_l$.

[5]The *different quantities* of the variable resource refer to *alternative quantities* used with constant amounts of other resources, not to a chronological application of additional units.

[6]Whether or not we assume that diminishing returns occur at the outset is not important. For expository purposes we usually assume first increasing and then decreasing returns as the quantity of the variable resource is increased.

PRODUCT CURVES AND TECHNICAL EFFICIENCY

The three product curves defined and described earlier show the *technical efficiency of resources* for various resource combinations that may be used in making a product. The technical efficiency of any given resource is defined as the ratio of the product output to the resource input—that is, it is the average product of the resource. The greater the product output per unit of resource input, the greater the technical efficiency of the resource is said to be.

A production function with *constant returns to size* is commonly used to illustrate technical efficiency conditions for a firm. It has the virtues of directness and simplicity; however, the results obtained are in no sense restricted to such a production function. Constant returns to size mean that changes of a given proportion in the quantities of all resources used change product output in the same proportion. A 50 percent increase in the quantities of all resources used to make the product will result in a 50 percent increase in the output of the firm; doubling the quantities of all resource inputs will double the product output. Assume that both capital and labor are completely divisible with respect to quantities used and that the same technology will be used for any given ratio of labor to capital, regardless of the absolute amounts of resources used. The same technology will be used if 2 units of labor work 1 unit of capital as are used if 1 unit of labor works ½ unit of capital or if 4 units of labor work 2 units of capital. Mathematically the **production function** in this case is **homogeneous of degree one.**[7]

production function homogeneous of degree one
A production function with characteristics such that an increase of a given proportion in all resource inputs will increase output in the same proportion.

We are concerned with the *ratio* of the resources as we establish the firm's product curves; we are not really limited to 1 unit of capital, or to any fixed amount. We can think of the firm as using any amount of capital it wishes to use; but in establishing the product curves, we convert our observations into terms of product obtainable from 1 unit of the capital resource. For example, if 10 units of labor working 2 units of capital produce 38 units of product per unit of time, for purposes of establishing the product curves we would convert the data to an equivalent of 1 unit of capital—that is, 5 units of labor working 1 unit of capital produce an output of 19 units of product per unit of time.[8] An

---

[7]The production function $x = g(k, l)$ is homogeneous of degree n if $\lambda^n x = g(\lambda k, \lambda l)$. It exhibits

1. Constant returns to scale, or is homogeneous of degree one, when $n = 1$.

2. Increasing returns to scale when $n > 1$.

3. Decreasing returns to scale when $n < 1$.

[8]If the production function of Footnote 7 is homogeneous of degree one, it takes the form $\lambda x = g(\lambda k, \lambda l)$, which exhibits the following properties:

1. AP_l and AP_k are functions of the *ratio* of capital to labor. Letting $\lambda = \frac{1}{l}$, then

$$\frac{1}{l} x = g\left(\frac{1}{l} k, \frac{1}{l} l\right) = g\left(\frac{k}{l}, 1\right) = h\left(\frac{k}{l}\right); \quad \text{that is,}$$

$$AP_l = h\left(\frac{k}{l}\right) = h(r) \quad \text{where} \quad r = \frac{k}{l}, \text{ and } AP_k = \frac{x}{k} = \frac{x}{l} \times \frac{l}{k} = AP_l \times \frac{1}{r} = \frac{h(r)}{r}.$$

(continued on page 238)

increase in the quantity of capital used, with the quantity of labor held constant, is equivalent to a decrease in the quantity of labor, with the quantity of capital held constant, when we think in terms of the ratio of the two resources used.

The Three Stages for Labor

Letting the product schedules of Table 9.1 and the product curves of Figure 9.3 be those of the firm under consideration, we can divide each into three stages. In all three, the average product curve and the total product curve of labor provide information on how efficiently the resources are being used for various labor-capital ratios. As the ratio of labor to capital is increased—that is, as more and more labor per unit of capital is used—the average product curve yields information regarding the amount of product obtained per unit of labor for the various ratios. The total product curve depicts the amount of product obtained per unit of capital.

Stage I is characterized by increases in the average product of labor as more labor per unit of capital is used. These increases mean the technical efficiency of labor—the product per worker—is rising. The total product obtained per unit of capital as larger quantities of labor are applied to it is also rising in Stage I. The increases in total product mean the technical efficiency of capital is also increasing in Stage I. Thus, increases in the quantity of labor applied to a unit of capital in Stage I increase the technical efficiency with which *both* labor and capital are utilized.

Stage II is characterized by decreasing average product and shrinking marginal physical product of labor. But the marginal physical product is positive, since total product continues to increase. In Stage II, as larger quantities of labor per unit of capital are used the technical efficiency of labor—product per worker—decreases; however, the technical efficiency of capital—product per unit of capital—continues to increase.

In Stage III the application of larger quantities of labor to a unit of capital reduces the average product of labor still more. In addition, the marginal physical product of labor is negative, and total product is falling. The efficiency of both labor and capital decreases when the firm pushes into Stage III combinations.

(*continued from page 237*)

Thus, both AP_l and AP_k are functions of the capital-labor ratio only. They are constant for all changes in K and L in equal proportions, since such changes do not alter the k/l ratio.

2. The MPP_k and MPP_l are also functions of the k/l ratio only. Since

$$AP_l = \frac{x}{l} = h(r), \quad \text{then} \quad x = l \times h(r). \quad \text{Therefore,}$$

$$MPP_l = \frac{\partial x}{\partial l} = h(r) + l\frac{dh(r)}{dr} \times \frac{\partial r}{\partial l} = h(r) + l \times h'(r) \times \frac{-k}{l^2}$$

$$= h(r) - \frac{k}{l} \times h'(r) = h(r) - r \times h'(r), \text{ and}$$

$$MPP_k = \frac{\partial x}{\partial k} = l\frac{\partial h(r)}{\partial k} = l\frac{dh(r)}{dr} \times \frac{\partial r}{\partial k} = l \times h'(r)\left(\frac{1}{l}\right) = h'(r).$$

In looking over the three stages we note two things: (1) the combination of labor and capital that leads to maximum technical efficiency of labor lies at the boundary line between Stages I and II, and (2) the combination of labor and capital leading to maximum technical efficiency of capital is the one at the boundary line between Stages II and III.

The Three Stages for Capital

If the production function of the firm is homogeneous of degree one, we can rework Table 9.1 and Figure 9.3 to determine the product schedules and product curves for alternative quantities of capital applied to one unit of labor. We can show that Stage I for labor is Stage III for capital, that Stage III for labor is Stage I for capital, and that Stage II for labor is also Stage II for capital.

To facilitate comparison of the product curves of labor with those of capital, it will be convenient to set up the product schedules of Table 9.2 and the product curves of Figure 9.4 in an unorthodox way. Table 9.2, which shows the effects of increasing the ratio of capital to labor, should be read from bottom to top. Figure 9.4, read in the conventional way from left to right, shows the effects of increasing the ratio of labor to capital, but read from right to left, it shows the impact of increasing the ratio of capital to labor.

The Product Schedules   To see the results of the reworking of Table 9.1 in Table 9.2, look at the bottom of Table 9.1, where 10 units of labor are used per unit of capital. In terms of a ratio, this combination means the same thing as using $\frac{1}{10}$ of a unit of capital per unit of labor. These numbers are shown in columns (1) and (2) in the last row of Table 9.2. Similarly, in terms of ratios 9 units of labor per unit of capital are the same as $\frac{1}{9}$ of a unit of capital per unit of labor, and so on up through the table until we reach the top row, where

Table 9.2
Product Schedules for Capital

(1) Capital	(2) Labor	(3) Total Product (capital)	(4) Marginal Physical Product (capital)	(5) Average Product (capital)	
1	1	3	(−)1	3	Stage III
$\frac{1}{2}$	1	$3\frac{1}{2}$	(−)3	7	
$\frac{1}{3}$	1	4	0	12	
$\frac{1}{4}$	1	4	4	16	Stage II
$\frac{1}{5}$	1	$3\frac{4}{5}$	9	19	
$\frac{1}{6}$	1	$3\frac{1}{2}$	15	21	
$\frac{1}{7}$	1	$3\frac{1}{7}$	22	22	
$\frac{1}{8}$	1	$2\frac{3}{4}$	30	22	Stage I
$\frac{1}{9}$	1	$2\frac{1}{3}$	75	21	
$\frac{1}{10}$	1	$1\frac{1}{2}$	15	15	

**Figure 9.4
Product Curves
for Capital**

Using a linearly
homogeneous production
function cross section,
reading the Labor/Capital
axes from left to right,
the familiar TP_l, AP_l, and
MPP_l are generated and
the diagram can be
divided into Stages I, II,
and III for labor. Reading
from right to left,
increasing the ratio of
capital to labor, the TP_l
curve becomes the AP_k
curve, and the AP_l curve
becomes the TP_k curve.
The MPP_k is then drawn
in correct relationship to
the AP_k and TP_k curves.
The three stages for
capital are symmetrical to
the three stages for labor.

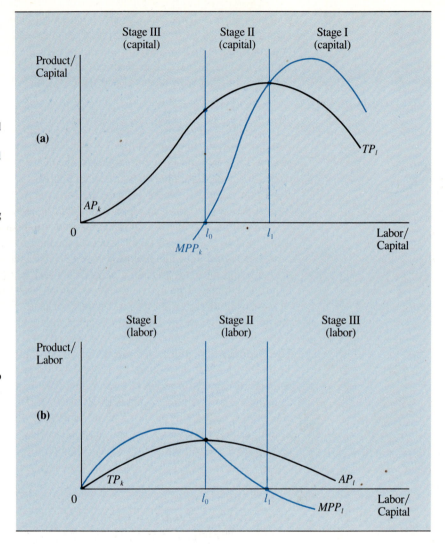

1 unit of capital is used with 1 unit of labor. The ratios of capital and labor are
the same throughout Tables 9.1 and 9.2.

The total product schedule for various amounts of capital applied to 1 unit
of labor is determined from column (3) of Table 9.1. Ten units of labor applied
to 1 unit of capital produce 15 units of product. Obviously, then, $\frac{1}{10}$ of a unit
of capital applied to 1 unit of labor should produce a total product of $\frac{15}{10}$, or
$1\frac{1}{2}$, units of product. This result is listed in the last row of column (3) in Table
9.2. Since in Table 9.1 9 units of labor applied to 1 unit of capital produce 21

units of product, then in Table 9.2, $\frac{1}{9}$ of a unit of capital applied to 1 unit of labor will produce a total product of $2\frac{1}{3}$. Total product of the larger quantities of capital used with 1 unit of labor is computed in a similar way to complete column (3) of Table 9.2.

The marginal physical product schedule for capital should show the increments in total product per full unit increment in capital at the various ratios of capital to labor used. The first $\frac{1}{10}$ of a unit of capital used increases total product from zero to $1\frac{1}{2}$ units. Therefore, at this ratio of capital to labor the marginal physical product of a unit of capital is $1\frac{1}{2} \div \frac{1}{10} = \frac{3}{2} \times 10 = 15$ units of product. This quantity is listed in column (4) in the last row of Table 9.2.

An increase in capital from $\frac{1}{10}$ of a unit of $\frac{1}{9}$ of a unit increases total product from $1\frac{1}{2}$ to $2\frac{1}{3}$. The product increment is $\frac{7}{3} - \frac{3}{2} = \frac{14}{6} - \frac{9}{6} = \frac{5}{6}$ of a unit of product. The capital increment is $\frac{1}{9} - \frac{1}{10} = \frac{10}{90} - \frac{9}{90} = \frac{1}{90}$ of a unit of capital. Marginal physical product of a unit of capital at this point is $\frac{5}{6} \div \frac{1}{90} = \frac{5}{6} \times 90 = 75$ units of product. Column (4) of Table 9.2 is calculated by similar computations on up through columns (1) and (3).

Column (5) of Table 9.2, read from bottom to top, presents average product per unit of capital for the various capital-labor ratios. The average product of capital for each ratio is obtained by dividing the total product of capital by the quantity of capital used. Since $\frac{1}{10}$ of a unit of capital produces $1\frac{1}{2}$ units of product, the average product of capital equals $1\frac{1}{2} \div \frac{1}{10} = 15$ at this point. Similarly, $2\frac{1}{3}$ units of product divided by $\frac{1}{9}$ of a unit of capital equals an average product of capital of 21 units. The other figures of column (5) are determined by similar computations.

When Table 9.1 is compared with Table 9.2, two columns of Table 9.1 turn out to be identical with two columns in Table 9.2. First, the total product schedule of labor applied to 1 unit of capital [see Table 9.1, column (3)] has become the average product schedule of capital applied to 1 unit of labor [see Table 9.2, column (5)]. Second, the average product schedule of labor applied to 1 unit of capital [see Table 9.1, column (4)] has become the total product schedule of capital applied to 1 unit of labor [see Table 9.2, column (3)]. A little reflection will reveal that these relationships should be expected. The total product of more and more labor applied to 1 unit of capital is the average product of capital (or the product per unit of capital) as the ratio of labor to capital is increased. Likewise, the average product of labor (product per unit of labor) is necessarily the total product of various quantities of capital applied to 1 unit of labor.

A further observation can be made. Stages I, II, and III are marked off approximately for labor in Table 9.1; Stages I, II, and III for capital are marked off approximately in Table 9.2.[9] That which is Stage I for labor in Table 9.1 has become Stage III for capital in Table 9.2. That which is Stage III for labor in Table 9.1 has become Stage I for capital in Table 9.2. Stage II for labor is also Stage II for capital in both tables.

_____

[9]The boundary lines between stages must be approximations when product schedules are set up in table form. Only on continuous graphs can the exact boundaries between the stages be established.

The Product Curves In Figure 9.4, product curves for capital per unit of labor, as well as those for labor per unit of capital, are shown. The product curves for both labor applied to a unit of capital and capital applied to a unit of labor are drawn in the diagram. Reading the horizontal axes of both panels from left to right, the ratio of labor to capital is increasing, giving rise to the three familiar product curves for labor [TP_l in panel (a) and AP_l and MPP_l in panel (b)]. Reading the horizontal axes from right to left, the ratio of capital to labor is increasing; however, equal distances do not measure equal increments. The total product curve of labor when the ratio of labor to capital is increased becomes the average product curve for capital when the ratio of capital to labor is increased. The average product curve for labor when the ratio of labor to capital is increased becomes the total product curve for capital when the ratio of capital to labor is increased. Note that the marginal physical product curve for capital, reading from right to left in panel (a), lies above the average product curve for capital when average product is increasing, cuts the average product curve at its maximum point, and lies below the average product curve when that curve is decreasing. Note also that the marginal physical product curve for capital reaches zero at the ratio of capital to labor at which the total product of capital is maximum. The marginal physical product of capital is negative where increases in the quantity of capital per unit of labor lead to decreases in the total product of capital. The three stages for both capital and labor are shown in Figure 9.4.

Stage II Combinations

Stage II contains all the relevant ratios of labor to capital for the firm. The three stages, with their relationships and their characteristics, are summed up in Table 9.3. In Stage I for labor, labor is used too sparsely on the capital, and increases in the ratio of labor to capital will raise its average product. The firm should boost the ratio of labor to capital used at least to the point at which the average product of labor will no longer rise. Such an increase will place the firm in Stage II. In Stage III for labor, the marginal physical product of labor is negative, meaning that too much labor is used per unit of capital. The ratio of labor to capital should be decreased at least to the point at which the marginal physical product of labor is no longer negative. Now only Stage II ratios remain with us.

Table 9.3 The Three Stages for Labor and Capital	Labor Productivity When the Ratio of Labor to Capital Is Increased		Capital Productivity When the Ratio of Capital to Labor Is Increased	
	Stage I	Increasing AP_l	Negative MPP_k	Stage III
	Stage II	Decreasing AP_l and MPP_l, but MPP_l is positive	Decreasing AP_k and MPP_k, but MPP_k is positive	Stage II
	Stage III	Negative MPP_l	Increasing AP_k	Stage I

The main points emerging from the foregoing discussion are worth emphasizing. The combination of labor and capital that yields maximum efficiency for labor lies at the boundary between Stage I and Stage II for labor; the one that yields maximum efficiency for capital lies at the boundary between Stage II and Stage III for labor.

The introduction of resource costs into the picture puts the economic issues facing the firm into proper perspective. Suppose that capital is so plentiful that it costs nothing at all while labor is scarce enough to command some price. Because whatever cost outlay the firm makes will go for labor, the firm will achieve its greatest economic efficiency (lowest cost per unit of product) at that ratio of labor to capital which maximizes product per unit of labor. This ratio occurs at the boundary between Stages I and II for labor. The output per unit expenditure will increase through Stage I and decrease through Stages II and III.

Suppose that labor can be had for the asking and that capital is a scarce resource that commands a price. In this case the entire cost outlay goes for capital, and economic efficiency is greatest when the ratio of labor to capital is such that product per unit of capital is maximum. Throughout the first two stages, product per unit of capital (and per unit expenditure) increases as the ratio of labor to capital is increased. At the boundary between Stages II and III for labor, product per unit of capital and product per unit of expenditure are maximum. In Stage III they decrease.

Suppose next that both labor and capital are economic resources, that is, both are scarce enough to command a price. Increases in the ratio of labor to capital in Stage I for labor increase the product per unit of both labor and capital. These increases also raise the product obtained per unit of expenditure on both; hence the firm will move at least to the boundary between Stages I and II. If the firm moves into Stage II, increasing the ratio of labor to capital, the product per unit expenditure on labor drops while that per unit expenditure on capital increases. (Which is more important, the rising efficiency of capital or the dwindling efficiency of labor? We shall return to the question in a moment.) If the firm moves into Stage III for labor, the product per unit expenditure on capital and on labor both decrease; hence when both resources have costs, the firm should not go beyond the boundary line between Stages II and III for labor.

Labor-to-capital ratios of Stage I and Stage III are ruled out of the firm's consideration under all circumstances. The firm will not operate in Stage I for either resource when capital is free and when labor has costs, or when labor is free and capital has costs, or when both resources command prices. The same reasoning applies to Stage III. Stage II is left as the possible range of relevant ratios of labor to capital.

Which of the ratios of labor to capital falling within Stage II will the firm use? The answer depends on the comparative costs or prices per unit of capital and labor. We have already observed that if capital is free and labor must be paid for the firm will use the ratio at which Stage II for labor begins. If capital must be paid for and labor is free, the firm will use the ratio at which Stage II for labor ends. From these points, we can deduce that the lower the price of capital relative to the price of labor, the closer the ratio should be to the beginning of labor's Stage II, while the lower the price of labor relative to the price of capital, the closer the ratio should be to the end of labor's Stage II. Thus, for any resource that a firm employs we can say that the firm should use some ratio of that resource to other resources that falls within Stage II for it.

A Generalized Stage II

Isoquant diagrams enable us to establish a generalized Stage II—one not restricted to a production function homogeneous of degree one. Consider the isoquant map in Figure 9.5. From it we can read off the set of resource combinations that will produce any given level of output. In addition, we can locate the total product curves for resource A—a different one for each different level of resource B with which alternative quantities of A are used. We can also locate the total product curves for resource B—one for each different quantity of A with which alternative quantities of B are used.

On any given isoquant, the marginal rate of technical substitution of A for B is measured by the ratio of the marginal physical product of A to the marginal physical product of B. Suppose that in Figure 9.5 combination M of A and B is used to produce x_6 of X. In moving from combination M to combination Q, holding the output level constant at x_6, the firm gives up MN of resource B for

**Figure 9.5
Stage II on an
Isoquant Diagram**

The combinations of resources A and B lying between ridge lines $0C$ and $0D$ are Stage II combinations. For combinations lying above $0C$ the MPP_b is negative, indicating Stage III for B. The MPP_a is negative for combinations to the right of $0D$, meaning that they are in Stage III for resource A.

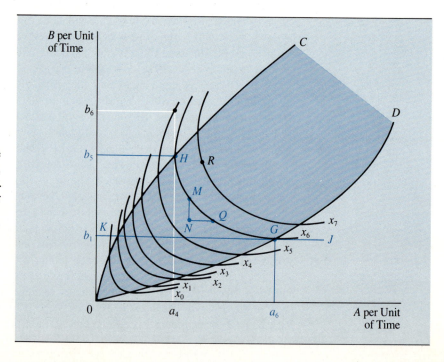

NQ of resource A. The reduction in output from giving up MN of B is $MN \times MPP_b$; the increase in output from NQ of A is $NQ \times MPP_a$. Since the reduction in output from giving up B must equal the increase in output from the additional A, then

$$MN \times MPP_b = NQ \times MPP_a, \quad \text{or} \quad \frac{MN}{NQ} = \frac{MPP_a}{MPP_b}.$$

(9.2)
$$\text{Since} \quad MRTS_{ab} = \frac{MN}{NQ}, \quad \text{then} \quad MRTS_{ab} = \frac{MPP_a}{MPP_b}.$$

If the $MRTS_{ab}$ is 2, then MPP_a is twice as large as MPP_b, meaning that an additional unit of A will compensate for the loss of 2 units of B.[10]

The line $0D$ joining the points at which isoquants become horizontal is called a *ridge line*. Consider point G on isoquant x_6. Since the slope of the isoquant, or $MRTS_{ab}$, is zero, it is apparent that MPP_a is also zero at this point. For a movement to the right from point G along line b_1J, the total product of A will decline, that is, MPP_a is negative for such a movement. This situation means that the firm is moving into Stage III for resource A. The same thing can be said for a movement to the right from every point along $0D$: any combination of A and B to the right of $0D$ is in a generalized Stage III for resource A. The upward slopes of those portions of the isoquants lying to the right of $0D$ reflect the negative MPP_a in Stage III for A.

Line $0C$ joining the points at which isoquants become vertical is also a ridge line. At point H, an increase in resource B along line a_4H as extended will decrease the total product of B, that is, MPP_b is negative for the increase. The same thing can be said for any increase in B from a point on $0C$. Consequently any combination of A and B that lies above $0C$ is in Stage III for resource B.

The combinations comprising this area between ridge lines $0D$ and $0C$ thus constitute a generalized Stage II for both resources. These are the combinations that are relevant for the production decisions of the firm. We need not restrict our thinking to a linearly homogeneous production function or to a production function in which one resource is fixed in quantity. A change in the quantity of either resource from a combination such as R in the generalized Stage II area will show diminishing returns for that resource.

---

[10]The marginal rate of technical substitution of A for B on any given isoquant is found by differentiating the isoquant equation as follows: $x_0 = f(a, b)$, and $dx_0 = f_a da + f_b db = 0$. Therefore,

$$-\frac{db}{da} = \frac{f_a}{f_b} = MRTS_{ab}.$$

The partial derivatives f_a and f_b are, respectively, MPP_a and MPP_b. If an isoquant is to be convex to the origin, then

$$\frac{d^2b}{da^2} > 0; \text{ that is,}$$

$$-\frac{d^2b}{da^2} = \frac{d}{da}\left(\frac{f_a}{f_b}\right) = \frac{d}{da}(MRTS_{ab}) < 0, \text{ or, the } MRTS_{ab} \text{ is diminishing.}$$

The Least-Cost Resource Combination

least-cost resource combination
A combination of resources for a firm at which the marginal rate of technical substitution between the resources is equal to the ratio of their prices or, what amounts to the same thing, the marginal physical product per dollar's worth of one resource is equal to the marginal physical product per dollar's worth of every other.

isocost curve
A curve showing all combinations of two resources that a firm can purchase for a given cost outlay, given the prices of the resources.

Which of the Stage II combinations should a firm use in turning out its product? We assume that the firm's objective is to use the **least-cost resource combination** in order to minimize the cost of producing any given output level—that is, the resource combination should be the one that keeps its cost outlay for that output as low as possible. Another way of stating that objective is to say that whatever cost outlay the firm makes, it should use the resource combination that will produce the greatest amount of product for that outlay.

The problem facing the firm is essentially the same as that facing a consumer. Isoquants show the outputs that the firm gets from "consuming" various combinations of resources. These are analogous to indifference curves, which show the "outputs" of satisfaction a consumer gets from consuming various combinations of goods and services. To complete the analogy, we need the firm's counterpart of the consumer's budget line.

This counterpart is called an **isocost curve**, or "equal cost" curve. In Figure 9.6, let the firm's total cost outlay on resources A and B be T_1 dollars and the resource prices be p_a and p_b, respectively. The amount of B that the firm can get if it buys no A is T_1/p_b; the amount of A that the firm can get if it buys no B is T_1/p_a. A line joining these two points shows all combinations of the two

**Figure 9.6
Cost Minimization, Output Maximization, and the Expansion Path**

For a given cost outlay T_1 the firm maximizes output with the resource combination F at which $MPP_a/MPP_b = p_a/p_b$, or at which the isocost curve for that cost outlay is tangent to the highest possible isoquant, x_3 in this case. Given p_a and p_b, changes in the cost outlay shift the isocost curve parallel to itself, generating the expansion path GH.

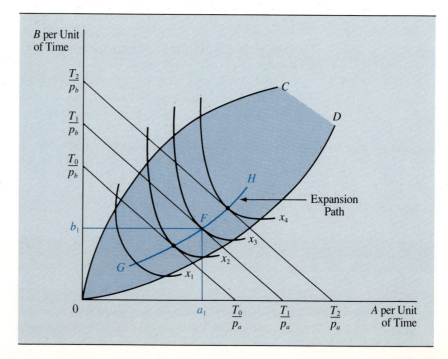

that cost outlay T_1 will purchase. This line is the isocost curve.[11] Its slope will have an absolute value of

(9.3)
$$\frac{T_1/p_b}{T_1/p_a} = \frac{T_1}{p_b} \times \frac{p_a}{T_1} = \frac{p_a}{p_b}.$$

The maximum output obtainable with a given cost outlay is that of the highest isoquant touched by the isocost curve. In Figure 9.6, given the firm's production function, resource prices of p_a and p_b, and a cost outlay of T_1, the maximum amount of X that can be obtained is x_3. This is produced at point F, with a_1 of A and b_1 of B. Any other combination that will produce x_3 lies above the isocost curve generated by cost outlay T_1; and as long as p_a and p_b remain constant, other combinations can be obtained only by increasing the cost outlay.

Changes in the firm's cost outlay, given the prices of resources A and B, will shift the isocost curve parallel to itself. If the cost outlay were a smaller amount, say, T_0, the isocost curve would shift to the left; thus T_0 would be the least possible cost of producing output x_2. If the cost outlay were a greater amount, say, T_2, the isocost curve would shift to the right, and T_2 would be the least possible cost of producing output x_4. The line GH joining all points of equilibrium (least-cost resource combinations) for each possible cost outlay is called the **expansion path** of the firm.

expansion path
A curve showing the firm's least-cost (maximum output) resource combinations for all possible output levels (cost outlay levels).

For a firm to minimize the costs of producing a given output level, the marginal rate of technical substitution between any two resources must be equal to the ratio of the prices of those resources. In Figure 9.6, cost outlay T_1 is the minimum cost of producing output level x_3. However, resource combination F, containing a_1 of A and b_1 of B, is the only resource combination that will achieve this result.

What are the conditions that prevail at F? The slope of the isocost curve for outlay T_1 is p_a/p_b throughout its entire length. The slope of isoquant x_3 at point F is measured by MPP_a/MPP_b. Thus at point F:

(9.4)
$$\frac{p_a}{p_b} = \frac{MPP_a}{MPP_b} = MRTS_{ab},$$

which can be rewritten as

$$\frac{MPP_a}{p_a} = \frac{MPP_b}{p_b}.$$

---

[11]An isocost curve for a firm using two resources, A and B, can be represented by the equation $p_a a + p_b b = T_0$, or $p_b b = T_0 - p_a a$. Dividing through by p_b we obtain

$$b = \frac{T_0}{p_b} - \frac{p_a}{p_b}a,$$

in which T_0/p_b is the intercept on the B axis and p_a/p_b is the slope of the curve.

Treating T as a parameter and assigning different values to it generates a family of parallel isocost curves.

To secure a given output at the least possible cost, the marginal physical product of a dollar's worth of one resource must be equal to the marginal physical product of a dollar's worth of every other resource used.[12]

PRODUCTION POSSIBILITIES FOR THE ECONOMY

Once we have determined the production functions of individual firms or producing units, we can easily expand the analysis to show what constitutes efficient allocations of resources among producing units. We shall look first at the conditions leading to Pareto optimality in the allocation of resources among alternative uses. Then we shall consider the whole range of combinations of goods that an economy may produce efficiently. We shall limit ourselves to a simple economy that produces two goods, X and Y, using two resources, A and B.

Resource Allocation among Products

efficient distribution of resources
A distribution of resources among products or uses such that the marginal rate of technical substitution between any two resources is the same for each product or use.

When two resources, A and B, are used to produce two commodities, X and Y, some distributions of the resources between the two uses will be more efficient than others. An **efficient distribution of resources** is a Pareto optimal distribution—one from which an increase in the output of one good can take place only if the output of the other is decreased. In the discussion that follows, it makes no difference whether the products are produced by the same or by

---

[12]To minimize costs,

(1) $$T = p_a a + p_b b$$

for a given level of output, or

(2) $$x_1 = f(a, b),$$

differentiate (2), obtaining

(3) $$-\frac{db}{da} = \frac{f_a}{f_b}.$$

Then take the first partial derivative of T with respect to a, obtaining

(4) $$\frac{\partial T}{\partial a} = p_a + p_b \frac{db}{da}.$$

Substituting (3) in (4) and setting the derivative equal to zero, we have

(5) $$\frac{\partial T}{\partial a} = p_a - p_b \frac{f_a}{f_b} = 0,$$

and the first-order minimum cost condition becomes

(6) $$\frac{p_a}{p_b} = \frac{f_a}{f_b};$$

that is,

$$MRTS_{ab} = \frac{p_a}{p_b}, \text{ or } \frac{MPP_a}{p_a} = \frac{MPP_b}{p_b}.$$

The second-order condition for minimum cost is that at the point of tangency of the isoquant curve and the isocost line the isoquant curve be convex to the origin, or

(7) $$\frac{d^2 b}{da^2} > 0.$$

different firms. The isoquant map for product X shows the composite production function for all firms making X; similarly, the isoquant map for product Y shows the composite production function for that product. We assume that the supplies of resources A and B are fixed amounts per unit of time, that is, the resource supply curves are perfectly inelastic.

The Edgeworth box in Figure 9.7 provides a convenient method of determining which distributions are most efficient. Let the quantity of resource A be $0_x a_5$ or $0_y a_5'$ and the quantity of resource B be $0_x b_5$ or $0_y b_5'$. Isoquants showing production levels of X are convex to the 0_x origin, and those showing production levels of Y are convex to the 0_y origin. Suppose the initial distribution of the two resources is shown at F, with $0_x a_1$ of A and $0_x b_1$ of B used in the production of X and with $a_1 a_5$ of A and $b_1 b_5$ of B used in the production of Y.

Are these the most efficient combinations of available resources for the production of X and Y? The output levels are 100 units of each. The slope of the $x = 100$ isoquant at point F, or MPP_a/MPP_b, in the production of X is greater than the slope of the $y = 100$ isoquant, or MPP_a/MPP_b, in the production of Y. This information means that if a unit of A is transferred from the production of Y to the production of X, with the output of X held constant at 100 units, the quantity of B released from the production of X is more than enough to compensate in the production of Y for the release of the unit of A. Suppose, for example, that ED in Figure 9.7 represents the unit of A transferred from the production of Y to the production of X. If the production of X is held at the 100-unit level, EF units of B are released from the production of X. But to hold the output of Y constant at the 100-unit level, only CF units of B are needed to compensate for the unit of A transferred out. Thus we have a surplus of EC units of B if production of X and Y is held at the original levels.

Figure 9.7
Efficient Resource
Distributions

Distribution F of resources A and B between a producer of X and a producer of Y is not efficient. The producer of X could give up units of B to the producer of Y for units of A in such amounts that the producer of X could gain or the producer of Y could gain with the other losing nothing, or such that both could gain. This is the case at any point to the left of the contract curve GH. To the right, exchanges in the other direction can result in output gains with no losses. Any distribution on the contract curve, where $MRTS_{ab}^x = MRTS_{ab}^y$, is Pareto optimal.

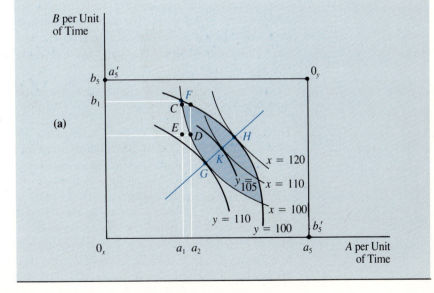

The released units of B can be used to increase one or both of the product outputs. If the output of X is held at 100 units and the surplus B is turned to the production of Y, this usage constitutes a movement downward to the right around isoquant $x = 100$ and to a Y isoquant above the 100-unit level. Transfers of A from the production of Y to the production of X and of B from the production of X to the production of Y, carried from point F to point G, increase the output of Y to 110 units *without* decreasing the amount of X produced. If the released units of B were used to increase the output of X, holding Y constant at 100 units, a movement from F to H could take place, increasing the production of X to 120 units. The released B could be used to increase the production of both X and Y, moving from point F to some point, K, between G and H, where an X isoquant is tangent to a Y isoquant. As we have located it, point K represents output levels of 110 units of X and 105 units of Y. Clearly, in all of these cases the efficiency with which resources are used is enhanced.

Any one of the points—G, H, or K—is Pareto optimal. Resource redistributions from F to any one of these points increase the output of at least one of the products without decreasing the output of the other. Once the resource distribution becomes G, H, or K, however, no further transfer of *any* kind can be made without reducing the output of at least one of the goods. A Pareto optimal distribution of resources is said to be an *efficient* distribution.

The condition that must be met for an efficient resource distribution is that $MPP_{ax}/MPP_{bx} = MPP_{ay}/MPP_{by}$—that is, the point locating the efficient distribution in the Edgeworth box must be a point of tangency between an isoquant of one product and an isoquant of the other. In Figure 9.7, the contract curve GKH extended is the locus of all such points. Any point on it, once reached, is Pareto optimal.

The analysis tells us nothing about how much X and how much Y the society wants produced. More information is needed to handle this problem. All we have learned is that any distribution of resources, like F, that is not on the contract curve is inefficient. The output of one or both products can be increased by a redistribution of the resources between the two uses to a distribution that lies on a segment of the contract curve like GH—within the arcs of the isoquants that pass through F.

Transformation Curves

transformation curve
A curve showing the maximum production possibilities for two products given the resources available to produce them.

The information provided by the contract curve of Figure 9.7 is commonly displayed in the form of a **transformation curve** for the two products, showing the combinations of them that can be produced efficiently given the resource supplies and the state of technology available for producing them. In Figure 9.7, if all the resources available in the economy are used to produce Y, the total output of the product is shown by the Y isoquant that passes through 0_x. If this amount of Y is y_5, we can plot the combination as point M in Figure 9.8. Product X can be produced only if some of product Y is given up with resources being transferred from the production of Y to the production of X. In Figure 9.7 the process of giving up successively more Y to produce successively more X

**Figure 9.8
Transformation
Curve for Two
Products**

Transformation curve *MN* shows all combinations of *X* and *Y* that can be produced efficiently with given quantities of resources *A* and *B* and a given state of technology. The quantities of *X* and *Y* plotted are obtained from the isoquants of an Edgeworth box along the contract curve. $\Delta y/\Delta x$ measures the marginal rate of transformation, MRT_{xy}.

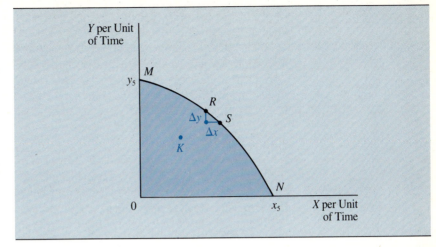

marginal rate of transformation
The quantity of one product that must be given up in order to produce an additional unit of another; measured by the slope of the transformation curve for any given combination of products on it.

is represented by a movement along the contract curve from 0_x toward 0_y. Each pair of tangent isoquants provides the *X* and *Y* output combinations that are plotted as the transformation curve in Figure 9.8. The larger the output of *X*, the smaller the amount of *Y* that can be produced; thus the transformation curve must slope downward to the right. If all of the available resources are used to produce *X*, the total output is x_5 units per unit of time, as is shown by point *N* in Figure 9.8.

The average slope, $\Delta y/\Delta x$, of the transformation curve between two points close together, such as *R* and *S*, measures the **marginal rate of transformation** of *X* for *Y*, or MRT_{xy}.[13] This is defined as the amount of *Y* that must be given up to produce an additional unit of *X*. The MRT_{xy} is shown as increasing in Figure 9.8, meaning that the less *Y* and the more *X* the economy chooses to produce, the more *Y* it must give up to produce an additional unit of *X*. The primary explanation of this relationship is that some of the economy's resources tend to be more specialized to the production of *X* while others are much more useful in producing *Y*. When all of the economy's resources are used in producing *Y* not much *Y* need be sacrificed to produce a unit of *X*, since those resources more specialized to the production of *X* are the ones that are transferred. However, the larger the output of *X* and the smaller the output of *Y* become, the more necessary it is to transfer those resources more specialized to the production of *Y* to production of the additional *X*. Consequently, larger and larger amounts of *Y* must be given up for one-unit increases in the output of *X*.

The transformation model of Figure 9.8 provides an excellent summary of the production choices available to a society. If some of its resources are unemployed, the combination of goods will be one, such as *K*, lying below the

---

[13]In terms of calculus, MRT_{xy} at any given point on the transformation curve is the slope of the curve at that point, that is, dy/dx.

transformation curve. The output of one or both products can be increased without decreasing the output of any other good. An inefficient distribution of resources brings about the same result. The combinations on the curve show the production possibilities or alternatives when resources are fully employed and distributed or allocated efficiently. These are Pareto optimal production possibilities. We will return to this model in the welfare analysis of Chapter 18.

SUMMARY

The principles of production lay the foundation for the analyses of costs, supplies, resource pricing and employment, resource allocation, and product distribution. These topics will be considered in later chapters.

The term *production function* is applied to the physical relationship between the resource inputs and product output of a firm. Product output is determined partly by the quantities of resource inputs and partly by the technology used by the firm. The production function can be summed up graphically as a production surface and displayed in two dimensions as an isoquant map.

Holding the quantities of all other resources constant, the quantity of any one resource can be varied, and the effects on product output can be observed. As the quantity of the variable resource is increased the law of diminishing returns will become effective. We distinguished among total product, marginal physical product, and average product of the variable resource. The product schedules or product curves of the variable resource were divided into three stages. Stage I is characterized by increasing average product. In Stage II, average and marginal physical products of the variable resource are decreasing, but its marginal physical product is still positive. In Stage III, the marginal physical product of the variable resource is negative. We deduced that only those ratios of the variable resource to other resources lying within Stage II may be economically efficient for the firm to use.

The precise combination of variable resources that the firm should use depends on the marginal rate of technical substitution among those resources and on their respective prices. To maximize product with a given cost outlay, or to minimize cost for a given amount of product, resources should be combined in ratios such that the $MRTS_{ab} = p_a/p_b$—that is, such that the marginal physical product per dollar's worth of one equals the marginal physical product per dollar's worth of every other resource used.

An Edgeworth box is useful in showing the distributions of resources among products that are efficient in a Pareto optimal sense. The resulting contract curve provides the necessary information for establishing a transformation curve, which shows the optimal production possibilities for the economy.

APPLICATIONS

Each of the following applications illustrates important properties of isoquant maps, isocost curves, and expansion paths by using recent events with which many students will be familiar.

TECHNOLOGICAL CHANGE AT COCA-COLA

America still has a sweet tooth, although the 80 pounds of beet and cane sugar eaten for every man, woman, and child in 1981 was down from the 102 pounds of a decade earlier. Ten percent of this sugar binge was consumed in soft drinks. Part of the cut in sugar use was due to a desire to cut calories and the consequent rising popularity of diet drinks despite the health concerns over saccharin that we noted in Chapter 5. In 1985, the average American consumed 460 twelve-ounce soft drinks, 110 of which were sugar-free.[14]

The soft drink producers were among the last to adjust to the soaring sugar prices in the 1970s that led makers of ice creams and baked goods to substitute cheaper corn sweeteners such as dextrose, glucose, and fructose. Soft drink producers advertised competitively on the basis of taste differences and feared that even the slightest change in their beverages would cause consumers to react adversely. Some substitution of fructose for sugar occurred in Coca-Cola's *diet* soft drinks, but no major change occurred in Coke until 1980—and then the change was gradual, as described in the accompanying article.

Apparently corn sweeteners initially altered the traditional taste of Coke, owing to the chemical composition of Coke syrup, which Coca-Cola makes and sells to independently owned bottling firms throughout the world. This formula is one of the most famous secrets in the history of American entrepreneurship and is known to only a few top people in the cloisters of Coca-Cola's headquarters in Atlanta. Substantial laboratory testing was required to make sure that fructose would not change Coke's taste. It is also possible that subtle adjustments were made in the syrup formula to compensate for using fructose. In 1980 Coca-Cola started using 50 percent fructose in its syrup formulas both for soda fountains and for bottles and cans. In 1983 it adjusted the formula for fountain syrup to 75 percent fructose.[15] PepsiCo soon followed suit.[16] By mid-1984, Coca-Cola increased the fructose content of its bottled and canned drinks to 75 percent and of its fountain syrup to 100 percent. By late 1984, the nondiet drinks of

---

[14]Gene Bylinsky, ''The Battle for America's Sweet Tooth,'' *Fortune,* July 26, 1982, 28; Nancy Yoshihara, ''NutraSweet: A Big Taste of Success,'' *Los Angeles Times,* April 12, 1985.

[15]L. Erik Calonius, ''Coca-Cola Allows More Corn Sweetener to Replace Sugar in Coke Fountain Syrup,'' *The Wall Street Journal,* March 2, 1983.

[16]Janet Guyon, ''PepsiCo to Permit Use of Corn Sweetener in Two Brands, Raising Funds to Fight Coke,'' *The Wall Street Journal,* May 22, 1983.

both producers were made from 100 percent fructose, a move that was expected to save Coca-Cola $28 million and PepsiCo $60 million per year.[17]

The isoquant analysis in the four panels of Figure 9.9 shows the gradual before-and-after adjustment process for fountain syrup. In each panel, fructose per unit of time is plotted along the horizontal axis and sugar per unit of time along the vertical axis. Technological progress in the use of fructose is shown by the changing shapes of the isoquant curves as we move from panel (a) to panel (b).

In panel (a) Coke isoquants are horizontal before any technological change is accomplished, indicating that fructose cannot be substituted for sugar without altering Coke's original taste. The marginal physical product of fructose is zero. The initial cost outlay on sweeteners is T_1, and the prices of sugar and fructose are p_{s1} and p_{f1}, respectively. The rise in the price of sugar to p_{s2} simply lowers the Coke syrup output obtainable with that cost outlay from x_5 to x_1.

Panel (b) shows Coke's isoquants after technological adjustments and testing permit the substitution of fructose for sugar. The marginal physical product of fructose in Coke syrup production is now positive, so the isoquants have the usual convex-to-the-origin shape. Using fructose in syrup lowers production costs and means that a higher output, x_3, can now be produced with cost outlay T_1, whereas only x_1 was possible before. Apparently the isoquant map and p_{f1}/p_{s2} were such that the company settled initially on a 50-50 mix. The short-run expansion path is UV.

Over the longer run, fructose producers increased output. By mid-1984, each pound of fructose was about 25 percent cheaper than sugar. We show this in panel (c) by decreasing the price of fructose to p_{f2}. The expansion path now is WN with about a three-to-one mix of fructose to sugar. By late 1984, the two inputs were close substitutes, and the price of fructose was p_{f3}, about one-third cheaper than sugar. We show this in panel (d), with isoquants that are almost flat and isocost lines that are flatter than in panel (c). Syrup is made entirely of fructose, so the long-run expansion path becomes YZ along the X axis. The cost outlay T_1 yields as much output as before sugar prices rose.

Coca-Cola again acted gradually in replacing saccharin with aspartame in Diet Coke. Aspartame, a new chemical, is about 200 times sweeter than sugar, lacks saccharin's metallic aftertaste, and does not require a label warning. Initially, most producers retained some saccharin because aspartame's price was 20 times greater. Eventually, most switched totally to aspartame when its price declined by about half and they were sure that consumers preferred it to sac-

[17]From *The Wall Street Journal:* Sonia L. Nazario, ''Coke Raises Level of Corn Sweetener Allowed in Product,'' February 9, 1984; Wendy L. Wall and Scott Kilman, ''Coca-Cola Increases Corn-Syrup Content to 100% at Fountains; Millers Helped,'' May 9, 1984; Thomas E. Ricks and Delia Flores, ''Pepsi, Coke Raise to 100% the Corn Syrup Bottlers Can Use to Sweeten Cold Drinks,'' November 7, 1984.

Figure 9.9 Technological Change in the Production of Coke Syrup

Panel (a) shows that fructose cannot be substituted for sugar and Coca-Cola uses all sugar in its syrup. In panel (b) technology allows substitution of fructose for sugar and the price of fructose relative to sugar is such that it is used 50-50 with sugar. In panel (c) the price of fructose has dropped enough to induce about a three-to-one use of fructose to sugar. Panel (d) shows that a further decrease in the relative price of fructose and improved substitution possibilities cause the company to use fructose only.

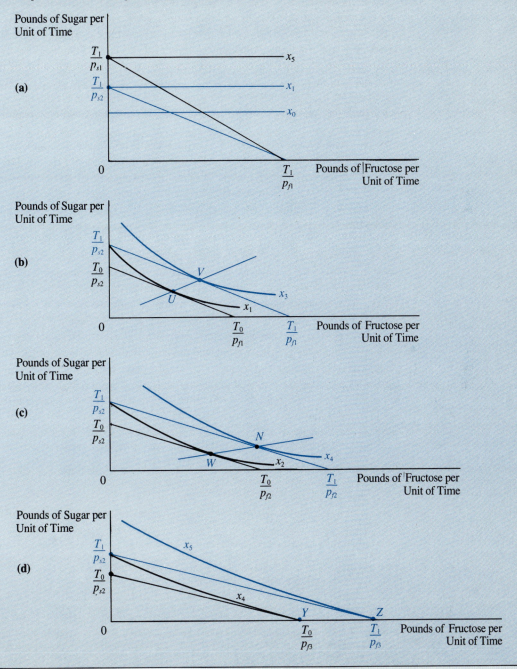

charin. But Coca-Cola still used both sweeteners to avoid a sudden change in the taste of its Diet Coke.[18]

In 1985, however, Coca-Cola abruptly and materially changed the flavor of Coke, one of the most successful products in history. Coke's formula had been altered slightly a few times during its 99-year reign, and it was losing market share to sugared rivals and diet drinks. After four and one-half years of elaborate planning, Coca-Cola decided Coke should have a sweeter, smoother, less-filling taste. In taste comparisons involving 190,000 persons, the new flavor was preferred to either the traditional Coke or its close rivals by a 55 percent to 45 percent margin. Ominously, some advertisers warned that fickle customers could defect if a "little bit of Americana" were lost. Even the New York Stock Exchange was worried, bidding Coca-Cola shares down a bit in anticipation of the change.

The bold move was announced with enough hoopla and flair to get the message across to two-thirds of the nation within 24 hours. Before long it became perhaps the largest public *faux pas* in the history of marketing. Sales declined 15 percent. Customers called on hot lines and signed petitions to bring back the old Coke. Some stockpiled what they could buy. PepsiCo, of course, gloated mercilessly. About two months after the change, a beleaguered Coca-Cola management decided to sell both flavors. Having misestimated their demand curve badly, Coca-Cola management nevertheless rallied quickly. In one week the price of a Coca-Cola share rose about 8 percent in active trading.

Coca-Cola's experience shows that brand loyalty, especially for consumer goods, is difficult to measure and risky to tinker with. As one advertising executive put it, "Can you imagine a new and improved Chanel No. 5?" The experience also demonstrated that consumer demand determines what entrepreneurs produce, not the other way around as some neophytes believe. Information about consumer demand is expensive to get, however. Entrepreneurs cannot dial up AT&T, Sprint, or MCI to determine quickly what consumers want. Instead, a series of trial-and-error steps is often required, and skill or luck separates the winners from the losers. In retrospect, a 55 percent to 45 percent vote was too little information on which to bet an entire company's future, particularly when only 53 percent of Coke's *regular* customers liked the new flavor.[19]

---

[18]From *The Wall Street Journal:* Carolyn Phillips, "Searle Fights to Keep Red-Hot Aspartame Hot for a Long Time," September 18, 1984; Trish Hall, "Pepsi to Use Only Aspartame to Sweeten Diet Soft Drinks in Effort to Improve Taste," November 2, 1984; "Seven-Up to Sweeten Its Diet Soft Drinks Only with Aspartame," November 14, 1984.

[19]"Coke Tampers with Success," *Newsweek,* May 6, 1985, 50; Anne B. Fisher, "Coke's Brand-Loyalty Lesson," *Fortune,* August 5, 1985, 44–46. From *The Wall Street Journal:* Scott Kilman and Thomas E. Ricks, "Coke Formula of Main Brand Is Seen Altered," April 22, 1985; Scott Kilman, "Coke Is Altering Its Sugar-Based Drink Formula," April 24, 1985; Scott Kilman, "Coca-Cola Co. to Bring Back Its Old Coke," July 11, 1985; John Koten and Scott Kilman, "Coca-Cola Faces Tough Marketing Task in Attempting to Sell Old and New Coke," July 12, 1985.

COCA-COLA DECIDES TO USE CORN SWEETENER IN COKE, SENDING SUGAR PRICES TUMBLING

by John Koten and Gay Sands Miller, *The Wall Street Journal*

Coca-Cola Co. decided to use high-fructose corn sweetener in Coke, a move likely to send significant ripples through the entire sweetener industry.

The move by the nation's largest sugar buyer sent sugar prices tumbling yesterday while stock prices of corn sweetener makers soared.

Coca-Cola has allowed bottlers to use a high level of high-fructose corn sweetener in its noncola products since June 1978, but the decision to use it in its best-known brand has been eagerly awaited by the fructose producers. Their product is normally at least 10% less expensive than the beet and cane sugars long used to sweeten Coke.

Supplies Are Limited   Coca-Cola said as much as 50% of the sweetener used in its Coke brand will contain fructose, though that level can't be reached immediately since supplies of the sweetener are limited. "For the time being, we'll take all we can get," a spokesman said.

Coca-Cola had resisted using the sweetener in its Coke drink because of taste problems. A few years ago, J. Paul Austin, the company's chairman and chief executive officer, was quoted as saying that when high-fructose sweeteners are mixed with the ingredients used to make Coke a chemical reaction is produced that throws off the taste.

Solved the Problem   But the company apparently has been able to solve that problem. Coca-Cola said lab tests and an 18-month consumer test market at a company-owned bottling plant showed there wasn't any difference in taste or quality between fructose-sweetened Coke and regular Coke.

Observers predicted the Coke move would soon spread to its arch-rival, Pepsi. "We're studying it carefully," said a Pepsi spokesman in Purchase, N.Y.

Corn sweetener makers were jubilant, and appeared likely to accelerate their expansion plans. A. E. Staley Manufacturing Co., for example, said it will expand capacity for the product Coca-Cola will use "well beyond" its previously proposed doubling of capacity to 1.2 billion pounds this year.

Allowed in Noncola Brands   High-fructose sweeteners are already used in Coca-Cola's other soft-drink brands—Mr. Pibb, Sprite and Fanta. A fructose product, containing 42% fructose and about 55% dextrose, was first allowed in the company's noncola brands in 1974, when sugar prices soared. Bottlers could use it for as much as 25% of total sweeteners.

Then, in mid-1978, Coke allowed a second fructose product, containing 55% fructose, to provide as much as 75% of the sweetener in noncola drinks. The latest move extends these sweeteners to the Coke brand.

Sugar has been so important to Coca-Cola that, by one calculation, a change of one cent a pound in sugar prices can cause a $20 million swing in the operating profits of the company and its bottling empire. Coca-Cola has been vital to the sugar industry, too, buying about a million tons a year, or 10% of the sugar sold in the U.S.

Sugar Prices Fell Sharply   Sugar prices, which have nearly tripled in the past year, fell sharply on the news. Speculators have treated sugar as an alternative to high-priced gold

and silver in hedging against political and economic worries. Yesterday, however, the price of raw sugar in the world market fell 1.6 cents a pound to 18.11 cents for March delivery on the New York Coffee, Sugar & Cocoa Exchange.

It's understood that the management of Coca-Cola U.S.A., the company's domestic soft-drink division, has been under considerable pressure from the parent company to improve sales and profitability of the Coke brand. Observers said the move to fructose could be a major step in that direction.

But it probably won't be possible immediately. Fructose-industry capacity for the so-called "second-generation" product to be used by Coca-Cola is about 1.8 billion pounds a year. Analysts said the company this year may only be able to secure 200 million to 300 million pounds of the estimated 1.2 billion pounds its decison could require.

Steven Vannelli, an analyst with Davis Skaggs & Co., San Francisco, said the Coca-Cola move could spark a fructose price boost of three cents to four cents a pound for the second-generation commercial product, which currently sells in the Midwest for 12⅔ cents a pound. This, he said, could boost annual per-share earnings $1 at Staley, 30 cents a share at Archer-Daniels-Midland Co. and about 22 cents a share at Standard Brands Inc.

Despite all the speculative interest in Coca-Cola's announcement, it could be three years before all the company's bottlers are using 50% corn sweetener, said Joseph Frazzano, an analyst with Oppenheimer & Co.

ROAD SALT USE IN MIDWESTERN CITIES

Relatively little salt is manufactured for table consumption. Most of it is sold to cities and counties to be spread on roads for the removal of winter ice, an activity that may strike Californians as odd but is well understood by most mid-westerners. A series of strikes and natural disasters during the summer of 1979 caused the manufacture of salt to decline by about 10 percent, as described in the accompanying article. This reduction in supply squeezed many midwestern cities, owing to the higher prices they had to pay for deicing salts for the coming winter. The isoquant/isocost analysis presented in this chapter helps us conceptualize the consequences that the higher salt prices had and sheds light on which of the cities mentioned—Chicago, Cincinnati, and McKeesport, Pa.—adjusted to the new constraint in the most economical manner.

Municipal governments are generally responsible for maintaining public roads and streets in safe driving conditions. In a sense, cities are in the "business" of "producing," among other things, safe travel for motorists and pedestrians alike. Safety—avoiding accidents with their costs in lost property and lives—is the "output" and such "inputs" as labor, machines, bulldozers, ambulances, and road salts are used in its production. This process is conceptualized in Figure 9.10 for a single city, let us say, Cincinnati. The two substitute inputs are road salts, measured along the X axis, versus sand (or other resources), measured along the Y axis. The isocost curves show alternative road maintenance budgets that may be spent entirely on salt, entirely on sand, or on some combination of the two inputs. The different levels of road maintenance budgets are indicated by T_0, T_1, and T_2. The initial price of salt is p_{s1}, and the price of sand is p_0. The different levels of road safety that can be achieved with different combinations of salt and sand are indicated by such isoquants as x_1^{Ci} and x_2^{Ci}. The tangencies between isoquants and total outlay lines show the least-cost combinations for obtaining given levels of safety, or the maximum amounts of road safety that can be obtained for given levels of outlay. If the price of salt before the price increase was p_{s1}, and the price of sand p_0, the relevant expansion path for Cincinnati was GH. If T_1 was the original budget level, the city's optimum combination was H, achieving safety level x_2^{Ci}.

When the price of salt rose from p_{s1} to p_{s2}, the total outlay line shifted from AB to AC. For the same T_1 budget, Cincinnati's optimum combination of salt and sand was S, which contained less salt; road safety declined to x_1^{Ci}. By increasing its budget from T_1 to T_2, the city could remain on isoquant level x_2^{Ci} with combination J, buying less salt than it was originally. Judging from the article, this appears to be what the city officials decided to do. They bought less salt at the higher price and decided to stretch it by using more sand than previously. They also increased the budget. But they kept road safety at approximately its previous level.

A somewhat different adjustment seems to have occurred in Chicago. The Chicago officials appeared determined to purchase the same quantity of salt after the price increase as they did before, and their solution to the higher salt price

ROAD DEPARTMENTS FIND PRICE FOR SALT
HAS AS MUCH AS DOUBLED FROM LAST YEAR
by Thomas Petzinger, Jr., *The Wall Street Journal*

To hundreds of highway purchasing agents in the Midwest, lowly salt has suddenly become white gold.

In recent weeks, state and municipal road departments have discovered they'll be paying as much as double last year's prices for de-icing salt, or be forced to go without it altogether. While salt producers say they're sympathetic to the problem, one acknowledges that "as a company, we're delighted with the effect this situation is having on prices."

The situation is this: In 1977, the Department of Energy took over a huge rock-salt mine in Louisiana from Morton-Norwich Products Inc.'s Morton Salt Co. for use as a "strategic" crude-oil storage facility. Then, last June, there was an explosion that halted production at another Louisiana mine owned by Cargill Inc. As a result of the explosion, in which five persons were killed, mining regulations were tightened at other Louisiana salt-mining operations, thus reducing their productivity.

Also this summer, workers at Akzona Inc.'s International Salt Co. operation in Cleveland began a three-month strike. And earlier this month, Hurricane David wiped out a huge crop of salt being extracted from seawater at a solar-salt farm in the Bahamas owned by Diamond Crystal Salt Co.

Thus, the highway salt market will be 10% short on supplies this winter, the Salt Institute, a trade group, estimates.

Road Maintenance   Wintertime road maintenance is by far the nation's biggest salt market, accounting for about 11 million tons, or roughly 44% of the industry's annual output of 25 million tons. Table salt and food processing account for less than one million tons a year, and water conditioning and agriculture just two million tons each, so the current shortage isn't expected to have any serious effect on those markets.

The chemical industry consumes about four million tons a year in chlorine and soda ash production and in some quarters is experiencing a supply problem. Pennwalt Corp., for example, was "cut off" by Cargill after the mine explosion and hasn't yet arranged an alternative supply, according to a spokesman.

Among users of de-icing salt, the impact varies widely. The city of Chicago, for example, advertised for bids from salt producers early in the May-to-September bidding season and, as a result, arranged for delivery of the 202,000 tons it will require this winter. However, the city is paying Morton $15.96 a ton, up 27% from last year.

Things are far worse among government units that entered the bidding process later on. Cincinnati, for example, advertised for bids in August, two weeks earlier than in prior years but still late enough that the big suppliers were sold out. The city finally did arrange a winter supply—which it will have to stretch with

sand—but only by paying $30 a ton, or double last year's price. And when McKeesport, Pa., opened its bids last week, the low offer was $29.48 a ton, up from $22 a ton paid for each of last year's 1,800 tons.

Stay Out of McKeesport   "Council flatly rejected the bids" as out of line, says Patricia Monoyoudis, McKeesport's Finance Administrator. "We're just going to have to play it by ear day by day until the snow starts flying. My advice to you is: Stay out of McKeesport this winter," she says.

Part of the high cost of salt this year, according to the producers, is a heavy increase in shipping charges, which in many cases account for one-half of the total cost. Most Louisiana salt goes to the Midwest, via barges along the Mississippi and Ohio rivers and then by rail or truck. According to Diamond Crystal, barge rates between Louisiana and southern Ohio have jumped 65% in the last year, partly because of heavy demand by grain shippers.

Some big salt users have been forced to turn overseas for salt, which is high in price to begin with and also must be shipped at an added cost. The Ohio Department of Transportation, for example, recently had to arrange a supply from Chile and Mexico for 22 of the state's 88 counties. The average price was about $37 a ton, compared with an average of about $23 a ton for the domestic variety.

**Figure 9.10
Salt versus Other
Inputs in Cincinnati**

At prices p_{s1} and p_0,
respectively, for salt and
sand, the expansion path
is GH extended. With an
outlay of T_1 dollars, the
maximum level of safety
achieved is x_2^{Ci} with
combination H. An
increase in the price of
salt to p_{s2} results in
expansion path SJ
extended, and T_1 dollars
will buy safety level x_1^{Ci}
only. Combination S,
containing more sand and
less salt, is used. Outlay
T_2 is needed to achieve
the former safety level.

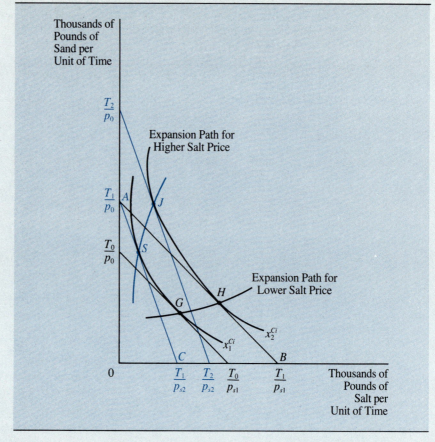

dilemma appears to be economically inefficient. Chicago went straight into the salt market and purchased its full "requirement" of road salts, presumably based on the amount it had needed the previous year, and paid a stiff price for that requirement. Figure 9.11 shows, however, that it would be inefficient for Chicago to use the same quantity of salt after the price increase as it did before *unless* it simultaneously wanted to increase the level of road safety that it produced. Before the price of salt went up from p_{s1} to p_{s2}, Chicago spent T_1 dollars and achieved the x_2^{Ch} level of road safety with combination J of salt and sand. To buy the same amount of salt and sand after the price of salt rises, it must increase its budget to T_3, and the total outlay line GH would pass through J. Since GH has the same slope as AC, Chicago could have achieved the higher level of road safety x_3^{Ch} with an outlay of T_3 and combination M of salt and sand. By using combination J after the price increase in salt, it wasted resources. It would have done better with combination L, using less salt and more sand to produce safety level x_2^{Ch}.

Figure 9.11   Salt versus Other Inputs in Chicago

With expenditure T_1 and prices p_{s1} and p_0 for salt and sand, respectively, Chicago purchases combination J. Purchasing the same combination after a rise in the price of salt to p_{s2} requires an outlay of T_3. Efficiently spent, T_3 will buy combination M and provide a higher safety level x_3^{Ch} than would the continued purchase of combination J after the price rise.

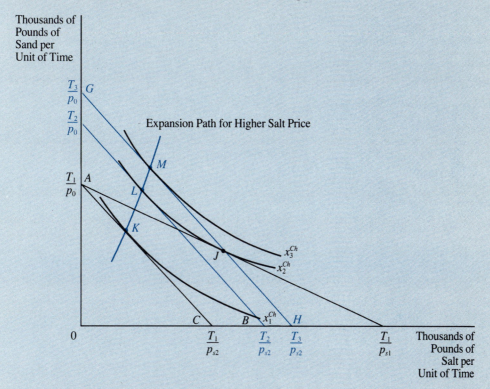

The city of McKeesport, Pa., entered the road salt market very late in the year, well after Chicago and Cincinnati and after salt prices had climbed substantially. The city found the price to be so high that it decided not to buy road salts at all but simply "tough it out" and hope for a mild winter. As Figure 9.12 demonstrates, the city necessarily accepted a lower level of road safety because of this decision.

Prior to the increase in the price of salt, McKeesport would have used combination U of salt and sand, achieving a safety level of x_2^M. If the council correctly understood the city's production function for road safety, then its decision to buy no salt at all after the price increase indicated at best a corner solution at W and a lower safety level x_1^M. The city's financial expert was wise in advising motorists to stay out of McKeesport that winter!

**Figure 9.12
Salt versus Other
Inputs in McKeesport**

With outlay T_1 and prices p_{s1} and p_0, respectively, for salt and sand, McKeesport would have bought combination U. The increase in the price of salt to p_{s2} induced the city to eliminate salt altogether, reducing its safety level to x_1^M.

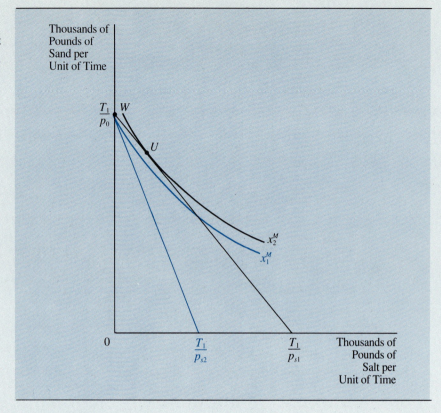

Suggested Readings

For more advanced treatments of production theory, see

Baumol, William J. *Economic Theory and Operations Analysis*. 4th ed., 267–289. Englewood Cliffs, N.J.: Prentice-Hall, 1977.

De Alessi, Louis. "The Short Run Revisited." *American Economic Review* 57 (June 1967): 450–461.

Friedman, Milton. *Price Theory*, Chaps. 6 and 9. Chicago: Aldine Publishing Co., 1976.

Problems and Questions for Discussion

1. The Acme Manufacturing Company has been engaged in the production of metal spools, all of a uniform type, for many years. Production schedules for labor and machinery are independent of each other and of other resources. On a monthly basis they are estimated as follows:

Labor Employed	Spools per Month	Machinery (physical units)	Spools per Month
1	200	1	300
2	370	2	430
3	500	3	500
4	600	4	545
5	675	5	570
6	740	6	586
7	800	7	600
8	855	8	612
9	900	9	622
10	940	10	630
11	970	11	635

The company is currently employing 7 workers and 7 units of machinery.

a. What is the average product of workers? Of machinery? Explain.

b. What is the marginal physical product of workers? Of machinery? Explain.

c. If one additional worker were to be employed, how many units of machinery could be given up without loss of production? Explain.

d. If a monthly cost outlay of $5,100 is to be made and the respective monthly prices of workers and units of machinery are $600 and $100, what combination of workers and machinery should be used?

2. During World War II, the United States built a number of airstrips on mainland China utilizing local labor. Both men and women sat around rock piles breaking up rock into gravel with hammers. Concrete was mixed by hand and was carried to the runway forms in baskets on the heads of long lines of workers. Would it have been more efficient to have brought in rock crushers and concrete mixers to do the job? Explain carefully.

3. Demonstrate with the aid of isoquants and isocost curves that the combination of inputs that maximizes output for a given cost to the firm is the

same combination that minimizes cost for that level of output. Explain the logic of this result.

4. College seniors can improve their job prospects after graduation either by raising their grades or by devoting time to interviews with several prospective employers (it is risky to interview with only one).
   a. Use the isoquant-isocost diagram to conceptualize this problem. What is plotted on each axis? How is output defined?
   b. What determines the isocost line's slope and position?
   c. Would you expect many seniors to adopt a ''corner solution,'' in which they spent all their time on either grades or interviewing but never a combination of the two? Explain.

5. Congress and the Reagan administration argued for several years over Urban Mobility Block Grants. Under this proposal, communities would get fewer federal transportation dollars, but with fewer ''strings'' attached. They would no longer have to spend some amount on highways and another amount on mass transit as individual federal grants required. (Rich Connell, ''Meet the Obstacle to L.A. Rail,'' *Los Angeles Times*, April 11, 1986.)
   a. Assume that highways and mass transit are competing inputs to ''transportation.'' Show how a community could be made better off with a block grant than with individual grants.
   b. Now show how another community could be made worse off with a block grant than with individual grants.
   c. The answers you gave in (a) and (b) indicate why the block grant proposal is controversial. Explain.

6. If a fixed amount of labor and a fixed amount of capital are available to produce tractors and airplanes, illustrate and explain
   a. The conditions for an efficient allocation of the resources between the two products.
   b. How a transformation curve for the two products is developed.
   c. The probable slope of the transformation curve.

7. In 1983, American Airlines and Pan American World Airways swapped equipment so that each had aircraft of only a single type, permitting economies on spare parts, training, maintenance, and scheduling. Both initially had 747s and DC-10s. The 747s were too large for many of American's domestic routes, but they were ideal for Pan Am's international flights. American gave up all eight of its 747s for all fifteen of Pan Am's DC-10s. (''American Air Agrees to Swap Eight 747s for 15 Pan Am DC-10s,'' *The Wall Street Journal,* November 7, 1984.)

   Use an Edgeworth box to analyze this trade. Substitute isorevenue curves for isoquants, with each isorevenue curve showing different combinations of 747 and DC-10 flight hours needed to yield a given level of revenue. Show and explain the pretrade situation and the incentives for trade. What must the isorevenue curves look like for each airline to wind up with only one kind of equipment after the trade?

*8. Draw the necessary diagrams to show the substitution of aspartame for saccharin in diet drinks for PepsiCo and for Coca-Cola according to the facts that are summarized on pages 254–256.

*9. Research is under way for new low-calorie chemicals sweeter than aspartame. A University of Illinois team sponsored by the National Institute of Dental Research isolated a chemical 1,000 times sweeter than sugar from a mint-like plant in Mexico. A pharmaceutical company derived a chemical 600 times sweeter than sugar from sugar itself. (From *The Wall Street Journal:* "A Mint from Mexico Is Sweeter than Sugar," January 18, 1985; "Johnson & Johnson Tests a New Sugar Substitute," February 8, 1985.)

  a. Searle, a major pharmaceutical firm, holds the patent on aspartame. What policy of Searle's is probably stimulating the search for new sweeteners?

  b. Searle's patent on aspartame expires in 1992. It was estimated in 1985 that commercial development of new sweeteners would require five to ten years. In the meantime, aspartame accounted for about half of Searle's annual profits. Does the Searle policy analyzed in part (a) seem sensible now?

  c. Assume rival sweeteners eventually become commercial and are as effective as aspartame in soft drinks. Use diagrams like Figure 9.9 to show the potential substitutions away from aspartame. Upon what will the degree of substitution depend?

*10. When gasoline prices were rising, Detroit planned to make lighter cars by substituting more aluminum for steel. As the price of aluminum rose relative to steel, however, Chrysler switched back to steel for some parts in its cars. (Amal Nag, "Detroit's Switch to Small-Car Production Dashes Expectations of Aluminum Makers," *The Wall Street Journal,* November 18, 1980.) Draw a before-and-after isoquant-isocost diagram to show this result.

*11. In 1980, the U.S. Environmental Protection Agency (EPA) imposed extra fines on companies that violated the pollution standards of the federal Clean Air Act (mainly steel producers and electric utilities). A violator had to estimate for the EPA how much it saved by not installing pollution-control equipment. A company that did not submit an estimate, or submitted an estimate that the EPA rejected, would be fined whatever the EPA determined until the violation ceased. ("Air Polluters to Be Fined Additionally to Offset Any Savings by Noncompliance," *The Wall Street Journal,* July 17, 1980.)

  a. Assume that a typical steel producer can choose between inputs that pollute and those that do not. Show how the EPA's lump-sum fine alters the cost-minimizing input combination.

  b. Assume that the EPA prohibited industrial processes that polluted instead of taxing them. How would this change your answer to (a)?

---

*Denotes an application-oriented problem.

Chapter 10 _____

COSTS OF PRODUCTION _____

Chapter Outline _____

Basic Cost Concepts
    The Alternative Cost (*Opportunity Cost*) Principle
    Explicit and Implicit Costs
    Cost, Resource Prices, and Efficiency
The Short-Run and Long-Run Viewpoints
    The Short Run
    The Long Run
Short-Run Cost Curves
    Total Cost Curves
    Per Unit Cost Curves
    Relationship of *MC* to *AC* and to *AVC*
    Most Efficient Rate of Output
Long-Run Cost Curves
    Long-Run Total Costs
    Long-Run Average Costs
    Economies of Size
    Diseconomies of Size
    Most Efficient Size of Plant
    Long-Run Marginal Cost
    Relationships between *LMC* and *SMC*

Applications _____

Costs of Obtaining a Higher Education
Cost Minimization by a Multiple-Unit Firm
Economies of Size in the Beer Industry

Chapter 10 Appendix _____

The Geometry of Short-Run Per Unit Cost Curves

Costs of production constitute a major determinant of the quantities of a good or service that will be placed on the market. To understand supply and quantities supplied, we must understand costs, which in turn are rooted in the principles of production. We consider first the meaning of costs and, second, the short-run and long-run cost curves of the individual firm or production unit.

BASIC COST CONCEPTS

The concept of costs of production as used in economic analysis differs somewhat from common usage of the term. Common usage conveys some idea of the *expenditures* of a firm necessary in turning out a product but it is not always clear which categories of expenditure are included and which are not. The economic concept is more precise and consistent. To build up the concept as it is used in economics, we discuss first the alternative cost principle and then the implicit and explicit aspects of costs.

The Alternative Cost (Opportunity Cost) Principle

The basic idea of the alternative cost principle is contained in the transformation curve of Chapter 9. Under conditions of full employment and an efficient allocation of resources among goods and services, an increase in the output of any one product requires the sacrifice of some amounts of alternative products. If a certain kind of labor is used in making both washing machines and refrigerators, an increase in the output of refrigerators entails a reduction in the quantity of washing machines available, since labor must be withdrawn from the latter use. If steel is used in making automobiles and football stadiums, an increase in football stadiums leaves less steel available for making automobiles, reducing the number of cars that can be manufactured. Thus, an increase in the production of any commodity requires the sacrifice of some value of alternative products.

Economists define the costs of production of a particular good as the value of the forgone alternative items that resources used in its production could have turned out. This principle is called the **alternative cost principle,** or the **opportunity cost principle.** The costs of resources to a firm are their values in their best alternative uses. To secure the services of resources, the firm usually must pay for them amounts equal to what they can earn in those alternative uses. In the earlier example, the cost of the labor in the manufacture of washing machines is the value of refrigerators that the labor could have produced. Unless the manufacturer of washing machines pays approximately that amount for the labor, it will go into or remain in refrigerator production. The steel example is similar. Automobile manufacturers must pay enough for steel to attract or hold the desired amounts away from alternative employments of steel—and its value in the alternative employments is its cost in automobile manufacturing from the economist's point of view.

alternative cost principle (opportunity cost principle) The principle stating that the underlying basis of cost—the cost of producing a unit of any good or service—is the value of the resources needed to produce that item in their best alternative use.

Explicit and Implicit Costs

explicit costs of production
The costs of resources hired or purchased by a firm to use in its production process.

The outlays made by a firm (which we usually think of as its expenses) are the **explicit costs of production.** They consist of explicit payments for resources bought outright or hired by the firm. The firm's payroll, payments for raw and semifinished materials, payments of overhead costs of various kinds, and costs charged against sinking funds and depreciation reserves are examples of explicit costs. They are the costs that accountants list as the firm's expenses, and they tend to be determined by the alternative cost principle.

implicit costs of production
The costs of self-owned, self-employed resources used by a firm in its production process.

Implicit costs of production are the costs of self-owned, self-employed resources frequently overlooked in computing the expenses of the firm. The costs of a single proprietor who sets aside no salary for himself or herself but who takes the firm's ''profits'' as payment for services rendered is an excellent example. A still more common implicit cost is the return to the owners of a firm on their investment in plant, equipment, and inventories.

The consideration of the firm owner's salary as a cost can be easily explained. In accordance with the alternative cost principle, the cost of the single proprietor's services in producing the firm's product is the value of the forgone alternative product that would have resulted had the owner worked for someone else in a similar capacity. We consider as a part of the firm's costs, then, a salary for the proprietor equal to the value of the owner's services in his or her best alternative employment. This cost is an implicit cost, which does not take the form of an ''expense'' outlay.

The consideration of a return on investment as a cost of production is more tricky. Return on investment usually is thought of as coming from the firm's profits rather than as being a cost of production. A simple case is that of a single proprietor who has invested in (purchased) the land, building, and equipment for the business establishment. A return on the investment equal to what the proprietor could have earned had the same amount been invested elsewhere in the economy is an implicit cost of production. Had the proprietor invested elsewhere, the investment would have been used to purchase resources to produce other goods. What those resources could have earned in those alternative uses would determine the return on investment that could have been realized had the proprietor invested there.

The same principle applies on a larger scale to a corporation. Stockholders are the real owners of the corporation's land, plant, equipment, and inventories[1]—they have invested money in resources used by the corporation. Dividends equal to what stockholders could earn had they invested elsewhere in the economy are implicit costs of production from the point of view of the economist. The costs of resources obtained by the firm with stockholders' investments are, according to the alternative cost principle, the value of the al-

---

[1]In addition, the corporation may have borrowed money by selling bonds to increase the amounts of its plant and equipment. Thus, bondholders too have invested money in the corporation. But interest payments on the bonds—the return on the bondholders' investments—are explicit payments and are recorded as costs by the corporation, as well as by the economist.

ternative products forgone by holding the investment where it is. To hold the investment where it is, the corporation must pay a return to stockholders about equal to what they could earn if they invested elsewhere in the economy.

Cost, Resource Prices, and Efficiency

Costs of production incurred by the firm consist of both explicit and implicit obligations to resource owners. These obligations are just large enough to obtain and hold resources in the employment of the firm. Usually the firm's "expenses" include the explicit obligations only. Thus, costs of production as viewed by the economist differ somewhat from (and will usually be larger than) the firm's accounting "expenses."

The foregoing discussion of costs is oversimplified. We shall be concerned with a firm's costs of production at various alternative product outputs. Costs at each output depend on (1) the values of the resources the firm uses—that is, resource prices—and (2) the technology available for combining resources to produce the output. Initially we shall eliminate the problem of resource pricing by assuming that the firm is a pure competitor in the purchase of resources—that is, the single firm takes such a small proportion of the total amount of any given resource in existence that it cannot by itself influence the resource price. The firm can get all it wants of any one resource at a constant price per unit. Thus differences in costs at different output levels will result from differences in the efficiency of the technology the firm can use at each of those outputs. We examine the effects on costs of possible changes in resource prices as a result of output changes on the part of a firm after resource pricing has been considered (Chapter 14).

THE SHORT-RUN AND LONG-RUN VIEWPOINTS

In conceptualizing a firm's costs of production a distinction is made between the short-run and long-run viewpoints. These are essentially planning rather than calendar time concepts; they refer to the time horizon over which the firm's planning stretches. We examine them in turn.

The Short Run

short run
A planning period so short that the firm is unable to vary the quantities of *some* of the resources that it uses; usually thought of as the time horizon during which the firm cannot change its size of plant.

A planning period so short that the firm is unable to consider varying the quantities of *some* resources used is called the **short run.** It is possible to think of a period so short that no resource can be varied in quantity. Then, as the planning period is lengthened, it becomes possible to adjust the quantity of one. A progressive lengthening of the period permits more and more resources to become variable in quantity until ultimately they all fall into the variable category. Any period between that in which the quantity of no resources can be changed and that in which all resources but one are variable can legitimately be called the short run. However, to facilitate exposition we use a more restricting definition.

The possibilities of varying the quantities of different resources depend on their nature and the terms of hire or purchase. Some, such as land and buildings, may be leased by the firm for given time periods; or, if they are owned outright, it may take some time to acquire additional amounts or to dispose of a part of the quantities already owned. The number of top management personnel is not ordinarily readily variable; amounts of heavy machinery especially designed for the firm's use cannot be quickly increased or decreased. Typically, the period required for variation in the quantities of such resources as power, labor, transportation, raw materials, and semifinished materials will be shorter than that required for variation in the amounts of land, buildings, heavy machinery, and top management.

The usual interpretation of the short-run concept is a planning period sufficiently brief that the firm does not have time to vary the quantities of such resources as land, buildings, heavy machinery, and top management; these are the firm's short-run **fixed resources.** This concept of the short run *does* allow changes in the quantities of such resources as labor, raw materials, and the like; these are the firm's **variable resources.**[2]

The calendar time length of the short run will vary from one market to another. For some, the short run may be very short indeed. Such will be the case where the quantities of fixed resources used by a firm in the market are typically small or can be added to or subtracted from in a short period of time; various textile and many service industries are cases in point. For others, the short run may be several years; for example, the automobile or basic steel industries.

The quantities of fixed resources used determine the size of the firm's plant.[3] The size of plant sets the upper limit to the amount of output per unit of time that the firm is capable of producing. The firm can vary its output up to that limit, however, by increasing or decreasing the quantities of variable resources used in the fixed size of plant.

The fixed resources, or the plant, may be compared with a meat grinder. The variable resources will be analogous to unground meat. In this case, the output of ground meat per unit of time can be varied by changing the input of unground meat. There will be some upper limit beyond which the output cannot be increased, regardless of how much unground meat is on hand to push through the grinder.

fixed resources
Those resources used by a firm whose quantity it cannot change in the short run.

variable resources
Those resources used by a firm that it can change in quantity in either the short run or the long run.

---

[2]A clear distinction between resources that are fixed and resources that are variable is not always possible. For some firms several of the resources listed here as "variable" may require more time for alterations in quantity taken than some listed as "fixed." For example, contractual arrangements for the purchase of power or labor may be such that quantities of these resources cannot readily be varied; yet it may be possible for the firm to lease out, sublease, or sell some part of its "fixed" resources on short notice.

[3]The term *plant* is used here in a broad context to cover the whole scope of the firm's operations. A firm may operate several establishments at different locations; we shall view these all together as the firm's "plant."

The capital and labor example of Chapter 9 can also be viewed in a short-run context. We can think of the fixed amount of capital as the fixed size of plant and the variable quantities of labor as the variable resources used with it.

The Long Run

long run
A planning period long enough for the firm to be able to vary the quantities of all the resources it uses.

No definitional difficulties are presented by the **long run.** It is a planning period long enough for the firm to be able to vary the quantities per unit of time of all resources used. Thus all resources are variable; no problem of classifying resources as fixed or variable exists. The firm can vary its size of plant as it desires, from very small to large or vice versa.

SHORT-RUN COST CURVES _____

fixed costs
The costs of the fixed resources used by a firm in the short run.

variable costs
The costs of the variable resources used by a firm in either the short run or the long run.

Classification of resources in the short run as fixed and variable enables us to classify their costs as fixed and variable also. **Fixed costs** are the costs of fixed resources. **Variable costs** are those of variable resources. The distinction between fixed and variable costs is basic to the discussions of total, average, and marginal costs that follow.

Total Cost Curves

In the short run, the total costs of an enterprise depend on the firm's size and on the output level produced. The component parts of total costs are total fixed costs and total variable costs. We examine these in turn.

Total Fixed Costs   The costs per unit of time of all of its fixed resources constitute the firm's *total fixed costs*. They include the salaries that must be paid top management to keep it intact over time. They include the costs of holding and maintaining its land—that is, what the land would be worth in alternative uses over time. They include the costs of keeping investment in plant and equipment from shifting away from the firm. Short-run total fixed costs are thus the *alternative costs* of the fixed resources. They are the obligations that the firm must incur to keep those resources from slipping away in the long run. Note that total fixed costs depend on the size of the firm's operation—its size of plant—and not on the output level at which the plant is operated. We can therefore say that a firm's short-run total fixed costs are constant for all possible levels of output, given its size of plant.

A hypothetical total fixed cost schedule is presented and the corresponding total fixed cost curve is plotted in Figure 10.1. Note that the total fixed cost curve is independent of the output level, is parallel to the quantity axis, and lies above it by the amount of the total fixed costs.

Total Variable Costs   The alternative costs, or the total obligations that a firm incurs for its variable resources, constitute its *total variable costs*. Unlike its total fixed costs, the firm's total variable costs must vary directly with its output.

Figure 10.1 Total Costs for a Firm

(a) Schedules

Quantity of X	Total Fixed Cost	Total Variable Cost	Total Cost
1	$100	$ 40	$140
2	100	70	170
3	100	85	185
4	100	96	196
5	100	104	204
6	100	110	210
7	100	115	215
8	100	120	220
9	100	126	226
10	100	134	234
11	100	145	245
12	100	160	260
13	100	180	280
14	100	206	306
15	100	239	339
16	100	280	380
17	100	330	430
18	100	390	490
19	100	461	561
20	100	544	644

(b) Curves

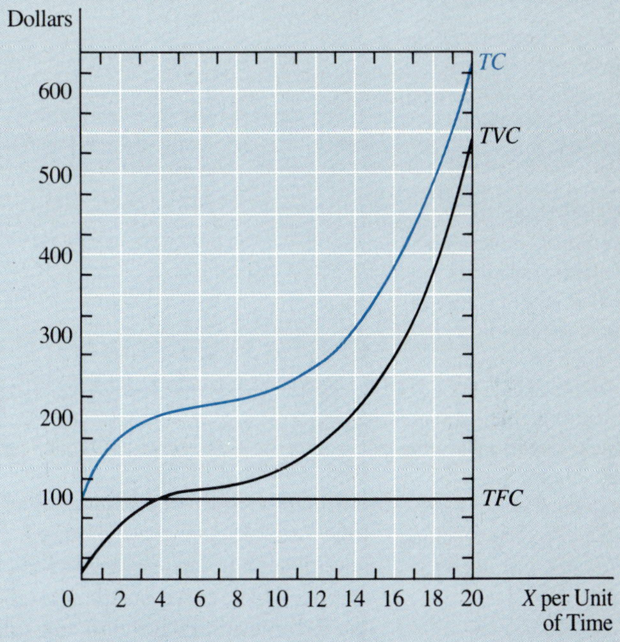

Panel (a) lists schedules of the total cost components for a hypothetical firm. These are plotted as total cost curves in panel (b).

Larger outputs require greater quantities of variable resources and hence larger cost obligations. For example, the larger the output of an oil refinery, the more crude oil input it must use and the larger will be its crude oil costs.

The shape of the total variable cost curve with respect to the firm's output will depend on whether increasing or diminishing returns to variable resources exist as larger and larger quantities of them are used with the firm's given size of plant. Consider the simple case in which a firm uses only one variable resource, resource A. A conventional total product curve for A is drawn on the right-hand side of Figure 10.2, showing increasing returns to A for quantities up to a_3 and diminishing returns for larger quantities. The point of inflection on the TP_a curve is at F.

The TP_a curve is easily converted into the total variable cost curve of the firm once the price of the variable resource A is known. Let the price of A be p_{a1}, so that for any given input of A total variable cost is that quantity of A multiplied by its price. Measure total variable cost (dollars' worth of A) on a horizontal axis stretching to the left of the origin. Total variable cost when a_1

**Figure 10.2
Relationship between
the *TVC* Curve and
the *TP* Curve of
Variable Resources**

Letting resource *A* be the firm's only variable resource, TP_a is the total product curve for *A*. It shows increasing returns to *A* between 0 and a_3 units of *A* and diminishing returns for still larger quantities used. If each quantity of *A* is multiplied by p_{a1}, the price of *A*, quantities of the resource can be shown to the left of 0 as dollars' worth, measuring total variable costs for each output level of the output axis. The resulting *TVC* curve is a mirror image of TP_a.

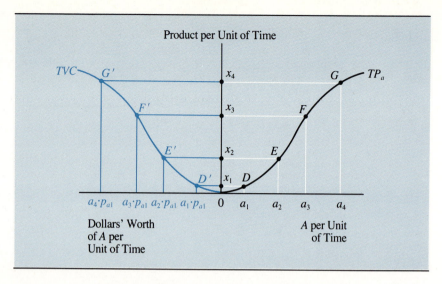

of *A* is used is $a_1 \times p_{a1}$, and the corresponding output of product is x_1. On the left-hand side of the diagram, these coordinates locate point D' on the firm's total variable cost curve. Points E', F', and G' are located in a similar manner, and all such points together trace out the firm's total variable cost curve.

The *TVC* curve on the left-hand side of the diagram is a mirror image of the TP_a curve on the right-hand side. If, for example, p_{a1} is 1 dollar and we let the distance on the horizontal axis that measures 1 unit of *A* to the right of the origin be equal to the distance that measures 1 dollar's worth of *A* to the left of the origin, the reflection is exact. The point of inflection, F', on *TVC* is the precise counterpart of *F* on TP_a. Both curves are concave upward from the origin to their respective inflection points and are concave downward beyond the inflection points because of increasing returns to *A* for quantities up to a_3 and decreasing returns for still greater quantities. If we rotate the left-hand side of the diagram 90 degrees clockwise, letting the product axis become the horizontal axis, the *TVC* curve is concave downward out to the inflection point and concave upward beyond that point.

Usually a firm uses several variable resources rather than only one, but the principles at work are the same as those of the single resource example. With a given size of plant—a given complex of fixed resources—we can think of increasing the complex of variable resources used. Since we start from a very small complex, increasing returns to the variable resources may occur—equal increments in outlays on the entire complex may result in larger and larger increments in output—and the *TVC* curve, consequently, will slope downward. As larger and larger outlays are made, however, diminishing returns to the complex come into play—equal increments in *TVC* result in smaller and smaller increments in output—and the *TVC* curve becomes concave upward. At some output level the fixed size of plant will have reached its absolute maximum capacity to produce. Now the total variable cost curve turns straight up. Increased obligations incurred for still larger quantities of variable resources will lead to no increases in output at all. The total variable cost schedule and the *TVC* curve of Figure 10.1 reflect the results of increasing and diminishing returns to variable resources.

Total Costs   The summation of total fixed costs and total variable costs for various output levels comprise the *total costs* of the firm for those output levels. The total cost column of Figure 10.1 is obtained by adding total fixed cost and total variable cost at each level of output. Likewise, the total cost curve is obtained by summing the *TFC* curve and the *TVC* curve vertically. The *TC* curve and the *TVC* curve must necessarily have the same shape, since each increase in output per unit of time raises total costs and total variable costs by the same amount. The output increase does not affect total fixed costs. The *TC* curve lies above the *TVC* curve by an amount equal to *TFC* at all output levels.[4]

Per Unit Cost Curves

In price and output analysis, *per unit cost curves* are used extensively—more so than are total cost curves. Per unit cost curves show the same kind of information as total cost curves, but in a different form. The per unit cost curves are the average fixed cost curve, the average variable cost curve, the average cost curve, and the marginal cost curve. The appendix to this chapter supplements the following discussion, showing the geometric derivations of the per unit cost curves from their total cost counterparts.

Average Fixed Costs   The fixed costs per unit of product at various levels of output, or the *average fixed costs,* are obtained by dividing total fixed costs by those outputs. Thus the average fixed cost column of Figure 10.3 is computed by dividing the total fixed cost column of panel (a) in Figure 10.1 by the different quantities of X. The average fixed cost schedule is then plotted as the *AFC* curve.

The greater the output of the firm, the smaller average fixed costs will be. Since total fixed costs remain the same regardless of output, fixed costs are spread over more units of output, and each unit of output bears a smaller share. Therefore, the average fixed cost curve is downward sloping to the right throughout its entire length. As output per unit of time increases, it approaches—but never reaches—the quantity axis. Thus, it becomes apparent that firms with large fixed costs—for example, the railroads, with their tremendous fixed charges on roadbeds and rolling stock—can substantially reduce their per unit fixed costs by producing larger outputs.

_____

[4]The short-run total cost function can be represented mathematically as $C = k + f(x)$, in which
$$TC = C$$
$$TFC = k$$
$$TVC = f(x).$$

Figure 10.3   Per Unit Costs of a Firm

(a) Schedules

Quantity of X	Average Fixed Cost	Average Variable Cost	Average Cost	Marginal Cost
1	$100.00	$40.00	$140.00	$40
2	50.00	35.00	85.00	30
3	33.33	28.33	61.66	15
4	25.00	24.00	49.00	11
5	20.00	20.80	40.80	8
6	16.67	18.33	35.00	6
7	14.29	16.43	30.72	5
8	12.50	15.00	27.50	5
9	11.11	14.00	25.11	6
10	10.00	13.40	23.40	8
11	9.09	13.18	22.27	11
12	8.33	13.33	21.66	15
13	7.69	13.85	21.54	20
14	7.14	14.72	21.86	26
15	6.67	15.93	22.60	33
16	6.25	17.50	23.75	41
17	5.88	19.41	25.29	50
18	5.55	21.67	27.22	60
19	5.26	24.27	29.53	71
20	5.00	27.20	32.20	83

(b) Curves

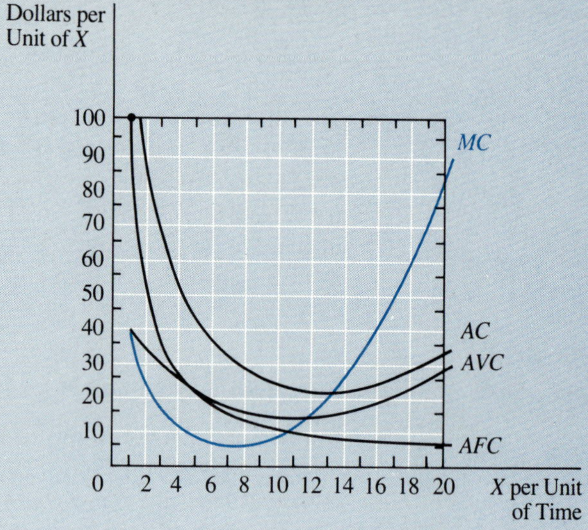

The average cost columns of panel (a) are computed from the corresponding total cost columns of Figure 10.1. The marginal cost column lists the increase in the total costs of Figure 10.1 for each one-unit increase in the firm's output level. These schedules are plotted as the *AFC*, *AVC*, *AC*, and *MC* of panel (b).

Average Variable Costs   Variable costs per unit of output are computed in the same way as fixed costs per unit of output. The average variable cost column of panel (a) in Figure 10.3 is obtained by dividing total variable costs in Figure 10.1 at various outputs by those outputs. Plotted graphically, the average variable cost column of Figure 10.3 becomes the *AVC* curve.

The *average variable cost* curve usually will have a U shape. This shape can be explained by the principles of production. Suppose, for example, that a factory is designed to employ approximately 100 workers. The size of plant is fixed, and labor is the only variable resource. The amount of product if only one worker is employed will be extremely small, but if an additional person is hired the two can divide the jobs to be performed and more than double the single worker's output. In other words, the average product of labor increases with the employment of the additional worker. If a doubling of labor (variable) costs will more than double output, labor costs per unit of output (average variable costs) will decrease. Thus throughout Stage I for labor, the average product per worker increases and the average variable costs decrease. When enough workers are employed to go into Stage II, average product of labor decreases or, what amounts to the same thing, average variable costs increase. The average variable cost curve in this case is a sort of monetized mirror reflection of the average product curve for labor.

The same general principles apply when a complex of several variable resources is used by the firm. At small input levels of the complex, product per unit of cost outlay or "average product" of the complex will be increasing, meaning that average variable costs will be decreasing. As input levels are increased, "average product" reaches a maximum and then decreases. Average variable costs correspondingly reach a minimum and then increase.

When the firm uses a complex of variable resources, combinations of ratios of the variable resources to one another must also be considered. Suppose that the firm for which the cost curves of Figure 10.3 are drawn uses three variable resources—A, B, and C—with its given size of plant, and resource prices are p_a, p_b, and p_c, respectively. If the firm's output is to be 6 units of product, and if its average variable costs are to be as low as possible ($18.33) for that output, the variable resources must be combined in such proportions that

$$\frac{MPP_a}{p_a} = \frac{MPP_b}{p_b} = \frac{MPP_c}{p_c}.$$

If they are not so combined, average variable costs for that output will exceed $18.33. Similarly, each point on the average variable cost curve can be attained only if the firm combines variable resources in the proper proportions for each and every output at which those points are located. Failure to do so will result in higher costs.

Average Costs   The overall costs per unit of output, the *average costs,* can be obtained in either of two ways. If total costs at various outputs in Figure 10.1 are divided by the respective outputs, the result will be the average cost column of Figure 10.3. Alternatively, in Figure 10.3 average fixed costs and average variable costs added together at each of the output levels produce the average cost column. Graphically, the *AC* curve in Figure 10.3 represents the average cost column plotted against outputs. The *AC* curve is also the vertical summation of the *AFC* and *AVC* curves.

The average cost curve too is usually thought to be U shaped. This shape depends on the efficiency with which both fixed and variable resources are used. Given the size of plant, the greater the firm's output, the greater the efficiency of the fixed resources will be as a group—that is, the smaller average fixed costs will become. In Figure 10.3 variable resources are used more and more efficiently until output reaches 11 units. Up to this level average costs must be decreasing, because the efficiency of both fixed and variable resources is increasing. Between 11 and 13 units of output, average fixed costs decrease, but average variable costs increase as variable resources become less efficient. However, the decreases in average fixed costs more than offset the increases in average variable costs so that average costs continue to decrease. Beyond 13 units of output per unit of time, decreases in the efficiency of variable resources more than offset increases in the efficiency of fixed resources, and average costs rise. We should note an obvious fact in passing: the minimum point on the average variable cost curve lies at a lower output level than does the minimum point on the average cost curve.[5]

Marginal Cost   The change in total costs resulting from a one-unit change in output is called **marginal cost.** It can be defined just as accurately as the change in total variable costs resulting from a one-unit change in output, since a change in output changes total variable costs and total costs by exactly the same amounts. Marginal cost depends in no way on fixed costs. The marginal cost column of panel (a) in Figure 10.3 can be computed from either the total variable cost column or the total cost column of Figure 10.1. It is plotted graphically as *MC* in Figure 10.3

marginal cost
The change in a firm's total costs per unit change in its output level.

Figure 10.4 shows the relationship between a marginal cost curve and the total cost curve from which it is derived. Consider output x in the total cost diagram in panel (a); total costs at that output are T. Now let output be increased by 1 unit to x_1; total costs increase to T_1, and marginal cost is TT_1. The marginal cost of a unit of output at any output level can be found in the same way. The marginal cost values plotted against outputs in panel (b) form the marginal cost curve. At any given output level, marginal cost is measured by the distance from the base line up to the marginal cost curve; thus marginal cost of the x_1 unit is x_1m_1 or $0M$ dollars. This represents the same number of dollars as does TT_1 in panel (a).

The marginal cost curve usually is U shaped, and this shape comes from the *TC* curve. Up to the x_2 level of output the *TC* curve is concave downward, or, each one-unit increase in output per unit of time up to that point will increase total costs by a smaller amount than did the preceding one. Marginal cost is decreasing as output is increased to that level. Point E on the *TC* curve at output level x_2 is the point of inflection, at which point marginal cost takes on its minimum value. At outputs greater than x_2, the total cost curve is concave upward, meaning that each one-unit increase in output per unit of time raises total costs by more than the preceding one. Therefore, marginal cost will be increasing for outputs beyond that level.

Marginal cost at any given output can be thought of geometrically as the slope of the total cost curve at that output. The approximate slope of the total cost curve of panel (a) between B and D is CD/BC. BC is equal to one unit of

---

[5]The average cost function is derived from Footnote 4 by dividing the total cost function by output and is

$$AC = \frac{C}{x} = \frac{k}{x} + \frac{f(x)}{x}, \text{ in which } AFC = \frac{k}{x} \text{ and } AVC = \frac{f(x)}{x}.$$

Since $AFC = \frac{k}{x}$, then $x \times AFC = k$, and the AFC curve is thus a rectangular hyperbola.

Figure 10.4 The Relationship Between *MC* and *TC*

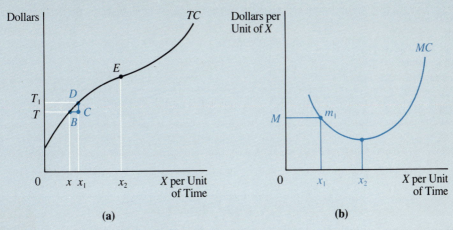

For the increase in output from x to x_1 in panel (a), total cost increases from
T to T_1. CD/BC, or the approximate slope of the *TC* curve between x and x_1,
measures marginal cost for output x_1, and this amount, say $0M$ dollars, is
plotted as x_1m_1 in panel (b). At other output levels, similar measurements on
the *TC* curve provide the data for plotting the *MC* curve.

output, and CD is equal to $T_1 - T$, or marginal cost of the x_1 unit. The slope
of the total cost curve between B and D is thus equal to the marginal cost of
the x_1 unit. For the typical firm, one unit of output is measured by an infinitesimal distance along the quantity axis; the large size of the unit of output (x to
x_1) in panel (a) is for purposes of illustration only. If one unit of output is
measured by an infinitesimal distance along the quantity axis, marginal cost at
any given output is numerically equal to the slope of the total cost curve at that
output. The slope of the *TC* curve of panel (a) is decreasing between zero and
output x_2 (although *TC* is rising) and increasing beyond x_2. Thus marginal cost
first decreases and then increases as output climbs.

Relationship of *MC* to *AC* and to *AVC*

The marginal cost curve bears a unique relationship to the average cost curve
derived from the same total cost curve. Up to output x_2 in Figure 10.5 where
AC is decreasing, *MC* is less than *AC*. Beyond x_2 where *AC* is increasing as
output increases, *MC* is greater than *AC*. It follows that at the output x_2 at which
AC is minimum, *MC* is equal to *AC*.

For example, suppose that the firm's output is x and its average cost is $0C$.
We know that average cost at any output equals the total cost of that output
divided by the output; therefore, $0C = TC/x$ at output x. Suppose that the

Figure 10.5
The Relationship between MC and AC

Between the 0 and x_2 output levels, where AC is decreasing, MC is less than AC. At x_2, where AC is minimum, MC equals AC. At outputs above x_2, where AC is increasing, MC is greater than AC.

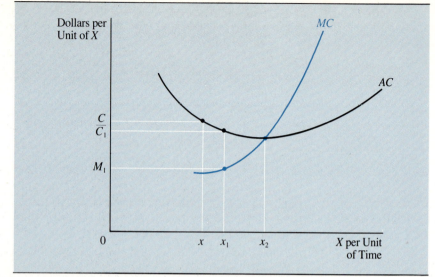

output is increased by 1 unit to x_1 and that the addition to total costs is $0M_1$, which is the marginal cost of the x_1 unit. Suppose further, as we show in Figure 10.5, that marginal cost of the x_1 unit is less than the average cost $0C$ of x units. Since the additional unit of output per unit of time adds a lesser amount to total costs than was the average cost of x units, the average cost of x_1 units must be less than the average cost of x units. However, the average cost of x_1 units will not be pulled down as low as the marginal cost of the x_1 unit. Thus $0C_1 < 0C$, but $0C_1 > 0M_1$—that is, when average costs are decreasing, marginal cost is necessarily less than average cost. Similarly, when an additional unit of output adds an amount to total costs equal to the old average cost, as it does at x_2, the new average cost will equal the old and will also equal the marginal cost of the additional unit of output. Also, when an additional unit of output adds a greater amount to total costs than was the original average cost, the new average cost will be greater than the original but will be less than the marginal cost of the additional unit. These relationships can be verified by reference to Figure 10.3.

The relationships between marginal cost and average variable cost will be identical with those between marginal cost and average cost—and for the same reasons. When average variable cost is decreasing, marginal cost will be less than average variable cost. When average variable cost is minimum, marginal cost and average variable cost will be equal. When average variable cost is increasing, marginal cost will be greater than average variable cost. These relationships can also be verified in Figure 10.3.

The complete set of short-run per unit cost curves is pictured in Figure 10.3. The marginal cost curve cuts the average variable cost curve and the average cost curve at their respective minimum points. An increase in fixed costs would shift the average cost curve upward and to the right in such a way that the marginal cost curve would still intersect it at its minimum point. No change in the marginal cost curve would be involved, since marginal cost is independent of fixed cost.[6]

As we have presented them, the variations in the component parts of short-run costs as the firm varies output do not depend on changes in the price paid per unit for each of the various resources used. We assumed at the outset that the firm can get all it wants of any resource at a constant price per unit, that is, it buys resources under conditions of pure competition. The shapes of the short-run curves reflect the efficiency with which resources can be used at the alternative output levels obtainable with a given plant size.

In the real world, we observe such things as quantity discounts on resources purchased in large amounts by the firm. This represents a departure from pure competition in the buying of resources; it is a departure from the assumptions on which our cost curves are based. Should quantity discounts occur, the total variable cost curve and the total cost curve will increase less as output is increased than they would otherwise. Correspondingly, quantity discounts will cause the average variable cost curve and the average cost curve to show greater decreases, then smaller increases, than they would otherwise show as output is increased. Further modifications of short-run cost analysis will be developed in Chapter 14.

Most Efficient Rate of Output

most efficient rate of output
The output level at which a firm's short-run average costs are minimum; the most efficient of all possible short-run output levels given the firm's size of plant.

The output at which the firm's short-run average cost is lowest is the output at which any given size of plant is most efficient. Here the value of the inputs of resources per unit output of product is least. As we shall see later, the **most efficient rate of output** for a given plant size is not necessarily the output at which the firm makes the greatest profits. Profits depend on revenue as well as costs.

---

[6]Starting from the total cost function, $C = k + f(x)$, the marginal cost function becomes

$$MC = \frac{dC}{dx} = f'(x)$$

and is thus seen to depend in no way on k. Further, if average cost is decreasing, then

$$\frac{d\left(\frac{C}{x}\right)}{dx} = \frac{x\frac{dC}{dx} - C}{x^2} < 0, \text{ or, dividing each term of the fraction by } x,$$

$$\frac{dC}{dx} - \frac{C}{x} < 0 \quad \text{and} \quad \frac{dC}{dx} < \frac{C}{x},$$

which means that $MC < AC$. Similarly, it can be shown that if AC is increasing, then

$$\frac{d\left(\frac{C}{x}\right)}{dx} > 0, \text{ or } \frac{dC}{dx} > \frac{C}{x}, \text{ or } MC > AC.$$

If AC is constant, then $\dfrac{d\left(\frac{C}{x}\right)}{dx} = 0$, or $\dfrac{dC}{dx} = \dfrac{C}{x}$, or $MC = AC$.

LONG-RUN COST CURVES

In the long-run planning period, any size of plant is a possibility for the firm. All resources are variable: the firm can change the quantities used per unit of time of land, buildings, machinery, management, and all other resources. There will be no fixed costs. We need to concern ourselves here with the long-run total cost curve, the long-run marginal cost curve, and the long-run average cost curve.

Long-Run Total Costs

We would expect the long-run total cost curve to look like *LTC* in panel (b) of Figure 10.6, starting at the origin of the diagram and moving upward to the right in much the same fashion as a total variable cost curve. This curve, as we have drawn it, reflects first decreasing and then increasing long-run average costs.

The long-run total cost curve of panel (b) originates in the isoquant-isocost map of panel (a). The production function represented by the isoquant map generates a typical long-run total cost curve. Let numbers on the isoquants indicate the levels of output. The prices of resources A and B are constant at p_{a1} and p_{b1}, respectively, and determine the slope $(-p_{a1}/p_{b1})$ of the family of isocost curves. Alternative possible total cost outlays are shown as the numerators of the various fractions (TCO/p_{b1} and TCO/p_{a1}) along both the A and the B axes. Note that the isocosts showing \$100 increments in total cost outlay are spaced equally from one another.

The spacing of the isoquants reflects first economies and then diseconomies of size as the firm's plant size is increased. To state it another way, the spacing reflects increasing efficiency and then decreasing efficiency in the use of resources as the plant is expanded. As we move along the expansion path, equal increments in the firm's output require decreasing increments in total cost outlay until point H is reached. Beyond point H, increasing increments in cost outlay are required to bring about equal increments in output. The resulting total cost is that of panel (b).

Long-Run Average Costs

The long-run average cost curve is derived from the long-run total cost curve in the same way as any "average" curve is derived from any "total" curve. At each level of output we divide *LTC* by output to find *LAC* for that level. The result is the *LAC* curve.

It is instructive, however, to build up the *LAC* curve in an alternative way. Think of the long run as a set of alternative short-run situations into any one of which the firm can move. At any given time we can adopt the short-run viewpoint and consider the alternative output levels that can be produced with the size of plant in existence at that time. Yet, from the point of view of a long-run planning period, the firm has opportunities to change the short-run picture.

Figure 10.6 From Isoquants to the *LTC* Curve

This diagram bridges the gap between a firm's production function and its *LTC* curve. Note first in panel (a) that isocosts for $100 increments in total cost outlays are identified along the *A* axis and are equidistant from one another. Then note that moving out along the expansion path to point *H*, isoquants for 10-unit increments in output are closer and closer together. Beyond point *H* they are farther and farther apart. Next note along the *B* axis the outlays necessary to produce the outputs identified by the isoquants. These outlays, plotted against the corresponding outputs, form the *LTC* curve.

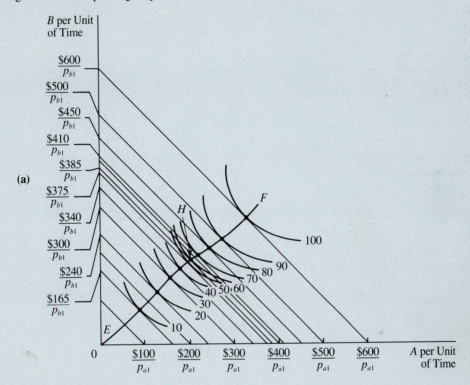

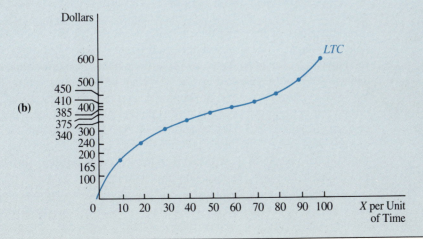

**Figure 10.7
The Long-Run
Average Cost Curve:
Three Alternative
Plant Sizes**

At output x, plant SAC_1 will produce at a lower average cost than will SAC_2 or any other size of plant. At x', plants SAC_1 and SAC_2 are equally efficient. At x_1, SAC_2 will produce at lowest average cost. At x_3, SAC_3 is most efficient. Consequently, the blue lower portions of the SAC curves form the LAC curve.

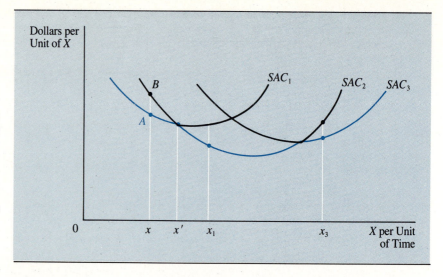

The long run may be compared with the action sequence of a motion picture: if we stop the film and look at a single picture, we have a short-run concept.

Suppose now that it is technically possible for the firm to build only three alternative sizes of plant. These are represented by SAC_1, SAC_2, and SAC_3 in Figure 10.7. Each SAC curve is the short-run average cost curve for a given plant size. In the long run the firm can build any one of these, or it can shift from one to another.

Which one should the firm build? The answer depends on, and will vary with, the long-run output per unit of time to be produced. Whatever the output is to be, the firm will want to produce at an average cost as low as possible for that output.

Suppose the output level is to be x. The firm should construct the plant represented by SAC_1, which will produce output x at a smaller cost per unit (xA) than will either of the other two. If SAC_2 were used, costs would be xB per unit. For output x' the firm would be indifferent between SAC_1 and SAC_2, but for output x_1, it would prefer to use SAC_2. For output x_3 the firm would construct and use the plant represented by SAC_3. We are now in a position to define the *long-run average cost curve*. It shows the least possible cost per unit of producing various outputs when the firm is able to plan to build any desired size of plant. In Figure 10.7 the blue portions of the SAC curves form the long-run average cost curve. The black portions of the curves are irrelevant; the firm would never operate in these portions in the long run, because if it were to do so it could reduce costs by changing plant size instead.

The possible plant sizes that a firm can build as a long-run undertaking usually are unlimited in number. For every conceivable size there will be another infinitesimally larger or infinitesimally smaller. Their SAC curves are those shown in Figure 10.8; any number of additional SAC curves can be drawn between any two of those in the diagram. The outer portions of the SAC curves

**Figure 10.8
The Long-Run
Average Cost Curve:
Infinite Alternative
Plant Sizes**

The *LAC* curve is made
up of infinitesimal parts
of all *SAC* curves of the
firm—at each output, that
part of an *SAC* curve that
produces the output at the
lowest possible average
cost. The *LAC* curve is
thus the envelope curve
to all possible *SAC*
curves.

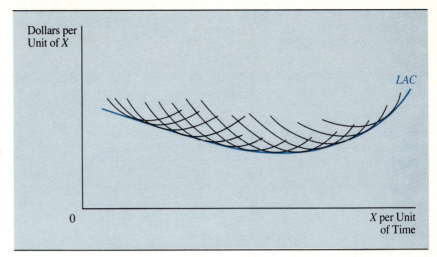

form the blue line, which is the long-run average cost (*LAC*) curve. Since this curve is made up of very small segments of the various *SAC* curves, it can be considered as a curve just tangent to all possible *SAC* curves representing the plant sizes that the firm conceivably could build. Mathematically it is an envelope curve to the *SAC* curves.

Every point on the long-run average cost curve—or the long-run total cost curve, for that matter—requires that the firm be using a least-cost combination of resources. For any given output, long-run total cost and long-run average cost are least when *all* resources used are combined in proportions such that the marginal physical product per dollar's worth of one equals the marginal physical product per dollar's worth of every other. This statement means that the last dollar increment in spending on management must add the same amount to total product as the last dollar increment in spending on raw materials. A dollar spent on labor and a dollar spent on machinery must both yield the same addition to total product, and so on for all resources. Should these conditions not be fulfilled—should a dollar spent on management add less to total product than a dollar spent on machines—then some shifts in expenditure from management to machines will increase total product without increasing total costs; or, if we consider the matter another way, the shifts will provide a decrease in total cost or a decrease in average cost, holding total product constant. Thus the cost levels shown by the long-run average cost curve for various outputs can be attained by the firm only if the least-cost resource combination is used for each output.

Economies of Size

The long-run average cost curve is usually thought to be U shaped. Such will be the case if a firm becomes successively more efficient up to some specific size or range of sizes and if it then becomes successively less efficient as the

Figure 10.9
Economies and Diseconomies of Size

Greater efficiency resulting from economies of size causes the *SAC* curves of larger plant sizes to lie at lower levels than those of smaller ones up to some plant size such as SAC_3. Plant sizes still larger, such as SAC_4, lie at progressively higher levels because of diseconomies of size. Economies and diseconomies of size give the *LAC* curve its U shape.

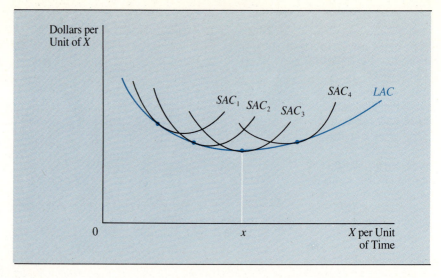

economies of size
The forces causing a firm's long-run average costs to decrease as its output level and size of plant are increased; usually thought to be (1) increasing possibilities of division and specialization of labor and (2) greater possibilities of using more efficient technology.

range of plant sizes—from very small to very large—is considered. Increasing efficiency associated with larger and larger plant sizes is reflected by *SAC* curves lying at successively lower levels and farther to the right. Examples are provided by SAC_1, SAC_2, and SAC_3 in Figure 10.9. Decreasing efficiency, associated with still larger plant sizes, would be shown by *SAC* curves lying at successively higher levels and farther to the right, such as SAC_4. The resulting *LAC* curve would thus have a general U shape.

We call the forces causing the *LAC* curve to decrease for larger outputs and plant sizes **economies of size.** The discussion of the beer industry at the end of this chapter shows how important economies of size can be in shaping the sizes and number of firms that a market contains. These forces are referred to frequently as *economies of scale,* but strictly speaking this latter term is correct only if the production function is homogeneous, that is, if all resources are increased in the same proportion to obtain greater outputs and larger plant sizes. Usually different plant sizes employ different proportions in the resource mix— all resources are *not* increased in the same proportion—for larger plant sizes. Consequently, we use the less restrictive term economies of size. Two important economies of size are (1) increasing possibilities of division and specialization of labor and (2) increasing possibilities of using advanced technological developments and/or larger machines. These economies will be discussed in turn.

Division and Specialization of Labor   The advantages of division and specialization of labor have long been known to both economists and the general public.[7] A small plant employing few workers cannot specialize the workers on particular operations as readily as can a larger plant employing more people. In

---

[7]See Adam Smith, *The Wealth of Nations,* ed. Edwin Cannan (New York: Modern Library, 1937), Bk. 1, Chaps. 1–3.

the small plant the typical worker performs several different operations in the process of producing the commodity and may not be particularly proficient at some of them. In addition, time may be lost in the worker's changing from one set of tools to another in carrying out different operations.

In a larger plant greater specialization may be possible, with the worker concentrating on that process at which he or she is most adept. Specialization in a particular process eliminates the time lost in changing from one set of tools to another. Also, the worker engaged in a single type of operation develops shortcuts and speed in performing it. The efficiency of each worker is likely to be higher and cost per unit of output correspondingly lower where division and specialization of labor are possible. A word of warning may be necessary, though: in some cases it may be possible to carry specialization to the point at which the monotony of the task begins to counteract increases in the efficiency of the individual's performance.

Technological Factors   The possibility of lowering costs per unit of output by mass production technology increases as the plant size is increased. In the first place, the cheapest way of producing a small output will usually not be one that employs the most advanced technological methods. Consider, for example, the production of automobile hoods. If the output were to be two or three hoods per week, large automatic presses would not be used. The cheapest way to produce the hoods would probably be to hammer them out by hand. With this method the cost per unit would be comparatively high; there would be no inexpensive way of producing the small output or of operating the small plant for the production of a limited output.

For larger outputs and plant sizes, mass production technological methods can be used to effect reductions in per unit costs. In this example, if output were to be several thousand units per week, then a larger plant with automatic presses could be installed, and costs per unit would be substantially lower than is possible with the small plant.

In the second place, technological considerations are usually such that in order to double the capacity of a machine to produce, a doubling of material, construction, and operating costs of the machine is not necessary. For example, it is cheaper to build and operate a 600-horsepower diesel motor than it is to build and operate two 300-horsepower diesel motors; the 600-horsepower motor has no more working parts than a single 300-horsepower unit. In addition, the 600-horsepower engine does not require twice the amount of materials used in building a single 300-horsepower motor.

The same type of example can be made for almost any machine. Technological possibilities represent a very important explanation for the increasing efficiency of larger and larger plant sizes up to some limit.

Diseconomies of Size

The question arises as to why, once the plant is large enough to take advantage of all economies of size, still larger sizes are likely to result in less efficiency. It would appear offhand that the firm would be able to at least maintain the

diseconomies of size
The forces causing a firm's long-run average costs to increase as its output level and size of plant are expanded; usually thought to be the increasing difficulties of coordinating and controlling the firm's activities for larger outputs and sizes.

economies of size. The usual answer to this question is that there are limitations to the efficiency of a single management in controlling and coordinating a single firm. These limitations are called **diseconomies of size.**

As the size of the plant is increased, management, like the lower echelons of labor, may become more efficient through division of tasks and specialization in particular functions; but the argument commonly made is that beyond some certain size the difficulties of coordinating and controlling the firm multiply rapidly. The contacts of top management with the day-to-day operations of the business become more and more remote, causing operating efficiency in production departments to decrease. Decision-making responsibility must be delegated, and coordination must be established among the decision-making subordinates. The paperwork, travel expenses, telephone bills, and additional employees necessary for coordination pile up. Occasionally plans of separate decision-making subordinates fail to mesh, and costly slowdowns occur. To the extent that greater difficulties of coordination and control reduce the efficiency per dollar outlay on management, as the size of the plant is increased per unit costs of production will increase.

The discussion so far may be interpreted to mean that as the size of plant expands economies of size cause the long-run average cost curve to fall, and then, when all economies of size are realized, diseconomies of size begin straightaway. Such is not necessarily the case. Once the plant is large enough to take advantage of all economies of size, there may be a range of larger plant sizes in which diseconomies are not yet evident. As a result, the long-run average cost curve will have a horizontal series of minimum points rather than the single minimum point of the conventional long-run average cost curve. When the plant has become sufficiently large for diseconomies of size to occur, the long-run average cost curve turns upward to the right. Another possibility is that some diseconomies begin to occur in a plant too small to realize all economies of size. If the economies of size for larger plants more than offset the diseconomies, the long-run average cost curve slopes downward to the right; where diseconomies of size more than offset economies of size, it slopes upward to the right.

Most Efficient Size of Plant

most efficient size of plant
That size of plant for which the firm's short-run average cost curve forms the minimum point of its long-run average cost curve; the most efficient of all possible plant sizes for a firm.

The **most efficient size of plant** is the one generating the short-run average cost curve that forms the minimum point of the long-run average cost curve. It can also be thought of as that size of plant having a short-run average cost curve tangent to the long-run average cost curve at the minimum points of both. The short-run average cost curve of the most efficient size of plant in Figure 10.10 is SAC.

Firms will not invariably construct plants of most efficient size and operate them at the most efficient rates of output. As we shall see, they will do so under conditions of pure competition in the long run but likely not under pure monopoly, oligopoly, and monopolistic competition. The size of plant that will operate at the lowest cost per unit for given outputs will vary with the output to be produced. For example, in Figure 10.10, plant SAC will produce output

**Figure 10.10
The Most Efficient
Size of Plant**

The size of plant with
short-run average cost
curve *SAC*, lying at the
bottom of the *LAC* curve,
is the most efficient of all
possible sizes; that is, it
will produce at the lowest
possible cost per unit.

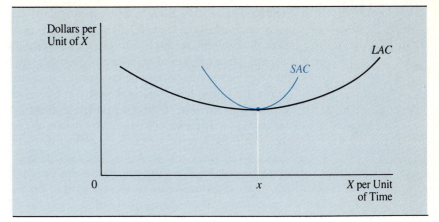

x more cheaply than will a plant of any other size, and output x can be produced
at a lower cost per unit than can any other output. But for outputs greater or
smaller than x, per unit costs will necessarily be higher. Plants other than those
of most efficient size will produce such outputs at lower costs per unit than will
the plant of most efficient size.

How can we determine the appropriate size of plant to be constructed for
a specific output? Consider Figure 10.11. Suppose that the firm is producing
output x_1 with plant SAC_1. Plant SAC_1 is being operated at less than its most
efficient rate of output. Let the output level be increased to x_2, in either of two
ways: (1) by increasing the output rate with plant SAC_1 or (2) by changing to a
larger plant size. Either method will allow the firm to reduce costs per unit.

**Figure 10.11
Appropriate Plant
Size for a Given
Output**

The appropriate plant size
for a given output is that
with an *SAC* tangent to
the *LAC* at that output. If
the firm were to increase
output from x_1 to x_2, a
larger plant size, SAC_2,
should be used since it
will produce x_2 at a
lower cost per unit than
will SAC_1.

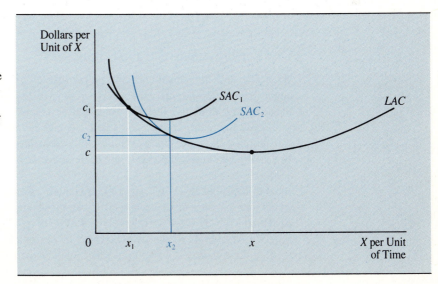

Method 1 will cause SAC_1 to be used at its most efficient rate of output, with costs lower than c_1. However, if the firm uses method 2, economies of size from the larger plant, SAC_2, will allow even greater per unit cost reduction for output x_2 than will method 1; here costs per unit will be c_2, which is the lowest cost at which the output can be produced. For outputs between zero and x, the firm will achieve lowest per unit costs for any given output by using a plant smaller than the most efficient size at less than the most efficient rate of output. Similarly, for any given output greater than x, the lowest cost per unit will be achieved if the firm uses a plant larger than the most efficient size at a greater than most efficient rate of output. The applicable general principle is this: To minimize cost for any given output, the firm should use the plant size for which the short-run average cost curve is tangent to the long-run average cost curve at that output. The importance of this principle can be seen in the discussion of the brewing industry at the end of this chapter.

Long-Run Marginal Cost

The *long-run marginal cost curve* shows the change in long-run total cost per unit change in the firm's output when the firm has ample time to accomplish the output change by making the appropriate adjustments in the quantities of all resources used, including those that constitute its plant. It measures the slopes of the *LTC* curve at various output levels.

From the *LTC* curve of panel (a) in Figure 10.12 we can deduce that *LMC* would be less than *LAC* where *LAC* is decreasing—that is, from zero to output x—and would be greater than *LAC* for output levels beyond x where *LAC* is increasing. At output x, *LMC* and *LAC* are equal. These relationships are shown in panel (b) by the *LAC* and *LMC* curves. The *LMC* curve bears the same relationship to its *LAC* curve that any given *SMC* curve bears to its *SAC* curve.

Relationships between *LMC* and *SMC*

When the firm has constructed the proper size of plant for producing a given output, short-run marginal cost will equal long-run marginal cost at that output. Suppose, for example, that the given output is x_2 in Figure 10.12. The firm would use the plant represented by SAC_2, which is tangent to the *LAC* curve at that output. The corresponding total cost curves are STC_2 and *LTC* of Figure 10.12. We can verify that STC_2 would lie above *LTC* at output levels below x_2 because SAC_2 is greater than *LAC* at those levels. At output x_2 STC_2 would be equal to *LTC*, because SAC_2 and *LAC* are equal. At outputs greater than x_2 STC_2 would again exceed *LTC*, because SAC_2 for those outputs again lies above *LAC*. At output x_2, where SAC_2 is tangent to *LAC*, curve STC_2 must also be tangent to *LTC*. At outputs in the neighborhood of but below x_2, STC_2 must have a smaller slope than *LTC*; at output levels greater than x_2, the STC_2 curve must

Figure 10.12
Relationship between Short-Run and Long-Run Costs

The SAC_2 curve of panel (b) is tangent to LAC at the output level at which the STC_2 of panel (a) is tangent to LTC. At outputs below x_2 the slope of STC_2 is less than the slope of LTC; therefore SMC_2 lies below LMC for those outputs. At x_2, where the slopes of STC_2 and LTC are the same, SMC_2 equals LMC. At greater outputs the slope of STC_2 exceeds that of LTC, and SMC_2 is greater than LMC.

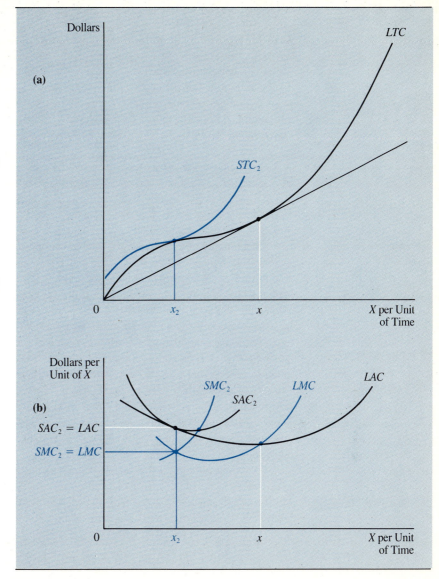

have a greater slope than LTC. At x_2, where STC_2 is tangent to LTC, both curves have the same slope.

Because the slope of the STC_2 curve is the short-run marginal cost for that size of plant and the slope of LTC is the long-run marginal cost, it follows that $SMC_2 < LMC$ at outputs just smaller than x_2, $SMC_2 > LMC$ at outputs just larger than x_2, and $SMC_2 = LMC$ at output x_2. These relationships are shown in Figure 10.12.

SUMMARY

Costs of production are the obligations incurred by the firm for resources used in making its product. The cost of any given resource is determined by its value in its best alternative use. This concept is called the alternative cost principle. Costs of production differ from the usual concept of the firm's "expenses," which usually coincide with explicit resource costs. In determining costs of production, implicit resource costs also must be included. The analysis of costs presented in the chapter assumes that the firm cannot by itself influence the price of any resource that it buys.

In the short run, resources used by the firm are classified as fixed and variable. The obligations incurred for them are fixed costs and variable costs. Total fixed costs and total variable costs for different outputs are the component parts of total costs. From the three total cost curves, we derive the corresponding per unit cost curves—average fixed cost, average variable cost, and average cost. The short-run average cost curve shows the lowest per unit cost of producing different outputs with a given plant size and is a U-shaped curve. In addition, we derive the marginal cost curve. The output at which short-run average cost is lowest is called the most efficient rate of output for a given size of plant.

All resources can be varied in quantity by the firm in the long run; consequently, all costs are variable. The long-run average cost curve shows the lowest per unit cost of producing various outputs when the firm is free to change its plant to any desired size. It is the envelope curve to the short-run average cost curves of all possible sizes of plant, and it is usually U shaped. The factors causing this shape are called economies of size and diseconomies of size. The long-run marginal cost curve shows the change in total costs resulting from a one-unit change in output when the firm is free to vary the quantities used of all resources.

For whatever output the firm produces in the long run, if the lowest per unit cost is to be obtained for that output, the plant size must be such that its short-run average cost curve is tangent to the long-run average cost curve at that output. For such a plant size, short-run marginal cost will equal long-run marginal cost at the output of tangency.

APPLICATIONS

From the many possible applications of cost analysis, three have been selected here for their illustrative content. The first is a common one for all college and university students. The second shows an important economic principle at work. The third is an intriguing case study of an important industry's costs.

COSTS OF OBTAINING A HIGHER EDUCATION

What are the annual costs to a student of attending a college or university? Or, to state the question in a slightly different way, what does it cost a student to invest in human capital to the extent of 30 hours of college or university credit over the course of an academic year? Most students and their parents will underestimate the cost.

The explicit costs to the student are fairly clear. Tuition is a prime consideration. Next in importance are books and supplies. Here the family's calculations are likely to stop.

At least two items of an implicit nature are frequently overlooked. The most important one—and the largest cost item in a year of academic training—is the student's forgone earnings. What could the student have earned if he or she had elected to join the labor force in lieu of enrolling in the college or university and investing such a large block of time in studying? The second is the forgone interest on tuition payments. If tuition is paid at the beginning of each semester, the student loses interest on one-half of one-half of the annual tuition for the academic year, since that amount could have been kept out on loan at the going interest rate. Similar forgone interest costs may occur if room and board payments are made in advance on a semester-by-semester basis. However, these latter interest costs can be avoided if a student lives off the campus and/or pays room and board on a monthly basis.

Let us summarize and provide perspective. Dollar amounts that may approximate the various cost items for a student at a private college or university for an academic year are listed in the following table.

Explicit Costs	
Tuition	$ 8,000
Books and supplies	500
Subtotal	$ 8,500
Implicit Costs	
Forgone earnings	$14,000
Forgone interest ($2,000 @ 8%)	160
Subtotal	$14,160
Total Costs	$22,660

COST MINIMIZATION BY A MULTIPLE-UNIT FIRM

We have derived the cost curves for the overall operation of a firm, aggregating the costs of production of the various production units that the firm may operate if it is indeed a multiple-unit firm. An interesting problem remains, however. How should such a firm allocate its total output level among its production units in order to minimize the cost of producing that output level? Should it always seek to produce in those units that have the lowest average costs?

Suppose that a firm producing crude oil is composed of two units, Unit 1 and Unit 2. The short-run average and marginal cost curves of each unit are illustrated in Figure 10.13. Let the firm's anticipated total output level be X barrels per day.

To minimize its costs, the firm should allocate the X barrels between Unit 1 and Unit 2 in such a way that the *marginal cost* of production in Unit 1 is equal to that of Unit 2—that is, Unit 1 should produce x_1 barrels and Unit 2 should produce x_2 barrels with $x_1 + x_2 = X$. Marginal cost in both units is M, or \$10. Note that the average costs for Unit 1 are higher than those for Unit 2 at these output levels.

Nevertheless, the firm's total costs are minimized. Suppose the output level of Unit 1 is reduced by 1 barrel while that of Unit 2 is increased by 1 barrel. Since marginal cost at the x_1 output level is \$10, a 1-barrel reduction in the

Figure 10.13   Cost Minimization by a Multiple-Unit Firm

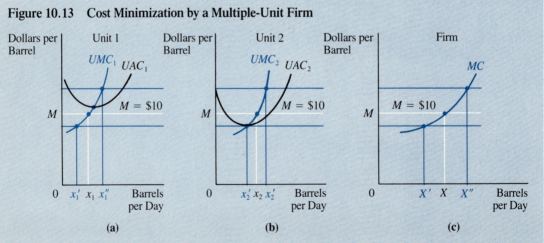

To minimize costs for a given output X the multiplant firm should allocate the output among the plants so that marginal costs in each of the plants are the same. Since MC is the horizontal summation of UMC_1 and UMC_2, each unit should be operated at the output level at which its marginal cost is $0M$. Unit 1 should produce x_1 and Unit 2 should produce x_2, and $x_1 + x_2 = X$.

output of Unit 1 reduces the firm's total costs by that amount. But a 1-barrel increase in the output of Unit 2 pushes marginal cost in Unit 2 above $10—say, to $10.25. By the definition of marginal cost, this amounts to a $10.25 increase in the firm's total costs. The *net* effect of a shift of a barrel of oil per day from Unit 1 to Unit 2 is a $.25 increase in the firm's total costs. Similarly, from the original output levels, x_1 and x_2, a shift in production from Unit 2 to Unit 1 would increase the firm's total costs. Total costs are thus minimum when production is allocated so that the marginal cost is the same in each unit.

These conditions for minimizing the firm's total costs are applicable for any total output level. If the firm were to produce X' barrels per day, x_1' should be produced by Unit 1 and x_2' by Unit 2. If the total output were to be X'', then x_1'' should be produced by Unit 1 and x_2'' by Unit 2. In each instance the total output is so allocated that marginal costs (UMC_1 and UMC_2) are the same for the two production units. If these two costs are summed horizontally, we obtain the firm's overall marginal cost curve, MC. This curve shows the marginal cost at alternative total output levels when each of those levels is allocated among production units so as to minimize total costs.

ECONOMIES OF SIZE IN THE BEER INDUSTRY[8]

As economist Kenneth Elzinga has observed, there has long been a special economic relationship between college students and beer. The fortunes of commercial brewers helped to endow Harvard and Vassar, for example, and college students have taken a keen interest in the nature and extent of the industry's output.[9] Watchful consumers of beer may have noticed, however, that the number of brands from which they may choose has been declining—indeed, the beer industry in the twentieth century, and especially in the period since World War II, has undergone one of the most dramatic shakeouts in American economic history.

The industry reached its peak in this century in 1914, when 1,392 brewery plants were operating. Prohibition reduced it to 331 in 1933, but it rallied temporarily to 756 in 1934 after repeal.[10] Table 10.1 shows the decline from 1946 to 1976, which has been concentrated among small local or regional breweries. Elzinga found that of the 182 plants eliminated during 1950–61 a total of 119 simply closed their doors while in another 41 cases the company that bought the brewery continued to operate it from another location.[11] The shakeout was

---

[8]Helpful comments on the materials in this section were given by George W. Hilton, editor, *The Breweriana Collector,* and Peter H. Blum, historian, Stroh Brewery Co.

[9]Kenneth Elzinga, ''The Beer Industry,'' in *The Structure of American Industry,* 4th ed., ed. Walter Adams (New York: Macmillan, 1971), 189.

[10]See Ira Horowitz and Ann R. Horowitz, ''Firms in a Declining Market: The Brewing Case,'' *Journal of Industrial Economics* 13, no. 2 (March 1965): 130.

[11]Elzinga, ''The Beer Industry'' (1971), 199; and Elzinga, ''The Beer Industry,'' in *The Structure of American Industry,* 6th ed., ed. Walter Adams (New York: Macmillan, 1982), 221.

**Table 10.1
Number of Breweries
and Brewery Firms
in the United States,
1946–1976**

Year	Plants	Firms
1946	471	
1947	465	404
1948	466	
1949	440	
1950	407	
1951	386	
1952	357	
1953	329	
1954	310	263
1955	292	
1956	281	
1957	264	
1958	252	211
1959	244	
1960	229	
1961	229	
1962	220	
1963	211	171
1964	190	
1965	179	
1966	170	
1967	154	125
1968	149	
1969	146	
1970	137	
1971	134	
1972	131	108
1973	114	
1974 (June)	108	
1976	94	49

Source: Charles F. Keithahn, *The Brewing Industry,* Staff Report of the Bureau of Economics, U.S. Federal Trade Commission (Washington, D.C.: December 1978), 11.

caused by a combination of hostile changes in both demand and supply conditions, although in retrospect the changes in supply conditions appear to have been of the greater importance.

Changes in Demand Conditions

One reason why so many firms and breweries closed during the 1940s and 1950s is that demand for beer declined. Per capita consumption in 1908–17 (the decade before Prohibition) was 19.9 gallons per person annually but fell to 15 gallons in 1958.[12] Apparently beer was not an inferior good during this era; its income elasticity during 1956–59 was estimated to be 0.4,[13] indicating that the rise in

_____

[12]Elzinga (1971), 192.

[13]Thomas F. Hogarty and Kenneth G. Elzinga, "The Demand for Beer," *The Review of Economics and Statistics* 59, no. 2 (May 1972): 195–198.

real incomes during the 1940s and 1950s was not the cause of the decline in demand. A better explanation is found in demographic data; persons in the 21–44 age group account for 69 percent of all beer consumption, and this group was roughly of constant size until the 1960s, when the "baby boom" generation born after 1945 came of drinking age.[14] Moreover, legal drinking ages declined in over half the states, "dry" states were shrinking in number, and drinking became more common among women.[15]

By 1968, per capita beer consumption increased to 16.7 gallons per year and was growing at more than twice the rate of population growth in the 21–44 age cohort. Part of the explanation for the rise in beer consumption was a sharp shift in tastes away from distilled liquors to beers and wines and, within each group, toward the beverages that were light in color, dry in taste, and lower in calories. Many of the smaller breweries specialized in the stronger-flavored beers, and by the 1980s the light beers were the fastest-growing segment of the market.[16]

A second profound change in drinking habits was the rise in home or off-premises consumption and the corresponding decline in tavern and saloon drinking. Taverns usually were supplied with kegs from local or regional breweries, owing to the high costs of shipping the product relative to its value. (Beer is over 90 percent water and is heavy and awkward to transport.) By 1979, however, 88.4 percent of beer was sold in cans or bottles for nontavern consumption,[17] and these products had to be pasteurized to kill the bacteria that would cause spoilage at ambient temperatures (keg beer does not require pasteurization because it is chilled continuously). The per barrel cost of pasteurization was greater for the smaller brewers due to their lower output.

A third change in demand conditions was the shift in preferences to disposable containers, which is, of course, related to the rise in home consumption. The shift from kegs to returnable bottles required an investment that caused some local brewers to go out of business. But the advantage for the survivors was limited by the cost of collecting the empties for refilling; this kept down the mileage radius within which brewers could profitably ship their product. Bottles had to be shipped by trucks rather than less expensive railroad boxcars, owing to the greater rate of breakage on rails. The surviving smaller breweries finally lost even their limited advantage when consumers' preferences shifted to cans, which could be shipped with less breakage by either rail or truck. By 1979, canned beer amounted to more than 60 percent of all the beer produced in the United States.

A fourth change in demand was toward a greater variety of types and sizes of containers. Beer drinkers are fussy. Some prefer only bottles, because they

[14]Charles F. Keithahn, *The Brewing Industry,* Staff Report of the Bureau of Economics, U.S. Federal Trade Commission (Washington, D.C.: December 1978), 29.

[15]Elzinga (1971), 192; (1982), 221.

[16]Keithahn, *The Brewing Industry,* 30–31; and Carl Cannon, "Miller Tries Harder but It's Still Busch's League," *Los Angeles Times,* May 3, 1981.

[17]*Brewers Digest* 40, no. 5 (May 1980): 11.

are convinced that cans alter the taste. Others prefer cans, because they believe that an iced can will chill the liquid faster (a bottle retains heat longer), which improves the flavor. Within each group customers differ in their favorite sizes— 12- or 16-ounce cans plus bottles of various sizes up to a quart. Each different type and size of container requires a separate "closing line"—the complex and highly expensive machinery that fills each container with liquid and then seals it. To maintain between four and six bottling and canning lines, and to operate them at optimal speeds, would require an enormous liquid flow-through and would have imposed on small brewers an additional capital cost in an industry that already was extremely capital intensive.

Sources of Plant Economies

Technological changes in the 1960s and 1970s markedly increased the rate of operation of the closing line. In 1965, the machinery could move about 500 bottles or 900 cans per minute; by 1971, this had increased to either 750 bottles or 1,200 cans;[18] and by the late 1970s the speed of the 12-ounce canning line had risen to about 1,500 cans per minute.[19] With these developments, the minimum efficient size of a brewery increased terrifically. Economist Frederick M. Scherer found that a brewery plant, to utilize the modern closing lines at their optimal rates, would have to produce 1.5 million barrels per year to operate the canning line efficiently, between 0.6 and 0.8 million barrels for the bottling line, and 1 to 1.2 million barrels for the kegging line. The minimum brewery size for just one size of each type of container was therefore at least 3.3 million barrels and the minimum size of a brewery designed to produce beer in a variety of container sizes was 4 to 5 million barrels.[20]

Scherer described the options that brewers with small plant capacities faced:[21]

1. Operating slower but higher–unit cost packaging lines for low-volume products

2. Operating additional high-speed lines at rates below their optimal (that is, cost-minimizing) rate

3. Operating a limited number of packaging lines and thereby incurring appreciable changeover costs

4. Doing without special package sizes and hence suffering loss of sales

5. Building a brewery with a capacity of 4 to 5 million barrels so that one could achieve a better balance with respect to utilization of filling equipment.

---

[18]Charles G. Burch, "While the Big Brewers Quaff, the Little Ones Thirst," *Fortune*, November 1972, 104.

[19]Keithahn, *The Brewing Industry*, 34.

[20]Scherer's unpublished study is described in Keithahn, 34–37.

[21]As cited in Keithahn, 36.

Comparisons between the new beer "factories" that have been designed for high annual capacities versus older and smaller plants are startling. In 1972, for example, Schlitz's modern plant at Memphis, with an annual capacity of 4.4 million barrels, employed only 483 production workers. Falstaff had four out-of-date plants, with a combined annual capacity of 4.1 million barrels and about 1,800 production workers. Each Schlitz worker at the Memphis plant produced 9,110 barrels in 1972, whereas each of the Falstaff workers produced only 2,277. The labor cost of the Schlitz-Memphis beer was estimated at $1.08 per barrel versus $4.39 for Falstaff.[22] Scherer concluded that the labor crew for a modern brewery with an annual capacity of 4 million barrels could be the same size as that for an older plant of 1 million and that the savings in unit labor costs in moving from the smaller plant to the larger would be $.06 per barrel.[23]

Sources of Firm Economies

Brewing firms grew in size during the 1946–76 era not only because of increased economies to the operation of a single plant but owing to greater economies in the operation of a multiplant firm. One of the greatest economies of nationwide production and sales came from lower advertising costs per barrel. The shelf life of approximately three months for bottles and cans gave brewers increased incentives to advertise when their inventories grew.

Brewers also are subject to stringent regulation by the federal government and each state authority, and the cost of compliance can be cut on a per barrel basis by increasing production. The industry is also subject to a federal tax of $.65 per case and various state taxes that averaged $.41 per case in 1985. Taxes represent the single largest cost item in beer—about 12 percent of its price in 1985.[24] From the analysis of tax incidence in Chapter 4, we know that it is unusual for a seller to be able to shift *all* of the burden of taxes onto consumers. The likelihood that taxes pinch smaller brewers inordinately is consistent with a rule that makes smaller brewers eligible for a remission of up to $180,000 per year in federal alcohol taxes.

Scherer estimated that in 1977 a brewing firm needed three to four plants to exhaust all of the available multiplant economies of size and thus to minimize average cost. A firm having four breweries of minimum efficient size (roughly 4.5 million barrels of annual capacity) could produce a total of 18 million barrels per year. Such a firm in 1977 would have brewed 11.5 percent of all the beer sold in the United States, and four such firms would have produced 46 percent. To wit, four optimally sized firms in 1977 could have supplied about half of the market at minimum long-run average cost.[25]

---

[22]Burch, "While Big Brewers Quaff," 104–106.

[23]As cited in Keithahn, *The Brewing Industry*, 37.

[24]Brooks Jackson, "Brewing Industry Organizes Lobbying Coalition to Head Off Any Increase in U.S. Tax on Beer," *The Wall Street Journal*, July 11, 1985.

[25]Keithahn, *The Brewing Industry*, 59.

Table 10.2
Changes in Annual
Capacities of Brewing
Firms: 1962, 1979,
and 1985

	1962	1979	1985
Total brewing firms in operation	156	47[a]	44
Annual capacity above 100,000 barrels	80	32	21
Annual capacity below 100,000 barrels	76	15	23[b]

[a]Of these, 12 firms were still in operation after having been absorbed by another brewing firm.

[b]Includes 12 microbreweries.

Sources: For 1962: *World Directory of Breweries, 1963–64* (Mount Vernon, N.Y.: American Brewer Publishing Corporation, 1963), 334–335; and *American Brewer,* 1963, 1964.
For 1979: "Buyers Guide and Brewery Directory for 1980," *Brewers Digest* 50, no. 1 (January 1980, pt. 2): 10–28.
For 1985: *Brewers Digest* 61, no. 2 (February 1986): 18–19.

What is just as surprising as the huge minimum efficient size of the brewery firm in the late 1970s is the extent to which the minimum efficient size has increased. Ira and Ann Horowitz studied the period 1947–62 and estimated that the range of minimum average cost for a firm began at 1.5 million barrels of annual capacity and was exhausted at about 3 million barrels.[26] On the strength of this estimate, the Horowitzes predicted in 1965 the coming slaughter of the smaller brewers:

> . . . [T]here are still some 40 out of the 148 companies in the brewing industry with production capacity of less than 100,000 barrels a year, the minimum efficient size of plant, and we can look for these firms to leave the industry in the near future. An additional 33 firms have production capacities of less than 200,000 barrels which, while greater than the minimum efficient size of plant, is well below the level necessary to achieve economies of scale. The future for these firms, too, would appear to be none too bright.[27]

Table 10.2 shows how correct the Horowitzes were and how great the slaughter was. Brewing firms with less than 100,000 barrels of annual capacity made up half the industry in 1962 but less than 30 percent in 1979. In 1962 there were 27 firms between 100,000 and 200,000 barrels, but in 1979 there were 4.[28]

These dramatic changes can be illustrated in the following pair of cost diagrams. Figure 10.14(a) shows the relevant long-run planning possibilities facing a brewery firm for the period 1947–62, based on the Horowitzes' estimates, before the technological advances permitting a sharp increase in the speeds of the bottle- and can-closing lines. Cost curve $SAC_{1947-62}$ reflects the minimum estimated efficient plant size of 0.1 million barrels per year; long-run planning curve $LAC_{1947-62}$ shows the exhaustion of economies of firm size at a range of output rates between 1.5 and 3 million barrels per year. The position

---

[26]Horowitz and Horowitz, "Firms in a Declining Market," 150.

[27]Ibid., 152.

[28]See sources for Table 10.2.

**Figure 10.14
Minimum Plant Sizes
(*SAC*) and Firm Sizes
(*LAC*) for Efficient
Production, 1947–
1962 and 1977**

In panel (a) $SAC_{1947-62}$
shows the minimum one-
plant firm size compared
with $LAC_{1947-62}$ for a
multiplant brewing firm
as estimated by the
Horowitzes. The
introduction of new
technology in the
brewing industry after
that period results in the
panel (b) comparison in
1977 as estimated by
Scherer.

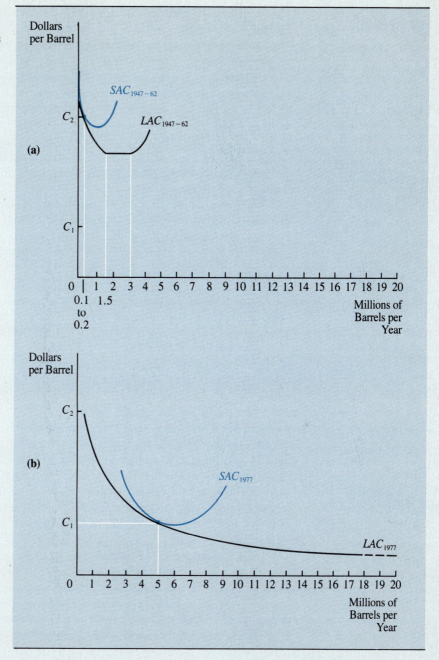

of $SAC_{1947-62}$ clearly shows that a firm having a single plant of minimum efficient
size could not compete with the beer sold at lower costs by efficiently sized
larger firms during this period. These smaller breweries either were abandoned
or were merged into more efficient, larger configurations that allowed their
owners to take advantage of economies of advertising, transportation, and use

of cans that were available for firms of at least 1.5 million barrels' annual capacity.

The technological changes that came about with the development of faster closing lines caused a downward shift in the long-run planning curve to the position shown by LAC_{1977} in Figure 10.14(b). Brewery firms in the 1947–62 era had to plan their output rates within the options shown by $LAC_{1947-62}$. But by 1977 they had to contemplate the most efficient adjustment away from the point on $LAC_{1947-62}$ at which they had been operating to a prospective rate of output selected from the long-run possibilities on the new planning curve, LAC_{1977}. The minimum sizes necessary to exhaust available economies in 1977 were estimated by Scherer at about 5 million barrels per year for the individual plant, which is illustrated by SAC_{1977}, and about 18 million barrels per year for the firm, which is illustrated by LAC_{1977}. (Scherer's data are not clear about the shape of LAC_{1977} for output rates greater than 18 million barrels per year, so we have drawn that segment of the curve as a dashed line to reflect this uncertainty.)

Effects of Size Economies

Has the decline in brewing firms encouraged monopoly or collusive pricing among those that remain? This was the suspicion of the U.S. Department of Justice, which attacked mergers in the 1960s and again in the early 1980s. If the department's theory was correct, then mergers would have led the surviving firms to reduce output and raise prices. But if mergers were induced by economies, then the surviving firms would raise output and lower prices. Beer prices are difficult to adjust for changes in levels of quality owing to the growth in premium beers. But in general they rose during the 1970s by less than the consumer price index, and the biggest brewers increased prices by less than the industry average.[29] In a study of mergers in the 1980s, William S. Lynk found that total output was higher in areas where the major brewers directed their supplies. He concluded that the "shift in sales from small to large brewers [was] accomplished, not by interference with the supply of the small, but by expansion of supply from the large," and that the largest brewers cut prices as their output increased.[30]

These data support the hypothesis that the industry's shakeout was promoted by economies rather than attempts to monopolize, and that the Department of Justice's theory was wrong. Early on, the stronger national brewers spotted the trends toward larger- and multiple-plant operations, placed big bets on the accuracy of their forecasts, and reaped substantial returns while moving their industry toward a more efficient position via the price system.[31] Size alone was

[29]Cannon, "Miller Tries Harder"; and "Growth of Anheuser-Busch, Miller Puts Squeeze on Smaller Brewers," *The Wall Street Journal,* January 5, 1982.

[30]William S. Lynk, "Interpreting Rising Concentration: The Case of Beer," *Journal of Business* 57, no. 1 (1984): 53–54.

[31]Donald Alan Norman, *Structural Change and Performance in the U.S. Brewing Industry* (Los Angeles: University of California, doctoral dissertation, 1975), 50, 66, 103.

insufficient to guarantee survival, however. Success required quality of product and effectiveness in marketing as well as low production costs.

Recent Adjustments

By the early 1980s, the sharp rise in beer consumption was over. The country was undergoing what historians may call the second temperance movement of this century. Concerns over alcohol and drunk driving were rising, and some states were raising the legal drinking ages that they lowered in a more permissive era. Happy hours were "out"; health was "in." As one wag put it, "It's hard, after all, to jog with a hangover." People were switching to such low-alcohol products as wine coolers and nonalcoholic "beer" and fruit juices. Ritzy hotels started to serve expensive afternoon "teas" in cocktail lounges. The population was aging: in 1983, males 18–24—the main beer-drinking cohort—declined for the first time in decades. Per-capita annual beer consumption peaked in 1981 at 35.6 gallons, and declined 7 percent by 1983. In Britain, pub consumption fell 12 percent from 1979 to 1985, although wine coolers appear to be making pub drinking more fashionable again.[32]

Demand changes were translated into production changes. Output fell in 1984 less than 1 percent, but it was the first drop ever. Miller never opened the huge plant it built in Ohio in 1980 when its demand was growing 14 percent a year.[33] The demise of even more breweries and reduced industry profits were in the cards, but with smaller penalties for the entrepreneurs who made the necessary adjustments quickly.

Two recent developments bear watching. Table 10.2 indicated that the number of brewing firms with capacities of less than 100,000 barrels per year increased between 1979 and 1985, reversing the trend between 1962 and 1979. The reversal is due to the growth of "microbreweries"—small firms making specialized beers selling at prices to compete with imports rather than major brewing firms. Some produce draft beer for restaurants or on-premises "brew-pub" consumption. They sell mainly in local markets and avoid the investment in closing lines that are efficient only for larger operations. A dozen microbreweries were operating in 1985, and none before 1980. A few are almost backyard operations, producing under 1,000 barrels per year, that may have sprung from hobbies. Their success has been mixed and their prospects are uncertain.[34]

[32]"Water, Water Everywhere," *Time,* May 20, 1985, 69–73; David F. Musto, "New Temperance vs. Neo-Prohibition," *The Wall Street Journal,* June 25, 1984; Trish Hall, "Americans Drink Less, and Makers of Alcohol Feel a Little Woozy," *The Wall Street Journal,* March 14, 1984; U.S. Department of Commerce, Bureau of the Census, *Statistical Abstract of the United States, 1985,* 105th ed. (Washington, D.C.: U.S. Government Printing Office, December 1984), 765; Lisa Wood, "Brewing: The Customer Calls the Tune," *Financial Times (London),* May 15, 1985.

[33]*Modern Brewery Age,* March 25, 1985, MS-55; Peter Nulty, "Living with the Limits of Marlboro Magic," *Fortune,* March 18, 1985, 24–33.

[34]New York City used to be the brewery capital of the nation, owing to its huge population and restaurant trade. But production ceased in the 1950s because of high taxes, labor costs, and levels of chlorine and other pollutants in its water supply. Since 1984, however, two new microbreweries have catered to restaurants. ("Big Apple Now Has Two Breweries," *Los Angeles Times,* December 27, 1985.)

The second development is the introduction by Heileman, in a new Milwaukee brewery, of a low-capital technology from Britain and Germany. By unifying equipment at two stages of the usual brew kettle operation, the plant is operated by only six employees, and is intended eventually to produce about 72,000 barrels per year. It makes only draft brands, thereby avoiding the expensive closing lines. Heileman expects these beers to be cost-competitive with higher-priced imports but not with the major U.S. brands.[35] How much this new technology reduces plant economies remains to be seen.

_____

[35]George W. Hilton, correspondence, September 18, 1986.

Suggested Readings

The classic statement of cost-curve analysis is

Viner, Jacob. "Cost Curves and Supply Curves." *Zeitschrift für Nationalökonomie* 3 (1931): 23–46. Reprinted in American Economic Association, *Readings in Price Theory*, edited by George J. Stigler and Kenneth E. Boulding, 198–232. Homewood, Ill.: Richard D. Irwin, 1952.

For more advanced treatments of the cost-curve apparatus, see

Friedman, Milton. *Price Theory*, Chap. 5. Chicago: Aldine Publishing Co., 1976.

Stigler, George J. *The Theory of Price*, 3rd ed., Chaps. 6 and 9. New York: Crowell-Collier and Macmillan, 1966.

Problems and Questions for Discussion

1. It is often argued that the reason for being of state universities is that they provide higher education at a lower cost than do private universities. Assuming that the quality of output is the same for each type of university, discuss this issue in terms of the annual costs
   a. To a student and his or her family
   b. To the society as a whole

2. Some developing countries have asked for compensation from Western

countries for those of their talented people who go to universities in the West and remain because of better job prospects. After studying the issue, the United Nations has offered three alternative economic concepts for valuing the loss to the home country:

(1) "Historic cost," or the actual expenses of educating the student, based on prevailing prices of educational services in the host country. This measure does not take into account differing qualities of education obtained at different universities, the extent of financing by the home country or subsidization by the host country, or any income earned by the student while attending a university.

(2) "Opportunity cost," defined by the U.N. as the expense that the host country would incur to duplicate the foreign student's skills by educating one of its own citizens. This measure does not take into account whether the person would have been employed if he or she had returned to the home country or whether a portion of income earned in the host country would be remitted to relatives or others in the home country.

(3) "Discounted present value" of the income actually earned or expected to be earned by the student in the host country. ("UNCTAD Takes on the Brain Drain," *Regulation,* November/December 1982, 8–11.)

    a. Which measure has the most logical economic rationale?

    b. Which measure would require the most compensation?

    c. If forced to choose among them, which would you choose? Why?

3. In 1983 falling interest rates caused a surge in trading of commodities on the Chicago Mercantile Exchange. However, as trading volume increased, the errors that traders typically make rose at an even greater rate. During one hectic nine-day period, 42 percent more errors were generated than during a similar period of light trading. On some particularly pressing days, 10 percent of the transactions had errors; hurried hand signals on the trading floor confused buy orders with sell orders (when talk is rapid, "fifteen" can easily be mistaken for "fifty"). Traders are responsible for their mistakes—during this period one trader lost $36,750 in one day. (Thomas Petzinger, Jr., "As Activity Rises in Financial-Futures Pits, Expensive Mistakes by Brokers Proliferate," *The Wall Street Journal,* November 23, 1982.)

    a. Why would trading increase when interest rates fall?

    b. How would you depict with cost curves of a trading firm the fact that trading errors tend to rise faster than the volume of trading? Explain carefully.

4. A steel mill uses labor and capital to produce tons of steel. The prices of labor and capital are p_{l1} and p_{k1}, respectively. With an isoquant-isocost diagram show how:

    a. Its long-run total cost curve is generated and explain the shape of the curve.

    b. Its short-run total cost curve is generated and explain the shape of the curve.

5. Show with appropriate diagrams and explain the effects of each of the following situations on (1) the firm's least-cost combinations of resources and (2) the firm's long-run total cost curves:

   a. The Department of Agriculture eliminates regulations preventing producers of meat from using tuberculosis-infected hogs in such intensely cooked products as bologna, frankfurters, and sausages. (Richard L. Hudson, "Move to Cut Regulation of Meat Stirs Criticism," *The Wall Street Journal,* November 2, 1981.)

   b. Prices of Chinese goose down increased by 75 percent in 1981 (400 percent relative to 1976). Consequently, U.S. makers of winter clothing were induced to substitute in part cheaper feathers and/or synthetic fibers for down in jacket insulation. Yet down parkas costing only $50 a few years ago cost $130 in the winter of 1981–82, even though the later ones were not pure down. (Frederick Rose, "High Costs of Down Insulation Send Some Winter Clothing Makers Ducking," *The Wall Street Journal,* June 4, 1981.)

6. Diagram and explain the effect on total, average, and marginal cost curves of the changes in isoquants or expansion paths in each of the following problems from Chapter 9:

   a. The substitution of fructose for sugar in sugared soft drinks from Figure 9.9

   b. The substitution of new sweeteners for aspartame in diet soft drinks from Problem 9(c)

7. Diagram and explain the effect on total, average, and marginal cost curves of the changes in isoquants or expansion paths given in each of the following problems from Chapter 9:

   a. The substitution of steel for aluminum in Chrysler cars from Problem 10

   b. The choice between inputs that pollute and inputs that do not pollute for a steel producer confronted with the EPA fines described in Problem 11(a) and (b)

8. The long-run average cost curve of a firm is given. Locate an output rate to the left of its minimum point. What size of plant should the firm use to produce that output? Show these points diagrammatically, and draw in the long-run and short-run marginal cost curves. Explain your answers.

*9. Assume that your university has two dormitories with different levels of average cost. How should a given number of students per year be assigned between the two to minimize total costs? Explain without drawing a diagram.

*10. Most of the firm average cost curves in Chapter 10 are U-shaped, implying a unique output rate that minimizes average cost. But in Figure 10.14, the

_____

*Denotes an application-oriented problem.

middle segment of the beer industry's long-run average cost curve is flat, implying a range of equally efficient firm sizes. Does this imply that more industries have firm average cost curves that are U-shaped than have a flat segment? (George J. Stigler, "The Economies of Scale," *Journal of Law and Economics* 1 (October 1958): 54–71.)

*11. Using the scheme in Figure 10.14(b), draw the U-shaped *SAC* curves for the new Heileman plant and for a microbrewery, based on the factual discussion in the text. Explain the output rates and average cost levels that appear to be associated with these plants relative to the SAC_{1977} curve for a major brewery plant in Figure 10.14(b).

Chapter 10 Appendix _____

THE GEOMETRY OF SHORT-RUN PER UNIT COST CURVES_____

The relationships between total cost curves and per unit cost curves can be shown geometrically. Using the three total cost curves as starting points, we shall derive from them the corresponding per unit cost curves. Then we shall show geometrically the relationship between the average cost curve and the marginal cost curve.

The Average Fixed Cost Curve

In Figure 10.15 the average fixed cost curve in panel (b) is derived from the total fixed cost curve of panel (a). The quantity scales of the two diagrams are the same. The vertical axis of panel (a) measures total fixed costs, whereas that of panel (b) measures fixed cost per unit.

Consider output x in panel (a), where total fixed cost is measured by xA. Now consider the straight line $0A$; its slope is $xA/0x$, which is numerically equal to average fixed cost $0R$ in panel (b). Likewise, at output x_1 average fixed cost $0R_1$ in panel (b) equals the slope of $0A_1$, or $x_1A_1/0x_1$.

Figure 10.15   The Geometry of *TFC* and *AFC* Curves

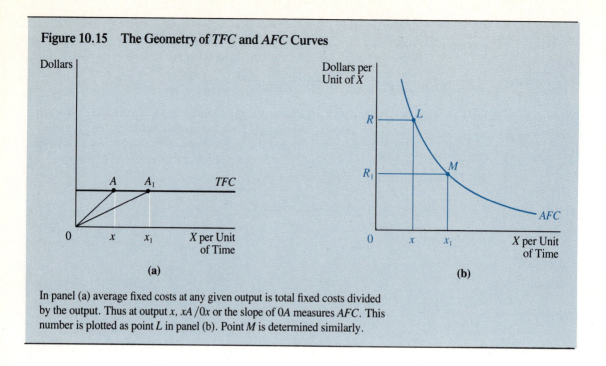

In panel (a) average fixed costs at any given output is total fixed costs divided by the output. Thus at output x, $xA/0x$ or the slope of $0A$ measures *AFC*. This number is plotted as point L in panel (b). Point M is determined similarly.

At successively larger outputs the slopes of the corresponding $0A$ lines become smaller and smaller, showing that average fixed cost decreases as output increases; however, it can never reach zero. The numerical slopes of the $0A$ lines plotted against the respective outputs for which they are drawn comprise the average fixed cost curve of panel (b).

Geometrically, the *AFC* curve is a rectangular hyperbola. It approaches, but never reaches, both the dollar axis and the quantity axis and is convex to the origin of the diagram. The distinguishing feature of a rectangular hyperbola is that at any point on the curve, such as L, the values represented on each axis, when multiplied together, produce the same mathematical product as results when the corresponding values at any other point on the curve, such as M, are multiplied together—in other words, $0x \times 0R = 0x_1 \times 0R_1$. Such must necessarily be the case for the average fixed cost curve. Because total fixed costs are constant and because average fixed cost at any output multiplied by that output equals total fixed cost, the mathematical product of any output times its corresponding average fixed cost must equal the mathematical product of any other output times its corresponding average fixed cost.

The Average Variable Cost Curve

In Figure 10.16 the average variable cost curve in panel (b) is derived from the total variable cost curve in panel (a). The process of derivation is similar to that used in obtaining the *AFC* curve. At output x, *TVC* equals xB; hence *AVC* at

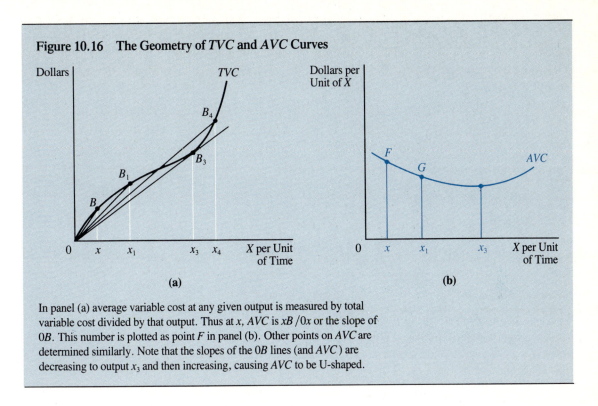

Figure 10.16 The Geometry of *TVC* and *AVC* Curves

In panel (a) average variable cost at any given output is measured by total variable cost divided by that output. Thus at x, *AVC* is $xB/0x$ or the slope of $0B$. This number is plotted as point F in panel (b). Other points on *AVC* are determined similarly. Note that the slopes of the $0B$ lines (and *AVC*) are decreasing to output x_3 and then increasing, causing *AVC* to be U-shaped.

output x equals $xB/0x$, which equals the slope of line $0B$. At x_1, *AVC* equals $x_1B_1/0x_1$, which equals the slope of $0B_1$. At x_3, *AVC* equals $x_3B_3/0x_3$, which equals the slope of $0B_3$. At x_4, *AVC* equals $x_4B_4/0x_4$, which equals the slope of $0B_4$. The numerical slopes of the $0B$ lines plotted against their respective outputs trace out the *AVC* curve of panel (b).

The geometric derivation of the *AVC* curve makes it clear that the curve takes its shape from the *TVC* curve. Between output 0 and output x_3, the $0B$ line for each successively larger output must have a smaller slope than the one for the preceding output; hence between 0 and x_3, the *AVC* curve must be decreasing. At output x_3, line $0B_3$ is just tangent to the *TVC* curve and thus has a smaller slope than any other $0B$ line can possibly have. At x_3, *AVC* is as low as it can get. At outputs greater than x_3, the $0B$ lines will increase in slope, meaning that *AVC* is increasing. The *AVC* curve must have a U shape if we have correctly established the shape of the *TVC* curve.

The Average Cost Curve

In Figure 10.17 the average cost curve in panel (b) is derived from the total cost curve in panel (a) in the same way that the *AVC* curve is derived from the *TVC* curve. At output x, *TC* equals xC, so *AC* equals $xC/0x$, which equals the

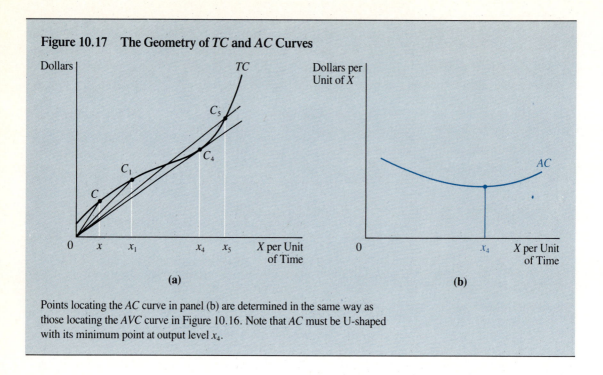

Figure 10.17   The Geometry of *TC* and *AC* Curves

(a)   **(b)**

Points locating the *AC* curve in panel (b) are determined in the same way as those locating the *AVC* curve in Figure 10.16. Note that *AC* must be U-shaped with its minimum point at output level x_4.

slope of line $0C$. At output x_1, *AC* equals $x_1C_1/0x_1$, which equals the slope of $0C_1$. At output x_4, *AC* equals $x_4C_4/0x_4$, which equals the slope of $0C_4$. At output x_5, *AC* equals $x_5C_5/0x_5$, which equals the slope of $0C_5$. The slopes of the $0C$ lines plotted against the corresponding outputs locate the *AC* curve in panel (b).

If the shape of the *TC* curve is correct, the *AC* curve must be a U-shaped curve. The $0C$ lines decrease in slope as output increases up to output x_4. At output x_4, $0C_4$ is tangent to the *TC* curve and consequently is the one of least slope. Here *AC* is minimum. At greater outputs, the slopes of the $0C$ lines are increasing, that is, *AC* is increasing.

The Relationship between *AC* and *MC*

The relationship between *AC* and *MC* can be shown geometrically with the aid of the *TC* curve of Figure 10.18. Consider output x_1, where average cost is equal to the slope of line $0C_1$. Marginal cost at output x_1 is equal to the slope of the *TC* curve at that output. The line $0C_1$ has a greater slope than does the *TC* curve at that output; hence average cost is greater than marginal cost at x_1. This will be the case for any output up to x_4. At output x_4, the slope of line $0C_4$ is equal to the slope of the total cost curve, meaning that average cost and marginal cost are equal at that output. As we have already seen, average cost is minimum at output x_4. At output x_5, the slope of line $0C_5$ is less than the

Figure 10.18
The Geometry of *AC* and *MC* Curves

At successively higher output levels from 0 to x_4, the $0C$ lines and average costs are necessarily decreasing. Also, at points such as C_1 the slope of the *TC* curve, or marginal cost, must be less than the slope of the $0C$ line, or average cost. Thus from 0 to x_4, $MC < AC$. At x_4 the slope of $0C_4$ equals the slope of *TC* so $MC = AC$. Similarly, at outputs greater than x_4, $MC > AC$.

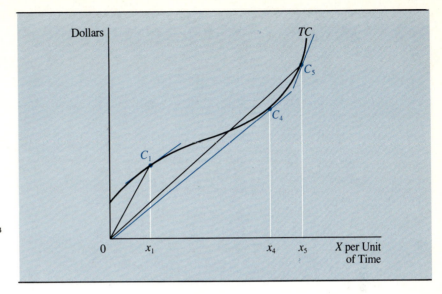

slope of the *TC* curve, meaning that marginal cost is greater than average cost at that output. This relationship will hold at any output above x_4—that is, at outputs for which average cost is increasing. Thus when average cost is decreasing, marginal cost is less than average cost. When average cost is increasing, marginal cost is greater than average cost.

PRICES AND OUTPUT LEVELS OF GOODS AND SERVICES

WE bring demand and costs together in Part Four. Building on the foundations laid in Parts Two and Three, we develop models of the market mechanism to show how prices and output levels of goods and services are determined under each of the basic selling market structures that were introduced in Chapter 8.

Chapter 11

PRICING AND OUTPUT UNDER PURE COMPETITION

The purely competitive model of prices and outputs is constructed in this chapter. It explains how production is organized by prices and profits in a purely competitive, or frictionless, private enterprise economy. Ways in which monopoly elements modify the operation and the results of the system are taken into account in Chapters 12 and 13.

Pure competition was defined in Chapter 3. Its prime characteristics are (1) product homogeneity among the sellers in the market; (2) many buyers and sellers of the product—that is, enough of each so that no one is large enough relative to the entire market to influence product price; (3) an absence of artificial restraints on demand, supply, and product price; and (4) mobility of goods and resources.

THE VERY SHORT RUN

The *very short run,* or *market period,* refers to situations in which supplies of products are already in existence. For example, demand for a product may be seasonal, with production scheduled ahead of the months in which the item is to be sold. The clothing industries are cases in point; spring, summer, fall, and winter production is based on estimated seasonal demands and occurs well in advance of the sales season. Other examples include retail markets for fresh fruit and vegetables: retailers purchase stocks of perishable goods; once the stocks are on hand, they must be disposed of before they spoil. Still another example is that of a product produced seasonally for a demand that continues year round; production of wheat and other farm crops typifies this situation. Two basic problems must be solved by the economy in the very short run: (1) How are existing supplies of goods to be allocated or rationed among the many consumers who want them? (2) How are given supplies to be rationed over their entire very-short-run periods?

Rationing among Consumers

Price is the mechanism for rationing or allocating a fixed supply among the consumers who want it. Suppose that the period during which the supply is fixed is one day and that the demand curve of Figure 11.1 shows the different quantities per day that consumers will take from the market at different possible prices. The supply curve is vertical, since supply for the day is fixed. Price *p* will clear the market. Everyone who wants the commodity at that price will receive it in the desired amounts. At a price below *p* a shortage will develop, and consumers will drive the price up. At a price above *p* surpluses will exist, and individual sellers will lower their prices to get them off their hands. At price *p* consumers voluntarily ration themselves to the fixed supply.

Rationing over Time

Prices also serve to ration a fixed supply over time, but this process is more complex and uncertain. Suppose that in Figure 11.2 the market period is one year, but the demand curve is for four-month time units. To simplify matters,

**Figure 11.1
Very-Short-Run
Rationing among
Consumers**

With a fixed supply of x, the equilibrium price p will ration the good so that there are no surpluses or shortages. Every buyer receiving the good values it at p per unit or more.

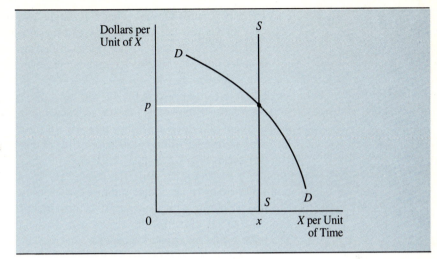

imagine further that the demand curve per four-month period remains constant. Sellers try to anticipate the market for each period and sell or hold their supplies accordingly.

Since the diagram applies to four-month periods only, the supply curve for the first period will not be vertical, because sellers have the option of selling in any or all of the three periods. During the first period, sellers would be willing to sell more at higher prices than at lower prices, given their expected future price possibilities. The supply curve would be upward sloping to the right, like S_1S_1, yielding a market price of p_1 and a quantity exchanged of x_1.

**Figure 11.2
Very-Short-Run
Rationing over Time**

Letting the very short run be 12 months and the time unit of the diagram be 4 months, S_1S_1, S_2S_2, and S_3S_3 represent the successive supply curves for the time periods of the year. With the constant demand for the three time periods, product price will be p_1 for the first period, p_2 for the second period, and p_3 for the third, if sellers correctly anticipate market forces.

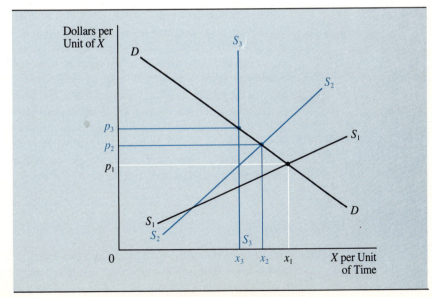

The supply curve for the second four-month period would usually lie above S_1S_1 and tend to be less elastic. It would lie above S_1S_1 because of sellers' expectations of sufficiently higher prices in that period as compared with the first to cover storage costs plus a return on investment in the goods carried over. There is a possibility—but not a certainty—that at relatively lower prices the supply curve for the second period will lie to the right of S_1S_1, as docs S_2S_2. This may occur if something happens to change sellers' evaluations of what will happen in the third period. If they now expect lower prices in the third period, they may in turn be willing to dispose of larger quantities in the second period at lower prices than in the first. Their opportunities for disposing of held-over supplies have been narrowed. The smaller elasticity at various prices is also a result of the narrowing of opportunities for disposing of the supplies held over. The periods during which supply can be disposed of now have been reduced to two. The supply curve for the second period would look something like S_2S_2. The price would be p_2 and the quantity sold x_2.

The third four-month period will be identical with the case shown in Figure 11.1. The remaining supply must be disposed of in this period; consequently, the supply curve in Figure 11.2 will be S_3S_3. Note that S_3S_3 lies above S_2S_2 except at low prices and that it is less elastic than S_2S_2—in fact, S_3S_3 is completely inelastic. The price will be p_3, and the quantity sold will be x_3.

The successively higher prices for the four-month periods will occur as shown only if sellers correctly anticipate demand and the amounts that should be held over. If sellers misjudge the future market and hold large quantities over to the second and third periods, the prices during those periods may fall below that of the first period. If sellers' anticipations are correct, the price for each successive period should be sufficiently higher than that of preceding periods to pay storage costs, a normal rate of return on investment in held-over supplies, and compensation for the risks in holding supplies over to succeeding periods.

Thus price is the rationer of fixed supplies over time. Sellers or speculators, as the case may be, in holding supplies off the market during the early part of the overall very-short-run period cause the price to be higher during that time than it would otherwise be. By their speculative activity they smooth out both the prices and the quantities sold over the entire period. In the absence of any speculative activity, relatively large quantities would be placed on the market early in the period, holding the price down; relatively small quantities available in the latter part of the period would cause the price to be high. The speculative activity described, while not eliminating the upward price trend over time, does much to narrow the differential between the early and late parts of the period. Activity of this type occurs regularly in the markets for those storable farm products lying outside the price support program.

sunk costs
Historical expenditures that are irrelevant for current or future decisions about what to exchange or produce.

Sunk Costs

Once a good is on the market in fixed quantities, costs of production play no part in the determination of its price. The price will be determined solely by the fixed supply, together with demand for the product.[1] It is futile for holders of such a product to try to recoup production costs. A purely competitive seller, who cannot consume the product, will prefer to dispose of the holdings at any price above zero rather than keep it indefinitely. Old bread and overripe bananas are cases in point. Costs of production enter the picture only when there is some possibility of varying the supply produced over the time period under consideration. Such a possibility exists in both the short and the long run, which we shall consider next.

THE SHORT RUN

As we saw in Chapter 10, the short run is a time period in which a firm can vary its output but does not have time to change its size of plant. The number of firms in a market is fixed, because new firms do not have time to enter and existing firms do not have time to leave. Any changes in market output must come from the fixed plant capacity of existing firms. Since each firm is too small relative to the market in which it sells to be able to affect the market price of the product, the problem facing it is that of determining what output to produce and sell. For the market as a whole, the market price and market output must be determined.

The Firm

As a starting point, we use the premise that a firm's objective is to maximize its profits or minimize its losses if it cannot make profits. This premise can be modified to include such objectives as sales maximization with a minimum profit constraint, concern for the environment, enhancement of community cultural activities, and the like. But usually we expect a firm to make those choices that will enable it to make more profits rather than less, and such choices lead toward profit maximization.

profits
The difference between a firm's total receipts and its total costs when the former exceed the latter, including as costs the alternative costs of all resources used.

Profits   Since the concept of profit is ambiguous enough to require explicit definition, a note on profits is in order before proceeding further. Economic **profits** are a pure surplus or an excess of total receipts over *all* costs of production incurred by the firm. Included as costs are obligations incurred for all resources used equal to what those resources could earn employed in their next best alternative uses, that is, the opportunity or alternative costs of all resources used. These costs include returns to the owners of capital used equivalent to what they could get had they invested in capital elsewhere in the economy. They include implicit returns to labor owned by the operator of the business. Thus profits are so much "gravy" for the firm.

---

[1]Note that in the example of Figure 11.2 market supply is fixed at an absolute quantity for the third period only.

The contrast between the concept of economic profits as just defined and the accountant's concept of a corporation's net income or "profits" should help make this definition clear. (Corporation income taxes will be ignored.) A corporation's "profits" are determined by the accountant as follows:

Gross income − Expenses = Net income or "profits."
(including interest
payments on bonds,
amortization expenses,
depreciation expenses,
and so on)

However, from the point of view of economics, certain costs have been left out of consideration. Obligations to the owners of the corporation's capital (its stockholders) are as much costs of production as are those incurred for labor or raw materials. Corporations are thought to pay dividends to stockholders *from their profits.* But from the point of view of economic theory, this is not correct. To arrive at *economic profits,* returns to investors, *including dividends,* equal to what those investors could have earned elsewhere in the economy must be subtracted from the corporation's net income as follows:

$$\begin{matrix} \text{Net income} \\ \text{or ``profits''} \end{matrix} - \begin{matrix} \text{Returns} \\ \text{to investors} \end{matrix} = \begin{matrix} \text{Economic} \\ \text{profits} \end{matrix}$$

What happens to profits made by an individual firm? They accrue to the firm's owners in either or both of two forms: (1) higher direct money payments or (2) increases in the value of the owners' holdings. The former means higher-than-average dividends to corporation stockholders, or, in the case of partnerships and proprietorships, higher money payments than would have been received if the individuals had worked or invested elsewhere in the economy. The latter means that the firm keeps some of the profits as retained earnings to expand or improve itself, to use as working capital, or for other purposes. Retained earnings are expected to increase the value of the owners' holdings.

Profit Maximization: Total Curves   Profit maximization requires a comparison of total costs with total receipts at various possible output levels and choice of the output at which total receipts exceed total costs by the greatest amount. Total receipts, or total revenue at different outputs, are plotted against short-run total costs at various levels of output in Figure 11.3. The curve labeled π in panel (b) shows profits at those output levels. The total cost curve here is the short-run total cost curve of Chapter 10. The total receipts curve needs further elaboration.

Since the purely competitive firm can sell either large or small outputs at the same price per unit, its total receipts curve will be a linear, upward-sloping curve starting at zero. If sales of the firm are zero, so are total receipts; if sales are one unit of output per unit of time, the firm's total receipts are equal to the price of the product; at two units of output and sales, total receipts will be twice

**Figure 11.3
Short-Run Profit
Maximization:
Total Curves**

A firm's profits (or
losses) are measured by
the vertical distance
between *TR* and *TC*. At
x', losses are *FG*. At *x*,
profits are *AB*. Panel (b)
shows the profit curve.

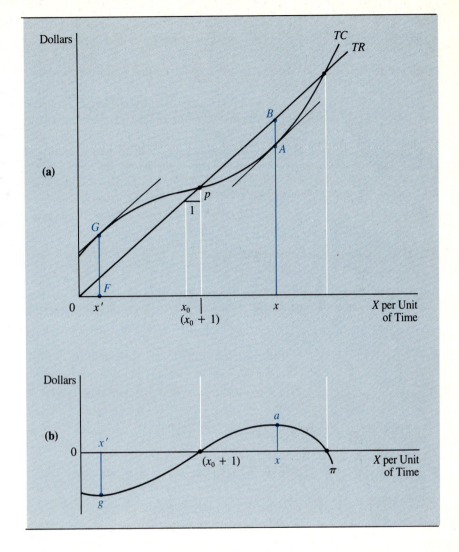

the price of the product. Each one-unit addition to the firm's sales per unit of time will increase total receipts by a constant amount—the price per unit of product. Hence the total receipts curve is upward sloping and linear.[2]

Profits of the firm are maximum at output *x*, where in panel (a) the vertical distance of *TR* above *TC* is greatest. The amount is measured by *AB*. At output *x*, the slopes of the two curves are equal. At outputs just smaller than *x*, the slope of *TR* exceeds that of *TC*; hence the two curves spread farther and farther

_____

[2]The total receipts curve can be written as

$$R = f(x) = px.$$

marginal revenue
The change in a firm's
total revenue per unit
change in its sales level.

apart as output increases. At outputs just greater than x, the slope of TC exceeds that of TR; hence the two curves come closer and closer together as output rises.

The amount by which the firm's total receipts change when its sales are changed by one unit is called **marginal revenue.** Under conditions of pure competition, since the product price is fixed in the firm's view the change in total receipts brought about by a one-unit change in sales is necessarily equal to the product price—marginal revenue and the product price for the purely competitive seller are the same thing. In panel (a), an increase in sales from x_0 to $(x_0 + 1)$ increases TR by an amount equal to p. Thus both marginal revenue and product price are equal to the slope of the TR curve.[3]

The necessary conditions for profit maximization can be restated in terms of marginal revenue and marginal cost. Since marginal cost is equal to the slope of the TC curve and marginal revenue is equal to the slope of the TR curve, profits are maximized at the output at which marginal cost equals marginal revenue.[4] At outputs between x' and x, we can see that marginal revenue is greater than marginal cost. Therefore, larger outputs in this range up to x will add more to the firm's total receipts than to its total costs and consequently will make net additions to profits or net deductions from losses. Beyond output x, marginal cost is greater than marginal revenue. Larger outputs beyond x add more to total costs than to total receipts and cause profits to fall.[5]

Profit Maximization: Per Unit Curves   Analysis of the firm's profit-maximizing output is usually put in terms of per unit cost and revenue curves. The basic analysis is the same as before, but the diagrammatic treatment is in a different form. The firm's short-run average cost curve SAC and short-run marginal cost curve SMC are shown in Figure 11.4, as is the demand curve dd

---

[3]The relationship between marginal revenue and total revenue is the same as that between marginal utility and total utility, between marginal physical product and total product of a resource, and between marginal cost and total cost. Since
$$R = f(x) = px,$$
in which p is a constant, then
$$MR = \frac{dR}{dx} = f'(x) = p.$$

[4]This statement must be used with caution. Consider output x' in Figure 11.3. At this output losses rather than profits are maximized, although marginal cost equals marginal revenue. The relationship between the TR curve and the TC curve at the output of equality between MR and MC must be considered carefully.

[5]Denoting profits by π and letting the total cost function be $C = g(x)$, then $\pi = R - C = f(x) - g(x)$.
The first-order conditions for profit maximization are
$$\frac{d\pi}{dx} = f'(x) - g'(x) = 0, \quad \text{or} \quad f'(x) = g'(x); \quad \text{that is,} \quad MR = MC.$$
If the second-order conditions show $\dfrac{d^2\pi}{dx^2} < 0$, the output is one of maximum profit—like x in Figure 11.3(b). If the second-order conditions show
$$\frac{d^2\pi}{dx^2} > 0,$$ losses are maximized. This is the case at x' in Figure 11.3(b).

**Figure 11.4
Short-Run Profit
Maximization: Per
Unit Curves**

A firm's profits are
maximized at the output
at which *SMC* = *MR*. Its
total profits are the blue
area *cpmn*.

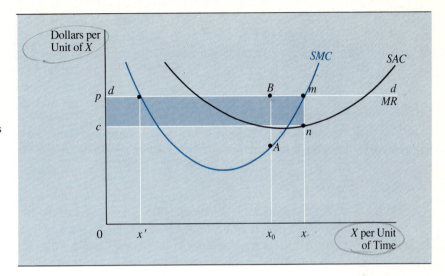

faced by the firm. Since marginal revenue is equal to the price per unit, the
marginal revenue curve *MR* coincides with *dd*. Both are horizontal at the level
of the market price of the product.

Profits are maximum at the output level at which marginal cost equals
marginal revenue—that is, at x, where *SMC* equals *MR*.[6] At any output less
than x, say, x_0, marginal revenue x_0B exceeds marginal cost x_0A. Larger outputs
up to x will increase total receipts more than they do total costs; hence profits
will rise up to that point. Beyond output x, *SMC* is greater than *MR*, and
movement to those larger outputs will increase total costs more than it does total
receipts, causing profits to decrease. Therefore, x is the output of maximum
profits.

Total profits of the firm appear in Figure 11.4 as the area of the rectangle
cpmn. Profit per unit is price p minus average cost c at output x. Total profit is
equal to profit per unit multiplied by sales—that is, total profit equals $cp \times x$.
Note that at output x profit per unit is not maximized, nor is there any reason
why it should be. The concern of the firm is with total profits, not with profit
per unit.

losses
The difference between a
firm's total costs and its
total receipts when the
latter are less than the
former, including as costs
the alternative costs of all
resources used.

Loss Minimization   If it should happen that the market price of the product is
less than short-run average costs at all possible output levels, the firm will incur
losses instead of making profits. Since the short run is defined as a time period
so short that the firm cannot change its size of plant, liquidation of the plant in
the short run is not possible. The choices open to the firm are whether to (1)

_____

[6]Note that *MC* equals *MR* at output x', but this is an output of maximum loss. For profit maximization
MC must equal *MR* and, *additionally, MC* must intersect *MR* from below.

produce at a loss or (2) discontinue production. Fixed costs will be incurred even if the second alternative is chosen.

The firm's decision rests on whether or not the price of the product covers average variable costs (or whether total receipts cover total variable costs). Suppose the market price of the product is p_0 in Figure 11.5. If the firm produces x_0, at which SMC equals MR_0, total receipts equal $p_0 \times x_0$. Total variable costs also equal $p_0 \times x_0$; hence total receipts just cover total variable costs. Total costs are equal to total variable costs plus total fixed costs; therefore, if variable costs are just covered, the firm's loss will be equal to total fixed costs. It makes no difference whether the firm produces or not—in either case, losses equal total fixed costs.

If the market price is less than minimum average variable costs, the firm will minimize losses by discontinuing production. The loss will equal total fixed costs when the firm produces nothing. If the firm produced at a price less than p_0, average variable costs would be greater than price and total variable costs would be greater than total receipts. Losses would equal total fixed costs plus that part of total variable costs not covered by total receipts. Price p_0 is called the **shutdown price.**

At a price greater than minimum average variable costs but lower than minimum SAC, it pays the firm to produce. At a price such as p_1, an output of x_1 results in losses that are less in amount than total fixed costs. Total receipts are $p_1 \times x_1$, and total variable costs are $v_1 \times x_1$. Total receipts exceed total variable costs by an amount equal to $v_1 p_1 \times x_1$. The excess of total receipts over total variable costs can be applied against total fixed costs, thus reducing losses to an amount less than total fixed costs. Loss in this case equals $p_1 c_1 \times x_1$.

Suppose, for example, that the producer under consideration is a wheat farmer who owns his farm and machinery. The farm is mortgaged and the machinery not yet paid for. Mortgage and machinery payments constitute fixed

shutdown price
The price below which a firm would cease to produce in the short run.

Figure 11.5
Short-Run Loss Minimization

A firm minimizes losses if price is below AC but above AVC by producing the output at which $SMC = MR$. If price were below p_0, the firm would shut down. That portion of the SMC curve lying above the AVC curve is the firm's short-run supply curve.

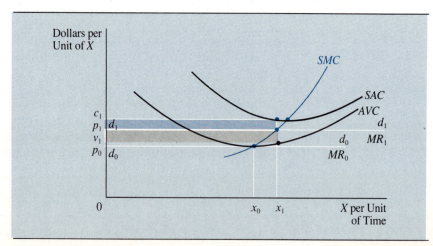

costs and must be met whether or not the farmer produces wheat. Outlays for seed, gasoline, fertilizer, and his own labor represent variable costs. If the farmer produces nothing, there will be no outlays on variable resources.

Under what circumstances should the farmer produce nothing at all and hire his labor out to someone else? If expected receipts from the wheat crop are not sufficient to cover the costs of seed, gasoline, fertilizer, and his own labor, he should not produce. If he produces under these circumstances, his losses will equal his mortgage and machinery payments plus that part of his variable costs not covered by his receipts. If he does not produce, his losses will equal mortgage and machinery payments only. Thus he should not produce.

Under what circumstances will it be to his advantage to produce even though incurring losses? If expected receipts will more than cover the variable costs, the excess can be applied to the mortgage and machinery payments, and production should be undertaken. Under these circumstances a decision not to produce means that the loss will be the full amount of the fixed costs, while if the farmer produces the loss will be less than the total fixed costs.

In Figure 11.5, at output level x_1 and market price p_1, equality between SMC and MR shows that losses are minimum. At a lower output, MR is greater than SMC, and increases in output will add more to total receipts than to total costs, thus reducing losses. Beyond x_1, SMC is greater than MR, meaning that increases in output will add more to total costs than to total receipts, thus increasing the losses. Hence losses are minimum at the output where SMC equals MR.

To summarize, the firm maximizes profits or minimizes losses by producing the output at which SMC equals MR, or the market price. There is one exception: if the market price is less than the firm's average variable costs, losses will be minimized by stopping production altogether, leaving losses equal to total fixed costs.

Short-Run Supply Curve of the Firm   That part of the firm's SMC curve that lies above the AVC curve is the **short-run firm supply curve** for the product. The SMC curve shows the different quantities that the firm will place on the market at different possible prices. At each possible price, the firm will produce the amount at which SMC equals p (and MR) to maximize profits or minimize losses. Supply drops to zero at any price below AVC.

Producer's Surplus   Since a firm's marginal cost, or supply curve, of a product usually slopes upward to the right, it appears that we should be able to identify a measure of producer's surplus analogous to the consumer's surplus measurement of Chapter 6. This is indeed the case. A **producer's surplus** is defined as the difference between the market value of the product at the profit-maximizing output level and the alternative costs of producing that output—the value of other products that could have been produced had the producer elected not to produce at all.

Consider a firm, such as that in Figure 11.6, with a resource endowment that can produce as much as x_6 units of X or, alternatively, v_4 dollars' worth of

short-run firm supply curve
A curve showing the different quantities per unit of time of a good or service that a firm will place on the market at all possible prices; that part of the firm's short-run marginal cost curve that lies above its average variable cost curve.

producers' surplus
The difference between the total amount producers (a producer) receive for any given quantity of product and the minimum amount they would have been willing to accept for it; represented diagrammatically by the area above the supply (marginal cost) curve and below the price at which that quantity is sold.

Figure 11.6
Measurement of
Producer's Surplus

A firm's producer's surplus in the production of x_1 of X is measured in panel (a) by v_4v_5, the difference between the market value of x_1 units of X and the cost of producing that quantity. In panel (b) it is measured by the blue area above the MC curve and below price p_{x1}.

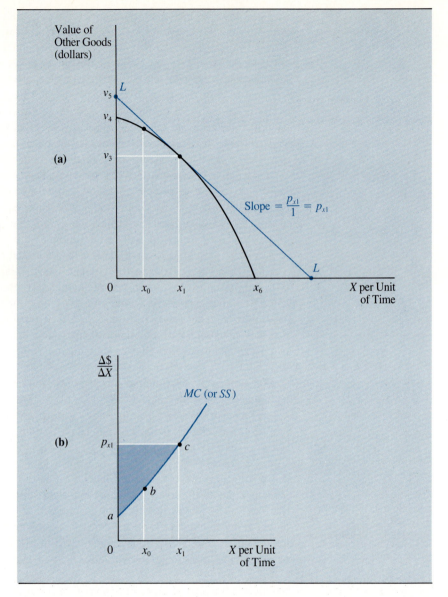

other goods and services. In panel (a), the vertical axis measures value of other items in dollars and the horizontal axis measures quantity of X. The transformation curve, v_4x_6, shows all possible combinations of X and the values of other goods and services that could be produced.

The firm's marginal cost curve in panel (b) is constructed from v_4x_6. At any given level of production, say, x_0, marginal cost is measured by the slope of the transformation curve at that point—that is, the marginal rate of transformation of X for dollars, or MRT_{xv}. The MRT_{xv} is the amount of dollars (or value of other goods and services) that must be given up to increase production of X by one unit at that production level. We plot that number of dollars as x_0b in panel (b); other points comprising the MC curve are obtained in the same way. Note that an increasing MRT_{xv} translates into a rising MC curve as the output of X is increased.[7]

At any given market price p_{x1}, the firm maximizes profits by producing the output at which marginal cost equals that price, or marginal revenue. In panel (b), the profit-maximizing output is x_1. Suppose now that we draw a straight line, LL, in panel (a) tangent to the transformation curve at output level x_1. Since the slope of the transformation curve equals marginal cost, and since marginal cost equals price at output x_1, the slope of LL equals p_{x1}. The market value of x_1 units of X is thus represented as v_3v_5—output x_1 multiplied by p_{x1}.

We can now measure producer's surplus at production level x_1. The market value of x_1 units is v_3v_5 in panel (a), or $0p_{x1}cx_1$ in panel (b). The total value of other products given up to produce x_1 is v_3v_4 in panel (a), or $0acx_1$ in panel (b). Producer's surplus is v_4v_5 in panel (a), or $ap_{x1}c$ in panel (b).[8] Whereas consumer's surplus in Chapter 6 was represented by the area under the demand curve and above the level of market price, producer's surplus is represented in panel (b) by the area above the marginal cost curve and below the level of market price.

The Market

Thus far the market price has been taken as given, but we now have the tools necessary to see how it is determined. Market price emerges from interactions between demanders of a good on the one hand and its suppliers on the other. We discussed the forces underlying a market demand curve in previous chapters, but we have yet to establish the market supply curve. The short-run market supply curve for a commodity is a short step beyond the individual firm supply curve. After we establish it, we shall consider short-run equilibrium for an entire market.

Short-Run Market Supply Curve As a first approximation, we can think of the **short-run market supply curve** as the horizontal summation of the short-run supply curves of all firms in the market. This supply curve shows the quantities of the commodity that all firms together will place on the market at various possible prices. Such a short-run market supply curve is valid if resource supplies to the group of firms in the market are perfectly elastic—that is, if changes in resource inputs and product output by all firms simultaneously have no effect on resource prices. We shall return to this point shortly.

short-run market supply curve
A curve showing the different quantities per unit of time of a good or service that all firms together will place on the market in the short run at various possible prices.

———————————

[7]Letting the transformation curve be $v = t(x)$, then $MRT_{xv} = -\dfrac{dv}{dx} = -t'(x) = MC_x$.

For a rising MC curve, $t''(x) < 0$.

[8]Representing marginal cost in panel (b) as $MC = g'(x)$, then at output level x_1 producer's surplus can be expressed as $x_1 \cdot p_{x1} - \int_0^{x_1} g'(x)dx$.

Short-Run Equilibrium   Figure 11.7 shows diagrammatically the determination of market price, market output, and the output of one representative firm of the market. The output axis of the market diagram is considerably compressed as compared with that of the firm diagram; the price axes of the two diagrams are identical. The market demand curve for the product is shown as *DD* in panel (b), and the *SAC* and *SMC* curves of the representative firm are shown in panel (a). The horizontal summation of all individual firm supply curves establishes the short-run market supply curve, *SS*. The short-run equilibrium market price is *p*, and the demand curve (*dd*) and the marginal revenue curve (*MR*) faced by the firm are horizontal at that level. To maximize profits, the respective firm—and each firm in the market—produces the output at which *SMC* = *MR* = *p*. The firm output is *x*. The combined outputs of all firms are the market output *X*. The market as a whole and each individual firm in it are in short-run equilibrium.

An increase in market demand for the product to D_1D_1 will increase the short-run equilibrium price and output. The increase in demand will cause a shortage of the good at the old price, *p*, which will be driven up by consumers to *p'*. The demand curve and marginal revenue curve faced by the firm shift up

Figure 11.7   Short-Run Equilibrium: Firm and Market

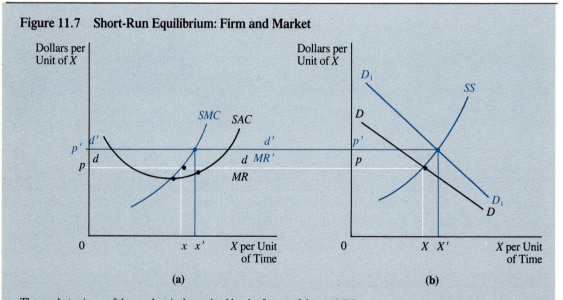

The market price *p* of the product is determined by the forces of demand *DD* and supply *SS*. The demand curve *dd* facing the firm, together with the marginal revenue curve *MR*, is horizontal at that price. To maximize profits the firm produces output *x*. Market output *X* is the summation of firm outputs. What are the results if the market demand curve is D_1D_1?

to the level of the new market price, to $d'd'$ and MR', respectively. To maximize profits, each firm will expand its output up to the level at which its SMC equals its new marginal revenue and the new market price. The new output level for the representative firm will be x', and the new market output will be X'.

Supply Curve Modifications   When an expansion or contraction of resource inputs by all firms acting simultaneously causes resource prices to change, the short-run market supply curve is no longer the horizontal summation of individual firm supply curves. Even though one firm cannot affect resource prices through expansion or contraction of the quantities it buys, all firms acting at the same time may be able to do so. If the expansion of the market output and resource inputs raises resource prices, individual firm cost curves will shift upward, while the reverse is true if expansion reduces resource prices. The possibility exists too that some resource prices will rise and some will fall. The effect may be to change the shape of the cost curves slightly and cause some shift up or down, depending on whether resource price increases or decreases are predominant.

The net effect of resource price increases when expansion occurs will be to make the short-run market supply curve less elastic than it would otherwise be. In panel (a) of Figure 11.7 the rise in demand increases price and marginal revenue, inducing firms to expand output. But suppose the output expansion pushes resource prices up, shifting SAC and SMC upward. The upward shift in SMC is also a shift to the left, meaning that the new SMC curve will equal marginal revenue or price at a smaller output than would be the case had it not shifted. Similarly, in panel (b), resource price decreases resulting from expansion of the market output will cause the market supply curve (SS) to be more elastic than the one shown in Figure 11.7. The short-run market supply curve in this case is obtained by summing individual firm's profit-maximizing outputs at each possible level of the market price.

THE LONG RUN

The possibilities of output variation in a purely competitive market are much greater in the long run than in the short run. In the long run, output can be varied through increases or decreases in the utilization of existing plant capacity—as is the case in the short run. More important, however, in the long run firms have time to alter their plant sizes, and there is ample time and opportunity for new firms to enter, or for existing ones to leave, the market. The two latter possibilities greatly increase the elasticity of the long-run market supply curve as compared with that of the short-run. Long-run adjustments in the size of plant by individual firms will occur simultaneously with the entrance or exit of firms to and from the market, but they can be more easily understood if they are considered first by themselves.

The Firm: Size of Plant Adjustments

The firm's determination of the size of plant to use can be put into proper focus by assuming that entry into the market is blocked in some way. Suppose that the firm is faced with a certain market price, say, p, in Figure 11.8. Its long-run average cost curve and long-run marginal cost curve are LAC and LMC, respectively. To maximize long-run profits the firm should produce output x, at which long-run marginal cost equals marginal revenue. The plant size that enables the firm to produce output x at the least possible cost per unit is SAC, and for that size of plant short-run marginal cost also is equal to marginal revenue. Profits of the firm are $cp \times x$.

The Firm and the Market

For the market as a whole, long-run adjustments to a disturbance depend on whether the market is one of increasing costs, constant costs, or decreasing costs.

Long-Run Equilibrium   For a firm, *long-run equilibrium* means that it has either no incentive or no opportunity to change what it is doing. If profit maximization is the objective, the firm of Figure 11.8 is in long-run equilibrium. Its $LMC = MR = p$, so there is no incentive to change the size of its plant. Its $SMC = MR = p$, so there is no incentive to move from an output level of x per unit of time.

Long-run equilibrium for a market implies more than long-run equilibrium for individual firms. There must also be no incentive for new firms to enter or for existing firms to leave. In other words, there must be no lure of economic profits to induce the entry of new firms or threat of losses to prompt present firms to leave.

If entry into the market is open—and in pure competition it is not blocked—profits like those made by the firm of Figure 11.8 will attract new firms. The

**Figure 11.8
Plant Size
Adjustment in
the Long Run**

Faced with price p the firm's long-run output will be x. The appropriate size of plant for that output is SAC, which is tangent to LAC at x. At the output of tangency, $SMC = LMC$ and the firm is maximizing both short-run and long-run profits.

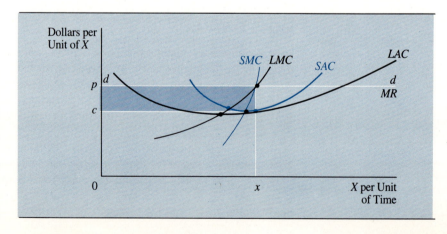

market promises a rate of return to investors greater than that they can earn on the average elsewhere in the economy. The entry of new firms increases the supply of product X and causes the price to move downward from its original level p. Each individual firm already in the market, faced with downward-shifting demand and marginal revenue curves, will cut its output level below x and will reduce its size of plant below SAC. In the interest of maximizing profits, outputs will be cut to levels at which the long-run marginal cost curve cuts the successively lower marginal revenue curves.

Economic profits can be made by firms in the market until enough producers have entered to drive the price down to p_1, as is the case in Figure 11.9. At that point individual firms will have cut their plants back to the most efficient sizes, as is shown by SAC_1, and they will operate at the most efficient rate of output. Economic profits have been eliminated by the entry of new firms, and there is no inducement for more firms to enter. No losses are being incurred, and thus there is no incentive for firms to leave the market. The individual firms in the market are doing satisfactorily; they are earning returns for all resources equal to what those resources could earn in alternative employments.[9]

The market is in long-run equilibrium when all its firms are in the position shown in Figure 11.9. In general terms, for every firm $LAC = SAC = p$ at the output being produced, and at no other output can lower average costs be obtained. Also, for each firm there is no incentive to increase or decrease the size of plant or output, since $LMC = SMC = MR$.

For long-run market equilibrium to exist, individual firms must also be in long-run equilibrium. However, the converse of this assertion will not hold. An individual firm could be in long-run equilibrium while making profits—as in Figure 11.8, for example. But in this case, the market would not be in equilib-

---

[9]In our discussion of the long run we shall assume that for all firms, both already in the market and potentially in it, the minimum points of the LAC curves lie at the same level. This condition is a necessary one for defining the long-run equilibrium position of a market.

In reality long-run equilibrium is never likely to be achieved in any market—it is a will-o'-the-wisp that is forever chased but never caught. Before a market can reach equilibrium, conditions defining that position change. Demand for the product changes, or costs of production change as a result of resource price changes or new technology. Thus the chase goes on toward a new equilibrium position. The long-run (and other) equilibrium concepts are important, however, because they show us the motivation for, and direction of, the chase. In addition, they show us how the chase works toward (in most cases) solution of the economic problem.

The argument usually made regarding equality of minimum long-run average costs of firms in the market rests on the alternative cost doctrine. Initial inequalities in such costs may result from superior management of particular firms, from favorable locations of certain firms with respect to power, markets, and sources of raw and semifinished materials, or from other similar causes. According to the alternative cost doctrine, these differentials will not persist. The superior manager who can make profits for the firm could do the same for other firms in the market and, perhaps, in others outside it. The manager's prospective value to other firms becomes his or her cost to the firm in which he or she works; thus the cost of the manager's services to the one firm increases to the point at which he or she can make pure profits for none. The same argument applies to a favorable location: The cost of the favorable location becomes its value to other firms that could use it to advantage, that is, the capitalized value of the returns it could earn for them. Hence the profits a desirable location can earn for any one firm disappear as its cost is correctly determined.

**Figure 11.9
Long-Run
Equilibrium**

Long-run market
equilibrium means no
profits or losses can be
made by individual firms
in the market. Therefore,
$SAC_1 = LAC_1 = p_1$ at
the minimum points of
both average cost curves.
Simultaneously, $SMC_1 =
LMC_1 = MR_1$ at output
x_1, and the firm, as well
as the market, is in long-
run equilibrium.

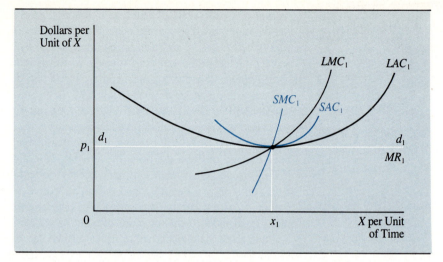

rium. The existence of long-run market equilibrium requires long-run individual
firm equilibrium at a no-profit, no-loss level of operation.

Similarly, long-run equilibrium for both a market and an individual firm
requires that short-run equilibrium exist at the same time. Short-run equilibrium
for an individual firm and a market can exist even if there is long-run disequilibrium for the individual firm and/or market. Long-run equilibrium for a market
is a more general concept than is either long-run equilibrium for a firm or short-
run equilibrium for both a firm and a market.

Although this analysis serves to introduce the concept of long-run equilibrium in a purely competitive market, it is by no means a complete analysis of
the long-run adjustments that occur within the market as a result of some disturbing force. Usually changes in cost as well as price will take place as new
firms, attracted by profits, enter the market. The nature of the cost adjustments,
if any, will depend on whether the market is one of increasing costs, constant
costs, or decreasing costs. Each of these will be analyzed in turn.

Increasing Costs   Consider first a market of increasing costs. The nature of
increasing costs will become evident as we move through the analysis. Suppose
the market is initially in long-run equilibrium. Then suppose that the disturbing
force is an increase in demand for product X.[10] We shall first trace through the
short-run and long-run effects of the increase in demand; then we shall establish
the long-run market supply curve for the product.

Long-run equilibrium diagrams for the market and for a representative firm
are shown in Figure 11.10. In panel (b), the market demand curve is DD and
the short-run market supply curve is SS; in panel (a), the firm's long-run average

---

[10]It could just as well be an improvement in technology. An excellent student exercise is to show
and trace through the effects of such a disturbance.

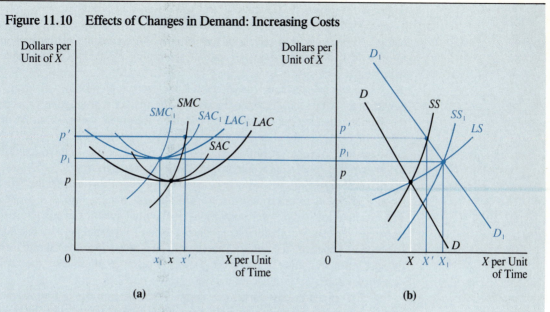

Figure 11.10   Effects of Changes in Demand: Increasing Costs

Starting from long-run equilibrium at market output X, let demand increase to D_1D_1. Firm output increases to x' and profits attract new firms into the market. The entry of new firms increases resource prices, shifting the set of cost curves upward, and decreases the market price as market supply increases. Long-run equilibrium is reestablished at some price p_1 and market output X_1 at which profits are again zero. Firm output is x_1.

cost curve and short-run average cost curve are *LAC* and *SAC*, respectively, and its short-run marginal cost curve for size of plant *SAC* is *SMC*. The long-run marginal cost curve is omitted; it is not essential for the analysis and unduly complicates the diagram.

Since the market and the firm are in long-run equilibrium, they are necessarily in short-run equilibrium, too. Therefore, we can think of the market demand curve and the short-run market supply curve as establishing the industry price p. The demand curve and the marginal revenue curve faced by the firm are horizontal and are equal to price p at all levels of its output. The firm produces the output at which *SMC* (and *LMC*) equals marginal revenue or price. Individual firm output is x; market output X is the summation of individual firm outputs at price p. There are just enough firms in the market to make the price equal to minimum short-run and long-run average costs for the firm at output x. The firm is using the most efficient size of plant at the most efficient rate of output. There are no economic profits or losses being incurred.

What will be the short-run effects of an increase in market demand to D_1D_1? The market price will rise to p', and the firm, to maximize profits, will increase output to x', the output at which *SMC* equals the new marginal revenue. Market output will increase to X', and the firm will be making profits equal to output x' multiplied by the difference between price p' and short-run average costs at output x'. The short-run effects of the increase in demand are (1) an increase in price and (2) some increase in output as existing plant capacity is worked with greater intensity.

Consider now the long-run effects. The existence of profits will bring in new firms. As these firms enter, increasing the market's productive capacity, the short-run market supply curve will shift to the right; the more firms that enter, the farther to the right the curve will move. The increases in supply will cause price to move downward from the short-run high of p'. As the price falls, individual firms will reduce output from the short-run high of x'.

increasing cost industry
An industry in which the entry of new firms causes resource prices to rise, which in turn causes the cost curves of existing firms to shift upward.

In an **increasing cost industry,** the entry of new firms causes the whole set of cost curves for existing firms to shift upward. Such a shift will occur in a market that uses significant proportions of the total supplies available of the resources necessary for making its product. Suppose, for example, that one such resource is a special steel alloy. The entry of new firms increases the demand for such resources, thus raising their prices. As resource prices rise, the set of cost curves shifts upward accordingly.

Any given set of cost curves presupposes that the firm can get all it wants of any one resource at a constant price per unit. No single firm causes the prices of resources to change, since it does not take a large enough amount of any resource to be able to affect its price. It is the greater demand for resources brought about by the entry of new firms and, perhaps, by the simultaneous expansion of output by existing firms that causes resource prices to rise. The forces causing resource prices to rise lie completely outside the control of the individual firm and are said to be *external* to it. The increases in resource prices and the consequent upward shifts of the cost curves are thus the result of **external diseconomies** of increasing production in the market.

external diseconomies
Forces outside the activities of any single firm that cause resource prices to rise and cost curves of the firm to shift upward as new firms enter the market.

A two-way squeeze is put on profits by the entry of new firms as the price falls and costs rise. New firms enter until the price decreases enough and costs rise enough for the price to be again equal to minimum long-run average costs for individual firms. All profit is squeezed out. In panel (a) of Figure 11.10, the new price is p_1 and the new cost curves are LAC_1, SAC_1, and SMC_1. The entry of new firms stops, and the market is once more in long-run equilibrium. The new long-run market price of p_1 lies between the original long-run price of p and the short-run high of p'. The new firm output is x_1, at which SMC_1 is equal to the new long-run marginal revenue and price. Market output will have increased to X_1, since the increased capacity of the market has moved the short-run supply curve to SS_1.[11]

---

[11]To keep an already complex exposition as simple as possible, a long-run development of a transitory nature has been ignored in the argument of the text. The short-run high price, resulting from the increase in demand for the product, not only attracts profit-seeking new firms into the market but also creates an incentive for existing firms to increase their plant sizes beyond the most efficient. This situation will be the case in Figure 11.8, since for the individual firm maximum long-run profits are obtained at the output at which long-run marginal cost equals marginal revenue and price. Then, as the entrance of new firms lowers price, the output at which long-run marginal cost equals price becomes smaller, and the firm is induced to reduce its plant size. When enough firms have entered to eliminate profits, the firm once more will be building the most efficient size of plant.

Will the new long-run output of the firm be equal to, greater than, or less than the old long-run output x? The answer depends on the way in which the cost curves shift upward. Whether these curves shift straight up, a little to the left, or a little to the right depends on the comparative price increases of different classes of resources. If all resource prices increase proportionally, the same combinations of resources will be the least-cost combinations. The cost curves will shift straight up, and the new long-run firm output will be equal to the old. Suppose, however, that short-run fixed resources go up relatively more in price than do those that are considered variable in the short run. The firm will want to economize on the now relatively more expensive fixed resources. The proportions of these resources to the relatively cheaper variable ones will be decreased to secure least-cost combinations. The most efficient size of plant will tend to be slightly smaller in the new long-run equilibrium position than it was in the old. Hence the new long-run equilibrium firm output will tend to be less than the old, as is shown in Figure 11.10. If short-run fixed resources increase proportionally less in price than do short-run variable resources, least-cost combinations will favor larger sizes of plant. The firm will want to economize on the now relatively more expensive resources and use larger proportions of those that constitute the plant. The new most efficient size of plant and the new output will tend to be larger than the old.

The *long-run market supply curve* in Figure 11.10 is *LS*. It joins all points of long-run equilibrium for the market. This curve can be thought of as the horizontal summation of the minimum points of all individual firm *LAC* curves as the entry of new firms shifts their cost curves upward. The long-run market supply curve shows the outputs that will be forthcoming at different possible prices when there is ample time for size-of-plant adjustments as well as for the entry and exit of firms.

Constant Costs   The pattern of analysis for a market of constant costs is basically the same as that for a market of increasing costs. Starting from the position of long-run equilibrium shown in Figure 11.11, suppose that an increase in demand occurs. The short-run effects are the same as before: The price will increase to p', the firm's output will increase to x', and the market output will increase to X'. Economic profits will be made by individual firms.

New firms will be attracted into the market in the long run. As before, the short-run market supply curve will shift to the right as new firms enter, causing the price to fall.

constant cost industry
An industry in which the entry of new firms causes no changes in resource prices or in the cost curves of existing firms.

In a **constant cost industry,** the entry of new firms does not increase market demands for resources sufficiently to cause their prices to rise. Of the total supplies of resources necessary for the production of X, it takes a part small enough so that no influence is exerted on resource prices by the new firms coming in. If the entry of new firms has no effect on resource prices, the cost curves of existing firms will remain as they were before. Profits will be made until enough firms have entered to bring the price back down to p. Price and minimum long run average costs will be equal, and long-run equilibrium will be reestablished. The new short-run market supply curve will be SS_1. Individual firm output will be that at which *SMC* equals marginal revenue and price p. The

Figure 11.11   Effects of Changes in Demand: Constant Costs

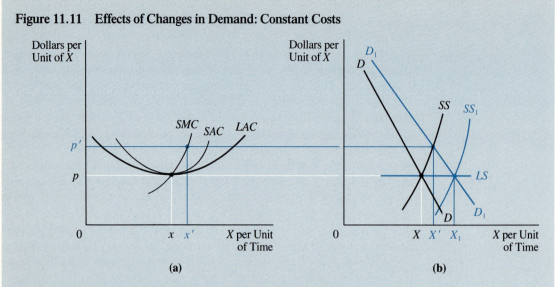

(a)   **(b)**

Starting from long-run equilibrium at market output X, let demand increase to
D_1D_1. Firm output increases to x'. Profits attract new firms into the market,
shifting the supply curve to the right and decreasing the market price. When
enough have entered to reduce profits to zero, long-run equilibrium is reestablished at market price p, market output X_1, and firm output x.

entry of new firms will have increased market output substantially, to X_1. The
long-run supply curve will be LS and will be horizontal at the level of minimum
long-run average costs.

Decreasing Costs   Cases of decreasing costs are probably rather rare. Analytically they parallel increasing and constant cost cases. As before, we start with
a market and its firms in long-run equilibrium and then assume demand increases. The short-run effects are the same as before. In Figure 11.12, the market
price increases to p', firm output goes up to x', and the market output increases
to X'. Pure profits equal to x' times the difference between p' and SAC at output
x' will be made by the representative firm.

New firms will be attracted in the long run because of the pure profits
available. The short-run market supply curve moves to the right as new firms
add to the market's productive capacity. Price goes down as these new firms
enter.

decreasing cost industry
An industry in which the
entry of new firms causes
resource prices to fall,
which in turn causes the
cost curves of existing
firms to shift downward.

In a **decreasing cost industry,** the entry of new firms must cause resource
prices to fall. The decrease in resource prices as new firms enter causes the cost
curves to shift downward. Both the price of X and the costs of production are
decreasing. Eventually the declining product price overtakes the declining cost
curves, and profit is squeezed out. The new long-run equilibrium price is p_1,

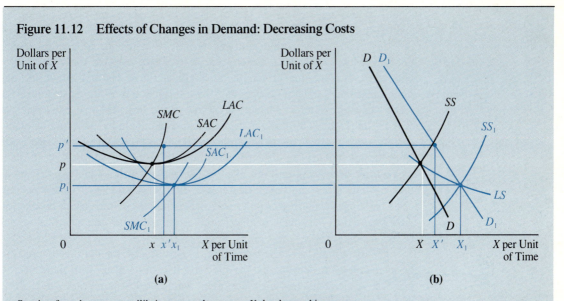

Figure 11.12   Effects of Changes in Demand: Decreasing Costs

Starting from long-run equilibrium at market output X, let demand increase to D_1D_1. Individual firm profits induce new firms to enter, causing resource prices to fall, shifting the firm's cost curves downward, and causing product price to fall because of increasing supply. Long-run equilibrium is re-established when the falling price overtakes the downward-shifting cost curves at some market price p_1, market output X_1, and firm output x_1.

which is less than the original price of p. Individual firm output is x_1, at which both short-run and long-run marginal costs equal marginal revenue or price. The new industry output is X_1. The long-run supply curve, LS, will be downward sloping to the right.

What are the circumstances that could conceivably give rise to decreasing costs? Suppose the market in question is a young one growing up in a new territory.[12] Transportation facilities and the organization of markets, both for resources and the final product, may not be well developed. An increase in the number of firms in the market, and consequently in its size, may make feasible the development of improved transportation and marketing facilities that will substantially reduce the costs of individual firms. For example, industrial growth of an area may stimulate development and improvement of railway, highway, and air transportation service into and out of that area. However, good explanations of decreasing costs are rather hard to find; whatever the explanations given for particular cases, they usually stem basically from improvements in the

_____

[12]In this case, the chances of its being one of pure competition are small.

quality of resources furnished or from greater efficiencies developed in the re-source-furnishing industries.

external economies
Forces outside the activities of any single firm that cause resource prices to fall and cost curves of the firm to shift downward as new firms enter the market.

Decreasing costs, or **external economies,** of increasing production should not be confused with the *internal economies* of size possible for a single firm with a size of plant smaller than the most efficient one. The individual firm has no influence over external economies; these result solely from expansion of the market or from sources outside the control of the firm. Internal economies of size *are* under the control of the firm—it can secure them by enlarging its plant.

Increasing cost markets are probably the most prevalent of the three cases analyzed and decreasing costs the most unlikely to occur. Markets of constant cost and of decreasing cost are likely to become markets of increasing cost as they become older and better established. If it is possible to have decreasing costs once the decreasing costs or external economies of increasing production have been taken advantage of, the market must surely become one of constant or increasing costs.

The disturbing force triggering these chains of adjustments was assumed to be an increase in demand for the product. It could just as well have been a decrease in demand, in which case there would be losses for individual firms and exit from the market would have occurred until long-run equilibrium was again established. Or, in lieu of changes in demand, we could have assumed that major technological developments caused disequilibrium, inducing new firms to enter the market until long-run equilibrium was reestablished.

THE WELFARE EFFECTS OF PURE COMPETITION

In a private enterprise economic system, what are the welfare implications of purely competitive market structures? A complete assessment of the expected effects must wait until we have examined resource pricing and employment in detail. However, some tentative statements can be made at this point.

The welfare impacts of purely competitive forces can be brought out by summarizing how the purely competitive mechanism operates. Suppose that initially disequilibrium exists; there is a random array of prices, outputs, and distribution of productive capacity (resources). There are two givens throughout the following discussion: (1) pure competition exists in all markets, and (2) the distribution of purchasing power does not change. We focus attention on two goods, food (F) and clothing (C).

The Very Short Run

In the very short run, consumers—confronted with the initial prices of goods and services—attempt to allocate their incomes so as to maximize satisfaction. Since supplies are initially fixed, prices move to the levels that will just clear the markets and create no surpluses. All exchanges that are mutually beneficial to buyers and sellers occur as prices move toward their equilibrium levels. Since such exchanges benefit the exchanging parties without decreasing the welfare of any external parties, community welfare increases. Community welfare with fixed supplies is maximum when for each consumer

$$MRS_{fc} = \frac{p_f}{p_c}; \quad \text{or, in marginal utility terms,}$$

$$\frac{MU_f}{MU_c} = \frac{p_f}{p_c} \quad \text{or} \quad \frac{MU_f}{p_f} = \frac{MU_c}{p_c}.$$

All consumers are on their contract curves, and the distribution of goods is complete.

The Short Run

If the plant capacity in food and clothing production is fixed and outputs of both commodities are not at short-run profit-maximizing levels, will the consequent adjustments increase welfare? Suppose that firms producing food are operating at outputs such that $SMC_f < p_f$ and that clothing firms are producing outputs at which $SMC_c > p_c$. The production of clothing will be reduced, and the production of food will be increased. Community welfare will be increased in the process, because consumers value variable resources being used in producing F more than they value them being used in making other goods. This differential valuation is the meaning of $SMC_f < p_f$. The price p_f is the value that consumers place on any one unit of F at the current supply level. At current production levels of F, the short-run marginal cost of F is the value of the products that the resources used in producing the last one-unit increment in F can turn out in their best alternative uses. Consequently, consumer welfare can be increased by transfers of resources from those other uses into the production of F—that is, from uses in which those resources produce a smaller value of product into the use where their output is of greater value. Similarly, $SMC_c > p_c$ means that consumers value resources being used in producing C less than they value them being used in producing other goods. Consumer welfare can be increased by transferring resources from C into the production of other goods.

The purely competitive market mechanism induces producers to accomplish the output changes that consumers desire. To maximize profits or to minimize losses in the short run, producers of F want to increase their outputs to levels at which $SMC_f = p_f$. Producers of C desire to contract their outputs to levels at which $SMC_c = p_c$. Producers of F offer slightly higher prices for the necessary variable resources. Output contraction decreases demand for variable resources used for clothing, which in turn depresses the prices offered for them. To the extent that F and C use the same kinds of variable resources, voluntary reallocation by resource owners, from the lower-paying to the higher-paying uses sufficient to equalize their remuneration in the two uses, will occur. If the two markets use different kinds of variable resources, a general reallocation of variable resources may take place throughout the economy. Reallocation may occur from market C to other markets that can use the kinds of variable resources needed in producing C. In turn, reallocation of the kinds of resources used in market F, from other markets to market F, may occur. The overall short-run resource reallocation that occurs will be limited, however, by the existing plant capacity in the two markets. Short-run equilibrium exists when $SMC_f = p_f$ and $SMC_c = p_c$.

The Long Run

Although the short-run reorganization of production increases the welfare of consumers, it stops short of maximizing it because of fixed plant capacity in each market. In the long run there is ample time for productive capacity to move, that is, for firms to enter and to exit whenever incentives to do so occur.

Suppose that short-run equilibrium exists and that firms in F show profits while those in C incur losses. The profits in F and the losses in C mean that consumers value investment in plant and equipment more in F and less in C than they value it in other uses; their welfare will therefore be increased by transfers of investment out of C and into F. The incentives motivating producers bring about this result.

The short-run losses in C mean rates of return on investment in that market below what investment elsewhere in the economy will earn. Consequently disinvestment in C will occur—through failure to take care of depreciation on plant and equipment and through the eventual liquidation of some existing firms. As firms leave C the supply of product decreases, causing its price to rise. The decreased demands for resources in C lower their prices, decreasing costs of production for the remaining firms. The exit of firms will cease when the decreasing supply of product has raised its price and lowered costs enough so that losses are no longer being incurred. Now a smaller number of firms in C will be producing with plants of most efficient size and most efficient rates of output, but in total they will produce a smaller combined output at a higher price than in the short run.

At the same time, short-run profits in F attract resources (productive capacity) into that market. The profits indicate a higher return on investment than investors can earn elsewhere in the economy; this is a lucrative field in which to invest. New firms are established in the market. Increasing demands for resources raise their prices and the cost curves of both entering firms and firms already in the market. The entry of new firms increases market supply, driving the price down. New firms enter until the increasing supply reduces the price of F to the level of the higher average costs. Entry stops when profits no longer appear to be obtainable to entering firms. Existing firms are forced to use most efficient plant sizes and operate them at most efficient rates of output to avoid losses. Now more firms are in the market, their combined outputs are greater, and the product price is lower than it was in the short run.

The reallocation of resources may be direct or indirect. If the plant capacity of firms in C can be easily converted to the production of product F, firms in C may simply switch over to producing the more profitable F. Or, if the production processes of the two markets are unrelated, reallocations will be of the indirect nature just described, with firms folding in *C* and new firms emerging in *F*. In either case, profits and losses, and differential prices for resources in the two markets, bring about the desirable reallocation of resources or productive capacity.

With the establishment of long-run equilibrium, the economy is operating at maximum economic efficiency. Individual firms in each market operate most efficient plant sizes at most efficient rates of output. Consumers receive units of each product at prices equal to the minimum obtainable average cost per unit. Each consumer is induced to consume those quantities of goods at which the marginal rate of substitution between any two is equal to the price ratio of the two. Thus the marginal rate of substitution between any two goods is the same for all consumers. Producers are induced to produce those quantities of each good at which long-run marginal costs are equal to their respective prices. Marginal rates of transformation between any two goods are thus equal to their price ratios and, in turn, are equal to consumer marginal rates of substitution between them.

The achievement of long-run equilibrium conditions in purely competitive markets appears to lead to maximum consumer welfare. As we examine the other market structures we shall find that they fall short of reaching the summit. One of our tasks is to assess the extent to which they fall short. The purely competitive model provides an excellent benchmark for this purpose, and several conditions resulting from long-run purely competitive equilibrium that have welfare implications are worth noting.

First, pure competition leads to that organization of productive capacity at which *prices of products are equal to their per unit costs—marginal and average*. There are no profits or losses. Productive capacity (resources) is so allocated that it is valued equally by consumers in all its alternative uses, and no reallocation can increase welfare.

Second, *each firm operates at peak efficiency,* producing its output at the least possible cost per unit. In long-run equilibrium the firm is induced to operate a most efficient plant size at the most efficient rate of output in order to avoid losses. It takes advantage of all possible economies of size and uses the most efficient resource combination for the output level it produces.

Third, *resources are not diverted into sales promotion efforts*. No necessity exists for individual firms to engage in aggressive activities to promote sales when they sell in purely competitive markets. One firm alone cannot influence a product's price, and the products of all firms in that market are homogeneous. Since the individual firm can sell all it wishes to at the going market price, sales promotion to increase its volume is unnecessary. Buyers have so many alternative sources of supply that price increases on the part of one seller reduce that firm's sales to zero.

SUMMARY

This chapter draws together the analyses of demand and of costs to show how the price system organizes production under the special conditions of pure competition. Pricing and output are discussed from the time viewpoints of the very short run, the short run, and the long run.

Supplies of goods are fixed in amount in the very short run. Price serves to ration existing supplies as well as fixed supplies among consumers over the duration of this period.

In the short run, individual firm outputs can be varied within the limits of their fixed sizes of plant. To maximize profits, individual firms produce the outputs at which their short-run marginal costs equal marginal revenue or product price. Market price of a product is determined by the interactions of all consumers and all producers of the good. Individual firms may make profits or incur losses in the short run.

In the long run, additional firms will enter markets that make profits, and some existing firms will leave markets in which losses occur; thus productive capacity expands in the former markets and contracts in the latter. Expansion of productive capacity lowers market price of the product and decreases individual firm profits; contraction of productive capacity increases market price and reduces firm losses. Long-run equilibrium exists in each market when the number of firms is just sufficient for neither profits nor losses to be incurred. When a market is in long-run equilibrium, product price equals average cost of production. Each firm must be operating at most efficient size of plant and rate of output if losses are to be avoided.

A market may be characterized as one of increasing, constant, or decreasing costs. Increasing costs occur when the entrance of new firms into the market raises the price of resources used to produce the product; the resulting higher costs are called external diseconomies. In constant cost markets, the entrance of new firms does not increase demand for resources enough to raise their prices; consequently no changes in the costs of existing firms occur. Decreasing costs, which must be rare in the real world, occur when the entrance of new firms causes resource prices and costs of production to fall; these declines are termed external economies.

Pure competition has certain important welfare effects or implications. First, consumers get products at prices equal to their per unit costs of production. Second, pure competition, where it can exist, results in the greatest economic efficiency. Third, there is little need for sales promotion efforts on the part of individual firms.

APPLICATIONS

Competitive markets are not always left free to remain competitive over time. First, in a market of many firms, single smaller firms may be unable to protect themselves from efforts of larger firms to eliminate them from the market through political means. Second, firms in a competitive market may be able to reduce competition among themselves—that is, to become an effective cartel—through legislative or government regulatory activities. We illustrate each of these possibilities in the competitive markets for personal transportation by car: the jitneys of the World War I era and taxis in the Great Depression of the 1930s. Then we present a case, ocean shipping, in which competitive firms are faced with either producing at a loss or shutting down.

JITNEYS[13]

Jitneys were unlike any present-day form of transportation. In the form of the Ford Model T, the first "family car" that was the rage of its day, they combined the features of buses, taxis, and delivery vehicles. Jitneys could hold about five seated passengers plus a few more standing on the running boards. Typically the owner of a car would pick up fares who were heading in the same direction as he was during the morning and evening home-to-work commute at $.05 each. In this sense, jitneys were the first carpools. However, some owners drove jitneys on a full-time basis. A few would follow well-known routes and schedules, but most would select their "routes" according to the destination of the first passenger(s) to board (indicating the destination by posting a sign on the windshield much like modern buses do) and then solicit other passengers who were headed in that general direction.

Jitneys were highly competitive among themselves, but most of their patrons came from the street railway lines. The trolleys dominated American urban transportation during this period, but they operated with fixed schedules and, of course, their routes were absolutely inflexible. An automobile trip often was more direct, quicker, and like present-day taxi services, permitted lateral mobility away from main thoroughfares into residential areas. Moreover, the jitneys were aided by the trolleys' pricing scheme—$.05 per passenger regardless of distance. Although this was a bargain for a ten-mile trip, it was a relatively high price for a short jaunt of two to three miles. It was these shorter trips for which jitneys were in greatest demand. Jitneys regularly worked the trolley lines, too, and often drove just ahead of the streetcar, soliciting passengers at rail stops. Beginning in Los Angeles in July 1914, the use of jitneys spread quickly until

[13]This discussion is drawn from Ross D. Eckert and George W. Hilton, "The Jitneys," *The Journal of Law and Economics* 15 (October 1972): 293–325.

a nationwide peak of 62,000 units were in service a year later. The financial losses to the trolleys were huge, running at a rate of about $2.5 million annually in California alone in 1916.

The trolley companies initially viewed the jitneys as a fad that would quickly pass once the vehicle owners began making economically rational calculations of their operating and ownership costs. The street railways estimated these costs in a businesslike manner, including the expenses of depreciating cars and the implicit wages that jitney drivers could earn elsewhere. They concluded that most drivers were operating their vehicles at a ''loss.'' But this was a serious miscalculation, for two reasons.

First, the implicit wage that jitney drivers assigned themselves as a part of the costs of their enterprises was nonexistent or low, since most of them were either fully or partially unemployed. Unemployed jitney owners would put their vehicles into service if revenues were sufficient to pay them implicit wages equal to or above the money value they placed on their leisure time. Those to whom part-time employment was available would require implicit wages from jitney operations equal to or above what they could earn in alternative employments. Consequently, during periods of recession more jitneys would be available than during periods of higher employment and better alternative earning opportunities. Trolley companies overestimated the implicit wages that would be required to induce persons to operate in the jitney trade, especially during the 1914–15 recession.

The trolley companies' second miscalculation was assuming that the family car, when used as a jitney, would be depreciated as an investment expense just as if it had been purchased for strictly jitney-driving purposes. The usual accounting calculation of profit-or-loss, the so-called bottom line, would produce an erroneous economic result by failing to take into account that the family car had been purchased and would continue to be used for nonjitney purposes whether or not the head of the household also drove the car as a public conveyance. The trolley companies failed to recognize that the costs most jitney drivers had to cover to remain in business were relatively low and that the potential supply of jitneys was almost as great as the supply of family cars for part-time driving.

By the spring of 1915, the trolley companies had switched from a policy of benign neglect to one of active hostility, and their trade press referred to jitneys as ''a malignant growth'' and ''this Frankenstein of transportation.'' Most cities had only one trolley firm, and few had more than two or three. Typically trolley companies received monopoly franchises from the city in exchange for tax payments of 1 or 2 percent of gross receipts. Thus the city officials and the trolley firms had a mutual interest in annihilating the jitney, and they formed alliances for this purpose. The jitney drivers were numerous, but they were transient and wholly lacking in political clout.

Instead of prohibiting jitneys outright, the cities and trolley companies pushed through ordinances restricting jitney operations, thereby taking away the advantages that made them popular. Basically they raised the typical jitney's average costs to a point at which it became unprofitable to operate. Some of these ordinances were diabolically clever. Requiring that jitneys take out official licenses and pay annual fees (and in some cases take out franchises and pay direct taxes as a percentage of gross receipts) sharply raised jitney operating costs. Compelling them to operate full eight-hour days eliminated most of the part-timers. Establishing fixed routes for the small vehicles reduced their attractiveness to many passengers, and in many cities these routes were not permitted to parallel those of trolleys. Requiring that jitneys follow long routes all the way to suburban areas unprofitable for jitneys and trolleys alike eliminated even more. Many cities prohibited jitneys from soliciting passengers at rail stops, and some even forbade them from entering downtown business areas. In some cities, jitneys reacted by forming "car clubs" that did not charge fees for travel but did accept "donations" from their "members." But the courts held that this was an attempt to evade the law. By the end of 1915 the jitney fleet had been cut in half, and by the early 1920s it was gone.

TAXICABS

The jitneys' survivors were called taxicabs. They provided personalized door-to-door services for fewer people at higher fares and did not threaten the trolley systems. Taxicab markets in most major cities were relatively unregulated before 1929. In that year major fleet owners established a nationwide trade association to lobby for ordinances to restrict additional entry to "their" markets.[14] With the Depression of the early 1930s, more and more unemployed people were flooding taxi markets just as they had the jitney markets two decades earlier. Entry costs were low and the competition was keen, and this time the injured parties were the established taxi firms rather than the transit companies. These firms lobbied their local city councils for ordinances to limit the number of licenses that could be issued, give preferential rights for new licenses to existing firms rather than new entrants, and set minimum fare levels to diminish price competition.[15]

In New York City, for example, a 1937 ordinance limited the number of taxi licenses to 13,566—the total of cabs then on the streets—as compared with about 11,900 in operation since 1961. The license, called a "medallion" because it consists of a steel plate bolted to the vehicle's front hood, may legally be sold. Through the years the demand for taxi service and the fares that cabs may charge have increased, but the supply of cabs has declined, largely because of restrictions on the use of automobiles and tires during World War II, which caused some licensees to abandon their medallions. The exchange value of the medallion reached $68,000 in 1980, although the annual license fee that the city charges is only $150; and banks, expecting that the city will not reissue dormant

---

[14]Edmund W. Kitch, Mark Isaacson, and Daniel Kasper, "The Regulation of Taxicabs in Chicago," *The Journal of Law and Economics* 14 (October 1971), 317.

[15]Ross D. Eckert, "On the Incentives of Regulators: The Case of Taxicabs," *Public Choice* 14 (Spring 1973): 83–99.

medallions or create new ones, have been willing to finance more than half the purchase price.[16] A similar licensing system exists in Chicago, where the number of cabs has been limited since the 1930s. In 1970 a maximum of 4,600 licenses was allowed; a license exchanged in the market then for about $25,000.[17] In Los Angeles a different system of regulation evolved. Licenses were limited in the late 1920s. In the early 1930s, there was a series of bankruptcies and mergers among taxi firms. In 1934 the city created five territories and gave each of five remaining firms a franchise to operate exclusively in one of the territories. That system of territorial monopolies endured for nearly 50 years.

The taxicab market in Washington, D.C., is a prominent exception to the producer pattern that we have seen. It is a competitive market organized to benefit customers. Washington taxi firms faced the same problems during 1930–33 as did other cities. The number of operators swelled owing to unemployment, and the preexisting firms urged the local government to protect them from the influx of competitors. But Washington is a federal city, governed chiefly by members of Congress who are elected in the states and who are not beholden to local businesses for political support or other favors. Members of Congress keep the taxi market competitive by refusing to restrict entry; therefore, supply is high and the fares (which Congress also determines) are low. This suits the self-interests of members of Congress, since they use cabs intensively for business trips around town. Congress has forbidden taxi operators to install taxi meters, out of a concern that this would raise the cost of trips, and has instead maintained a system of zone fares which, as one might expect, has the lowest per mile prices on the trips that congresspersons take most often—generally, the run between Capitol Hill and the federal offices downtown. Not surprisingly, a political system in which the interests of producers are relatively strong will yield outcomes in favor of those producers, just as a political system in which consumers hold the trump cards will tend to accommodate consumer self-interests.

CHRISTINA ONASSIS IS SCRAPPING SOME OF HER SHIPS _____

The accompanying article gives a glimpse of Christina Onassis' painful, meat-ax dismemberment of the superb fleet that her father had assembled in the heyday of the oil tanker market. It was ironic but predictable that the fortunes of the tanker firms would move opposite to those of OPEC. When OPEC prices were low, energy consumption and oil shipments from the Middle East were high. Onassis and his competitors had bet on rising shipments right up to 1973, so

---

[16]Joe Mysak, "Trafficking in Taxis: The Market for Medallions Is a Two-Way Street," *Barron's*, February 23, 1981, 15–18.

[17]Ibid.

higher OPEC prices and reduced exports forced major adjustments in the resulting shakeout. The article partially describes the adjustment process; some of it fits the analysis illustrated in Figure 11.5.

In the short run, Christina Onassis and her employees took steps to minimize losses. Tanker owners can either make long-term leases (charters) with oil firms or let the ships shop (cruise) for business. Sometimes this means waiting in the Persian Gulf or Rotterdam for word from a cargo broker. Seasonal or short-notice business fetches higher rates, but it is expensive to keep the ships idle even for a week. Long-term charters tie up the ship for years, missing the extra profits that would occur if oil imports were to rise unexpectedly, but they do offer earnings stability. Onassis switched some ships to long-term charters at rates that clearly were greater than operating costs but not full costs. Ships were laid up when operating costs exceeded charter rates.

Liquidation of some of the Onassis plant became economical in the long run, and fleet size and composition were adjusted in several ways. First, Ms. Onassis' father, just before his death, paid $17 million to cancel the fixed-cost obligation he had made several years earlier to build three more huge tankers (VLCCs). The capital in this market—the ships—is mobile but highly specialized; not much can be done with a 200,000-ton oil tanker except haul oil. The huge ships became outmoded as energy use declined, refineries closed, and production increased in such non-OPEC countries as Mexico with ports too shallow to accommodate them. The reopening of the Suez Canal reduced the demand for ships to haul huge cargoes around the Cape of Good Hope and put a premium on smaller tankers that could use the canal. Second, Ms. Onassis exchanged big tankers for smaller, more economical vessels. Third, she diversified the plant to include some dry cargo carriers as well as specialized tankers. Fourth, she scrapped ships that had no prospect of earning more than operating costs.

By the end of 1982 the Onassis firm was much smaller, operating only 24 of the 56 ships it had in 1975. It was only eighth of the ten largest independently owned shipping firms, all of which compete extensively with a thousand other independent shipowners and, to some degree, with the large fleets owned by Exxon, Shell, Chevron, Standard Oil of Indiana, and Texaco. Thus, the industry appeared to be highly competitive. On scanty data, the author of the article estimated that Onassis earned 10 to 12 percent per year on the firm's invested capital in 1982, a modest return given the risks.

The shakeout continued well after the article was published. In 1985 alone, 105 superships in excess of 100,000 tons went to the wrecking yards. In 1979, 750 VLCCs were operating, but by mid-1986 there were only 425, one-third of which were idle. The greatest carnage was among the ultralarge crude carriers (ULCCs) of at least 300,000 tons. Of 120 ULCCs constructed since 1968, 27 had been scrapped, 39 were mothballed or under repair, 13 were in floating storage, and the rest were idle, hoping for charter at rates that covered operating costs. Shipyards were also idle, of course, so new ships could be constructed rapidly should demand suddenly surge. As a result, values of existing ships

CHRISTINA ONASSIS RIDES OUT THE TANKER STORMS
by David Fairbank White, *Fortune*

She is far from being the richest woman in the world, as she is sometimes billed, but she's not headed for the poorhouse either. Olympic Maritime S.A., the company that Aristotle Socrates Onassis built, has a solid core of ten tankers on long-term charter to major oil companies. They throw off a reliable stream of cash flow—the envy of weaker companies—and Olympic has used the cash plus new debt to modernize and upgrade its fleet, something few competitors have been willing and able to do. The Onassis fleet has shrunk from 56 ships in 1975 to 38 today, of which 14 are listed as laid up. Still, Olympic ranks as the world's eighth-largest independent tanker owner.

For most of his career, Onassis was, despite his flamboyance, a conservative shipowner who chartered vessels long term to oil companies before the ships came down the ways. But when inflation soured the take on some long-term charters, he committed his free tankers to the spot market in shipping's greatest year, 1973. A very large crude carrier

(VLCC) of 200,000 tons or more, which costs perhaps $50 million to build, could bring in over $15 million on one trip from the Persian Gulf to Rotterdam.

Ari is said to have pocketed $100 million in profits that year and plunged by ordering six more supertankers worth $360 million from French and Japanese yards. Other shippers were gambling just as recklessly. But soaring oil prices and falling consumption knocked the shipping industry into a depression from which it still hasn't recovered.

Today, nine punishing years later, more than a third of the world's 347 million deadweight tons of tanker capacity is unwanted excess. From Scandinavia to Greece to Southeast Asia, bays and fjords are filling up as ships come off time charter and fall into lay-up. Nearly 17% of the tanker supply, or 58 million tons, is now mothballed.

If owners care to gamble, they can pay the $4 million a year that it costs to keep a supertanker cruising in search of cargo. At any given time

as many as 40 supertankers are waiting in the Persian Gulf. Other hobo ships hover off Venezuela, off Nigeria, off the big Caribbean refineries that feed the U.S. market. Some are being used as floating tank farms. Dry-cargo ships are faring little better, with 21 million tons, or 10% of total capacity, laid up.

Most threatened of all by changing times are the gargantuan VLCCs, which have passed their day of greatest use. Only smaller tankers with shallow drafts are able to service many of the so-called local oil fields, such as the North Sea, Mexico's Bay of Campeche, and offshore California. "It seems that everybody is finding oil at their doorstep," says C. Y. Chen, a leading shipowner. Shipments to the U.S from Persian Gulf states have fallen by half in five years. Much of this oil now moves through three pipelines to the Mediterranean or through the Suez Canal, reopened in 1975 for tankers of up to 150,000 tons.

Some great fleets are sailing toward oblivion. Daniel K. Ludwig, an

collapsed. Vessels costing $100 million in the late 1970s brought $6 million as scrap.[18]

The Greek shipping industry has long been the world's largest. This is due in no small part to the reputations of its entrepreneurs for self-confidence—taking unusual risks and performing their obligations reliably. But their boldness in expanding during the late 1970s was ill-timed for the largest and most dev-

_____

[18]From *The Wall Street Journal:* Stephen Duthie, "As World Demand for Oil Shrinks, Big Cargo Ships Are a Dying Breed," November 25, 1985; and Ken Wells, "Life on a Supertanker Mixes Tedium, Stress for Kenneth Campbell," September 11, 1986.

American shipowner once in the Onassis league, has let his 54 ships dwindle to 17 since 1975. Ari's special rival, the Niarchos Group, owns only 33 ships, less than half the peak number. Neither Ludwig nor the Niarchos Group is among today's top ten independent tanker owners. In recent years the last melancholy journey for many behemoths of the seas—as well as older, smaller vessels that aren't fuel efficient—has been to scrapyards in Taiwan, Pakistan, and elsewhere.

Olympic Maritime seems to have come through these wrenching times in better shape than others. Sniffing the changing winds—he was always good at that—Onassis started the turnaround in his last year, reportedly paying a painful $17 million to cancel contracts for three of the six supertankers he had impulsively ordered. The swing back to more customary Onassis conservatism continued under Christina. The other three big ships were too far along to be stopped, but after the 270,000-ton *Olympic Breeze* slid into the gentle

waters off Yokohama in 1976, it was chartered to Mobil Oil. The rate was so low it would have made Ari whip out his large handkerchief and wipe his brow—a gesture he was famous for—but at least the charter covered operating costs.

Anderson [managing director], presumably with Christina's blessings, has been brutal in scrapping losers. Eleven supertankers have gone to the junkyard, six of them in the past two years. Four more are laid up and may not have long to live. Meanwhile, maritime sources say that Olympic has bought four additional dry-cargo ships—for a total of 15—and five fuel-efficient medium tankers, ranging from 82,000 to 113,000 tons, a handy size for the Bay of Campeche or the Suez run. Two of the new cargo ships (and two older ones) are listed as being laid up, but the new tankers are paying off. Three are on charter to Shell and the other two, just off charter to Pemex, the Mexican oil company, are active in the spot market.

Just how much money this secre-

tive company earns overall requires some educated guesswork. But the striking fact that emerges, after considerable allowance for error, is that the fabled Onassis empire is actually small potatoes among the world's great enterprises. Olympic may be earning $15 million to $20 million a year on a net worth of no more than $160 million.

World trade doesn't depend, of course, on the success or failure of Olympic Maritime. It isn't big or important enough to get anywhere near *Fortune's* list of the largest transportation companies. But all of us must gamble in small ways or large and so are fascinated by high rollers. Ari was one and his daughter looks like another. One of Ari's oldest associates, recently retired, predicts: ''She'll stay in shipping.'' She named her two newest and proudest vessels for her dead brother and dead father. She would probably sell her islands, her yacht, even her Saint Laurents and Givenchys before sending such ships to the beaches of Pakistan.

astating recession in shipping history. Ten percent of the 800 Greek firms went under during 1983–85, and perhaps another 25 percent of their fleet would have to be scrapped. Entrepreneurs like Christina Onassis, who boldly cut back when the handwriting was on the wall, managed to survive.[19]

---

[19]Roger Cohen, ''Bankers Keep Greek Shipping Afloat in a Sea of Bad Debts,'' *The Wall Street Journal*, July 12, 1985.

Suggested Readings

For an advanced treatment of the theory of a competitive industry, see

Friedman, Milton. *Price Theory,* Chap. 6. Chicago: Aldine Publishing Co., 1976.

The classic treatment is

Marshall, Alfred. *Principles of Economics,* 8th ed., Bk. 5, Chaps. 4 and 5. London: Macmillan, 1920.

For an excellent survey of the importance and role of the profit-maximization assumption, see

Machlup, Fritz. "Theories of the Firm: Marginalist, Behavioral, Managerial," *American Economic Review* 57 (March 1967): 1–33.

Problems and Questions for Discussion

1. In 1986, U.S. automobile producers offered car buyers attractive financing rates of between zero and 2.9 percent to reduce inventories of existing 1986-model cars to create room for new 1987 cars. But many "comparison shoppers" in big cities were surprised when some dealers refused discounts on the "window sticker" price. (Melinda Grenier Guiles, "Good News: Incentives on '86 Cars; Bad News: The Pickings Are Slim," *The Wall Street Journal,* September 9, 1986.) Would an economist have been surprised by these results? Explain.

2. A corporation's managers, contemplating a substantial increase in the company's plant and equipment, are puzzling over means of financing the new investment. The problem is whether they should float a bond issue to raise the money or sell additional shares of common stock. How will the corporation income tax affect their decision?

3. To maximize profits, the firm produces at an output level at which total revenue exceeds total costs by the greatest possible amount. At the same time, profits are maximized at the output level at which marginal cost equals marginal revenue. Can you reconcile these two statements?

4. Rising fuel costs in the late 1970s were decimating the U.S. shrimp-fishing fleet in the Gulf of Mexico. Many families who had owned boats for generations were taking losses or selling out. (Lynda Schuster, "Shrimp-Boat Owners, Pinched by Fuel Costs, Anchor for the Winter," *The Wall Street Journal,* December 15, 1980.) Associations of shrimpers have been asking the U.S. government to implement (1) low-interest, disaster relief loans to shrimpers from the Small Business Administration, (2) price ceilings on diesel fuel, and (3) a tariff of 20 percent on shrimp imported from Mexico. For a typical shrimp-fishing firm that is operating near its shutdown point assess the likely effects of each of these actions on its demand and cost curves and on its profits or losses.

5. The deregulation of the U.S. airline industry has led to myriad adjustments. Some carriers—such as Braniff and Continental—went bankrupt. Ozark, Frontier, and Eastern merged with stronger carriers. New carriers like People Express, formed after deregulation with lower operating costs owing to

favorable labor union agreements, were successful for a while but eventually were merged with other carriers as airline fares (adjusted for inflation) fell on the longest and most competitive routes.

    a. Draw the demand and cost curves of an airline that has decided either to go into bankruptcy or to merge.

    b. Do the same for an airline that is deciding whether or not to shut down.

    c. Do the same for an airline that shows promise of surviving.

6. Is the long-run supply curve of a purely competitive industry more or less elastic at each price level than the short-run supply curve? Explain.

7. In 1981, Mexico was selling its oil for $31.24 per barrel while Saudi Arabia was charging $32. Assume Mexico's marginal cost of lifting oil was constant at $3 per barrel and that Saudi Arabia's was constant at $.50 per barrel. Diagram and explain the per-barrel producer's surplus for each.

8. Assume that company *A* manufactures widgets in competition with those of several other manufacturers, and that the styles of widgets tend to change every few years to adjust to consumer demands. Competitors were selling their new widget models in January 1987, but *A* refused to sell its new model until it sold all 3,000 units of the old model left over from the previous production run. *A*'s widgets sold for $23.50 each, and *A*'s sales manager argued that selling the new models without having sold the 3,000 old units first was "just like throwing away" $70,500. What erroneous assumptions did the manager make about the nature of *A*'s costs by valuing the old widgets at $23.50 each? Explain.

9. In 1984, many department stores had sales before Christmas rather than after owing to unusually big inventories. Sales and earnings were down, and several chains filed for bankruptcy. Observers believed there were "too many shopping centers and too many retailers." They expected more price cuts and, eventually, a "shakeout." (Hank Gilman and Steve Weiner, "Oversupply of Retail Outlets Is Seen as Big Cause of Holiday Price Cuts," *The Wall Street Journal,* December 18, 1984.) Assume that a large city's retailing industry is highly competitive and of increasing cost. As demand declines, diagram and explain the resulting shakeout in terms of short-run adjustments and the restoration of a long-run equilibrium.

10. The wholesale lamb market is purely competitive—it has a homogeneous product, no restraints on price or supply, and many firms at each stage of production. Herds start on ranches, are fattened at feedlots, and are sent to slaughterhouses on reaching the optimum weight of 55 pounds. Usually lambs move from stage to stage at uneven rates from various regions, so supplies do not accumulate. But in 1980–81, a severe drought caused ranchers to sell to feedlots early, so more lambs reached the optimal weight early. Feedlot operators who bought extra lambs from drought-stricken ranchers were stuck with feed costs that did not create extra value (slaughterhouses figure the weight in excess of 55 pounds is mainly fat). To avoid losses, they sold to slaughterhouses early, and live lamb prices plummeted. ("Live

Lamb Prices Drop 26% in 5 Months, Putting a Big Squeeze on Feedlot Owners,'' *The Wall Street Journal,* January 5, 1981.)

a.   Draw diagrams for the wholesale lamb market and the situation of an individual feedlot operator facing a market price per pound above operating costs. What are his choices?

b.   Now diagram the situation where price is less than operating costs. What are his choices?

11.   Oklahoma was the last state to repeal Prohibition and has a substantial ''dry'' vote, but it has a highly competitive liquor market. Until recently, many states kept up liquor prices by limiting the number of distributors and excluding out-of-state distributors. Oklahoma law prevents price fixing, requires distributors to sell in Oklahoma at the lowest prices that they charge anywhere in the United States, and permits distributors to ship liquor anywhere—including big states like California, where shipments from the ''Oklahoma connection'' can be found in about half the package liquor stores. (Marilyn Chase, ''Cut-Rate Spirits from Bible Belt Delight California's Drinkers, Irk Liquor Giants,'' *The Wall Street Journal,* September 11, 1981.)

a.   Diagram and explain the effect of the ''Oklahoma connection'' on the market price of liquor in California.

b.   Diagram and explain the resulting loss in producer's surplus to the California liquor distributors.

Chapter 12 _____

PRICING AND OUTPUT UNDER PURE MONOPOLY _____

Chapter Outline _____

Applications _____

Chapter 12 Appendix I _____

Chapter 12 Appendix II _____

Although the nature of pure monopoly was explained in Chapter 8, we shall review briefly its essential characteristics before examining pricing and output in a pure monopoly situation. Pure monopoly is a market situation in which there is a single seller of a product for which no good substitutes exist; the product must be clearly different from other products sold in the economy. Changes in the prices and outputs of other goods leave the monopolist unaffected. Conversely, changes in the monopolist's price and output leave other producers in the economy unaffected.

Pure monopoly in the real world is rare. Local public utility markets approximate it. Other markets that approach this type of structure include the manufacturing of locomotives, telephone equipment, and shoe machinery, as well as the production of magnesium and nickel.[1] But monopoly is not pure unless substitutes are nonexistent. Even in the public utility field, gas and electricity are to some extent substitutes. Aluminum also has substitutes, as do the metal alloys produced with the aid of molybdenum and magnesium.

Nevertheless the pure monopoly model provides tools of analysis that are indispensable for the study of prices, outputs, resource allocation, and economic welfare. We shall discuss in turn basic monopoly concepts, short-run and long-run pricing and output, price discrimination, effects of monopoly on welfare, and public regulation of monopoly pricing.

COSTS AND REVENUES UNDER MONOPOLY

How, if at all, do monopolists' costs and revenues differ from those of pure competitors?

Costs of Production

The cost concepts that we developed in Chapter 10 are as applicable to pure monopoly as they are to pure competition. The difference between pure monopoly and pure competition lies in the conditions under which goods and services are *sold,* not in conditions under which resources are *purchased*. In this chapter we assume that the monopolistic seller of a product is a purely competitive buyer of resources and has no effect on resource prices.[2] The monopolistic firm can get as much of any resource as it desires without affecting its price per unit.

---

[1]F.M. Scherer, *Industrial Market Structure and Economic Performance,* 2d ed. (Chicago: Rand McNally, 1980), 67.

[2]Modifications of cost curves to take account of a single firm's influence on resource prices are deferred to Chapter 16; they would make no essential difference in the development of this chapter.

Revenues

What is the difference between the purely competitive firm and the monopolistic firm on the selling side? A purely competitive firm faces a horizontal demand curve and a marginal revenue curve that coincides with it, since the firm can sell any desired amount at the market price. However, the monopolist faces the market demand curve which, according to the law of demand, usually slopes downward to the right. This downward slope has important implications for the monopolist's marginal revenue in relation to its price.

Marginal revenue at different levels of sales per unit of time for the monopolist will be less than the price per unit at those levels. Consider Table 12.1. A typical demand schedule faced by a monopolist is shown by columns (1) and (2). Total revenue at different levels of sales is listed in column (3) and at any given level of sales equals the price multiplied by the quantity sold. Column (4) lists marginal revenue and shows the changes in total receipts resulting from one-unit changes in the sales level. With the exception of the first unit, marginal revenue is less than the price at each level. Suppose that the firm's current level of sales is 3 units of X; price per unit is $8, and total receipts are $24. If the firm desires to increase sales per unit of time to 4 units of X, it must reduce the price per unit to $7 in order to expand sales. The fourth unit brings in $7. However, the firm takes a $1 loss per unit on its previous sales volume of 3 units. The total loss of $3 must be deducted from the selling price of the fourth unit in order to compute the net increase in total receipts resulting from the 1-unit increase in sales. Thus marginal revenue at a sales volume of 4 units is $7 - $3 = $4 (also the difference between $28 and $24).[3]

---

[3]Let the demand curve be $p = f(x)$; then $TR = xp = xf(x)$, and

$$MR = \frac{d(TR)}{dx} = p + x\frac{dp}{dx} = f(x) + xf'(x).$$

A geometric method of finding the marginal revenue curve for a given demand curve is developed in Appendix I of this chapter.

**Table 12.1
Demand, Total
Revenue, and
Marginal Revenue
Schedules for X**

(1) Price	(2) Quantity per Unit of Time	(3) Total Revenue	(4) Marginal Revenue
$10	1	$10	$10
9	2	18	8
8	3	24	6
7	4	28	4
6	5	30	2
5	6	30	0
4	7	28	(−)2
3	8	24	(−)4
2	9	18	(−)6
1	10	10	(−)8

Figure 12.1 Implications of Demand Elasticity for Marginal Revenue

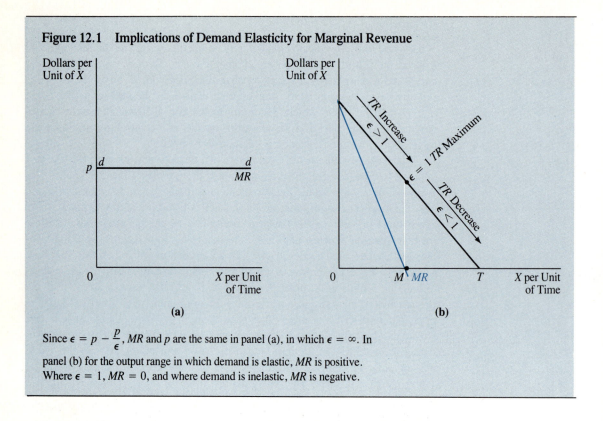

Since $\epsilon = p - \dfrac{p}{\epsilon}$, MR and p are the same in panel (a), in which $\epsilon = \infty$. In panel (b) for the output range in which demand is elastic, MR is positive. Where $\epsilon = 1$, $MR = 0$, and where demand is inelastic, MR is negative.

When the demand schedule and marginal revenue schedule of Table 12.1 are plotted on the same diagram, the marginal revenue curve lies below the demand curve—in fact, the marginal revenue curve bears the same relationship to the demand curve as does any marginal curve to its corresponding average curve. The demand curve is the firm's average revenue curve. When any average curve—average product, average cost, or average revenue—decreases as the firm's output increases, the corresponding marginal curve lies below it.

The relationship between a firm's marginal revenue and the price at which it sells is as follows:

$$MR = p - \frac{p}{\epsilon};$$

that is, marginal revenue is equal to price minus the ratio of price to the elasticity of demand at any given level of sales.[4] Consider the demand curve faced by a purely competitive firm, as is shown in Figure 12.1(a). Elasticity of demand at

---

[4]From Footnote 3,

$$MR = \frac{d(TR)}{dx} = p + x\frac{dp}{dx} = p + \frac{p}{\dfrac{dx}{dp} \times \dfrac{p}{x}} = p - \frac{p}{\epsilon}, \text{ since } \epsilon = -\frac{dx}{dp} \times \frac{p}{x}.$$

This proposition is proved geometrically in Appendix II of this chapter.

**Figure 12.2
Short-Run Profit
Maximization:
Total Curves**

Like the pure
competitor's, the
monopolist's profits at
various outputs are equal
to $TR - TC$. Profits are
maximum at x, where the
slope of the TR curve
equals the slope of the
TC curve.

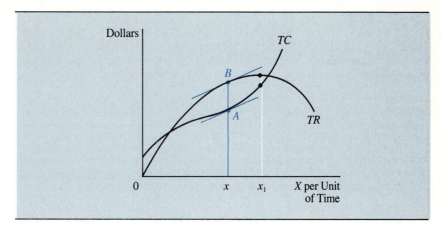

all outputs approaches infinity (∞). Because $MR = p - p/\epsilon$ and because $\epsilon \to \infty$, p/ϵ approaches zero and MR approaches p—that is, for all practical purposes $MR = p$ at all outputs. Now consider a monopolist faced by the straight-line demand curve of Figure 12.1(b). At output M, halfway between 0 and T, $\epsilon = 1$. At smaller outputs $\epsilon > 1$, and at larger outputs $\epsilon < 1$.[5]

We noted in Chapter 3 that when $\epsilon > 1$ an increase in sales causes TR to increase. This means that when $\epsilon > 1$, MR must be positive. The equation $MR = p - p/\epsilon$ states the same thing: if $\epsilon > 1$, then p/ϵ must be less than p and MR must be positive. The greater ϵ is, the smaller p/ϵ will be and the smaller will be the difference between p and MR. At the output where $\epsilon = 1$, TR is maximum and MR should be zero. The formula supports this point. If $MR = p - p/\epsilon$ and $\epsilon = 1$, then $MR = p - p = 0$.

In Chapter 3 we also learned that when $\epsilon < 1$ increases in sales cause TR to decrease. MR must be negative in this case: if $MR = p - p/\epsilon$ and $\epsilon < 1$, then $p/\epsilon > p$ and MR is negative. Thus the formula is consistent with the relationships between elasticity and total revenue when sales are increased.

THE SHORT RUN

What are the effects of the different set of demand and revenue curves on a monopolist's output level and price?

Profit Maximization: Total Curves

The rules for profit maximization are the same for a pure monopolist as they are for a pure competitor. When plotted, the total receipts schedule of Table 12.1 becomes a total receipts curve like that of Figure 12.2. Note the difference

---

[5]See pp. 59–60.

**Figure 12.3
Short-Run Profit
Maximization: Per
Unit Curves**

The monopolist's profits
are maximum at the
output at which $SMC = MR$. Profit per unit is cp.
Total profits are the blue
area $cp \times x$.

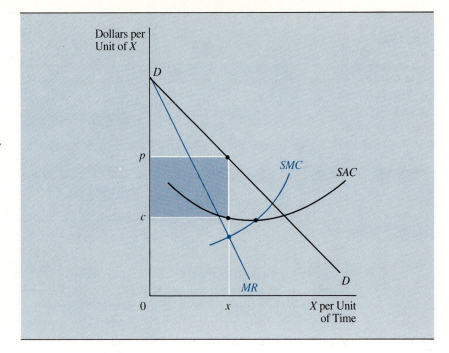

between the monopolist's *TR* curve and that of a purely competitive firm. The difference results from the fact that to sell greater outputs the monopolist must charge lower prices. Therefore, total receipts increase at a decreasing rate and at some output level, such as x_1, they reach a maximum. Still larger sales cause total receipts to fall rather than rise. The monopolist maximizes profits at output x, where the difference between *TR* and *TC* is greatest. The output at which the difference between the *TR* and *TC* curves is greatest is that at which their slopes are equal (tangents to the curves at this output are parallel). Since the slope of the *TC* curve is marginal cost and that of the *TR* curve is marginal revenue, profits are maximum at the output at which marginal revenue equals marginal cost.[6]

Profit Maximization: Per Unit Curves

Diagrammatic representation of short-run profit maximization by a monopolist in terms of per unit costs and receipts is presented in Figure 12.3. Profits are maximum at output x, at which *SMC* equals *MR*. The price per unit that the monopolist can get for that output is p. Average cost is c, and profits are equal to cp multiplied by x. At smaller outputs, *MR* is greater than *SMC*; thus larger outputs up to x add more to total receipts than to total costs and increase profits.

_____

[6]The mathematics of profit maximization for a monopolist are the same as for a purely competitive firm (see p. 322).

**Figure 12.4
Short-Run Loss
Minimization: Per
Unit Curves**

If the firm's *SAC* curve
lies above *DD* at all
outputs, the firm
minimizes losses at the
output at which *SMC* =
MR. Per unit losses are
pc. Total losses are the
blue area *pc* × *x*.

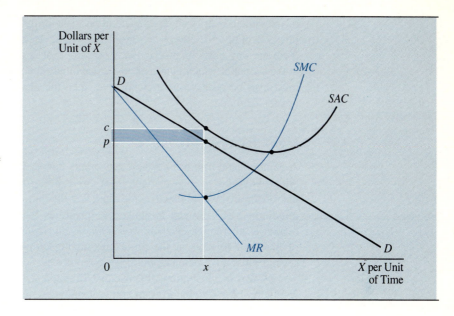

At larger outputs, *MR* is less than *SMC*; hence increases beyond *x* add more to
total costs than to total receipts and cause profits to shrink.[7]

Two Common Misconceptions

There is a common misconception that a monopolist always makes profits.
Whether or not this is so always depends on the relationship between the market
demand curve faced by the monopolist and the conditions of cost. The monopolist may incur losses in the short run and, like the purely competitive firm,
continue to produce if the price more than covers average variable costs. In
Figure 12.4, the monopolist's costs are so high and the market so small that at
no output will the price cover average costs. Losses are minimum, provided the
price is greater than the average variable costs, at output *x*, at which *SMC* equals
MR. Losses are equal to *pc* × *x*.

Another common misconception is that the demand curve faced by a monopolist is inelastic. Most demand curves, with the exception of those faced by
firms under conditions of pure competition, range from highly elastic toward
their upper ends to highly inelastic toward their lower ends[8] and cannot be said
to be either elastic or inelastic. They are usually both, depending on the sector

---

[7]The intersection of *MR* and *SMC* tells us nothing other than that profits are maximum or losses are
minimum at that output. The price is shown by the demand curve at that output and not by the *MR*
curve. Profits are determined by the price and *average cost,* not by the price and *marginal cost.*

[8]The situation could conceivably be reversed, but such an occurrence would be unusual. A demand
curve that is inelastic toward the upper end and elastic toward the lower end would necessarily be
one with a greater degree of curvature than that of a rectangular hyperbola.

of the demand curve under consideration. The output that maximizes a monopolist's profits will always be within the elastic sector of the demand curve if there are any costs of production. Marginal cost is always positive; therefore, at the output at which marginal cost equals marginal revenue, marginal revenue must also be positive. If it is positive, then the elasticity of demand must be greater than one.

Short-Run Supply

A monopolistic firm has no short-run supply curve. That part of the *SMC* curve lying above the average variable cost curve does *not* show the quantities that the monopolist would place on the market at the various alternative prices above minimum *AVC*—instead it shows the quantities that would be placed on the market at alternative levels of *marginal revenue* for that firm. Any given level of marginal revenue at the profit-maximizing output level is consistent with several alternative demand and price possibilities.

By way of illustration, suppose that a monopolist faces demand curve D_1D_1 in Figure 12.5. Profits are maximum at output x, product price is p_1, and the level of marginal revenue is r. Now suppose that the demand curve is D_2D_2 such that the marginal revenue curve MR_2 for the new demand curve also is equal to *SMC* at output level x and marginal revenue level r. The price at which output x will be sold is now p_2 instead of p_1. Thus the monopolist's output is

**Figure 12.5
Absence of the
Supply Curve in
Monopoly**

A monopolist has no short-run supply curve because the price at which it would be willing to produce any given output is ambiguous. Note that marginal revenue level r would induce the firm to produce output x. That level of marginal revenue is consistent with price p_1 if the demand curve is D_1D_1 and also with p_2 if the demand curve is D_2D_2.

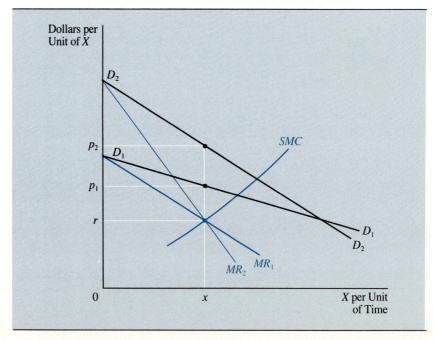

not determined by marginal cost and price; instead it is determined by marginal cost and marginal revenue. For purposes of comparison, consider again the discussion of a purely competitive firm's short-run supply on page 325.

THE LONG RUN

Long-run equilibrium conditions in a monopolized market differ somewhat from those in a purely competitive market. Monopoly profits, like competitive profits, create incentives for the entry of new productive capacity. But in a monopolized market, unlike in a competitive market, entry is blocked. If it were not, new firms would enter in response to profits, and the market would no longer be one of pure monopoly—it would become one of oligopoly.

Barriers to Entry

Barriers to entry come in many shapes and sizes. They may be inherent in the nature of a firm's production function and in the market for the product, or they may be deliberately established by the monopolist. These two types of barriers are often referred to as natural barriers and artificial barriers, respectively. The former are more or less inevitable. Presumably something can be done about the latter.

natural barriers to entry
Costs of entry into a market caused by technology that makes the minimum efficient size of a single firm large relative to the size of the market.

The important characteristics of the **natural barriers to entry** that result in natural monopoly are illustrated in Figure 12.6. The position of the market demand curve and the marginal revenue curve relative to the monopolist's LAC curve are such that MR lies below the downward-sloping part of the LAC curve. Long-run profits are maximized at the output level at which LMC equals MR. The output is x, and the price is p. The monopolist should use the size of plant that will produce output x at the least possible average cost for that output— that is, its short-run average cost curve, SAC, should be tangent to the LAC curve at output x. The SMC curve is necessarily equal to the LMC curve at the output of tangency between the average cost curves, so SMC also equals MR. The monopolist is in both short-run and long-run equilibrium. Profits are measured by $cp \times x$; any change in the size of plant or in the rate of output will decrease profits.

Any potential entrant must consider the effects of entry on the product price. Total sales volumes exceeding x can be sold only at prices below p. At such price levels, the horizontal distances from the vertical axis to the LAC curve show the minimum quantities the newcomer must produce to break even. These quantities, added to quantity x, may well cause the price to be below long-run average costs for both firms, as is the case in Figure 12.6, and entry by the new firm is forestalled. (More than one firm could survive in this case if all the firms colluded to hold the price at level p.) The original firm has the additional option of increasing its output, forcing the market price down, to preclude profit possibilities for the newcomer.

natural monopoly
A form of monopoly that occurs when technology makes the minimum efficient size of a single firm so large relative to market size that it would not be profitable for additional firms to enter. Economies of size occur through all profitable output levels.

Such a **natural monopoly,** stemming from natural entry barriers, rests on

**Figure 12.6
Long-Run Profit
Maximization: Less
than Most Efficient
Plant Size**

If the monopolist's
market is small relative
to the most efficient size
of plant, it will use a less
than most efficient plant
size at less than the most
efficient rate of output.
The output of long-run
profit maximization is x,
at which $LMC = MR$. At
this output $SAC = LAC$
and $SMC = MR$ also.
Profits are shown by the
blue area.

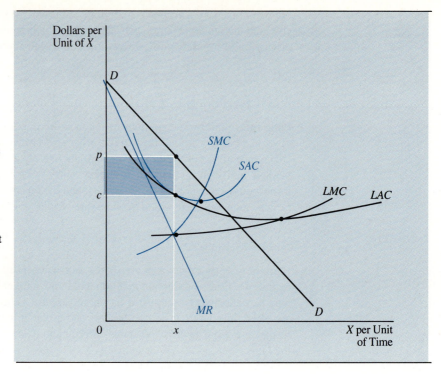

**artificial barriers
to entry**
Restraints on entry into a
market imposed by either
firms already in the mar-
ket or government poli-
cies, or by a combination
of both.

two conditions. First, the size of the market must be small relative to the most
efficient size of plant for a firm in that market. Second, the monopolist's production function must exhibit increasing returns to size, and its long-run average
cost curve must show economies of size throughout all profitable output levels.

The most important **artificial barriers to entry** are those supported or
enforced by the state. Monopoly positions are often established and maintained
through patent rights to key machines or processes. In the United States, a patent
gives its inventor exclusive rights to the patented item for a period of 17 years.
In the manufacture of shoe machinery, a single company once held patents
simultaneously on virtually all equipment used in the manufacture of shoes,
leasing the machinery out to shoe manufacturers instead of selling it to them in
order to maintain control.[9] Exclusive franchises to carry on particular lines of
business are frequently granted by governments. Taxicab and bus services, as
well as electric, gas, and telephone companies, are among the monopolies established in this way; local governments block entry through licensing regulations and building codes. The list goes on and on.

Monopolistic firms themselves can use artificial, or self-help, means of
blocking entry. A common way is through ownership or control of the sources

[9]Clair Wilcox, *Competition and Monopoly in American Industry,* Temporary National Economic
Committee Monograph No. 21 (Washington, D.C.: Government Printing Office, 1940), 72–73.

of raw materials from which a product is made. Prior to World War II, the Aluminum Company of America was reputed to own or control over 90 percent of the available supplies of bauxite, the basic raw material used in the making of aluminum.[10] This type of barrier will be most effective where raw material sources are highly concentrated geographically; magnesium, nickel, and molybdenum provide additional examples.

The requirement that entry be completely blocked if pure monopoly is to continue over time helps explain why this type of market is rare. Except in cases where the government blocks entry, it is extremely difficult for a monopolist to suppress the rise of substitutes when profits can be made in the field. Patents similar to those of the monopolist can be secured, although putting them to use in making substitute products may be difficult in some cases. Some patents may become obsolete as new ideas and processes supersede those of the past. Where sole ownership of raw materials is the monopolizing device used, substitute raw materials frequently can be developed to make a product that is a reasonably good substitute for the original.

Size of Plant Adjustments

Since entry into the market is blocked, the monopolist adjusts long-run output by means of size of plant adjustments. Three possibilities exist. First, the relationship between the monopolist's market and long-run average costs may be such that a plant smaller than the most efficient size will be built. Second, the relationship may be such that a most efficient size of plant will be appropriate. Third, the monopolist may, under certain circumstances, be induced to build a plant larger than the most efficient size.

Less than Most Efficient Size of Plant Suppose the monopolist's market is so limited that the marginal revenue curve lies below the long-run average cost curve or cuts it to the left of its minimum point, as illustrated in the natural monopoly case of Figure 12.6. The monopolist will build a less than most efficient size of plant and operate it at a less than most efficient rate of output. The market is not large enough to expand the plant sufficiently to take advantage of all economies of size. The size of plant used will have some excess capacity. If it were made smaller than SAC, so that no excess capacity occurred, there would be a loss of some of the economies of size that SAC offers. This loss would more than offset any gains from fuller utilization of a smaller plant size.

Local power companies in small- and medium-sized towns often operate plants smaller than the most efficient sizes at less than the most efficient rates of output. The relatively small local market for electricity limits the generating plant to a size too small to use the most efficient generating equipment and technology. Yet the well-planned plant will have some excess capacity—both to take advantage of economies of size and to meet peak output requirements.

---

[10]Ibid., 169–172.

Most Efficient Size of Plant   Suppose that the monopolist's market and cost curves are such that the marginal revenue curve hits the minimum point of the *LAC* curve, as in Figure 12.7. The long-run profit-maximizing output is *x*, at which *LMC* = *MR*; this will necessarily be the output at which *LAC* is minimum. To produce *x* at the least possible cost per unit for that output the monopolist should build plant *SAC*, the most efficient size of plant. In this case *SMC* = *LMC* = *MR* = *SAC* = *LAC* at output *x*. The firm is in both short-run and long-run equilibrium. The price is *p*, the average cost is *c*, and profits are equal to *cp* × *x*. Under the assumed conditions the firm operates a most efficient size of plant at the most efficient rate of output.

Greater than Most Efficient Size of Plant   Suppose that the monopolist's market is large enough for the marginal revenue curve to cut the *LAC* curve to the right of its minimum point. This situation is diagrammed in Figure 12.8. The long-run profit-maximizing output is *x*. The appropriate plant to build is *SAC*, which is tangent to *LAC* at that output. At output *x*, *LMC* = *SMC* = *MR*; hence the monopolist is in short-run as well as long-run equilibrium.

Under the assumed conditions the monopolist builds a plant larger than the most efficient size and operates it at more than the most efficient rate of output if profits are maximized. The plant is so large that diseconomies of size occur. It therefore pays to use a plant a little smaller than the one that would produce output *x* at its most efficient rate of output. By operating *SAC* at more than its most efficient rate of output, a lower per unit cost can be attained than would

Figure 12.7
Long-Run Profit
Maximization: Most
Efficient Plant Size

A monopolist would use a most efficient size of plant at its most efficient rate of output only if the market size relative to that size of plant happened to be such that the *MR* curve cut the *LAC* curve exactly at the bottom of the latter. Should this occur, *SMC* = *LMC* = *MR* = *SAC* = *LAC* < *p* at output *x*. Profits are the blue area.

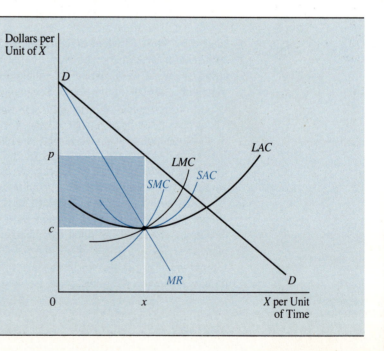

**Figure 12.8
Long-Run Profit
Maximization:
Greater than Most
Efficient Plant Size**

If a monopolist's market
relative to its most
efficient plant size is such
that the *MR* curve cuts
the *LAC* curve to the
right of its minimum
point, the monopolist will
use a larger than most
efficient size of plant
at a greater than most
efficient rate of output.
Profits are maximized at
output *x*, at which *SMC*
= *LMC* = *MR*. Profits
are shown by the blue
area.

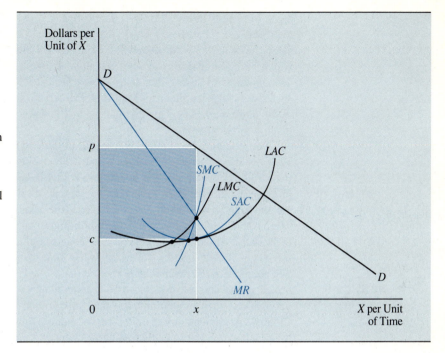

be possible with a larger plant. The diseconomies of size of a still larger plant
are of a greater cost magnitude than is the operation of *SAC* beyond its most
efficient rate of output.

PRICE DISCRIMINATION

In some cases a monopolist finds it possible and profitable to separate and keep
separate two or more markets for the same product, charging different prices in
each. This practice is called *price discrimination*. Its most common type is third-
degree discrimination, but we will also take a look at first- and second-degree
discrimination.

**third-degree price
discrimination**
A monopolistic practice
of charging different
prices in different mar-
kets for a product, not
accounted for by varia-
tions in production or
selling costs but based
primarily on differences
in demand elasticities and
prevention of resale
among the markets.

Third-Degree Price Discrimination

Three conditions are necessary in order for a monopolist to practice **third-degree
price discrimination.** First, the monopolist must be able to keep the markets
apart, otherwise the product will be purchased in the market with the lower
price and resold in the one with the higher price, ironing out the price differential
that the monopolist is attempting to establish. Second, the elasticities of demand
at each price level must differ among the markets. Third, the price differences
among the markets must have causes other than the variations in costs of producing and selling the product in the different markets.

Distribution of Sales   Consider first the way in which the monopolist would distribute sales between two (or more) markets. Up to any given volume of sales (ignoring costs for the moment), it always pays to sell in the market in which an additional unit of sales per unit of time adds most to total receipts. This amounts to saying that sales should be distributed among the markets in such a way that marginal revenue in each market is equal to marginal revenue in the other market(s). This distribution yields the greatest total receipts from a given volume of sales.

Suppose that the monopolist can sell in the two separate markets of Figure 12.9. Demand curves for Market 1 and Market 2 are D_1D_1 and D_2D_2, respectively. For convenience, the quantity axis of Market 2 is reversed, with units of X measured from right to left. If the volume of sales is less than x_0 the entire amount should be sold in Market 1, since the additions to total receipts from sales in that market will exceed any addition to total receipts made from selling in Market 2. If the total volume of sales equals x_1 plus x_2, the monopolist should sell x_1 in Market 1 and x_2 in Market 2 so that marginal revenue in Market 1 will equal marginal revenue in Market 2, that is, r. To show that this distribution brings in the greatest possible total receipts, suppose that the sales volume in one market is cut by one unit and that in the other it is increased by one unit. Cutting sales by one unit in either market reduces total receipts from that market by an amount equal to r. Increasing sales by one unit in the other market will add less to total receipts than r, since marginal revenue from an additional unit of sales per unit of time in that market will be less than r. With the proper distribution of sales, the price in Market 1 will be p_1 and the price in Market 2 will be p_2.

The reasons why elasticity of demand at each possible price must differ between the two markets now become clear. Since $MR = p - p/\epsilon$, if elasticities

**Figure 12.9
Distribution of Sales among Markets: Third-Degree Price Discrimination**

The distribution of a given sales volume between the two markets that will maximize total receipts for that sales volume is the one which will make marginal revenue in Market 1 equal to marginal revenue in Market 2. For example, x_1 in Market 1 and x_2 in Market 2 is the distribution of a sales volume equal to $x_1 + x_2$ that will maximize total receipts from that total amount of sales.

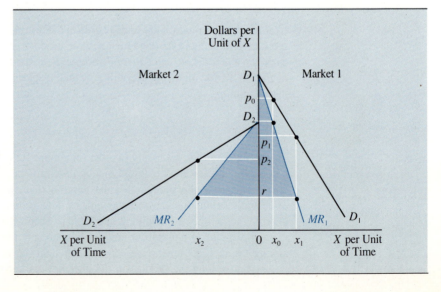

were the same in the two markets at equal prices, the corresponding marginal revenues would also be the same. The distribution of sales that makes marginal revenue in Market 1 equal to marginal revenue in Market 2 would make the price in Market 1 equal to the price in Market 2. If such were the case, there would be neither point nor profit in separating the markets.

Profit Maximization   The monopolist's cost curves, together with the marginal revenue curve for the total sales volume, are needed to solve the profit-maximizing problem. Let the average cost curve and the marginal cost curve be those of Figure 12.10. They depend in no way on how the monopolist's output is distributed among markets. The marginal revenue curve for the monopolist's total sales volumes when sales are properly distributed among markets is ΣMR in Figure 12.10. The demand curve and the marginal revenue curve for Market 2 have been drawn in the usual way. Then MR_1 and MR_2 are summed horizontally to obtain ΣMR.

The profit-maximizing problem is now reduced to a simple monopoly problem. The total output of the monopolist should be x, at which $MC = \Sigma MR$. The distribution of sales and the prices charged should be x_1, sold at price p_1 in Market 1, and x_2, sold at price p_2 in Market 2. With this distribution, $MR_1 = MR_2 = r$. If total output and sales were less than x, marginal revenue in one market or the other (or both) would be greater than r and marginal cost would be less than r. Increases in production up to x would therefore add more to total

**Figure 12.10
Profit Maximization:
Third-Degree Price
Discrimination**

To maximize profits the monopolist produces the output that equates its marginal cost to the marginal revenue for its entire output and sales level. The overall MR is determined by summing horizontally the MR_1 and the MR_2 curves. The resulting output x should be distributed so that marginal revenue in each market, as well as MC, is equal to r. Total profits are area $cp_1 \times x_1$ plus area $cp_2 \times x_2$.

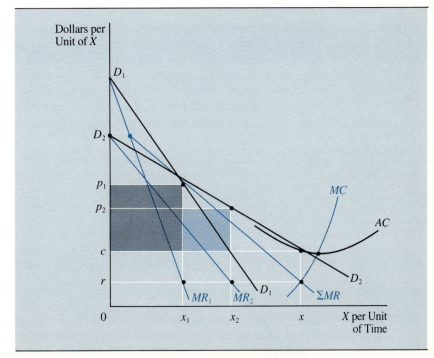

receipts than to total costs and would increase profits. If total output and sales were expanded beyond x, marginal cost would exceed r and marginal revenue in one market or the other (or both) would be less than r. Such increases in production would add more to total costs than to total receipts and would reduce profits. With output x properly distributed between the two markets, profits in Market 1 will equal $cp_1 \times x_1$ and profits in Market 2 will equal $cp_2 \times x_2$. Total profits will be $(cp_1 \times x_1) + (cp_2 \times x_2)$.[11]

Examples of Third-Degree Price Discrimination   Third-degree price discrimination is frequently encountered in public utility markets. Electric power companies usually separate commercial from domestic users of electricity and have separate meters for each. Elasticity of commercial users' demand for electricity is higher than that of domestic users; consequently a lower rate is charged commercial customers. This discrimination stems from the greater possibility of commercial users adopting substitutes for the power companies' product, although some of the rate differences may be accounted for by the lower costs of serving commercial users, who buy relatively larger quantities per day. Large commercial users may find it possible not only to find substitute sources of power but to generate their own. This has become increasingly common in New York City, where electricity rates and the frequency of blackouts are among the nation's highest.[12] Although domestic users may, and sometimes do, generate their own electric power, the generating plants that they use for their power needs are so small that costs per unit tend to be prohibitive.

Another example of third-degree price discrimination occurs in the field of foreign trade in the classic case of "dumping." Goods are sold abroad for a lower price than the domestic or home price even though production costs may be the same or higher for those units sold abroad. The markets are separated by transportation costs and tariff barriers. Elasticity of the demand curve facing the seller in the foreign market is usually higher than that in the domestic market. Although the seller may be a monopolist in the domestic market, it may find itself confronted abroad with competitors from other countries. Substitutes for the product on the world market increase the elasticity of the foreign demand curve faced.

---

[11]Let the monopolist's total receipts for both markets be $R = R_1 + R_2$, in which $R_1 = R_1(x_1)$ and $R_2 = R_2(x_2)$. Let the total cost equation be $C = C(x)$, in which $x = x_1 + x_2$.
The profit equation is $\pi = R - C = R_1(x_1) + R_2(x_2) - C(x_1 + x_2)$.
The necessary conditions to maximize profits are

$$\frac{\partial \pi}{\partial x_1} = R_1'(x_1) - C'(x) = 0$$

$$\frac{\partial \pi}{\partial x_2} = R_2'(x_2) - C'(x) = 0, \text{ or}$$

$R_1'(x_1) = R_2'(x_2) = C'(x)$, which means that marginal revenue in Market 1 equals marginal revenue in Market 2 equals marginal cost for the monopolist's entire output.

[12]Daniel Machalaba, "Idea of Producing Own Power Intrigues Many Companies; Utilities are Alarmed," *The Wall Street Journal*, March 1, 1979.

First-Degree Price Discrimination

first-degree price discrimination
A monopolistic practice in which the seller is able to sell each successive unit of product at the maximum price that any buyer is willing to pay, thus capturing the entire consumers' surplus.

Real-world examples of **first-degree price discrimination** are hard to find, but it is worth discussing as a limiting case. It requires the assumption that the monopolist is able to separate sales by one-unit increments, extracting the highest possible price for each unit sold. In Figure 12.11, suppose that a sales level of one unit, measured by an infinitesimal distance along the X axis, can be sold for A dollars. Each successive increment in the sales level is sold at the price shown by the demand curve at that sales level—for example, the x_0th unit sells for p_0, and the x_1th unit sells for p_1. Essentially the monopolist faces a constant real income demand curve. To simplify the discussion, assume further that there are no income effects from changes in the price of the product. The constant real income demand curve, D_r, coincides with the constant money income demand curve, D_m.

A comparison of the results of profit maximization by the discriminating monopolist with those of the nondiscriminating monopolist yields interesting results. In the absence of discrimination, the monopolist of Figure 12.11 produces an output of x_0 and sells at price p_0; profits are $c_0 p_0 \times x_0$. There is a consumers' surplus of $p_0 AB$.

For the discriminating monopolist, the marginal revenue curve MR_r coincides with the demand curve D_r, since each one-unit increment in the sales level adds an amount to total revenue equal to the price at which it sells. Profits are maximized at output level x_1, where MC equals MR_r. The profit picture is different from that to which we have become accustomed. Total receipts are measured by area $0AEx_1$ and total costs by area $0c_1 Fx_1$—so profits are $c_1 AEF$.

Figure 12.11
Profit Maximization: First-Degree Price Discrimination

With no discrimination the monopolist would produce x_0 and charge price p_0. Profits are $c_0 p_0 \times x_0$. There is a consumers' surplus of $p_0 AB$. With first-degree discrimination the monopolist would produce x_1 and charge price p_1. Profits would be $c_1 AEF$. There would be no consumers' surplus. The monopolist would have captured it.

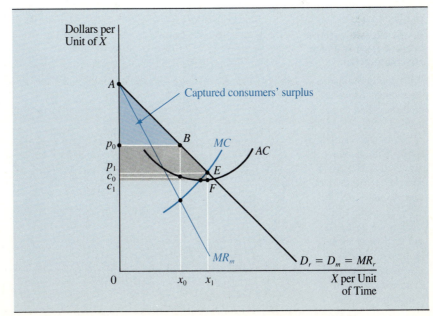

The monopolist has succeeded in capturing the entire amount of consumers' surplus—the blue area, p_0AB. In addition, since marginal revenue and product price are the same, marginal cost equals price, and this higher output level is closer to the "correct" one for the economy.

Second-Degree Price Discrimination

second-degree price discrimination
A monopolistic practice in which the seller is able to sell blocks of output, charging the maximum possible price for each block and selling the additional blocks at successively lower prices.

Second-degree price discrimination, like third-degree, is much more common than is first-degree. In the second-degree situation the monopolist places some given minimum block of product units on the market at the maximum per unit price obtainable. Additional blocks are priced at successively lower prices, with all units within any one block priced the same. A two-block illustration is presented in Figure 12.12. Again assume there are no income effects from price changes in the product, so that the constant real income demand curve, D_r, and the constant money income demand curve, D_m, are identical. Again we compare the economic effects of profit maximization by a nondiscriminating monopolist with those of a discriminating monopolist.

A nondiscriminating monopolist, faced with demand curve D_m and marginal revenue curve MR_m, maximizes profits at output level x_0. The price is p_0, and profits are $c_0p_0 \times x_0$. Consumers' surplus is p_0AB.

Now let the second-degree price-discriminating monopolist sell an initial block of goods at price p_2 and an additional block at price p_1. The marginal revenue curve faced is a stairstep curve, Ap_2EFH. Profits are maximum at output level x_1, total receipts are $0p_2EFGx_1$, and total costs are $0c_1Jx_1$. Total profits

Figure 12.12
Profit Maximization: Second-Degree Price Discrimination

With no discrimination the monopolist would produce x_0 and charge p_0, making profits of $c_0p_0 \times x_0$. Consumers' surplus is p_0AB. With second-degree discrimination, charging p_2 for the first x_2 units and p_1 for the next x_2x_1 units, total receipts are $0p_2EFGx_1$ and total costs are $0c_1Jx_1$. Profits are c_1p_2EFGJ. The monopolist has captured p_0p_2EK of consumers' surplus.

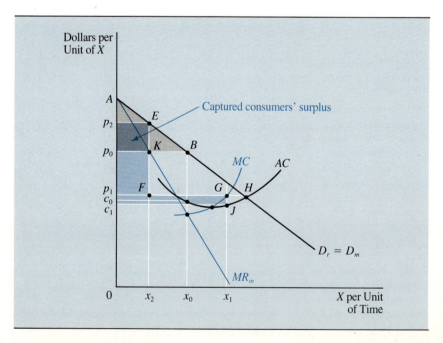

are therefore $c_1 p_2 EFGJ$, and the discriminating monopolist has captured $p_0 p_2 EK$ of consumers' surplus. Note that in this case, too, price discrimination induces an increase in output above the level that would be sold by a nondiscriminating monopolist, although it may or may not be the "correct" amount for the economy. It would be the "correct" amount only if the marginal cost curve were to cut the marginal revenue curve at the point where the latter joins the demand curve; i.e., at H.

Some public utility rate-making procedures utilize second-degree price discrimination. It is fairly common for electric power distributors to price electricity to consumers at a relatively high price per kilowatt hour for some minimum monthly rate of consumption and to charge a lower price for all that is consumed over that amount. Water rates are sometimes set in the same way. The practice is also quite common in private wholesale trade in the form of quantity discounts for all sales over some specified minimum quantities.

THE WELFARE EFFECTS OF PURE MONOPOLY

What impact would the introduction of pure monopoly into the purely competitive world discussed in Chapter 11 have on consumer welfare? The effects appear most striking when we assume that some markets are characterized by pure competition and others by pure monopoly. As in the purely competitive case, a complete statement of the welfare effects of pure monopoly must wait until resource pricing and employment have been discussed.

Short-Run Output Restriction

If all markets were initially purely competitive and were in long-run equilibrium, monopolization of one or more of them would reduce consumer welfare. Suppose, for example, that X in Figure 12.13 represents one market in a purely competitive economy. The market demand curve is DD, and the market short-run supply curve (the sum of the individual firm marginal cost curves) is SS. The market price is p, and the output level is X. Although the average cost curves are not drawn, suppose that the market is in long-run equilibrium and that Pareto optimality exists throughout the economy.

What would be the short-run impact of monopolization of product X? If the productive capacity of the market were brought under the control of a single firm, demand would look different to the monopolist than it did to the individual firms when the market was purely competitive. The purely competitive firms each saw a horizontal demand curve at the market price p. Each firm saw a marginal revenue curve that coincided with that demand curve and produced an output level at which short-run marginal cost was equal to marginal revenue or price p. The monopolist sees the new market demand curve sloping downward to the right and a marginal revenue curve that lies below the demand curve, like MR in Figure 12.13. When we assume that the monopolist takes over intact the physical facilities of the market and that no diseconomies of size are thereby

**Figure 12.13
Monopolistic Output
Restriction**

In a competitive market
the product price would
be p and the market
output would be X.
Consumers' surplus
would be pNB. If the
productive capacity of the
market were taken over
intact by one firm, the
marginal cost curve of
the monopolist would be
the same as the SS, or
ΣMC, of the previously
competitive firms, and its
marginal revenue curve
would be MR. Output
would be X_1 and price
would be p_1. Consumers'
surplus would be reduced
to p_1NA, but pp_1AF of
that amount is transferred
to producers as
producers' surplus, so the
net loss is FAB. The FBE
part of producers' surplus
is no longer available so
the total deadweight loss
to the economy is EAB.

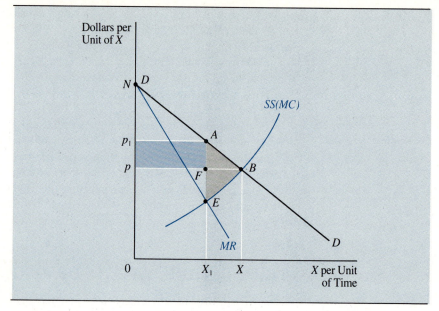

engendered, SS (the market supply curve or marginal cost curve under pure
competition) becomes the marginal cost curve of the monopolist. To maximize
profits, the monopolist would reduce the market output level to X_1 and raise the
price to p_1. The reduction in the output of X would release some of the resources
used to produce X, and these in turn would be used to increase the outputs of
other goods, reducing their prices in the process.

As resources are transferred out of X into other uses, welfare is reduced.
The marginal cost of X at any output level is the value in other uses that
consumers attach to the resources used to produce a unit of X. The price of X
at that output level is the value they attach to the same resource bundle used to
produce X. We note in Figure 12.13 that as the output level of X is reduced
from X toward X_1 the marginal cost of X falls below its price, indicating that
resources are being transferred from uses where their values to consumers are
greater to uses where their values to consumers are lower. This change must
necessarily reduce the level of well-being of at least some members of the
society.

The concepts of consumers' surplus and producers' surplus are often used
to measure the welfare loss of monopolization. If Figure 12.13 represents a
competitive market, product price is p and consumers' surplus is pNB dollars.
With monopolization the price becomes p_1, and consumers' surplus is reduced
to p_1NA, its total loss being pp_1AB dollars. However, pp_1AF of that amount has
been transferred to the monopolist, becoming additional producers' surplus, and
is thus not a loss to the society. The net loss to the society in this transfer process
is FAB, and the reduction in the output level from X to X_1 entails a subtraction
from producers' surplus of FBE. So the *total net loss* to the society in terms of

deadweight loss
The total net loss to society in terms of reduced consumers' surplus and producers' surplus owing to monopolization of the market.

both consumers' surplus and producers' surplus as a result of monopolization of the market is *EAB* dollars. This total net loss is referred to as **deadweight loss.**

Long-Run Output Restriction

Welfare will also be held below its optimum level in the long run by blocked entry into a market in which profits are being made. Where long-run profits occur the product price exceeds average costs, indicating that productive capacity in the market is too small relative to productive capacity elsewhere in the economy. Consumers value those resources making up plant capacity more when they are used in the profit-making market than when they are used elsewhere—therefore, welfare is less than it could be.

A major problem posed by monopoly in a private enterprise economy, then, is that it prevents the price mechanism from organizing production in a Pareto optimal way. The monopolized markets are induced to maintain output levels that are too small—marginal costs are less than the respective product prices—and the monopolies prevent productive capacity itself from expanding where consumers desire expansion, that is, where profits are made. The use of insufficient quantities of resources in the monopolized markets necessarily means the use of too much in the competitive ones if full employment of resources exists.

Inefficiency of the Firm

In addition to the welfare impact of output restriction, the monopolistic firm ordinarily will not use resources at their peak potential efficiency. The purely competitive firm in long-run equilibrium uses the most efficient size of plant at the most efficient rate of output. The size of plant and the output that maximizes the monopolist's long-run profits are not necessarily the most efficient ones.[13] However, if monopoly is to be compared with pure competition on this point, the comparison is legitimate only for markets in which pure competition can exist. In an industry with a limited market relative to the most efficient rate of output of the most efficient size of plant, monopoly may result in lower costs or greater efficiency than would occur if there were many firms each with a considerably less than most efficient size of plant. In such a case, even though monopoly may result in greater efficiency than any other type of market organization resources still will not be used at peak potential efficiency.

Sales Promotion Activities

It may be to the advantage of a monopolist to engage in some sales promotion activities, whereas under pure competition there is little point to activities of this kind. The monopolistic firm may use sales promotion to enlarge its market, that is, to shift its demand curve to the right. Also, if the firm can convince the

---

[13]See pp. 363–365.

public that consumption of its product is highly desirable or even indispensable, elasticity of demand at various prices may be decreased; in addition, such activities may be used to shield it from potential competition and to protect its monopoly position. Its objective in this case will be to get its name so closely tied to its product that potential competitors will find it futile to attempt to enter the market. At this point it is difficult to assess the impact of sales promotion activities on welfare. We shall be in a better position to analyze these effects when we have completed the study of oligopoly in Chapter 13.

REGULATION OF MONOPOLY

The tools of monopoly analysis so far discussed provide some indications of how monopoly could be regulated to offset, at least in part, its adverse effects on welfare. Two possible governmental regulatory devices are (1) direct regulation of monopoly price and (2) regulation through taxation.

Price Regulation

Authority is frequently vested in state regulatory commissions to govern the rates or prices charged by public utilities, such as gas and electric power companies. The economic problem involved is determination of the rate that will induce the monopolist to furnish the greatest amount of product consistent with its costs and with consumer demand.[14]

The profit-maximizing output of a monopolist in the absence of price regulation is shown in Figure 12.14.[15] The monopolist maximizes profits at output level x, where marginal cost equals marginal revenue. The price is p, and profits are $cp \times x$. Since entry into the market is blocked, the profits may persist over time.

By establishing a maximum price below p but greater than r, the regulatory commission can induce the monopolist to increase output. Suppose a maximum price of p_1 is established at the level at which the marginal cost curve cuts the demand curve; the demand curve faced by the monopolist becomes p_1AD. Between output levels of zero and x_1, sales will be made at p_1 per unit. The monopolist cannot charge more, but the public will take its entire output at that price. For output levels greater than x_1, the monopolist must lower the price below p_1 to clear the market; hence the market demand curve becomes relevant.

The change in the demand curve faced by the firm alters the marginal revenue curve as well. From zero to x_1, the new demand curve is infinitely elastic—it is the same as the demand curve faced by a firm under pure com-

---

[14]Economic aspects of the problem frequently are subordinated to political aspects, but we shall omit the latter.

[15]The analysis can be presented in either long-run or short-run terms. A short-run explanation has the virtue of being less complex.

**Figure 12.14
Regulation of
Monopoly by Price
Control**

Without regulation the
monopolist produces x
selling at p and making
profits of $cp \times x$. With a
regulated maximum price
of p_1 the marginal
revenue curve becomes
p_1ABC. Output increases
to x_1, and profits
decrease to $c_1p_1 \times x_1$.

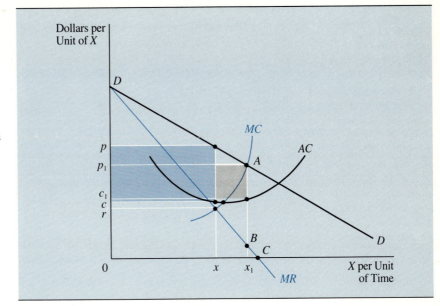

petition—and marginal revenue equals p_1. Beyond output x_1, the market demand curve and the original marginal revenue curve are relevant. After the maximum price is established, the marginal revenue curve of the monopolist is p_1ABC.

The monopolist's profit-maximizing position must be reexamined in view of the altered demand and marginal revenue situation. With the establishment of the maximum price, x is no longer the profit-maximizing output. Profits will be maximized at the level of output at which the marginal cost curve cuts the new marginal revenue curve. At x, marginal revenue exceeds marginal cost; consequently increases in output up to x_1 increase profits. At outputs beyond x_1, marginal cost exceeds marginal revenue—which drops off sharply, or is said to be "discontinuous" at x_1—causing profits to decrease. The new profit-maximizing output is x_1, a larger output than before. Even though profits of $c_1p_1 \times x_1$ occur, welfare has been increased.

Taxation

Taxes levied on monopolists are often thought to be appropriate regulatory devices to prevent them from reaping the full benefits of their positions. We shall consider two types: (1) a specific tax or a fixed tax per unit on the monopolist's output[16] and (2) a lump-sum tax levied without regard to output.[17]

---

[16] The general effects would be the same if an *ad valorem* tax, a fixed percentage of the product price, were levied.

[17] The general effects would be the same if the tax were a fixed percentage of the monopolist's profits.

**Figure 12.15
Regulation of
Monopoly by a
Specific Tax**

In the absence of taxation
the monopolist produces
x and sells at p with
profits of $cp \times x$.
Imposition of a specific
tax shifts the cost curves
upward by the amount
of the tax, and the
monopolist produces x_1
and sells at p_1 with
smaller profits of
$c_1 p_1 \times x_1$.

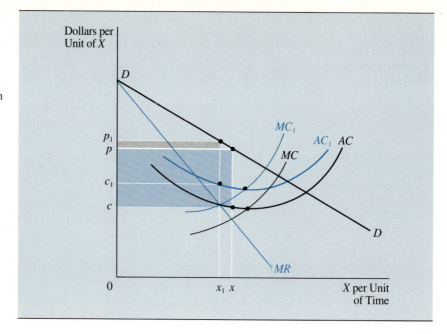

A Specific Tax   Suppose that a specific tax is levied on the monopolist firm
of Figure 12.15. Its original average cost and marginal cost curves are AC and
MC; the original price and output are p and x. The tax is a variable cost and
shifts the average and marginal costs upward by the amount of the tax. Faced
with the new cost curves, AC_1 and MC_1, the monopolist cuts output to x_1 and
raises price to p_1 in order to maximize profits.

  The monopolist is able to pass a part of the specific tax on to the consumer
through a higher price and a smaller output. At the same time its profits will be
smaller after the tax than before—pretax profits were $cp \times x$, while after-tax
profits are $c_1 p_1 \times x_1$. To make certain that after-tax profits are smaller than
pretax profits, think for a moment of the firm's total revenue and total cost
curves. Total receipts of the monopolist at various outputs are unchanged by
the tax, but total costs at all outputs will be greater. Profits at all possible outputs
will be smaller than before, and maximum profits after the tax will necessarily
be smaller than they were before. If all the monopolist's profits were taxed away
through specific taxes, prices still higher and outputs still smaller than those
shown in Figure 12.15 would result. It appears that a specific tax on the monopolist's product would reduce rather than increase welfare.[18]

_____

[18]Consider, however, the possible effects of specific taxes levied on the outputs of pure competitors
in the economy, which would induce them to reduce their output levels, releasing resources to the
monopolized markets and inducing the latter to expand their outputs. Or, consider the impact of
per unit subsidies paid to monopolists.

**Figure 12.16
Regulation of
Monopoly by a
Lump-Sum Tax**

A lump-sum tax imposed
on a monopolist is a
fixed cost and does not
change the marginal cost
curve. Consequently,
price and output are not
changed—profits are
smaller by the amount of
the tax.

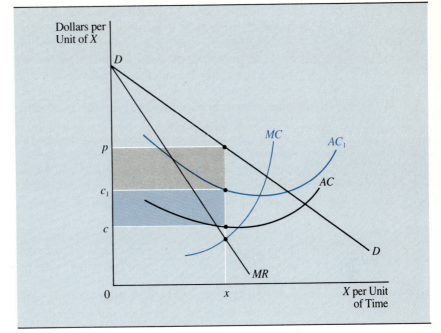

A Lump-Sum Tax Suppose that a lump-sum tax is imposed on the monopolist of Figure 12.16—for example, a license fee is imposed by a city on its only swimming pool. The original average and marginal cost curves are AC and MC; the original price and output are p and x. Since the lump-sum tax is independent of output, it is a fixed cost to the monopolist. It shifts the average cost curve to AC_1, but it has no effect on the marginal cost curve. Consequently the profit-maximizing price and output remain at p and x, but profits fall from $cp \times x$ to $c_1p \times x$.

The lump-sum tax must be borne by the monopolist alone. It is not possible to pass any part of it on to the consumer through higher prices and smaller outputs; attempts to do so will decrease profits even more. All of the monopolist's profits may be taxed away in this manner, with no effect whatsoever on output and price. The lump-sum tax by itself has no impact on welfare.

SUMMARY

Pure monopoly is rare in the real world; however, its theory is applicable to those markets in which it is approximated and to firms that act as though they were monopolists. In addition, the theory furnishes the tools of analysis necessary for the study of oligopoly and monopolist competition.

The differences between the theories of pure monopoly and pure competition rest on the demand and revenue situations faced by the firm and on the conditions of entry into markets in which profits are made. For the monopolist, marginal revenue is less than price, the firm's marginal revenue curve lies below the demand curve that it faces, and entry by new firms is blocked.

The monopolist maximizes short-run profits or minimizes short-run losses by producing the output and charging the price at which marginal revenue equals short-run marginal cost. It may incur losses and, if so, continue to produce if price exceeds average variable cost. The monopolist operates within the elastic sector of its demand curve.

In the long run, the monopolist maximizes profits at the output at which long-run marginal cost equals marginal revenue. The size of plant to be used will be the one whose short-run average cost curve is tangent to the long-run average cost curve at the profit-maximizing output. Short-run marginal cost will equal long-run marginal cost and marginal revenue at that output.

Monopolistic firms sometimes find it possible and profitable to engage in price discrimination. The most common type is third-degree discrimination; however, there are a number of examples of second-degree discrimination. First-degree discrimination is confined primarily to the realm of theory as a limiting case.

Monopoly has important implications for welfare in a private enterprise economy. Where it exists along with competitive markets, it leads to output restriction and prices that are higher than marginal costs. The possibility of long-run profits in a monopolized market exists because of blocked entry. Where profits occur, consumers are willing to pay more for a product than is necessary to hold the resources making that product in the market concerned. Blocked entry limits transfer of resources into and expansion of output of a monopolized profit-making market and thus reduces welfare. A monopolistic firm is not likely to operate most efficient-sized plants at most efficient rates of output. Some sales promotion efforts may be made to enlarge the market, to decrease elasticity of demand for its product, and to discourage potential competition.

The theory of monopoly sheds some light on effective means of monopoly regulation. A maximum price set below the monopoly price will benefit consumers through both the lower price and an increased product output. A specific tax levied on the monopolist's product will be partly shifted to consumers through output restriction and higher prices. A lump-sum tax must be borne entirely out of the monopolist's profits.

APPLICATIONS

Circumstances in the world around us are seldom as precise and as amenable to analysis as are those closeted in classroom theory. But the classroom theory enables us to discover causal relationships and to make sense out of them. We present some widely diverse aspects of monopoly-like behavior in the applications that follow.

FINDING THE RIGHT MONOPOLY PRICE

It is easy for other firms to look upon a monopolist's situation with envy. After all, the absence of competitors and product substitutes permits higher-than-competitive profits from higher prices and lower quantities. The exact price and quantity to maximize profits look easy enough from Figure 12.3. But the detailed information a monopolist must have to maximize profits is almost never available at zero cost.

How many times have we heard in casual conversation, or read in newspapers, that a monopolist "always will charge the highest price that the market will bear"? But the *right* price to maximize profits is not provided by the market automatically: the monopolist can set the market price because of control over quantity supplied. But which market price should be chosen?

A monopolist usually has more accurate information about the nature of costs than about demand. Is the demand curve straight or curved? Where does it lie? What are the elasticities at each price? In practice, most monopolists attempt to deal with the information-cost problem by shrewd guesses and estimates, trial-and-error changes in price as new conditions develop, and sometimes sophisticated market research to delineate specific arcs of the demand schedule. Sometimes expert consultants and brokers who specialize in acquiring this information about demand and in making better-than-average predictions about particular price elasticities are hired. Since such data are valuable to sellers, those managers, executives, or brokers who have successful records in choosing profit-increasing prices and quantities often command high fees.

The accompanying excerpts from a *Fortune* article show in a microcosm the basic problem that all monopolies face in attempting to find the price that maximizes profits. The famous persons listed in the lecture bureau of Harry Walker, Inc., all know from the start they could get big fees by giving talks to meetings of corporate executives, labor union conventions, college commencements, and the like. But which groups should they talk to and what prices should they charge? Mr. Walker, judging by the nature and number of his clients, has lower information costs about demand elasticities than anyone in the business. All of his clients save Henry Kissinger, whose bargaining power seems to have been stronger, pay Walker one-third of their earnings to choose suitable engagements, set their prices, and bargain with buyers on their behalf. This lessens

SPEECH IS GOLDEN ON THE LECTURE CIRCUIT
by Stephen Solomon, *Fortune*

Nearly all speakers hire agents who take a cut, usually one-third, of the lecture fee. The agent who first recognized and exploited the incipient demand for the new kind of speaker was Harry Walker, president of Harry Walker, Inc., of Manhattan, now probably the largest ''lecture bureau'' in the country. Walker claims he booked 2,000 dates this past year for a lineup of speakers that almost amounted to a shadow government: [Alexander] Haig, [Michael] Blumenthal, [Henry] Kissinger, Joseph Califano, James Schlesinger, William Simon, and Gerald Ford, to name a few. He also represents leading economists (e.g., Milton Friedman, Walter Heller) and prominent newsmen (e.g., Mike Wallace, Marvin Kalb, George Will).

Fees for such performers have practically kept pace with the price of OPEC oil. In 1970, the high was about $2,500; today it is around $15,000, and Kissinger once got $20,000. This tremendous increase, combined with the sharp growth in Walker's bookings—up more than 40 percent in 1979 alone—has enabled his family-owned company to triple its revenues and profits in the past five years.

Walker represents speakers from both political parties and holds them in equally high regard; above their heads he sees price tags that gradually melt into halos. He is a shrewd judge of talent. ''Milton Friedman,'' he says, comparing two economists, ''is worth two Joe Pechmans.''

''Genius'' is a word Walker uses frequently in describing how he built the business. He would have you believe he has no serious competition— ''Kissinger asked me why he shouldn't sign up with one of my competitors instead of with me. I said, 'I don't have any competitors.' '' The man who had handled Brezhnev and Chou En-lai signed on—but not before he had talked Walker into cutting his agent's commission well below the standard 33⅓ percent.

In truth, the notion that there is no serious competition in this business is nothing more than a facade. When he envisions reality, Walker sees himself as a Spanish galleon surrounded by pirates who are about to climb on board and carry away his treasure. There are ten or so major lecture bureaus around the U.S. and scores of one-person, one-room, one-telephone operations. ''It's a cutthroat business,'' Walker will admit. ''They try to contact my speakers and tell them they will take a lower commission.''

The predominant contractual arrangement in the business is called a ''listing,'' in which speakers allow more than one agency to advertise their availability and then choose among the offers. Walker handles financial commentator Louis Rukeyser and columnist Jack Anderson on this basis. But, wherever possible, he presses for exclusive management rights. His agreement with Kissinger and Ford stipulates that he is their only agent, though they may accept

the temptation to give price breaks to friends and former associates. The article in *Fortune* lists the fees that Walker obtains for some of his clients but does not mention the number of speeches that each client gives at his or her fee level. For example, among economists, Nobel laureate Milton Friedman is said to command twice the fee of Joseph Pechman, but it is possible that Pechman gives more speeches than Friedman and is thus at a point on the demand curve for his services representing a higher quantity but a lower price.

It is clear in the next to last paragraph of the article that Mr. Walker is keenly aware that the demand curves for his clients' services are downward sloping and that each captures some amount of monopoly gain. The article does not mention price discrimination, but the nonresalable character of each speech raises the possibility that Mr. Walker can obtain different fees for his clients, depending upon the particular audience or event and the travel or other costs involved for his speakers. Walker's own fees are constrained by competition speaking engagements on their own without paying him a commission. Blumenthal and Haig have agreed to make all their bookings through Walker and give him his cut.

In return, Walker and his staff aggressively "package" his clients, bombarding trade associations and *Fortune 500* companies ("I worship that list," he says) with brochures, biographical sketches, letters from satisfied listeners, and tapes of prior speeches. A new speaker will be trotted out to show his stuff at the annual convention of the American Society of Association Executives, which draws the presidents of nearly all the major trade associations. The exposure is as valuable to newcomers on the lecture circuit as an appearance on the *Tonight Show* is to budding show-business talent. Walker has three video recorders in his Long Island home to catch all the news programs, lest he miss something that might make one of his clients a particularly timely attraction. He handles itineraries and travel plans—all

of his speakers fly first class, stay at the best hotels, and ride in limousines (at the sponsoring group's expense).

The Economics of Talk   Why are the fees so high? One reason is that heavy demand is outstripping the supply of speakers. For trade-association conventions, a big-time attraction is worth his fee if he builds attendance that helps off-set the costs of rental space and food. Even at the prices they charge, top dogs on the circuit get many more offers than they have the time to fulfill. "I can't believe it," says Walker of clients who blithely turn down $10,000 fees. "I actually have to convince people to take the money."

The agents themselves tend to drive up prices. Speakers are reluctant to get involved in the gaucheries of haggling over fees, and might feel compelled to lower their price if they came under pressure from friends or acquaintances. The agent provides a convenient shield from such demands. The speaker need only say he

is under contract, and much as he would like to talk cheap, there is nothing he can do about it.

"There's very little bargaining," says Ken Gerbino, part owner of Corporate Seminars, Inc., a Beverly Hills company that puts on seminars for business. "Walker knows what the speakers' time and effort are worth—and that's what we pay." If a charity or nonprofit group pleads lack of funds, Walker is not about to cave in.

Walker has quasi-cartelized a major segment of the industry. As is the case in any other business, not all products are interchangeable in the lecture industry—warlocks don't compete with diplomats, for example. But lots of business groups might consider some former Cabinet officers fairly substitutable—say, Blumenthal and Simon. To the extent that Walker can sign interchangeable speakers to exclusive contracts, he can control their output and exercise a degree of monopoly power over prices.

from other lecture bureaus that have their own prestigious clients and may attempt to lure away some of Walker's.

Did you locate a technical error in this piece where the writer refers to "demand outstripping supply"? What does he mean by this remark? Would not higher lecture fees induce speakers to offer *higher quantities supplied*? How would you rephrase the author's point in precise economic terms?

PRICE DISCRIMINATION BY MEDICAL LABORATORIES AND PHYSICIANS

The accompanying article shows that the prices charged by medical laboratories to insurance carriers and Medicare in California for blood counts and other diagnostic tests in 1982 were not cost based and apparently were twice as high as the fees physicians and private patients paid for identical services. This appears to be a case of third-degree price discrimination between two markets. Discriminatory rates charged by hospitals for room, medicines, and surgery facilities are also common. Basic rates assume that patients have private or government insurance. Some hospitals post lower rates for patients without insurance, but in others patients must bargain or face potentially devastating financial losses for major illnesses.

Patients with insurance generally have less elastic and greater demands than those without it. Even nonprofit hospitals respond to pecuniary incentives of this kind. The growth of both public and private insurance programs means that fewer patients pay their own hospital and laboratory bills, and these patients have fewer incentives to scrutinize charges or to make inquiries about prices before requesting service.

The potential for price discrimination seems particularly large when the so-called "third-party payer" is the U.S. government, with its vast resources and high bureaucratic costs of monitoring its programs. Sometimes legislation permits health care providers to hamstring the cost-cutting efforts of hard-nosed bureaucrats by appealing their decisions through the courts (as happened in the California laboratory case presented here). In other cases, however, scrutiny by the government yields reverse discrimination. In 1982 federal officials reduced the percentage of hospital reimbursement costs for Medicare patients. Hospitals made up the revenue by increasing their charges to patients insured by private employers, costing businesses an extra $5 billion per year.[19] Such pricing practices are caused by the nature of medical insurance and the local monopoly positions that certain hospitals hold.

Economist Reuben A. Kessel argued that price discrimination was common among surgeons in the 1950s.[20] Established surgeons limited competition from younger medical graduates by extra specialty examinations required by state licensing boards and by county medical societies seeking to discourage competitive advertising or price cutting. In the latter case the penalty for "unethical" competitive behavior was expulsion from the local society, in which membership in good standing was required for remaining on a hospital staff. (Try to practice medicine, particularly surgery, without access to hospital facilities!) Kessel argued that restricting competition permitted established surgeons to price discriminate among patients of varied incomes. In some cases, surgeons charged zero to extremely poor patients—which if you think about it is also evidence for the price discrimination hypothesis. Does your local grocery store charge more for hamburger to wealthy customers and practically give it away to the poor, or does it base prices on costs and competitively charge the same to all?

Consistent with Kessel's hypothesis, the American Medical Association during the 1950s opposed Medicare, prepaid medical plans such as Kaiser Per-

---

[19]Michael Waldholz, "Businesses Are Forming Coalitions to Curb Rise in Health-Care Costs," *The Wall Street Journal*, June 17, 1982.

[20]Reuben A. Kessel, "Price Discrimination in Medicine," *The Journal of Law and Economics* 1 (1958): 20–53.

manente and other forms of insurance that did not allow doctors to bill patients individually. (Blue Cross and Blue Shield plans are based on individual billing and along with other insurance of this kind are popular among surgeons.) Also lending weight to Kessel's argument was evidence that county medical societies often were dominated by surgeons, who had more to gain from discriminatory pricing than nonsurgeons, and that noncompetitive restraints by dental and psychiatric societies were weaker. Neither dental nor psychiatric practice generally requires hospital affiliation, so those professional societies had much weaker enforcement devices against competitive behavior. Both professions are more likely to charge the same prices to all patients regardless of income.

Recent empirical research suggests that physicians did receive the higher-than-competitive returns that the price discrimination and entry limitation hypotheses would predict but that the extra returns were fairly small for general practitioners. Table 12.2 shows that between 1950 and 1964, when the medical

**Table 12.2
Return to Medical Training Relative to a Four-Year College Education at Alternative Rates of Discount, 1947–1973***

Year	Discount Rate 8%	10%	12%
1947	− $ 5,243	− $11,464	− $15,333
1948	− 1,122	− 9,258	− 14,345
1949	8,702	− 2,497	− 9,580
1950	9,973	− 2,374	− 10,158
1951	15,106	2,622	− 5,257
1952	11,312	− 960	− 8,714
1953	12,257	− 25	− 7,757
1954	16,159	1,917	− 7,101
1955	16,801	2,003	− 7,400
1956	18,622	3,037	− 6,867
1957	21,013	4,544	− 5,920
1958	24,250	7,256	− 3,713
1959	21,550	4,542	− 6,389
1960	29,178	9,742	− 2,731
1961	25,993	7,015	− 5,134
1962	27,103	7,946	− 4,324
1963	29,270	9,739	− 2,969
1964	38,857	16,535	1,972
1965	38,072	15,366	617
1966	41,218	17,267	1,789
1967	61,876	32,610	13,481
1968	55,712	28,230	10,262
1969	56,885	29,389	11,374
1970	67,252	37,904	18,571
1971	66,181	38,369	19,877
1972	49,142	26,040	10,588
1973	53,881	30,740	15,089

*Estimates are for the median general practitioner serving a one-year internship. All estimates are in real 1976 dollars.

Source: Keith B. Leffler, "Physician Licensure: Competition and Monopoly in American Medicine," *The Journal of Law and Economics* 21 (April 1978): 168. By permission of The University of Chicago Press © 1978 by the University of Chicago.

profession was undergoing relatively few major changes, the average general practitioner earned about $5,000 over what a person with a four-year college education would have earned when a discount rate of 10 percent was employed.[21] (Unfortunately data for surgeons are not available.) This return does not seem very high considering that the training for physicians is lengthy and arduous and requires a mix of skills that holds down the number of candidates. In addition, they work long and irregular hours, have higher-than-average mortality rates, are subjected to progressive tax rates, and, during 1950–64, had a better-than-average chance of being conscripted into the armed forces.

Table 12.2 also shows that the relative incomes of general practitioners increased substantially after the introduction of Medicare in 1966. (Many patients who previously could not afford private medical care and were confined to public hospital services were able to demand private services because of government financing. Ironically, the AMA had been among the strongest opponents of Medicare, perhaps because it failed to anticipate its potential for adding to physicians' incomes.) Partly as a result of this income increase, the supply of medical graduates and licensed physicians in the United States rose by about two-thirds between 1965 and 1982—a rate about triple the growth in the general population. Moreover, the number of board-certified specialists surged almost threefold between 1960 and 1977.[22] Over the longer run, the supply of practicing physicians was expected to increase from 492,000 in 1983 to 640,000 in 1994. Patients may view this so-called "doctor surplus" (at what wage?) as a blessing, but the AMA sees it as a curse. It favored reducing U.S. medical school admissions plus stiffer examinations and tighter state licensing standards for graduates of foreign medical schools. In 1983, 10,000 physicians, or one-third of all new U.S. physicians, were foreign medical school graduates. Many were Americans not admitted to U.S. medical schools; about two-thirds were from Canada.[23]

Price discrimination is likely to be less important in the late 1980s and 1990s owing to a variety of competitive forces. Along with the rise in medical graduates, some states have granted M.D. licenses to osteopaths.[24] In 1986, Florida pharmacists, over the objections of physicians' groups, won the right to prescribe mild drugs. Fourteen states have granted such rights to nurse practitioners, who give preventive and well-person care.[25] The use of pediatric nurse

[21]Keith B. Leffler, "Physician Licensure: Competition and Monopoly in American Medicine," *The Journal of Law and Economics* 21 (April 1978): 165–186.

[22]William B. Schwartz et al., "The Changing Geographic Distribution of Board-Certified Physicians," *The New England Journal of Medicine* 303 (October 30, 1980): 1032, 1036.

[23]From *The Wall Street Journal:* Becci M. Breining, "Blessings of a Doctor 'Surplus'," November 29, 1983; and Mark V. Pauly, "The Doctor Drawbridge," November 8, 1985. American Academy of Pediatrics, "Committee Reviews Decline of FMGs in Hospitals," *News and Comment* 33 (April 1982): 4–5.

[24]Paul Jacobs, "Medical Board to Allow MD Licenses for Osteopaths," *Los Angeles Times,* February 9, 1980.

[25]From *The Wall Street Journal:* Martha Brannigan, "Pharmacists Will Soon Prescribe Drugs in Florida, to the Chagrin of Physicians," April 3, 1986; and Cynthia Crossen, "Nurses, Tired of Answering to Doctors, Begin to Treat Patients on Their Own," January 7, 1986. Richard C. Paddock, "Nurses Back Bill to Let Them Prescribe Drugs," *Los Angeles Times,* August 26, 1984.

LABS BILLING MEDI-CAL, MEDICARE AT RATES ABOVE 'WHOLESALE,' CONGRESS PANEL TOLD
By Marlene Cimons, *Los Angeles Times*

Independent medical laboratories in California and elsewhere often have multiple price lists, billing physicians the "wholesale" cost of tests while charging private and federal programs a higher rate, federal investigators told a House subcommittee Friday.

In California, Medi-Cal, the state's Medicaid program for the poor, routinely reimburses more than the "wholesale" price for many lab tests, witnesses said.

"California spent $100 million on lab tests in 1980," Elliot A. Segal told members of the oversight and investigations subcommittee of the House Energy and Commerce Committee. "If, on average, $1 less per test were charged, the state could save close to $20 million a year. It's just wasting money."

Segal, a subcommittee staff member, investigated lab pricing in California and the District of Columbia.

Such labs, he said, bill about $100 million a year to Medicare—about one-fifth of all charges for medical tests. The other four-fifths are billed by physicians, he said.

Paul Keller, chief of the California Department of Health Services' surveillance and utilization review branch, said in a telephone interview that the state was aware of the problem and was attempting to correct it.

"The labs are supposed to charge us the amount they would charge the general public for the same or comparable services," he said. "When we find the lab billing us more than they charge physicians, we take an action to recoup the difference."

Segal said that the differences between the "wholesale" price—the one often charged to doctors—and the "retail" price—that billed to patients and third parties such as insurance companies and Medicare—often range from $4 to $6, regardless of the cost of the test.

"For low-cost tests, such as blood counts, where wholesale prices often range from $3 to $5, the retail price is often more than two times the wholesale price," he said.

The General Accounting Office, an investigative arm of Congress, already has reported that physicians themselves often mark up laboratory charges when billing Medicare for tests performed by independent laboratories.

Source: "Labs Billing Medi-Cal, Medicare at Rates Above 'Wholesale,' Congress Panel Told," Marlene Cimons, March 6, 1982, *Los Angeles Times.* Reprinted by permission.

practitioners was fostered by pediatricians to reduce their work loads in routine cases, and they became popular with patients and insurers because of lower fees. Some entrepreneurial nurse practitioners established successful freestanding businesses, billing patients and insurance companies directly. Physicians now worry about the degree to which nurse practitioners' services are substitutes rather than complements for their own. The fear is acute in pediatrics and obstetrics because of declining birthrates and more physicians. The American Academy of Pediatrics, a physician group, threatened to suspend all formal association with the pediatric nurse practitioners, including their right to publish in professional pediatric journals, unless the nurses agreed to refrain from independent practice and billing. Obstetricians who cooperate with nurse midwives and alternative birth centers may lose referrals, have difficulty scheduling surgeries at hospitals, or be denied malpractice insurance by physician-owned insurance companies.[26]

---

[26]American Academy of Pediatrics, *News and Comment* 33 (November 1982): 30; J. Robert Willson, "Can Professional and Institutional Conflicts Be Resolved?" National Association of Childbearing Centers, *NACC News,* vol. 2, no. 1 (Spring 1984): 12; Peggy Pagano, "Antitrust Enforcers Turn Attention to Service Sector," *Los Angeles Times,* April 7, 1985.

Hospitals are changing drastically. Medicare now reimburses according to a schedule of diagnostic categories on a fixed-price rather than cost-plus basis. For-profit chains now own over 10 percent of the nation's hospitals. To survive, local not-for-profit hospitals are increasingly being run like businesses: cutting costs, trying to collect overdue bills, and sending charity cases to public facilities. Some are trying to attract customers with day-care services plus clinics in personal fitness, stress management, and preventive medicine.[27] Others are slashing emergency room prices after losing business to neighborhood doctors who established cut-rate, freestanding "immediate medical care" centers for such routine ailments as sore throats and skinned knees. These "doc in the box" facilities grew from 180 in 1981 to 2,500 in 1986. Groups of physicians at big hospitals are establishing larger-scale "preferred provider organizations" that contract with insurance companies to provide comprehensive care at discount rates to large employers.[28]

In summary, patients are shopping more for medical services, have a greater variety of services to choose from, and get more services at competitive, cost-based prices. It is now common for physicians to have listed phone numbers, send thank-you letters to new patients and flowers to the patients who referred them, advertise, schedule more office hours, and make house calls.[29]

---

[27]Scott Kraft, "Hospitals for Profit: What Price Care?" *Los Angeles Times,* March 31, 1985; and Laralyn Sasaki, "Hospitals Offer Unconventional Services in Hopes of Attracting Future Patients," *The Wall Street Journal,* August 1, 1985.

[28]Michael Waldholz, "To Attract Patients, Doctors and Hospitals Cut Prices to Groups," *The Wall Street Journal,* July 19, 1983.

[29]Breining, "Blessings of a Doctor 'Surplus' "; Laurel Sorenson, "Hospitals and Doctors Compete for Patients, with Rising Bitterness," *The Wall Street Journal,* July 19, 1983.

Suggested Readings

Two classic treatments of the theory of monopoly are

Marshall, Alfred. *Principles of Economics,* 8th ed., Bk. 5, Chap. 14. London: Macmillan, 1920.

Robinson, Joan. *The Economics of Imperfect Competition,* Chaps. 2 and 3, 15–16. London: Macmillan, 1933.

Two modern treatments of the problems that must be overcome to achieve a monopoly are

Stigler, George J. *The Organization of Industry,* Chaps. 8 and 10. Homewood, Ill.: Richard D. Irwin, Inc., 1966.

McGee, John S. "Predatory Price Cutting: The Standard Oil (N.J.) Case," *The Journal of Law & Economics* 1 (October 1958): 137–169.

The problems involved in government regulation of monopoly are treated in

Posner, Richard A. "Natural Monopoly and Its Regulation," *Stanford Law Review* 21 (February 1969): 548–563.

Problems and Questions for Discussion

1. The lifework of Rembrandt van Rijn, the famous seventeenth century Dutch artist, amounted to some 600 paintings, 1,400 drawings, and 300 etchings. Each etching was made on a copper plate that could make numerous copies. Once successful, hoping to increase the prices of his etchings, Rembrandt "at intolerable prices . . . had them bought back all over Europe wherever he could find them, at any price." (Robert Wallace, *The World of Rembrandt: 1606–1669,* Amsterdam: Time-Life Books, 1968, 20 and 136.) Would you expect Rembrandt's attempt at monopolization to work?

2. In 1982 a federal grand jury was probing possible anticompetitive behavior on the part of American Airlines toward the now bankrupt Braniff International Airlines. American allegedly attempted to force out Braniff in order to create a near-monopoly on traffic at the huge Dallas–Fort Worth airport. It was accused of having performed such "dirty tricks" as dumping $9 million in tickets billed to Braniff all at once on the airline market's clearinghouse in New York, thereby creating severe cash-flow problems for Braniff. American strongly denied the allegation. Braniff later went bankrupt. (Brenton R. Schilender, "U.S. Grand Jury Anticompetitive Probe Centers on Dallas–Ft. Worth Air Traffic," *The Wall Street Journal,* April 22, 1982.) Whether or not these charges were true, do you think one airline could obtain a long-run monopoly or near-monopoly position at a given airport through behavior of this kind? Compare your thinking with that of John S. McGee ("Predatory Price Cutting: The Standard Oil [N.J.] Case," *The Journal of Law and Economics* 1 [October 1958]: 137–169).

3. Consider the transformation curve for a two-product world in which product *X* is manufactured and sold by a monopolist while product *Y* is manufactured and sold by pure competitors. If firms in each market maximize profits, what, if anything, can we say about the output mix in the economic system?

4. Suppose that there is a single supplier of natural gas in a community and that a regulatory commission is contemplating a ceiling price for the prod-

uct. The commission decides to use ''average cost pricing'' methods, that is, to set the ceiling at the level at which the firm's average cost curve intersects the demand curve. If there is more than one such intersection, the one occurring at the largest output level will be used. What can you say about (1) the regulated price and output versus the unregulated price and output and (2) the shortages or surpluses resulting from the price regulation under each of the following circumstances?

   a. The average cost curve is falling at its point of intersection with the demand curve.

   b. The average cost curve is rising at its point of intersection with the demand curve.

   c. The average cost curve is minimum at its point of intersection with the demand curve.

5. Are there *any* circumstances under which a monopolist would operate in the *inelastic* portion of its demand curve? Assume that the monopolist seeks to maximize profits, that price and quantity are not regulated, and that its output is not subsidized by the government or anyone else. Explain your answer with the help of an appropriate diagram.

6. In 1985, an official of a regional (monopoly) blood bank operated by the American Red Cross said that ''if the competition has neither the resources nor the desire to provide a full line of products and services [to hospitals], the pricing of Red Cross products can then be structured to reflect this weakness. The price of products not supplied by the competition can be increased. A charge can be added for service during nonregular hours. If only the large hospitals are being approached by the competition, volume discounts can be created for large institutions, while normal revenue levels continue from smaller hospitals.'' (D. O. Kasprisin, ''Innovation: The Risks, the Rewards,'' *Red Cross News,* vol. 1, no. 2 (December 1985); reprinted in American Association of Blood Banks, *Blood Bank Week,* January 17, 1986.) How would you describe, in technical economic terms, the pricing strategy advocated in this quotation?

7. In 1984, consumers spent about $1.8 billion to rent movie video cassettes but only $500 million to buy them. The Hollywood studios have kept the sales price to consumers high—a cassette for *Terms of Endearment* in 1984 sold for $39.95. The marginal cost per cassette is about $8 for home consumers or video stores. (Geoffrey Colvin, ''The Crowded New World of TV,'' *Fortune,* September 17, 1984, 160.)

   a. Could the studios sell each movie in separate packages—one to video stores for rental at a high price and another to consumers for sale at a lower price? What obstacle do they face?

   b. What further steps would be necessary to make this strategy profitable?

8. Which, if any, of the following college and university pricing practices constitute first-, second-, or third-degree price discrimination?

    a. The campus bookstore sells books to faculty at a 10 percent discount from the prices charged students.

    b. A private college has a fixed annual tuition rate but grants scholarships to some students from low-income families as determined by examination of tax returns.

    c. A university has a fixed annual tuition rate regardless of the number of courses taken.

    d. A private university granted $5,000 in financial aid to a senior and to a sophomore with identical grade point averages. It divided the sophomore's grant into a $3,000 gift and a $2,000 loan; the senior's was a $2,000 gift and a $3,000 loan.

    e. A university charges students only 5 percent more for a weekly 21-meal plan than it charges for a weekly 15-meal plan.

    f. A college permits students to buy meal plans even if they live off campus, but it does not permit students to live in campus residence halls without purchasing meal plans. The same price for the meal plan is charged to both groups.

9. Airlines used to give regular customers who had flown a certain number of miles discounts through coupons for free trips between designated cities. In 1985, coupons were replaced with frequent flier programs, in which each registered customer has a mileage account and gets first-class tickets at coach prices or free flights after reaching the mileage threshold.

    a. What degree of price discrimination do the frequent flier programs involve?

    b. What were the probable reasons for replacing the coupon scheme with the mileage-account scheme?

*10. Before resigning in 1985, U.S. Ambassador to the United Nations Jeane J. Kirkpatrick signed an agreement with Harry Walker for a major speaking tour for the following year. Her fees, Walker said, "rank with those of the most sought-after speakers in the world today." Another recent client of Walker's was vice presidential candidate Geraldine Ferraro. (Jennings Parrott, "Newsmakers," *Los Angeles Times,* April 2, 1985.) Make a list of factors that would affect the demand for speeches from a former public official.

*11. Insurance companies use a fee schedule to reimburse physicians according to the nature of their specialty and the type of service they performed. Surgeons or physicians using instruments in technical procedures get hourly rates from $200 to $600, but diagnosticians using only cognitive skills typically get less than $100. A major study at Harvard sponsored by the U.S. government is evaluating fee schedules and may propose changes.

---

*Denotes an application-oriented problem.

(Allan Parachini, "Examination of Medical Services," *Los Angeles Times,* April 27, 1986.) What would be the effect on the ability of physicians to engage in price discrimination of each of the following changes:
a. Equalizing hourly rates of diagnosticians and surgeons.
b. Paying each physician a per patient annual fee no matter what services were performed, out of which the patient's entire care would be provided.

DERIVATION OF THE MARGINAL REVENUE CURVE_____

The marginal revenue curve can be derived geometrically from a given demand curve. A linear demand curve will be used to develop the method, which will then be modified to cover the case of a nonlinear demand curve.

Linear Curves

Consider first what a marginal revenue curve is. In Figure 12.17 the quantity units are purposely large. Suppose a single unit of sales adds an amount $0K$ to the firm's total receipts. Both total receipts and marginal revenue are equal to area I, or $0K \times 1$. When sales are increased to 2 units of X per unit of time, suppose total receipts increase by an amount $0L$. Marginal revenue of a unit now equals area II, or $0L \times 1$. Area II does not overlap area I but lies entirely to the right of it. The dotted line from the top of area II to point L is a reference line only, to assist in reading marginal revenue from the dollar axis. Total revenue from the 2 units equals marginal revenue when sales are 1 unit plus marginal revenue when sales are increased to 2 units; in other words, total

**Figure 12.17
Marginal and Total
Revenue**

Areas I, II, and III are
the respective marginal
revenues of 1, 2, and 3
units of sales per unit of
time. The sum of these,
or the area under the
stairstep line *KN*, is the
total revenue of a sales
level of 3 units.

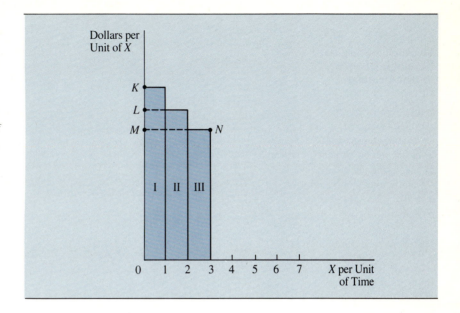

revenue equals area I plus area II. When sales are increased to 3 units per unit
of time, marginal revenue equals 0*M*—or, what amounts to the same thing,
equals area III. Total revenue is now equal to area I plus area II plus area III.
The stairstep curve from *K* to *N* is the marginal revenue curve for the firm
through 3 units of sales.

For a typical firm, a single unit of output is measured by an infinitesimal
distance along the *X* axis. If the distance measuring a single unit of output is
infinitesimal, the marginal revenue curve no longer looks like the discontinuous
or stairstep curve of Figure 12.17 but looks as smooth as the *MR* curve in Figure
12.18. The point to be made from Figure 12.17 is that at any given level of
sales total receipts are equal to the area under the marginal revenue curve up to
that quantity. In Figure 12.17 total receipts from 3 units of sales equal the sum
of areas I, II, and III, as we have said. The same is true in Figure 12.18, where
total receipts when sales are 0*M* are equal to area 0*ASM*.

Assume that the demand curve faced by a monopolist is the straight line
DD of Figure 12.18 and that we want to determine marginal revenue at sales
level 0*M*. (Ignore the *MR* curve temporarily.) Price at quantity 0*M* will be *MP*
or 0*N*. Suppose now that *MR* is drawn as a tentative marginal revenue curve.
It should start from the vertical axis at a common point with the demand curve.[30]
Reference to Table 12.1 shows that the marginal revenue curve for a straight-
line demand curve also will be a straight line spreading away from the demand
curve as the sales level increases.

---

[30]Actually it coincides with the demand curve at a sales level of 1 unit. However, if the distance
measuring a unit of sales on the quantity axis is infinitesimal, we can assume that both curves start
from a common point on the vertical axis.

Figure 12.18
Measuring Marginal
Revenue, Given a
Linear Demand
Curve

With a linear demand
curve *DD* marginal
revenue at a given sales
level 0*M* can be located
by measuring the distance
NA and setting point *S* so
that *SP* = *NA*. Marginal
revenue is *MS*.

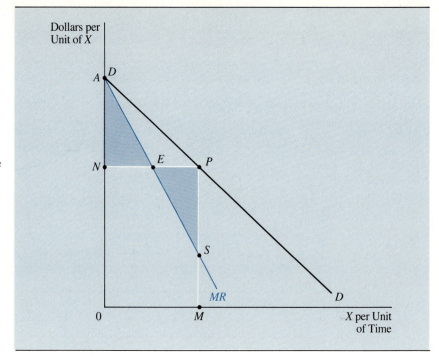

What conditions must be fulfilled if marginal revenue is to be correctly
measured at sales level 0*M*? If *MR* were the marginal revenue curve, area 0*ASM*
would equal total receipts. Area 0*NPM* (that is, price times quantity) also equals
total receipts. Hence area 0*NPM* must equal area 0*ASM*. Area 0*NESM* is common to both the larger areas and, if subtracted from each, the area of triangle
ANE must be equal to the area of triangle *EPS*. Angle *NEA* equals angle *SEP*
because the opposite angles formed by two intersecting straight lines are equal.
Since triangles *ANE* and *EPS* are right triangles, with an angle of one equal to
the corresponding angle of the other, they are also similar triangles. If *MR* is
correctly drawn, triangles *ANE* and *EPS* will be equal in area as well as similar
and thus will be congruent. If they are congruent, *SP* must equal *NA* since the
corresponding sides of congruent triangles are equal. Therefore, to correctly
locate marginal revenue at sales level 0*M*, we must measure the distance *NA*
and set point *S* below point *P* so that *SP* will equal *NA*. Marginal revenue at
0*M* will be *MS*.

Use of the geometric method of deriving marginal revenue from a given
demand curve is simpler than the proof. Suppose that we locate the marginal
revenue curve for demand curve *DD* in Figure 12.19. Select several points such
as *P*, P_1, and P_2 at random on the demand curve. The corresponding levels of
sales are 0*M*, 0M_1, and 0M_2; corresponding prices will be 0*N*, 0N_1, and 0N_2.
Now drop below *P* by an amount equal to *NA* and call the newly located point
S; marginal revenue at sales level 0*M* is *MS*. Drop below P_1 by an amount equal

Figure 12.19
Location of the *MR* Curve for a Linear Demand Curve

To locate the marginal revenue curve for the linear demand curve *DD* set several points such as *P*, *P*₁, and *P*₂. Locate points *S*, *S*₁, and *S*₂ by measuring *SP*, *S*₁*P*₁, and *S*₂*P*₂ so they are equal to *NA*, *N*₁*A*, and *N*₂*A*, respectively. The locus of these points forms the *MR* curve.

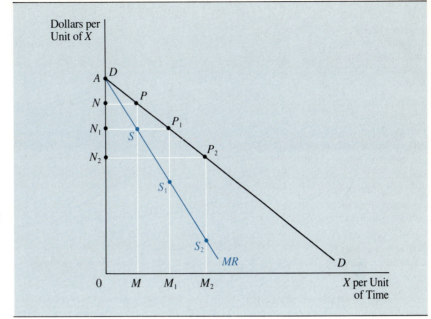

to N_1A, to point S_1; marginal revenue at $0M_1$ equals M_1S_1. Repeat the process at P_2 so that S_2P_2 equals N_2A. The line joining the S points is the marginal revenue curve.[31]

Nonlinear Curves

The procedure is slightly modified for locating the marginal revenue curve for a nonlinear demand curve. Suppose that the demand curve in Figure 12.20 is *DD*. This and the marginal revenue curve start from a common point on the vertical axis, and we should locate marginal revenue at several different sales quantities, say $0M$, $0M_1$, and $0M_2$. The corresponding points on the demand curve are P, P_1, and P_2; the corresponding prices are $0N$, $0N_1$, and $0N_2$. Draw a tangent to the demand curve at point P such that it cuts the vertical axis—call this point A. If the tangent were the demand curve, we could easily find marginal revenue for it at sales level $0M$; we would drop below P by an amount equal to NA and set point S so that SP equaled NA. Actually the tangent and demand curve DD are the same curve and have the same slope at the point of tangency.

---

[31]Let the demand equation be $p = a - bx$. Then $TR = xp = ax - bx^2$, and

$$MR = \frac{dTR}{dx} = a - 2bx.$$

Thus for a linear demand function the marginal revenue function is also linear, has the same intercept a on the price axis, and has twice the slope b of the demand function.

**Figure 12.20
Location of the
MR Curve for a
Nonlinear Demand
Curve**

To locate the marginal
revenue curve for a
nonlinear demand curve
DD set points such as P,
P_1, and P_2. Draw
tangents to DD at these
points. Locate points S,
S_1, and S_2 by measuring
SP, S_1P_1, and S_2P_2 equal
to NA, N_1A_1, and N_2A_2,
respectively. The MR
curve is the locus of
these points.

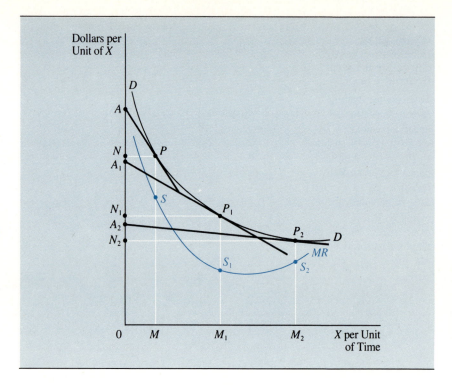

Therefore, MS will be marginal revenue for DD at sales level $0M$ as well as for
the tangent when the tangent is thought of as being the demand curve. Marginal
revenue at sales $0M_1$ can be found by drawing a tangent to DD at P_1 intersecting
the vertical axis at A_1. Drop below P_1 by an amount equal to N_1A_1; marginal
revenue at $0M_1$ is M_1S_1. Repeat the procedure at P_2, so that S_2P_2 equals N_2A_2;
marginal revenue at $0M_2$ is M_2S_2. The line joining the S points is the marginal
revenue curve for DD. Note that when the demand curve is not a straight line,
the A points on the vertical axis shift as different levels of sales are considered.[32]

_____

[32]A common mistake in locating the marginal revenue curve for a given demand curve is that of
drawing the marginal revenue curve so that it bisects the distance between the demand curve and
the vertical axis. This procedure will locate the marginal revenue curve accurately for a linear
demand curve only. If the demand curve has any curvature to it—that is, if it is convex or concave
when viewed from below—such a procedure is not valid. If the demand curve is convex from below,
the marginal revenue curve will lie to the left of a line bisecting the distance between the vertical
axis and the demand curve. If the demand curve is concave from below, the marginal revenue curve
will lie to the right of such a line.

Even in the case of a linear demand curve the procedure described here is correct in a mathematical sense only—it is not sound logically from the point of view of economics. For example,
in Figure 12.18 point E lies on the marginal revenue curve for demand curve DD. Sales level $0M$
(or NP) and price $0N$ (or MP) are used in locating point E. However, there is no economic reason
why sales level $0M$ or price $0N$ (or MP) should have any connection at all with marginal revenue
at one-half of sales level $0M$. The connection is purely a mathematical one stemming from the fact
that DD is a straight line. With regard to sales level $0M$ and price $0N$, the only marginal revenue
value that could be logically derived from them is marginal revenue at those levels.

PRICE, MARGINAL REVENUE, AND ELASTICITY OF DEMAND

The proposition that marginal revenue equals price minus the ratio of price to elasticity of demand at that price is proven geometrically with the aid of Figure 12.21. Suppose that the sales level is $0M$. The demand curve is either DD or D_1D_1—both of which are tangent at that level of sales. At sales level $0M$, the elasticity of both curves is the same, and the corresponding marginal revenues will also be the same. For convenience, let us draw the marginal revenue curve corresponding to D_1D_1; elasticity of demand at $0M$ equals $MT/0M$. However, $MT/0M$ is equal to PT/AP, since a line (PM) parallel to one side of a triangle ($A0$) cuts the other two sides into proportional segments; likewise, $PT/AP = 0N/NA$. Because $0N = MP$ and $NA = SP$, $0N/NA = MP/SP$. Elasticity of demand at $0M$ is equal to $MT/0M = PT/AP = 0N/NA = MP/SP$, or $\epsilon = MP/SP$. Dividing through by ϵ and multiplying through by SP, $SP = MP/\epsilon$. From the diagram it can be seen that $MS = MP - SP$. Because $SP = MP/\epsilon$, then $MS = MP - MP/\epsilon$, or:

$$\text{Marginal Revenue} = \text{Price} - \text{Price/Elasticity}.$$

**Figure 12.21
Price, Elasticity
of Demand, and
Marginal Revenue**

It can be shown with geometry that marginal revenue equals price minus price/elasticity at any given output. Geometrically, elasticity at output $0M = MT/0M = PT/AP = 0N/NA = MP/SP$. Or, $SP = MP/\epsilon$. Since price is MP, then marginal revenue $MS = MP - SP$, or $MP - MP/\epsilon$.

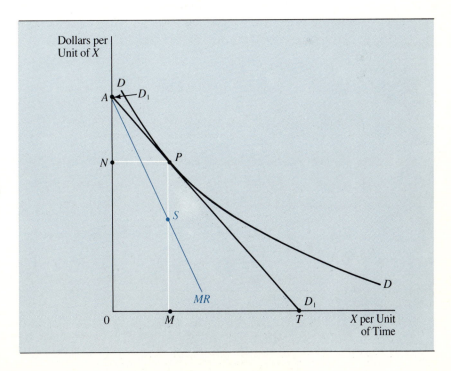

Chapter 13

PRICING AND OUTPUT UNDER IMPERFECT COMPETITION

Chapter Outline

Applications

A wide range of market structures falls between the limiting cases of pure competition and pure monopoly. The whole range is termed *imperfect competition*. A market in which there are many sellers of the product, but in which the output of each has characteristics that distinguish it from the output of the others, is one of *monopolistic competition*. However, if there are few enough sellers in a market for the sales of one to have some perceptible impact on the sales of others, the market structure is one of *oligopoly*. These imperfectly competitive market structures were defined in Chapter 8.

The theory of monopolistic competition provides few new analytical tools; it is similar to the theory of pure competition. Its strongest claim to separateness is that it furnishes a better description of many competitive industries—food processing, men's clothing, cotton textiles, and the service trades and health professions in large cities—by recognizing small monopoly elements stemming from product differentiation and consequent small differences in the prices that can be charged by the different sellers in any one such industry.

There is no single unique theory of oligopoly—nor is there likely to be. Oligopoly encompasses a broad spectrum of cases from two sellers, which distinguishes it from monopoly, to one less than "many," which distinguishes it from monopolistic and pure competition. The basic features of a single case or set of cases may be unique. In addition, oligopolistic uncertainty limits the ability of any one seller to determine accurately how other firms in the market will react to its marketing activities and in turn how their reactions will affect its own decisions. Analysis of pricing and outputs under oligopoly lacks the neatness and precision of the theories of pure competition and pure monopoly.

SPECIAL CHARACTERISTICS OF IMPERFECT COMPETITION

In what respects are markets of imperfect competition similar to other market structures, and in what respects are they different? On the cost side, the cost curves of the imperfectly competitive firm are like those of a monopolistic or a purely competitive firm. Differences among the market structures lie on the demand side.

In the first place, product differentiation always occurs in monopolistic competition and usually occurs in oligopoly. Market demand curves become difficult to locate with precision when differentiation occurs because product units may vary among the sellers in a market. Ounces of toothpaste are not the same as ounces of tooth powder. Meals differ among restaurants. Variation in skill levels makes the services of dentists or physicians nonhomogeneous within a market. Prices for a given type of product may vary because of product differentiation. Toasters may sell at prices from $20 to $40, with the different prices reflecting consumers' views of differences in quality and availability. So prices and quantities in a market become clusters, and the usual market demand curve is a band rather than a line.

Product differentiation causes the demand curve facing the individual firm to be somewhat less elastic than it would be if differentiation did not occur. This feature is most evident in monopolistic competition. Instead of being perfectly elastic, as is the case for the purely competitive firm, the demand curve facing the firm is less than perfectly elastic because of the attachments of consumers to particular sellers.

In the second place, in oligopolistic markets oligopolistic uncertainty in many cases makes the demand curve facing the firm conjectural. What one firm is able to do is conditioned by the ways in which its rivals react to its market activities. The degree of oligopolistic uncertainty is variable from market to market. In some cases a firm may be quite knowledgeable as to the reactions of other firms to its own price changes and can determine the demand curve facing it with some confidence. In others individual firms can make only educated guesses. Interdependence among firms and uncertainty about rivals' reactions give rise to a whole host of problems and strategies for oligopolistic firms that we do not find in the other market classifications.

COLLUSION VERSUS INDEPENDENT ACTION IN OLIGOPOLY

An oligopolistic market structure invites firms in the market to attempt collusion, but collusive arrangements are seldom perfect and are usually difficult to maintain over time. There are at least three major incentives leading oligopolistic firms to attempt collusion: (1) They can increase their profits if they can decrease the amount of competition among themselves and act monopolistically. (2) Collusion can decrease oligopolistic uncertainty. If the firms act in concert, they reduce the likelihood of any one firm's taking actions detrimental to the interests of the others. (3) Collusion among the firms already in a market may block newcomers from it. However, once a collusive arrangement is in existence any single firm has a profit incentive to break away from the group and act independently, destroying the collusive arrangement. We distinguish among cases of perfect collusion, cases of imperfect collusion, and situations characterized by independent action on the part of individual firms.[1]

Perfect Collusion

cartel
An organization of firms in a market in which certain management decisions and functions that would otherwise be performed independently by individual firms are transferred to a collusive group representing them.

Cartel arrangements may approach perfect collusion among the sellers in a market. A **cartel** is a formal organization of the producers within a given market. Its purpose is to transfer certain management decisions and functions of indi-

---

[1]Fritz Machlup, *The Economics of Sellers' Competition* (Baltimore: The Johns Hopkins Press, 1952), 363–365.

vidual firms to a central association in order to improve the profit positions of the firms. Overt formal cartel organizations are generally illegal in the United States, but they have existed extensively in other countries and, like OPEC, on an international basis. In the United States, covert collusion may result in cartel-like arrangements; the electrical equipment case of the 1960s provides an example.[2] In addition, the government itself may be enlisted to help support what are essentially cartel arrangements, as in the case of agricultural marketing orders discussed later. Oil prorationing by state commissions in the major petroleum-producing states has served this purpose.[3]

The extent to which functions are transferred to the central association varies in different cartel situations. We shall consider two representative cartel types. The first, selected to illustrate almost complete cartel control over member firms, will be called the **centralized cartel.** The second illustrates cases in which fewer functions are transferred to the central association; it will be designated as the **market-sharing cartel.**

In the centralized cartel, decision making with regard to pricing, output, sales, and distribution of profits is accomplished by the central association, which markets the product, determines prices, specifies the amount that each firm is to produce, and divides profits among member firms. Member firms are represented in the central association, and the cartel policies presumably result from exchanges of ideas, negotiation, and compromise. However, a single firm's power to influence cartel policies is not necessarily proportional to its representation in the central association; its economic power in the industry may significantly influence cartel policies.

The market-sharing cartel is a somewhat looser form of organization. The firms forming the cartel agree on market shares with or without an understanding regarding prices. Member firms do their own marketing but observe the cartel agreement.

centralized cartel
A cartel in which the central association or group makes decisions regarding prices, output, sales, and distribution of profits.

marketing-sharing cartel
A cartel in which the market shares of the member firms are determined mutually.

Imperfect Collusion

Imperfectly collusive cases are made up mostly of tacit informal arrangements under which the firms in a market seek to establish prices and outputs and yet escape prosecution under the U.S. antitrust laws. The price leadership arrangements that have existed in a number of industries—steel, tobacco, oil, and others—are typical of this class. However, tacit unorganized collusion can occur in many other ways. Gentlemen's agreements of various sorts with regard to pricing, output, market sharing, and other activities of the firms within the industry can be worked out on the golf course and at ''social'' occasions of different kinds.

---

[2]F.M. Scherer, *Industrial Market Structure and Economic Performance,* 2d ed. (Chicago: Rand McNally, 1980), 170–172.

[3]Walter S. Measday, ''The Petroleum Industry,'' in *The Structure of American Industry,* 5th ed., ed. Walter Adams (New York: Macmillan, 1982), 51–52.

Independent Action

Cases of independent action are just what the term implies: the individual firms in a market each go it alone. In some markets, independent action often touches off price wars when the reactions of rivals to the economic activities of one firm are retaliatory in nature. In other markets, independent action may be consistent with stability over time. Firms may have learned by experience what the reactions of rivals will be to moves on their part and may voluntarily avoid any activity that will rock the boat. Or, it may be that the management of each firm is reasonably well satisfied with current prices, outputs, and profits and is content to let things continue as they are rather than chance the start of a chain reaction.

Classification Limitations

Collusion is a matter of degree, with cases of perfect collusion and cases of independent action at the polar limits. We cannot with certainty say that all price leadership cases or all gentlemen's agreements fall under the heading of imperfect collusion. Ordinarily we would expect that to be the case, but in some instances the terms of agreement and adherence to those terms may be strict enough to present a case of perfect collusion. Similarly, cartel arrangements may not always be enforced strictly enough to warrant calling them perfect collusion, but rather they may fall in the category of imperfect collusion.

Reference to the number of firms in a market is conspicuously absent from the classification that we have made. Yet the degree of collusion achieved is not entirely divorced from the number of firms involved. The greater the number of firms in a given market, the harder it will ordinarily be to achieve a high degree of collusion. The smaller the number of firms involved, the easier it is for the activities of individual firms to come under the scrutiny of the others. Small numbers are more easily policed by the group as a whole; hence collusive arrangements are less likely to be violated by the individual firms.

THE SHORT RUN

We turn now to outputs and pricing in markets of imperfect competition. In monopolistic competition the analysis is very similar to that of pure competition and pure monopoly. Since there is no single oligopoly case, we examine typical examples under each of the three collusive classifications of the preceding section to obtain a general grasp of the fundamental problems and principles involved in oligopolistic situations. We should keep in mind that in the short run individual firms do not have time to change their plant sizes, nor is it possible for new firms to enter. The number of firms in a market is fixed.

Monopolistic Competition

Short-run profit maximization by a monopolistically competitive firm is shown graphically in Figure 13.1. The demand curve facing the firm, *dd*, is downward sloping to the right but is highly elastic for the reasons explained in Chapter 8.

Figure 13.1
Short-Run Profit
Maximization

The monopolistically
competitive firm
maximizes profits in the
short run by producing
the output at which
SMC = *mr*. Profits are
cp × *x*, the blue area.

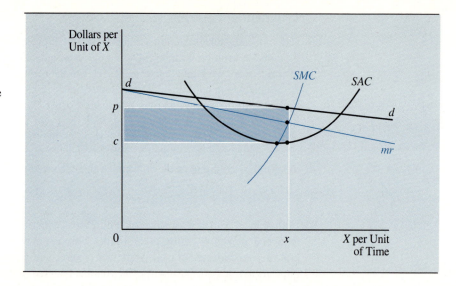

The marginal revenue curve, *mr*, lies below it. The firm's short-run average cost and marginal cost curves are *SAC* and *SMC*, respectively. The firm maximizes profits (or would minimize losses if the *SAC* were to lie above *dd* at all possible outputs) by producing output *x*, at which marginal cost equals marginal revenue. Profits per unit are *cp*; total profits are measured by the area *cp* × *x*.

Short-run equilibrium in the market does not imply that all firms charge the same prices. Identical prices would not be expected, since the firms of the industry do not produce homogeneous outputs. Each firm seeks its own profit-maximizing position and equates its own marginal cost to its own marginal revenue. Yet the prices charged by different producers will not be far apart. In short-run equilibrium we would expect prices to be clustered but not necessarily equal. Although each producer has some discretion in setting its own price, it is subject to the restrictive effects of the competition from many close substitutes for its product.

Oligopoly: Perfect Collusion

There are two major types of perfect collusion cases in oligopolistic markets. These are: (1) the centralized cartel and (2) the market-sharing cartel.

The Centralized Cartel   Collusion in its most complete form is exemplified by the centralized cartel. Its purpose is the joint or monopolistic maximization of profits by the several firms of the market. "Ideal" or complete monopolistic price and output determination by a cartel will rarely be achieved in the real world—although it may be approached in some instances.

Suppose that the firms of an industry have surrendered the power to make price and output decisions to a central association. Quotas to be produced are determined by the association, as is the distribution of industry profits; policies adopted are to be those that will contribute most to these profits. To simplify the analysis, we assume that the firms of the industry produce a homogeneous product.

Maximization of the cartel's profits is essentially a monopoly problem, since a single agency is making decisions for the industry as a whole. Profits are maximum where the market output and price are such that market marginal revenue equals market marginal cost. These two concepts need explanation.

The association is faced with the market demand curve for the product; the market marginal revenue curve is derived from it in the usual manner. The market marginal revenue curve shows how much each one-unit increase in the volume of sales per unit of time will increase total receipts. The market demand curve and the market marginal revenue curve are shown by DD and MR, respectively, in Figure 13.2.

The market marginal cost curve is constructed from the short-run marginal cost curves of the individual firms in the market. The two-firm case in Figure 13.2 shows how this is done. For any given output level the central agency should minimize market costs. This goal can be accomplished by allocating quotas to the member firms in such a way that the marginal cost of each firm when producing its quota is equal to the marginal cost of every other firm when each is producing its respective quota. If quotas are allocated to individual firms

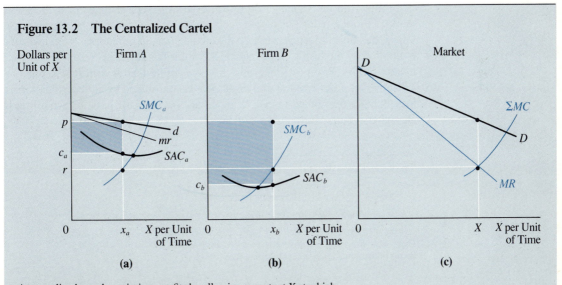

Figure 13.2   The Centralized Cartel

A centralized cartel maximizes profits by allowing an output X at which market marginal revenue MR equals market marginal cost ΣMC. Production quotas should be allocated to member firms so that each firm's SMC equals level r, or market MR. Market profits are the sum of firm profits shown in blue.

in any other way, industry costs for the given output will not be minimized. Suppose, for example, that the quota of firm A with respect to that of firm B is such that A's marginal cost is greater than B's; total market cost could be decreased by reducing A's quota and increasing B's. Reducing A's production rate by one unit will reduce industry total cost by an amount equal to A's (higher) marginal cost; increasing B's production rate by one unit will increase market total cost by an amount equal to B's (lower) marginal cost. Thus the reduction of firm A's quota will decrease total cost by more than the increase in firm B's quota will raise it. When quotas are correctly allocated for each possible output level, the market marginal cost curve will be the horizontal summation of the individual firm's short-run marginal cost curves. The market marginal cost curve in Figure 13.2 is ΣMC.[4]

The profit-maximizing price for the cartel will be p, and the market output will be X. Each individual firm should produce the quota at which its short-run marginal cost is equal to market marginal revenue r. The quota of firm A will be x_a, and that of firm B will be x_b. (Ignore dd and mr in the firm A diagram for the present.) If market output exceeds X, marginal costs of one or more firms will be greater than r and market marginal revenue will be smaller. More will be added to market total costs by these outputs than to market total receipts; hence profits will decrease. If market output is less than x, some or all firms' short-run marginal costs will be less than r, while market marginal revenue will exceed r. Larger outputs up to X will add more to market total receipts than to market total costs, and profits will increase.[5]

Profits can be computed on a firm-by-firm basis and totaled for the entire market. Profit per unit of output for a single firm will equal the market price minus the firm's average cost at the output that it produces. Profit per unit multiplied by the firm's output equals the profit that the firm contributes to total market profits. Profit of firm A is $c_a p \times x_a$, while that of firm B is $c_b p \times x_b$. Total market profits are the sum of the profits contributed by all individual firms; they may be distributed among firms on an "as earned" basis or according to any other scheme deemed appropriate.

---

[4]See the multiple-plant case discussed on pp. 294–295.

[5]Let π = profits:

$\quad R = f(x_a + x_b)$ = total revenue of the cartel

$\quad C_a = g(x_a)$ = total cost for firm A

$\quad C_b = h(x_b)$ = total cost for firm B.

Then, $\pi = R - (C_a + C_b) = f(x_a + x_b) - g(x_a) - h(x_b)$.
To maximize profits, the necessary conditions are

$$\frac{\partial \pi}{\partial x_a} = f'(x_a + x_b) - g'(x_a) = 0,$$

$$\frac{\partial \pi}{\partial x_b} = f'(x_a + x_b) - h'(x_b) = 0, \quad \text{or}$$

$$f'(x_a + x_b) = g'(x_a) = h'(x_b),$$

that is MR from cartel sales must equal the marginal cost of firm A's output and the marginal cost of firm B's output.

The "ideal" monopolistic determination of market output and price just described is seldom achieved in practice. Decisions made by an association result from negotiation and compromise among the points of view and interests of cartel members. Therefore, the association would probably not be able to act precisely as would a monopolist. Profits, for example, may be distributed according to production quotas assigned to individual firms. Some firms, being able to exert great pressure on the central association, may receive quotas that run their marginal costs above those of other firms, thus raising industry costs and lowering industry profits. In addition, pressure on the central association to increase the quotas of some firms may result in decisions to expand market output beyond the profit-maximizing level, which would result in prices and profits below the full monopolistic level. Inefficient, high-cost firms may be assigned quotas that run their marginal costs above market marginal revenue, even though principles of economy may indicate that such firms should be shut down completely. These possibilities by no means exhaust the field, but they do serve to illustrate the point that political decisions on the part of the association, made to placate certain member firms, may sometimes take precedence over economic considerations.[6] These possibilities also give us a glimpse of just how difficult it will be for even the most efficient central association to pursue a profit maximization strategy successfully.

In a cartel composed of several firms, individual firms have incentives to leave and operate independently. With the larger part of the industry adhering to the cartel price, an individual firm operating independently would be faced with a demand curve for its output that is much more elastic than the market demand curve in price ranges around the cartel price. Consider firm A in Figure 13.2. If it could break away from the cartel, it would be faced with a demand curve such as dd, provided other firms in the cartel adhered to price p. The demand curve facing any one individual firm under these circumstances would be much more elastic than the market demand curve at the cartel price, since a cut in price by this firm would attract buyers away from the rest of the cartel. Consequently marginal revenue for firm A, operating independently at output level x_a, would be higher than marginal revenue for the cartel at output level X. Firm A's marginal revenue would exceed its marginal costs at output x_a, and the firm could increase its own profits by expanding its output beyond x_a.

The incentives for price cutting for any one firm of a cartel are illustrated in Figure 13.3. In panel (a), the demand curve facing the firm for clandestine price cutting or price increasing is dd, generated on either side of point i, which represents the quota and price assigned the firm by the cartel central association. Operating in the cartel, the firm's total revenue is $0pix_a$. With a secret price cut to p_s, the firm's total revenue is increased by area $x_a jkx_s$ − area $p_s pij$. Its total costs are increased by the additional area under the marginal cost curve, that is, by $x_a lmx_s$. Therefore the firm's profits would be raised through secret price cutting by $(x_a jkx_s - p_s pij) - x_a lmx_s$.

---

[4]See the multiple-plant case discussed on pp. 294–295.

Figure 13.3   The Rewards for Secret Price Cutting by One Firm in a Cartel

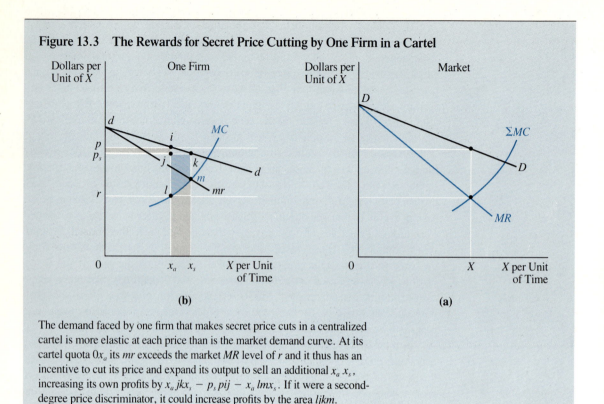

(b)

(a)

The demand faced by one firm that makes secret price cuts in a centralized cartel is more elastic at each price than is the market demand curve. At its cartel quota $0x_a$ its mr exceeds the market MR level of r and it thus has an incentive to cut its price and expand its output to sell an additional $x_a x_s$, increasing its own profits by $x_a jkx_s - p_s pij - x_a lmx_s$. If it were a second-degree price discriminator, it could increase profits by the area $ljkm$.

If the firm can practice second-degree price discrimination, separating the old from the new customers, it can obtain even larger gains. Suppose it can sell quota $0x_a$ at the cartel price and can then secretly cut price and sell an *additional* $x_a x_s$ units. Now area $ljkm$ represents the additional revenues minus the additional costs; it is not necessary for the firm to relinquish the revenues represented by the rectangle $p_s pij$. This price discrimination tactic can benefit the firm in two ways: (1) it results in greater profits than does price cutting without discrimination, and (2) it reduces the risk that the cartel central association will detect the price cutting, since the price break is given on fewer units of sales—$x_a x_s$ instead of $0x_s$. The less sold outside the cartel, the smaller will be the reduction in the total sales of the association and thus the lower will be the probability that other firms will realize what is happening. Smaller sellers in a cartel are more likely to avoid detection in secret price cutting than are large sellers. They tend to have disproportionate leverage in obtaining cartel quotas and use their strategic position within the cartel to grow at the group's expense.[7]

_____

[7]George J. Stigler, "A Theory of Oligopoly," *Journal of Political Economy* 72 (February 1964): 44–61.

The price-cutting incentives for one firm apply to each member of the group. Each firm is likely to recognize that its competitors have similar incentives to deal secretly, so for self-protection some may try to cut price by some amount first. These cuts increase industry output, lower industry price, and weaken the power of the central association. The gains from collusion tend to be destroyed. Cartels are apt to hold together best when there are few sellers and few buyers, thus reducing the costs of monitoring the participating firms.

The Market-Sharing Cartel   Market-sharing arrangements are more common than centralized cartels. The difficulties that a central association encounters in selecting a price that all members can agree on, dividing quotas equitably, and preventing secret dealing often make market-sharing arrangements emerge by default. Under certain circumstances, market sharing can result in an "ideal" monopoly price and output for the industry—that is, the industry profit-maximizing level of price and output. In most cases, however, it is likely to fall short of the monopoly position.

Suppose that the firms of an industry produce a homogeneous product and agree on the share of the market that each is to receive at each possible price. Homogeneity of the product will establish the rule of a single price in the product market. To simplify the analysis, assume further that there are only two firms in the industry, each having equal costs and agreeing to share the market half and half.

The two firms will have identical views regarding the price to charge and the output to produce. In Figure 13.4, the market demand curve for the product is DD, and each firm faces demand curve dd for its own output. Each has a

**Figure 13.4
The Market-Sharing
Cartel**

Two identical firms, sharing a market fifty-fifty, would maximize market profits where $\Sigma MC = MR$ if each maximizes its own profits. Each would produce an output of x at which $SMC = mr$. Market ΣMC is the horizontal summation of the firm SMCs and lies twice as far to the right as SMC. Since DD and dd are isoelastic, mr lies below dd by the same amount that MR lies below DD at each price. Consequently, the intersection of ΣMC and MR occurs at the same level and at twice the output of that of SMC and mr.

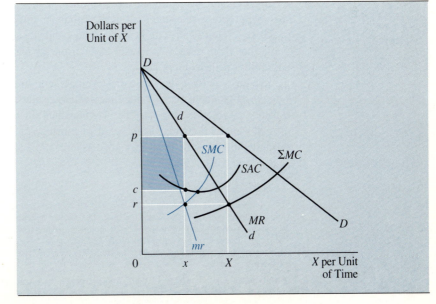

short-run average cost curve and a short-run marginal cost curve of *SAC* and *SMC*, respectively; the marginal revenue curve faced by each is *mr*. The profit-maximizing output for each firm will be *x*, at which *SMC* is equal to *mr*. Each will want to charge price *p*, and profits for each will equal *cp* × *x*. Together the firms will produce an industry output of *X* that will fill the market at price *p*, since *dd* lies halfway between the market demand curve and the price axis.

Under the assumed conditions the market-sharing cartel, like the centralized cartel, will arrive at price and output levels that a monopolist would set if in complete control of the producing facilities of the industry. Such a monopolist's marginal cost curve would be Σ*MC*, the horizontal summation of the two *SMC* curves of the two plants—it would lie twice as far to the right at each price level as the *SMC* curve of Figure 13.4. The monopolist would face the market demand curve *DD*, and at output *X* industry marginal revenue, *MR*, would be at level *r*—the same level as individual firm marginal revenue at output *x*. This would be so because *DD* has the same elasticity at price *p* as does *dd*.[8] At output *X*, industry marginal cost is also at level *r*, making it the profit-maximizing output for the monopolist. The monopolist would sell output *X* at price *p* per unit.

Several factors, however, may stand in the way of the achievement of an "ideal" monopolistic price and output. Costs of production for the individual firms are likely to differ rather than be identical, as we assumed that they were. Market sharing largely precludes the transferring of output quotas from firms with higher marginal costs to those with lower marginal costs at the outputs produced by each. Differing points of view and differing interests of the firms comprising the cartel may result in compromises that prevent maximization of industry profits. This is OPEC's core problem, as we will discuss later. Individual firms, assigned market shares and given a product price, may deliberately or in good faith overestimate the quantities of product that constitute their respective proportions of the total market; thus they may encroach on the markets of others.[9] Additionally, the degree of independent action left to individual firms may whet their desires to break away from the cartel and may increase the possibility of their doing so.

Under a market-sharing cartel arrangement, markets need not be shared equally. High-capacity firms may receive larger market shares than firms of low capacity. Market sharing may be accomplished on a regional basis, with each firm allocated a particular geographic area instead of sharing a common market. A whole host of difficulties may arise as a result of different demand elasticities

---

[8]Two demand curves with equal elasticities at each of various price levels are said to be isoelastic. Demand curves are isoelastic when the quantities taken at each of various prices form a constant ratio to each other. (Joan Robinson, *The Economics of Imperfect Competition* [London: Macmillan, 1933], 61.) Because *dd* lies halfway between *DD* and the price axis at different prices, the quantities taken as shown by *dd* are in constant ratio to the quantities taken as shown by *DD*. The ratio is one-half.

[9]To minimize sales in excess of market shares or quotas, most cartels exact penalties from the member that exceeds its quota.

at particular prices: different costs, inferior territories, encroachment upon one another's territories, and so on—all of which make pricing and output problems much more difficult than they appear to be in our model. The range and magnitude of the uncertainties imply that the number of collusive arrangements attempted generally will exceed the number that are successful.

Oligopoly: Imperfect Collusion

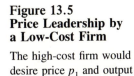

price leadership
A loose form of collusive arrangement in which one firm is identified as the price setter or leader whose prices are followed by the other firms.

Price leadership arrangements are the predominate forms of imperfect collusion. Two illustrative cases follow.

Price Leadership by a Low-Cost Firm   In the absence of formal cartel arrangements, price leadership by one firm in a market frequently provides the means of colluding. Suppose that there are two firms in the market, that a tacit market-sharing arrangement has been established with each firm assigned half the market, that the product is undifferentiated, and that one firm has lower costs than the other.

A conflict of interest will occur with regard to the price to charge. In Figure 13.5, the market demand curve is DD and each firm faces demand curve dd. The cost curves of the high-cost firm are SAC_1 and SMC_1; those of the low-cost firm are SAC_2 and SMC_2; the marginal revenue curve of each is mr. The high-cost firm will want to produce an output of x_1 and charge a price of p_1, whereas the low-cost one will want to produce an output of x_2 and charge a price of p_2.

Since the low-cost firm can afford to sell at a lower price than the high-cost firm can, the latter will have no recourse other than to sell at the price set

**Figure 13.5
Price Leadership by
a Low-Cost Firm**

The high-cost firm would desire price p_1 and output x_1, while the low-cost firm would want price p_2 and output x_2 in order to maximize profits. The low-cost firm can undercut the price of the high-cost firm and thus become the price leader.

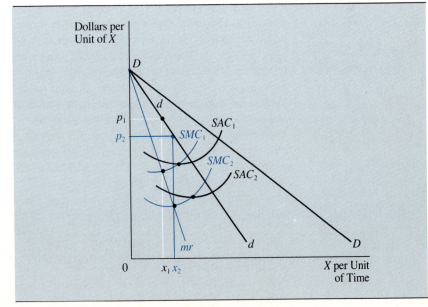

by the former—thus the low-cost firm becomes the price leader. This type of situation has several ramifications, depending on the comparative costs of the firms, the number of firms in the industry, the shape and position of the market demand curve, and the share of the market that each firm is to receive.[10]

Price Leadership by a Dominant Firm   Many oligopolistic markets are made up of one or more large firms together with a number of small ones. To avoid large-scale price cutting, tacit collusion may occur in the form of price leadership by one or more of the large firms.[11] To simplify the analysis, assume that there is a single large dominant firm and a number of small firms in the market. Suppose that the dominant firm sets the price for the market and allows the small ones to sell all that they desire at that price. The dominant firm then fills out the market.

Each small firm tends to behave as though it were in a competitive atmosphere. It can sell all that it wants at the price set by the dominant firm; it faces a perfectly elastic demand curve at the level of the established price. The marginal revenue curve of the small firm coincides with the demand curve faced by it; hence to maximize profits, the small firm should produce the output at which its marginal cost equals marginal revenue and the price set by the dominant firm.

A supply curve for all small firms combined is obtained by summing their marginal cost curves horizontally. It shows how much all small firms together will place on the market at each possible price; it is labeled ΣMC_s in Figure 13.6.

The demand curve faced by the dominant firm can be derived from this information. The market demand curve, DD, shows how much of the product consumers will take off the market at each possible price, whereas the ΣMC_s curve indicates how much the small firms combined will sell at each possible price. The horizontal differences between the two curves at all possible prices reveal how much the dominant firm can sell at those prices. The demand curve faced by this firm is dd and is obtained by subtracting the ΣMC_s curve from the DD curve horizontally. To see this in detail, suppose that the dominant firm sets the price at p'. At this or any higher price the small firms would fill the market, leaving no sales for the dominant firm. At a price of p'', the small firms would sell quantity $p''A''$, leaving $A''B''$ for the dominant firm to sell. In order to place the demand curve for the dominant firm's product in proper relationship to the quantity and dollar axes of the diagram, we can set point C'' so that $p''C''$ equals $A''B''$. This process can be repeated at various assumed prices. The line joining all points thus established will be dd, the demand curve faced by the dominant firm. At any price below their respective average variable costs the smaller firms will drop out of the market, leaving the entire market to the dominant firm.

---

[10]Kenneth E. Boulding, *Economic Analysis,* vol. I of *Microeconomics,* 4th ed. (New York: Harper & Row, 1966), 475–482.

[11]Price leadership has been common in the fabrication of nonferrous alloys, steel, agricultural implements, newsprint, and other industries. See Scherer, 176–184.

Figure 13.6
Price Leadership by
a Dominant Firm

The market demand curve is DD. The horizontal summation of small firm marginal cost curves is ΣMC_s. The demand curve facing the dominant firm, dd, is found by subtracting ΣMC_s from DD horizontally. Once the dd curve is determined, its marginal revenue curve MR_d can be found. To maximize profits the dominant firm's output would be x_d, at which its SMC_d intersects MR_d. The price would be p. At that price small firms collectively, each equating its marginal cost to p, would place x_s on the market. Total market output would be X.

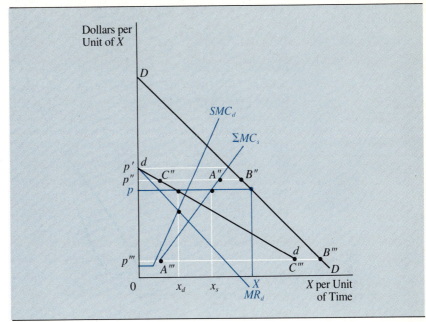

The profit-maximizing price and outputs are determined in the usual way. The marginal revenue curve of the dominant firm is MR_d, and its marginal cost curve is SMC_d. Profits are maximum for this firm at an output level of x_d, at which SMC_d equals MR_d. The price it charges is p. Each small firm maximizes profits by producing the output at which its marginal cost is equal to its marginal revenue, and marginal revenue for each small firm is equal to price p. Total output for the small firms combined is x_s, the output at which ΣMC_s equals p; total market output is x_d plus x_s and equals X. Profit for the dominant firm is x_d times the difference between price p and its average cost at output x_d; profit for each small firm is equal to its output times the difference between price p and its average cost at that output. (Average cost curves are omitted from Figure 13.6 to avoid cluttering the diagram.)

Many variations of the dominant firm model are possible. For example, if there are two or more large firms surrounded by a cluster of small ones, the small firms may look to one or to a group of the large firms for price leadership. The large firms collectively may estimate the amounts that the small firms will sell at various prices and proceed to share or divide the remaining market in any one of various possible ways. The present analysis assumes no product differentiation, but differentiation may occur in similar price leadership cases, causing price differentials for the products of the various firms. The gasoline industry furnishes a case in point. Retail prices of the major companies—one or more of which often serves as the price leader—will be very close together in a given locality, while those of small independents will tend to be a few cents per gallon below those of the majors.

Oligopoly: Independent Action

It would be a mistake to characterize all oligopolistic markets as collusive. In many, collusion has never existed; in others, collusive arrangements, when effected, have broken down. It appears too that the antitrust laws may have deterred concerns in some industries from engaging in collusion and may have forced firms in others to cease doing so. Empirical data on the extent to which collusion occurs in oligopolistic markets are not available, since this is the kind of information that colluding firms want to suppress rather than publicize. In any case, a very substantial segment of oligopolistic market structures is likely to contain firms that act independently of others.

price war
A situation in which rival firms drive prices down through attempts to undercut one another's prices.

Price Wars and Price Rigidity **Price wars** present a persistent danger to individual firms in oligopolistic markets characterized by independent action. Little of a precise analytical nature can be said about these. One seller may lower the price to increase sales—but this move takes customers away from rivals, who may retaliate with a vengeance. The price war may spread throughout the market with each firm trying to undercut others. The end result may well be disastrous for some individual firms.

The specific causes of price wars are varied, but they originate from the interdependence of sellers. A new filling station opening up in a given locality, or an existing one attempting to revive lagging sales, may be the initiating factor. Surplus stocks at existing prices and limited storage facilities have touched off price wars in the sale of crude oil in the petroleum industry. In a young industry, sellers may not have learned what to expect of rivals, or they may be scrambling to secure an established place in the industry, in the process inadvertently starting a price war.

Maturity on the part of an industry may substantially lessen the likelihood of price wars. Individual firms may have learned what not to do and may carefully avoid activities that could touch off hostilities. They may have established a price or a cluster of prices that is tolerable to all from the point of view of profits. Such prices are believed by many to be rather rigid over time, although there is no clear-cut evidence that this is the case. Individual firms are thought to engage in nonprice competition rather than in price rivalry in order to increase their respective shares of the market and profits. Soft drinks and cigarettes are often cited as examples of mature rigid-price industries.

kinked demand curve
The demand curve that a firm faces if other firms in the market follow price decreases but not price increases; it has a "kink" or corner in it at the initial price.

The Kinked Demand Curve An analytical device sometimes used to explain oligopolistic price rigidity is the **kinked demand curve.**[12] This case is thought to occur under a special set of conditions in a market and for a given firm. First, the industry sells a differentiated product and has established a satisfactory cluster of prices. Second, other firms in the market will follow any price decrease made by one firm in order to hold their market shares. Third, if the one firm

---

[12]Paul M. Sweezy, "Demand under Conditions of Oligopoly," *Journal of Political Economy* 47 (August 1939): 568–573.

Figure 13.7
The Kinked Demand
Curve: Cost Changes

The kinked demand curve
FDE facing a firm results
from rivals matching
price cuts made by the
firm but failing to react
to price increases. The
"kink" causes the *MR*
curve to contain the
discontinuous segment
AB. Changes in the
firm's costs that move its
SMC curve up or down,
still intersecting the *MR*
curve within the *AB*
segment, do not induce
the firm to change either
price *p* or output *x*.

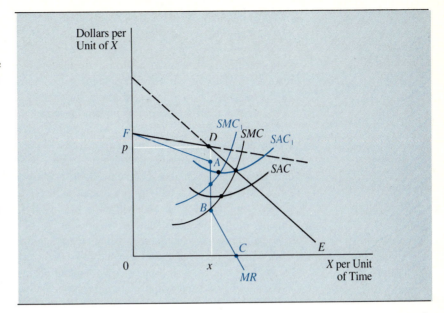

increases its price, other firms will not follow; they expect that firm to lose its market share as its price becomes relatively higher than their own.

The demand curve facing the single firm under these conditions is *FDE* in Figure 13.7. Initially the firm is selling quantity *x* at price *p*. If it decreases its price other firms will follow, and it will retain only its share of the market as represented by *DE*. Should the firm increase the price above *p* others will not follow, and it will lose its market share; for price increases, it will face demand curve *FD*. The entire demand curve faced by the firm, *FDE*, has a "kink" at the original price *p*.

This kink in the demand curve makes the marginal revenue curve discontinuous at output *x*. The *FD* portion of the demand curve generates the *FA* portion of the marginal revenue curve, and the *DE* segment generates the *BC* part. These two segments of the marginal revenue curve do not meet at output *x*, so the marginal revenue curve for the entire range of outputs is *FABC*. The vertical segment *AB* is a discontinuity at *x*.

We can also look at the discontinuity of the marginal revenue curve from the point of view of demand elasticity. The demand curve breaks at output *x*, creating an abrupt drop in elasticity between output levels infinitesimally below and infinitesimally above *x*. Since $MR = p - p/\epsilon$, marginal revenue must drop sharply at *x*.

If the firm's cost curves are *SAC* and *SMC*, profits are maximum at output *x* and price *p*, even though we have no information on how that price was determined originally. The marginal cost curve cuts the marginal revenue curve within its discontinuous part. At an output level less than *x*, marginal revenue would exceed marginal cost, and the firm's profits would be increased by expanding output to x. If output were increased above x, marginal cost would exceed marginal revenue for the increases, and profits would fall.

Discontinuous marginal revenue curves could result in price rigidity. Suppose that the firm's costs rise because of increases in the prices it must pay for resources. The cost curves shift upward to positions such as SAC_1 and SMC_1; but as long as the marginal cost curve continues to cut the discontinuous part of the marginal revenue curve, there is no incentive for the oligopolist to change either price or output. Similarly, resource price decreases shift the cost curves downward, but as long as the marginal cost curve cuts the marginal revenue curve in its discontinuous part, no price-output changes occur. If costs go up enough for the marginal cost curve to cut the FA segment of the marginal revenue curve, the oligopolist will restrict output to the point at which marginal cost equals marginal revenue and will raise the price. Likewise, if costs decrease enough for the marginal cost curve to cut the BC segment of the marginal revenue curve, the oligopolist will increase output up to the level at which marginal cost equals marginal revenue and will lower the price. But some leeway for the cost curves to shift up or down without changing the oligopolist's profit-maximizing price and output exists, because the marginal cost curve cuts the marginal curve in its discontinuous part.

Price rigidity would also survive some demand changes. The initial position of the oligopolistic firm is pictured in panel (a) of Figure 13.8. Assume its costs do not change and market demand for the product increases. The demand curve faced by the oligopolist shifts to the right to $F_1D_1E_1$, as is shown in panel (b), but it remains kinked at some price in the neighborhood of p. The marginal revenue curve moves to the right also, with its discontinuous segment always occurring at the output level at which the demand curve is kinked. If the increase in demand is limited enough so that the marginal cost curve still cuts the marginal revenue curve in the discontinuous segment B_1A_1, the firm continues to maximize profits at price p but at a larger output, x_1. If the increase in market demand should shift the firm's demand curve farther to the right than $F_1D_1E_1$, the marginal cost curve would cut the marginal revenue curve's F_1A_1 segment, and to maximize profits the firm should increase the price as well as the output. A decrease in market demand shifts the firm's demand curve to the left to $F_2D_2E_2$, as is shown in panel (c). Here there is no incentive to change the price, although output decreases until the demand curve shifts far enough to the left for the marginal cost curve to intersect the B_2C_2 segment of the marginal revenue curve. This amount of shift would induce the firm to lower the price along with output.

Although the logic underlying the kinked demand curve is intriguing, its empirical existence has not been borne out by research efforts.[13] It remains as only one of many oligopolistic possibilities.

---

[13]George Stigler, "The Kinky Oligopoly Demand Curve and Rigid Prices," *Journal of Political Economy* 55 (October 1947): 432–449; and Julian Simon, "A Further Test of the Kinky Oligopoly Demand Curve," *American Economic Review* 59 (December 1969): 971–975.

Figure 13.8
The Kinked Demand Curve: Changes in Demand

If the kinked demand curve *FDE* facing a firm increases or decreases as do $F_1D_1E_1$ or $F_2D_2E_2$, the firm is induced to change its output but not its price. In panel (b) the increase in demand causes the firm to increase its output to x_1. In panel (c) the decrease in demand results in a decrease in output to x_2. The price remains at p as long as the *SMC* curve cuts the *MR* curve's discontinuous segment.

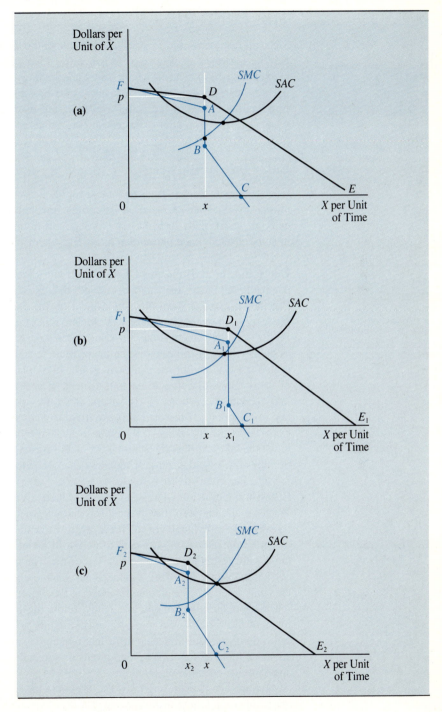

THE LONG RUN

Since all resources used by firms are variable in the long run, output in a market may be increased or decreased in two ways. First, the number of firms in the market may be increased or decreased, depending on the conditions of entry into the market—exit will almost always be possible. Second, any individual firm has the option of increasing or decreasing its size of plant and operating whatever size it has at any desired rate of output.

Entry into a Market

Incentives exist for new firms to enter or for old firms to leave a market whenever profits or losses are incurred by its current firm population. The conditions of entry are most likely to be at issue in oligopolistic markets, although they may in some instances become important in markets of monopolistic competition.

Entry and the Existence of Oligopoly   If entry into an oligopolistic market is comparatively easy, that market may not remain oligopolistic in the long run. Whether it does or does not will depend on the extent of the market for the product, as compared with the most efficient size of plant for an individual firm. Profits will attract new firms, lowering the market price or the cluster of prices as industry output increases; when the price no longer exceeds long-run average costs for individual firms, entry will cease. If the market is limited, the number of firms may still be small enough to make it necessary for each firm to take into account the actions of the others; if so, the market situation will remain one of oligopoly. If the market is extensive enough so that the number of firms can increase to the point at which each no longer considers that its activities affect the others or that the activities of other firms affect it, the market situation becomes one of either pure or monopolistic competition.

Entry and Collusion   Easy entry tends to break down collusive arrangements. We have already seen that in a collusive arrangement a strong incentive exists for any one individual firm to break away from the group. The same sort of incentive operates to attract new firms into a cartelized market and to induce those same firms to remain outside the cartel. The entering firm, if it remains outside the group, will face a demand curve more elastic at various price levels than that of the group and, consequently, will be confronted with higher marginal revenue possibilities. At prices slightly below the cartel price, it can pick up many of the cartel's customers. At prices slightly above the cartel price, it can sell little or nothing. Entering firms that remain outside the collusive group will encroach more and more on group profits or will cause the group to incur losses and force its eventual dissolution.

Even when the entering firms are taken into the cartel, a strong presumption exists that dissolution of the cartel will follow eventually. Refer to Figure 13.9. Suppose curve ΣMC is the horizontal summation of individual firm short-run marginal cost curves. The price will be p, and market output will be X. The

**Figure 13.9
Long-Run Cartel
Equilibrium and the
Effects of Entry**

Suppose that initially just enough firms are in the cartel to make ΣMC the cartel marginal cost curve. Minimum marginal cost for any firm is $0M$. Cartel profits, if made, are maximized at output X and price p and new firms have an incentive to enter. Entry moves the cartel ΣMC curve to the right. At ΣMC_1 cartel output would become X_1, price would be p_1, and all firms would produce. If still more firms enter, moving cartel marginal cost toward ΣMC_2, cartel profit is maximized by holding output at X_1, not allowing these additional firms to produce.

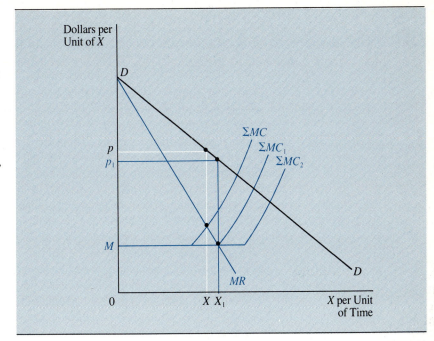

entry of new firms will move the ΣMC curve to the right,[14] increasing the profit-maximizing output and lowering the profit-maximizing price. When enough firms have entered to shift the market marginal cost curve to ΣMC_1, forcing the price down to p_1 and increasing the level of output to X_1, profits for the market may still exist. More firms will enter, shifting the market marginal cost curve to some position such as ΣMC_2; however, profits will decrease if output is expanded beyond X_1. Market marginal revenue for the additional output will be less than marginal cost. The more profitable course of action for the cartel is to keep the additional firms idle and simply cut them in on the profits. Plant costs of additional firms augment total costs of the cartel, and eventually enough firms will have entered to cause all profit to be eliminated. A strong incentive now exists for individual firms to break away from the cartel. Any single firm, if it markets its own output, faces a more elastic demand curve in the neighborhood of the cartel price than does the cartel. Marginal revenue for the firm exceeds marginal revenue for the cartel; also, average cost for the firm is lower than that for the cartel.[15] The firm that can break away can make profits, provided others remain in the cartel and the cartel price is maintained. The temptations facing each individual firm are likely to result in a breakup of the cartel.[16]

---

[14]Assume that M is the minimum price at which any firm will enter the industry.

[15]The individual firm's average cost is lower since the cartel is holding the plant capacity of a number of firms idle, thus adding to cartel average costs.

[16]Don Patinkin, ''Multiple-Plant Firms, Cartels, and Imperfect Competition,'' *Quarterly Journal of Economics* 41 (February 1947): 173–205.

Barriers to Entry   As we noted in Chapter 12, barriers to the entry of new firms into a market may be inherent in the nature of the market or they may be erected by existing firms and governmental units—that is, they may be natural or artificial. Natural oligopoly is similar to natural monopoly: It exists when the entry of a new firm would cause losses to be incurred by all firms in the market. It appears to be a rather rare species in the U.S. economy.

Among the artificial barriers to oligopolistic markets, several are worth emphasizing. First, federal government regulatory commissions have restrained entry. The Federal Communications Commission controls access to radio frequencies and television channels. Until a decade ago the Civil Aeronautics Board controlled entry into air transport. Second, product differentiation is itself a barrier to some markets. An industry's product becomes closely identified with the names of particular sellers, and consumers shun the "off brands" of firms attempting to enter. Standard brands that are well known are thought to be best, while new, unknown brands are considered inferior. Product differentiation has been an important barrier to the automobile and to the pharmaceutical industries.

Entry into an oligopolistic market may or may not be completely blocked, as it is in the case of pure monopoly, but even restricted entry makes it possible for profits to exist in the long run for individual firms. This is not to say that pure profits will always exist in oligopolistic markets—losses can and do occur, or the firms may be just covering average costs, showing neither profit nor loss. When no profits are being made entry will not be desired regardless of whether it is restricted or open. The possibility of profits provides the motivation for entry, and when entry is restricted profits may persist over time. Restricted entry prevents profits from playing their essential role in the organization of productive capacity in a private enterprise economy.

Adjustments with Entry Restricted

Barriers to the entry of new firms into profit-making markets occur mostly in oligopoly, but they sometimes occur in monopolistic competition as the result of legislative activity of one kind or another. Owners or operators of the firms in a particular industry may belong to a trade association that has political influence on a local, statewide, or perhaps even nationwide basis. If the firms in the industry are fairly profitable, the trade association may foresee the possibility of wholesale entry. Therefore, it may use its influence to secure the enactment of entry-blocking legislation, rationalized as insuring an "adequate" supply of the commodity at prices allowing those in the trade to make fair and reasonable profits. In the service trades in a particular city or state, one can easily find laws that tend to block entry.[17]

In such situations individual firms seek to adjust their respective plant sizes to those required for long-run profit maximization. The long-run average cost curve and the long-run marginal cost curve are the relevant ones for the firm.

---

[17]Milton Friedman, *Capitalism and Freedom* (Chicago: University of Chicago Press, 1962), Chap. 9.

**Figure 13.10
Long-Run Profit
Maximization:
Entry Restricted**

In the long run with entry restricted, profits may not be eroded away by the entry of new firms. The individual firm maximizes profits by producing the output at which *LMC* = *mr*. The size of plant for that output is *SAC*. Profits are *cp* × *x*.

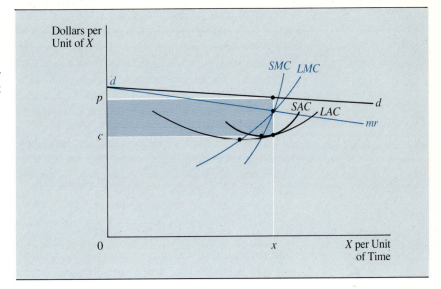

These are shown as *LAC* and *LMC* in Figure 13.10. The demand curve faced by the firm is *dd*, and the marginal revenue curve is *mr*. Profits will be maximum at output *x*, at which long-run marginal cost equals marginal revenue. Output *x* can be sold for price *p* per unit. To produce output *x* at the least possible cost per unit, the firm should build the plant size at which its short-run average cost curve is tangent to its long-run average cost curve at that output. Since *SAC* is tanget to *LAC* at output *x*, short-run marginal cost is equal to long-run marginal cost and to marginal revenue at that output. Profits are equal to *cp* × *x*.

If the firm should deviate from output *x* by increasing or decreasing its rate of output with the given size of plant, *SMC* would be greater than or less than *mr*, and profits would decline. If it should raise or lower its rate of output by changing the size of plant, *LMC* would be greater than or less than *mr*, and profits would decline. Long-run equilibrium for the firm, when entry into the industry is blocked, means that the firm produces the output at which *SMC* equals *LMC* equals *mr* and at which *SAC* equals *LAC*. The size of plant that an oligopolistic firm should build depends on its expected rate of output. For any given rate of output we can say, as a first approximation, that the firm should produce that output at the least possible average cost—that is, build the plant size that makes its short-run average cost curve tangent to its long-run average cost curve at that output.

Under perfect collusion—and often under imperfect collusion—quotas, market shares, and outputs of individual firms may be predictable with some degree of accuracy. In such cases the firm would be expected to adjust its size of plant accordingly. Not much can be said with regard to whether the size of plant would be of most efficient size, less than most efficient size, or greater than most efficient size; it may be any one of the three, depending on the nature of the oligopolistic situation involved. There is no reason to expect that the firm would automatically construct a most efficient size of plant.

For a firm in a market characterized by independent action, there will be no more certainty regarding the size of plant to build than there will be regarding the output to produce and the price to charge. Growth possibilities of the industry may influence the decisions of the firm to a large extent. The existence of a large growth potential would make the individual firm optimistic with respect to anticipated sales and would result in plant enlargements. "Live-and-let-live" policies or fear of "rocking the boat" on the part of individual firms may lead to fairly determinate outputs and, consequently, to some degree of certainty as to the sizes of plant to build. Again, there is no reason for believing that most efficient sizes would be built.

Adjustments with Entry Open

Ordinarily we would expect entry into a monopolistically competitive market to be easy. Existing firms without the benefit of a trade association are likely to feel unconcerned about a few firms more or less in the industry; or, in the event they are concerned about the entry of new firms, they feel powerless to do anything about it. The mere fact that a large number of firms exist suggests that the size of each is something less than gigantic and that effective collusion without government support would be extremely difficult. Thus most of the barriers to entry that occur in oligopolistic markets are not effective in markets of monopolistic competition.

When pure profits exist for firms in the market and potential entrants believe that they too can make pure profits, entry will be attempted. As new firms enter they encroach on the markets of existing firms, causing the demand curve and the marginal revenue curve faced by each to shift downward. The downward shift of each firm's demand curve results from the increase in market supply of the product as new firms enter. The increase in supply (and in the number of suppliers) pushes the whole cluster of price ranges for individual firms downward.

The entry of new firms will affect costs of production for existing ones. As in pure competition (and in oligopoly to the extent that entry is possible), a market classification of increasing cost, constant cost, and decreasing cost can be used. If the market were one of increasing costs, the entry of new firms would cause resource prices to rise, which would shift the cost curves of existing firms upward and would raise the level of costs of entering firms. Under constant costs, the entry of new firms would have no effects on resource prices or on the cost curves of individual firms. In the unlikely case of decreasing costs, the entry of new firms would cause resource prices to decrease and the cost curves to shift downward. We shall examine only the case of increasing costs.

The entry of new firms will shift the demand curves faced by individual firms downward and their cost curves upward. These shifts will cause profits to decrease, but new firms will continue to enter so long as profit possibilities remain. Eventually enough firms will have entered to squeeze out pure profits.

**Figure 13.11
Long-Run Profit
Maximization:
Entry Open**

In the long run with entry open, profits attract new firms and losses induce existing firms to leave. Profits are eroded by entry and losses erased by exit. In long-run equilibrium the LAC_1 curve is tangent to d_1d_1 and $LMC_1 = SMC_1 = mr$ at an output level such as x_1.

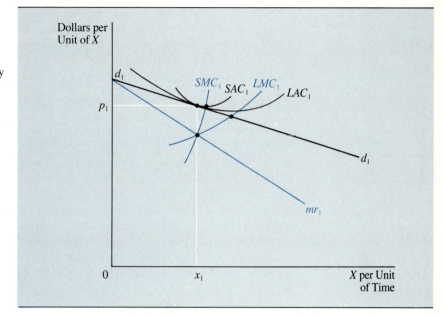

This situation for the individual firm is pictured graphically in Figure 13.11. Compared with that of Figure 13.10, the demand curve faced by the firm has shifted downward as new firms enter, from dd in Figure 13.10 to d_1d_1 in Figure 13.11; the long-run cost curves have shifted upward to LAC_1 and LMC_1; the short-run cost curves have also shifted upward, and adjustments in the size of plant have occurred. When enough firms have entered to cause the demand curve faced by each firm to be just tangent to its long-run average cost curve, firms of the market will no longer be making profits, and entry will stop.

Long-run equilibrium will be achieved by individual firms and by the market as a whole when each firm is in the position shown in Figure 13.11. For each individual firm long-run marginal cost and short-run marginal cost equal marginal revenue at some output such as x_1. Any deviation from that output with size of plant SAC_1 will cause losses, as will any change in the size of plant. Short-run average cost equals long-run average cost at that output, and both are equal to the price per unit received by the firm for its product. The market as a whole will be in equilibrium, since no profits or losses will occur to provide the incentive for entry into or exit from it.

NONPRICE COMPETITION

Although oligopolists may be reluctant to encroach upon one another's market shares by lowering the product price, they appear to have little hesitancy in using other means to accomplish the same results. While open undercutting of the price(s) of rivals raises the specter of price wars that may be disastrous to

nonprice competition
Activities by a firm intended to enlarge its market share without cutting the price of the product; major forms are advertising and variation in product design and quality.

some firms, certain forms of **nonprice competition,** in particular product differentiation, offer more subtle and much safer ways of accomplishing the same objectives. Product differentiation occurs in two major forms: (1) advertising and (2) variation in design and quality of product. Both forms may, and do, occur simultaneously, but for purposes of analysis we shall treat them separately.

Advertising

The primary purpose of advertising is to shift the demand curve faced by the single seller to the right and to make it less elastic. Thus the seller can sell a larger volume at the same or a higher price without the danger of touching off a price war. Each seller tries to encroach on the markets of others through advertising. When one firm launches an ingenious and successful advertising program, there will ordinarily be a time lag before rivals can embark on similar programs. Profits can result for the campaigning firm during this interval.

Frequently the products of sellers in an industry can be differentiated effectively by advertising alone. Each seller attempts to attract customers to its particular brand name, although basically the product of each seller may be the same as that of the others. The success of sellers in this respect is especially evident in the aspirin industry. All 5-grain aspirin tablets conform to certain U.S. pharmacopoeia specifications, and one is as effective for the patient as another; nevertheless, some nationally known sellers are able to attract and hold customers at prices far greater than those of other aspirin producers.

In some instances, rival advertising campaigns succeed only in increasing the costs of individual sellers. Attempts on the part of a single seller to encroach on the markets of others may be anticipated by the other sellers. They in turn launch counteradvertising campaigns of their own, and all sellers succeed only in holding their original places in the market. The overall market for the product may not be expanded at all by advertising activity—the present-day cigarette industry is a case in point. Once rival advertising is started, however, no single seller can withdraw without losing its place in the market. The advertising outlays become "built in" to the cost structures of individual firms and lead to higher product prices than would otherwise prevail.

How far should nonprice competition through advertising be carried by the individual seller seeking to maximize profits? The same principles that have guided us thus far in profit maximization apply in this case. Advertising outlays are expected to add to the seller's total receipts, but successively larger outlays per unit of time beyond some point will add successively less to total revenues— that is, marginal revenue from advertising will decrease as outlays increase. Similarly, larger advertising outlays add to the seller's total costs—that is, marginal costs of advertising are positive. The profit-maximizing outlay on advertising will be that at which the marginal cost of advertising is equal to the marginal revenue received from it.[18]

---

[18]In practice, probably less is known about the effects of advertising outlays than about the effects of any other cost outlays made by the firm. Nevertheless, any intelligent approach by management to the "correct" magnitude of the advertising budget must be made on the basis of estimated marginal revenue and estimated marginal cost resulting from that budget's contraction or expansion.

Differences in Quality and Design

Variations in quality and design of particular products are usually used by a seller, along with advertising, to differentiate its product from its competitors'. The object of these variations is to cause consumers to prefer its product over those of other sellers—that is, to shift its demand curve to the right (or to enlarge its share of the total market) and to make its demand curve less elastic. In addition, quality variation may be used to extend the market vertically—different qualities to appeal to different classes or groups of buyers.

When quality and design variations are used to increase an individual firm's market shares, rival firms are not expected to sit by idly while their markets shrink—retaliation will occur. Successful innovations will be imitated and improved on. Individual firms may succeed in increasing their market shares temporarily, but if they seek to maintain these increases they must be able to keep ahead of their rivals.

The automobile industry has furnished an excellent example of using product variation to increase market shares of particular firms. One producer initiated power steering; consumers took to the innovation, and other producers followed to regain their market positions. Another mounted the motor on rubber, and the process was repeated. Low-pressure tires, automatic transmissions, front wheel drive, and many other improvements, both real and fancied, were introduced initially to enlarge the market share of one producer and in turn copied by others to regain or hold their shares of the market.

When quality differences are introduced to extend the market for a product vertically, we may find the same firm producing a range of product qualities to sell to different groups of buyers at various prices, or we may find different firms specializing in particular qualities of the product. Initially a product, say, deluxe garbage disposals, may be produced for middle income group markets. Sellers find that by producing "super deluxe" models the market can be expanded into upper income levels. Likewise, by stripping the deluxe model of fancy gadgets, a standard model can be sold to lower income groups at a lower price. When different firms specialize in particular qualities of the product, these quality differences may become the basis for market sharing.

Product variation often operates in the best interests of consumers. When it passes along the fruits of industrial research in the form of an improved product to the consuming public, consumer desires may be more adequately met than before. The electric mixer in lieu of the old hand-driven egg beater, the more portable and more versatile tank type of vacuum cleaner in lieu of the upright model, the no-frost refrigerator, compact disk record players, the self-starter on the automobile, and many other variations in product probably represent improved fulfillment of consumer wants.

Some product variation falls in the same class as retaliatory advertising: it increases costs but adds little to the fulfillment of consumer desires. Design changes adding nothing to the quality of the product may occur—for example, their purposes may simply be to differentiate last year's from this year's model. Each seller believes that other sellers will make some changes and decides it should do the same to hold its share of the market.

The principles of profit maximization with respect to design and quality changes are the familiar ones. Any changes that will add more to total receipts than to total costs will increase profits (or reduce losses); conversely, any changes that will reduce total costs more than total receipts will increase profits (or reduce losses). To maximize profits with respect to changes in the product, the firm should carry these changes to the point at which the marginal revenue obtained from them is equal to the marginal cost of making them.

THE WELFARE EFFECTS OF IMPERFECT COMPETITION

Market structures of imperfect competition as compared with pure competition appear to have some adverse effects on consumer welfare. There may be some output restriction with concomitant higher prices, internal inefficiency of the firm, wastes from cartelization, and some resource waste in sales promotion activities. There may, however, be some welfare gains from product differentiation.

Output Restriction

An imperfectly competitive firm usually faces a downward sloping demand curve—one that is less than perfectly elastic. Consequently, its marginal revenue at each sales level is less than the price of the product. Marginal cost will be equal to marginal revenue at an output less than that at which marginal cost equals price, and, at the profit-maximizing output, marginal cost will be less than price. This means that resources used in producing this product are less valuable in other uses than in this use. Consumers would prefer that additional resources be transferred into it up to the output level at which marginal cost equals (a lower) price.

In monopolistic competition with entry open, output restriction is not likely to be significant. New firms will enter profit-making markets until the average costs of firms equal price and zero profits result. Organization of the economy's productive capacity can follow consumers' tastes and preferences with a high degree of accuracy.

An additional factor restricting output comes into play in oligopolistic markets: firms may make profits in the long run because entry restrictions keep prices permanently above average costs. Additional productive capacity, desired by consumers, cannot come into the market.

Efficiency of Individual Firms

The maximum potential economic efficiency for an individual firm is realized when the firm is induced to build the most efficient size of plant and operate it at the most efficient rate of output. No automatic mechanism brings about this state of affairs in imperfect competition.

In the long run in monopolistic competition, with freedom of entry, the firm is forced into a less than most efficient size of plant operated at less than the most efficient rate of output. If firms are making profits, as is illustrated in Figure 13.10, those profits will attract new firms into the market. Entry will continue until the long-run average cost curve is tangent to the demand curve for each firm and profits are zero. When this occurs, as Figure 13.11 shows, the point of tangency must be on the downward-sloping part of the long-run average cost curve since the demand curve facing the firm is downward sloping throughout its length.

In oligopoly, in the long run the firm's output depends upon its quota, its market share, or its anticipation of its marginal revenue and its long-run marginal costs. Once a long-run output is decided upon, the firm will want to produce that output as cheaply as possible—that is, it will build the size of plant whose short-run average cost curve is tangent to the long-run average cost curve at that output. Coincidence of the desired output with the output of the most efficient size of plant operated at the most efficient rate of output would be sheer accident.

It is worth noting that firms in an oligopolistic market, even if they do not use most efficient plant sizes operated at most efficient rates of output, may be producing more efficiently than would firms of other market structures. The size of the market, along with technological factors confronting firms, may be such that only a few can survive. Atomizing the firms to obtain a semblance of pure or monopolistic competition could result in higher costs and prices.

Cartelization Wastes

One of the implications of our analysis of cartels is that they will almost always misallocate resources by generating idleness.[19] The group of firms attempts to achieve the monopoly price and output but without the coordination and control that a single firm could provide. In the short run, the higher prices require that each member reduce output. Even so, some firms may expand the number and size of their plants just to obtain leverage for a larger quota from the association in the case of a centralized cartel or from the informal meetings of the group in the case of a market-sharing cartel. These moves increase the idleness of resources even more. In the long run, cartel profits attract new entrants, which reduces the sales of existing firms (assuming no reduction in price) and raises excess capacity even more. The cartel may in the end achieve the monopoly level of equilibrium price and output, but if this occurs it will typically carry with it a total industry plant that exceeds the resources that a monopoly would have employed. In other words, the cartel may finally reach the monopoly price and output, but it will do so with less efficiency. These extra resource misallocations justify a harsher public policy against cartels relative to monopolies,

---

[19]W. H. Hutt, *The Theory of Idle Resources: A Study in Definition,* 2d ed. (Indianapolis, Ind.: Liberty Press, 1977), 145–154.

and it is probably for this reason that the U.S. antitrust statutes (primarily the Sherman Act) provide stiffer penalties against cartels and collusive arrangements.

Sales Promotion Effects

Firms in oligopolistic markets engage in extensive sales promotion activities designed to extend their own markets at the expense of their rivals'. As we have seen, the major forms of such activities are advertising and changes in product quality and design. To the extent that they add nothing to consumer satisfaction, resources used in these activities are obviously wasted. However, they often yield certain satisfactions to consumers in the forms of entertainment and improved product quality. In these instances the important question with regard to economic efficiency and welfare is whether or not the values of the additional satisfactions obtained from resources used in sales promotion activities are equal to their marginal costs, that is, equal to the satisfactions that the resources could have produced in alternative employments. A strong case can be made that since decisions regarding entertainment and product quality variations are made by business firms rather than by consumers in the marketplaces of the economy, expenditures on resources so used will be too large and will be misdirected. The value of the additional consumer satisfaction obtained will consequently be less than the marginal costs of providing it. To the extent that this phenomenon occurs, economic waste will be the result—welfare will be less than optimum.

Some waste due to advertising or design changes may occur also under monopolistic competition. Efforts on the part of individual firms to expand their markets in this way may be counteracted by similar efforts on the part of the others, and the resources so used will merely add to costs of production. Any such waste of resources will be much smaller under monopolistic competition than under oligopoly, where efforts on the part of one firm to expand its share of the market induce others to put forth similar efforts to prevent such expansion. Such rivalries do not exist under monopolistic competition. Advertising done by one firm provokes no retaliatory action by others. When the advertising of one is counteracted by that of others, it is simply the result of all firms trying to do the same thing—expand their own markets. None are reacting to encroachments of other firms on their particular markets.

But advertising may also have certain beneficial consequences for consumers. It may lower the costs of acquiring knowledge about prices and other characteristics of the differentiated products the market makes available. The application in the following section shows that restraints on advertising in certain health service trades can prevent the price competition that would occur even with restricted entry. What little evidence we have about the impact of advertising in the real world suggests that the benefits it provides to consumers in the form of better and cheaper price information outweigh its costs. Thus advertising may on net improve buyer welfare.

Range of Products

Product differentiation provides each consumer with a broader range of products from which to choose than does either pure competition or pure monopoly. Rather than being limited to a single kind and quality of automobile, each consumer can choose the kind and quality that best suits his or her needs and income. The same observations apply to television receivers, washing machines, refrigerators, and even entertainment. Gradations in product qualities, with each lower quality selling at a correspondingly lower price, increase the divisibility of the consumer's purchases of particular items. Consequently the opportunities for allocating income among different products may be so enhanced that the consumer can achieve a higher level of want satisfaction than would otherwise be possible. In addition, product differentiation enables a consumer to give vent to individual tastes and preferences with regard to alternative designs for a particular product. The range of products available under differentiated oligopoly and monopolistic competition appears to work in the consumer's favor—to increase individual welfare over what it would otherwise be.

On the other hand the different brands of a specific product may be so numerous that they prove confusing to the consumer, and problems of choice may then become very complicated. Ignorance with regard to actual differences of quality results in a willingness by the consumer to pay higher prices for particular brands that in reality are not superior to lower-priced brands of the same product in order to reduce search time and costs of obtaining information. What shopper can possibly be familiar with the comparative qualities of all the many different brands of soaps and detergents, floor waxes, electric irons, and so on, to say nothing of the differences in skills and locations of dentists and physicians?

SUMMARY

Imperfect competition covers the whole range of market structures between pure competition and pure monopoly. Within it firms face demand curves that are downward sloping to the right because of product differentiation in monopolistic competition and because of fewness of sellers as well as product differentiation in oligopoly.

We classified oligopolistic markets according to the degree of collusion that exists among firms in each of the industries. Under perfect collusion, we included groups of firms such as cartels. Under imperfect collusion, we included situations typified by price leadership and gentlemen's agreements. Under independent action, we included noncollusive cases.

Short-run profit maximization in markets of monopolistic competition has output and price results that approach those of pure competition. Perfectly collusive oligopolistic cases approximate the establishment of monopoly price and monopoly output for the market as a whole. The less the degree of collusion, usually the lower the price and the greater the output. In markets characterized by independent action on the part of individual firms, price wars are likely to be common occurrences. As the industry matures the situation may become collusive, or it may develop into a "live-and-let-live" attitude on the part of the firms in the market. In the latter case, price rigidity may occur; firms may be afraid to change price for fear of touching off a price war.

In the long run, the firm can adjust its plant size as desired and new firms can enter the market, unless entry is restricted. Barriers to entry may be classified as natural or artificial. Restricted entry may enable firms in the industry to make long-run pure profits and is common in oligopoly. Entry into monopolistically competitive markets is usually unrestricted and will erode any profits that occur.

The firms in oligopolistic markets frequently engage in nonprice competition, through product differentiation, to avoid touching off price wars. Nonprice competition takes two major forms: advertising and variation in quality and design. To the extent that firms using them succeed only in holding their respective market shares, costs of production and product prices will tend to be higher than they would be otherwise. The firm desiring to maximize profits will use each to the point at which the marginal revenue from it equals its marginal cost.

Some of the welfare effects of oligopolistic markets on the economy are the following.

1. Outputs are restricted below, and prices are increased above, the levels that will yield Pareto optimality, since product price tends to be higher than marginal cost. With entry partially or completely blocked, pure profits and additional output restrictions occur.

2. Individual firms are not induced to produce at their maximum efficiency plant sizes, although in many cases they produce more efficiently than they would if the industry were atomized.

3. Imperfect collusive arrangements and cartels may generate underutilized, or even unused, plant capacity.

4. Some sales promotion wastes occur.

5. The range of products available to consumers is broader under differentiated oligopoly than it would be under pure competition or pure monopoly.

APPLICATIONS

The greater the coordination of price and output decisions among oligopolistic firms, the greater the likelihood that they will generate a higher-than-competitive return. Attempts at collusion are more common than successful collusions, however, owing to the costs of enforcement. But these costs can be reduced by governmental participation. To illustrate these principles, we have taken three examples from a large and varied population of collusions. First is OPEC—the most famous and most important attempt at cartelization in the twentieth century, and for a while the most successful in spite of its lack of any centralized structure. Second are the agricultural marketing orders enforced by U.S. and Canadian authorities in what would otherwise be highly competitive industries. These arrangements range from very loose to tight, centralized cartels. Third are the restraints on advertising of eyeglass prices in some U.S. states. This practice reduces competition in an industry that would otherwise fit the monopolistic competition model, and illustrates the importance of advertising to consumers.

OPEC: A CARTEL?

The Organization of Petroleum Exporting Countries (OPEC) is frequently referred to as a cartel, but this is an exaggeration. OPEC colludes to achieve a higher-than-competitive price, which it did with great success in the late 1970s. But over the long run OPEC was unable to overcome the obstacles to successful collusion that we discussed in the materials accompanying Figures 13.2 and 13.3. First, it was unable to agree on a unified structure of prices for each grade of oil over a sustained period. Second, it failed either to prevent entry by nonmember countries or to induce them to join OPEC. Third, it was unable to establish centralized arrangements to limit each member's output. Fourth, it usually failed to prevent individual members from selling more by cutting price secretly. By 1986, OPEC's combined failures led to a precipitous decline in oil prices, the risk of a confrontation between its two most influential members, and wasteful oil production on a global scale.

Reaching Price Agreements

OPEC has always been deeply divided over what price would maximize profits for the group—the key problem facing any collusion or monopolist (as described in the lecture circuit application in Chapter 12). OPEC is a shell organization for thirteen sovereign, competitive governments: six in the Middle East, two in Northern Africa, two in Southwestern Africa, two in South America, and one in Southeast Asia. It meets several times a year and makes decisions by unanimity; membership is voluntary. Most members view price, production, and sales information almost as ''state secrets'' that are not reported even to OPEC headquarters in Vienna, where a small staff sometimes relies on newspaper reports to learn what members are doing. The various grades of crude oil are homogeneous and easy to identify, a *sine qua non* for successful collusion. But the group has been too large and diverse to make and keep agreements.

OPEC has two factions. The nine *short-run profit maximizers*—Algeria, Ecuador, Gabon, Indonesia, Iran, Iraq, Libya, Nigeria, and Venezuela—want a higher price *now* because of the low short-run elasticity of demand in consuming countries. This low elasticity is due to the high short-run costs of altering consumers' machinery to reduce energy use, designing and constructing plants to produce synthetic fuels, developing new oil fields, or switching to nuclear fuels wherever it is politically feasible to do so. The short-run maximizers have large populations with low per-capita incomes, and a high demand for cash to pay the interest on enormous foreign debts incurred in the heyday of rising oil prices. Most important, they have relatively low oil reserves and thus have less to lose when higher prices increase the rate of fuel substitution.

The four *long-run profit maximizers*—Kuwait, Qatar, Saudi Arabia, and the United Arab Emirates— have small populations, high per-capita incomes, and huge financial deposits. Their enormous oil reserves will last for at least 50 years at maximum output rates and into the twenty-second century at average output rates for 1980–86. Saudi Arabia has about one-fourth of the world's proven inventories of hydrocarbons, already located and waiting to be lifted from the ground. High prices move consumers up their existing demand curves via conservation, and each energy-saving investment reduces future oil sales permanently. (Would you be likely to discard the insulation or fuel-efficient car you purchased last year just because prices come down a bit this year?) Thus, these countries focus on the long-run elasticity and oppose prices that would cause enough fuel switching to reduce the future values of their reserves.

The long-run elasticity exceeds the short-run elasticity at each price, so the self-interests of the factions are impossible to reconcile. As Saudi Arabia's oil minister, Sheik Ahmed Zaki Yamani, said in January 1981 in an oft-quoted speech, "If we force Western countries to invest heavily in finding alternate sources of energy, they will. This would take no more than seven to ten years, and would result in reducing dependence on oil as a source of energy to a point which will jeopardize Saudi Arabia's interests. Saudi Arabia will then be unable to find markets to sell enough oil to meet its financial requirements." He added, "If I were an Algerian, I would certainly wish the price per barrel of oil to reach $100 this very day."[20]

Each faction has leverage. The long-run maximizers have enormous wealth and can lower oil prices whenever they want. But they lack geopolitical security owing to small populations and indefensible borders. Four of the short-run maximizers—Algeria, Iran, Iraq, and Libya—are militarily strong, unpredictable, and within easy striking range of the long-run maximizers.

A per-barrel price of $14 in 1986 was about the same as $6 in 1973 net of inflation, but prices moved on a roller coaster in the intervening period. From

---

[20]S. Fred Singer, "On an Oily Sea, a Bobbing Throne," *Los Angeles Times,* August 27, 1981.

Table 13.1
Percentage Shares
of World Crude
Oil Production,
1979 and 1984

	1979	1984
OPEC	49.5	32.5
USSR	18.3	22.0
United States	13.7	16.4
China	3.4	4.1
United Kingdom	2.5	4.6
Canada	2.4	2.7
Mexico	2.3	5.1
Other	7.9	12.6
Total	100.0	100.0

Source: Stanley Meisler, "OPEC Faces Crucial Bid for Survival," Los Angeles Times, June 30, 1985, citing data from the U.S. Department of Energy.

1973 to 1981, prices rose 5.5 times net of inflation, due to U.S. gasoline price controls and the reductions in supply caused by the Iranian revolution and the Iran-Iraq war. Consuming countries stockpiled oil to hedge against catastrophe, which briefly drove prices up to $40 per barrel. The short-run maximizers were gleeful but Saudi Arabia was alarmed. In 1979 and again in 1980, it pushed prices down by sharply increasing production. As Sheik Yamani boasted on American television in 1981, "We engineered the glut." Even after OPEC reached a temporary agreement on output quotas in August 1986, it was divided over price: the short-run maximizers wanted between $20 and $28 per barrel while the long-run maximizers wanted $15.[21]

New Entry

Price rose sharply in the late 1970s because non-OPEC countries could not produce what OPEC held back. But by 1984, the relative shares between OPEC and major non-OPEC producers changed drastically, as shown in Table 13.1. Because of new discoveries, Angola, Argentina, Australia, Benin, Brazil, Brunei, Cameroon, China, Colombia, Congo, Egypt, India, Malaysia, Mexico, Oman, Peru, Syria, Tunisia, and Zaire had become either almost self-sufficient in oil or exporters. By 1985 Mexico was the world's fourth largest producer. Between 1980 and 1986, Britain's output doubled and Norway's rose 60 percent. As OPEC reduced output, non-OPEC countries expanded production to fill the gap.[22]

[21]"Daily Saudi Oil Boost Expected to Hit 10.5 Million Barrels to Ease Shortfalls," Los Angeles Times, October 7, 1980. From The Wall Street Journal: James Tanner, "OPEC Indicates Some Oil Prices Will Keep Rising," December 21, 1979; Youssef M. Ibrahim, "Yamani, Pressured by Arab Producers, Backs Off on Call for Lower Oil Prices," May 7, 1981; "Oil-Production Pact Could Increase Prices, But Accord Is Shaky," August 6, 1986.

[22]Tyler Marshall, "British Resist Saudi Push to Ease Oil Glut," Los Angeles Times, February 2, 1986. From The Wall Street Journal: Youssef M. Ibrahim, "OPEC's Old Iron Grip on World's Oil Prices Becomes Ever Weaker," January 11, 1985; "Discovery in Colombia Points Up Big Change in World Oil Picture," May 13, 1985; "OPEC Postpones Talks on Output Quotas as Saudis Push Heavy-Crude Price Cut," July 23, 1985; Stephen D. Moore, "Oil-Price Crisis Strains Policies of Go-It-Alone Producer Norway," February 10, 1986.

OPEC's membership did not increase after 1973, but not for lack of trying. Mexico and Egypt occasionally attended meetings but refused membership, often setting their prices slightly below OPEC's. Saudi Arabia forced a price war in 1986 to induce Britain and Norway either to join OPEC or to cut production, but the gambit failed. A new producer's usual profit-maximizing tactic is to increase sales outside the collusion by chiseling.[23]

Output Quotas

OPEC, *as a group,* cannot sell more without lowering price, although *each individual member* has an incentive to chisel secretly. Thus, at the collusive price, some mechanism is needed to limit total production *and* to ration that limit among members. No member wants to be the only, the first, or the most generous to cut back. In a centralized cartel, low-cost producers would get larger quotas from which they would compensate high-cost producers for cutting back, thus equalizing marginal costs among all and minimizing total costs for the group.

In OPEC, each member's *national sovereignty* interfered with the need to cooperate to achieve maximum profits for the group. The short-run maximizers wanted Saudi Arabia to bear the brunt of the cutback, which for years it refused to do without a guarantee that others would abide by the quotas they agreed to. OPEC bickered over quotas for over two years before reaching in March 1983 the first of a series of highly political compromises, shown in column (1) of Table 13.2. For a price cut of 15 percent that the long-run maximizers wanted, Saudi Arabia became the "swing producer" (dominant firm), cutting output as necessary to maintain the limit of 17.5 million barrels per day that OPEC believed would hold prices steady. Sheik Yamani called it "bitter medicine."[24]

Price Cutting

OPEC was powerless to prevent chiseling from undermining the quota agreement. The higher OPEC's price, the more elastic its demand, and therefore the more elastic the demand of a secret price cutter. Incentives to cheat were enormous because a market price of, say, $20 per barrel was several times in excess of average extraction costs (probably under $2 for Saudi Arabia and the Persian Gulf states, and $5 to $10 for others) and many times in excess of marginal extraction costs (probably under $.50 for Persian Gulf countries, and $3 to $4 for others). Initially, chiseling was confined to the short-run maximizers who were strapped for cash. They gave relatively small discounts on inferior qualities

---

[23]"OPEC Discovers the Perils of Price-Fixing," *Fortune,* July 22, 1985. From *The Wall Street Journal:* Youssef M. Ibrahim, "OPEC Ministers Gather Again for Talks, Fearing Post-Winter Surplus, Price Drop," December 6, 1985; "Major Exporters Reject Request Made by OPEC," December 12, 1985.

[24]Youssef M. Ibrahim, "Saudis Threaten to Cut Oil Price Alone If OPEC States Won't Agree on Reduction," *The Wall Street Journal,* February 11, 1983.

Table 13.2
OPEC Quotas
and Production,
1983–1986 (in
thousands of
barrels per day)

	(1) March 1983[a]	(2) October 1984[b]	(3) October 1986[c]
Short-run Maximizers			
Algeria	725	663	669
Ecuador	200	183	221
Gabon	150	137	160
Indonesia	1,300	1,189	1,193
Iran	2,400	2,300	2,317
Iraq	1,200	1,200	2,000
Libya	1,100	990	999
Nigeria	1,300	1,300	1,304
Venezuela	1,675	1,555	1,574
Long-run Maximizers			
Kuwait	1,050	900	999
Qatar	300	280	300
Saudi Arabia	5,000*	4,353*	4,353
United Arab Emirates	1,100	950	950
Total	17,500	16,000	17,039

*Implicit quota as "swing producer."

Sources: [a]Youssef M. Ibrahim, "OPEC Cuts Oil Price for First Time, Lowering Its Bench Mark $5 a Barrel," *The Wall Street Journal,* March 15, 1983.

[b]Youssef M. Ibrahim and Richard B. Schmitt, "OPEC Says 11 of 13 Members to Reduce Oil Production Ceilings to Bolster Prices," *The Wall Street Journal,* November 1, 1984.

[c]Youssef M. Ibrahim, "OPEC Ministers Patch Up Their Pact, But Oil Markets Show Little Faith in It," *The Wall Street Journal,* October 23, 1986.

of oil, better credit terms, or lower taxes for oil companies. It escalated in 1984 when Iraq, Iran, and Libya began to barter oil for arms from the Soviet Union. Then Saudi Arabia bought ten Boeing 747s for enough oil to run the noncommunist world for a full day, and in 1985 it bartered more oil for French jet fighters. Each time, price cuts were necessary to make oil more attractive than cash. When sold, the bartered oil competed with regular OPEC sales.[25]

As conservation and non-OPEC production rose, OPEC's price structure collapsed. More sales by one member meant less for others, which they could only recoup by cutting price. Expectations of price cuts led buyers to postpone purchases, further reducing current demand. By late 1984, price cutting was widespread and OPEC production was about 6 percent above the agreed limit. Nigeria, which derived almost all of its export earnings from oil, threatened to

[25]From *The Wall Street Journal:* Amity Shlaes, "Soviets Help OPEC Members Undercut Minimum Price; Fudging for Andropov?" January 27, 1984; Youssef M. Ibrahim, "Saudi Prince Said to Overrule Yamani in Ordering Stepped Up Oil Production," July 31, 1984; "Production of Oil by OPEC Is Dropping Below Cartel's Daily Ceiling, Sources Say," August 21, 1984; Youssef M. Ibrahim and Allanna Sullivan, "Strength in Oil Prices Isn't Likely to Last, Many Analysts Think," April 23, 1985.

leave OPEC unless it got a larger quota. This time, Sheik Yamani observed, "we are sick and dying."[26]

OPEC again attempted to reduce production and ration it with the quotas shown in column (2) of Table 13.2. The new limit of 16 million barrels a day was about half what OPEC produced five years earlier. Saudi Arabia, the swing producer, absorbed 43 percent of the reduction. OPEC hired an accounting firm to monitor quotas. "We have decided to act like an effective cartel," one oil minister said, but it wasn't true. Price-cutting countries refused to provide the accountants with accurate information on prices or other terms, and some even refused them visas. The monitors were eventually allowed to inspect shipments of crude oil through all 50 ports. But they were denied information about either pipeline shipments or sales of refined products, on which chiseling was extensive. Moreover, no one could fine or punish violators. As economist Steve H. Hanke put it, "the probability of a meaningful agreement [on quotas] that could be monitored is just about zero."[27]

How Things Came Apart

OPEC's problems worsened. By mid-1985, about 80 percent of its sales were discounted. Quotas were flaunted openly, given Saudi Arabia's willingness to be swing producer. OPEC's production limit of 16 million barrels per day was about half its production capacity, so each member's incentives to sell more by secret dealing were enormous. Saudi Arabia's sales fell to 2.2 million barrels—one-fifth of its sales in 1979 and less than Britain's in 1985. Saudi oil revenues were one-third their 1982 level, its foreign bank reserves were about half, and it had a $20 billion budget deficit for the second straight year. Saudi Arabia, Sheik Yamani warned, had "no room to swing downwards."[28]

---

[26]Patrick Boyle, "OPEC Chiefs Vow to Hold $29 Oil Price," *Los Angeles Times,* October 24, 1984; Edward Boyer, "Winners and Losers from Cheaper Oil," *Fortune,* November 26, 1984. From *The Wall Street Journal:* Youssef M. Ibrahim, "Nigeria to Seek Oil Quota Rise from OPEC," January 17, 1984; "OPEC Expects to Keep Prices, Output the Same," July 9, 1984; "OPEC Members Criticize Britain, Norway Amid Renewed Warnings of Oil Price War," December 19, 1984; "OPEC Ministers Start Oil-Price Talks with Members Criticizing Each Other," December 20, 1984.

[27]William Tuohy, "OPEC Near Accord on Self-Policing Plan to Stave Off Oil Price War," *Los Angeles Times,* December 28, 1984. From *The Wall Street Journal:* Youssef M. Ibrahim, "OPEC Weighs Audits to Police Its Quotas, Prices," December 21, 1984; "OPEC Members Near Agreement on Plan to Audit Production Quotas and Prices," December 28, 1984; "Algeria and Nigeria Refuse to Endorse Internal Pricing Pact Reached by OPEC," December 31, 1984; Paul Hemp, "Dutch Accountants Take on a Formidable Task: Ferreting Out 'Cheaters' in the Ranks of OPEC," February 26, 1985; Youssef M. Ibrahim, "Most OPEC Members Seen Near Accord on Price Cuts for Two Grades of Crude," July 25, 1985; Michael Siconolfi, "Oil Analysts See Price Volatility Likely to Persist," July 21, 1986.

[28]"Yamani Says Price of Oil Could Fall to $20 a Barrel," *Los Angeles Times,* June 17, 1985. From *The Wall Street Journal:* Youssef M. Ibrahim, "Saudis Stiffen Threat to Start Oil-Price War," July 10, 1985; "Saudis Decide to Raise Output of Petroleum; Price War May Follow," September 16, 1985.

Apparently Sheik Yamani reasoned that a price war would halt chiseling and force outside producers to cut output or join OPEC. Saudi Arabia would gain by selling 4 million barrels a day at $15 per barrel relative to 2.5 million barrels at $20. It might even gain by selling 6 million barrels at $10, provided price did not decline further. Apparently he thought lower prices also would stimulate consumption and thus undo in part the 1980 error in letting price climb above $30. The short-run maximizers thought he was bluffing, but he wasn't. Saudi Arabia bartered more oil for arms and priced it to big oil companies on a "netback" basis—figuring price retroactively, after refinement into products, to protect buyers from further price cuts. The price war was, Sheik Yamani said, a calculated risk: "We are entering an unknown phase. Anything can happen." One OPEC minister feared that "the cancer is spreading. Now the fire is in the house."[29]

The same forces that gave OPEC leverage when supplies were falling gave the consuming countries leverage when supplies were rising. Short-run demand is inelastic, so lower prices would not reverse fuel switching soon even if buyers expected them to stay low. Netback pricing spread quickly: chiseling by the largest producer is easier to detect. OPEC output soared to 21 million barrels. One oil trader said, "I smell catastrophe. This circus is getting completely out of control." Prices, in a free-fall, touched $6 in mid-1986. Saudi Arabia could maintain income by increasing output up to a point. But selling 6 million barrels at $6 was inferior to selling 2.5 million at $15. Other OPEC members, already at maximum production, were "bleeding," one minister said. Another likened OPEC to "a club of cannibals eating each other." "The pain must go on to get real cooperation [from non-OPEC members]," another observed, but it didn't. Falling prices hurt Britain as an oil producer, but its exports were diversified and it benefited as a consumer from lower prices. Britain flatly refused OPEC's invitation to join.[30]

---

[29]Donald Woutat, "Growing Oil Glut Drives Down Prices," *Los Angeles Times,* January 17, 1986; Peter Nulty, "Saudi Arabia's No-Lose Oil War," *Fortune,* February 17, 1986. From *The Wall Street Journal:* Youssef M. Ibrahim, "OPEC Poised to Forfeit Role as Arbiter of Oil Prices as Big Output Boosts Loom," October 7, 1985; "Major Exporters Reject Request Made by OPEC," December 12, 1985.

[30]From *The Wall Street Journal:* Barbara Rosewicz and Gerald F. Seib, "After Years of Plenty, Saudis Face Recession as Oil Output Drops," January 8, 1985; Allanna Sullivan, "Oil Prices Plummet Over $1 a Barrel Amid Expectations of Producers' War," December 11, 1985; Youssef M. Ibrahim, "Global Oil Price War Is Expected to Affect the Industry for Years," February 11, 1986; "OPEC Begins New Parley Amid Tension and Desire to End Collapse of Oil Prices," March 17, 1986; Youssef M. Ibrahim and Michael Siconolfi, "Oil Prices Drop Amid Widespread Doubts that OPEC Meeting Will Produce Accord," April 15, 1986; Youssef M. Ibrahim, "Saudi Aide Doubts OPEC Will Steady World Oil Markets," April 23, 1986; "Saudi Arabia Is Trying to Boost Oil Demand and Curb Competition," May 13, 1986; "Oil Price Fall to $6–$8 a Barrel Seen Unless OPEC Trims Output Soon," July 23, 1986; "OPEC Splits Over Plans to Trim Output; Saudis Favor Moderate, Voluntary Cuts," July 30, 1986.

Apparently part of Saudi Arabia's strategy was to reduce Iran's ability to finance its war with Iraq. Saudi Arabia had helped Iraq financially and allowed Iraq to construct a pipeline across Saudi Arabia to the Red Sea. But in an early 1986 meeting in Tripoli, Libya, Iran, and Algeria threatened Saudi Arabia with sabotage, terrorism, and further attacks on its shipping. These risks the Saudi leadership was not prepared to take.[31]

After the most acrimonious series of meetings in its history (one lasting over two weeks), OPEC agreed in October 1986 to the new quotas shown in column (3) of Table 13.2, effective through December 1986. Three years of hard bargaining could not yield an agreement on permanent quotas. Total production was cut from 21 million to 17.039 million barrels per day, three-fourths of it by the long-run maximizers. Saudi Arabia promised to end its netback deals and the price war—what one oil trader called a "high-level game of chicken." Saudi Arabia underscored that commitment by relieving Sheik Yamani of his duties. Large percentage increases in quota went to Ecuador and Iraq, and small increases to all but Saudi Arabia and the United Arab Emirates. Smaller, higher-cost producers with political leverage gained at Saudi expense, but also at their own expense as total production rose.

How OPEC could raise price during a glut by raising total production remained to be seen. Some non-OPEC countries said they too would restrain production, but seeing is believing. As another oil trader put it, "you can't pull higher prices out of thin air." In the long run, OPEC probably will repeat the cycle of production limits and quotas followed by chiseling and overproduction—especially if the Iran-Iraq war ends.[32]

The Wastes of Collusion

The world would have been vastly better off with competitive oil pricing. Initially, low-cost producers in the Persian Gulf would have sold until their reserves declined. As price rose to signal greater scarcity, producers with slightly higher marginal costs in the Middle East and elsewhere would have entered. High-cost wells in the North Sea and Alaska would only have been drilled when they were justified by a higher *competitive* price.

With collusive pricing, a tight, centralized cartel that attempted to equalize marginal costs would be less inefficient than an imitation. Ideally, Saudi Arabia would lift 10 million barrels per day and compensate higher-cost producers who

---

[31]From *The Wall Street Journal:* Youssef M. Ibrahim, "Saudis Decide to Raise Output of Petroleum: Price War May Follow," September 16, 1985; "OPEC Leaders Affirm Support for Price War," February 4, 1986; "OPEC Confronts Paralysis," April 2, 1986.

[32]From *The Wall Street Journal:* Youssef M. Ibrahim, "OPEC Agrees on Pact to Cut Oil Production," August 2, 1986; "OPEC Delegates See the Bottom Line in Extending Output Pact: Better Prices," October 9, 1986; "OPEC Ministers Patch Up Their Pact, But Oil Markets Show Little Faith in It," October 23, 1986; "Yamani Ousted As Oil Minister, Saudis Report," October 30, 1986; "Kuwait Joins OPEC's Higher-Price Call, But Conflict Looms on Production Issue," November 12, 1986; Michael Siconolfi, "U.S. Oil Prices Fall Below $15 a Barrel as Saudis Balk at Reducing Production," November 25, 1986.

agreed to cut back, thus minimizing total costs for all. But over the long run even a tight cartel would fail without entry restrictions.

OPEC's experience shows not only how difficult a profit-maximizing collusive strategy is to pursue, but how wasteful incomplete cartelization can be. Too many petroleum fields were discovered too soon, only to produce too little or sit idle. High-cost producers sold too much, low-cost producers too little. Too many energy-saving investments were made too early, and too many perfectly good "gas-guzzling" cars scrapped prematurely.[33]

AGRICULTURAL MARKETING ORDERS[34]

The agricultural price supports we discussed in Chapter 4 are only the most prominent legacy of the New Deal's attempt to cure the farm depression of the 1930s. The other legacy is the agricultural marketing orders which, like price support programs, have expanded with prosperity rather than contracted. In 1985, 34 fruits, nuts, and vegetables in the United States were covered by 47 orders: about half the fruits and 15 percent of the vegetables by value. (A similar legacy in Canada created over 100 cartels that covered about 60 percent of crops.) These cartels have solid political support: each year, Congress forbids the Federal Trade Commission or the Office of Management and Budget (OMB) to review them.

Collusion in agriculture is tempting because products are so homogeneous, but enforcement costs are high because there are so many growers. These costs are reduced in this country by governmental authorities that grant antitrust immunity and enforce collusive arrangements at public expense. In the United States, the centralized authority of each cartel is called a *marketing board*. Membership is divided among growers, handlers (packinghouses), and usually one consumer—all nominated by growers. Board sizes range from 6 to 47 members; growers hold a majority on 40 boards, and on 6 only growers are represented. After the cartel's procedures are negotiated and ratified by a referendum of two-thirds of growers (by number or crop), they are published in the *Federal Register* and enforced by the U.S. Department of Agriculture (USDA) with civil and criminal penalties.

The purpose of marketing orders is to maximize profits via third-degree price discrimination. Sales are restricted in the primary market for fresh produce

---

[33]Refer to the discussion on gasoline price controls in Chapter 4, pp. 87–93.

[34]These materials are drawn from Thomas Borcherding with Gary W. Dorosh, *The Egg Marketing Board: A Case Study of Monopoly and Its Social Costs* (Vancouver, B.C.: The Fraser Institute, 1981); Jonathan Cave and Stephen W. Salant, "Cartels that Vote: Agricultural Marketing Boards and Induced Voting Behavior," in Elizabeth E. Baily, ed., *Regulation at the Crossroads: Challenges of the Coming Decade,* Proceedings of a conference sponsored by the National Science Foundation and Carnegie-Mellon University, Airlie House, Va., September 12–14, 1985 (Cambridge, Mass.: MIT Press, 1986); William S. Hallagan, "Contracting Problems and the Adoption of Regulatory Cartels," *Economic Inquiry* 23 (January 1985): 37–56; and Thomas M. Lenard and Michael P. Mazur, "Harvest of Waste: The Marketing Order Program," *Regulation,* May/June 1985: 19–26.

(grocery stores and restaurants), which has a lower demand elasticity. What remains is sold in the secondary market for export, freezing and processing, or animal feed. Equating marginal revenue in each market yields higher-than-competitive profits. Unless entry is restricted, which is rare, gains in the primary market are eventually offset by losses from secondary sales and unsold crops. Cartels with large and small growers have OPEC-type problems deciding how much to withhold from the primary market.

About half the 47 U.S. boards attempt to regulate the quantity of produce sent to the primary market. (The other half purportedly regulate only quality.) Lenard and Mazur divide the restrictions into the following four categories.

Producer allotment cartels allocate rights to produce among existing growers. Total capacity is restricted and new entrants must purchase quotas from existing producers. This occurs only if new growers have lower marginal costs, so inefficient producers are effectively paid to reduce output or shut down. If quotas are exchangeable, growers have incentives to equalize their marginal costs and therefore minimize the group's total costs.

Allotment schemes apply to four U.S. crops—hops, spearmint oil, cranberries, and Florida celery. Limiting production at any moment discriminates against smaller firms, so agreements are difficult to arrange. Getting sufficient votes for a Washington State hops marketing order in 1966 required making concessions to growers who planned to expand.[35] It is difficult to limit output even in relatively tight cartels.

Market allocation schemes limit primary market sales for almonds, filberts, walnuts, and raisins. In recent years, over 20 percent of walnuts and over half of raisins were withheld from primary markets. In 1985, one-sixth of California's almond crop and a full year's crop of raisins was held in storage.[36]

Reserve pools require each grower to store a certain fraction of the crop for destruction or later sale in secondary markets. In 1982, over the USDA's protest, the OMB turned down a request to put 20 percent of the tart cherry crop in storage.

Prorates are weekly limits on the amount of fresh California-Arizona citrus that packinghouses may sell in primary markets. The total limit is prorated among packers, who then cut the shipments they accept from growers. The remaining crop may be sold in secondary markets or stored on trees for later primary sales. Prorates, like market allocation and reserve pool schemes, do not limit entry or expansion by existing growers.

Allotments: Canadian Eggs

The workings of the British Columbia Egg Marketing Board (BCEMB) and the Canadian Egg Marketing Agency (CEMA) have been studied by Borcherding and Dorosh. BCEMB was formed in 1968 and consists of four grower-elected

---

[35]Hallagan, "Contracting Problems," 46, 55–56.

[36]Jeffrey H. Birnbaum, "Farm, Budget Officials Clash on Supply Curbs by Marketing Boards," *The Wall Street Journal,* December 7, 1982; Bruce Keppel, "State's Almond Growers in Bind," *Los Angeles Times,* September 29, 1985; Peter H. King, "Ups, Downs on Life in Raisinland," *Los Angeles Times,* May 15, 1986.

producers who set weekly marketing quotas. To prevent reductions in output by one province from being replaced by sales from other provinces, CEMA was formed in 1973. It consists of one representative of each of the ten provincial egg boards plus two federal officials. It sets nationwide output limits for fresh (or "shell") eggs and divides them among the provinces. Severe fines are imposed if quotas are violated, so the provincial boards compete for quotas. To keep the shell price up, production within quotas but in excess of what the shell market will absorb is diverted to the secondary domestic (and international) "breaker" market for liquid, powdered, and frozen eggs. The difference between the closed-market shell price and the free-market breaker price is made up by a fund created by a tax on every dozen fresh eggs sold. Together, BCEMB and CEMA have the powers of a central association in a centralized cartel.

Until 1976, BCEMB's quotas were transferable only as entire farms were sold. Now they are divisible and exchangeable up to a limit as part of a Canadian policy that favors small farms. Table 13.3 shows annual marketings and annual quotas between 1968 and 1979. The steady decline in the number of farms suggests the presence of economies of size.

If quotas were effective, shell prices in British Columbia would exceed those in Washington State (with similar production costs), and Table 13.4 shows that they did. In 1961–67, the competitive era before BCEMB, the average differential was 1.4 cents (Canadian). In 1968–72, when BCEMB set quotas without CEMA's aid, the average was 9.1 cents. After CEMA established a nationwide cartel in 1973, the average was 12.4 cents. Tariff and transportation costs amount to 6 to 8 cents, so differentials this great could not persist without quotas.

Borcherding and Dorosh used statistical techniques to estimate the resulting welfare gains and losses. They calculated that the value of the right to sell one

Table 13.3 **British Columbia Egg** **Marketing Board,** **Total Annual** **Marketing (TAM)** **and Annual** **Marketing Quota** **(AMQ), 1968–79**	Year	Numbers of Producers	AMQ (cases per week)[a]	TAM (cases per week)[a]	% AMQ Marketed
	1968	463	37,182	31,864	85.9
	1969	418	37,604	33,477	89.0
	1970	391	37,386	33,909	90.7
	1971	362	37,487	34,315	91.5
	1972	324	37,740	33,425	88.6
	1973	272	36,462	31,367	86.0
	1974	267	36,852	31,486	85.4
	1975	227	36,228	30,978	85.5
	1976	224	36,700	32,987	89.8
	1977	217	36,700[b]	33,406	91.3
	1978	198	36,700[b]	34,062	92.8
	1979[b]	193	36,700	34,900	95.1

[a]One case is 30 dozen.

[b]Estimates.

Source: Thomas Borcherding with Gary W. Dorosh, *The Egg Marketing Board,* 1981, 11. Reprinted with permission from The Fraser Institute, 626 Bute Street, Vancouver, Canada V6E 3M1.

Table 13.4
British Columbia and
Washington State
Egg Prices per
Dozen, 1961–78

		(1)	(2)	(3) Washington State Price in Canadian $	(4)	(5)
	Year	B.C. Price	Washington State Price		Differences (1) minus (3)	(4) Adjusted for CPI (1975 prices)
	1961	35.9	35.0	35.4	0.5	0.9
	1962	35.4	32.6	34.9	0.5	0.9
	1963	38.1	33.4	36.1	2.0	3.6
	1964	32.1	31.9	34.4	−2.3	−4.0
	1965	36.2	30.7	33.2	3.0	5.2
	1966	38.5	36.9	39.8	−1.3	−2.2
	1967	30.7	28.9	31.2	−0.5	−0.8
	1968	37.1	29.7	32.1	5.0	7.7
	1969	40.3	34.4	37.2	5.9	8.7
	1970	37.9	32.6	33.9	4.0	5.6
	1971	37.4	33.7	34.0	3.4	4.7
	1972	40.8	26.7	26.4	14.4	19.0
	1973	54.3	50.3	50.3	4.0	4.9
	1974	66.5	47.0	46.1	20.4	22.6
	1975	61.8	46.6	47.5	14.3	14.3
	1976	67.1	54.1	53.6	13.5	12.6
	1977	65.8	49.5	54.3	11.5	9.9
	1978	66.6	47.3	53.9	12.7	10.0

Source: Thomas Borcherding with Gary W. Dorosh, *The Egg Marketing Board,* 1981, 21. Reprinted with permission from The Fraser Institute, 626 Bute Street, Vancouver, Canada V6E 3M1.

30-dozen case in 1975 was worth between $550 and $800 (Canadian). Quotas transferred 11 cents per dozen or $5.3 million per year from consumers to producers (shown in Figure 12.13 by area pp_1AF). They estimated the dead-weight loss to consumers at $0.3 million per year (area AFB in Figure 12.13). The deadweight loss to producers was only $0.03 million (area FBE) since the supply of resources to the industry was highly elastic. Other welfare losses included $1.8 million per year in lost economies owing to BCEMB's limit on farm sizes, and $0.3 million in excess diversions to the breaker market. Per-household net losses from the cartel were only $10 per year, but per-grower gains were $14,500. Growers paid about $0.7 million in annual lobbying costs to maintain their privileges, however.[37]

Prorates: California-Arizona Citrus

In the 1920s and 1930s, the largest California citrus growers formed an asso-ciation to limit shipments. But their efforts failed because of chiseling and entry. Over the objections of smaller growers, marketing boards eventually were es-tablished for three types of citrus: valencia oranges (for juice), navel oranges

---

[37]Borcherding and Dorosh, *The Egg Marketing Board,* 44–52.

Table 13.5
Disposition of
California-Arizona
Navel Oranges
(annual averages)

	Domestic Fresh	Export Fresh	Processed	Total
1963–68				
Carloads	23,622	1,045	5,517	30,833
Percentage of total	76.6	3.4	17.9	100
1968–73				
Carloads	28,728	1,607	10,045	41,719
Percentage of total	68.9	3.9	24.1	100
1973–78				
Carloads	34,272	3,559	12,484	51,560
Percentage of total	66.5	6.9	24.2	100
1978–83				
Carloads	39,425	5,128	19,804	66,041
Percentage of total	59.7	7.8	30.4	100

Sources: U.S. Department of Agriculture; Thomas M. Lenard and Michael P. Mazur, "Harvest of Waste: The Marketing Order Program," *Regulation*, May/June 1985, 24.

(for peeling), and lemons. Dividing the crop between primary and secondary markets is tricky since citrus can be stored on trees for four months. Some boards have at times been candid about using sophisticated econometric techniques to determine the division that maximizes revenue.[38]

But whose revenue will be maximized? Within the Navel Orange Advisory Committee (NOAC), smaller packinghouses want the greatest reduction to be made by the biggest—Sunkist Growers, Inc., a cooperative of 6,000 growers controlling over half the California crop. Smaller packers want to ship more, which would cut Sunkist's price, too. These diverse interests occasionally yield deadlock, and newspaper stories have referred to NOAC as "the OPEC of oranges." In 1981, one renegade grower defied NOAC by giving oranges away to a food cooperative for low-income families. The USDA went to federal court to force the grower to open his books to establish whether these gifts exceeded his prorated share. In 1982, the USDA sued a tiny packinghouse that admitted to overshipping lemons because its quota was too small to "make ends meet." It stopped two Sacramento, Calif., college students from earning tuition money by selling undersized fruit at roadside stands.[39] Transferable quotas would give growers stronger incentives to resolve disagreements and equalize marginal costs.

The USDA cannot prevent new entry or expansion by existing growers. Before prorates, 90 percent of California-Arizona citrus was sold fresh. Table 13.5 shows that primary navel orange shipments declined to under 60 percent in 1978–83. Between 1950 and 1980, navel orange acreage in California in-

[38]Lenard and Mazur, "Harvest of Waste," 23–24; Bruce Keppel, "Oranges: Growers Split Over Need to Control Flow," *Los Angeles Times*, November 3, 1985.

[39]Cave and Salant, "Cartels that Vote"; Ronald B. Taylor, "Citrus Rebel Challenges U.S. Quotas," *Los Angeles Times*, June 10, 1981; Birnbaum, "Farm, Budget Officials Clash."

creased by 65 percent while total production doubled (although part of this growth is attributable to tax-shelter investing).

Under the rules of the Lemon Administrative Committee (LAC), growers must produce three or four fruits to get the right to sell one fresh. Japanese consumers get U.S. lemons at lower prices than Americans pay, but Canadians pay U.S. prices because the LAC counts exports to Canada against growers' prorated shares. High U.S. prices have stimulated production in Chile and Spain, and secondary prices have declined until it does not pay for some fruit to be picked. The LAC uses fruit that is unsold but "certified on tree" to fix each grower's prorated share of fresh sales. Apparently half a billion lemons (23 percent of the crop) were left to rot in 1982–83—more than were sold fresh.[40]

A new technique for shrink-wrapping prevents dehydration and allows the winter lemon crop to be preserved at least six months for sale in the higher-demand summer months. The LAC counts wrapped lemons as part of each grower's share, so the incentives to incur extra wrapping costs now are weak. Three percent of southern California lemons were left to rot in 1981–82, compared to 16 percent in Arizona and 28 percent in northern California. Arizona growers want to wrap additional lemons up to 10 percent of their quota. Obviously this would hurt southern California growers, who sell 80 percent of summer lemons, and these growers appear to have clout on the LAC.[41]

If transferable quotas were established for citrus as for Canadian eggs, Arizona growers could pay southern California growers to cut back or shut down. Letting perfectly good lemons freeze on trees and reducing incentives to adopt a technology that appears to be economical mainly because of third-degree price discrimination are typical of the welfare losses caused by weak cartels.

RESTRAINTS ON ADVERTISING
EYEGLASS PRICES _____

Economists have long debated the question of whether consumers *on net* gain or lose welfare as a result of advertising. Advertising is a selling expense to a firm and requires the use of resources; consequently the higher costs may cause prices to be higher than without advertising. But advertising may benefit consumers by saving them search costs. The better informed consumers are about prices, the smaller price differences among sellers should be. Searching for better prices is expensive in the time, trouble, and transportation required for visiting or communicating with sellers. Consumers who do enough searching often can find a seller who will quote a lower price, but the costs of the extra search may not be worth the money savings.[42] Advertising, by increasing the

---

[40]Lenard and Mazur, 25.

[41]From *The Wall Street Journal:* James Bovard, "Can Sunkist Wrap Up the Lemon Industry?" January 24, 1985; "The Squeeze on OLEC," August 20, 1985.

[42]George J. Stigler, "The Economics of Information," *Journal of Political Economy* 69 (June 1961): 213–225.

amount of information that consumers have at hand, lowers search costs and should, to some extent, reduce price differences. Whether or not the extra value of these benefits to consumers exceeds the extra costs of resources that firms devote to advertising budgets is a matter that cannot be settled *a priori*. Economic theory alone cannot predict whether the net of these two conflicting forces caused by advertising will be to raise prices or to lower them, and the debate among economists cannot be settled without some hard evidence.

Professor Lee Benham attacked this problem by comparing the prices found in markets in which advertising is allowed with those found in markets for similar products in which it is prohibited.[43] Restraints on advertising are common in most of the health service professions. Advertising increases knowledge and competition. The trade associations of physicians, nurses, and pharmacists (with regard to prescription drugs) have convinced most state legislatures to prohibit advertising and enforce that restraint with the threat of withdrawing or suspending licenses to practice. The professions typically have too many members to be able to establish and enforce their own restraints on advertising without governmental assistance. But restraints on advertising by optometrists and opticians vary considerably among states, so Benham used the prices of eyeglasses in markets of each type to determine whether advertising on net would cause prices to be higher or lower.

Benham's study is important for expanding our understanding of monopolistic competition as well as of advertising. The market for eyeglasses in most large cities fits the monopolistically competitive market structure rather well. There are a number of sellers, but each may have a sufficiently differentiated product to make its demand curve less than perfectly elastic. Small monopoly elements could be caused by differences in office location (especially in prime shopping centers), variations in the brands of lenses and frames that are stocked, and even differences in optical skills. These distinctions may be important to some buyers in spite of the fact that the number of substitutes available is very large. Without advertising, the cost to consumers of acquiring information about these differences is relatively high.

Benham's data base was a sample of eyeglass prices collected from a survey of the uses of and expenditures on health services in 1963. In that year, three-fourths of the states had regulations of some type against eyeglass advertising; some restraints applied only to price advertising, while others prohibited advertising of any kind. Two jurisdictions, Texas and the District of Columbia, had no restraints whatsoever. In general, Benham found that eyeglass prices were between 25 percent and 100 percent higher in states where advertising was completely forbidden than in states having no restrictions. The wide range is caused by the fact that some states impose restrictions other than advertising that sharply increase eyeglass prices, whereas other states have adopted a policy of almost complete *laissez-faire* in eyeglass markets. The nature of Benham's

---

[43]Lee Benham, "The Effect of Advertising on the Price of Eyeglasses," *The Journal of Law and Economics* 15 (October 1972): 337–352.

results did not change when the cost of an eye examination was included in the price of eyeglasses. But he did discover disparities in eyeglass prices between states that permitted nonprice advertising and those that prohibited advertising of all kinds. The resulting price differentials were still in favor of the states with the fewer restraints on advertising, although the differentials were much smaller than those reported here.

Benham concluded that his results were "... consistent with the hypothesis that, in the market examined, advertising improves consumers' knowledge and that the benefits derived from this knowledge outweigh the price-increasing effects of advertising."[44] This result came as a surprise to his university colleagues. A poll he had taken before the study showed that 40 percent of the economists and 100 percent of the professors of marketing polled expected prices to be the same or lower where advertising was prohibited!

---

[44]Ibid., 349.

Suggested Readings

For a modern statement of the theory of collusion, see

Stigler, George J. "A Theory of Oligopoly," *Journal of Political Economy* 72 (February 1964): 44–61.

An excellent statement of both the theory of and evidence for the kinked oligopoly demand curve is

Stigler, George J. "The Literature of Economics: The Case of the Kinked Demand Curve," *Economic Inquiry* 16 (April 1978): 185–204.

The intriguing story of the origins and demise of the infamous electrical industry collusions of the 1950s is

Smith, Richard Austin. *Corporations in Crisis*, Chaps. 5 and 6. Garden City, N.Y.: Doubleday & Co., Inc., 1963.

A case study of the archetypical example of oligopolistic interdependence is

White, Lawrence J. "The Automobile Industry." In *The Structure of American Industry*, edited by Walter Adams, 6th ed., Chap. 5. New York: Macmillan, 1982.

The classic statement of monopolistic competition is

Chamberlin, Edward H. *The Theory of Monopolistic Competition*, 8th ed., Chaps. 4 and 5. Cambridge, Mass.: Harvard University Press, 1962.

One of the strongest critiques of the theory of monopolistic competition is

Stigler, George J. "Monopolistic Competition in Retrospect." In *Five Lectures on Economic Problems*, 12–24. New York: Macmillan, 1947. Reprinted in George J. Stigler, *The Organization of Industry*, 309–321. Homewood, Ill.: Richard D. Irwin, 1958.

For an analysis of retailing as monopolistic competition, see

Weiss, Leonard W. *Case Studies in American Industry*, 3d ed., Chap. 5. New York: John Wiley & Sons, Inc., 1980.

Problems and Questions for Discussion

1. Suppose that the auto repair shops in Universityville form an association. They agree to, and post, a schedule of minimum hourly labor charges for shop work.
   a. How, if at all, could this action be advantageous to them as a group?
   b. If it is advantageous to them as a group, why may it be necessary for them to police the arrangement—that is, why may some shops want to "chisel?"
   c. How might collusion be disadvantageous to them in the long run?

2. The demand for college football games, particularly those between major metropolitan universities, is great relative to their supply; consequently, good players are valued highly by competing schools. To prevent paying relatively high "salaries" to amateurs and to help hold down the costs of athletic programs, the National Collegiate Athletic Association (NCAA) limits "laundry money," support for players from booster clubs, the number and value of football scholarships, recruiting expenses, number of years of athletic eligibility, and transfers of athletes between schools. Schools that violate the rules can be fined or suspended from their regular season schedule or post-season bowl games, both lucrative because of television coverage. (James V. Koch, "The Economics of 'Big-Time' Intercollegiate Athletics," *Social Science Quarterly* 52 [September 1971]: 248–260; *Microeconomic Theory and Applications* [Boston and Toronto: Little, Brown and Company, 1976], 289–292.)

   The NCAA claimed exclusive rights to sign TV contracts on behalf of members and to divide revenues among athletic conferences and individual schools. Its contracts with two TV networks and one cable network for the 1982–85 seasons were estimated to be worth more than $281 million. The contracts forced the networks to cover games of at least 82 schools over a two-year period, suggested what each school should be paid, and capped the number of times a team could be televised. In 1983, two universities with nationally prominent teams challenged the contracts as antitrust violations, and the U.S. Supreme Court agreed. (Steven Wermiel, "NCAA Pacts to Televise College Football Violate Antitrust Law, High Court Rules," *The Wall Street Journal*, June 28, 1984.)
   a. What conclusions can you draw from the NCAA's preferred division of TV revenues between universities that have strong football programs and those that do not?
   b. Is the NCAA a cartel? A centralized cartel? Explain.
   c. What would you predict were the effects of the Supreme Court's ruling on televised football coverage the following season?

3. In 1979, the United States imposed an embargo on grain sales to the Soviet Union and encouraged other countries to support it. Nevertheless, 1979–80 worldwide grain sales to the USSR doubled over 1978–79 sales. The largest sellers were Canada and Australia (both major grain producers), which previously had announced that they would support the embargo. Minor grain producers in the European Economic Community apparently adhered to the embargo as they said they would. U.S. sales of grain to the USSR increased during the embargo year, however, and U.S. sales of soybeans as "livestock" food, which was not covered by the embargo agreement, were characterized as "massive." (Ronald Koven, "EEC Finds Russia Doubled Grain Imports Despite Embargo; U.S. Disputes Analysis," *The International Herald-Tribune,* October 24, 1980.) Use the theory discussed in this chapter to explain the effectiveness of the U.S. embargo.

4. In August 1983, five of the United States's eight leading steelmakers raised prices an average of 7 percent on the product lines for which demand was strongest. All announcements were made on the same day and were to go into effect on the same day of the following week. One of the remaining three firms, which was the most profitable, refused to follow the price rise; the other two were studying it. (Thomas F. O'Boyle, "Steel Prices are Raised 7 Percent by 5 Big Makers," *The Wall Street Journal,* August 26, 1983.) Would you characterize this episode as perfect collusion, imperfect collusion, or independent action? Explain.

5. From World War II to the mid-1970s, no new automobile manufacturing firms have been able to enter the industry and survive. What possible explanations can be offered in view of the fact that established firms in the industry, except for Chrysler and American Motors in some years, were generally profitable during that period?

* 6. Assume that OPEC members agree to reduce rivalry among themselves by establishing a joint sales agency. The independent agency staff would deal with buyers directly and exclusively on behalf of OPEC members. Sales would be divided between OPEC members according to the prices and quotas that the group had previously agreed to. Assume further that the agency staff could not be induced to shade prices because of bribes from buyers or to violate quotas because of bribes from individual OPEC members. Which of OPEC's problems would these hypothetical procedures resolve? Which would they perpetuate? Explain.

* 7. When Saudi Arabia began its netback pricing, it concentrated on the major oil companies. It asked them not to resell the discounted oil in the "spot" market for short-term deliveries, where prices can change drastically on a daily basis. It also asked them to use the extra oil in their own refining systems only. (Youssef M. Ibrahim, "Saudis Decide to Raise Output of

_____

*Denotes an application-oriented problem.

Petroleum: Price War May Follow,'' *The Wall Street Journal,* September 16, 1985.)

    a. In economic terms, how would you characterize this pricing tactic? Explain.

    b. Would you expect the restrictions placed on these sales by Saudi Arabia to be effective? Explain.

*8. Some American oil industry observers argued in 1986 that the OPEC price war would cause higher-cost wells to be closed, and that this would set the stage for later monopoly pricing by OPEC. Evaluate this argument.

*9. Saudi Arabia's strategy to cut prices until non-OPEC countries joined OPEC's effort to reduce supplies obviously failed. What could Saudi Arabia have done to enhance the odds of its success?

*10. Within the Lemon Administrative Committee, Sunkist Growers, Inc., has been referred to as ''the Saudia Arabia of OLEC, the organization of lemon-exporting countries.'' (''The Squeeze on OLEC,'' *The Wall Street Journal,* August 20, 1985.) Is this analogy apt? Explain.

*11. In 1983, the Reagan administration's Office of Management and Budget, over the USDA's objection, proposed to phase out the ''closed shop'' or producer allotment cartels for spearmint oil and Washington State hops, but proposed to leave alone the prorate cartels for California-Arizona citrus. (Jeffrey H. Birnbaum, ''Reagan Moves to Curb Power of Farm Boards,'' *The Wall Street Journal,* May 4, 1983.) Explain the welfare implications of these proposals.

*12. In early 1986, the USDA held hearings on establishing an egg marketing board in the United States based on the Canadian model. The board could compensate growers for reducing the number of laying hens, and its activities would be financed by an initial tax of one cent per dozen eggs that would be increased to two cents at the end of four years. Tax proceeds would amount to $48 million initially. Demand is believed to be inelastic. (Jerome Ellig, '' 'Henocide' Looms Under Marketing Order,'' *The Wall Street Journal,* March 4, 1986.)

    a. If an egg board is created, what problems would it encounter in the short run? The long run? Explain.

    b. If an egg board is created, which of the models discussed in this chapter would you prefer? Explain.

    c. Would you favor creating an egg board or maintaining a competitive egg market? Why?

*13. Casual observations in most cities and towns indicate new automobile service stations being built. At the same time we hear people say, ''We don't really need all those stations.'' In terms of the theory of monopolistic competition, can you put analytical content into observations and comments of these kinds?

* **14.** Dentists began setting up practices in shopping centers in the late 1970s, usually in the spaces occupied by large general merchandise chains. They cut prices some 25 percent below prevailing dental rates, used the stores' credit card mailing lists to announce their openings, and avoided direct advertising, relying instead on word of mouth. For the most part they have been quite successful both financially and in reaching new patients. One reported that half of her patients had not seen a dentist for over two years because of prevailing high rates. One state has passed a law limiting any one dentist to not more than two offices and prohibiting dentists from working for nondentists. Consequently dentists in this state rent their spaces and maintain their own identities.

    a. Do dental services in sizable communities belong in the market classification of monopolistic competition, pure competition, or oligopoly? Explain.

    b. Why do you think the state legislature passed the law?

THE DETERMINATION OF AND THE FUNCTIONS OF RESOURCE PRICES

IN analyzing markets for goods and services, we have assumed that resource prices were given without much concern for how those prices are determined or for the functions they perform in a market economy. The purpose of Part Five is to fill the void, examining resource markets in detail. It will be useful to review Chapter 9, "The Principles of Production," since Part Five builds on the foundation established there.

Resource prices play a key role in the operation of a private enterprise economy. First, they are an essential element in determining the levels of employment of different kinds of labor and capital. Second, they serve to allocate resources among different uses. Third, they provide the inducements or incentives for individual firms to use efficient resource combinations. Fourth, as the organized pressures for higher wages, farm price supports, and the like illustrate, they are important to us personally. All of us are resource owners, and the prices we get for the resources that we own affect our incomes and our shares of the economy's output.

Chapter 14

PRICING AND EMPLOYMENT OF RESOURCES: THEORY

Chapter Outline

What are the forces at work in resource markets that determine resource prices and levels of employment? To identify and analyze these we first examine resource market structures. Next we consider the relationship between a firm's costs and the resources it employs. Then we look closely at the market for any given resource—the demand for it, the supply of it, and the interactions of buyers and sellers that influence its price and employment level. The area of resource pricing and employment is so rich in application materials that we depart from our usual format in this and the next chapter. This chapter will cover the theory with no applications section. Chapter 15, like Chapter 4, will be devoted entirely to applications.

RESOURCE MARKET STRUCTURES _____

A simple definition of the market for a resource will suffice for most purposes. The market for a resource is the area within which the resource is free to move (or is mobile) among alternative employments. The extent of the market for a given resource will vary, depending on the time span under consideration. The longer the period of time, the broader the market will be.

Markets for resources can be classified in a manner parallel to that of product markets. The product market classifications of pure competition, pure monopoly, and imperfect competition are based on the number of *sellers* in each market and whether or not product differentiation is present. Resource markets are classified according to the number of *buyers* in each market and whether or not any differentiation among the resource units in any given market occurs. Resource markets may be purely competitive, purely monopsonistic, or imperfectly competitive, but for our purposes it will be sufficient to refer only to markets of competition and monopsony.

Competition in the buying of resources implies several things. First, no one firm takes enough of any given resource to be able to influence its price. Second, resources are mobile among different employments. Third, resource prices are free to change—no price fixing occurs.

monopsony
A market situation in which there is a single buyer of an item for which there are no good substitutes.

Monopsony in the purchase of a given resource exists when there is a single buyer of it.[1] Again, parallel to product-selling markets, we can distinguish among buying markets of oligopsony and monopsonistic competition in the imperfect competition category. In *oligopsony* there are a few buyers of a given resource for which units may or may not be differentiated, and one buyer takes a large enough proportion of the total supply to be able to influence the price. In *monopsonistic competition* there are many buyers of the resource but there is differentiation that causes specific buyers to prefer the resource of one seller over that of another.

---

[1]The term *monopsony* is applied also to cases in which there is a single buyer of a particular product; however, our discussion will be confined to monopsony in resource markets.

RESOURCE PURCHASES AND COSTS OF PRODUCTION

In the analysis of product pricing and output in Chapters 11, 12, and 13, little attention was given to the determination of resource prices. We assumed that each firm could get as much as it desired of each resource it used at a constant price per unit; that is, that it was a pure competitor in the purchase of each resource, taking the market prices of resources as given. In this section we look explicitly at how resource prices and resource purchases by the firm affect costs of production.

Least-Cost Resource Combinations

A firm that uses several variable resources must determine the combinations of resources necessary to produce alternative outputs at the least possible costs. The least-cost combination for a given output was defined in Chapter 9 as that at which the marginal physical product per dollar's worth of one such resource is the same as the marginal physical product per dollar's worth of every other variable resource used; that is, if only two resources, A and B, were used

(14.1)
$$\frac{MPP_a}{p_a} = \frac{MPP_b}{p_b}.$$

But (14.1) applies only to purely competitive resource purchasing in which each one-unit change in the quantity of a resource used changes the firm's costs by an amount equal to the price of the resource; that is, the resource supply curve facing the firm is horizontal at that price. We can make the case more general by substituting the **marginal resource cost** of each resource for its price in the formula. Marginal resource cost of a resource is the technical name given to the change in the firm's total costs for a one-unit change in the employment level of the resource. Therefore, (14.1) becomes

marginal resource cost
The change in a firm's total costs resulting from a one-unit change per unit of time in the purchase of a resource.

(14.2)
$$\frac{MPP_a}{MRC_a} = \frac{MPP_b}{MRC_b}.$$

The significance of the substitution will become apparent when we consider monopsony in resource purchasing.

The use of the least-cost combination for a given output does not ensure that the firm is maximizing profits. It only ensures that the firm's total costs and average costs are as low as possible for that output only. In Figure 14.1(a) consider the competitive seller of panel (a) or the monopolistic seller of panel (b). If either produces an output of x_0 it must use resources A and B in quantities such that MPP_a/MRC_a equals MPP_b/MRC_b in order to hold average variable costs down to v_0. For either firm at output x_0, MC_x is less than MR_x and profits are not maximized.

Figure 14.1   Least-Cost Combinations and Profit Maximization

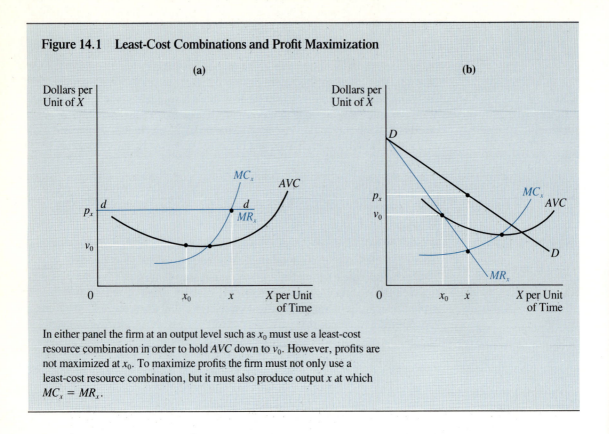

In either panel the firm at an output level such as x_0 must use a least-cost resource combination in order to hold AVC down to v_0. However, profits are not maximized at x_0. To maximize profits the firm must not only use a least-cost resource combination, but it must also produce output x at which $MC_x = MR_x$.

Marginal Physical Products, Marginal Costs, and Profit Maximization

The marginal cost of a product is simply the reciprocal of the least-cost resource combination conditions for producing it. Consider product X produced with variable resources A and B. Any one unit of resource A contributes an amount to the firm's total cost equal to MRC_a and adds an amount to the firm's total product equal to MPP_a. Thus the fraction MRC_a/MPP_a should be read as "the change in the firm's total costs per unit change in the product." This is the same thing as the marginal cost of product X. Hence we can state that MC_x equals MRC_a/MPP_a; likewise, MC_x equals MRC_b/MPP_b. Since MPP_a/MRC_a equals MPP_b/MRC_b, when the firm is using a least-cost combination of A and B we can state that

$$(14.3) \qquad \frac{MPP_a}{MRC_a} = \frac{MPP_b}{MRC_b} = \frac{1}{MC_x};$$

or, we can consider the reciprocals of the foregoing terms and state that

(14.4)
$$\frac{MRC_a}{MPP_a} = \frac{MRC_b}{MPP_b} = MC_x.$$

The latter statement means that at whatever output the firm is producing, if it uses the least-cost combination of resources the amount of A or the amount of B or the combined amounts of both necessary to add a single unit to its output bring about the same addition to its total costs.

Suppose that the product is men's suits and the variable resources used are labor, machines, and materials. The last one-unit increment in quantity produced per unit of time should increase total costs of the firm by the same amount, regardless of whether the increment in product is obtained by increasing the ratio of labor to materials and machines, materials to labor and machines, or machines to labor and materials. Total costs should be raised by the same amount if the increment in product is obtained by simultaneous increases in the quantities of all three resources. When resources are used in the correct combination, they are equally efficient at the margin. The last dollar outlay on one resource adds the same amount to total product as the last dollar outlay on any other resource. The increment in cost necessary to bring about the last unit increase in product output per unit of time is the marginal cost of the product.

Suppose that we again consider profit maximization by the firm in terms of the quantities of resources that should be used. With reference to Figure 14.1 for either firm at output x_0, MC_x is less than MR_x, or

(14.5)
$$\frac{MPP_a}{MRC_a} = \frac{MPP_b}{MRC_b} = \frac{1}{MC_x} > \frac{1}{MR_x}.$$

The firm is using the resources in correct proportions to produce output x_0. However, output x_0 is too small for profit maximization, since MC_x is less than MR_x. In the pursuit of maximum profits, the firm will add to its output by increasing the inputs of A and B. Additional quantities of A and B used with the constant quantities of fixed resources cause the marginal physical product of each to fall. The prices and marginal resource costs of A and B remain constant (and equal) if the firm purchases them under conditions of pure competition; consequently MPP_a/MRC_a and MPP_b/MRC_b decrease, as does $1/MC_x$.

A decrease in $1/MC_x$ is an increase in MC_x. Thus decreases in the marginal physical products of A and B are the same as increases in the marginal cost of product X. Larger quantities of A and B will be employed to expand the firm's output up to the point at which

(14.6)
$$\frac{MPP_a}{MRC_a} = \frac{MPP_b}{MRC_b} = \frac{1}{MC_x} = \frac{1}{MR_x},$$

or up to the point at which the firm's marginal cost equals its marginal revenue.

At this profit-maximizing output the firm will be using its variable resources both in the correct combination and in the correct absolute amounts.

PRICING AND EMPLOYMENT OF A VARIABLE RESOURCE: PURE COMPETITION IN PURCHASING

Market structures in product sales are independent of market structures in resource purchases. Sellers in markets from pure competition on the one hand to pure monopoly on the other may purchase resources competitively. We assume in this section that all firms purchase resources competitively. First, we construct the individual firm demand curve, the market demand curve, and the market supply curve for the resource. Then we determine the market price, the firm's employment level, and the market level of employment of the resource.

The Demand Curve of the Firm: One Resource Variable

The demand curve of a firm for a given variable resource should show the different quantities of it the firm will take at various possible prices. But the factors influencing the quantities that a firm will take when confronted by various alternative prices of the resource differ when the given resource is the only variable resource used from those that prevail when it is one of several variable resources used. Assume for the present that the given resource is the only variable one used—that is, the quantities of all other resources employed remain constant.[2] Assume also that the firm's objective is to maximize its profits.

The firm considers different quantities of the resource—for example, resource *A*—with regard to their effects on its total receipts and total costs. If larger quantities of *A* per unit of time will add more to the firm's total receipts than to its total costs, their use will increase profits (or decrease losses). On the other hand, if larger quantities of *A* will add more to the firm's total costs than to its total receipts, their use will cause profits to fall (or losses to increase). The firm should employ that quantity at which a one-unit increase in its employment level increases both total receipts and total costs by the same amount.

marginal revenue product
The value to a firm of a change in output when the firm changes the level of employment of a resource by one unit; expressed mathematically by marginal physical product of the resource multiplied by marginal revenue of the output.

Marginal Revenue Product   The change in a firm's total receipts when it changes the employment level of some resource *A* by one unit is called the **marginal revenue product** of that resource to the firm, or MRP_a. To compute it, note first that the change in the output of the firm caused by a one-unit change in the employment level of *A* is the marginal physical product of resource *A*, or

_____

[2]The assumption is the same as that made in defining the law of diminishing returns in Chapter 9.

MPP_a. This change in output alters the firm's total receipts by an amount per unit equal to the marginal revenue the firm receives from its sale. Thus a one-unit change in the employment level of A changes the firm's total receipts by the marginal physical product of A multiplied by the marginal revenue received from the sale of the product. If X is the product and A is the resource under consideration, then

(14.7)
$$MRP_a = MPP_a \times MR_x.$$

Marginal revenue products for both a competitive seller and a monopolistic seller[3] of product are computed in Table 14.1. In both parts of the table let the resource quantities be in Stage II for resource A. For the competitive seller in part (a) marginal revenue from the sale of the product is the same as the product price. Marginal revenue product of A at each possible level of employment is determined either by multiplying marginal physical product at that level by marginal revenue, or by simply looking at the change in total revenue resulting from a one-unit increase in the employment of A. For the monopolistic seller in part (b) the marginal revenue product of A is computed in the same way, but note that as the firm's output and sales increase, the marginal revenue from its sales decreases and is always less than the price of the product.[4] Marginal revenue product of a resource is the measure of the value of any one unit of it *to the firm*. As we shall see, it shows the price the firm would be willing to pay per unit at each possible level of employment.

The marginal revenue product of a resource decreases as the employment level of it increases if the firm is employing Stage II quantities of it. For a competitive seller of product the decreases result from the operation of the law of diminishing returns—decreases in marginal physical product. For a monopolistic seller of product, decreasing marginal revenue from increasing sales levels reinforces the effects of the law of diminishing returns.

---

[3] In this chapter we use the term *monopolistic seller* to mean any seller facing a downward-sloping product demand curve, except where we explicitly indicate otherwise.

[4] In Table 14.1(b), a fifth unit of A per unit of time increases output and sales of X from 28 units to 35 units and total receipts of the firm from \$280 to \$343. The increment in revenue per unit increment in sales, or MR_x, equals \$63 ÷ 7, or \$9 per unit, for each of the 7 units. Marginal revenue product of A when 5 units are employed must therefore equal $MPP_a \times MR_x$—that is, 7 × \$9 = \$63.

In terms of calculus, $x = f(a) =$ the firm's production function,

and $\dfrac{dx}{da} = f'(a) =$ marginal physical product of A;

$p_x = h(x) =$ the demand curve facing the firm.

Thus $R = x \times p_x = x \times h(x) =$ the firm's total revenue,

and $\dfrac{dR}{dx} = p_x + x \times h'(x) =$ marginal revenue.

Therefore, $MRP_a = \dfrac{dR}{da} = \left(\dfrac{dR}{dx}\right)\left(\dfrac{dx}{da}\right) = [p_x + x \times h'(x)]f'(a) = MR_x \times MPP_a$.

Table 14.1   **Marginal Revenue Product and Value of Marginal Product**

	(1) Quantity of A (a)	(2) Marginal Physical Product (MPP$_a$)	(3) Total Product (x)	(4) Product Price (p$_x$)	(5) Total Revenue (TR$_x$)	(6) Marginal Revenue (MR$_x$)	(7) Marginal Revenue Product (MRP$_a$)	(8) Value of Marginal Product (VMP$_a$)
(a) **Competitive** **Seller**	4	8	28	$10.00	$280.00	$10.00	$80.00	$80.00
	5	7	35	10.00	350.00	10.00	70.00	70.00
	6	6	41	10.00	410.00	10.00	60.00	60.00
	7	5	46	10.00	460.00	10.00	50.00	50.00
	8	4	50	10.00	500.00	10.00	40.00	40.00
(b) **Monopolistic** **Seller**	4	8	28	$10.00	$280.00	—	—	—
	5	7	35	9.80	343.00	$9.00	$63.00	$68.60
	6	6	41	9.60	393.60	8.43	50.60	57.60
	7	5	46	9.40	432.40	7.76	38.80	47.00
	8	4	50	9.20	460.00	6.90	27.60	36.80

value of marginal product
The market value of the change in output when a firm changes the employment level of a resource by one unit; expressed mathematically as the marginal physical product of the resource multiplied by the product price.

Value of Marginal Product   When the employment level of some resource A is changed by a firm producing some product X, it is often important to consider the *market's* valuation of the change as well as the impact of the change on the firm's total receipts. Again, in Figure 14.1, a one-unit change in the employment level of A changes the output level of X by MPP_a. The change in the output of X is valued by the market, or by buyers of the product, at its per unit price. The market's valuation of the employment level change, or the **value of marginal product** of A, is the marginal physical product of A multiplied by the product price; that is,

$$(14.8) \qquad VMP_a = MPP_a \times p_x.$$

The marginal revenue product of a resource to a monopolistic seller of product is less than the value of marginal product of the resource. This means that buyers of the product of a monopolistic seller value a unit of any resource used by the firm more highly than does the firm itself. We will explore the implications of this situation later on in the chapter. For any resource used by a competitive seller of product, marginal revenue product and value of marginal product are the same because marginal revenue from the sale of product is the same as the product price.

The Demand Curve   The marginal revenue product curve of Figure 14.2 is the firm's demand curve of resource A, since it shows the quantities the firm will take at different possible prices as the firm attempts to maximize profits. For example, in panel (a) if the price of A, and its marginal resource cost, were $4, a fourth unit of A per unit of time adds $14 to the firm's total receipts but

Figure 14.2

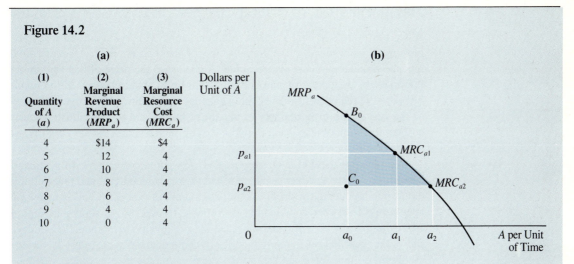

	(a)		
(1)	**(2)**	**(3)**	
	Marginal	**Marginal**	
Quantity	**Revenue**	**Resource**	
of A	**Product**	**Cost**	
(a)	**(MRP_a)**	**(MRC_a)**	
4	$14	$4	
5	12	4	
6	10	4	
7	8	4	
8	6	4	
9	4	4	
10	0	4	

In panel (a) the firm should employ 9 units of A to maximize profits if p_a (marginal resource cost) is $4. If p_a were $8 the firm should employ 7 units per unit of time. Similarly, in panel (b) at price p_{a2} the firm should employ a_2 units. At price p_{a1} it should employ quantity a_1.

only $4 to its total costs; therefore, it adds $10 to the firm's profits. A fifth, sixth, seventh, and eighth unit of A each adds more to total receipts than to total costs and, consequently, makes a net addition to profits. A ninth unit of A adds the same amount to both total receipts and total costs. A tenth unit, if employed, will decrease profits by $4. Hence when p_a is $4, profits are maximized with respect to resource A at an employment level of 9 units. We can write the profit-maximizing condition in either of the following forms: $MRP_a = MRC_a$ or

$$(14.9) \qquad MPP_a \times MR_x = MRC_a.$$

The second form is simply an elaboration of the first. If p_a were $10 per unit, 6 units would be employed; if it were $14 per unit, the employment level would be 4 units.

In panel (b) of Figure 14.2 if the price of A were p_{a2}, the firm would maximize profits by using quantity a_2. If the firm were to use quantity a_0, that unit would add a_0C_0 to the firm's total costs but would add a_0B_0 to its total receipts and C_0B_0 to its profits. Increasing the employment level of A up to a_2 adds more to total receipts than to total costs and therefore increases profits; beyond a_2, larger quantities add more to the firm's total costs than to its total receipts and cause profits to decline. If the price of A were p_{a1}, the firm would maximize profits by using that quantity at which the marginal revenue product of A equals its price per unit.

The Demand Curve of the Firm: Several Resources Variable

When a firm uses several variable resources along with given amounts of fixed resources, its demand curve for any one of them is no longer the marginal revenue product curve of that resource. A change in the price of one, assuming the prices of the others remain constant, will bring about changes in the quantities used of the other resources; these changes will, in turn, affect the utilization of the one as the firm attempts to maximize profits and to reestablish a least-cost combination of resources. Suppose we call such changes the *firm* or *internal effects of a resource price change.*

To illustrate these effects, suppose that we want to derive the firm's demand curve for resource A, which is one of several variable resources, and that initially the firm is producing the profit-maximizing output of product X and is using the appropriate least-cost combination of variable resources. As shown in Figure 14.3, the price of A is p_{a1} and the quantity employed is a_1. The MRP_{a1} curve shows the marginal revenue product of A when the quantity of A only is varied.

Suppose that for some reason the price of A falls to p_{a2}. Since $MRP_a > MRC_a$, the firm will tend to expand employment of A toward a_1'. This greater utilization of A will shift the marginal physical product and marginal revenue product curves of variable resources complementary to A to the right; the corresponding curves of substitute resources will be shifted to the left. Since the prices of other resources remain constant, the utilization of complementary resources will increase while that of substitute resources will decrease. Such changes in the utilization of other resources will shift the marginal physical product and the marginal revenue product curves of A to the right. Each different

Figure 14.3
The Firm's Demand Curve for One of Several Variable Resources

Initially, at point N, the firm is using a least-cost combination of resources, and MRP_{a1} is its marginal revenue product curve for A. A decrease in the price of A induces the firm to use smaller quantities of resources competitive to A and larger quantities of those complementary to A. Consequently, the marginal revenue product curve for A will shift to the right to some position MRP_{a2}, and the quantity of A employed will increase to a_2 when the firm is again using a least-cost combination. Points such as N and M comprise the firm's demand curve for A.

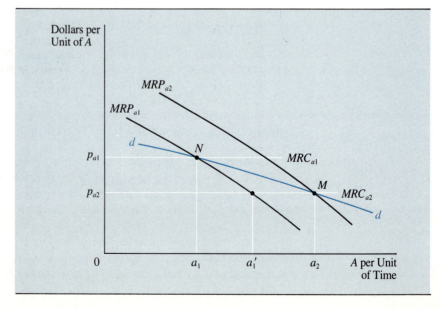

level of utilization of each other variable resource will result in a different marginal physical product curve and marginal revenue product curve for A.

When these and higher-order complementary and substitute effects have worked themselves out, the firm will be on some such marginal revenue product curve as MRP_{a2} and will be employing that quantity of A at which its marginal revenue product equals its marginal resource cost or price—that is, quantity a_2.[5] The employment levels of other variable resources will also be such that for each one its value of marginal product equals its own marginal resource cost or price when the firm is again maximizing profits and using the appropriate least-cost combination.

Points N and M are on the firm's demand curve (dd) for resource A. They show the quantities of A that the firm would take at alternative prices of A when the prices of all other resources are held constant and their quantities are adjusted appropriately for each price of A. Other points on the firm's demand curve for A can be established in a similar fashion and trace out the dd curve. Ordinarily the firm's *demand curve for a resource* will be more elastic than will any single marginal revenue product curve of that resource. The better the substitutes available for that resource, the more elastic that curve will be.

The Market Demand Curve

A first approximation to the market demand curve for a resource is the horizontal summation of individual firm demand curves for it. However, a straight-forward horizontal summation leaves out what we shall call the *market* or *external effects of a resource price change*.

In purely competitive selling markets each individual firm is small enough relative to the markets in which it operates to anticipate that its actions will have no effect on the price of anything it buys or sells. Consequently a firm's demand curve for a resource should show the different quantities that it would take at various alternative resource prices when it anticipates that its actions will have no effect on the price of whatever product it sells. The firm considers only the firm, or internal, effects of resource price changes.

The market, or external, effects come about as a result of simultaneous expansion or contraction of industry outputs of products by all firms using a given resource as the price of the resource changes. If industry X is one of those using resource A, a decrease in the price of that resource will cause all firms using it to increase their employment of it. Although no one firm's increase in output is sufficient to cause a reduction in the price of X, the simultaneous increases in output of all firms may cause such a price decrease to come about. Each such fall in the price of X and the marginal revenue from X will cause shifts to the left or decreases in the whole family of individual firm marginal

---

[5]The increasing ratios of resource A to fixed resources of the firm will ensure that the marginal physical product and the marginal revenue product of A decline even though the changing utilization of other variable resources tends to shift the curves for A to the right.

Figure 14.4   The Market Demand Curve for a Resource

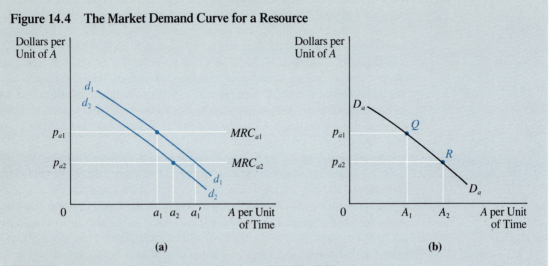

(a)   **(b)**

The market demand curve D_aD_a is the summation of quantities that all firms will employ at each possible price of A. In all cases other than pure monopoly in selling, a decrease in the price of A will cause product price to fall farther than individual firms anticipate, thus shifting their MRP_a curves and demand curves for A to the left and dampening the increase in their employment levels of A below what their original demand curves indicated it would be.

revenue product curves and consequent shifts to the left or decreases in individual firm demand curves for resource A.

The external effects of changes in the price of a resource and the construction of the market demand curve for the resource are illustrated in Figure 14.4. Suppose that the firm of the diagram, and every other firm that uses resource A, is in equilibrium and that the price of A is p_{a1}. The firm's demand curve for A in panel (a) is d_1d_1; the firm is employing a_1 of A. By summing the amounts that all firms employ at price p_{a1}, we determine the total amount taken off the market at that price, A_1. Thus Q is a point on the market demand curve for A in panel (b).

Suppose next that the price of A falls to p_{a2}. Each firm will expand its employment of A—but as the firms in each industry that uses A expand employment of it and, consequently, expand their outputs of products, market prices of products decrease. Individual firm demand curves for resource A shift to the left toward positions such as d_2d_2. Thus the individual firm employment levels of A will increase toward such quantities as a_2 rather than toward a_1'.

Dampening of the expansion in the employment of A results from the market or external effect of the decrease in the resource price. When each individual firm has made the necessary adjustments to achieve a least-cost combination of resources and a profit-maximizing product output, and when each firm's level of employment is one such as a_2, the amounts that all employ together at price p_{a2} can be totaled to obtain quantity A_2, establishing R as a second point on the market demand curve for A. Other points on the market demand curve can be found in a similar way and all together trace out the market demand curve D_aD_a.

However, if all purchasers of resource A were purely monopolistic sellers of product, the market demand curve for A would be the horizontal summation of all individual firm demand curves for it. There would be no external or market effects resulting from a decrease in the price of A, for each monopolist would be the sole supplier of product for its market. The effect of a decrease in the price of A on the quantity of product turned out by any given industry and, consequently, on the price of the commodity has already been taken into account in the marginal revenue product curves and in that monopolist's demand curve for the resource.

If the purchasers of resource A are oligopolists or monopolistic competitors, the market demand curve for the resource is no longer the horizontal summation of individual firm demand curves for it. A change in the resource price changes not only the output that any single firm in a given market will produce but the outputs of all other firms in the market as well. These adjustments will occur in every such industry that uses the resource. As in the purely competitive case, changes in product outputs of other firms in the industry will shift the product demand curve facing any given firm and, consequently, that firm's demand curve for resource A. Thus at any given price the quantities employed by all firms in all industries using A when each firm is maximizing its profits must be totaled to locate a point on the market demand curve for A. Other points on the market demand curve can be obtained in the same fashion.

The procedure just outlined is applicable for establishing the market demand curve for a resource regardless of the type of product market in which the firms using the resource sell. The usual case will be that in which some of the firms using resource A will sell in one type of product market and some will sell in other types. The only market structure requirement to be met is that all firms purchase the resource competitively.

The Market Supply Curve

The _market supply curve for a resource_ shows the different quantities per unit of time that owners of the resource will place on the market at different possible prices. Generally it will be upward sloping to the right, indicating that at higher prices more of it will be placed on the market than at lower prices. Nonhuman resource inputs used for any one product are in general the outputs of other industries. Their supply curves, then, will be the appropriate market supply curves of those markets. Except in cases of constant cost and decreasing cost, they will slope upward to the right. In the petroleum industry, for example, increases in crude oil prices lead to a more rapid rate of recovery, and vice versa. The precise shapes of resource supply curves are not of paramount importance for our purposes, although for certain types of economic problems they will be. They may be upward sloping to the right; they may be absolutely vertical; or, in unusual circumstances, they may bend back on themselves at high prices. The basic analysis is the same in each case.

The labor supply curve of an individual is an interesting analytical case. People do not always offer to work more hours when wage rates rise; this is because of possible trade-offs between work and leisure. Any one hour of the day can be devoted to either leisure activities or work; the alternative or opportunity cost of an hour of leisure time is the additional income that could have been earned from using it for work, and the opportunity cost of an hour of work is the value of the satisfaction that could have been obtained from devoting it to leisure. Thus both income and leisure are items that people would usually prefer more of rather than less. An increased wage rate permits a person either to obtain more income by working the same number of hours or to obtain the same income by working fewer hours. Thus the effect of the increase on the quantity of labor supplied depends upon the individual's preferences.

The indifference curve techniques of Chapters 5 and 6 lend themselves to the analysis of choices between income and leisure time. Suppose, for example, that the indifference map in Figure 14.5(a) shows a person's preference structure

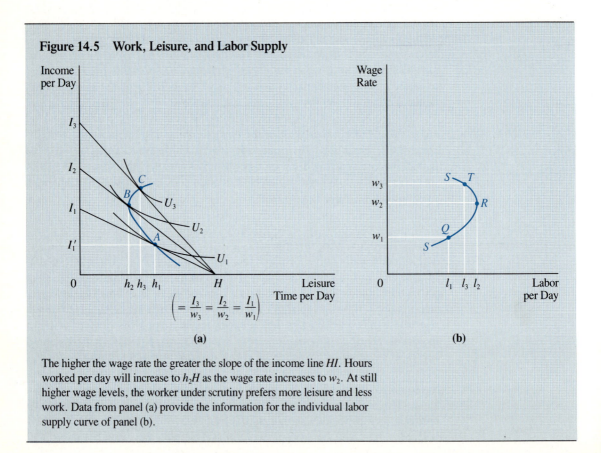

Figure 14.5   Work, Leisure, and Labor Supply

The higher the wage rate the greater the slope of the income line HI. Hours worked per day will increase to h_2H as the wage rate increases to w_2. At still higher wage levels, the worker under scrutiny prefers more leisure and less work. Data from panel (a) provide the information for the individual labor supply curve of panel (b).

for combinations of daily income and leisure. Income (I) is measured on the vertical axis, and leisure (H) on the horizontal axis. Any one indifference curve shows combinations of income and leisure that are equivalent to the individual. Higher indifference curves show preferred sets of income-leisure combinations.

A budget line, or income line, shows the income level that can be obtained by working (giving up leisure) different numbers of hours at a given wage rate. The distance $0H$ represents the maximum number of hours of leisure per day that it would be possible for the individual to trade for work. Some minimum number of hours is required for eating and sleeping. If this number were 10 hours per day, then $0H$ would be 14 hours. At a wage rate of w_1, the individual can earn an income of I_1 ($= 0H \times w_1$) by working $0H$ hours per day, keeping his or her tradable leisure at zero. If h_1H hours per day are worked, income earned is I_1' ($= h_1H \times w_1$) and the tradable leisure time is $0h_1$ hours. Note that the slope of the income line is the wage rate w_1.

The individual would be expected to seek out the most preferred combination of income and leisure from all the combinations that the income line will permit. Given the wage rate w_1, combination A is preferred over all of the others available; this is the highest indifference curve that can be reached. The person will work h_1H hours, earning an income of I_1' dollars per day. At this point the marginal rate of substitution of leisure for income is equal to the wage rate—the amount of income that the individual would be willing to sacrifice to obtain an additional hour of leisure is the amount that he or she would be required to sacrifice in the labor market.

By considering the income lines generated for different wage rates, points on the individual's labor supply curve can be determined. At wage rate w_1 the amount of labor supply (L) will be h_1H ($= 0l_1$) per day, and this point is plotted as point Q in Figure 14.5(b). A higher wage rate, w_2, will shift the income line clockwise to I_2H, increasing the amount of labor supplied to h_2H ($= 0l_2$); this is plotted as point R. A still higher wage rate, w_3, generates income line I_3H and induces the individual to supply h_3H ($= 0l_3$) hours of labor per day, giving rise to point T. These and other points located in a similar fashion trace out the labor supply curve SS.

The total impact of a wage rate change on the amount of labor supplied (or leisure demanded) is the combined result of an income effect and a substitution effect. A higher wage rate increases the income that an hour of work provides and thus makes an hour of leisure more expensive. The individual has an incentive to work more hours and indulge in less leisure time—the substitution effect. But the higher wage rate also generates an income effect: it enables the person to obtain the same income with less work than before, providing an incentive to reduce the number of hours of work. In the theory of consumer behavior, the substitution and income effects of a price change operate in the *same* direction for goods that are not inferior. In the case of income-leisure choices, however, the income and substitution effects of a wage rate change operate in *opposite* directions.

The substitution and income effects of a wage change are illustrated in Figure 14.6 which is essentially the same diagram as Figure 14.5(a). As before,

**Figure 14.6
Substitution and
Income Effects of a
Wage Rate Change**

The $h_1 h_2$ increase in hours worked when the wage rate is increased from w_1 to w_2 can be broken down into a substitution effect $h_1 h'$ and an income effect $h' h_2$. The income effect operates in the opposite direction from the substitution effect.

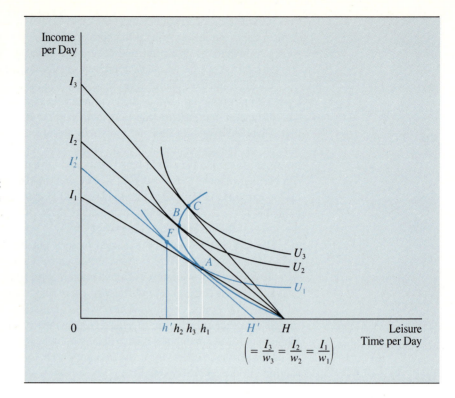

the time available for work each day is $0H$, and the indifference curves show the individual's preference structure between income and leisure. At wage rate w_1, the individual selects the combination of work hours and leisure hours indicated by point A on indifference curve U_1. At a higher wage rate, say, w_2, the person selects combination B on indifference curve U_2. To decompose the movement from combination A to combination B into the substitution effect and the income effect, we first eliminate the latter. To accomplish this we take away the real income increase generated by the wage rate increase, leaving only the substitution effect. The appropriate compensating decrease in income is $I_2' I_2$, which shifts the income line from $I_2 H$ parallel to itself to $I_2' H'$ and makes it tangent to indifference curve U_1 at some point, F. The pure substitution effect of the wage rate increase is thus an increase in the hours of work the individual would offer, amounting to $h_1 h'$. The income effect is now obtained by returning the withdrawn income to the individual, moving the income line from $I_2' H'$ back to $I_2 H$. The pure income effect of the wage rate increase is a decrease in work effort amounting to $h' h_2$ hours. In Figure 14.6 we show the substitution effect outweighing the income effect for the wage rate increase from w_1 to w_2, so that the net impact of the raise is an increase of $h_1 h_2$ in the hours of labor offered.

In some cases, the income effect of a wage change may outweigh the substitution effect so that a wage rate increase results in a *decrease* in the amount of labor offered. We show this in Figures 14.5 and 14.6 for an increase in the wage rate from w_2 to w_3. To avoid clutter in the diagram, the income effects of the wage rate increase have not been separated from the substitution effects; however, the decomposition can be easily accomplished. The increase in the wage rate from w_2 to w_3 brings about a *net reduction* in hours of labor offered of h_2h_3. Since the substitution effect of an increase in wage rates is *always* toward more hours of work offered, this result can be obtained only if the income effect, working in the opposite direction, is greater. As we show in Figure 14.5(a), between points B and C, where the income effect of wage rate changes outweighs the substitution effects, the corresponding labor supply curve of Figure 14.5(b) bends backward, or upward to the left, for wage rate increases.

The importance of backward-bending individual labor supply curves should not be exaggerated. Within relevant wage rate ranges, they may not be backward bending for many persons. Further, even if individual labor supply curves do bend back above some wage rate level, there is no assurance that the market supply curve will show the same characteristic. Increases in wage rates that may cause some individuals to place fewer hours of labor on the market will also induce new individuals to enter the labor market. The entrance of new workers into the market at higher wage rate levels may very well affect tendencies of workers to reduce their individual offerings. Nevertheless, empirical investigations show that historically (1) as wage rates have risen and affluence has increased, average working hours per week have declined for individuals and (2) workers earning relatively high wage rates tend to work fewer hours per week than those earning relatively low rates.

Resource Pricing and the Level of Employment

The conditions of market demand and market supply, as summed up in the market demand curve and the market supply curve, determine the market price of the resource. Its equilibrium price will be that at which resource buyers are willing to take the same quantity per unit of time that sellers want to sell.

In panel (b) of Figure 14.7, the market demand curve and the market supply curve for resource A are D_aD_a and S_aS_a, respectively; its price is p_a. At a higher price, sellers will want to sell more than buyers will want to take at that price. Some unemployment will occur, and the owners of idle units will undercut one another to secure full employment of their particular supplies. Thus the price will be driven down to the equilibrium level of p_a. At prices lower than p_a, there will be a shortage of the resource; resource buyers will bid against one another for the available supply, driving the price up to the equilibrium level.

An individual firm purchasing resource A competitively can get as much as it wants at a price of p_a per unit. A single construction firm in Chicago will not be able to influence the market price of steel. The supply curve of the resource from a single firm's point of view is shown in panel (a) as a horizontal line (MRC_a) at the equilibrium market price. The dollars-per-unit axes in both panels are identical; the scale of the quantity axis of panel (b) is greatly compressed as compared with that of panel (a). The level of employment of the resource by

Figure 14.7   Determination of Market Price, Market Level of Employment, and Firm Level of Employment of a Resource

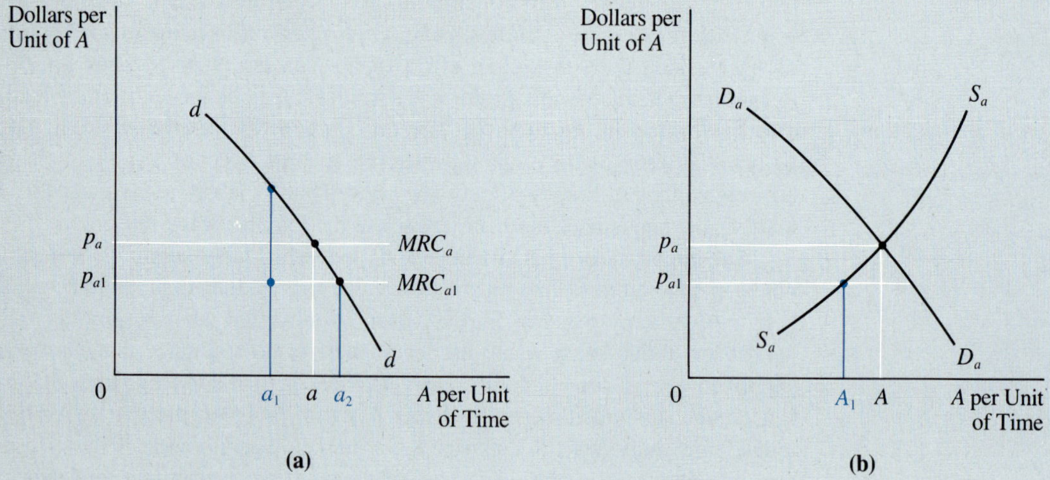

Under pure competition in resource buying, the price of the resource is determined by the market demand for and supply of it. The firm faces a horizontal supply curve for the resource at the equilibrium price p_a, and to maximize profits, employs quantity a. If the price were less than p_a a shortage would occur, inducing buyers to bid it back up to p_a.

the single firm is quantity a, assuming that dd is the demand curve of the firm associated with price p_a, and at that quantity marginal revenue product is equal to its price per unit. The market level of employment of the resource is the summation of the quantities employed by the individual firms and is shown as quantity A in panel (b).

The belief that resources are often paid lower than equilibrium prices is widespread enough to warrant its consideration in some detail. In Figure 14.7, suppose that resource A is priced at p_{a1}. At that price individual firms want quantities such as a_2 in order to maximize their profits with respect to the resource, but they cannot get as much as they desire since the entire quantity placed on the market at that price is only A_1. Some firms will necessarily get quantities even less than a, say, a_1. For such firms the marginal revenue product of A is greater than the resource price. If these firms expand their employments of the resource, they will increase their profits. Each firm believes that by offering a price slightly higher than p_{a1} it will be able to get as much of the resource as it desires. In the absence of collusion among the firms employing the resource—and in pure competition there is no collusion—each attempts the same strategy, but no firm succeeds in getting as much as it wants until the price has been driven up to p_a. Under pure competition in resource buying independent action on the part of each firm, together with the incentive to maximize profits, precludes the permanent location of a resource price below its equilibrium level.

Monopolistic Exploitation of a Resource

monopolistic exploitation
The difference between what a unit of a resource is worth to a firm and what it is worth to consumers because of monopoly in product sales.

Monopoly in a product market is said to result in exploitation of the resources used by the monopolist. In this respect **exploitation** means that units of a resource are paid less than the value of the product that any one of them adds to the economy's output. A monopolist employs that quantity of a resource at which its price equals its marginal revenue product—marginal physical product multiplied by marginal revenue from the sale of the product. But the value of product added to the economy's output by a unit of the resource is its value of marginal product—marginal physical product multiplied by price per unit at which the product is sold. The marginal revenue product of the resource to a particular firm facing a downward-sloping product demand curve is less than the value of marginal product of the resource, since marginal revenue is less than product price in such cases. Hence the prices paid resources used by monopolistic firms are less than the values of the products that they add to the economy's output.

Nevertheless, the price paid a resource must be equal to what it can earn in its alternative employments. Exploitation does not mean that the monopolist pays units of the resource less than do competitive firms. Exploitation under monopoly occurs because the monopolist, faced by the market price of the resource, stops short of the employment level at which the value of marginal product of the resource equals the resource price. Units of the resource contribute more to the value of the economy's output when employed by the monopolist than they do when employed by the purely competitive firm, but they are paid the same price in each market situation. Thus market forces will not induce resources to move into their more valuable uses.

It is worth noting that under pure competition a given resource receives a price per unit equal to both its marginal revenue product and its value of marginal product. Thus a unit of resource *A* is paid just what it contributes to the value of the economy's product. The market demand curve for *A* shows the value of marginal product for *A* in all its uses combined. The market demand curve and the market supply curve determine the price; hence the resource price is equal to its value of marginal product in any one, or in all, of the firms that use the resource. Any one firm takes the market price as given and adjusts the quantity it employs of the resource in such a way that its marginal revenue product and value of marginal product in that firm are equal to its market price. This point is frequently misconstrued. A firm is said to pay for a resource a price equal to its marginal revenue product—implying that the firm determines the marginal revenue product of the resource, then pays it accordingly. This implication misrepresents the nature of marginal productivity theory under pure competition in resource buying. The firm has nothing to say about the price. It must pay the market price, but it adjusts the quantity taken to the point at which the marginal revenue product equals that price.

PRICING AND EMPLOYMENT OF A VARIABLE RESOURCE: MONOPSONY

Monopsony in the purchase of a resource introduces several unique features into the determination of its price and employment level. These will be explained in this section.

Resource Supply Curves and Marginal Resource Costs

As the only buyer of a resource, a monopsonist faces the market supply curve for it. Ordinarily that supply curve is upward sloping to the right. A producer who furnishes the entire source of employment in an isolated area would be in this position, at least in the short run. Contrast the supply curve faced by a monopsonist with that faced by a firm that buys a resource under conditions of pure competition. Under pure competition the firm can get as many units of the resource per unit of time as it desires at the going market price; hence it is faced with a horizontal or perfectly elastic resource supply curve even though the market supply curve may be upward sloping to the right or less than perfectly elastic.

The upward slope of the resource supply curve faced by the monopsonist gives monopsony the characteristics that distinguish it from pure competition. To obtain larger quantities of the resource per unit of time, the monopsonist must pay higher prices. Columns (1) and (2) of Table 14.2 present a portion of a typical resource supply schedule illustrating this situation. Column (3) shows the total cost of resource A to the firm for different quantities purchased. Column (4) shows marginal resource cost of A to the firm.

Marginal resource cost, as we saw in the chapter, is defined as the change in the firm's total costs resulting from a one-unit change in the purchase of the resource per unit of time. When the resource supply curve faced by the firm is upward sloping to the right, marginal resource cost will be greater than the resource price for any quantity purchased by the firm. This relationship is illustrated in Table 14.2.

Suppose that the firm increases the quantity of A that it purchases from 10 to 11 units. The eleventh unit costs the firm $0.65. However, to obtain 11 units per unit of time, the firm must pay $0.65 per unit for *all 11 units*. Therefore, the cost of obtaining the other 10 units has increased from $0.60 to $0.65 per unit. An additional cost of $0.50 is incurred on the 10. Add this to the $0.65

Table 14.2 The Computation of Marginal Resource Cost	(1) Quantity of A	(2) Resource Price (p_a)	(3) Total Resource Cost (TC_a)	(4) Marginal Resource Cost (MRC_a)
	10	$0.60	$6.00	—
	11	0.65	7.15	$1.15
	12	0.70	8.40	1.25
	13	0.75	9.75	1.35

**Figure 14.8
Marginal Revenue
Product, Marginal
Resource Cost, and
Profit Maximization
for a Monopsonist**

The profit-maximizing
quantity of A for the
monopsonist is a, at
which $MRP_a = MRC_a$.
The price of the resource
is p_a, as shown by the
supply curve S_aS_a.

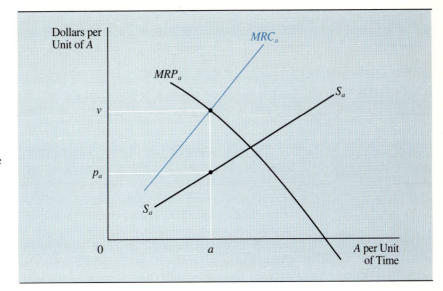

that the eleventh unit costs and the increase in the firm's total cost is $1.15. The marginal resource cost of the twelfth and thirteenth units can be computed in a similar way.[6]

A graphic illustration of the resource supply curve and the marginal resource cost curve faced by a monopsonist is shown in Figure 14.8. The market supply curve for resource A is S_aS_a; the marginal resource cost curve is MRC_a and lies above the supply curve. The marginal resource cost curve bears the same relationship to the supply curve that a marginal cost curve bears to an average cost curve—in fact, the market supply curve of A is the average cost curve of A, and the marginal resource cost curve of A is its marginal cost curve. Obviously, then, if the supply (average cost) curve of A is increasing, the marginal resource cost (marginal cost) curve must lie above it.

Pricing and Employment of a Single Variable Resource

Profit maximization with respect to resource A is governed by the same general principles for the monopsonist as for firms buying resources competitively. Larger quantities of A per unit of time will be purchased if they add more to the firm's total receipts than to its total costs. Additions to the monopsonist's

---

[6]Let the supply curve for resource A be $p_a = \phi(a)$. Then $TC_a = a \times \phi(a)$, and

$$MRC_a = \frac{dTC_a}{da} = \phi(a) + a \times \phi'(a) = p_a + a \times \phi'(a);$$

that is, marginal resource cost of A at the a level of employment is equal to the price of A at that level of employment plus the incremental cost of A for the entire a units of the resource.

If the firm buys resource A under conditions of pure competition, the supply curve of A to the firm is horizontal—that is, $\phi'(a) = 0$, and $MRC_a = p_a$.

total receipts as more A is employed are shown by the curve MRP_a in Figure 14.8; additions to total costs are shown by the marginal resource cost curve. Profits are maximized when quantity a of the resource is employed. Larger quantities would add more to total costs than to total receipts and would cause profits to decline. When the monopsonist's profits are maximized, that quantity of A is employed at which $MRP_a = MRC_a$, or

$$(14.9) \qquad MPP_a \times MR_x = MRC_a.$$

The monopsonist differs from the competitive buyer of the resource with respect to the price paid for it at the profit-maximizing level of employment. For quantity a of the resource, it is necessary for the monopsonist to pay a price of only p_a, although the marginal revenue product of the resource at that level of employment is v. Should the monopsonist employ that quantity of A at which its marginal revenue product is equal to its price—as does the competitive resource buyer—less profit will be made. To maximize profits, the quantity of the resource used is restricted, and it is paid a price per unit that is less than its marginal revenue product. The important consideration for profit maximization is the employment of that quantity at which the marginal resource cost equals the marginal revenue product—and for the monopsonist, the resource price is less than the marginal resource cost. Monopsony profits, resulting from the excess of the marginal revenue product of the resource over its price per unit, are equal to $p_a v \times a$.

Simultaneous Employment of Several Variable Resources

The conditions that must be met by the monopsonist to employ least-cost combinations of variable resources for given outputs are the same as those that apply to purely competitive resource buyers. The least-cost combination for the monopsonist is that combination at which the marginal physical product per dollar's worth of one resource is equal to the marginal physical product per dollar's worth of every other resource used; that is,

$$(14.2) \qquad \frac{MPP_a}{MRC_a} = \frac{MPP_b}{MRC_b}.$$

Since the reciprocal of either or both of the fractions in the equation represents the marginal cost of the product the conditions necessary for profit maximization are the familiar ones:

$$(14.6) \qquad \frac{MPP_a}{MRC_a} = \frac{MPP_b}{MRC_b} = \frac{1}{MC_x} = \frac{1}{MR_x}.$$

Conditions Giving Rise to Monopsony

Monopsony results from either or both of two basic conditions. First, monopsonistic purchases of a resource may occur when units of the resource are specialized to a particular user. This statement means that the marginal revenue product of the resource in the specialized use is enough higher than it is in any alternative employments in which it conceivably can be used to eliminate those alternative employments from the consideration of resource suppliers. Thus the resource supply curve facing the monopsonist will be the market supply curve of the resource and usually will be upward sloping to the right. The more the user is willing to pay for the resource, the greater will be the quantity placed on the market.

A situation of the kind described may occur when a special type of skilled labor is developed to meet certain needs of a specific firm. The higher the wage rate offered for the special category of labor, the more individuals there will be who are willing to undergo the necessary training to develop the skill. No other firm utilizes labor with this or similar skills; consequently, once trained, the workers' only options are to work for this firm or to work elsewhere at jobs where their marginal revenue products and wage rates are significantly lower.

Specialization of resources to a particular user is not confined to the labor field. A large aircraft or automobile manufacturer may depend on a number of suppliers to furnish certain parts used by no other manufacturer. In the tightest possible case, such suppliers sell their entire outputs to the manufacturer, and complete monopsony by the manufacturer therefore exists. Given time, the suppliers may be able to convert production facilities to supply other types of parts to other manufacturers, and the degree of monopsony enjoyed by the one may be decreased correspondingly.

The second condition from which monopsony may result is the immobility of certain resources. It is not necessary that resources in general be immobile but only that their mobility out of certain areas or away from certain firms be lacking, thus creating unique monopsonistic situations. Various forces may hold workers in a given community or to a given firm, including emotional ties to the community together with a fear of the unknown; ignorance regarding alternative employment opportunities; insufficient funds to permit job seeking in, and movement to, alternative job areas; seniority and pension rights accumulated with a firm. Specific cases of immobility among firms within a given geographic area may result from agreements among employers not to ''pirate'' one another's work forces. For many years the most famous of all ''no-pirating'' pacts between employers occurred in organized professional baseball. Formal collusion among the clubs, sanctioned by an antitrust immunity from Congress, reduced substantially wage competition for players and resulted in a sizable redistribution of income from players to clubs. This case will be examined in the next chapter.

Monopsonistic Exploitation of a Resource

Monopsony in the purchase of a resource also is said to result in exploitation of that resource. Monopsonistic exploitation can be understood best by comparing monopsony with pure competition in resource buying. In a purely competitive purchasing situation, each firm will add to its profits by taking larger quantities of the resource up to the point at which the marginal revenue product of the resource is equal to the resource price since the resource price is the same as its marginal resource cost. The resource receives a price per unit equal to what any one unit of it contributes to the firm's total receipts.[7]

In contrast, the monopsonist maximizes profits by stopping short of the resource employment level at which marginal revenue product of the resource is equal to its price per unit. This situation is shown in Figure 14.8. The profit-maximizing level of employment is that at which the marginal revenue product equals the marginal resource cost. Since the marginal resource cost exceeds the resource price, the marginal revenue product of the resource does also. Hence units of the resource are paid less than what any one of them contributes to the total receipts of the firm. This situation is called **monopsonistic exploitation** of the resource. The monopsonist restricts the quantity of the resource used and holds down its price.

monopsonistic exploitation
The difference between what a unit of a resource is worth to a firm and what it is paid because of monopsony in the purchase of the resource.

Measures to Counteract Monopsony

What can be done to counteract monopsonistic exploitation of resources? Two alternatives will be considered. First, minimum resource prices can be used. Second, measures successful in increasing resource mobility will reduce the monopsonistic power of particular resource users.

Minimum Resource Prices   Minimum resource prices can be established by the government or by organized groups of resource suppliers. The typical monopsonistic situation is pictured in Figure 14.9. The level of employment of resource A is quantity a. Its price per unit is p_a; however, marginal revenue product is v, and the resource is being exploited. Suppose that a minimum price is set at p_{a1} and that the firm must pay a price of at least p_{a1} per unit for all units purchased. Should the firm want more than a_1 units, it will face the mn sector of the resource supply curve. The entire supply curve then faced by the firm will be $p_{a1}mn$.

The alteration in the resource supply curve facing the firm also alters the marginal resource cost curve. For quantities between zero and a_1, each additional unit of A employed per unit of time adds an amount equal to p_{a1} to the firm's total costs. The new marginal resource cost curve coincides with $p_{a1}m$, the new supply curve, out to quantity a_1. For quantities greater than a_1, the regular supply curve mn is the relevant one, and the corresponding sector of the marginal resource cost curve becomes lk. The altered marginal resource cost curve is $p_{a1}mlk$; at quantity a_1, it is discontinuous between m and l.

The quantity of A that the firm should now employ to maximize profits will differ from that used before the minimum price was set. The firm should use quantity a_1, at which the new marginal resource cost is equal to the marginal revenue product of A. The minimum price not only eliminates monopsonistic exploitation of the resource, it also increases the level of employment in the process.

_____

[7]Monopolistic exploitation will occur if the resource-buying firms face downward-sloping product demand curves, but there will be no monopsonistic exploitation.

**Figure 14.9
Control of
Monopsony by
Minimum Resource
Prices**

The imposition of a
minimum resource price
of p_{a1} on the
monopsonist will
eliminate monopsonistic
exploitation of A. The
supply curve facing the
firm becomes $p_{a1}mn$ and
the marginal resource
cost curve becomes
$p_{a1}mlk$. Profits are
maximized at
employment level a_1, at
which marginal revenue
product equals the
modified marginal
resource cost.

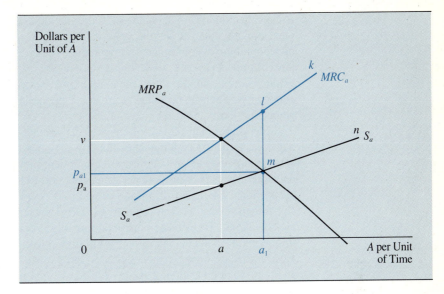

This analysis assumes that the minimum price of resource A is set at just the correct level to counteract monopsony completely. Such precision may or may not be achieved in fact; however, any minimum price between p_a and p_{a1} will counteract monopsony to some extent. The nearer to p_{a1} the price is set, the more nearly will exploitation be eliminated. Prices set between p_{a1} and v will also counteract exploitation, but at the expense of employment. Unemployment will occur since at any price level above p_{a1} resource sellers will want to put more on the market than buyers are willing to buy.

Countering of monopsony by price regulation is at best a difficult job. The precise price level at which monopsony is offset completely is hard to determine. In the labor field—where monopsony is most publicized—minimum wage laws may be the counteracting device used. However, different degrees of monopsony for different kinds of labor and for different situations make blanket price fixing of this type impractical as an overall monopsonistic offset. Collective bargaining on a firm-by-firm basis could more nearly meet and offset individual monopsonistic cases, but even here the problem of determining—let alone the difficulty of obtaining—the "correct" minimum price for the resource remains.

Enhanced Mobility   Measures to increase resource mobility among alternative employments get directly at the causes of monopsony. Immobility of resources is thought by many economists to be most serious in labor markets; hence our discussion will be centered on the labor resource. We shall present a few general lines of approach rather than specific and detailed programs. With regard to the labor resource, mobility among geographic areas and firms, horizontal mobility among occupations at the same skill level, and vertical occupational mobility to higher skill classifications will be of value in counteracting monopsony.

An efficient system of federal employment exchanges should provide one avenue of attack on labor immobility. An important function of such a system is the collection and dissemination of information regarding alternative employment opportunities. It should make data available to the entire labor force—including those in now isolated communities—with regard to high-wage, scarce-labor-supply areas and give descriptions of the requisite skills for obtaining employment in such localities. In addition, the system should perform the more common function of bringing together job opportunities and workers seeking alternative jobs.

The educational system offers a second avenue of attack. It can increase both the vertical and horizontal mobility of labor resources. With regard to vertical mobility, the availability and use of educational opportunities can channel larger numbers of the younger generation toward higher-paying, higher-level occupations. By means of vocational and trade schools the educational system can provide older workers with training for upward movement through skill classifications. To increase horizontal mobility, vocational guidance can assist in steering the potential labor force away from lower-paying occupations toward those providing higher remuneration at approximately the same skill level. In addition, adult education programs can furnish the retraining necessary for escape from particularly low-paying occupations that are no longer in demand.

Still a third line of attack is that of judiciously subsidizing worker migration out of areas characterized by monopsony, since one of the causes of immobility is lack of funds needed by workers to move into alternative employment areas. Subsidization of worker relocation may occur in the form of government loans or outright grants of funds.

The Concept of Mobility

A few observations regarding the meaning of mobility are in order to avoid misconceptions. To some people a mobile labor force may imply a drifting one with a high job turnover rate—an undesirable social situation. Mobility, as the term is used in economics, does not mean a lack of ties to communities and social institutions, nor does it mean that all workers must be ready to pack up and move at the slightest provocation. The amount of actual movement necessary to prevent monopsony usually will be quite small. The possibility or likelihood of migration is the important factor. Also, there is at all times considerable change and turnover of the labor force—workers changing jobs, new workers entering the labor force, and old workers retiring. This constant change constitutes mobility. The primary problem is that of directing the mobility that already exists into economically desirable channels.

GENERAL PROFIT-MAXIMIZING CONDITIONS: ALL MARKET STRUCTURES _____

We can now summarize the profit-maximizing conditions, applicable to all market structures, for the operations of firms in both product markets and resource markets. Suppose two resources, A and B, are used to produce product X. Without regard to product and resource market structures a firm would employ resource A at the level at which

(14.9)
$$MPP_a \times MR_x = MRC_a, \text{ or } \frac{MPP_a}{MRC_a} = \frac{1}{MR_x}.$$

Likewise, B should be employed up to the point at which

(14.10)
$$MPP_b \times MR_x = MRC_b, \text{ or } \frac{MPP_b}{MRC_b} = \frac{1}{MR_x}.$$

Equations (14.9) and (14.10) can then be combined as follows:

(14.11)
$$\frac{MPP_a}{MRC_a} = \frac{MPP_b}{MRC_b} = \frac{1}{MR_x}.$$

Since MPP_a/MRC_a and MPP_b/MRC_b are the same as $1/MC_x$, then

(14.6)
$$\frac{MPP_a}{MRC_a} = \frac{MPP_b}{MRC_b} = \frac{1}{MC_x} = \frac{1}{MR_x}.$$

For a purely competitive seller of product X who is also a purely competitive purchaser of resources A and B, MR_x is the same as p_x, and MRC_a and MRC_b, respectively, are equal to p_a and p_b. But for the product seller enjoying some degree of monopoly in selling product and monopsony in buying resources, MR_x is less than p_x, and MRC_a and MRC_b, respectively, are greater than p_a and p_b.[8] Note that when a firm employs each of its variable resources in the correct absolute amount for profit maximization, it necessarily will be using them in the correct or least-cost combination.

_____

[8]In terms of calculus, the general solution to the problem of profit maximization by a firm with respect to several variable resources is as follows:

$x = f(a, b) =$ the firm's production function;

$p_x = h(x) =$ the product demand curve facing the firm;

$p_a = \phi(a) =$ the supply curve facing the firm for resource A;

$p_b = \psi(b) =$ the supply curve facing the firm for resource B.

On the revenue side, $R = x \times p_x =$ total revenue of the firm,

$$\frac{dR}{dx} = p_x + x \times h'(x) = \text{ marginal revenue of the firm, and}$$

$$\frac{\partial R}{\partial a} = \left(\frac{dR}{dx}\right)\left(\frac{\partial x}{\partial a}\right) = [p_x + x \times h'(x)]\frac{\partial x}{\partial a} = \text{ marginal revenue product of } A \text{ to the firm.}$$

Similarly, $\dfrac{\partial R}{\partial b} = \left(\dfrac{dR}{dx}\right)\left(\dfrac{\partial x}{\partial b}\right) = [p_x + x \times h'(x)]\dfrac{\partial x}{\partial b} =$

marginal revenue product of B to the firm.

On the cost side,

$C = k + a \times p_a + b \times p_b =$ total costs of the firm; where $k =$ total fixed costs,

$$\frac{\partial C}{\partial a} = p_a + a \times \phi'(a) = \text{ marginal resource cost of } A;$$

$$\frac{\partial C}{\partial b} = p_b + b \times \psi'(b) = \text{ marginal resource cost of } B.$$

(continued)

ECONOMIC RENT

economic rent
The residual left for the fixed resources of a firm after the variable resources have been paid amounts equal to their alternative costs.

Perfect mobility of all resources does not occur in the short run even under conditions of pure competition. Those resources constituting the firm's size of plant are not mobile—they are fixed in quantity for particular uses or users. The longer the time period under consideration, the fewer will be the fixed resources.

The returns received by fixed resources are not determined according to the principles explained in this chapter. Since those resources are not free to move into alternative employments, their short-run remuneration will be whatever is left over after the mobile resources have been paid whatever it takes to hold them to the particular firm. The mobile resources must be paid amounts equal to what they can earn in alternative employments—that is, amounts equal to the values of their marginal product in alternative employments. The residual left for the fixed resources is called **economic rent.**[9]

A short-run cost-price diagram for an individual firm should help make clear the concept of economic rent. The short-run average cost curve, average variable cost curve, and marginal cost curve are drawn in Figure 14.10. Suppose that the market price of the product is p. The firm's output will be x, and total cost of the variable (mobile) resources will be $0vAx$. This is the outlay necessary if the firm is to hold its variable resources.

Should the firm attempt to reduce the payments made to variable resources, some or all of them will move into alternative uses where their marginal revenue products and remunerations are greater. Thus the average variable cost curve

---

To maximize profits,

$$\pi = R - C = x \times p_x - (k + a \times p_a + b \times p_b).$$

The necessary conditions are:

$$\frac{\partial \pi}{\partial a} = [p_x + x \times h'(x)] \frac{\partial x}{\partial a} - [p_a + a \times \phi'(a)] = 0,$$

$$\frac{\partial \pi}{\partial b} = [p_x + x \times h'(x)] \frac{\partial x}{\partial b} - [p_b + b \times \psi'(b)] = 0$$

or

$$[p_x + xh'(x)] \frac{\partial x}{\partial a} = p_a + a\phi'(a), \text{ and}$$

$$[p_x + xh'(x)] \frac{\partial x}{\partial b} = p_b + b\psi'(b);$$

that is,

$$MRP_a = MRC_a, \quad \text{and} \quad MRP_b = MRC_b.$$

If the firm is a purely competitive seller of product, then

$$p_x = h(x) = \bar{p}_x, \quad \text{and} \quad h'(x) = 0.$$

If it is a purely competitive purchaser of A, the supply curves of A and B are horizontal; so

$$\phi'(a) = 0, \quad \text{and} \quad \psi'(b) = 0.$$

Thus, the profit-maximizing conditions can be stated as

$$p_x \times \frac{\partial x}{\partial a} = p_a \quad \text{and} \quad p_x \times \frac{\partial x}{\partial b} = p_b, \text{ or}$$

$$VMP_a = p_a \quad \text{and} \quad VMP_b = p_b.$$

[9]These returns are sometimes called *quasi rents*. This term, introduced by Alfred Marshall, is used so ambiguously in economic literature that we shall avoid it altogether.

**Figure 14.10
Economic Rent**

Economic rent, the
residual left to fixed
resources after variable
resources have been paid
their alternative costs, is
measured by the area
vpBA. It is equal to total
receipts of the firm minus
total variable costs.

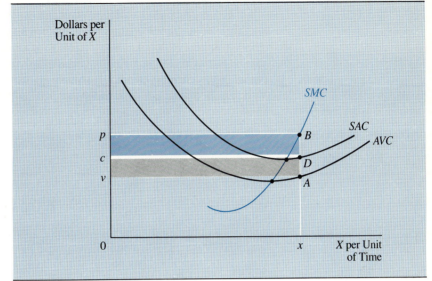

shows the necessary outlays per unit of product output that the firm must make
for variable resources. The fixed resources get whatever is left from the firm's
total receipts—that is, they receive economic rent. Total rent for the fixed resources is *vpBA*. The lower the market price of the product, the lower the rent
will be; the higher the market price, the higher the rent will be.

A problem now arises with regard to the nature of the *SAC* curve; what
does it show? To get at the problem, suppose that we consider the firm's investment in the fixed resources. The rent represents the return on investment in
the firm's fixed resources. Only that part of the rent which represents a return
on investment equal to what that amount of investment could earn elsewhere in
the economy or in alternative uses constitutes fixed costs for the firm. Thus
letting the part of rent represented by *vcDA* be the fixed costs for the firm, the
rest of the rent is what we have defined previously as pure profits. Average cost
at any output is equal to average fixed cost plus average variable cost at that
output.

Economic rent may be equal to, greater than, or less than enough to cover
the firm's fixed costs. When investment in the firm yields a higher rate of return
than investment on the average elsewhere in the economy, rents will be greater
than total fixed costs; we then say that the firm is making pure profits. When
rents equal total fixed cost—that is, when investment in the firm yields the same
rate of return as investment elsewhere—the firm's profits are zero. When product
price is not sufficient for rents to equal total fixed costs or when investment
elsewhere in the economy yields a higher rate of return than it does with the
firm, we say that the firm is incurring losses.

SUMMARY

In this chapter the pricing and employment of resources are incorporated into the theory of profit maximization by the individual firm. A firm using several variable resources solves two problems simultaneously in the process of maximizing its profits. It must use those resources in the correct absolute amounts, and in doing so it also uses them in a least-cost combination; that is,

$$\frac{MPP_a}{MRC_a} = \frac{MPP_b}{MRC_b} = \cdots = \frac{MPP_n}{MRC_n} = \frac{1}{MC_x} = \frac{1}{MR_x}.$$

Under pure competition in resource purchasing, the market price, individual firm level of employment, and market level of employment of a resource are determined simultaneously. Resource units receive a price equal to their marginal revenue products. If the resource user is also a pure competitor in the sale of product, the price paid a resource is equal to its value of marginal product as well, since its marginal revenue product and value of marginal product are the same. If the user has some degree of monopoly in product sales, it exploits resource units monopolistically—the value of marginal product of the resource exceeds its marginal revenue product.

Where monopsony in resource purchasing occurs, the level of employment is that at which marginal resource cost equals marginal revenue product of the resource. Since the monopsonist faces an upward-sloping supply curve of the resource, marginal resource cost exceeds the resource price, and units of the resource are exploited monopsonistically.

Resources that are immobile, or fixed in quantity supplied to the firm, receive economic rent, the difference between the firm's total receipts and its total variable costs.

Suggested Readings

Two classic statements of the economics of resource pricing are
Hicks, J. R. *Value and Capital,* 2d ed., Chaps. 6–7. Oxford: The Clarendon Press, 1946.
Hicks, J. R. *The Theory of Wages.* New York: Macmillan, 1932.

An advanced treatment of marginal productivity and the demand and supply of resources is
Friedman, Milton. *Price Theory,* Chaps. 11–13. Chicago: Aldine Publishing Co., 1976.

For a modern contribution to labor market analysis, see
Stigler, George J. "Information in the Labor Market," *Journal of Political Economy* 70, Supplement to Part 2 (October 1962): 94–105.

One of the early analyses of monopsony is found in
Robinson, Joan. *The Economics of Imperfect Competition.* London: Macmillan, 1933.

Problems and Questions for Discussion

1. "Rising marginal costs result from the operation of the law of diminishing returns." Analyze this statement in detail.

2. The relationship between a commercially mixed feed for dairy cows and the quantity of milk produced per day by a cow, holding all other inputs constant, is as follows:

Feed	Milk
2	1.0
4	2.0
6	2.8
8	3.5
10	4.0
12	3.9

The price of milk is $1 per gallon; the price of the feed is $.35 per pound. Determine the most profitable quantity of feed to use. Explain your reasoning.

3. In 1982, General Motors, which purchased about 7.5 percent of the U.S. steel output, announced that it would subsequently buy steel only on the basis of manufacturer bids. GM used to buy from over a dozen suppliers on the basis of published prices. The new system was expected to result in lower prices and fewer suppliers. (Amal Nag, ''GM Is Adopting Bidding System for Buying Steel,'' *The Wall Street Journal*, March 23, 1982.)
   a. Explain GM's adjustment to a lower steel price in terms of Equation 14.3.
   b. Would you expect GM to buy steel only from the single manufacturer that bid the lowest?

4. In 1983, a professor at the Harvard Business School estimated that the Ford Motor Company would have to cut its 1978 labor force of 256,600 persons by half to remain competitive with Japanese car producers. (''The New Economy,'' *Time,* May 10, 1983, 63.) In terms of two variable resources, labor (L) and steel (S), explain the effects of such a reduction on Ford's marginal costs.

5. In 1956, 60 percent of Harvard Business School graduates took their first jobs in manufacturing and 10.4 percent in investment banking and consulting. In 1986, 20 percent took their first jobs in manufacturing and 55.7 percent in investment banking and consulting. In 1986, starting salaries for jobs in real estate, computer-related jobs, and commercial banking were an average of $55,000, whereas starting salaries in manufacturing were $40,000 to $45,000. (Floyd A. Oliver, ''At Harvard, High Pay and Some Bad Omens,'' *Los Angeles Times,* November 2, 1986.)

   Generally, the demand for manufactured products declined and the demand for services increased between 1956 and 1986. Use the theory developed in the chapter to explain and diagram the declines in wages and employment in manufacturing and the increases in service industries.

6. Commutative justice is said to be attained when units of a resource are paid what they are worth to the society. Consider two of many purchasers of

common (unskilled) labor. One sells the product as a monopolist; the other sells it as a pure competitor. Explain the wage rate that each would pay, the level of employment in each firm, and whether or not commutative justice would be attained. Illustrate your answer with a diagram.

7. In 1985, the average workweek in Sweden was 28.8 hours, probably the lowest in the industrialized world. Based on interviews, many Swedes appeared to work fewer hours in order to enjoy more leisure. (Philip Revzin, "Swedes Gain Leisure, Not Jobs, by Cutting Hours," *The Wall Street Journal*, January 7, 1985.) What additional information would be necessary before interpreting this evidence as being consistent with the backward-bending supply of labor curve in Figure 14.5?

8. Would you expect that there is much monopsony in the purchase of common labor in the United States? Why or why not?

9. Could GM's new steel bidding system lead to its having monopsony power over steel producers? Explain.

10. Explain and illustrate how setting minimum resource prices can be used to counteract (1) monopolistic exploitation of a resource and (2) monopsonistic exploitation of a resource. Would you expect this tactic to be successful? Explain.

11. What kinds of government policies other than price fixing might be used to counteract monopsonistic exploitation of resources?

12. A purely competitive manufacturer of product X uses two variable resources, A and B, to turn out its product. State and explain the complete set of conditions, both with respect to the level of product output and the levels of resource inputs, that must be met if profits are to be maximized.

13. Explain how the concept of economic rent differs from the concept of economic profit.

Chapter 15

PRICING AND EMPLOYMENT OF RESOURCES: APPLICATIONS

This chapter consists entirely of applications of the theory developed in the preceding chapter. The theory of resource pricing and employment is a powerful device for understanding contemporary events and public policies. Newspapers and other media abound with stories about complex phenomena in markets for labor and other resources, the importance of which can best be comprehended by those who have a sharp grasp of the fundamentals of economic analysis.

From a wide range of possibilities, we have selected five applications to illustrate several of the most important principles developed in Chapter 14. To show that the position of the firm's demand curve for a resource is affected by the availability of complementary resources, we present the debate over use of the short-handled hoe in the farming fields of the western United States. To illustrate the process by which wages are determined in competitive labor markets, we discuss the controversy over illegal aliens (undocumented workers) in southern California, which has also become a matter of concern in Chicago, Miami, New York, and other cities. To illustrate monopsony, we describe the origins, consequences, and eventual elimination of the reserve clause in the contracts between professional baseball players and baseball clubs—for almost a century the most prominent monopsony in the American economy.

We illustrate the concept of economic rent with two applications. The first shows how economic rents arise normally from natural resource scarcities—strategically located straits and the Suez Canal, which sharply reduce the costs of ocean shipping. The second shows how monopoly rents can arise artificially because of governmental restraints on entry—the monopoly rents created by U.S. quotas on the importation of textiles from Hong Kong.

THE EFFECTS OF COMPLEMENTARY CAPITAL ON FARM LABOR WAGES

Truck farm laborers for generations have suffered from weeding rows of lettuce, melons, and other crops with short-handled hoes (between 12 and 18 inches) that cause backaches and other orthopedic problems. They prefer long-handled hoes (four feet) that can be employed standing up. Growers have insisted that the short-handled device is more effective because working close to the ground discloses more weeds, damages fewer plants, and does a given job in less time. Few individual growers would have incentives to substitute the long-handled hoe if it would reduce labor productivity while competitors continued to require short-handled ones, so the farm unions have sought industrywide prohibitions by law. This prompted a bitter feud between growers and unions. California outlawed the "inhumane" *cortito* in 1975, and the accompanying article describes the farm workers' union's 1983 victory in Arizona.

Fields are tilled with a combination of labor and capital, which may have complementary as well as substitute relationships. In Figure 15.1, the marginal revenue product curve for labor used with a given amount of capital on one farm is MRP_{l1}. The smaller the amount of capital used, or the less productive capital is, the farther to the left the MRP_l curve will be. Now if the short-handled

ARIZONA'S PROHIBITION OF THE SHORT-HANDLED HOE IS CALLED A 'VICTORY FOR HUMANITY'

by Bill Curry, *Los Angeles Times*

Down the long, dirt row he went, stooped at the waist and moving methodically and almost mechanically into the heat shimmering above an awakening field of cantaloupes. With a stubby hoe in his right hand, he thinned the sprouts and cut away the weeds.

Then he would pause to straighten, as best he could, and rest his bent back. He pressed the handle of the little hoe across his lower back in brief and ironic relief: The farm workers say it is the short-handled hoe that causes the pain in the first place and ruins their backs.

For more than half a century, farm workers have complained about the short-handled hoe, and for more than a decade they have sought to banish it from America's fruit and vegetable fields. They have burned it in protest, dropped it in waste cans in contempt, and fought it in court. It has become a symbol of oppressive stoop labor, a rallying point for union organizers.

And now the workers have claimed yet another victory over the tool. It happened in Arizona, one of the last places where it is still used on a large scale. On June 1, Arizona will ban the short-handled hoe as hazardous. It will be the third state to do so since 1975, when California became the first in the farm workers' war to rid the nation's fields of what they and many doctors say is an inherently harmful and inhumane tool.

"It's overwhelming, the evidence is overwhelming that it's hazardous," said Larry Etchechury, director of occupational safety and health in Arizona. "There is no doubt the farm worker is hurt by the short-handled hoe."

It is a tool, however, that growers say is the most efficient and economical available. Arizona's ban, they add, may well produce an increase in farm mechanization leading to farm worker unemployment.

'It's Going to Cost Money' "It's going to cost (growers) money one way or the other, either crop damage or (the work) will take twice as long," said Cecil Miller Jr., president of the Arizona Farm Bureau Federation. "There is no question we can do a more efficient job with the short-handled hoe. The ban sure makes it tough. Someone is going to go to court to challenge it."

Like so many grower-worker issues, the battle over the hoe here was tainted by long-standing hard feelings between the two groups. The hoe has a handle perhaps 12 to 18 inches long, compared to a four-foot handle on a regular hoe. It requires field workers to bend at the waist as they hack at the earth at their feet to thin and weed, in an unbroken pass down the seemingly endless rows.

The short hoe is used primarily for lettuce, which accounts for about one-half of this state's $150-million vegetable industry, but has also been used for melons, sugar beets and other crops.

So close to the ground, the workers can better see the small sprouts, causing less crop damage while destroying each and every unwanted plant, the growers say.

California is the nation's No. 1 lettuce-producing state, with 72% of the market, and Arizona is second, with 16%. The short-handled hoe still is used in scattered lettuce fields in such states as Colorado and New Mexico. Texas banned the hoe in 1981.

Will Issue Citations It is unknown how many of Arizona's 35,000 farm workers will be affected, but beginning June 1, occupational safety and health inspectors will make unannounced farm inspections and issue citations, carrying up to a $1,000 penalty, to growers using the hoe.

"There is a substitute for the short-handled hoe—the long-handled hoe is available," said Etchechury, adding that there are no alternatives for many other stoop labor jobs. "There is nothing you can do instead of stoop labor in lettuce harvesting."

Sam Kanemura, harvesting supervisor for the J. A. Wood Co.'s operations here in Scottsdale, said workers who earn about $4.50 an hour, including benefits, cultivating, "can make more progress with the short-handled hoe. I guarantee you it's over double (the cost) with the long-handled hoe.

'Doesn't Damage Crops' "The short hoe doesn't damage the crops. The long hoe damages the crops and takes double, triple the time. It (the short hoe) hurts the first two or three days, but after that they get used to it," he said.

"It's better to be working with the long-handled hoe," countered Jose Burciaga, a young lettuce worker, from Chandler, Ariz. "The growers think the short-handled hoe is much faster. They're just thinking about how much money they make. But it hurts people, it hurts their health. After the first day, your whole body hurts, especially in the waist area. It continues 'til the season is over."

"Give me a long-handled hoe and I'll do the same job," says Beatrice Martinez, 37, another Chandler farm worker. "The *cortito* has left me with bad memories. It's just inhuman."

Source: "Arizona's Prohibition of the Short-Handled Hoe Is Called a 'Victory for Humanity'," Bill Curry, May 27, 1983, *Los Angeles Times.* Reprinted by permission.

**Figure 15.1
Effects of Outlawing
the Short-Handled
Hoe**

With the short-handled
hoe, MRP_{l1} shows the
marginal revenue product
of labor. A shift to the
long-handled hoe, which
actually represents a
decrease in the capital
with which labor works,
shifts the marginal
revenue product curve to
the left to MRP_{l2}.

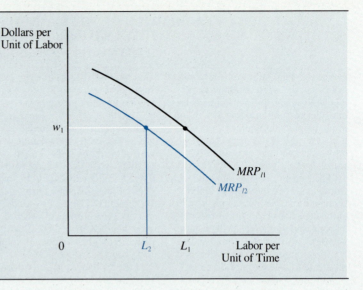

hoe is really more productive (which is not contested in the article), the substitution of the inferior long-handled hoe will shift the marginal revenue product curve for labor to the left to MRP_{l2}, reducing the employment level on the farm from L_1 to L_2. If this happens on all farms, a smaller total demand for labor will decrease wage rates; or, if wage rates are held at w_1, unemployment will result.

Every job has pecuniary as well as nonpecuniary elements, and it is possible that farm workers would be willing to accept a lower wage as the cost of getting rid of the hated *cortito*. As one of the Arizona state health officials said, "even if there are some decreases in production, we still have to consider the effects on people."

JOB COMPETITION FROM UNDOCUMENTED ALIENS

The debate over whether the influx of undocumented aliens is a bounty or an incubus has raged for years in California and Texas. Citizens of Mexico enter these states surreptitiously along the lengthy and lightly populated border between the two countries, seeking and getting such menial jobs as field hands or busboys in hotels and restaurants. The question is whether or not this reduces the employment of low-skilled American workers. Each side of the issue is discussed in the accompanying article.

The labor demand and supply curves underlying the argument that undocumented workers reduce the employment levels of U.S. workers are shown in Figure 15.2. Suppose that units of both U.S. and Mexican low-wage workers are more or less homogeneous. Suppose also that we distinguish between the agricultural market of panel (b) and the nonagricultural market of panel (a) for labor. In the nonagricultural market the demand curve is D_nD_n, the supply of

WITHOUT ILLEGAL ALIENS, INDUSTRIES IN SOME STATES COULDN'T SURVIVE
by Sam Allis, *The Wall Street Journal*

Asked about the burden of illegal aliens on his state's economy recently, California Gov. Jerry Brown replied that a number of industries there couldn't function without them. That may be an understatement.

The garment industry, hotels and restaurants, agriculture, health care and assembly operations in California rely heavily on the cheap, often exploited labor of the undocumented worker, the term used to identify the illegal alien working in this country. Many say that these people, most of whom are from Mexico, will ease a shortage of unskilled labor in the future.

Some people believe many Hispanics who live near the poverty level are "screaming" to have undocumented workers deported. Others say the jobs the undocumented take in the construction industry would be attractive to American workers. But no one really knows because so little hard data exist on illegal aliens.

Estimates of their numbers range from one million to more than eight million nationally. By all accounts, California receives the most, followed by Texas. Chicago has been a magnet for undocumented Mexicans for decades, while natives of Caribbean countries flock to Miami, New York and Washington, D.C.

In California, illegal aliens pour by the thousands each year through the sieve-like border at San Ysidro, about 20 miles south of San Diego. Without valid papers, they head for the best place to find work and anonymity—the barrio in East Los Angeles.

Edgar, an undocumented worker from Nicaragua, paid what's known as a "coyote" $400 to take him across the Mexican border into California six years ago. He went to Los Angeles and stayed with relatives until he found work as a bundler in a garment shop paying $60 a week in cash for 55 hours work. He had never heard of overtime or social security benefits.

According to a still incomplete two-year study by two University of California professors, 82% of the 500 Hispanic garment workers they interviewed were undocumented, as were more than 70% of 326 restaurant and hotel workers interviewed.

The professors, Sheldon Maram and Stewart Long, also found that few of the nearly 1,200 black and Hispanic unemployed whom they interviewed in Los Angeles this spring said they would accept the kinds of minimum-wage jobs held by undocumented workers. Although 60% said they were willing to do the work, hardly any would do it at the $3.10-an-hour minimum wage.

domestic workers is S_dS_d, and the supply of both U.S. and Mexican workers is S_nS_n. The horizontal difference between S_nS_n and S_dS_d shows the amounts that aliens are willing to supply at each wage rate. In the agricultural market, made up mostly of aliens, the demand and supply curves are D_aD_a and S_aS_a, respectively.

In the absence of any barriers to immigration, the equilibrium wage rate would be w_1 in both markets. The employment level in the agricultural market would be L_{a1}, and that in the nonagricultural market would be L_{n1}. In the nonagricultural market the employment level for U.S. workers would be L_{d1} and that of Mexicans would be $L_{d1}L_{n1}$.

What happens if a law is passed prohibiting undocumented aliens from working in the United States? In point of fact, aliens are much more easily found and deported in nonagricultural than in agricultural areas. Suppose that enforcement policies effectively block them from nonagricultural employment. Panel (a) shows that the effective supply curve is now S_dS_d. The wage rate for domestic workers rises to w_2, and their employment level expands to L_{d2}. U.S. nonagricultural workers gain, but their employers lose.

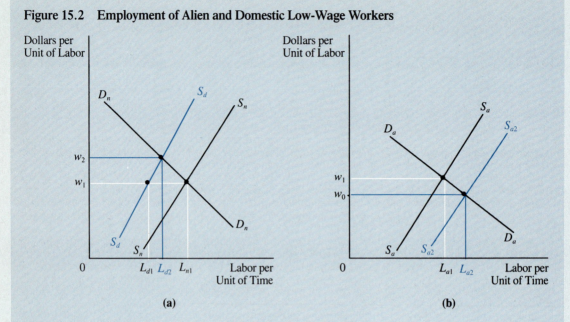

Figure 15.2   Employment of Alien and Domestic Low-Wage Workers

(a)

(b)

In the absence of immigration barriers the equilibrium wage rate is w_1. With immigration barriers, effective in the nonagricultural market of panel (a) but not in the agricultural market of panel (b), the total labor supply curve will be composed of domestic workers only, and is $S_d S_d$. The wage rate becomes w_2. Aliens who would have come into the nonagricultural market come into the agricultural market instead, increasing the labor supply to $S_{a2} S_{a2}$ and reducing the agricultural wage rate to w_0.

Just the reverse is likely to happen in the agricultural sector in panel (b). Many aliens now blocked from working in the nonagricultural sector shift to the agricultural sector, where they can hide more easily. The supply curve in that sector may well shift to the right, depending on how well or how poorly the law can be enforced. If it does shift to the right to some position such as $S_{a2} S_{a2}$, the wage rate falls to w_0 and the employment level rises to L_{a2}. Workers lose, and growers of agricultural products gain.

MONOPSONY IN PROFESSIONAL BASEBALL[1]

Professional baseball players officially were "liberated" in 1975—liberated from a monopsonistic restriction in their contracts that indentured them to the

[1]These materials are based on Simon Rottenberg, "The Baseball Players' Labor Market," *Journal of Political Economy* 64 (June 1956): 242–258; David S. Davenport, "Collusive Competition in Major League Baseball—Its Theory and Institutional Development," *The American Economist* 14 (Fall 1969): 6–30; and Gerald W. Scully, "Pay and Performance in Major League Baseball," *American Economic Review* 64 (December 1974): 915–930.

employers holding their contracts for the duration of their athletic careers. The restriction, dating back to 1879, survived for 96 years and might have endured indefinitely had it not been for a strategic miscalculation by the club owners. This era in the baseball players' labor market has been carefully studied by several economists and represents a "textbook case" of monopsony.

The Reserve Clause

The incentives of baseball clubs to collude on wages were enormous owing to the players' large economic rents—the difference between the values of their skills in baseball as compared with their next best employments. Players like Ruth, Feller, Spahn, Koufax, and Mays had superb skills that made them worth a great deal in baseball, but the next best alternative for most of them would have been a relatively low-wage job. Thus the clubs, by suppressing wage competition, could capture for themselves some of the economic rents that would otherwise have gone to the players.

The baseball players' labor market actually consisted of three separate markets, depending upon each individual player's contractual status. Players who had never signed a contract with any team in organized baseball—usually youngsters out of high school—were called *free agents*. They were free to sell their services to whichever club bid highest, and the clubs competed in this market by offering bonuses to those signing up. Bonuses were usually modest and represented the portion of the player's economic rent that he retained.[2]

Once a player signed a contract his market options changed drastically. All players were required to sign a *uniform contract* that was drawn up by organized baseball and used by all clubs. The contract had a one-year duration, and it could be terminated unilaterally by the club. But its key feature was a clause that reserved the club's unilateral right to renew the contract for another year at a wage established by the club, subject to the condition that next year's salary could not be less than 75 percent of the current year's figure. In addition, there was and still is an absolute minimum annual salary. This arrangement tied each player's baseball services to the club with which he initially signed, and it gave the club an exclusive right to deal with him. Some athletes occasionally bargained with their clubs by threatening to quit baseball altogether unless they were paid higher wages. Such "holdouts" gained attention on the sports pages, but the club's "final" offer would signal that the player either could accept it or withdraw from baseball to his next best employment. In fact, very few athletes withdrew.

The third labor market consisted of *player contracts*. The uniform contract gave the club the unilateral right to transfer the player to one of its own minor league teams, sell his contract to another team, or trade it for the contract of another player(s). Players whose contract was sold or traded were required by the uniform contract rules to report for work to the acquiring club within 72

---

[2]Rottenberg notes that during the 1940s and 1950s bonuses of as much as $100,000 were not unknown, but they usually were much smaller.

hours. By acquiring the player's contract, the new club also gained the reserved right to renew the contract every year at a noncompetitive wage. Clubs seeking to purchase or trade for a player's contract could deal only with the club that owned it. Tampering, or negotiating directly with players, was prohibited by general agreement among clubs, and the Commissioner of Baseball would levy a substantial fine on an offender. Club owners took tampering so seriously that some were, and still are, unwilling to discuss even with sportswriters their plans to deal for player contracts without first opening formal negotiations with the controlling club.

As Gerald W. Scully put it, "The (reserve clause) restriction grants some monopsony power to the owner and the exercise of that power results in a divergence between *MRP* and salary. The marginal revenue product continues to be an essential factor in player salary determination, but under the reserve clause, players and owners share the player's *MRP*."[3] This portion of the monopsony gain equals the economic rent that is lost by the players, which could be capitalized into the prices that clubs could obtain by trading or selling contracts to other teams. The bonus, as we noted earlier, is the portion of the player's economic rent that he retains.

The Extent of Exploitation

Ideally each baseball club would use its monopsony power in the labor market to engage in salary discrimination in the same manner that other firms use their monopoly power in the product market to engage in price discrimination. Each player logically should be presented a take-it-or-leave-it offer reflecting his next best alternative, his outside income from product endorsements and other pecuniary activities, and changes in his marginal revenue product to the team. However, it is difficult for many monopsonists to arrive at this lowest possible salary offer. Moreover, to reduce salaries to such a level could destroy team morale, result in a poorer season win-loss record, and hence reduce gate receipts. Thus we should expect that the salaries of players would exceed somewhat their next best earning possibilities. This expectation is clearly supported by data from a variety of sources.

The reserve clause was first introduced in the National League in late 1879 after a season of intense wage competition among teams.[4] David S. Davenport reports that about 68 percent of one of the team's total expenses in 1878 went for team salaries but that it had declined to 54 percent in 1880. From 1883 to 1950, the gross receipts of baseball clubs rose by 80 times the initial level, but player salaries increased only 7 times. Increases in baseball salaries also have lagged behind the trend increases in salaries in motion pictures and other recreation industries.[5]

_____

[3]Scully, "Pay and Performance," 916.

[4]Rottenberg, "Baseball Labor Market," 247.

[5]Davenport, "Collusive Competition in Baseball," 17.

COLLUSIVE COMPETITION IN MAJOR LEAGUE BASEBALL—
ITS THEORY AND INSTITUTIONAL DEVELOPMENT
by David S. Davenport

It is difficult to determine if a player is economically exploited. I made an attempt with one particular player—Sandy Koufax. I chose Koufax because as a starting pitcher, he only plays in one quarter or fifth of all games, providing an opportunity to assess individual drawing power and to try to determine whether he was "exploited.". . . I made a "guesstimate" of the value of Koufax's *MRP* by comparing the attendance at Dodger games when he pitched with that at games when he did not. I also made a rough estimate of his indirect contribution by comparing the attendances and overall playing records in two consecutive years—one in which he played and the next in which he was retired. The results . . . are dramatic, although admittedly inexact. Koufax in 1966 drew an average of 6,000 more customers per game in nineteen games at home and 7,000 more in nineteen road games. Taking $2.00 as the average ticket price and figuring the Dodgers' percentage of receipts to be 80% at home and 20% on the road, the additional revenue from games which Koufax started is $236,178. Since his salary was reported to be $120,000, later said to be $130,000, it appears that Koufax's wage was far below the value of his *MRP*. But this $236,000 is in no rational sense

the extent of the Dodgers' marginal revenue from Koufax. In 1966, he won 27 and lost 9, leading the Dodgers to the pennant with a 95–67 record for a winning percentage of .586. Koufax retired. The following season, the Dodgers finished in eighth place with a record of 73-89 and a .451 percentage. For 36 games, the number pitched by Koufax in 1966, the average Dodger pitcher (a .451 winner) would have won 16 and lost 20.

The difference between this record and that of Koufax in '66 is eleven victories and losses, or half the difference between the club's season records in 1966 and 1967. The difference in Dodger home attendance alone was 953,430. One might argue that with Koufax pitching, the improved playing record would recover half the attendance difference. I think this is a high estimate, as I suspect club attendance increases at an accelerated rate as the club gets closer to first place. And there is probably some duplication from the direct analysis above. But if we only credit his pitching with recovering, say, a fourth of the attendance difference, he would increase Dodger home attendance by 238,360 and revenues (attendance times $1.60, the Dodger share of the $2.00

average ticket) $381,376. His total marginal revenue, then, could be guesstimated at $617,554.

Compared with Koufax's salary of $130,000, the Dodgers received almost $500,000 of his marginal revenue. And Koufax did not get his $130,000 through his own bargaining power alone. . . . Koufax got his $130,000 only through a bargaining coalition with fellow star pitcher, Don Drysdale. The importance of their combined talent to Dodger playing fortunes was so high that the Dodgers were forced to increase their offer, especially since Koufax and Drysdale were not in the position of having nowhere else to go but had already signed movie contracts. Even with the help of this added bargaining strength, Koufax was exploited for an estimated $500,000. It is reasonable to argue that this was not all exploitation. . . . Other portions could be assigned to interest on the original investment in the franchise, rent from the use of the club's own stadium, return on the club's favorable franchise location, and part of the salaries for other players who through cooperation contributed to [his] value. But it remains most doubtful that Sandy Koufax came anywhere close to realizing the value of his marginal product.

Source: The American Economist, vol. 14, no. 2 (Fall 1969), 17–18. Reprinted by permission.

The accompanying excerpt from Davenport's article offers a back-of-the-envelope calculation of the *MRP* versus the wage paid to Sandy Koufax, the ace pitcher of the Los Angeles Dodgers during the 1960s. He estimates that the Dodgers obtained about $500,000 of the annual economic rent that would have accrued to Koufax under a regime of competitive wages—an amount about four times his highest salary.

Gerald W. Scully's research shows how sophisticated statistical techniques, when cleverly applied to basic economic concepts, can yield a striking estimate of the monopsony gain in baseball.[6] To do this Scully had to compare salaries with *MRP*s for players of different qualities. Organized baseball keeps extensive historical data on player productivities (for example, batting averages or strike-outs), and salaries are announced publicly, although there is no assurance that they are accurate. Scully estimated the productivities of players based on the productivities of entire teams. This required a comparison between each team's revenues from attendance and broadcasting on the one hand and the team's win-loss percentage in that season on the other. Using data for 1968–69, Scully estimated that a one-point rise in the team's win-loss percentage would increase revenues by $10,330.

Table 15.1 shows Scully's estimates of the strength of the wage collusion. The differences between his estimates of gross versus net marginal revenue product reflect his attempt to remove the costs of training, operating farm clubs, and search activities that clubs engage in as they develop players. Thus his comparisons between net *MRP* and salary yield his estimate of the gain to clubs from wage collusion only. The gains are large and are probably understated because Scully was generous in his estimate of the training and search costs—the difference between gross *MRP* and net *MRP*. Based on different assumptions about career lengths and productivities not shown in Table 15.1, Scully concluded that "average players receive salaries equal to about 11 percent of their gross and about 20 percent of their net marginal revenue products. Star players receive about 15 percent of their net marginal revenue products. . . . On the whole, therefore, it seems that the economic loss to professional ballplayers under the reserve clause is of a considerable magnitude."[7] Interestingly enough, Scully's estimate of the portion of Sandy Koufax's economic rent that the Dodgers obtained based on these complex statistical techniques was only about $125,000 (or 25 percent) more than the estimate given by David Davenport using a simple arithmetic procedure.[8]

Baseball's Defense of the Reserve Clause

The baseball club owners long had argued that the reserve clause was necessary to equalize the distribution of player talent within the league and to prevent a single team from dominating league play. Without the clause, the club owners claimed, the financially strongest teams—usually those in the largest metropolitan areas—could buy up all the best players, win pennants perpetually, and wreck the value of franchises in other cities.

The fallacy of this argument was exposed in 1956 in a classic article on baseball economics by Simon Rottenberg, from which an excerpt is reprinted here. Rottenberg argues that teams have an incentive to be balanced relatively evenly because attendance receipts are maximized by barely winning a pennant, not by mopping up the league. He uses the concept of diminishing returns to

---

[6]Scully, "Pay and Performance," 920–921.

[7]Ibid., 929.

[8]Ibid., 922.

**Table 15.1
Scully's Estimates of
the Strength of the
Wage Collusion by
Baseball Clubs
against Players**

Performance[a] (SA or SW)	Gross Marginal Revenue Product[b]	Net Marginal Revenue Product	Salary
	Hitters		
270	$213,800	$ 85,500	$31,700
290	230,000	101,700	34,200
310	245,200	116,900	36,800
330	261,400	133,100	39,300
350	277,500	149,200	41,900
370	292,700	164,400	44,400
390	308,900	180,600	47,000
410	325,000	196,700	49,600
430	340,200	211,900	52,200
450	356,400	228,100	54,800
470	372,600	244,300	57,400
490	387,800	259,500	60,000
510	403,900	275,600	62,700
530	420,100	291,800	65,300
550	435,300	307,000	67,900
570	451,400	323,100	70,600
	Pitchers		
1.60	$185,900	$ 57,600	$31,100
1.80	209,200	80,900	34,200
2.00	232,400	104,100	37,200
2.20	255,700	127,400	40,200
2.40	278,900	150,600	43,100
2.60	302,200	173,900	46,000
2.80	325,400	197,100	48,800
3.00	348,600	220,300	51,600
3.20	371,900	243,600	54,400
3.40	395,100	266,800	57,100
3.60	418,400	290,100	59,800

[a]*SA* is the lifetime slugging average of hitters and differs from the "batting" averages that are usually
calculated in that the slugging average takes into account the number of bases advanced on each hit rather than
simply the number of hits. *SW* is the lifetime strikeout-to-walk ratio of pitchers, the clearest measure of the
productivity of pitchers in isolation from the rest of the team. The average life of hitters is assumed by Scully
to be 8 years and of pitchers 6 years.

[b]The estimated average cost of player development and training is $128,300 per year. This is the difference
between the column of gross marginal revenue products and the column of net marginal revenue products.

Source: Gerald W. Scully, "Pay and Performance in Major League Baseball," *American Economic Review* 64
(December 1974): 923. Reprinted by permission.

make his point. Rottenberg demonstrates in the excerpt that the distribution of
playing talent around the league will be the same with the reserve clause as
without it, although the incomes of the clubs relative to those of the players
will be larger with the clause.

David S. Davenport has shown that the effects of the reserve clause have
been just the opposite from the clubs' stated intention:

> *In practice, the reserve clause has made possible what it was theoret-
> ically designed to prevent—it has allowed dominant clubs to control player*

THE BASEBALL PLAYERS' LABOR MARKET
by Simon Rottenberg

Is it clear that the reserve rule is necessary to achieve more or less equal quality of play among teams? Assume that teams are distributed among locations, as they are in fact, so that the revenues of some are very much larger than those of others. Assume a free players' labor market, in which players may accept the offer of the highest bidder and teams may make offers without restraint.

At first sight, it may appear that the high-revenue teams will contract all the stars, leaving the others only the dregs of the supply; that the distribution of players among teams will become very unequal; that contests will become less uncertain; and that consumer interest will flag and attendance fall off. On closer examination, however, it can be seen that this process will be checked by the law of diminishing returns, operating concurrently with each team's strategic avoidance of diseconomies of scale.

Professional team competitions are different from other kinds of business ventures. If a seller of shoes is able to capture the market and to cause other sellers of shoes to suffer losses and withdraw, the surviving competitor is a clear gainer. But in baseball no team can be successful unless its competitors also survive and prosper sufficiently so that the differences in the quality of play among teams are not "too great."

If the size of a baseball team is thought of as the number of players under contract to it, each player being weighted by some index of his quality, then diseconomies of scale set in at some point when a team too far outstrips its competitors, and they become larger in proportion to the size of the differences.

Two teams opposed to each other in play are like two firms producing a single product. The product is the game, weighted by the revenues derived from its play. With game admission prices given, the product is the game, weighted by the number of paying customers who attend. When 30,000 attend, the output is twice as large as when 15,000 attend. In one sense, the teams compete; in another, they combine in a single firm in which the success of each branch requires that it be not "too much" more efficient than the other. If it is, output falls.

A baseball team, like any other firm, produces its product by combining factors of production. Consider the two teams engaged in a contest to be collapsed into a single firm, producing as output games, weighted by the revenue derived from admission fees. Let the players of one team be one factor and all others (management, transportation, ball parks, and the players of the other team), another. The quantity of the factor—players—is measured by making the appropriate adjustment for differential qualities among players, so that a man who hits safely in 35 per cent of his times at bat counts as more than one who hits safely only 20 per cent of the time. Given the quantity of the other factors, the total product curve of the factor—players of one team—will have the conventional shape; it will slope upward as the "quantity" of this factor is increased, reach a peak, and then fall. It will not pay to increase this factor without limit. Beyond some point—say, when a team already has three .350 hitters—it will not pay to employ another .350 hitter. If a team goes on increasing the quantity of the factor, players, by

hiring additional stars, it will find that the total output—that is, admission receipts—of the combined firms (and, therefore, of its own) will rise at a less rapid rate and finally will fall absolutely. At some point, therefore, a first star player is worth more to poor Team B than, say, a third star to rich Team A. At this point, B is in a position to bid players away from A in the market. A's behavior is not a function of its bank balance. It does what it calculates it is worthwhile to do; and the time comes when, in pursuing the strategy of its own gains, it is worthwhile, whatever the size of its cash balance, to forgo the services of an expert player and see him employed by another team.

The wealthy teams will usually prefer winning to losing. If they do, they will prefer winning by close margins to winning by wide ones. If their market behavior is consistent with this objective—that is, if they behave like rational maximizers—playing talent will be more or less equally distributed among teams.

It does not require collusion to bring about this result. It is not senseless to expect it to be produced by a free labor market in which each team is separately engaged in gainful behavior. The position of organized baseball that a free market, given the unequal distribution of revenue, will result in the engrossment of the most competent players by the wealthy teams is open to some question. It seems, indeed, to be true that a market in which freedom is limited by a reserve rule such as that which now governs the baseball labor market distributes players among teams about as a free market would.

Source: *Journal of Political Economy*, vol. 64, no. 3 (June 1956), 254–55, by permission of The University of Chicago Press. © 1956 by The University of Chicago.

talent and competition through such practices as the farm system and the buying of player contracts, while the control and lowering of cost curves for labor have allowed weaker clubs to survive. An empirical look at the competition supposedly promoted is indicative of the failure of a policy that does not attack the problem source. Between 1920 and 1968, the rich market area Yankees have won 29 American League flags in 48 seasons. In the National League, three teams—St. Louis, . . . and the rich market area New York-San Francisco Giants and Brooklyn-Los Angeles Dodgers—have won 33 of 48 pennants.[9]

Rottenberg's analysis is consistent with the evidence that Davenport gathered.

Competition Replaces Monopsony

Baseball, for one reason or another, has always enjoyed an antitrust immunity. Initially that immunity was established by a 1922 case in which the Supreme Court employed an archaic definition of interstate commerce that removed baseball "games" from the ambit of the Sherman Act. Although the Court's definition of interstate commerce was broadened over time, Congress never intervened to remove the original immunity granted baseball clubs. In Curt Flood's challenge of the reserve clause, the Supreme Court in 1972 refused to overturn it on grounds that although Congress realized the inconsistency between baseball's immunity and the general antitrust policy, it deliberately chose to maintain the inconsistency.

The Baseball Players Association never attacked the reserve clause through a strike. They obtained increases in the minimum salary paid to players from the $7,500 level that prevailed in the early 1950s to $30,000 in the early 1970s. The Association also strove for better pensions and grievance procedures that would benefit all players.

In 1973 the clubs acceded to a request by the players to allow outside arbitration of a broad range of contractual disputes. This was a major blunder. Within two years, Andy Messersmith mounted a challenge of the reserve clause on the ground that it ought to apply for only one renewal year rather than in perpetuity at the discretion of the club. Defending the reserve clause with the same "equal distribution" arguments that Simon Rottenberg's article had debunked, the clubs adamantly refused to negotiate with the players over this issue and demanded that the arbitrator give an immediate, all-or-nothing answer. On December 23, 1975, impartial arbitrator Peter Seitz ruled that the reserve clause was indeed a fit subject for negotiation between the clubs and the players, an outcome that was upheld on each of two occasions in which the clubs appealed the ruling to federal courts. Organized baseball had lost the reserve clause even though its antitrust exemption was still intact! Mr. Seitz, for his part, was fired by the clubs.[10]

---

[9]Davenport, "Collusive Competition in Baseball," 9.

[10]Jerome Holtzman, "Summation of Year's Activities," *Official Baseball Guide—1976* (St. Louis: *The Sporting News*, 1976), 283–292.

Within a year the clubs and the players had reached the type of agreement that Seitz's ruling required. In effect, the players could become free agents after six years of play by playing out their contracts plus one additional year; players after five years could demand to be traded. They could veto any six clubs they did not want to be traded to. Any player taking either step would have to wait an additional five years before asking to be traded again. This was a collective bargaining compromise in which the players got less than complete freedom of contract on an annual basis and the owners gave up on the reserve clause for fear the players would strike.[11]

The effects of the Seitz ruling were dramatic. Bidding for the initial group of 24 free agents occurred in a New York hotel in November 1976. The owners spent a total of $23 million. Reggie Jackson won the sweepstakes with $3 million for his new contract. Gene Autry, owner of the California Angels, put down $5.2 million for three players. Charlie Finley, owner of the Oakland "A's," whose controversial contracts with several of "his" players—mainly Catfish Hunter—may have led to the challenge of the reserve clause,[12] apparently emerged from the bidding room in a state of gloom. He said, "This is the worst thing that's ever happened to baseball. It was like a den of thieves in there . . . everyone trying to cut one another's throats (*sic*). It's like having someone come in your house and snap up all your children. I feel I was contributing to the demise of baseball. I don't have the money to get into the bidding but then I don't have an alternative either."[13] Bowie Kuhn, Commissioner of Baseball, observed: "That the weaker clubs are trying to improve through this system is gratifying. And it may be that we are going to see the beginning of a process where the stronger clubs will be outbid by the weaker clubs. The important concept of preserving some sort of balance will be benefited by the process."[14] This observation was, of course, 180 degrees away from the old "equal distribution" argument that the clubs had used to defend the reserve clause.

By 1980 the results of the new competition were plain. At the end of 1979 more than 100 players had changed club uniforms since 1975, and the average player's salary had increased from $51,000 in 1976 to between $130,000 and $150,000 in 1980. Salaries also had risen for players who had not yet become free agents. In November 1980, Dodger left-fielder Dusty Baker signed a five-year contract with the Dodgers for $4 million after eight months of negotiations and just a few minutes before the moment that he was scheduled to become a free agent. A month later Dave Winfield signed with the Yankees for $1 million plus $1.5 million per year for each of ten years with cost-of-living increases. As Winfield contentedly observed, "There's a market value for everything." About a year later, Dodger Steve Garvey went to the San Diego Padres for $6.6 million over five years that was reported to be $7.5 million after incentive

---

[11]Ron Rapoport, "Baseball's Free Agent Jitters," *Los Angeles Times,* November 23, 1976.

[12]Ross Newhan, "Baseball's Golden Era, " *Los Angeles Times,* December 6, 1976.

[13]Ross Newhan, "Baseball's Free Agent Scramble Is On," *Los Angeles Times,* November 5, 1976.

[14]Newhan, "Baseball's Golden Era."

Table 15.2
Average Nominal Player Salary, Average Real Player Salary (in 1972 dollars), and Percentage of Change in Average Real Player Salary, 1971–1980

Year	Average Nominal Salary[a]	Average Real Salary	Change in Average Real Salary (%)
1971	31,543	41,918	—
1972	34,092	43,860	4.63
1973	36,566	44,285	0.97
1974	40,839	44,570	0.64
1975	44,676	44,676	0.24
1976	51,501	48,692	8.99
1977	76,066	67,560	38.75
1978	99,876	82,392	21.95
1979	113,558[b]	84,204	2.20
1980	130,592[c]	85,299	1.18

[a]Average nominal salary data are from *Sports Illustrated,* January 5, 1981.

[b]This was the first year that the Players Association discounted deferred payments. They used a 9 percent rate to discount deferred payments without interest.

[c]This figure is based on the Players Association's estimate that salaries increased by about 15 percent in 1980. The Player Relations Committee's estimate of the average 1980 salary is $146,500.

Source: Kenneth Lehn, "Property Rights, Risk Sharing, and Player Disability in Major League Baseball," *The Journal of Law and Economics* 25 (October 1982), 348, by permission of The University of Chicago Press. © 1982 by The University of Chicago.

bonuses were taken into account.[15] Future years' income in such contracts must be discounted to present value—which rarely occurs on the sports pages—but it is clear that baseball wages went up sharply after 1975.

Table 15.2, published by Kenneth Lehn in 1982, supports the hypothesis that ending the reserve clause redistributed income from the clubs to the players. Adjusting wages by the CPI, Lehn found that the average real salary increased more than 38 percent in 1977 and another 22 percent in 1978. He found that ending the reserve clause also changed the nature of contracts and thus the nature of resource allocation of baseball teams. Before 1976 all players were on one-year contracts, but in 1980 35 percent had at least three guaranteed years.

In addition, longer contracts reduced the costs of being disabled to players. Lehn found that at a given moment players with guaranteed long-term contracts were more likely to be disabled than players with short-term contracts and that players experienced more disability days after signing long-term contracts than in previous seasons. However, bonuses for frequency and quality of performances reduced disability rates.[16]

[15]Frederick C. Klein, "Baseball is Prospering Despite Shifts Caused by New 'Free Agents'," *The Wall Street Journal,* April 4, 1979; Mike Littwin, "The Free-Agent Draft: Baseball's No-Star Wars V," *Los Angeles Times,* November 13, 1980; Mike Littwin, "Baker Signs 5-Year Dodger Contract," *Los Angeles Times,* November 11, 1980; "The Man with the Golden Bat," *Fortune,* January 26, 1981, 25; Dave Distel, "$6.6 Million Contract; Garvey Accepts Padres' Offering," *Los Angeles Times,* December 22, 1982.

[16]Kenneth Lehn, "Property Rights, Risk Sharing, and Player Disability in Major League Baseball," *The Journal of Law and Economics* 25 (October 1982):343–366.

The 1981 season produced a 49-day strike by the Major League Players Association—effectively a labor union—against the club owners in a textbook-like standoff between monopsony and monopoly situations. The sole issue was the compensation that clubs losing players as free agents would receive from clubs hiring them. The owners as a group wanted an industrywide rule to limit their individual incentives to compete for free agents. In professional football, for example, the commissioner levies a discretionary ''tax'' on the club hiring a free agent to compensate the club losing him. This discourages the hiring of free agents, lowers their wages, and leads fewer players to seek free agent status. The players saw the compensation issue as an attempt by the owners to recapture some of the economic rents they had lost to the players when the reserve clause was eliminated. The owners initially wanted as compensation what would amount to the sixteenth-best person on the hiring club's 40-man roster, and 18 months later they agreed to the twenty-fourth-best person on the roster. The settlement came only a week before the benefits from the owners' $50 million strike insurance policy with Lloyd's of London would have been exhausted.[17]

The experience was costly to both sides but particularly so to the owners. The strike insurance benefits were smaller than the attendance revenues they lost from 710 games, or 38 percent of the season, in one of baseball's most popular eras. This happened the year after the clubs had come close to setting an attendance record. The owners had been divided over the strike from the start, but a group of ''hawks'' hoped it would discourage unionization and the use of free agent status. Neither occurred, and the owners had compounded the miscalculation they had made six years earlier when they threw away the reserve clause.

Competition among owners continued to push up player salaries. The average doubled from $185,000 in 1981 to $363,000 in 1985; 37 players were paid over $1 million per year, and 2 over $2 million. An attempt by the owners to limit salaries led to another strike just as the 1985 season opened. Without the reserve clause, the players were in the stronger position. After two days the owners agreed to a new five-year contract that did little to limit salary bids.[18] The owners' antitrust immunity was still intact, but rivalry among them made it almost worthless.

---

[17]Mark Heisler, ''Baseball Can't Make Up those 50 Days,'' *Los Angeles Times,* August 1, 1981.

[18]Thomas Moore, ''Baseball's New Game Plan,'' *Fortune,* April 15, 1985, 19; Steve Springer, ''Baseball Lurches Toward New Strike; The Questions Appear Simple but Answers are Complicated,'' *Los Angeles Times,* August 6, 1985; Kenneth Reich, ''Ueberroth Pitches Near-Perfect Game,'' *Los Angeles Times,* August 8, 1985; and Hal Lancaster, ''Baseball Players, Owners, Gear Up for New Fight Over Free Agency,'' *The Wall Street Journal,* October 20, 1986.

STRAITS, THE SUEZ CANAL, AND ECONOMIC RENT FROM OCEAN SHIPPING[19]

The age-old doctrine of "freedom of the seas," a principle of international law first set down in the time of Elizabeth Tudor, has been transformed during the past 40 years. Through the first half of this century, coastal nations generally asserted control over foreign shipping and fishing out to the three-mile limit only. By the late 1970s, however, all but a handful of coastal states asserted control out to twelve nautical miles. At present there are 121 straits that are international waterways under a three-mile limit but would be overlapped by a twelve-mile limit and thus be under the exclusive control of the adjacent coastal nations. Such control could be used either to collect tolls or to exact political concessions from maritime and oil-importing countries.

The gains that states can capture from the straits they control are in the form of economic rent. The available data suggest that such gains are not especially large. The maximum amount that any one state can extract from a shipowner is the difference between the costs of taking the next best, but more circuitous, route and the costs of traveling the direct route through the strait. Economists at the U.S. Treasury in 1974–75 attempted to estimate some of these available rents. Closing off the English Channel, through which between 22 and 27 percent of U.S. imports pass, would have cost the United States only $35 million to $45 million per year extra in shipping costs. This is the maximum rent that the controlling country or countries could extract from the United States. Closing off all four of the straits that link the Pacific and Indian oceans without circumnavigating Australia would have increased the cost of U.S. oil imports to the West Coast by about $.35 per barrel, or about 30 percent of the cost of the shorter trip. This would have amounted to an extra $137 million per year in 1975 for the United States; again the $137 million figure is the maximum rent that could have been extracted from this country. The figure pertaining to Japan would have been larger, since almost all of its oil imports come through these straits from the Persian Gulf. These data are not conclusive, but they do suggest that the economic power of straits states, if they were to exercise it fully, is far from overwhelming.

The inherent limits on the rents that stem from such a geographical monopoly are clear from the experience of Egypt with the Suez Canal. The canal was closed when ships were sunk in it during the 1973 Six Day War, but the Egyptians cleared and reopened it in 1975 with the intention of profiting from its operation. The director of the Egyptian canal authority declared his policy on tolls in 1974: "We expect to be able to set dues that will make it in the interest of a ship to use the canal if it physically can,"[20] a policy that is about as oriented toward profit maximization as one could imagine. The actual tolls in 1976 were about $200,000 for the passage of a tanker of 249,000 deadweight

---

[19]This material is based on Ross D. Eckert, *The Enclosure of Ocean Resources: Economics and the Law of the Sea* (Stanford, Calif.: Hoover Press, 1979), Chapter 3.

[20]Ibid., 77.

tons, or something close to $1 per ton. But revenues collected at these prices were far short of the $400 million annually that the canal authority anticipated, and ship traffic was only about one-third of the prewar levels. What explains the director's miscalculation in setting tolls?

The key error was his failure to estimate correctly the extra cost of the detour—circumnavigating Africa via the Cape of Good Hope. The cost of circumnavigation declined after 1974 owing to a reduction in oil shipments out of the Persian Gulf. As oil-consuming nations cut their imports the demand for tankers declined, and the cost of tanker charters dropped markedly. Lower daily costs of hiring tankers reduced the opportunity costs of the longer trip, causing more shipowners to choose the lower-cost alternative. Using the canal cuts about 12 days off the length of a trip between the Persian Gulf and Rotterdam; at the time, the daily operating costs of a large tanker were about $7,000. The canal toll of about $1 per ton meant that tankers of more than 100,000 deadweight tons could usually save by taking the longer trip. The experience evidently weighed heavily in the decision of the Egyptians in 1976 to deepen the canal in order to accommodate larger tankers and at the same time to adjust downward the schedule of tolls. As the director of the canal authority put it, "After the improvement [canal deepening] program we have to reexamine the toll structure because perhaps it may be a bit high."[21]

MONOPOLY RENTS FROM QUOTAS ON HONG KONG TEXTILES

Economic rents arise from natural scarcities, as in the case of the Suez Canal, or from contrived scarcities caused by governmental policies or other devices used to limit market entry. Rents in the latter case are called "monopoly rents," since the returns to the protected investors are in excess of competitive levels. The accompanying article describes the quotas on textile exports from Hong Kong to the United States. Figure 15.3 shows the manner in which this policy helps U.S. textile producers by increasing their sales at the expense of Hong Kong while hurting U.S. consumers through smaller supplies and higher prices of textiles.

Assume a constant U.S. demand for textiles of D_u and a total supply of S_t. The quantities that U.S. textile producers supply on the U.S. market at various prices are shown by S_u, with Hong Kong producers supplying the difference between S_u and S_t. At the equilibrium market price, p, X_t is sold, with X_1 supplied by U.S. producers and $X_1 X_t$ made up by imports from Hong Kong. Consumers' surplus is measured by the area pTA, and producers' surplus is shown by area pAR.

The quotas established by the United States change the supply curve from S_t to RJS_t^1 as imports are restricted. Welfare losses are created, since the higher

---

[21]Ibid., 78.

**Figure 15.3
Monopoly Rents from
Hong Kong Textile
Quotas**

In the absence of quotas, total supply is S_t and domestic supply is S_u. The price per unit of textiles is p with imports amounting to X_1X_t. With quotas on imports of HB, the effective supply becomes RJS_t^1 and price rises to p'. A deadweight loss of MBA occurs. Domestic producers receive a gain in producers' surplus of $pp'HG$. Consumers lose consumers' surplus of $pp'BA$. Rent-seeking activities would shift the after-quota supply curve to $RJ'S_t^1$, reducing somewhat the gain in domestic producers' surplus.

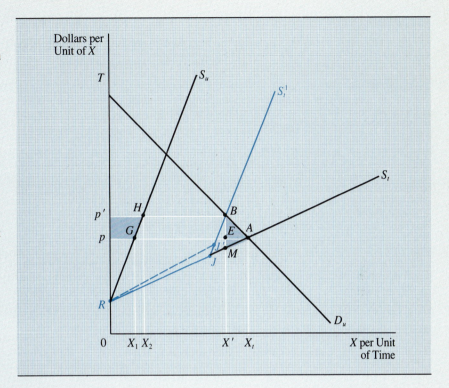

monopoly rent
A greater-than-competitive rate of return to producers caused by artificial protections from new entry contrived by the state or by existing producers.

market price p' reduces total sales to X'. The consequent welfare loss to consumers has two elements. The first is the deadweight loss in consumers' surplus equal to the value represented by triangle EBA. The second is the value represented by the rectangle $pp'BE$, which is transferred from consumers to producers by the higher price p'. The total loss to consumers is thus $pp'BA$.

   The losses to consumers are not precisely offset by gains to producers. Producers capture rectangle $pp'BE$ from consumers, an amount they were not earning previously. However, the lower output X' reduces producers' surplus by a deadweight amount equal to the triangle EAM. The gain minus the loss is defined as the **monopoly rent** to producers resulting from the quota restriction. U.S. producers receive monopoly rent equal to the shaded area $pp'HG$ owing to a production level of X_2 rather than X_1. Losses to consumers and gains to producers will be greater the *less* elastic D_u is.

   Exchangeable quotas, the article shows, are valuable property rights. The chief beneficiaries are producers who had been awarded quotas when the system was first established. They have received valuable windfall gains either from selling their textiles at higher-than-expected market prices or from selling their quotas to other producers. These other producers have received smaller gains, because they must pay for their rights. The quota's value is the present discounted value of the stream of sales that can be made at the above-market price

U.S. TEXTILE QUOTAS: THEY SUIT HONG KONG
by Jacques Leslie, *Los Angeles Times*

Textile quotas may sound like a dull subject but they inspire passion in Hong Kong, the world's leader in textile exports, and jack up the price of clothing in the United States.

The British colony's textile quota system, an American importer said, is "an infection that started very small and over the years built up into what could become an epidemic."

Most people involved in textiles here agree that the quota system is a disease. American importers complain that in addition to the inherent cost of the products they buy, they must additionally pay high premiums for the quotas which give them the right to ship the products to the United States. Hong Kong manufacturers also battle to obtain production quotas while trying to keep abreast of the latest changes in fashion in their foreign markets. Further compounding the picture, the Hong Kong government must administer a complex and costly licensing system.

In the end, American consumers also suffer. The quota for one woolen sweater made in Hong Kong currently costs between $1.25 and $1.50. Under the industry rule of thumb that retail prices reflect a quadrupling of basic costs, U.S. buyers pay an estimated $5–$6 more for a Hong Kong sweater because of the quota system.

Hong Kong is the world's biggest textile supplier to the United States, last year exporting 887 million square yards of cloth, or 17% of all fabric shipped to the United States. Hong Kong and two other Asian textile exporters, Taiwan and South Korea, which run similar quota systems, together account for 42% of all cloth exported to the United States last year.

Hong Kong's quota system developed in the late 1950s and early 1960s as industrialized nations, including the United States, began putting up barriers to protect waning domestic textile industries. Hong Kong now has quota agreements with 17 textile-importing nations.

In the case of the United States, exporting nations were assigned maximum shares of the total volume—or quotas—of textiles that they could ship each year. Separate categories were established for hundreds of different kinds of clothing and fabric. It was left up to the exporting nation to decide how the quotas should be distributed.

The Hong Kong government divided the quotas among manufacturers and shippers who had previously dealt in the U.S. market. If the quota holders were unable to use all their quota in any given year, they were allowed to sell the quota either for that year or permanently.

When the system was devised, an experienced American importer here asserted, the Hong Kong government "honestly, sincerely didn't realize that it was giving a tremendous windfall to quota holders." But that is what happened. As the demand for Hong Kong textile products grew, quotas —particularly in "hot" categories dictated by changing fashions—became valuable commodities.

In some instances, American importers claim, quotas became so lucrative that holders closed down their factories and simply lived off the proceeds of their annual quota sales. Alluding to such people, Sam Benson, an American importer for Outlander Group Ltd., said, "Quotas are making millionaires out of people who don't deserve it—not people who work or produce."

In order to prevent such abuses of

---

p' rather than at p. The article says that this amounted to between $1.25 and $1.50 per sweater in 1977.

Exchangeability of quotas encourages more efficient resource use and reduces welfare losses. Some Hong Kong firms respond better to the changing tastes of American consumers, and not all firms will be equally efficient in production. Thus exchangeability allows firms with greater sales potential or lower production costs to purchase quotas held by firms with lower sales potential or higher production costs. Certain brokers who assist in these exchanges thus also profit.

The high levels of monopoly rent that quotas cause have led to several the quota system, the Hong Kong government last fall instituted reforms requiring quota holders to use some of their quotas themselves or else forfeit a portion of it. But many observers believe the reforms did not go far enough, and could be circumvented by underground quota transactions.

In addition to the quota holders, the other chief beneficiaries of the present system are mysterious men known as quota brokers. As their name suggests, they buy and sell quotas, and, by skillful speculation, they can make fortunes. For this reason they have been called "sharks" and "parasites."

Their unpopularity probably explains why they prefer to stay out of the public eye. Asked for a list of quota brokers, one government official said none existed, and asserted that he did not even know how many quota brokers work in Hong Kong. He said only that the number is well below 10%.

To some extent quota brokers are scapegoats for the inadequacies of the system. Although they are not productive in the strictest sense, they probably are, as one observer said, "totally necessary" because quota transactions here are so numerous and varied.

"Quotas are a highly perishable commodity," said a Hong Kong government official. "If a broker makes any money, he's just getting recompense for the risk he's taking."

Some American importers here argue that the United States should abandon the present system of allotting a given amount of quota to each exporting nation. Instead, the importers say, the United States should administer the system itself. They argue that they should be given the quotas so that they can seek the most efficient foreign producers.

This proposal obviously contains a large element of self-interest, since the importers who now must struggle to find quotas to cover their purchases would become quota holders themselves.

Importers claim that textile retail prices would drop because the system would force manufacturers of different nations to compete against each other more intensely. But it is not clear whether this would happen, since substantial competitive pressures already exist.

The major drawback to the United States of an importer-based system is that it would require an extensive bureaucracy to administer. But importers deny that this is a grave problem.

The advantages of the current system to exporters such as Hong Kong are clear. Since each exporting nation is allotted a quota, the system effectively protects that nation's share of the total export market. While this may encourage complacency, it also enables manufacturers to plan in advance. Hong Kong manufacturers argue that if an importer-based system were adopted, the industry would be ravaged by uncertainty.

The most effective way to benefit the American consumer would be to abandon quotas entirely. This would allow foreign textile manufacturers to compete on a more even basis with American producers, who now enjoy tariff protection in addition to quotas. But this option is considered unfeasible because of the political strength of textile-related unions in the United States. The unions are believed to be more vehement advocates of protectionism than U.S. manufacturers, many of whom have factories abroad.

Source: "U.S. Textile Quotas: They Suit Hong Kong," Jacques Leslie, March 13, 1977, *Los Angeles Times.* Reprinted by permission.

proposals for changing policy. One would keep the allocation of quotas under Hong Kong administration but eliminate the exchangeability feature for a portion of them. Without exchangeability, quotas allocated to less efficient firms could not be sold to more efficient ones, and the RJ portion of the S_t supply curve in Figure 15.3 would twist upward and become $RJ'S_t^1$. The market price of textiles would rise only if the twist in the supply curve caused J' to lie above B. The winners and losers among producers would be different from those in existence when quotas were fully exchangeable.

Another proposal would transfer administration of the program from Hong Kong to the United States. Not surprisingly, this proposal comes from the United

States, and its main beneficiaries would be American textile importers, lobbyists, and government officials, who would decide which Hong Kong firms got quotas. This plan would not reduce deadweight losses or monopoly rents unless the total quota were increased. At best, it would merely change the distribution of welfare gains and losses while maintaining their present size; at worst, it would reduce monopoly rents to Hong Kong producers (as long as the total quota did not change) if U.S. administrators had a poorer understanding of which producers were more efficient. Once quotas were set, American consumers would be locked into the mistakes that U.S. administrators would make assuming continued prohibition of exchanges. The major losers would be Hong Kong brokers, who otherwise undoubtedly have a comparative advantage over their U.S. counterparts.

In Figure 15.3, we calculated the welfare losses to consumers as being equal to the deadweight loss of consumers' surplus EBA owing to the reduction in output plus the surplus transferred to producers in the amount of $pp'BE$. In one sense, it is correct to view the sum of these two areas, or $pp'BA$, as the total cost of the quota *monopoly*. The total costs of *monopolization*, however, are greater than $pp'BA$ by the value of the scarce resources that competitive would-be monopolists or quota holders would spend to acquire rights to a part of $pp'BE$.[22]

Artificial, government-created monopoly rents do not spring from thin air. They arise as persons seek preferential treatment for themselves and exclusion of their rivals through lobbying and other activities. Spending scarce resources to acquire part of the monopoly rent $pp'BE - EAM$ is what economists call *rent seeking*. It is a normal feature of economic life wherever governments restrict or offer to restrict market entry and thus create monopoly rents. Examples include quotas on textile imports, taxicab licenses, off-the-air or cable television franchises, and liquor licenses in various states. Restrictions on entry create rents like $pp'BE - EAM$ in Figure 15.3 and give people incentives to compete for them. The costs of rent seeking take various forms. They could be paid as license fees if it were government policy to hold auctions for quotas. They could be paid in wages to lobbyists or lawyers if it were government policy not to hold auctions. They could also be paid as bribes to corrupt officials, depending upon law and cultural traditions.

The monopoly rent represents a loss to consumers from transfers of consumers' surplus to producers. It also involves some deadweight loss to society as a whole. Yet a seeker of a monopoly rent would allocate scarce resources to this effort up to the point at which the marginal cost of his or her payment and effort equaled the expected marginal gain. If buying and selling quotas were the mode of competition, aspiring quota holders would pay cash plus brokers' commissions up to the point at which the marginal payments were equal to the value of the rent from the extra quota obtained. If advocacy were the mode of com-

---

[22]This discussion is drawn from Gordon Tullock, "The Welfare Costs of Tariffs, Monopolies, and Theft," *Western Economic Journal* 5 (June 1967): 224–232; and Robert D. Tollison, "Rent Seeking: A Survey," *Kyklos* 35 (1982, Fasc. 4): 575–602.

petition for rents, attorneys in the short run would be reallocated toward helping aspiring monopolists argue their cases with governmental authorities and away from more productive pursuits. The losses from this type of competitive rent seeking would grow through duplicative lobbying efforts if a group of would-be monopolists were competing for a monopoly right that would be awarded to just one of them. This is because neither the winning nor the losing rent seekers would get their sunk costs refunded by the government.

The article does not describe how the quota system came about. U.S. textile producers and labor unions no doubt lobbied Congress for the necessary legislation. The resulting rents they acquired were partly dissipated through rent seeking by the lobbyists they hired. The losses to society from monopoly rents resulting from reduced textile consumption plus rent seeking could be avoided only if the U.S. government's restrictions on the importation of textiles were relaxed.

SUMMARY

The theory of resource pricing and employment is applicable to a variety of contemporary events. The short-handled hoe is a complementary capital resource that apparently enables farm workers to earn a higher wage than they would with a tool that requires more time to do the same job, although a different tool apparently reduces painful back and spine injuries.

Immigration into a competitive labor market by undocumented workers affects wages in that labor market and related markets. Controversies surrounding illegal aliens figured prominently in the important legislation aimed at controlling immigration across the lengthy border between the United States and Mexico that Congress adopted in 1986.

The effect of collusion among buyers was illustrated in the application concerning professional baseball. Wages of players soared after monopsony arrangements among clubs were eliminated.

Economic rents come about through natural resource scarcities, as in the case of the Suez Canal. Monopoly rents come about through artificial restraints on supply, as in the case of quotas on the importation of Hong Kong textiles into the United States. Monopoly rents, unlike economic rents, are not dissipated because entry is restricted. The welfare losses to consumers are understated by the rent seeking that accompanies the creation and perpetuation of restrictive public policies.

Suggested Readings

Two excellent analyses of labor markets are

Rees, Albert. *The Economics of Trade Unions*. Chicago: University of Chicago Press, 1962.

Rees, Albert. *The Economics of Work and Pay*, Part 2. New York: Harper & Row, 1973.

For an analytical treatment of discrimination in labor markets, see

Becker, Gary S. *The Economics of Discrimination*. Chicago: University of Chicago Press, 1971.

Sports enthusiasts will benefit from

Noll, Roger G., ed. *Government and the Sports Business.* Washington, D.C.: The Brookings Institution, 1974.

Noll, Roger G. "Major League Sports." In *The Structure of American Industry,* edited by Walter Adams, 6th ed., Chap. 10. New York: Macmillan, 1982.

A readable and useful exposition of the theory of rent seeking is

Tollison, Robert D. "Rent Seeking: A Survey," *Kyklos* 35 (1982, Fasc. 4): 575–602.

Problems and Questions for Discussion

1. California's prohibition of the short-handled hoe to weed and thin crops did not prevent the use of knives and other sharp implements to harvest lettuce, broccoli, and celery. These tools also result in worker injuries and require bending at the waist. (Harry Bernstein, "GM Contracts with UAW Setting Precedents; Ban on Short-Handled Hoe," *Los Angeles Times,* July 17, 1985.) Explain the consequences of prohibiting the use of these tools as well as of the *cortito*.

2. Assume that an enforceable law is enacted requiring the owners of farms to buy medical insurance for occupational injuries to farm workers. Diagram and explain how this would affect the number of workers hired and their wage rate.

3. In 1811 British textile handicraftsmen in Nottingham and the surrounding areas rioted and smashed newly introduced textile machines that produced competitive goods, lowering their wages. They issued proclamations in the name of a mythical "King Ludd" and were known as Luddites, the name given to any group seeking from short-run self-interest to prevent the introduction of labor-saving technology. In 1983 a member of a state legislature said, "The economy is moving toward dependence on machines instead of human labor as a means of producing goods in each plant, and toward high-technology, capital-intensive industries in place of older, established craft or labor-intensive processes. As this 'progress' rolls on, fewer and fewer jobs are created per dollar invested. Each recovery from recession involves a greater investment of capital in expensive, high-tech industry, and this in turn makes greater unemployment a growing likelihood." (Bruce Bartlett, "The Luddite Answer to Unemployment," *The Wall Street Journal,* July 18, 1983.)

   a. Analyze with the aid of diagrams the effects of the Luddites' riots on the wages of other workers in the British textile industry of the period.

   b. Analyze with the aid of diagrams the effects of the introduction of computers and robots on each of the following groups of workers:

      (1) Those with complementary skills

      (2) Those with substitute skills

      (3) Those employed in making computers and robots.

4. In the discussion of alien workers, it was assumed that additional immigrants meant fewer jobs for domestic workers. However, some U.S. work-

ers were of the opinion that the jobs aliens took often were "dead-end, demeaning, and underpaying" jobs that stigmatized people and reduced their "upward mobility." (Merle Linda Wolin, "Americans Turn Down Many Jobs Vacated by Ouster of Aliens," *The Wall Street Journal,* December 7, 1982.) Redraw the diagrams of Figure 15.2 to reflect these underlying views of labor supply; explain your work.

5. The narrow Strait of Hormuz is the only waterway connecting the Persian Gulf and the Indian Ocean. Through it pass all the tankers carrying oil from Iran, Kuwait, Saudi Arabia, and other countries. Officials of the U.S. government from time to time have been concerned that the Persian Gulf countries might block the strait deliberately to reduce the quantity of oil shipped and raise its price. Assess the economic logic of this argument. Is it in the economic self-interests of oil-exporting countries? (Ignore the separate issue of terrorist organizations attempting to block the strait for political purposes.)

6. In 1982, about 5,800 airline pilots were grounded or furloughed because of airline mergers, bankruptcies, and replacement of three-pilot aircraft by two-pilot aircraft. Some sold cars or operated small businesses. A few stayed in aviation: about 10 percent got jobs as pilots of corporate jets; some worked as part-time air traffic controllers for drastically reduced salaries, and some flew for foreign air carriers that they never heard of before. (Roy J. Harris, Jr., "Squadrons of Furloughed Airline Pilots, Finding Few Jobs Aloft, Grapple with Life on the Ground," *The Wall Street Journal,* July 9, 1982.)
    a. What economic term would you use to describe the reductions in salaries or wages that the pilots have incurred?
    b. Explain what determined which pilots took the greater reductions.

7. In the 1960s, an agreement was made among the institutions of higher education in California that prevented a department head from proceeding with recruitment of associate and full professors from other campuses in the state "without first notifying . . . the head of his own institution. The head of the recruiting institution [was required], in turn, [to] discuss the matter with the head of the institution from which recruitment [was] contemplated. Negotiations [could] begin only after the head of the recruiting institution . . . authorized his department head to proceed." (J. F. Barron, "Restrictive Hiring Practices in Institutions of Higher Learning in California," *The Journal of Law and Economics* 4 [October 1961]: 186–193.)
    a. Had you been a professor at one of the state's institutions seeking to move to another, would you have favored or opposed the rules? How would your views have differed if you had been a professor from outside the state seeking employment in that state? Explain.
    b. What resource market model is illustrated here? Explain.
    c. If the rules were effectively enforced, what effects would you expect them to have on academic salaries? Why?

d. For what reasons might rules of this kind be established? Which qualities of schools would benefit? Which would lose?

8. The "Help Wanted" ads for registered nurses in a large metropolitan newspaper seldom mention salary rates offered for regular hospital nursing jobs. Over 100 hospitals place such advertisements in any given Sunday edition of the paper, so it does not appear that the omission is accidental. Salary rates for engineers, accountants, managers, mechanics, and many other occupations are listed.

   a. What circumstances might lead hospitals not to mention salary rates for ordinary nursing positions?

   b. Check the Sunday edition of your closest metropolitan newspaper to see if it bears out our observation.

   c. Nurses in some cities have formed unions. Could there be a connection between unionization and your findings in (a) and (b)?

9. Suppose that bricklayers' labor is purchased competitively and that the bricklayers' union is able to push wage rates above the equilibrium level. Show and explain the effects on

   a. The market level of employment

   b. The total wage bill for bricklayers.

10. In the bricklayers' unionization diagram, identify the areas that correspond to each of the following gains or losses:

   a. The gains to workers who stay employed and the losses to those who do not

   b. The deadweight loss of buyer's surplus to employers

   c. The deadweight loss of producer's surplus to workers

   d. The net buyer's surplus to employers.

11. In 1980, losses to all U.S. auto producers were $4 billion, but in 1984 and 1985 they earned $8.8 billion per year. Much of the difference is attributable to the "voluntary restraint" on the exportation of new cars to the United States that Japan adopted in 1981 at the urging of the U.S. government. (Robert W. Crandall, "Detroit Rode Quotas to Prosperity," *The Wall Street Journal,* January 29, 1986.) Based on the discussion of the Hong Kong textile quotas, would the Detroit auto producers be the only beneficiaries of quotas on Japanese cars? Diagram and explain.

12. In 1985, the U.S. International Trade Commission proposed quotas to cut the importation of shoes by 35 percent. Quotas were expected to cost U.S. consumers about $2.5 billion per year—$50,000 to $80,000 per job for each of about 30,000 U.S. jobs. Each job carries an average annual wage of $14,000. Quotas would be assigned to importers by auction. Under the usual quota system, importers never know when they place orders with foreign firms whether the goods can be sold, since the total quota limit may have been reached by the time the goods arrive. The auction would remove this uncertainty, and the monopoly rents would be captured by the U.S.

Treasury. (Jane Seaberry, "Shoe Quotas a Costly Idea to Save Jobs," *Los Angeles Times,* June 17, 1985.)

a.   Using Figure 15.3, assume that shoes are measured along the horizontal axis. S_u is the domestic supply. The difference between S_u and S_t at each price is what importers supply. RJS_t^1 is the supply curve after quotas have been adopted. What area approximates the estimated $2.5 billion annual cost of quotas to consumers?

b.   What area approximates the estimated value of 30,000 domestic jobs preserved at an average wage of $14,000 per job (about $420,000,000 per year)?

c.   If consumers lose $2.5 billion per year from the program and workers gain only $420 million, what purpose do quotas serve?

d.   How does the bidding system benefit consumers?

Chapter 16

RESOURCE ALLOCATION

Chapter Outline

Applications

One of the most important functions performed by the price system in a private enterprise economy is that of allocating resources among different uses and different geographic areas. If a high level of efficiency is to be attained in the economy, constant reallocation of resources must be in process in response to changes in human wants, the kinds and quantities of resources available, and the available technology. In developing the principles of resource allocation, we shall first discuss the conditions of "correct" or efficient allocation. Then we shall consider the concept of resource markets and the allocation of resources among them that leads to maximum efficiency in resource use. Finally, we shall examine certain circumstances that prevent resources from being efficiently allocated.

RESOURCE ALLOCATION AND WELFARE

What are the allocation conditions that must be met if units of any given resource are to make their maximum contributions to welfare? In general terms, the requirement is that the value of marginal product of the resource in any one of its uses be the same as its value of marginal product in all of its other uses. Suppose that some other allocation prevails—for example, that a tractor used on a farm contributes at the margin $2,000 worth of farm products anually to the economy's output and that an identical tractor used in construction can contribute a yearly $3,000 worth of products to it. If a tractor were switched from farming to construction, there would be a net gain to consumers of $1,000 worth of product. Obviously some consumers can be made better off without making anyone worse off. Transfers of resources from lower value of marginal product uses to higher value of marginal product uses always yield a welfare increase. Maximum welfare results when these transfers have been carried to the point at which the value of marginal product for each resource is the same in all its alternative uses.

RESOURCE MARKETS

When the price system is used to allocate resources, the concept of a resource market becomes important. The extent of a resource market depends on the nature of the resource under consideration and on the time span relevant to the problem at hand. Within a given time span some resources are more mobile than others, and consequently their markets tend to be larger. Mobility depends on a number of things—shipping costs, perishability, social forces, and the like—and resources differ with respect to these characteristics.

Ordinarily the mobility of any given resource varies with the time span for which its owners are making decisions. Over a short period of time its mobility is more limited than over a longer period. Consider a certain kind of labor, say, machinists. Over a short time period of a few months, or perhaps a year, machinists in the United States will not move readily from one geographic area to another, although they may be fairly free to move from one employer to another within a single locality. The longer the period of time under consideration, the larger the geographic area within which they are free to move. Over a period of 25 years, they will be fairly mobile throughout the entire economy.[1]

Over short periods of time all the machinists, or all the units of any other resource in the economy, do not necessarily operate in the same market. The economy can be divided into a number of submarkets, each being the area within which units of a resource are mobile in the given time span. The longer the time span being considered, the greater the interconnections among the submarkets. Over a sufficiently long period, the submarkets tend to fuse into a single market.

Short-run submarkets for a resource are conceptual rather than real in the sense that boundaries between them are blurred—each submarket overlaps others. Nevertheless it is useful to distinguish between (1) a short period during which the submarkets for a given resource are entirely separate and (2) a long period in which resources have sufficient time to move freely among the submarkets and fuse them into a single market.

RESOURCE ALLOCATION UNDER PURE COMPETITION

Will the price system allocate resources among their various uses such that optimal welfare will be approached? If pure competition exists in both product markets and resource markets, and if there are no externalities in consumption and production, such an allocation will tend to occur; therefore, the competitive model with no externalities provides a convenient starting point. We begin with the short-period allocation of a resource within a given submarket; then we extend the analysis to include long-period allocation among submarkets or over the entire economy.

Allocation within a Given Submarket

When units of a resource are so allocated that its value of marginal product in one use is greater than it is in other uses, the allocation is incorrect from the point of view of economic efficiency and welfare. The resource units would be worth more to the society in the higher value of marginal product use; if they were transferred from the lower to the higher value of marginal product uses, the total value of the economy's output would be increased.

Resource prices furnish the mechanism for reallocation when resources are incorrectly allocated under a purely competitive system. Suppose that units of a given resource are allocated between two industries in quantities such that its

---

[1]Mobility does not require the physical transference of a machinist from one area to another or even from one employer to another. As old machinists retire from the work force and new ones enter mobility can exist, for in certain areas the retiring machinists may not be replaced while in others the number of entries into the trade may exceed retirements.

value of marginal product is higher in one than in the other. Given this allocation, firms in the industry in which the value of marginal product is higher will also be willing to pay more per unit for the resource because in each industry it will be paid an amount equal to its value of marginal product. Consequently resource owners, seeking maximum income, transfer resource units from the lower-paying to the higher-paying uses.[2] As units of the resource are transferred, its value of marginal product decreases in the employments to which it is moved and increases in the employments from which it is taken. The transfer continues until the resource's value of marginal product is equalized in all its uses and all firms in the submarket are paying a price per unit equal to that value of marginal product. At this point the resource is being efficiently allocated and, within the submarket, is making its maximum contribution to net national product.

To illustrate the technical economics of the allocation process, suppose that the firms in two different industries, X and Y, operate in the same submarket for resource A. Suppose also that, initially, units of A are efficiently allocated among the firms of both industries. The VMP_{ax}, or value of marginal product of A in the firms of the industry producing X, is equal to VMP_{ay}, or the value of marginal product of A in the firms of the industry producing Y. Suppose further that there is neither a surplus nor a shortage of A on the market, so that

$$VMP_{ax} = VMP_{ay} = MRP_a = p_a, \quad \text{or}$$
$$MPP_{ax} \times p_x = MPP_{ay} \times p_y = MRP_a = p_a,$$

where p_a is the price per unit of resource A, and p_x and p_y are the respective prices of product X and product Y.

Suppose that an increase occurs in the market demand for X while demand for Y remains unchanged. The level of aggregate demand remains constant, and the increase in demand for X is offset by decreases in demand for commodities other than X and Y. The price of X rises, thereby increasing VMP_{ax}; resource A has become more valuable to society in the production of X than in the production of Y. The original allocation of A no longer maximizes welfare—that is, this allocation is no longer the correct one. At price p_a for the resource, employers in the industry producing X find that a shortage of A exists. Consequently they will bid up the price of A enough to cause owners of A to transfer units of it from the industry producing Y to that producing X. As the quantity of A employed by firms in the industry producing X increases relative to the quantities of other resources used, MPP_{ax} declines, and as the output of X increases, p_x declines; thus VMP_{ax} declines.

Changes within the industry producing Y will accompany changes in that producing X. As units of A are transferred from the production of Y to X the proportions of A to other resources used by firms in the industry producing Y

---

[2]New resource units just entering the market, say, college graduates, may be attracted to the jobs offering higher pay. This attraction, together with the failure to replace resource units retired from the market in lower-paying employments, provides an important method of transfer.

fall, and MPP_{ay} increases. Smaller amounts of Y are produced and sold; consequently p_y rises. Increases in MPP_{ay} and p_y mean higher VMP_{ay}.

Reallocation of A from the production of Y to X continues until units of the resource are again efficiently distributed between the two industries. Units of A move from the industry producing Y to that producing X until the VMP_{ax} has gone down enough and the VMP_{ay} has gone up enough for the two to be equal. The new price per unit of A will be somewhat higher than the old one, for its value of marginal product is now higher in both industries than it was previously. In bidding against each other for the available supply of A, firms in both industries have raised its price to the level of its value of marginal product in both uses.

Resource A will again be making its maximum contribution to net national product. When VMP_{ax} was greater than VMP_{ay}, every movement of a unit of A from the industry producing Y to that producing X increased A's contribution to net national product. Withdrawal of a unit of A from the industry producing Y decreased its contribution to net national product by an amount equal to VMP_{ay}. Putting the unit of A to work in the industry producing X increased A's contribution to net national product by VMP_{ax}. Hence a net gain in A's contribution to net national product resulted from such transfers until A's value of marginal product was once more equalized among firms in the two industries.

Allocation among Submarkets

We turn now to allocation of resources among submarkets. Consider two resources: (1) a certain kind of labor and (2) capital. All units of labor are homogeneous. Capital is fixed in specific forms and is immobile for the short period; but over the long period it is mobile, can change its form, and can be reallocated from one use to others.[3]

Allocation of Labor   In Figure 16.1, suppose that Area 1 and Area 2 initially constitute separate, short-period submarkets. The goods produced in the two submarkets are the same, as are capital facilities. Their labor demand curves, D_1D_1 and D_2D_2, are also the same. However, labor supplies for the two areas differ. Area 1 has a larger labor supply than Area 2; the labor supply curve S_1S_1 of Area 1 lies farther to the right than S_2S_2 of Area 2.

---

[3]Capital is usually considered in two contexts: (1) as concrete agents of production and (2) as a fluid stock of productive capacity. The first context is a short-run concept, with capital taking such specific forms as buildings, machinery, wheatland, and so on. The second is a long-run concept. Concrete pieces of equipment have time to wear out and be replaced, but replacement of the same kind and in the same place does not necessarily occur. Replacement can be in the form of new and different kinds of concrete agents. In agriculture, horse-drawn machinery was allowed to depreciate as the use of tractors became widespread and special machinery adapted to the tractor gradually came into use. Or capital may flow from one industry to another and from one location to another through depreciation in the one and the building of new equipment in the other. Thus while capital may be almost completely immobile in the short run, in the long run it becomes quite mobile. See Frank H. Knight, *On the History and Method of Economics* (Chicago: University of Chicago Press, 1956), 56–57.

Figure 16.1   Allocation of Labor between Submarkets

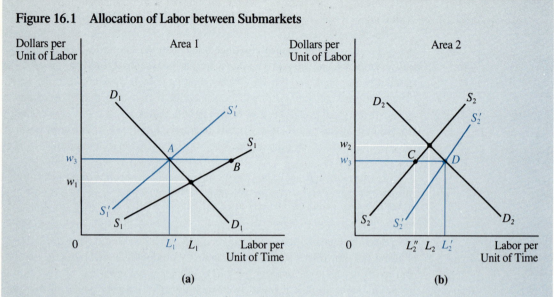

If the supply of labor is S_1S_1 in Area 1 and S_2S_2 in Area 2, labor is not efficiently allocated. Wage rates will be w_1 and w_2, respectively, inducing labor migration to Area 2. Supply decreases in Area 1 and increases in Area 2 until the wage rate is w_3 in both. The price system brings about the more efficient allocation of labor and increases GNP in the process.

Labor is inefficiently allocated, and its distribution causes its value of marginal product and its price to differ between the two areas. The price of labor, or the wage rate, in Area 1 will be w_1, and in Area 2 it will be w_2. The level of employment in Area 2 is L_2, while that in Area 1 is higher at L_1. The higher ratio of labor to capital in Area 1 causes the marginal physical product and value of marginal product of labor to be lower there. The reverse holds in Area 2: the ratio of labor to capital is smaller, and consequently the marginal physical product and value of marginal product of labor are higher.

The disparate submarket prices for labor furnish the incentive for long-period movement or reallocation of labor from Area 1 to Area 2, and reallocation tends to eliminate the wage differential. As workers leave Area 1, the short-period supply curve for that submarket shifts to the left; as they enter Area 2, its short-period supply curve shifts to the right. As the ratio of labor to capital declines in Area 1, labor's value of marginal product and wage rate increase, while in Area 2 the increasing ratio of labor to capital decreases labor's value of marginal product and wage rate. Reallocation continues until wage rates of the two submarkets are equal at w_3. The labor supply curve of Area 1 is now $S_1'S_1'$, and that of Area 2 is $S_2'S_2'$.

The reallocation of labor between Areas 1 and 2 increases real net national product and welfare. Before the movement began, the value of marginal product of labor in Area 1 was w_1; in Area 2 it was substantially higher, at w_2. The movement of a unit of labor from Area 1 to Area 2 causes a loss of w_1 dollars' worth of product in Area 1 and a gain of almost w_2 dollars' worth of product in Area 2. This gain more than offsets the loss in Area 1 and creates a net increase in total value of product produced in the economy. Each transfer of a unit of labor from Area 1 to Area 2 brings about such a net increase until the values of marginal product and the wage rates of labor are the same in the two submarkets. Labor is then efficiently allocated between the two areas—it is making its maximum contribution to welfare. No further transfer of labor in either direction can increase net national product but will decrease it instead. Also, equalization of the wage rates will have removed the incentive for labor migration to occur.

Allocation of Capital   The entire burden of adjustment will not be thrown on labor in the long period as the foregoing analysis suggests; it will be partly absorbed by reallocation of capital. The high ratio of labor to capital in Area 1 amounts to the same thing as a low ratio of capital to labor; likewise, the low ratio of labor to capital in Area 2 means a high ratio of capital to labor. Therefore, we would expect the value of marginal product of capital in Area 1 to exceed that in Area 2. Differing productivities of capital and returns on investment between the two areas furnish the incentive for capital to migrate from Area 2 to Area 1.

Long-period capital migration affects the short-period labor demand curves and the wage rates of the two areas. As units of capital leave Area 2, the demand curve (value of marginal product curve) for labor in that area shifts to the left, augmenting the decline in wage rates caused by the increasing labor supply. As units of capital enter Area 1, the demand curve for labor there increases; these increases in demand join the decreases in supply in raising the wage rates of Area 1.

When the reverse migrations of labor and capital have been sufficient to equalize wage rates and returns on investment between the two areas, both labor and capital will have been correctly allocated. Further transfers of either resource in either direction will reduce the real net national product yielded by the two submarkets combined.

CONDITIONS PREVENTING EFFICIENT ALLOCATION _____

In the real world a number of forces prevent the price system from allocating resources efficiently. Even with the price system free to operate and with resource prices free to guide resource allocation, three important causes of inefficient allocation can be cited: (1) monopoly in product markets, (2) monopsony in resource markets, and (3) certain nonprice impediments to resource movements. In addition, direct interference with the price mechanism by the government or by private groups of resource owners and resource purchasers constitutes a cause of incorrect allocation. We shall consider these causes in turn.

The term *monopoly* is used in a broad context to include pure monopoly, oligopoly, and monopolistic competition—all cases in which individual firms face downward-sloping product demand curves. Similarly, the term *monopsony* is used broadly. Complete monopsony in resource purchases precludes any real-location whatsoever. With less than complete monopsony, units of a given resource may be free to move along a limited number of buyers, any one of which can influence its market price.

Monopoly

Monopoly in product markets may not affect resource movements directly. Resources may be free to move among alternative employers even though the firms using them enjoy a degree of product monopoly. Steel, common labor, certain raw materials, and other resources are employed by many firms and may flow readily from one to another without regard to the types of product market in which individual firms sell. Where price discrepancies for any such resource exist within or among submarkets, long-period reallocation of the resource tends to occur to whatever extent necessary to eliminate the discrepancies. Every firm in every submarket has an incentive to employ that quantity of the resource at which its marginal revenue product equals its marginal resource cost. Reallocation tends to occur until the price of the resource is the same in all its alternative employments.

When some degree of product monopoly exists for different products, real net national product and welfare will not be maximized even if all resources are so allocated that the marginal revenue product of each is the same in all its alternative employments. For any given resource, the value of marginal product will differ in different uses even if the marginal revenue product is everywhere the same. Discrepancies among the values of marginal product of the resource will occur because of differences in elasticities of product demand for profit-maximizing firms. Differing demand elasticities mean that product prices and corresponding marginal revenues are not proportional to each other among the different products. Hence values of marginal products of the resource in its various uses are not proportional to its marginal revenue products. When the latter are equal, the former will be unequal. Inequalities among values of marginal product of a resource in its various uses show that net national product could be increased by transferring units of the resource from lower value of marginal product uses to higher value of marginal product uses.

It is the *value of marginal product* of a resource that measures the contribution of a unit of it to the value of the economy's output—its marginal physical product multiplied by the price of the final product. *Marginal revenue product* shows the contribution that a unit of the resource makes to the total receipts of a single firm. Where monopoly exists, this is less than the value of the product added to the economy's output by the resource unit. Thus when a resource is so allocated that its price is equalized in all alternative uses, the price system has done its job. Even though further reallocation from lower value of marginal product uses to higher value of marginal product uses will increase net national product, there is no automatic motivation for it to occur.

Figure 16.2 Monopoly Misallocation of a Resource

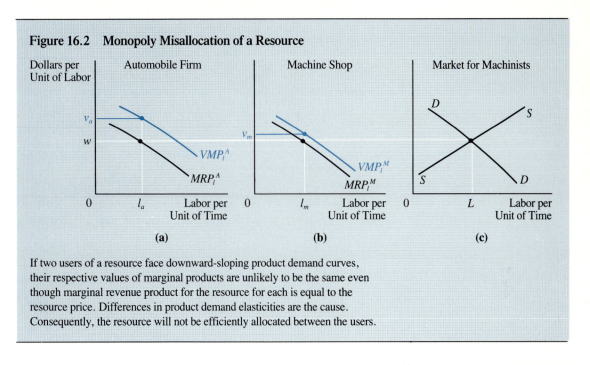

If two users of a resource face downward-sloping product demand curves, their respective values of marginal products are unlikely to be the same even though marginal revenue product for the resource for each is equal to the resource price. Differences in product demand elasticities are the cause. Consequently, the resource will not be efficiently allocated between the users.

In Figure 16.2, suppose that machinists in Detroit work both for automobile firms (A) and for independent machine shops (M). The latter tend to be subject to more competition than the former; thus the product demand curve facing A would likely be less elastic than that facing M. Assuming that this is so, we show the VMP_l^A exceeding the VMP_l^M even though MRP_l is the same for both. Society would gain in terms of net national product if some machinists transferred from machine shops to automobile manufacturers. However, since both pay a wage rate of w, the price system will not motivate the transfers.

In addition, partially or completely blocked entry into monopolistic industries may prevent other resources from being so allocated that their respective marginal revenue products and prices are equalized within and among submarkets. We can think of such resources as being inseparable from the existence of individual firms—they are short-run "fixed" resources. They can enter industries only in the form of plant for new firms. The existence of long-run profits for the firms in an industry indicates that the marginal revenue products of such resources are greater in that industry than they are elsewhere in the economy.

Monopsony

The existence of monopsony in resource purchases may also prevent the price system from allocating resources efficiently. Where some degree of monopsony is present, an individual firm purchases that quantity of a resource at which its marginal revenue product equals its marginal resource cost. When the resource supply curve to the firm slopes upward to the right, marginal resource cost exceeds the price that the firm pays the resource. When equilibrium in the

Figure 16.3   Resource Misallocation When Some Degree of Monopsony Is Present

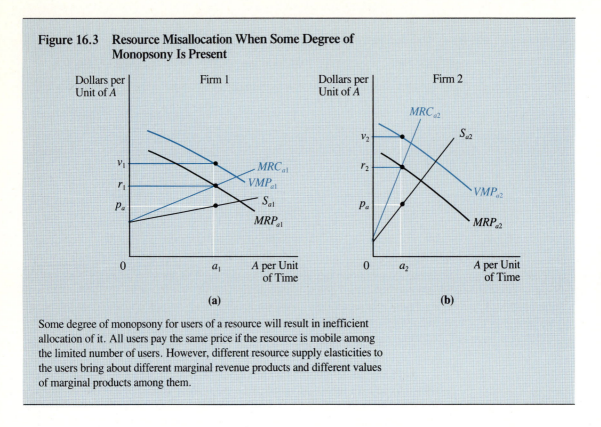

Some degree of monopsony for users of a resource will result in inefficient allocation of it. All users pay the same price if the resource is mobile among the limited number of users. However, different resource supply elasticities to the users bring about different marginal revenue products and different values of marginal products among them.

purchase of the resource is reached on the part of any single firm, the price paid the resource is below its marginal revenue product.

Differential prices of the resource guide its allocation among the few firms using it, just as they did in the monopoly analysis. Voluntary reallocation of the resource will cease when its price is the same in its alternative uses. In Figure 16.3, p_a is such a price. Resource owners will have no incentive to transfer units of it from one employment to another, and an equilibrium allocation of it will have been achieved.

Even though an equilibrium allocation may be achieved and all firms may be paying the same price for the resource, it is not likely that it is making its maximum contribution to net national product. To the extent that the supply curves of the resource facing different firms have differing elasticities, marginal resource costs and marginal revenue products of the resource among the different firms will not be equal. In Firm 1, $MRC_{a1} = MRP_{a1}$ at employment level a_1; in Firm 2, the profit-maximizing level of A is a_2. Marginal revenue product in Firm 1, which faces supply curve S_{a1}, is r_1; in Firm 2, which faces the less elastic supply curve for A, S_{a2}, it is r_2.

Differing degrees of monopoly in product markets may create even further distortions in the pattern of values of marginal products. Certainly there is no reason for believing that the values of marginal products of the resource will be the same among its alternative employments even though it is everywhere paid the same price. About the most that we can say on this point is that resource transfers from lower value of marginal product uses to higher value of marginal product uses would increase real net national product. However, since the resource price is the same in its alternative employments, resource owners will not make such transfers voluntarily.

Nonprice Impediments

Resources may be inefficiently allocated for reasons other than discrepancies among prices, marginal resource costs, marginal revenue products, and values of marginal product. Some of the important nonprice factors follow.

Ignorance   Lack of knowledge on the part of resource owners may prevent resources from moving from lower-paying to higher-paying uses. In the most obvious case, resource owners may lack information concerning the price patterns of the resources over the economy as a whole. Bricklayers may not be aware of the areas and firms paying the highest wages for that service. Farmers may sell products in some areas at unnecessarily low prices when they are not aware of the higher prices that can be obtained elsewhere. Investors make mistakes when they are ignorant of alternative investment opportunities throughout the economy.[4]

Lack of knowledge may also prevent potential resources from being channeled into the resource supply categories in which they will contribute most to net national product. Various kinds of labor resources illustrate the point. For what trade or profession should potential entrants to the labor force be trained? Do those responsible for influencing or selecting the vocation possess full knowledge of the future returns to be derived from alternative vocations? Usually they do not. Children may follow parents as sharecroppers or machine operators, when alternative occupations would be more lucrative—or, where children do not follow parents' occupations, the information on which their employment decisions are made is often sketchy. Frequently the potential entrant and his or her advisers do not discover until the training program is well advanced or completed that the choice of occupation has been an unfortunate one economically—and at this point it may be too late to change.

Sociological and Psychological Impediments   Sociological and psychological factors may throw blocks in the way of the allocation of resources that will maximize net national product.[5] They include those ties to particular communities, to friends, and to family that restrict mobility regardless of the monetary

---

[4]The classic examples here are the many single proprietorships that fail in such endeavors as neighborhood grocery stores, eating and drinking establishments, and filling stations.

[5]We are not saying that such blocks constitute mistakes on the part of society. The "good life" is not necessarily achieved through maximization of net national product—it may be desirable to sacrifice some product, if necessary, for the achievement of other objectives or values.

incentives to move. Or, the virtues of a particular occupation, community, or way of living may be so extolled by various social groups that mobility is restricted. Glorification of the family farm, or of southern California, or of the teaching profession may be cases in point.

Institutional Factors   Various institutional barriers to reallocation of resources are evident in the economy. In the industrial world, workers accumulate certain rights with particular firms, including pensions and seniority. In some cases labor unions may restrict entry directly into particular occupations. Patent rights held by one firm or a group of firms in an industry may block the entry of new firms into it and thus condemn quantities of certain resources to other occupations in which their values of marginal products and rates of pay are lower. The list can be extended considerably, but these cases illustrate the point.

Price Fixing

Sometimes the price mechanism is not allowed to perform its function of signaling the spots where quantities of certain resources should be transferred in or out. Some resource prices are fixed or controlled by the government. Control may be exercised through such devices as minimum wage legislation, agricultural price supports, or the general price and wage controls that many advocate during inflation. Some resource prices may be partially or completely controlled by organized private groups of resource owners and purchasers. A number of labor unions fall within this category, as do certain farm marketing cooperatives and employer associations. Three hypothetical examples will illustrate some of the effects of controlled resource prices on the equilibrium allocation of resources and on net national product. We shall assume that in the absence of control pure competition would exist; however, even if some degree of monopoly in product markets were to be found, the results would be approximately the same.

Two submarkets for a given resource are shown in Figure 16.4. As a matter of convenience we shall call the resource labor (L). The two submarkets are alike except for the initial distribution of labor. They produce the same products and have identical supplies of capital. The demand curves for labor are the same for each submarket. Since Area 1 has a greater labor supply than Area 2, the short-period price of labor will be lower in Area 1 and the employment level will be higher. We shall consider three possible cases.

Case I   Assume that the workers of Area 2 are organized and that those of Area 1 are not. The initial labor demand and labor supply situations are shown in Figure 16.4. The equilibrium wage rate and employment level in Area 1 are w_1 and L_1, respectively; in Area 2 they are w_2 and L_2. Assume further that organized workers, through collective bargaining, succeed in placing a floor of rate w_2 under Area 2 wage rates. The immediate or short-period effects of the minimum wage rate of w_2 in that area will be nil. Since w_2 is initially the equilibrium wage rate there, the union should have little difficulty in obtaining

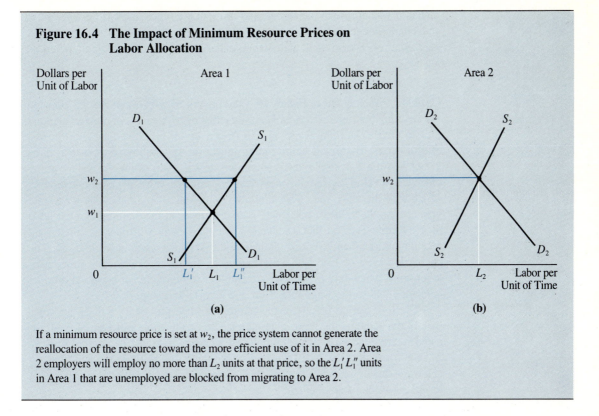

Figure 16.4 The Impact of Minimum Resource Prices on Labor Allocation

If a minimum resource price is set at w_2, the price system cannot generate the reallocation of the resource toward the more efficient use of it in Area 2. Area 2 employers will employ no more than L_2 units at that price, so the $L_1' L_1''$ units in Area 1 that are unemployed are blocked from migrating to Area 2.

it. At that rate of pay, employers of Area 2 are willing to employ as much labor as is willing to go to work. The wage differential between the two areas continues to reflect the existence of the initial maldistribution of labor.

The effects of the minimum wage rate set in Area 2 are felt in the long period. The wage differential creates an incentive for workers to migrate from Area 1 to Area 2. However, if additional workers were hired in Area 2, the ratio of labor to capital would increase, the marginal physical product of labor would decrease, and the value of marginal product of labor would decrease. Since the wage rate of such additional workers would be w_2 and since this rate would exceed their values of marginal product, they would not be hired. Any workers migrating from Area 1 to Area 2 would find themselves unemployed, and this prospect would keep migration from occurring. Employment in Area 1 at the lower wage rate of w_1 would be preferable to no employment at all in Area 2, regardless of how high wage rates were. Labor would remain poorly allocated between the two areas, and welfare would be permanently below its optimum level.

This situation sets the stage for interesting repercussions with regard to capital. An incentive for capital to migrate in the long period will be present in this case also—in fact, capital migration is the only adjustment in resource allocation that can occur. As capital migrates from Area 2 to Area 1, demand for labor will shrink in the former and grow in the latter, increasing wage rates and employment there. However, unemployment will develop among the organized workers of Area 2, and welfare will still be below its maximum potential level.[6]

Case II   Assume that in Figure 16.4 the organized workers of Area 2 succeed in extending their union to Area 1. Assume that once Area 1 is organized workers in both places can bring wage rates in Area 1 up to w_2. Immediate short-period effects occur. There will be no initial impact on the employment level in Area 2, but in Area 1 unemployment amounting to $L_1'L_1''$ will occur. In Area 1 at the old wage level of w_1, employment level L_1 equates value of marginal product of labor to the wage rate. The minimum wage rate of w_2 makes the wage rate greater than the value of marginal product of labor at the old employment level of L_1. Employers find that a reduction in employment will decrease their total receipts by less than it reduces their total costs; hence workers are laid off. The decreasing ratio of labor to capital increases the value of marginal product of labor until, when only L_1' workers are employed, their value of marginal product is again equal to the wage rate. Here the layoffs will stop.

The long-period effects of the minimum wage rate of w_2 will be approximately the same as the immediate effects. Since the wage differential is eliminated, there is no incentive for employed workers of Area 1 to migrate to Area 2. Employers of Area 2 will not find it profitable to hire more workers than L_2 at a wage rate of w_2; hence unemployed workers of Area 1 will not find migration to Area 2 to be of any benefit.

With regard to capital, the minimum wage rate of w_2 in Area 1 and the reduced ratio of labor to capital (increased ratio of capital to labor) eliminate the incentive for capital to migrate there in the long period. The ratio of capital to labor in Area 1 is increased sufficiently by the worker layoffs to make the value of marginal product of capital there equal to that in Area 2.[7] Thus the minimum wage rate of w_2 extended to both areas prevents the effects of the initial misallocation of resources from being alleviated by either labor or capital migration; in addition, it creates unemployment.

Case III   A third possibility, in which controlled resource prices may not affect resource allocation adversely, deserves some consideration. Assume that both areas are organized or, alternatively, that the government sets a minimum wage

[6]The women's full-fashioned hosiery industry furnishes an excellent example of the migration of capital from high-cost union areas to low-cost nonunion areas. See Sumner H. Slichter, *Union Policies and Industrial Management* (Washington, D.C.: The Brookings Institution, 1941), 353–360.

[7]Since the initial capital facilities and products produced in the two areas were assumed to be the same, the labor demand curves are also the same. At wage rate w_2, each market employs the same quantity of labor—that is, L_1' units of labor equals L_2 units of labor in Figure 16.4. Consequently ratios of labor to capital in the two areas, when the wage rate for both is w_2, will be the same, as will the value of marginal product of capital.

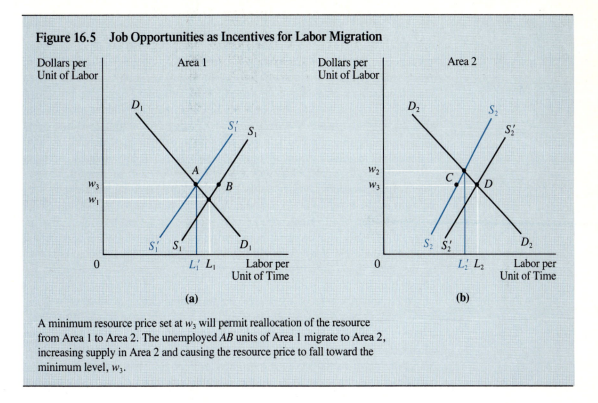

Figure 16.5   Job Opportunities as Incentives for Labor Migration

A minimum resource price set at w_3 will permit reallocation of the resource from Area 1 to Area 2. The unemployed AB units of Area 1 migrate to Area 2, increasing supply in Area 2 and causing the resource price to fall toward the minimum level, w_3.

rate applicable to both. The wage rate is set through collective bargaining or by the government at level w_3, as is shown in Figure 16.5—that is, at precisely the level that would prevail in free markets in the long period after workers have had sufficient time to migrate. The initial demand and supply relationships are D_1D_1 and S_1S_1, respectively, in Area 1 and D_2D_2 and S_2S_2 in Area 2. In Area 1 the minimum wage rate of w_3 will cause unemployment equal to AB. In Area 2 a labor shortage equal to CD will occur at w_3, and the wage rate in that submarket will rise to w_2.

Unemployment will assist the price system in reallocating labor from Area 1 to Area 2 in the long period. The unemployed and the lower-paid workers of the former will seek the higher-paying jobs of the latter. The supply curve for labor in Area 1 will shift leftward to $S_1'S_1'$, and that of Area 2 will shift rightward to $S_2'S_2'$. Labor will be reallocated so that its value of marginal product is equalized between the two submarkets, allowing it to make its maximum contribution to net national product.

Again, some migration of capital from Area 2 to Area 1 may occur in the long period. At wage rate w_3, the initial employment level is L_1' in Area 1 and is greater than that of L_2 in Area 2. Therefore, the ratio of capital to labor is smaller, and the marginal revenue product of capital is greater in Area 1 than in Area 2. Capital migration will reduce the demand for labor in Area 2 and increase it in Area 1, thus reducing the amount of labor migration necessary to secure full employment and maximum net national product.

SUMMARY _____

Any given resource is "correctly" allocated—makes its maximum contribution to economic welfare—when its value of marginal product is the same in all of its alternative uses. In a private enterprise economic system, resource prices serve the function of directing the allocation of resources.

Only if there could be and were pure competition in product markets and resource markets would resources tend to be allocated automatically so as to maximize net national product. If purely competitive market structures were all that existed, a misallocation of units of any given resource would cause its values of marginal product to vary from one employment to another. Consequently employers for whom its value of marginal product is higher bid resources away from those for whom it is lower. Transfers of resource units from lower to higher value of marginal product uses increase the contributions of the resource to welfare. Its maximum contribution occurs when its value of marginal product is the same in all its possible uses. The price of the resource will also be the same in all its alternative uses; therefore, no incentive will exist for further transfers to be made.

With some degree of monopoly in product markets, a resource will be reallocated among its alternative uses until its price is the same in all of them. However, employers who are monopolists to some degree will employ those quantities of the resource at which its marginal revenue product equals its price. Marginal revenue products of the resource will be the same in alternative employments. But since differing product demand elasticities cause values of marginal products of the resource to differ in alternative employments, the resource will not make its maximum contribution to net national product.

Where employers have some degree of monopsony but there is no resource differentiation, a resource will again be reallocated until its price is the same in alternative employments. But a monopsonist employs the resource up to the point at which marginal revenue product equals marginal resource cost. Different monopsonists may face resource supply curves of varying elasticities, and, if so, marginal resource cost will be different for each even though all pay the same price per unit for the resource. With equilibrium allocation of the resource achieved, marginal revenue products will differ. The usual case will be that differences in values of marginal product also occur, and the resource will not be making its maximum contribution to net national product.

Nonprice impediments to efficient allocation of resources include ignorance, sociological and psychological factors, and institutional restrictions. In some instances, the achievement of noneconomic values may be of more importance to society than efficient resource allocation.

Direct interferences with the price mechanism by the government and by private groups may prevent resources from being efficiently allocated in some cases; in others, such interference may not lead to adverse effects.

APPLICATIONS

From many possible illustrations of the important effects of federal government policies on the pricing and allocation of resources, we have selected three. First is the establishment of landing and departure slots at congested airports by the Federal Aviation Administration. Second is the creation of "pollution rights" by the Environmental Protection Agency. Third is the Davis-Bacon Act, which establishes above-market wage rates on federal construction projects.

ALLOCATING AIRPORT LANDING SLOTS WITHOUT PRICES

Airport congestion on the ground and in the air is common these days. The "airport problem" dates from 1968 when delays of up to two hours in runway takeoff queues and landing approach "stacks" unexpectedly occurred in Chicago, New York, and Washington. Lesser but significant delays now occur in many cities, and almost all travelers can recall the frustrations and concerns of delays during the 1981 air traffic controllers' strike. Congestion wastes resources through excessive waiting time, missed appointments and connecting flights, inefficient use of fuel and equipment, and generally lower public confidence in the air transportation system. One study placed a conservative estimate of these costs of over 100 million 1983 dollars for just the three New York airports in 1968.[8]

Airport space and time slots are scarce resources that must somehow be rationed among potential users. They are especially critical at the busiest airports at peak demand hours in the mornings and late afternoons, particularly on Mondays, Fridays, and holidays. Congestion occurs when the number of landings and takeoffs demanded exceeds the number that the runways can safely handle and when the excess is rationed by the first-come, first-served method rather than with prices.

Why don't airports reduce congestion by raising prices? Most airport authorities are nonprofit, government organizations that base landing fees on aircraft weight rather than the hour of day that runways are used. These fees are set by contract between airports and airlines. They are kept low through the common practice among airport managers of cross-subsidizing airfield operations from the revenues obtained from renting space to those restaurants, gift shops, car rental agencies, and flight insurance stands that bid the most. Ironically, the fees from airfield use—the airport's *raison d'être*, for which airline demand is often relatively inelastic—is a small fraction of its income.[9]

[8]A. Carlin and R. E. Park, *The Efficient Use of Airport Runway Capacity in a Time of Scarcity* (Santa Monica, Calif.: The Rand Corporation, Memorandum RM-5817-PA, 1969).

[9]Michael E. Levine, "Landing Fees and the Airport Congestion Problem," *The Journal of Law and Economics* 12 (October 1969): 79–108.

The rights to runway use at given times of the day without anticipated delays constitute a valuable resource to an airline. Allocating landing rights efficiently at a given airport requires reassignment from airlines with lower-valued flights to those with higher-valued flights to the point at which the marginal revenue product for each flight is equal. Airlines serving the more popular cities and carrying the most passengers would likely bid more for landing rights than less advantaged ones if auctions for those rights were held.

Rationing runway use by the principle of first-come, first-served will yield an efficient allocation only by sheer coincidence. The fees airlines actually pay are such a small fraction of their total costs that they are usually ignored in calculating where and when to fly. This system fails to give preference to higher-valued flights and causes inefficiently high levels of congestion—just like freeway rush hours.

The airport congestion problem could be solved by employing either of two economic devices: peak-hour landing charges or exchangeable property rights in a given number of landing "slots." The first approach, raising landing fees at peak times for popular airports, would give airlines running lower-valued flights incentives to adjust their schedules. The potential effectiveness of this device was tested in 1968, when minimum peak-hour landing fees for general aviation aircraft, those other than airline and military aircraft, were raised from $5 to $25 at each of the three main New York City airports, causing use by these planes to decline some 30 percent. However, most airport authorities are loathe to raise fees, and that is the only case where this approach has been attempted.

In the second approach, the airport has the authority to set the safe maximum number of landing slots for each hour of the day, sell them to users, and let the users exchange them like any other resource, equating marginal revenue products at higher levels to higher prices for prime time slots and at lower levels to lower prices for other time slots. This approach has been more common, but it has contained impediments to exchange that have restricted efficiency.

In response to the heavy congestion of 1968–69, the FAA established maximum numbers of slots at four highly congested airports—Washington National, O'Hare International in Chicago, and La Guardia and John F. Kennedy International in New York. Slots at each were allocated by a scheduling committee consisting of representatives of each airline. The committees were given antitrust immunity by the FAA as long as they abided by rules that encouraged agreement by voting rather than by market-type exchange. Their meetings were attended and studied by three economists, who concluded that this system yielded inefficient slot allocations.[10]

Prior to each semiannual meeting, members submitted to the FAA their requests for slots, which usually exceeded the number available at prime times. Members then bargained, attempting to induce other carriers to shift operations

---

[10]David M. Grether, R. Mark Isaac, and Charles R. Plott, "The Allocation of Landing Rights by Unanimity Among Competitors," *American Economic Review, Papers and Proceedings* 71 (May 1981): 166–171.

to off-peak times and generating hypothetical packages of slots that everyone hoped they could vote for. The FAA gave the committees strong incentives to reach "agreement," which was generally interpreted as requiring unanimity. This strengthened the bargaining position of any single airline, which potentially could frustrate agreement by withholding its consent, but uncertainty over what the FAA might do if it were required to intervene encouraged cooperation.

The key FAA rules that distorted the efficient allocation of slots were prohibitions on discussing (1) side payments; (2) origins and destinations, fares, profitability, or other forms of competition; (3) allocations at any one airport beyond a six-month period; and (4) allocations at any of the other three airports. The economists concluded that

> *These restrictions make it difficult if not impossible for the airlines to trade slots either across the high density airports or over time. Side conversations can take place but the public nature of the bargaining situation would make any 'under-the-counter' sales of slots difficult. Carriers have no property rights in slots and do not have the contractual authority to make sales or trades. Carrier A may be willing to pay carrier B for slots, but if B were to reduce its slots, some other carrier (not A) may end up with them through the committee process. . . .*[11]

The FAA rules made it difficult for airlines to allocate slots at a given airport among themselves according to their respective marginal revenue products. Airlines for whom slots had high marginal revenue products and who would have bought extra slots under different rules could not get them through committee bargaining, making their uses of slots inefficiently small. Carriers for whom slots had low marginal revenue products had few incentives to release slots they could maintain through committee skills and that they had no right to sell. Their operations were inefficiently large. Slots could not be loaned or rented on a short-term basis, and abandoned slots would be diverted back to the committee for reallocation without compensating the carrier that was relinquishing them. These slots would then become part of the "historical shares" of the carrier obtaining them and thus work to the future bargaining advantage of that carrier relative to the one that had given them up.

Efficient matching of slots among airports was distorted by the FAA's prohibition on discussions of flight origins or destinations or other indicators of the different values that individual airlines placed on available slots. Airline representatives on the committees understood these relationships and from time to time attempted surreptitiously to move slots around toward equalization of their marginal revenue products among carriers. But the FAA's rules made these arrangements awkward and less efficient than would have been the case in straightforward exchange. Allowing side payments between airlines or trading slots between committees would weaken this distortion of maximum economic welfare.

_____

[11]Ibid., 167.

Dissatisfaction with the slot allocations that scheduling committees made led the Federal Aviation Administration to create exchangeable property rights in landing and departure slots at the four high-density airports.[12] Airlines holding slots on April 1, 1986, could use them or sell, trade, or lease them to other carriers at their sole discretion. Within two months, airlines made 15 separate deals for slots at prices that consisted mainly of monopoly rent. The largest was Pan Am's purchase of three gates and 32 slots at La Guardia airport from Texas Air for $65 million.[13] Such sales indicate that previous allocations between submarkets by scheduling committees had not assigned slots to their highest-valued users and uses.

CREATING AND EXCHANGING PROPERTY RIGHTS TO POLLUTE

The U.S. Environmental Protection Agency preceded the FAA in implementing exchangeable property rights. The accompanying article describes how rights to pollute that were established and enforced by the EPA may be exchanged among firms (sometimes with the aid of brokers) subject to the overall limits on pollution that it sets. Evidence suggests that these rights have been bought by users who value them more highly and sold by those who value them less. Structuring property rights in this manner gives polluting firms better incentives to economize on scarce resources—including the use of the planet as a ''sink'' for wastes. They also have incentives to reduce the total amount of pollution since they can sell to others the unused portion of their rights. Allocation of resources with this property rights system is likely to be relatively efficient.[14]

THE DAVIS-BACON PREVAILING WAGE LAW

The Davis-Bacon Act was passed during the Great Depression to prevent northern contractors constructing federal buildings or public works from importing lower-wage southern labor without paying it the higher prevailing wage in the northern private sector. The accompanying article shows that the law is strongly favored by unions in the building trades because it ties wages and fringe benefits for federal construction work to union levels and thus limits competition from nonunion labor.

The Department of Labor sets Davis-Bacon standards through procedures that bias wage rates upward and raise the cost of federal construction unneces-

---

[12]For the importance of exclusive property rights in avoiding resource misallocations, refer to Chapter 2, pp. 24–25.

[13]From *Fortune*: ''Battle for Air Slots,'' March 3, 1986, 80; and ''A Bull Market in Slots and Gates,'' June 9, 1986, 8–9.

[14]J. H. Dales, *Pollution, Property, and Prices* (Toronto: University of Toronto Press, 1968), Chap. 5.

MARKET BOOMS FOR 'RIGHTS' TO POLLUTE

by Andy Pasztor, *The Wall Street Journal*

Stuart Rupp of Richmond, Calif., proudly calls himself a "broker." But he doesn't sell stocks, bonds, or futures.

Instead, Mr. Rupp, a partner in an environmental consulting firm, helps companies trade the "right" to spew additional pollutants into the atmosphere.

Such transactions are part of a new approach to reducing air pollution that relies on the marketplace rather than on federal regulations. A company that closes a plant or installs improved pollution-control equipment can receive "emission credits" for its clean-up efforts. These credits, in turn, may be purchased by another firm to offset increased air pollution caused by construction or expansion. The idea is to allow industry to negotiate the price and details of the trade-offs as long as the overall level of air pollution in an area isn't increased.

Hydrocarbons at $50,000 Times Mirror Co. was able to complete the $120 million expansion of a paper-making plant near Portland, Ore., after purchasing the right to emit about 150 tons of extra hydrocarbons into the air annually. A local dry cleaning firm and the owners of a wood-coating plant that had gone out of business sold the necessary credits for about $50,000. Without the credits, Times Mirror couldn't have persuaded state and federal regulators to permit the expansion, says Rod Schmall, manager of environmental and energy services for the subsidiary that runs the plant.

Companies are "just beginning to realize in large numbers that they actually can turn a profit by reducing pollution by a certain amount" and then striking a deal to sell off the resulting credits at handsome prices, says Bob Fuller of First Wisconsin Corp., a Milwaukee bank holding company that started experimenting with pollution credits for its clients three years ago.

The Carter administration promoted the notion first, but President Reagan's environmental advisers have endorsed it, too, as a way to simplify and loosen clean-air regulations: The General Accounting Office estimates that a "viable market in air pollution rights" could cut pollution-control costs at least 40% and perhaps as much as 90% for many businesses. After nearly two years of study, the GAO concluded that trading credits substantially increases industry flexibility in complying with clean-air laws and encourages the use of innovative technologies.

Practical and legal problems remain. But many companies are already starting to acquire and trade pollution rights in various ways.

VW's Approach When Volkswagen of America built its first car and truck assembly plant in Pennsylvania several years ago, the company needed a lot of credits. It received some from Jones & Laughlin Steel Co., apparently on the promise that the plant would buy some of its steel from the company each year in return. Volkswagen also persuaded the state transportation department to sharply curtail the use of certain road asphalts that give off hydrocarbon fumes when they dry. That estimated reduction in pollution also was credited to VW's account.

When General Motors Corp. built a plant in Oklahoma City, the chamber of commerce persuaded officials at four local oil company facilities to spend more than $500,000 to reduce air pollution coming from storage tanks. Their credits were then donated to GM, though the oil companies benefited from recapturing petroleum products that otherwise would have been wasted.

Despite such successes, it's often difficult to put the concept into practice, especially where the air is heavily polluted. Wickland Oil Co., an independent West Coast petroleum marketer, spent more than $25,000 and two years of bargaining to satisfy federal officials and round up enough credits to build a gasoline blending and distribution plant outside San Francisco.

Problems in California "I hate to discourage anybody from following in our footsteps," says Roy Wickland, the company's executive vice president. "But if a large firm from the outside" wants to trade emission credits anywhere in northern California, "their chances of success are pretty poor" because "only a few companies have them and fewer still" are willing to part with them.

Supporters of the offset principle hope to overcome that problem through improved marketing. First Wisconsin is setting up a computer system to track available credits for a nationwide trading system. And earlier this year, the Illinois chamber of commerce and state environmental officials established a clearing-house to handle market-style trading of pollution rights.

Another hurdle is corporate skepticism about disclosing details regarding company plants to prospective purchasers. Nevertheless, more than 40 states have adopted regulations or issued permits allowing some form of air-pollution offsets.

Many environmental groups support the offset trading concept but are concerned about how the Environmental Protection Agency intends to monitor and enforce private deals to ensure that air quality is improved in the long run. Jack McKenzie, an environmental official with Pacific Gas & Electric Co., complains that a few environmentalists "appear absolutely paranoid that someone will make money from cleaning up a facility."

DAVIS-BACON PAY LAW MAY FACE BIG CHANGES DESPITE UNION SUPPORT

by Robert S. Greenberger, *The Wall Street Journal*

CHARLESTON, S.C.—
John Moore, an electrician here, is shocked by the size of the wage increase that the federal government just gave him.

Mr. Moore says the $8.25 an hour that he normally earns working for Cullum Construction Inc. is the going rate for electricians here. But under the federal Davis-Bacon Law, which requires that an area's "prevailing wage" be paid to workers on projects receiving some federal funding, the Labor Department recently decided that Mr. Moore and other electricians here must be paid $11.85 an hour on federally backed projects. That includes about half the work done by Cullum and many other local contractors.

Critics in business and Congress have been questioning the construction-trade wage rates set under the Davis-Bacon Act for almost as long as the 50-year-old measure has been on the books. But now prospects are growing for major changes in the Depression-spawned program. The Reagan administration promises to alter the way the law is administered. And on Capitol Hill, where the Senate Labor Committee recently held hearings on the law, pressure for outright repeal is building.

Critics' Charges   Critics see Davis-Bacon as an example of outmoded and inflationary federal regulation. They charge that rather than protecting the prevailing wage structure in a community, many of the 12,000 area wage surveys taken each year by the Labor Department under the Davis-Bacon Act set artificially high rates that then put upward pressure on all wages.

Davis-Bacon wage changes can send economic tremors through cities such as Charleston because of the federal government's ubiquitous presence.

This city's scenic downtown, which sits on a narrow peninsula, is crowded with the red, white and blue signs that identify federally assisted construction. A Commerce Department sign on the antebellum Exchange Building, where slaves were once traded, proclaims that the restoration work is being done by an equal-opportunity employer. A few blocks away, on Meeting Street, fed-eral money helps build a municipal parking garage.

Wide Effects Seen   Thus, a sharp rise in the federally required rates has wide effects throughout this seaport city. John Brady, project manager at Ruscon Corp.'s construction of the Liberty National Bank Building, recalls that last winter four carpenters on the private project were sent across the street to work on the federally funded municipal garage. Their wages jumped from $5.50 an hour to $6.90.

Contractors argue that the Labor Department's survey methods and rules guarantee that the highest wage in each job category will emerge as the "prevailing wage." Often, the survey rate reflects the union wage—even here in Charleston, where about 80% of the construction workers are nonunion.

The Davis-Bacon rate for this area was raised twice as it moved through the government bureaucracy. The wage survey was taken last summer by Texas Jackson, a Labor Department employee who then worked in the area. Mr. Jackson says

sarily. The department requires that the Davis-Bacon standard be based on the precise wage rate that is received by at least 30 percent of the workers in a given skill category in the project area. Unions negotiate wage rates that apply to all their members, whereas nonunion wages usually vary by at least a few cents per hour from employer to employer. Thus the 30-percent rule usually ensures that the department's judgment about which wage rate "prevails" in the market will be a high union rate even if 70 percent of the construction work in the area is performed at lower nonunion rates. The Davis-Bacon rates that the department sets are usually 30 to 70 percent, and in some cases 100 percent, above the open-shop rate and raise the cost of federal construction activities by he surveyed 226 construction projects. His work sheet, dated Nov. 3, 1980, shows entries for 690 electricians and a recommended hourly wage of $8.51.

But after the information was forwarded to Washington for review, a second work sheet shows entries for 490 electricians and a recommended rate of $9.35 an hour, plus fringe benefits. Finally, in December, the department determined that the prevailing wage for electricians in Charleston was $11.85 an hour.

Anthony Ponturiero, director of the department's Division of Government Contracts, explains that the number of electricians was reduced to 490 from 690 because some of the survey information "wasn't supportable." And he says that under the regulations, the prevailing wage was set at $11.85—the union wage—because 211 of the 490 electricians were union members.

Arthur Mitchum, business manager of Local 776 of the International Brotherhood of Electrical Workers, says about 10% of the electricians in Charleston belong to unions.

The 30% Rule In determining the prevailing wage, the department used its 30% rule. If it doesn't find a clear majority of workers at one wage, it may set a wage paid to at least 30% of the workers surveyed in each category. However, nonunion workers often are paid a range of rates, depending on skill and experience. Mr. Cullum, for example, pays his 20 electricians hourly wages ranging from $7 to $9.25. Because union members are paid a negotiated wage, the 30% rule often reflects the union wage even when union members are in the minority.

In a 1979 report, the General Accounting Office found that the act was inflationary. "The Davis-Bacon Act is no longer needed and should be repealed," the GAO told Congress.

Administrative Changes The Reagan administration is reviewing the Davis-Bacon Law. But rather than repeal, it will focus on changing the way the wage surveys are conducted in order to make them more accurate. One possible change: elimination of the 30% rule so that the federal wage standard would be less influenced by union wages.

Under the best of circumstances, the department has trouble compiling accurate wage information. Thomas Phalen, a Washington attorney and member of the Davis-Bacon Wage Appeals Board, says department officials are "passive collectors of data." He notes that most surveys are taken by mail and that submitting information always is voluntary. In addition, the department has only 80 full-time staff people nationwide collecting data. Even with other field personnel pitching in, it is difficult to do a complete job, department officials say.

Furthermore, many of the contractors screaming the loudest about Davis-Bacon also contribute to the problem. For example, several major contractors here refused to participate in the survey; they protested that they didn't want the government involved in their businesses. In contrast, Mr. Phalen says, "Unions know exactly what the department is looking for, and they send it in as a matter of course."

5 to 20 percent. This welfare loss to the economy has been estimated at $200 to $500 million annually.[15]

The coverage of the Davis-Bacon Act has been extended from direct federal construction to federally assisted construction for such projects as highways, airports, housing, hospitals, and schools. In addition, all but nine states have adopted similar statutes of their own. These statutes strengthen unions, reduce

---

[15]John P. Gould and George Bittlingmayer, *The Economics of the Davis-Bacon Act: An Analysis of Prevailing-Wage Laws* (Washington, D.C.: The American Enterprise Institute for Public Policy Research, 1980).

Figure 16.6   The Impact of the Davis-Bacon Act

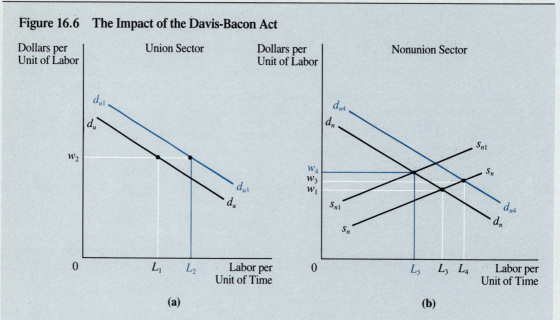

In a given locale the labor market is segmented into union and nonunion sectors with wage rates w_2 and w_1, respectively. The federal government now initiates a substantial construction project, increasing the demand for union labor under the Davis-Bacon Act to $d_{u1}d_{u1}$. At the union rate employment opportunities amounting to L_1L_2 open up, drawing new union members from the nonunion sector. Nonunion supply decreases, raising nonunion wage rates to w_4.

the amount of construction work that smaller nonunion firms bid for, and reduce employment opportunities for minorities, which tend to be underrepresented in unions. The U.S. General Accounting Office has studied the matter thoroughly and has recommended the statute's repeal.

The impact of the Davis-Bacon law in a given labor market is illustrated in Figure 16.6. Suppose that initially there is no federal construction in the area and that the labor force is partially unionized. Panel (b) represents the nonunion segment of the market, with a demand curve d_nd_n, a supply curve s_ns_n, wage rate w_1, and employment level L_3. The union segment is shown in panel (a), where demand is d_ud_u and the wage rate, established through collective bargaining, is w_2. Unionized employers can, of course, get as much labor as they desire at the union wage rate, so the effective supply of union labor is horizontal at wage rate w_2.

Now suppose that substantial federal construction is initiated in the area. The question is whether or not contractors on the federal projects will hire workers at union or at nonunion rates. It is important to the construction unions that workers be hired at union rates whether or not they are union members, although it would certainly be preferable to them for only union labor to be hired. If the contractors hire union labor, the demand curve in panel (a) shifts to the right to $d_{u1}d_{u1}$, increased employment opportunities enable the unions to attract new members, and the level of unionized employment expands to L_2. It becomes easier for the unions to maintain wage level w_2, because the labor supply of the nonunion sector has shifted to the left, raising nonunion wage rates to w_4. Even if the contractors had hired L_1L_2 nonunion workers at w_2, the same increase in nonunion wage rates to w_4 would have occurred, decreasing the union-nonunion wage differential and strengthening the unions' position in the market. The losers in this game are the general public. The costs of government projects are escalated, to be paid for by higher taxes, larger deficits, inflation, or all three combined.

Economist Martin Feldstein has argued that in hiring employees the federal government would do well to determine first the level of skill needed and then to set the *lowest* wage rate that would yield the desired number of workers.[16] In Figure 16.6, this would have the effect of increasing demand in the nonunion sector to $d_{n4}d_{n4}$ and raising the nonunion wage rate to w_3 and the employment level to L_4. There would be no losers, except that unions, faced with the somewhat larger union-nonunion wage differential, may have a little more difficulty maintaining and/or increasing the union wage scale. The general public would gain by getting more government projects built for the same cost, the same number of projects at lower cost, or some of both.

_____

[16]Martin Feldstein, "The Job of Controlling Public Sector Pay," *The Wall Street Journal*, October 1, 1981.

Suggested Readings

For further discussion of the airport landing slot problem, see

Eckert, Ross D. *Airports and Congestion: A Problem of Misplaced Subsidies.* Washington, D.C.: American Enterprise Institute for Public Policy Research, 1972.

Two opposite positions on the most efficient solutions to pollution and other spillover problems are

Coase, R. H. "The Problem of Social Cost," *The Journal of Law and Economics* 3 (October 1960): 1–44.

Pigou, A. C. *The Economics of Welfare,* 4th ed., Pt. 3, Chap. 9. London: Macmillan, 1932.

An excellent discussion of various distortions introduced into labor markets is

Rees, Albert. *The Economics of Work and Pay,* Pt. 3. New York: Harper & Row, 1973.

Problems and Questions for Discussion

1. Suppose that coal miners in Kentucky are initially unorganized and that an equilibrium wage rate, w_1, prevails. Then suppose that a union is formed and succeeds in organizing approximately one-half of the miners while the rest remain unorganized. The union succeeds in raising wage rates in unionized mines to w_2. Explain the effects on
   a. Resource allocation
   b. National income.

2. Much of the nation's crude oil is produced in Louisiana, Texas, and Oklahoma. In an uncontrolled market, the price per barrel of crude oil to buyers in New York is typically greater than it is in one of the producing states—for example, Oklahoma.
   a. What explanation can you offer for the price difference?
   b. Does the price difference to users mean that crude oil is being misallocated? Why or why not?
   c. What would be the effect on the allocation of crude oil if a ceiling price equal to the initial Oklahoma market price were placed on the resource?

3. One of the traditional objectives of labor unions is to obtain "equal pay for equal work" for their members. Suppose that all carpenters belong to the Carpenters' Union and that initially this objective has been attained. Assume that at this union wage scale equilibrium exists in the market for carpenters in both Oldtown and Newcity. Over time Newcity grows and expands, while Oldtown deteriorates. What mechanism exists for reallocating carpenters
   a. If the union loses members and the wage scale is no longer enforced?
   b. If the union wage scale is strictly maintained?

4. Apartment rents in the city of Alpha are controlled, while in adjacent Omega they are not. Show with appropriate diagrams and explain in each of the following cases
   a. Rent levels, shortages, surpluses, and quantities supplied of apartments in each city
   b. The effects of population growth in Alpha on the same variables in each city

c.   The effects of exemption of newly constructed apartment units from controls.

5. For over a hundred years, Arkansas has prohibited interest rates greater than 10 percent on consumer loans and has imposed on violators the stiffest penalties in the nation. In 1981 the rates charged in many states were close to 20 percent per year for loans of this kind. The Arkansas usury law applied not only to consumer finance lenders but to sellers of furniture, appliances, and automobiles. Some of these firms tightened credit requirements, raised prices, shortened payoff periods, and discontinued such services as "free" delivery. Others went out of business. (Brenton R. Schlender, "Arkansas Retailers Say Usury Law Threatens Wholesale Closedowns," *The Wall Street Journal,* May 22, 1981.)

   a.   Show with demand and supply curve diagrams the effects of the Arkansas interest rate limit on the interest rate charged consumers in that state as compared with those charged consumers in adjacent Texas, where there are no such controls. What will you measure along each axis of your diagrams?

   b.   Explain with diagrams the effects of the Arkansas limit on the interest rates that "loan sharks" can charge to those natives of the state who cannot obtain consumer loans from financial institutions or retailers at the controlled rate.

   c.   In Texarkana, which spans the border, would automobile dealers be more likely to open new dealerships on the Arkansas side of town or on the Texas side? Explain.

6. In 1979, California's usury limit was 10 percent while the market rate was over 12 percent. But the limit applied only to loans by individuals, mortgage bankers, insurance companies, and pension funds. Commercial banks, savings and loan associations, pawnbrokers, and some consumer finance companies were exempt from the usury limit. (John A. Jones, "Lender Logic: Up Usury Limit, Cut Mortgages," *Los Angeles Times,* August 19, 1979.)

   a.   Diagram and explain the effect of the usury limit on both exempt and nonexempt lenders in California.

   b.   The sources of many funds for consumer loans are investors throughout the country, such as insurance companies, who were not exempt from California's usury law. Diagram and explain the effect on lending in Arizona and Oregon, for example.

   c.   California voters raised the usury limit late in 1979. Diagram and explain the results in exempt and nonexempt markets.

7. As in the wheat program described in Chapter 4, the U.S. government "loans" money on the crops of U.S. sugar producers (in California, Hawaii, and Louisiana) whenever price falls below 18 cents per pound. The world sugar price is usually about one-third the domestic price, so the potential obligation is large. To keep down the deficit, the government places quotas on imports from Brazil, Costa Rica, the Dominican Republic,

and the Philippines. The domestic sugar price in 1986 was about 21 cents and the quota for 1987 was set at about 1 million tons, one-third the 1984 level. ("Sugar Quotas: A Guide for the Economically Perplexed," *Regulation,* July/August 1982, 4–6; Art Pine, "Sugar-Import Cuts of 41% Ordered by U.S. for 1987," *The Wall Street Journal,* December 16, 1986.)

    a. Diagram and explain the effect of the quota program on the U.S. market and the world market.

    b. Diagram and explain the effect of sugar quotas on the U.S. market for fructose, the sugar substitute used for soft drinks that was discussed in Chapter 9.

    c. Explain the position of each of the following groups toward sugar quotas: corn growers, fructose manufacturers, and the U.S. Department of Agriculture.

    d. Explain the position of each of the following groups: sugar refiners, soft drink manufacturers, ketchup and bakery goods manufacturers, and the U.S. State Department.

8. Physicians practicing in metropolitan areas of over 1,000,000 population appear to earn incomes about 15 percent lower than physicians in smaller communities with the same specialties and comparable training. (Joseph P. Newhouse et al., "Does the Geographical Distribution of Physicians Reflect Market Failure?" *Bell Journal of Economics* 13 (Autumn 1982): 493–505.) How could an income differential of this magnitude persist? Does it signify a misallocation of resources? Explain.

9. All but one Canadian province place a cap on the income each physician may earn and prohibit physicians from billing patients for anything over what the government pays. In 1986, the province of Quebec was considering legislation requiring physicians who wanted to practice in a city or to receive post-graduate medical training first to spend four years in "the northern bush." (David Frum, "Canada Puts Heat on 'Coldhearted' Doctors," *The Wall Street Journal,* August 11, 1986.)

    a. Diagram the wage rate and equilibrium quantity of physician services in an urban market and a rural market before either wage or location controls were imposed.

    b. Assume that physician incomes in both markets are capped at the market-clearing level in the urban market. Modify diagrams for both markets accordingly. What happens in each?

    c. Modify the diagrams in (b) to account for the effects of the rural service requirement on the supply of physicians in the urban market. What happens in each market?

*10. The U.S. Federal Aviation Administration placed the following conditions on the market in landing rights that it created in 1986. Analyze the impli-

---

*Denotes an application-oriented problem.

cations of each for achieving an efficient allocation of slots among submarkets:

   a.   A certain number of slots allocated to international air carriers may not
        be sold.
   b.   A certain number of slots allocated to private and corporate small air-
        craft (general aviation) may not be sold.
   c.   Airline slots not used at least 65 percent of the time during a two-month
        period must be relinquished to the FAA.

*11. Explain which of the following mechanisms for allocating airport landing
     and departure slots is likely to result in fewer resource misallocations. As-
     sume in each case that slots are fully salable or exchangeable once assigned
     among airlines:

   a.   Assigning slots initially via a lottery
   b.   Assigning slots initially via an auction
   c.   Assigning slots initially according to their allocation on April 1, 1986
        (which is what the FAA did).

*12. In 1976, California adopted a system for transferable air pollution rights
     similar to the EPA system described in the chapter. California authorities
     expected polluting firms that closed down or cleaned up high-emission
     sources to sell or trade their rights to other polluting firms that wanted to
     begin business in California. What happened instead was that many of the
     initial rightsholders ''hoarded'' rights for new polluting sources of their
     own. (Richard O'Reilly, ''Air Quality District Seeks More Access to Pol-
     lution 'Bank','' *Los Angeles Times,* July 8, 1982.) Explain whether you
     agree with California officials that hoarding misallocates pollution rights.

*13. In 1986, the Reagan administration apparently planned to propose elimi-
     nating application of the Davis-Bacon prevailing wage requirements to mil-
     itary construction projects of less than $1,000,000 and other federal con-
     tracts of less than $100,000. This would exempt 90 percent of military
     contracts from the scope of the law. (''Reagan Wants to Weaken Davis-
     Bacon Wage Rules,'' *The Wall Street Journal,* May 2, 1986.) Use a dia-
     gram similar to Figure 16.6 to explain the probable effects of this proposal.

Chapter 17

DISTRIBUTION OF INCOME AND PRODUCT

Of the four functions of an economic system with which we are concerned, we have yet to consider the distribution of the economy's product or income. Income distribution among the families and individuals of economic systems has been an age-old source of unrest and concern. A promise always extended by socialist economic systems is that they will improve the distribution of income. In recent years the governments of most private enterprise countries have been promising the same thing. In this chapter we examine the way in which a private enterprise system distributes income, the possibilities of redistribution, and the welfare implications of both.

INDIVIDUAL INCOME DETERMINATION

marginal productivity theory
The theory stating that in a private enterprise economy resource units are paid prices equal to either their values of marginal product or their marginal revenue products.

The principles of individual income determination and of income distribution in a private enterprise economic system are called the **marginal productivity theory.** These principles were set out in previous chapters; in this one we draw them together and summarize them.

Under pure competition in resource purchasing, the owner of a given resource is paid a price per unit for the units employed equal to the marginal revenue product of the resource. The price of the resource is not determined by any single employer or by any single resource owner. It is determined by the interactions of all buyers and all sellers in the market for the resource.

If for some reason the price of a resource is less than its marginal revenue product, a shortage occurs. Employers want more of it at that price than resource owners are willing to place on the market. Employers, bidding against one another for the available supply, drive the price up until the shortage disappears and each is hiring (or buying) that quantity of the resource at which its marginal revenue product equals its price.

A price high enough to create a surplus of the resource sets forces in motion to eliminate that surplus. Employers take only those quantities sufficient to equate its marginal revenue product to its price. Resource owners undercut one another's prices to secure employment for their idle units. As price drops, employment expands. The undercutting continues until employers are willing to take the quantities that resource owners want to place on the market.

Where some degree of monopoly[1] exists in product markets, the monopolistic firm employs those quantities of the resource at which its marginal revenue product is equal to its price. However, the price per unit received by owners of the resource is less than its value of marginal product, and the resource is exploited monopolistically.

Some degree of monopsony in the purchase of a given resource will cause it to be paid still less than its marginal revenue product. The monopsonist, faced with a resource supply curve sloping upward to the right, employs that quantity of the resource at which its marginal revenue product is equal to its marginal

---

[1]Again we use the term to refer to all cases in which the firm faces a downward-sloping product demand curve. They include cases of pure monopoly, oligopoly, and monopolistic competition.

resource cost, which in turn is greater than its price. Monopsonistic exploitation of the resource occurs to the extent that its marginal revenue product exceeds its price. If the resource purchaser is also a monopolist, marginal revenue product of the resource will in turn be less than its value of marginal product, and the resource will be exploited monopolistically as well as monopsonistically.

As we noted in Chapter 2, an individual's income per unit of time is the sum of the amounts earned per unit of time from the employment of the various resources that the person owns. If a single kind of resource is owned, the income will be equal to the number of units placed in employment multiplied by the price per unit that the individual receives. If the individual owns several kinds of resources, the income from each one can be computed in the same manner, and all can be totaled to determine that person's entire income.

PERSONAL DISTRIBUTION OF INCOME

personal distribution of income
The distribution of income among households of the economy.

The **personal distribution of income** refers to income distribution among spending units of the economy. We survey the distribution of income by size and then point up some of the problems involved in measuring income differences and equality.

Distribution among Spending Units

Some idea of the distribution of income in the United States is provided by Table 17.1. It is worth noting that 86.7 percent of the families had incomes of $10,000 or more per year in 1985. Note that 13.3 percent of families fell below

**Table 17.1
Distribution of Total Money Income in the United States before Taxes, 1985**

Total Money Income	Families Number (thousands)	Families Percent	Unrelated Individuals Number (thousands)	Unrelated Individuals Percent
Under $5,000	3,060	4.8	6,003	19.1
5,000 to 9,999	5,429	8.5	7,474	23.8
10,000 to 14,999	6,495	10.2	5,240	16.7
15,000 to 19,999	6,671	10.5	4,025	12.8
20,000 to 24,999	6,534	10.3	2,756	8.8
25,000 to 29,999	6,205	9.8	2,096	6.7
30,000 to 34,999	5,607	8.8	1,339	4.3
35,000 to 39,999	4,844	7.6	779	2.5
40,000 to 44,999	3,993	6.3	490	1.6
45,000 to 49,999	3,103	4.9	306	1.0
50,000 to 59,999	4,570	7.2	405	1.3
60,000 to 74,999	3,523	5.5	211	0.7
75,000 and over	3,525	5.5	228	0.7
Total	63,558	100.0	31,351	100.0
Median Income	27,735		11,808	

Source: U.S. Department of Commerce, Bureau of the Census, Consumer Income, Series P-60, No. 154 (August 1986), pp 10, 11.

the $10,000 per year level. Among unrelated individuals—persons 14 years of age or over who are not living with any relatives—almost one-fifth had incomes under $5,000 per year. Using the poverty thresholds defined by the federal government for 1985—roughly $11,000 for an urban family of four, with appropriate adjustments for other sizes of households—some 33.1 million persons lived in poverty in 1985. These constitute about 14 percent of the total population of the United States. Median family income was $27,735; the median income for unattached individuals was $11,808.

Income Equality and Income Differences

Lorenz curve
A device used to measure the extent of inequality in the distribution of income among households.

Inequality in the distribution of income among households is of great concern to many people. The device usually used to indicate the extent of inequality is the **Lorenz curve** of Figure 17.1, in which we measure the percentage of the total number of families and unrelated individuals on the horizontal axis and the percentage of total family and unrelated individuals' income on the vertical axis. If income were equally distributed among families, the relationship between the percentage of families and the percentage of income would form the straight diagonal line 0A—20 percent of the families would have 20 percent of the income, 50 percent of the families would have 50 percent of the income, and

**Figure 17.1
Inequality in the
Before-Tax
Distribution of
Income, 1985**

Equal distributions of income among all economic units would trace out the straight line 0A. The actual distribution in 1985 for families is shown as the solid blue line and for unrelated individuals as the dashed blue line.

Source: U.S. Department of Commerce, Bureau of the Census, Consumer Income, Series P-60, No. 140, 11.

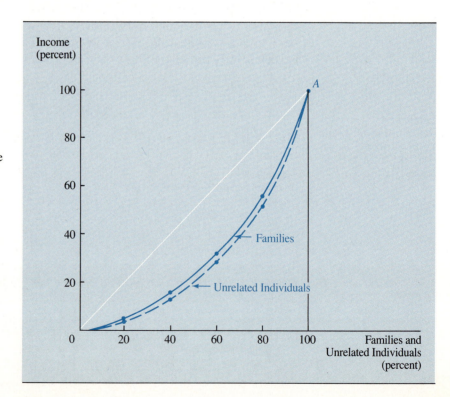

so on. But the actual distribution of income is not an equal apportionment. The actual distribution of family income in 1985 is shown by the solid blue line. Note that the lower 20 percent of families received only 4.6 percent of total income and the lower 60 percent only 32.4 percent of total income. The extent to which the actual income distribution deviates from a perfectly equal one is reflected by the curvature of the Lorenz curve. The dashed blue line shows the distribution of the total income of unrelated individuals among that group. Note that incomes of unrelated persons were even more unequally distributed than was family income.

Even if the Lorenz curves show perfect equality in the distribution of income, there is no assurance that all spending units are being treated equally by the economic system. Unrelated individuals vary in many ways; there are differences in ages, regional locations, cultural tastes, and the like. Therefore, equality of money income among them may lead to very different levels of fulfillment or of economic well-being. When we consider family spending units, the differences in family sizes and age distributions further compound the problem of lack of homogeneity among spending units.

The difficulties encountered in trying to define and measure income equality or income differences will not be of major importance for our purposes. We are interested in the causes of differences rather than in their normative implications. We shall have occasion to refer to "movements toward greater equality," but this phrase should be accepted for what it is—a loose statement meaning some mitigation of income differences among heterogeneous spending units. It means some lopping off of incomes at the top and some augmenting of incomes at the bottom. It does not mean that we can state with any precision the point at which income distribution is "equalized."

CAUSES OF INCOME DIFFERENCES _____

With reference to the determinants of individual[2] incomes, it becomes clear that differences in incomes arise from two basic sources: (1) differences in the kinds and quantities of resources owned by different individuals and (2) differences in prices paid in different employments for units of any given resource. The former are the more fundamental; the latter arise from various types of interference with the price system in the performance of its functions and from any resource immobilities that may occur.

It is convenient to use the broad classifications *labor* and *capital resource*. To enable us to see the importance of each in perspective, it is worthwhile to note the **functional distribution of income** in the United States—that is, distribution according to the classes into which resources are divided. In Table 17.2, compensation of employees represents income received by the owners of labor resources for the listed years, while corporate profits, interest, and rental

functional distribution of income
The distribution of income by kinds or classes of resources.

---

[2]The term *individual* will be used throughout the rest of the chapter to refer to a spending unit, regardless of its size or composition.

Table 17.2   National Income by Type of Income, 1939–1985

Type of Income	1939 Income (billions)	1939 Percent of Income	1949 Income (billions)	1949 Percent of Income	1959 Income (billions)	1959 Percent of Income	1969 Income (billions)	1969 Percent of Income	1979 Income (billions)	1979 Percent of Income	1985 Income (Billions)	1985 Percent of Income
Compensation of employees	$48.1	66.3	$140.8	64.7	$278.5	69.6	$565.5	72.8	$1,459.2	75.8	2,368.2	73.5
Business and professional proprietors' income	7.3	10.0	22.7	10.4	35.1	8.8	50.3	6.5	98.0	5.1	225.2	7.0
Farm proprietors' income	4.3	5.9	12.9	5.9	11.4	2.8	16.8	2.0	32.8	1.7	29.2	0.9
Rental income	2.7	3.7	8.3	3.8	11.9	3.0	22.6	2.9	26.9	1.3	7.6	0.2
Net interest	4.6	6.3	4.8	2.2	16.4	4.1	29.9	3.8	129.7	6.7	311.4	9.7
Corporate profits	5.7	7.9	28.2	13.0	47.2	11.8	78.6	12.0	178.2	9.3	280.7	8.7
Total[a]	$72.8	100.0	$217.7	100.0	$400.5	100.0	$763.7	100.0	$1,924.8	100.0	$3,222.3	100.0

[a]Columns may not total due to rounding.

Sources: Economic Report of the President (Washington, D.C.: Government Printing Office, 1965), 203; U.S. Department of Commerce, *Survey of Current Business* (May 1975, S-2, and July 1980, 14); Board of Governors of the Federal Reserve System, *Federal Reserve Bulletin*, Vol. 72, No. 11 (November 1986), A51.

income represent income received by capital owners. All are understated substantially, because proprietors' incomes include income both from labor and from capital. We can guess roughly that labor resources account for some 80 percent of national income and that capital resources account for some 20 percent.

In this section we first consider differences in the kinds and quantities of labor resources owned by different individuals. Next we discuss differences in capital resources owned. Finally we examine the effects on income distribution of certain manipulations of the price mechanism.

Differences in Labor Resources Owned

The labor classification of resources is composed of many different kinds and qualities of labor. These have one common characteristic—they are human. Any single kind of labor is a combination or complex of both inherited and acquired characteristics. The acquired part of a worker's labor power is generally referred to as human capital. We shall make no attempt to separate inherited from acquired characteristics.

Labor can be subclassified horizontally and vertically into many, largely separate resource groups. Vertical subclassification involves grading workers according to skill levels from the lowest kind of undifferentiated manual labor to the highest professional levels. Horizontal subclassification divides workers of a given skill level into the various occupations requiring that particular degree of skill. An example would be the division of skilled construction workers into groups such as carpenters, bricklayers, plumbers, and the like. Vertical mobility of labor refers to the possibility of moving upward through vertical skill levels.

Figure 17.2   Effects of a Shift in Demand on the Allocation of Bricklayers and Carpenters

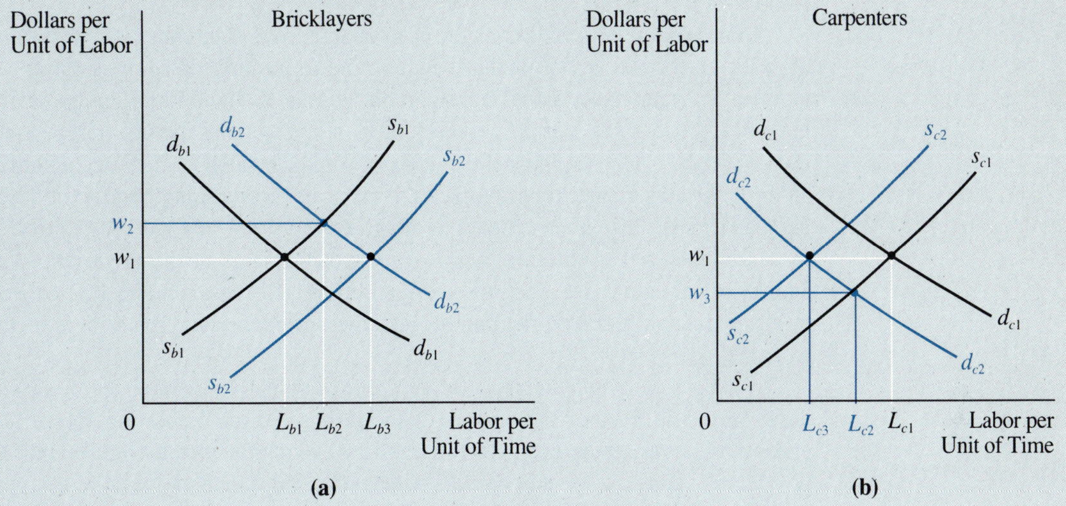

Suppose initially that both bricklayers' and carpenters' wage rates are w_1 and that L_{b1} bricklayers and L_{c1} carpenters are employed. An increase in demand for bricklayers to $d_{b2}d_{b2}$ and a decrease in demand for carpenters to $d_{c2}d_{c2}$ causes the wage rate for bricklayers to rise to w_2 and that for carpenters to fall to w_3. Over time more persons train as bricklayers and fewer train as carpenters, increasing the supply of the former and decreasing the supply of the latter until the wage rate is again approximately the same (shown here as w_1).

Horizontal mobility means the ability to move sideways among groups at a particular skill level.

Horizontal Differences in Labor Resources   At any specific horizontal level, individuals may receive different incomes because of differences in the demand and supply conditions for the kinds of labor that they own. A large demand for a certain kind of labor relative to the supply of it available will make its marginal revenue product and its price high. On the same skill level, a small demand for another kind of labor relative to the supply available will make its marginal revenue product and its price low. The differences in prices tend to cause differences in income for owners of the kinds of labor concerned.

Suppose, for example, in Figure 17.2 that the demand curves for bricklayers and carpenters are initially $d_{b1}d_{b1}$ and $d_{c1}d_{c1}$ and the supply curves $s_{b1}s_{b1}$ and $s_{c1}s_{c1}$, respectively. The wage rate is w_1. A shift in consumers' tastes occurs from wood to brick construction in residential units, causing demand for bricklayers to rise to $d_{b2}d_{b2}$ and that for carpenters to fall to $d_{c2}d_{c2}$. Bricklayers' wage rates thus rise to w_2, and those of carpenters fall to w_3. Over time horizontal mobility, resulting from the differences in wage rates, shifts the supply curves to $s_{b2}s_{b2}$ and $s_{c2}s_{c2}$, respectively, evening out the wage rates and increasing welfare in the process.

Some income differences result from quantitative differences in the amount of work performed by individuals owning the same kind of labor resource. A number of occupations afford considerable leeway for individual choice in the number of hours to be worked per week or month. Examples include independent professionals, such as physicians, lawyers, and certified public accountants, along with independent proprietors, such as farmers, plumbing contractors, and garage owners. In other occupations hours of work are beyond the control of the individual, yet in different employments of the same resource variations in age, physical endurance, institutional restrictions, customs, and so on can lead to differences in hours worked and to income differences among owners of the resource.

Within a particular labor resource group, qualitative differences or differences in the abilities of the owners of the resource often create income differences. Wide variations occur in the public's evaluation of individual dentists, physicians, lawyers, or automobile mechanics. Consequently within any one group variations in prices paid for services and in the quantities of services sold to the public will lead to income differences. Usually a correlation exists between the ages of the members of a resource group and their incomes. Quality tends to improve with accumulated experience up to a point.

Vertical Differences in Labor Resources   The different vertical strata themselves represent differences in labor resources owned and give rise to major labor income differences. Entry into high-level occupations, such as the professions or the ranks of business executives, is much more difficult than is entry into manual occupations. The relative scarcity of labor at top levels results from two basic factors: (1) individuals with the physical and mental characteristics necessary for the performance of high-level work are limited in number, and (2) given the necessary physical and mental characteristics, many lack either the opportunities for training or the necessary social and cultural environment for movement into high-level positions. Thus impediments to vertical mobility keep resource supplies low, relative to demands for them at the top levels, and abundant, relative to demands for them at the low levels.

Differences in labor resources owned because of disparities in innate physical and mental characteristics of individuals are accidents of birth; the individual has nothing to do with choosing them. Nevertheless they account partly for restricted vertical mobility and for income differences. The opportunities for moving toward top positions and relatively large incomes are considerably enhanced by the inheritance of a strong physical constitution and a superior intellect; however, these by no means ensure that individuals so endowed will make the most of their opportunities.

Opportunities for training are more widely available to individuals born into wealthy families than to those born to parents in lower-income groups. Some of the higher-paying professions require long and expensive university training programs that are often beyond the reach of the latter groups; the medical profession is a case in point. However, we often see individuals who have had the initial ability, drive, and determination necessary to overcome economic obstacles thrown in the way of vertical mobility.

Differences in social inheritance constitute another cause of differences in labor resources owned. These are closely correlated with differences in material inheritance. Frequently individuals born ''on the wrong side of the tracks'' face family and community attitudes that sharply curtail their opportunities and their desires for vertical mobility. Others more fortunately situated acquire the training necessary to become highly productive and to obtain large incomes because it is expected of them by the social group in which they move. The social position alone, apart from the training induced by it, may be quite effective in facilitating vertical mobility.

When vertical mobility would otherwise occur but is blocked, income differences persist and welfare is below its potential maximum. If those who are denied access to jobs and occupations with higher values of marginal products were able to attain these, the result would be higher real net national product as well as greater equality in income distribution.

Differences in Capital Resources Owned

In addition to inequalities in labor incomes, large differences occur in individual incomes from disparities in capital ownership. Different individuals own varying quantities of capital, such as corporation or other business assets, farmland, oil wells, or other property. We shall examine the fundamental causes of inequalities in capital holdings.

Material Inheritance   Differences in the amounts of capital inherited or received as gifts by individuals create disparities in incomes. The institution of private property on which private enterprise rests usually is coupled with inheritance laws allowing holdings of accumulated property rights to be passed from generation to generation. The individual fortunate enough to have a wealthy parent inherits large capital holdings which contribute much to the productive process, and the individual is rewarded accordingly. The child of a southern sharecropper—who may be of equal innate intelligence with the child of a wealthy parent but inherits no capital—contributes less to the productive process and receives a correspondingly lower income.

Fortuitous Circumstances   Chance, luck, or other fortuitous circumstances beyond the control of individuals constitute a further cause of differences in capital holdings. The discovery of oil, uranium, or gold on an otherwise undistinguished piece of land brings about a large appreciation in its value or its ability to yield income to its owner. Unforeseen shifts in consumer demand increase the values of certain capital holdings while decreasing the values of others. National emergencies, such as war, lead to changes in valuations of particular kinds of property and hence to differential incomes from capital. Fortuitous circumstances can work in reverse also, but even so their effects operate to create differences in the ownership of capital.

Propensities to Accumulate   Differing psychological propensities to accumulate and differing abilities to do so lead to differences in capital ownership among individuals. On the psychological side, a number of factors influence the will to accumulate. Stories circulate of individuals determined to make a fortune before they reach middle age. Accumulation sometimes occurs for purposes of security and luxury in later life; sometimes it stems from the desire to make one's children secure. The power and the prestige accompanying wealth provide the motivating force in some cases, while in others amassing and manipulating capital holdings is a gigantic game—the activity involved fascinates the players. Whatever the motives, some individuals have such propensities and others do not. In some instances the will to accumulate may be negative, and the opposite of accumulation occurs.

The ability of an individual to accumulate depends largely on his or her original holdings of both labor and capital resources. The higher the original income, the easier saving and accumulation tend to be. The individual possessing much in the way of labor resources initially is likely to accumulate capital with his or her income from labor; investments are made in stocks and bonds, real estate, a cattle ranch, or other property. Or, the individual possessing substantial quantities of capital initially—and the ability to manage it—receives an income sufficient to allow saving and investment in additional capital. In the process of accumulation, labor and capital resources of an individual augment one another in providing the income from which further accumulation can be accomplished.

Price Manipulations

Various groups of resource owners throughout the economy, dissatisfied with their current shares of national income, seek to modify income distribution through manipulation or fixing of the prices of resources that they own or the prices of products that they produce and sell. Groups of farmers—wheat, cotton, dairy, and others—have been able to obtain government-enforced minimum prices for their products. Groups of retailers have been able to secure state laws forbidding the sale of products at prices below some fixed percentage markup over cost. Labor organizations seek to increase, or in some cases to maintain, incomes of their members by fixing wages through the collective bargaining process. People throughout the economy, concerned with the small distributive shares of low-paid workers, support minimum wage legislation. We shall examine typical cases of price fixing in an attempt to assess their effects on income distribution.

Fixed Prices: Pure Competition   Suppose that owners of a given resource, dissatisfied with their shares of national income, seek and obtain a price above the equilibrium level for their resource. Will the incomes of the resource owners

Figure 17.3
Effects of a Minimum
Resource Price on
Income Distribution

A minimum resource
price of p_{a1} results in
unemployment of A_1A_1'.
The A_1 units that remain
employed receive higher
incomes while the
unemployed units receive
nothing. The distribution
of income becomes more
unequal.

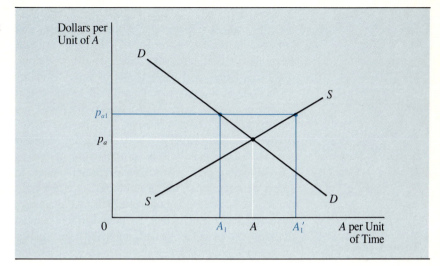

involved increase relative to the incomes of owners of other resources? In other
words, will the owners of the given resource receive a larger share of the
economy's product? Equally important, what will happen to the share of total
earnings of the resource received by each of its owners? What will be the effects
on the efficiency of the economy's operation or on welfare?

If demand for the given resource remains constant,[3] the effect of the minimum price on total income earned by the resource will depend on the elasticity
of demand. If elasticity is less than one, total income will rise and owners of
the resource as a group will have increased their distributive share. If elasticity
equals one, no change in total income will occur. If elasticity is greater than
one, total income and the distributive share of owners of the resource as a group
will decline.

Reference to Figure 17.3 will help to answer the second problem—the
effects of a minimum price on the distribution among the owners of the resource
of the total income earned by it. The demand and supply curves in the figure
for resource A are DD and SS, respectively; the equilibrium price is p_a, and the
level of employment is quantity A.

Suppose that a minimum price of p_{a1} is set for the resource—none can be
sold for less. Whether it is set by the government, through bargaining between

_____

[3]There seems to be no valid reason for assuming that a change in the price of the resource will
change the demand for it, especially if the resource concerned constitutes a small proportion of the
economy's total supplies of resources—and such is usually the case for any given resource. Even
if the fixed price raises the total income of the resource owners involved, it seems unlikely that
demand for the products that the resource assists in producing will be increased to any significant
degree. In a stationary economy, particularly, it seems logical to assume independence between
resource price changes and consequent changes in demand for the resource.

organized groups of buyers and sellers, or through unilateral action on the part of either resource buyers or resource sellers is of no consequence; the effects will be the same. Confronted by the higher price, each firm using resource A finds that if it employs the same quantity as before marginal revenue product for the resource will be less than its price. Consequently each firm finds that reductions in the quantity A used will lower total receipts less than they will decrease total costs and will increase the firm's profits. When all firms have reduced employment sufficiently for the marginal revenue product of the resource in each to equal p_{a1}, they will again be maximizing profits. The market level of employment will have dropped to A_1.

Minimum price p_{a1} will reduce employment, thus causing income differences between those whose resources are employed and those whose resources are not.[4] At price p_{a1} employers will take quantity A_1, but quantity A_1' of the resource seeks employment. Unemployment amounts to A_1A_1'. Those whose units of the resource remain employed gain greater distributive shares of the economy's product; however, those owning idle units now receive nothing for them. Units of the resource still are paid according to their marginal contributions to the total receipts of the firm. For the employed units, marginal revenue product is greater than formerly because of the reduction in the ratio of resource A to the other resources used by individual firms. The marginal revenue product of the unemployed units is zero.

The unemployed units of resource A may seek to be used in another resource classification. Suppose, for example, that units of resource A are carpenters. Carpenters denied employment in that skill category at a wage rate of p_{a1} may seek work as common laborers rather than remain jobless carpenters. Their marginal revenue product and their wage rate will be less in the lower skill classification. The minimum wage rate increases income differences in two ways: (1) employed carpenters receive higher wage rates and incomes than they would otherwise; and (2) the wage rates and incomes of common labor are lower than they would otherwise be as unemployed carpenters join their ranks and increase the supply of common labor.

The effects of the minimum price on welfare are clear. The units of A that no longer find jobs in their original occupations contribute nothing to the value of the economy's output—or, to the extent that they shift into lower productivity classifications, they contribute less than they would have otherwise. If the resource price were allowed to drop to its equilibrium level, greater employment in the uses with higher value of marginal product would raise the real value of the economy's output—and at the same time would contribute toward greater income equality among owners of the resource.

Supply Restrictions: Pure Competition   Resource prices in given employments may be increased indirectly through restriction of the resource supplies that can be used in those employments. Examples are furnished by governmental

---

[4]Unless the unemployment is shared equally by all owners of the resource.

acreage restrictions placed on cotton and wheat farmers. The same result may be obtained by labor union activity: the milk truck drivers' union in a large city may succeed in making union membership a condition of employment while at the same time restricting entry into the union. The effects on income distribution and total output of the economy are about the same as those resulting from fixing prices. The employment level of the resource in its restricted use is decreased, leaving some of the resource units either unemployed or seeking employment in alternative uses. Land excluded from cotton and wheat farming may be switched to the production of other products. Light truck drivers excluded from driving milk trucks may secure such alternative employments as delivery truck or taxi driving. Value of marginal product and price of resource units in the restricted use increase,[5] while value of marginal product and price of those placed in other employments decrease. These changes lead to differential prices for the resource and to greater income differences. At the same time they lead to a net national product smaller than the economy is capable of producing.

Fixed Prices: Monopoly   Do minimum resource prices set above the equilibrium level offset the restrictive effects of monopoly when resource buyers sell a product as monopolists? The argument is frequently made that they do and that the advance in resource prices comes from the monopolists' profits. Suppose that initially the equilibrium price for a given resource prevails. Firms with some degree of monopoly in product markets are among those who buy the resource, and the resource is so allocated that its price is the same in its alternative uses. The resource price equals its marginal revenue product in its various employments, and those units of the resource employed by monopolistic sellers are exploited monopolistically—they receive less than they contribute to the value of the economy's output.

   Will a minimum resource price set above the equilibrium level regain for resource owners what they lose from monopolistic exploitation? Consider Figure 17.4. A monopolistic seller of product purchases common labor at wage rate w_1, taking quantity L_1; monopolistic exploitation is w_1v_1 per unit. Now suppose that through a minimum wage law or through collective bargaining the wage rate is raised to w_2. The employer, in the interest of maximizing profits, reduces the amount of labor purchased to L_2, and exploitation becomes w_2v_2. Instead of recapturing the amount lost through exploitation, L_2L_1 workers have lost their

_____

[5]In the case of wheat land or cotton land, the ratio of land to other resources is decreased both through decreased acreage allowances and through more intensive application of labor and fertilizer. Greater marginal physical product of the land and possibly higher prices for smaller crops increase the value of marginal product of land.

   About the same thing happens with regard to milk truck drivers. Firms faced with restricted supplies attempt to make each driver as productive as possible. Slightly larger trucks may be used to minimize the number of trips back to the plant for reloading. Trucks may be made more convenient to get into, to get out of, and to operate. Idle truck time is avoided through better maintenance and repair facilities for trucks. Such measures increase the marginal physical product of the drivers. Additionally, the employment of fewer drivers may lead to smaller milk sales and higher milk prices. Thus, the value of marginal product of milk truck drivers will be higher than before.

Figure 17.4
Effects of a Minimum Wage Rate on the Exploitation of Labor

An effective minimum wage rate does not counteract monopolistic exploitation of labor. Let the initial wage rate be w_1. Exploitation is w_1v_1. Now let a minimum be set at w_2. The monopolist reduces the employment level to L_2 and exploitation of w_2v_2 occurs.

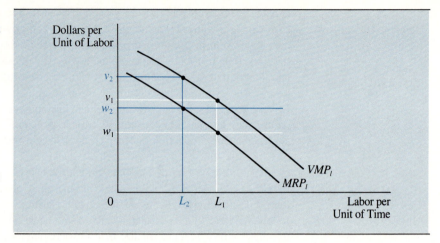

jobs. The L_2 workers who remain employed are, of course, better off, but monopolistic exploitation of them still occurs.[6]

In addition, the level of employment of the resource by monopolistic firms, already too low for maximum welfare, is reduced still further. At the higher price the firms employ fewer units of the resource. More units seek employment. Unemployment and even greater differences in income among owners of the resource occur. If the unemployed units then find employment in resource classifications or uses with lower marginal revenue product, income differences will be mitigated to some extent, but they will still occur.

Fixed Prices: Monopsony   In monopsonistic cases, minimum resource prices can offset monopsonistic exploitation of a resource. The employment level of the resource can be increased at the same time that its price is raised above the market level. The income and the distributive shares of the owners of the resource are increased relative to those of other resource owners in the economy. At the same time the level of real net national product and welfare will be increased.

The detailed explanation of how a minimum resource price offsets monopsonistic exploitation was presented in Chapter 14.[7] To recapitulate the analysis, a price set above the market price makes the resource supply curve faced by the firm horizontal at that price. For prices higher than the minimum, the original supply curve is the relevant one. For the horizontal section of the resource supply curve, marginal resource cost and resource price will be equal. By judicious

---

[6]Thus measures to offset monopolistic exploitation of resources must attack the monopolistic product demand situation. They must eliminate the difference between marginal revenue and price for the monopolist and hence between marginal revenue product and value of marginal product of resources.

[7]See pp. 474–475.

**Figure 17.5
Effects of Minimum
Resource Price
Increases When
Minimum Price
Equals Equilibrium
Price**

If the initial resource
price is p_{a1} and a
minimum price of p_{a2} is
negotiated, the price
increase will not cause
unemployment if demand
for the resource increases
sufficiently at the same
time so that the minimum
price does not exceed the
equilibrium level.

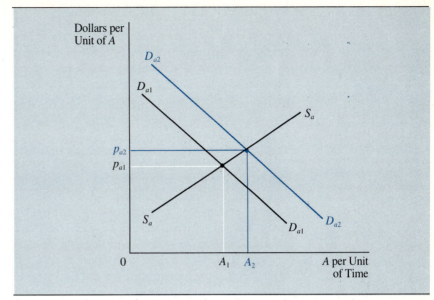

setting of the minimum price, the firm can be induced to employ that quantity
of the resource at which marginal revenue product equals resource price. Without
the minimum price, the firm restricts employment and pays units of the resource
less than their marginal revenue product.

Price Increases Accompanying Demand Increases   The effects of increasing
a minimum resource price when demand for the resource remains constant are
often confused with the effects of increases in minimum resource prices that
accompany increases in demand for the resource. Suppose, as in Figure 17.5,
that demand for a given resource is rising while simultaneously resource owners
organized as a group succeed in *bargaining out* a series of price increases with
the buyers of the resource. Suppose further that the contract prices at no time
exceed the rising equilibrium price. For example, when demand is $D_{a1}D_{a1}$ the
bargained price is p_{a1}, and when demand is $D_{a2}D_{a2}$ the bargained price is p_{a2}.
No adverse distributive effects for the owners of the resource arise; their positions are continuously improving as individual resource owners and as a group.
However, it is erroneous to conclude that raising minimum resource prices will
in general have no adverse effects on total income of the owners of the resource
in question or on the distribution of income within the group. We must distinguish carefully between those minimum price increases that are accompanied
by increases in demand for the resource and those that are not. Although the
former may have no adverse effects on total income of the owners of the resource
or on the distribution of income among such owners, such effects—except in
the case of monopsony—are likely to arise from the latter.

MOVEMENTS TOWARD LESS INEQUALITY _____

In most societies that rely heavily on the market mechanism to organize economic activity, there is a general belief that some reduction of income differences is desirable. The result has been a spate of antipoverty and income redistribution measures. What do we learn from microeconomics that will help us evaluate the effectiveness of alternative income redistribution policies?

Resource Redistribution

Since the market mechanism tends to reward households in proportion to their contributions to production processes, a major part of any redistribution program must consist of measures to improve the distribution of resource ownership. Some 80 percent of income is earned by labor resources, so it becomes apparent that differences in labor resources owned constitute the most important source of income differences. Differences in capital resources owned are also of some significance. How can these differences be reduced? In turn we shall look at: (1) redistribution of labor resources and (2) redistribution of capital resources.

Labor Resources   The ownership of labor resources can be redistributed through measures that enhance vertical mobility. Greater vertical mobility will increase labor supplies at higher skill levels and decrease them at lower levels. Greater supplies at the higher levels will reduce values of marginal product or marginal revenue products, thereby lowering the top incomes; smaller supplies at the lower levels will increase values of marginal product or marginal revenue products, thereby increasing incomes at the lower skill levels. The transfers from lower to higher skills will mitigate income differences and will add to net national product in the process.

At least two methods of increasing vertical mobility can be suggested. First, greater equality in educational and training opportunities for poor and rich alike can be provided. Second, measures may be taken to reduce the barriers to entry established by groups and associations of resource owners in many skilled and semiskilled occupations.[8]

Measures to enhance horizontal mobility also can serve to lessen income differences. These include the operation of employment exchanges, perhaps some government subsidization of movement, vocational guidance, adult education and retraining programs, and other, similar measures. The argument is really for a better allocation of labor resources, both among alternative jobs within a given labor resource category and among the labor resource categories themselves. Greater horizontal as well as greater vertical mobility will increase net national product at the same time that it decreases income differences.

---

[8]An example of such a barrier is provided by professional associations, which control the licensing standards that prospective entrants must meet in order to practice those professions.

Capital Resources   Policy measures to redistribute capital resources meet considerable opposition in a private enterprise economy. Many advocates of greater income equality will protest measures designed to redistribute capital ownership—even though these measures will contribute much toward such an objective. The opposition centers around the rights of private property ownership and stems from a strong belief that the right to own property includes the right to accumulate it and to pass it on to one's heirs.

Nevertheless if income differences are to be reduced, policy measures must include some means of providing greater equality in capital holdings among individuals. The economy's tax system pays lip service to this objective. In the United States, for example, the personal income tax and estate and gift taxes, both federal and state, are presumed to operate in an equalizing manner.

The personal income tax by its progressive provisions is supposed to reduce income differences directly; in so doing, it would reduce differences in abilities to accumulate capital. But that tax by itself is limited in the extent to which it can moderate income differences without seriously impairing incentives for efficient employment of resources and for reallocation of resources from less productive to more productive employments. In addition, over time a bewildering array of exemptions and loopholes has been incorporated into it, making its redistributive impact uncertain and random.

Estate and gift taxes will play major roles in any tax system seriously designed to reduce differences in capital ownership. The estate taxes in such a system would border on the confiscatory side, above some maximum amount, in order to prevent the transmission of accumulated capital resources from generation to generation. Gift taxes would operate largely to plug estate tax loopholes. They would be designed to prevent transmission of estates in the form of gifts from the original owner to heirs prior to the former's death.

Minimum Prices

Widespread use is made of minimum prices to accomplish the objectives of income redistribution. Examples include wage rates established through collective bargaining, legal minimum wage rates, price supports for farm products, rent controls, and crude oil price controls. Unfortunately many such measures miss their mark—we can seldom be certain that they will accomplish what they are intended to do. Wage rates set above equilibrium levels will reduce employment. Price controls may deprive some (poor) consumers of goods they would like to have. As we have seen, minimum prices in many cases add to rather than decrease income inequalities. In the process they often reduce economic efficiency.

The Negative Income Tax

Measures that redistribute the ownership of labor and capital resources may fall short of accomplishing the desired reduction in income inequalities among households. Supplementary income transfers from taxpayers to those at the bot-

Table 17.3
A Negative Income
Tax Plan

Income Base	Income Earned	Negative Tax (base − 50% of income earned)	Disposable income (income earned + negative tax)
$10,000	$ 0	$10,000	$10,000
10,000	2,000	9,000	11,000
10,000	4,000	8,000	12,000
10,000	18,000	1,000	19,000
10,000	20,000	0	20,000

tom of the income distribution scale may be necessary. *Negative income tax* proposals provide a means of making supplementary transfers with minimal effects on economic incentives. No widespread use has been made of negative income tax ideas; however, they constitute an interesting possible alternative to such current transfer programs as public assistance, unemployment compensation, food stamps, subsidized housing, and even social security.

The essence of a negative income tax plan is presented in Table 17.3. Two essential elements of it are (1) the income base and (2) the negative tax rate. The income base is the minimum level of income below which no household is allowed to fall. The negative tax rate is the percentage of income earned that is subtracted from the income base to determine the size of the subsidy or negative tax that is to be paid the household.

Suppose that the income base and the negative tax rate are set by the appropriate legislative body at $10,000 and 50 percent, respectively. There is nothing sacred about either of these figures—they can be whatever the society, acting through its legislature, wants them to be. If a household earns nothing at all during the year, this fact would be duly reported by an income tax return filed with the appropriate tax collection agency, say, the Internal Revenue Service. The tax collection agency, acting for the government, would then send a $10,000 check to the household, this amount becoming that household's disposable income. If the household reports an income earned of $2,000, the amount of the check mailed to it is $9,000, leaving it with a disposable income of $11,000. Similarly, an earned income of $4,000 results in a negative tax or subsidy of $8,000 and a disposable income of $12,000. At an earned income level of $20,000 or more per year, the household would receive no negative tax. Under the negative tax scheme a household can always have a larger disposable income if it earns income than it can have if it earns nothing. In addition, the more income it earns, the larger its disposable income will be. Thus positive incentives to earn are built into the plan. The larger the base and the smaller the negative tax rate, the larger will be the amount of income earned that the household will be allowed to keep and the higher will be the income level at which the amount of the subsidy to the household becomes zero.

The preservation of incentives to work and earn are important features of the negative income tax plan, but we should not overstate the case. To put it into proper perspective, suppose we subject a poor individual to three policy options. The first option provides the person with no subsidy whatsoever; the second provides a direct subsidy in which the welfare payments to the person are reduced dollar for dollar with his or her earnings; the third is the negative income tax option. How do the three compare with regard to incentives to work and earn?

The first option requires a straightforward use of the income-leisure time indifference map of an individual developed in Chapter 14. Consider panel (a) of Figure 17.6 first. The total daily hours of leisure time that could be available for work is $0H$. We draw a dashed vertical axis at H so that daily hours of work are measured to the left from the origin H. If the wage rate is w and the amount of labor performed per day is $l\ (=h_1H,\ h_2H,$ and so forth), then $l \cdot w$ generates the income line HK; the wage rate w determines and is equal to the slope of HK. Ignoring the other straight-line segments for the present, indifference curve U_1 is the highest the individual can reach. The daily work effort will be h_1H, and disposable income in the absence of any taxes will be $0D_1$.

To illustrate the second option, suppose in panel (a) that the individual can receive a daily welfare payment HE when not working. But if the individual works, the welfare payment is reduced one dollar for every dollar of income earned; the income line becomes EGK. Below work level h_3H the welfare payment exceeds any income the individual could earn, so the welfare payment generates the EG portion of the income line. At higher work levels income earned exceeds the welfare payment, so the GK portion of the income line becomes relevant. Indifference curve U_2 is the highest that the income line EGK will permit. To reach that level of satisfaction, the individual will elect not to work and will receive the daily welfare payment HE. The welfare payment has destroyed incentives to work. This will be the case for any welfare payment exceeding HJ.

Another possibility exists under the second option. Suppose the individual's indifference map is that of panel (b). Again the income line is EGK. If the individual does not work and receives the daily welfare check, the level of satisfaction depicted by indifference curve U_1' is reached. However, the higher satisfaction level of indifference curve U_2' is available if the individual works $h_1'H$ hours per day. Work is preferable to welfare in this case, or for any other case in which the welfare payment is less than HJ'.

Under the second option, in which welfare payments are reduced dollar for dollar by income earned, at least some individuals are likely to prefer welfare to work. Since the indifference maps of different individuals will not be the same, the critical welfare payment level HJ in panel (a) varies for different persons. Any given level of daily welfare payments will be above HJ for some persons and below HJ for others. Those in the former group will choose to receive welfare and not to work.

For analysis of the third, or negative income tax, option, consider again panel (a). Suppose the base income for every individual is HE—even if he or she does not work. If the individual works, income earned *without the negative tax* would trace out income line HK for different numbers of hours worked per

**Figure 17.6
Effects of Welfare
versus the Negative
Income Tax on
Incentives to Work**

In panel (a) a cash
subsidy of HE, greater
than HJ, would induce
the worker not to work,
putting her/him on
indifference curve U_2
rather than on U_1. A
negative income tax with
a floor of HE would
induce h_1H hours of
labor and an indifference
level of U_3. In panel (b)
a cash subsidy of HE,
less than HJ', would
induce the worker to
work h_1H hours, whereas
a negative income tax
with a floor of HE would
cause the worker to cut
back on hours worked to
$h_2'H$.

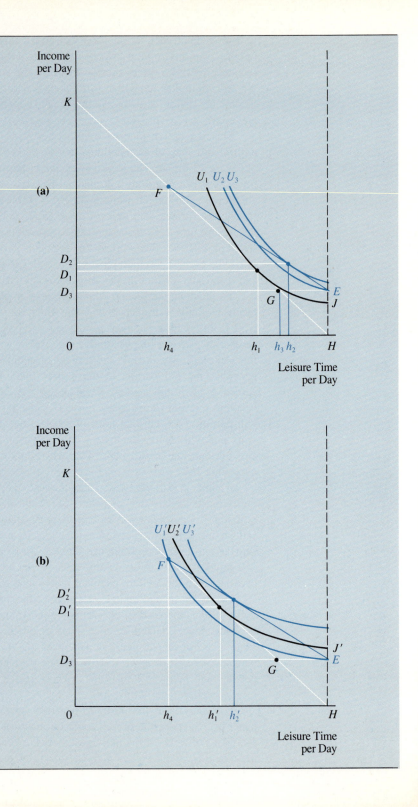

day. *With the negative income tax*, the income line becomes *EFK*. The *EF* segment of the income line has a smaller slope than *HK*. This is so because the negative tax decreases as income earned increases, reaching zero at some employment level h_4H.[9] With the negative income tax option, the individual chooses to work h_2H hours per day, receiving a disposable income of D_2.

We can now compare the options as they are displayed in panel (a). In the absence of any subsidization, the individual wants to work h_1H hours and have a disposable income of $0D_1$. A straight welfare plan in which the subsidy or welfare payment is greater than *HJ* induces the individual not to work. The negative income tax option with a base income of *HE* induces the individual to work h_2H hours, receiving a disposable income of $0D_2$. The negative income tax plan as compared with the welfare payment plan thus preserves some work incentives, but these incentives are not as strong as those provided by the market alone.

In panel (b) we compare the three options for an individual for whom either a welfare payment or a negative income tax would be less than *HJ'*. The welfare option drops out because the individual would never choose it, preferring instead to work $h_1'H$ hours per day. With the negative income tax the desired work hours are $h_2'H$ per day. Although the negative income tax preserves some work incentives, those incentives are not as great as the ones provided by the market.

The negative income tax idea has several appealing features in addition to that of preserving incentives for resource owners to employ their resources productively. It is simple in concept and could be administered easily by the existing tax collection mechanism; it does not require a separate bureaucratic agency. It attacks the problem of poverty directly by making subsidy payments only to the poor. If it were used, it would eliminate the need for many of the special income transfer programs now in existence.

Income Redistribution and the Price System

The foregoing discussion suggests that if a society that uses the price mechanism is not satisfied with the income distribution that mechanism generates, the most efficient way of redistributing income is to do it outside the operation of the

---

[9]Let: Y_e = income earned

  k = base income

  t = fraction of income earned subtracted from base income to determine negative tax

  N = negative tax

  w = wage rate

  l = hours of work per day

  Y_d = disposable income

Then: $Y_e = l \cdot w$

  $N = k - Y_e \cdot t = k - l \cdot w \cdot t$

  $Y_d = Y_e + (k - Y_e \cdot t) = l \cdot w + (k - l \cdot w \cdot t)$

  $= k + l \cdot w(1 - t)$ where $l \geqq h_4H$

price mechanism itself. Direct government intervention in the pricing of resources, goods, and services is likely to reduce the efficiency with which the economic system operates by distorting price signals and bringing about misallocations of resources. It may also generate unemployment and other surpluses—or, on the other hand, shortages. Redistributions of resource ownership and redistribution of money income by means of taxes and subsidies outside the price mechanism itself are less likely to have adverse effects on efficiency and can get directly at the heart of the problem—alleviation of poverty.

_____ ## SUMMARY _____

Individual claims to net national product depend on individual incomes; thus the theory of product distribution is really the theory of income distribution. Marginal productivity theory provides the generally accepted principles of income determination and income distribution. Resource owners tend to be remunerated according to the marginal revenue products of the resources they own, except in cases where resources are purchased monopsonistically.

Incomes are unequally distributed among spending units in the United States. Income differences stem from three basic sources: (1) differences in labor resources owned, (2) differences in capital resources owned, and (3) restrictions placed on the operation of the price mechanism. With regard to the same general skill level, we call these horizontal differences in labor resources. Different individuals also own different kinds of labor, graded vertically from undifferentiated manual labor to top-level professional labor. Differences in capital resources owned result from disparities in material inheritance, fortuitous circumstances, and propensities to accumulate.

Minimum prices for a given resource often lead to reduced employment or misallocation of some units of it and hence to differences in incomes among its owners. The case of monopsony provides an exception—minimum prices of resources can offset monopsonistic exploitation of the resources involved.

If society desires to mitigate income differences, it should use as its means of attack the redistribution of resources among resource owners. Attacks made by way of minimum prices are not likely to accomplish this task. The U.S. minimum wage, for example, has tended to improve the earnings of some low-wage persons at the expense of the employment and earnings of other low-income persons. Redistribution of labor resources can be accomplished through measures designed to increase both horizontal and vertical mobility; these will, in turn, increase net national product. The tax system offers one means of bringing about some redistribution of capital resources. Estate and gift taxes will bear the major burden of effective redistribution, but these may be supplemented by personal income taxes. A negative income tax plan shows much promise as an efficient means of making direct income transfers to the poor.

These measures can be accomplished within the framework of the price system of the private enterprise economy.

APPLICATIONS

From an imposing array of income transfer programs, we have chosen two. First we draw on an experiment with the negative income tax, a method of income transfer that appears to us to hold much promise. Next we examine the minimum wage, which seems to be universally approved—except by economists!

THE NEW JERSEY-PENNSYLVANIA EXPERIMENT[10]

The U.S. Office of Economic Opportunity, knowing the central importance of incentives in the debate over welfare reform, conducted a large-scale experiment in New Jersey and Pennsylvania between 1968 and 1972 to test the effect of income guarantees on work incentives. At the time most observers expected that the negative income tax proposal would reduce work incentives to some extent. The proposal not only provides grant income, but it lowers the effective market wage rate owing to the tax that is imposed. Both of these factors should cause some reduction in the amount of work supplied. But would the drop in labor supply be large enough to outweigh other advantages of the negative income tax proposal: for example, lower administrative costs than the present welfare system imposes in the form of fewer case workers needed to ensure that recipients comply with its rules and regulations? The key question to be determined was whether or not cash allowances, which decline as hours of work increase, reduce the amount of work done by the recipients *to any significant extent*.

The experiment involved 1,216 families, 725 in the experimental group and 491 in the control group. They were headed by males aged 18 to 58, had income levels at less than 150 percent of the poverty line, and lived in four urban communities in the two states. No families headed by women or families where the spouses were not together were included. The experiment lasted three years and cost $8 million, of which one-third was spent in the form of payments to the families involved. Most of the costs were accounted for by the research effort to determine the consequences of the program. Families in the experiment were placed in different groups according to the various combinations of guaranteed income level and tax rates that yielded the average four-week payments shown in Table 17.4. By way of comparison, in Figure 17.6 we assume a single combination of cash grant and tax rate. This was done to test two auxiliary hypotheses. First, the experimenters expected that the higher the tax rates the greater the substitution effects and thus the larger the reductions in labor supply at a given level of family satisfaction. Second, for a given tax rate they antic-

---

[10]This information is drawn from Joseph A. Pechman and P. Michael Timpane, eds., *Work Incentives and Income Guarantees: The New Jersey Negative Income Tax Experiment* (Washington, D.C.: The Brookings Institution, 1975).

Table 17.4
Average Four-
Week Payments to
Continuous Husband-
Wife Families
Participating in
the New Jersey
Income Maintenance
Experiment during
the Second of the
Three Years[a]

Guarantee Level (percent)	Tax Rate (percent)		
	30	50	70
125	—	$187.28	—
100	—	123.72	$66.07
75	$103.54	44.17	34.91
50	46.23	21.66	—

[a]There is substantial variation within each of the combinations of guarantee level and tax rate owing to differences in family size and earned income.

Source: Albert Rees and Harold W. Watts, "An Overview of the Labor Supply Results," in *Work Incentives and Income Guarantees: The New Jersey Negative Income Tax Experiment,* eds. Joseph A. Pechman and P. Michael Timpane (Washington, D.C.: The Brookings Institution, 1975), 76. Reprinted by permission.

ipated that plans having the more generous payments would show the bigger drops in labor supply.[11]

Some of the results of the experiment are shown in Table 17.5 for families subjected to the 50 percent rate of tax. Overall there was a decline in hours worked of between 5 and 6 percent; the effect was negative, as predicted, but not large. This finding very generally is consistent with the concept of a backward-bending labor supply curve. But Table 17.5 gave the researchers a big surprise in the degree to which the supply response differed among ethnic groups. There was a moderate and negative effect on the labor supply of white families, a strong and positive effect on the labor supply of black families, and a small but negative effect on the labor supply of Hispanic families. To date the researchers do not have a satisfactory explanation for these striking differences. Their expectation that greater tax rates would cause a greater reduction in labor supply was reflected by the data. The results might have been different if the experiment had been permanent. Three years may have been too short a time for some families to have adjusted to work situations that they could have fitted into if the duration of the experiment had been longer.

THE MINIMUM WAGE IN PRACTICE[12]

The legal minimum wage rate, first introduced in 1938 as an integral part of the New Deal, is among the most pervasive of American social programs. With reference to Tables 17.6 and 17.7, we divide time into two eras. In the first,

---

[11]Albert Rees and Harold W. Watts, "An Overview of the Labor Supply Results," in *Work Incentives and Income Guarantees: The New Jersey Negative Income Tax Experiment,* eds. Joseph A. Pechman and P. Michael Timpane (Washington, D.C.: The Brookings Institution, 1975), 60–77. See also Harold W. Watts and Albert Rees, eds., *The New Jersey Income-Maintenance Experiment: Volume II, Labor-Supply Responses* (New York: Academic Press, 1977).

Table 17.5
Labor Supply
Response of the
Family as a Whole
Based on Alternative
Computer Models,
According to Ethnic
Group, from Data
Generated by the
New Jersey Negative
Income Tax
Experiment over
Different Periods
of Time[a]

Model and Variable	Ethnic Group[b] (percent)		
	Whites	Blacks	Spanish-Speaking
Regressions pooled from eighth quarter			
Hours	−8	−3	−6
Earnings	−12	+9	−2
Regressions calculated from averages for twelve quarters			
Hours	−16	+1	−2
Earnings	−8	+13	−28

[a]Includes male heads, wives, and all other household members 16 years of age and over in continuous husband-wife families. The estimates cover the full three years of the work incentives experiment. The tax rate is 50 percent.

[b]Estimated coefficients are jointly significant at the 1 percent level for whites and blacks and at the 5 percent level for the Spanish-speaking.

Source: Albert Rees and Harold W. Watts, "An Overview of the Labor Supply Results," in *Work Incentives and Income Guarantees: The New Jersey Negative Income Tax Experiment*, eds. Joseph A. Pechman and P. Michael Timpane (Washington, D.C.: The Brookings Institution, 1975), 85. Reprinted by permission.

1938 to 1960, the minimum wage rate increased from $0.25 to $1.00 per hour, but the number of workers in firms covered by the law expanded from only 43.4 percent of the nonagricultural work force to 53.1 percent. Industries in certain product categories were deliberately excluded from coverage, and within covered industries certain small firms were exempt unless their sales reached a given threshold. In the second era, 1961 to 1981, the minimum wage rate was increased from $1.00 to $3.35 per hour and, more important, coverage was expanded to almost 84 percent of the nonagricultural work force.

The 1938–1960 Era

The likely consequences of a legal minimum wage rate have never been a mystery to economists. Owing to the law of demand, a wage floor that is imposed above the free-market rate and enforced by legislation should, if other conditions do not change simultaneously, cause a reduction in employment in the firms that are subject to coverage. Moreover, the reduction in employment in the covered sector will be larger the greater the elasticity of labor demand. The effect of the legislation in the first era can be illustrated with the diagrams of Figure 17.7. Although the wage floor is applied to the covered sector of panel (a), the effects spill over to the uncovered sector of panel (b).

---

[12]Much of this section is based on the excellent summary of the research on the effects of minimum wages by Finis Welch, *Minimum Wages: Issues and Evidence* (Washington, D.C.: American Enterprise Institute for Public Policy Research, 1978).

**Table 17.6
The Basic Minimum
Wage and Aggregate
Coverage, 1938–1981**

Month/Year of Change in Minimum	Basic Minimum Changed to	Basic Minimum as a Percentage of Average (Straight-Time) Manufacturing Wage	Percentage of All Nonsupervisory Employees in Private, Nonagricultural Work Covered
10/38	$0.25	41.7	43.4
10/39	0.30	49.5	47.1
10/45	0.40	42.1	55.4
1/50	0.75	54.0	53.4
3/56	1.00	52.9	53.1
9/61	1.15	51.2	62.1
9/63	1.25	52.7	62.1
2/67	1.40	51.5	75.3
2/68	1.60	55.6	72.6
5/74	2.00	47.2	83.7
1/75	2.10	45.1	83.3
1/76	2.30	46.0	83.0
1/78	2.65	48.4[a]	83.8[b]
1/79	2.90	49.7[a]	83.8[b]
1/80	3.10	49.9[a]	83.8[b]
1/81	3.35	51.9[a]	83.8[b]

[a]Manufacturing wages are extrapolated, based on log-linear trend, 1965–1976. During this period wages grew 6.3 percent a year (R^2 for the trend line is 0.989).

[b]Coverage rate under 1977 amendment estimated by Employment Standards Administration. The 1977 amendment did not significantly alter the definition of covered jobs, although provisions for reductions in minimum size for necessary coverage will inflate these levels.

Source: Finis Welch, *Minimum Wages: Issues and Evidence,* Washington, D.C.: American Enterprise Institute for Public Policy Research, 1978, 3. © 1978, American Enterprise Institute for Public Policy Research. Reprinted by permission.

**Table 17.7
Estimated
Percentages of
Nonsupervisory
Workers Covered
by Minimum Wage
Laws by Major
Industry: Selected
Years, 1947–1976**

Industry	1947–1960	1961–1966	1967–1968	1976
Mining	99%	99%	99%	99%
Contract construction	44	80	98	99
Manufacturing	95	96	97	97
Transportation and public utilities	88	95	97	98
Wholesale trade	69	69	72	80
Retail trade	3	33	49	72
Finance, insurance, and real estate	74	74	74	76
Services (excluding domestic)	19	22	63	72

Source: Finis Welch, *Minimum Wages: Issues and Evidence,* Washington, D.C.: American Enterprise Institute for Public Policy Research, 1978, 4. © 1978, American Enterprise Institute for Public Policy Research. Reprinted by permission.

Panel (a) shows a relatively low-wage group of firms that are initially in equilibrium at the free-market rate w_1 with the associated quantity of labor L_c. For simplicity we assume that all labor in the market is of equal quality so that it can be represented by a single demand schedule, either D_cD_c or $D_c'D_c'$. Now

Figure 17.7   Effects of a Legally Enforced Minimum Wage on Covered and Uncovered Industries

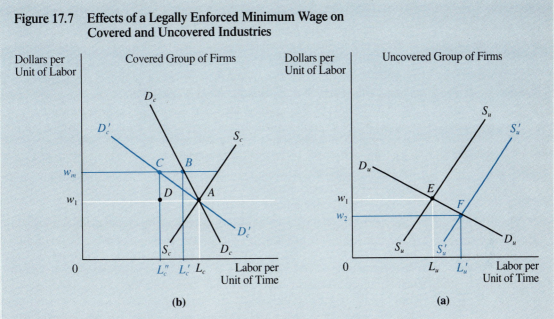

The unemployment effects of an effective minimum wage rate w_m in covered industries depend on the elasticity of demand for labor for the wage rate increase. For the less elastic demand curve D_cD_c in panel (a), the unemployment effects are least. Workers made unemployed by a minimum wage will tend to seek employment in uncovered firms and, as panel (b) shows, this increases the supply of uncovered workers and decreases their equilibrium wage rate.

assume that a legal minimum rate is established at w_m. The law guarantees the minimum to all who can get jobs at that rate, but it does not guarantee jobs. The wage rate w_m brings about a reduction in the quantity of labor hired. The economic question of importance is the extent to which employment in the covered industries falls, and this depends upon the elasticity of demand for labor. We draw two possible demand curves, in which $D'_cD'_c$ is more elastic than D_cD_c for each possible wage rate. The reduction in employment is $L_cL'_c$ if D_cD_c is the appropriate curve, but the reduction is the larger quantity $L_cL''_c$ if $D'_cD'_c$ is the demand curve.

Is demand likely to be relatively elastic for workers affected by the minimum wage? The elasticity of demand for labor generally has three major determinants. First, it tends to be greater the better the substitutes available for labor. Second, it tends to be greater the greater the elasticity of demand for the products for which the labor is employed. Third, it tends to be greater the higher the percentage of total costs that is accounted for by wages. All three suggest that labor demand curves are relatively elastic in the neighborhood of the minimum wage rate.

To test this hypothesis economists have investigated before-and-after employment in low-wage firms, industries, and regions each time the legal minimum wage has been increased and found predictable results. For example, a study of employment in sawmills and clothing plants that made men's garments and seamless hosiery in the 1950s showed that all suffered reductions in employment after a hike in the minimum wage, and the low-wage plants had the largest reductions.[13] In a county-by-county study in Florida, the minimum wage increases of the 1950s caused twice the reduction in employment in the low-wage counties as in the relatively high-wage ones. Further, the larger the difference between the legal minimum wage and the previously prevailing market wage, the greater the drop in employment.[14] Also, the low-wage firms having the largest difference between the new minimum wage and the previous free-market wage effected the more extensive substitution of capital for labor resources each time the minimum wage increased.[15]

Fast-food restaurants are probably one of the most important employers of low-wage labor—they employed 3.5 million people in 1985, of whom three-fourths were between the ages of 16 and 20. Increases in the minimum wage have predictable effects on this industry. Employment of teenagers declines in favor of older workers who are less mobile, more reliable, and need less training. Jobs and hours worked decline as positions are combined. Labor-intensive procedures also decline. When the minimum wage went to $2.65 in 1978, some hamburger restaurants continued to garnish with sliced pickles, for example, but they used fewer pickles and sliced them lengthwise. Packets of sugar and liquid dairy creamer replaced sugar pourers and cream pots. Fewer waiters and waitresses were hired as part of a trend toward self-service procedures, and chain restaurants were planning to open fewer new branches. Each observation is consistent with what one would expect from effective minimum wage rate changes in low-wage, competitive firms.[16]

We return to Figure 17.7 to consider what happens to people who must work fewer hours or take other jobs as a result of the higher minimum wage. In panel (a), the persons in group $0L_c''$ who continue to hold jobs in the covered sector after the minimum wage has been raised will gain the amount w_mCDw_1 over and above their former wage payments. But the position of the people in group $L_c''L_c$ is more difficult to determine. Basically they have three options.

First, they could continue to seek employment in the covered sector in a lottery-like queuing process for the reduced number of jobs that are now avail-

[13]J. M. Peterson, "Employment Effects of Minimum Wages, 1938–50," *Journal of Political Economy* 65 (October 1957): 412–430.

[14]Marshall R. Colberg, "Minimum Wage Effects on Florida's Economic Development," *The Journal of Law and Economics* 3 (October 1960): 106–117.

[15]David E. Kuan, "Minimum Wages, Factor Substitution, and the Marginal Producer," *Quarterly Journal of Economics* 79 (August 1965): 478–486.

[16]From *The Wall Street Journal*: Alecia Swasy, "Help Wanted: Burger Flippers, Teens Preferred," May 28, 1985; Paul Ingrassia, "Rise in Minimum Wage Spurs Some Firms to Cut Work Hours and Hiring of Youths," August 15, 1978.

able there. Searching for these jobs entails costs, and each person will have to make calculations a priori, weighing the expected search costs versus the probabilistic gains from obtaining one of the higher-paying jobs.

Second, after a period of unemployment while searching for jobs in the covered sector, they could cease their search for work and withdraw from the labor force. Persons making this decision are no longer "unemployed," as that term is defined by the U.S. Department of Labor, and are therefore not counted in the ranks of the unemployed—consequently we cannot equate the reduction in employment of $L_c'' L_c$ with a rise in unemployment as reflected in the Labor Department's official statistics. For this reason, the official statistics understate the real extent of *unemployment* that higher minimum wages cause; we can measure with confidence only the *reduction in employment*.[17]

The third alternative for people who end up in group $L_c'' L_c$ is to leave the covered sector for jobs in the uncovered sector. This is shown in panel (b). The supply of labor in the uncovered sector increases from $S_u S_u$ to $S_u' S_u'$, and the wage rate declines from w_1 to w_2. The lower wage rate gives firms an incentive to hire more labor until the marginal revenue product of labor once again is equal to the market wage rate. The new equilibrium quantity of labor is L_u'. The rise in employment in the uncovered sector, in the amount $L_u L_u'$, will be equal to the reduction in employment in the covered sector, in the amount $L_c'' L_c$, *only if no one chooses to become unemployed or to leave the labor force.*

The economic inefficiency caused by minimum wage rates is now apparent. The marginal revenue product of labor in the covered sector at w_m is greater than that in the uncovered sector at w_2. There is a strong presumption that the same relationship exists between values of marginal product. Inequality among values of marginal product means that society has suffered a reduction in real net national product. A higher value of marginal product in the covered sector has been given up in exchange for a lower value of marginal product in the uncovered sector. Society cannot achieve maximum welfare, since the allocation of labor resources in the economy is inefficient. Inefficiency will be least serious if the $L_c'' L_c$ units of labor losing jobs in the covered sector move to the uncovered sector; it will be more serious if some drop out of the labor force instead of taking jobs in the sector that is exempt. The waste will be larger in the latter case because a dropout from the labor force will yield society a negative value of marginal product.

Figure 17.7 is broadly consistent with what economists learned about the employment consequences of the minimum wage during the 1938–60 era when the coverage was relatively narrow. As economist Finis Welch put it, there was

---

[17]Jacob Mincer, "Unemployment Effects of Minimum Wages," *Journal of Political Economy* 84, pt. 2 (August 1976): S87–S104. The official statistics will overstate the rise in unemployment if people who formerly were not looking for work decide to reenter the labor force and search for jobs because they know that any job they find will pay a higher wage than previously, owing to the hike in the legal minimum. In any case, the official U.S. statistics are unreliable as a gauge of the effects of the minimum wage.

**Table 17.8
Percentage of
Employed Teenagers
Working in
Manufacturing,
Wholesale and Retail
Trade, and Services:
1930, 1940, 1955**

Industry	1930	1940	1955
Teenagers 14–17 years old			
Manufacturing	42%	26%	17%
Wholesale and retail trade	21	28	45
Services	22	36	33
Teenagers 18–19 years old			
Manufacturing	39	30	28
Wholesale and retail trade	18	26	31
Services	22	28	22

Source: Finis Welch, "Minimum Wage Legislation in the United States," *Economic Inquiry* 12 (September 1974): 298.

an enormous "run from cover."[18] This movement is apparent from Table 17.8. Teenagers, who are usually less skilled and lower paid, gradually shifted out of the covered manufacturing sector each time the legal minimum wage was increased and moved into such uncovered industries as services and the wholesale and retail trades. This movement would tend to reduce wage rates in the uncovered sector and produce the less efficient resource allocation described earlier. The minimum wage has also increased the vulnerability of teenagers to recessions. From 1954–68, teenagers were about four times more likely than adults to lose their jobs during an economic downturn. Marvin Kosters and Finis Welch concluded in 1972 that "minimum wage legislation has undoubtedly resulted in higher wages for some of the relatively low productivity workers who were able to obtain employment than these workers would have received in its absence. The cost in terms of lost employment opportunities and cyclical vulnerability of jobs, however, has apparently been borne most heavily by teenagers."[19]

A similar conclusion was drawn by Yale Brozen after studying the employment of household workers.[20] Employment in this industry usually displays a countercyclical pattern. When the economy is strong, people tend to avoid household jobs in favor of better-paying work elsewhere, but the reverse applies when the economy is in recession. This inverse correlation between economic fluctuations and employment in domestic work is broken, however, each time the legal minimum wage is raised. This is because household work has always been an uncovered activity. Domestic wage rates also tend to decline each time the legal minimum wage goes up.

[18]Welch, *Minimum Wages*, 29.

[19]Marvin Kosters and Finis Welch, "The Effects of Minimum Wages on the Distribution of Changes in Aggregate Employment," *American Economic Review* 62 (June 1972): 330.

[20]Yale Brozen, "Minimum Wage Rates and Household Workers," *The Journal of Law and Economics* 5 (October 1962): 103–109.

The 1961–1981 Era

The second era in minimum wage legislation, during which the legal minimum rate was increased and its coverage expanded sharply, can also be analyzed with the help of Figure 17.7(a). The more firms and industries covered by the legislation, the fewer "safety valves" there are available to accommodate the reduction in employment that minimum wage rate increases cause in the covered sector. For example, Finis Welch found that between 1961 and 1967 teenage employment in retail trade declined when coverage in this sector was increased from 30 percent to 58 percent.[21] But the precise extent of the fall in teenage employment, owing to post-1960 increases in the legal minimum wage rate and the expansion in its coverage, is difficult to measure. Over a half-dozen studies have been done on the post-1960 era, but they have produced diverse results as authors used different data bases and slightly different techniques. Still, several generalizations are possible.

One of the most important findings is that teenagers are not the only group adversely affected by the minimum wage.[22] Teenagers held only about one-third of the low-wage jobs in 1973. The remaining two-thirds were held by people of all ages, with those over 65 being an important group. Increases in the minimum wage rate seem to cause reduction in employment for males between the ages of 20 and 24, males over 65, and females over 20. Moreover, higher minimum wage rates also cause people who cannot find work to withdraw from the labor force rather than continue to search for the fewer jobs available in the covered sector. A reduction in full-time work tends to occur with only a partly offsetting rise in part-time work. For the economy, working hours decline relatively.

Our knowledge of the effects of minimum wage legislation has been built up gradually through a series of careful and complex empirical studies. The most obvious thing for economists to attempt to measure in covered markets is the rise in the average wage and the loss in employment in a before-and-after comparison each time the legal minimum wage is raised. But this sounds easier than it is. The increases in the legal minimum wage are usually relatively small, which makes the effects more difficult to find, especially when their consequences must be isolated from the effects of all the other forces operating simultaneously on the economy. Moreover, the *primary* effect of the higher legal minimum wage on employment loss in covered markets must be disentangled from the *secondary* or "ripple" effects. In covered markets, secondary effects include the substitution of capital for labor and the smaller number of "discouraged" low-wage workers who give up looking for work; in uncovered markets, they include the rise in employment and the fall in the average wage.[23]

---

[21]Welch, *Minimum Wages*, 32.

[22]Ibid., 34–38.

[23]John M. Peterson, *Minimum Wages: Measures and Industry Effects* (Washington, D.C., and London: The American Enterprise Institute for Public Policy Research, 1981), 18.

A series of over a dozen important studies of the economic effects of legal minimum wages published in 1980 and 1981 reinforce most of the conclusions drawn from the earlier theory. The following is a summary of their findings of the effects of U.S. minimum wage policy on employment in general and on teenagers in particular.

- The reduction in employment generally has been greater than expected in all industries, but particularly in such low-wage industries as retail trades and services, where labor demand is elastic.[24]

- Increases in the minimum wage during the 1960s raised wage rates in retail trade about 25 percent and firm labor costs as much as 5 percent and eliminated some 300,000 to 500,000 full-time jobs. Employment of 18- and 19-year-old men declined by 9 percent and of 14- to 17-year-old women by about 14 percent.[25]

- When employers must pay wage rates greater than workers' current marginal productivities, they adjust by increasing the pace of work, by letting workplace surroundings deteriorate, and by reducing fringe benefits, paid vacations and holidays, job security, and other amenities, with the result that many workers who keep their jobs lose more on net than they gain.[26]

- The minimum wage affects low-wage families neutrally across the wage structure rather than helping the lowest-wage families the most, so it is not an effective antipoverty program. It does appear to give very modest earnings increases to low-wage females at the expense of teenagers of both sexes.[27]

- Increases in the uniform minimum wage on a nationwide basis cause higher real wage rates in regions that have relatively low living costs. Paying the same wage rate for high- and low-skill workers raises the cost per unit of skill to employers and gives them incentives to substitute high- for low-skill workers. High-skill workers flow to low cost-of-living regions, such as the Sun Belt, and low-skill workers go to or remain in high cost-of-living regions, like the central cities of the Midwest and Northeast. This lessens the employment loss where the cost of living is low and makes it worse where the cost of living is high.[28]

- A 5 percent rise in the average wage of hired farm workers (a low-wage group) causes employment to fall by at least 5 percent. Higher legal min-

[24]Ibid.

[25]Belton M. Fleisher, *Minimum Wage Regulation in Retail Trade* (Washington, D.C., and London: The American Enterprise Institute for Public Policy Research, 1981).

[26]Walter J. Wessels, *Minimum Wages, Fringe Benefits, and Working Conditions* (Washington, D.C., and London: The American Enterprise Institute for Public Policy Research, 1980).

[27]Donald O. Parsons, *Poverty and the Minimum Wage* (Washington, D.C., and London: The American Enterprise Institute for Public Policy Research, 1980).

[28]Ronald J. Krumm, *The Impact of the Minimum Wage on Regional Labor Markets* (Washington, D.C., and London: The American Enterprise Institute for Public Policy Research, 1981).

imum wage rates explain 63 percent of the employment loss for seasonal farm workers in the late 1960s.

- Higher legal minimum wage rates reduce employment of teenagers relative to adults, reduce part-time as well as full-time work, and cause most of the employment loss among young workers. The negative effects are concentrated in such low-wage industries as retailing.

- The losses taken by youths who forfeit jobs exceed the gains by those who keep them. The productivities of teenagers are diverse, and more than half would earn wage rates greater than the minimum in its absence.[29]

- Higher minimum wage rates give employers incentives to reduce on-the-job training. Unless an employer captures 100 percent of the benefits of such training, a portion of its cost is usually paid for by the worker in the form of a lower wage (but not below the legally binding minimum). Thus younger workers not only get fewer job opportunities but have fewer opportunities in the jobs they do get to convert an essentially flat income stream through future years to one that is rising because of the improved productivity that on-the-job training stimulates.[30]

In 1977 the U.S. House of Representatives, during a debate over an increase in the legal minimum wage, established a Minimum Wage Study Commission consisting of seven of its members. Its agenda included such topics as the effects of higher legal minimum wage rates on employment and unemployment, poverty, and inflation and whether or not a subminimum should be established for teenagers. The commission produced a series of studies that essentially concurred with the results of the studies just described. In 1981 the commission voted (1) to reject the idea of a youth wage differential; (2) to reject a proposal to allow experimentation with differential wages for youth on a regional basis; (3) to index the legal minimum wage upward with inflation; (4) to restrict the differential wage rate then allowed for full-time students; and (5) to repeal a large number of narrowly drawn exemptions to the minimum wage law.[31]

Apparently the prospects that U.S. minimum wage policy will soon change are slight. Our nation's policy will continue to make some persons better off while at the same time making others worse off. As Finis Welch claims, "The minimum wage serves only as a tax from the poor to the poor."[32]

---

[29]Simon Rottenberg, ed., *The Economics of Legal Minimum Wages* (Washington, D.C., and London: The American Enterprise Institute for Public Policy Research, 1981).

[30]Masanori Hashimoto, *Minimum Wages and On-the-Job Training* (Washington, D.C., and London: The American Enterprise Institute for Public Policy Research, 1981).

[31]Mary Eccles and Richard B. Freeman, "What! Another Minimum Wage Study?" *American Economic Review, Papers and Proceedings* 72 (May 1982): 226–232.

[32]Welch, *Minimum Wages,* 25.

Suggested Readings

The economic literature on minimum wages is extensive. Three of the most readable and useful pieces are

Brown, Charles, Curtis Gilroy, and Andrew Kohen. "The Effect of the Minimum Wage on Employment and Unemployment." *Journal of Economic Literature* 20 (June 1982): 487–528.

Brozen, Yale. "The Effects of Statutory Minimum Wage Increases on Teen-Age Unemployment." *The Journal of Law and Economics* 12 (April 1969): 109–122.

Rottenberg, Simon, ed. *The Economics of Legal Minimum Wages.* Washington, D.C., and London: The American Enterprise Institute for Public Policy Research, 1981.

For opposing views on income redistribution by two prominent economists, see

Friedman, Milton. *Capitalism and Freedom,* Chaps. 10–12. Chicago: University of Chicago Press, 1960.

Okun, Arthur M. *Equality and Efficiency, the Big Tradeoff.* Washington, D.C.: The Brookings Institution, 1975.

Problems and Questions for Discussion

1. To what extent would you expect each of the following to contribute to the poverty problem in the United States?
   a. Monopolistic exploitation of resources
   b. Monopsonistic exploitation of resources
   c. Inequalities in labor resources owned
   d. Inequalities in capital resources owned

2. What impact would you expect licensing laws for particular occupations to have on
   a. Income distribution?
   b. Economic welfare?

3. Evaluate the income distribution consequences of the monopsony arrangements
   a. That previously existed against professional baseball players.
   b. That are used by NCAA-member schools to hold down wages of college athletes (as described in Problem 2 of Chapter 13).

4. In 1979, a strike by California lettuce workers apparently raised the price of lettuce by 400 percent and caused the profits of lettuce growers to nearly double. (Harry Bernstein, "Lettuce Strike Increased Grower Profits, Study Finds," *Los Angeles Times,* January 15, 1980.) Assume that the strike increased the wage rate of lettuce workers. With just these facts, analyze the likelihood that the strike improved the total wages received by lettuce workers.

5. Price controls and rationing by the government are often suggested as means of protecting the interests of the poor. Discuss the probable effects of this type of approach to redistribution of the economy's output on the following:
   a. The efficiency of consumption (*Hint:* Consider a two-good, two-person case in which one person is initially rich and the other is initially poor.)

    b. The efficiency of production

    c. The efficiency of the product mix in the economy

*6. Write a short essay on antipoverty programs, comparing a negative income tax with a uniform national minimum wage rate on the following points:

    a. Effectiveness in raising the earnings of low-income persons and in achieving the programs' goals

    b. How they look to a low-wage worker (put yourself in the shoes of such a worker, assuming that he or she is not sophisticated in economic analysis)

*7. Can increases in a country's legal minimum wage rate increase

    a. Its gross national product?

    b. The productivity of its labor force?

    c. The productivity of its stock of capital?

*8. How would you expect the members of Congress from states in each of the following areas of the United States to vote on a bill to make the minimum wage universal and to increase the rate? (Give your reasons in each case.)

    a. High-wage states

    b. Low-wage states

    c. Agriculturally oriented states

    d. Smokestack or conventional industrialized states

    e. High-tech states

*9. Available evidence suggests that an increase in the national minimum wage rate tends to decrease teenage employment and increase enrollments in high schools, colleges, and universities. (J. Peter Mattila, ''The Impact of Minimum Wages on Teenage Schooling and on the Part-Time/Full-Time Employment of Youths,'' in Simon Rottenberg, ed., *The Economics of Legal Minimum Wages*.) How would each of the following be affected by such an increase? (Give your reasons in each case.)

    a. The median ability of the entering college and university freshman class

    b. Employment in covered and uncovered industries

    c. Part-time employment in covered and uncovered industries

*10. Declining birthrates in the 1960s and 1970s caused fewer people to enter the job market in the 1980s even though the demand for labor was rising. ''Shortages'' of entry-level workers were expected to continue through the 1990s. Industries hardest hit were retailing, businesses using clerical skills, and hotels and restaurants—especially fast-food and convenience operations. (Martha Brannigan, ''A Shortage of Youths Brings Wide Changes to the Labor Market,'' *The Wall Street Journal,* September 2, 1986.)

    a. Explain what is probably meant, under these circumstances, by ''shortages.''

    b. ''The days of minimum wages are behind us forever,'' according to the manager of the branch of a nationwide chain of hotels in a fast-growing southern city, where entry-level wages increased over 35 percent in three years. Use supply and demand analysis to explain the effect of entry-level "shortages" in labor markets covered by legal minimum wage rates.

c.   Explain the probable effect of the "shortage" of entry-level labor on the distribution of income.

---

*Denotes an application-oriented problem.

Part Six

HOW THE PIECES FIT TOGETHER

W<small>E</small> try to bring the many facets of microeconomics together in Part Six. It contains little that is new, but it provides a focus and a consistent logical framework that will help us understand what microeconomics is all about. It is especially important that the concepts of *welfare* and general *equilibrium* be kept separate. Maximum welfare is the most desirable state of affairs that we can define objectively, and the conditions that will yield such a state are independent of the type of economic system that may exist. General equilibrium is the state of affairs that a price system will yield, and it may or may not be a maximum welfare situation. A major part of our task is to examine the price system in order to determine how well it performs in a welfare sense.

WELFARE AND EQUILIBRIUM

In this chapter we first review what is involved in the concepts of welfare and equilibrium. Then we examine the conditions that must be met in order to maximize welfare in the sense of Pareto optimality. Finally we consider the conditions required for general equilibrium to exist in a private enterprise economic system, and the implications of these conditions for economic welfare.

THE CONCEPTS OF WELFARE AND EQUILIBRIUM _____

Welfare and equilibrium are different concepts, although they are frequently confused with each other. We have defined *welfare* as the state of well-being of the persons comprising an economic system. We have defined **equilibrium** as a state of rest, a position from which there is either no incentive or no opportunity to move. We shall look at some of the principal aspects of each of these concepts.

equilibrium
A state of rest from which there is either no incentive or no opportunity to move.

Welfare

Most economic analysis is concerned with the welfare aspects of economic activity—how to achieve maximum or optimum welfare for the population in the economic system. An objective definition of optimum welfare constitutes a major problem. As we noted in Chapter 1, the concept is straightforward where only one person is being considered and is synonymous with that person's well-being. But when more than one individual is at issue, an objective definition of a unique optimum welfare position for the group as a whole becomes impossible, since such a definition would require interpersonal comparisons of satisfaction. The Pareto optimal situation, in which no one can be made better off without making someone else worse off, is the best solution that we can attain. There is no unique Pareto optimal situation for a group. A number of alternative such situations may exist, and we have no way of determining which is the "optimum" optimum.

Equilibrium

Equilibrium concepts are important, not because equilibrium positions are ever in fact attained but because these concepts show us the direction in which economic processes move. When equilibrium positions are *stable*—as they have been assumed to be throughout this book—economic units in disequilibrium move toward equilibrium positions. Even as they are doing so, however, changes in consumers' preference patterns, resource supplies, and technology alter the equilibrium positions themselves, thus redirecting the movements that are occurring. If equilibrium positions are *unstable*, disturbances will cause economic units to move farther away from rather than toward such positions.

Partial Equilibrium   A large part of the analytical structure that we have built

partial equilibrium
Equilibrium of an indi-
vidual unit and/or sub-
section of the economy
with respect to given data
or conditions external to
that unit or subsection.

up is called **partial equilibrium** analysis. It has been concerned with the movements of individual economic units toward equilibrium positions in response to
the given economic conditions confronting them. Thus the consumer, with given
tastes and preferences, is confronted with a given income and with given prices
of goods and services. Each consumer adjusts his or her purchases accordingly
to move toward equilibrium. The business firm—faced with given product demand situations, a given state of technology, and given resource supply situations—moves toward an equilibrium adjustment. The resource owner possesses
given quantities of resources to place in employment, for which there are given
alternative employment possibilities and resource price offers. The equilibrium
adjustment is made on the basis of the given data. The conditions of demand
and of cost in a particular industry engender profits or losses, and these motivate
the entry of new firms (if entry is possible) or the exit of existing firms, thus
leading toward equilibrium for that industry. Changes in the given data facing
economic units and industries alter the positions of equilibrium that each is
attempting to reach and motivate movements toward the new positions.

Partial equilibrium is especially suitable for the analysis of two types of
problems, both of which we have met time and again throughout the book.
Problems of the first type are those arising from economic disturbances that are
not of sufficient magnitude to reach far beyond the confines of a given industry
or sector of the economy. Problems of the second type are concerned with the
first-order effects of an economic disturbance of any kind.

As an illustration of the first kind of problem, suppose that the production
workers of a small manufacturer of plastic products go on strike. Suppose further
that the plant is located in a large city and that the workers are fairly well
dispersed among the residential areas there. The effects of the strike will be
limited largely to the company and the employees concerned. Partial equilibrium
analysis will provide the relevant answers to most of the economic problems
arising from the strike.

As an example of the second type of problem, suppose that a rearmament
program increases the demand for steel suddenly and substantially. Partial equilibrium analysis will provide answers to the first-order effects on the steel industry—what happens to its prices, output, profits, demand for resources, resource prices, and its resource employment levels. However, the first-order
effects by no means end the repercussions from the initial disturbance.

General Equilibrium   As individual economic units and industries seek equilibrium adjustments to what appear to be given facts their total group actions
change the facts that they face. If some units were in equilibrium and others
were not, those in disequilibrium would move toward equilibrium. Their activ-

general equilibrium
Simultaneous equilibrium
of all individual eco-
nomic units and subsec-
tions of the economy.

ities would change the facts faced by the units in equilibrium and would throw
the latter into disequilibrium. **General equilibrium** for the entire economy could
exist only if all economic units were to achieve simultaneous partial, or particular, equilibrium adjustments. The concept of general equilibrium stresses the

interdependence of all economic units and of all segments of the economy with one another.

A hard-and-fast line between partial equilibrium analysis and general equilibrium analysis is difficult to draw. Instead of establishing a dichotomy, it will be preferable to think of moving along a continuum from partial to general equilibrium, or from first-order effects of a disturbance into second-, third-, and higher-order effects. For example, in discussing pricing and output under market conditions of pure competition, we were concerned first with partial equilibrium, or equilibrium of the individual firm. Next we extended the analysis to an entire industry and observed the impact of individual firm actions on one another. Finally we observed how productive capacity is organized in a purely competitive private enterprise economy according to consumers' tastes and preferences. This series of topics represents progressive movement from the application of partial equilibrium analysis to that of general equilibrium analysis.

General equilibrium theory provides the analytical tools for accomplishing two objectives: (1) from the standpoint of pure theory, it provides the means of viewing the economic system in its entirety—the means of seeing what holds it together, what makes it work, and how it operates; and (2) it permits the determination of the second-, third-, and higher-order effects of an economic disturbance (this objective is really an application of the first one). When the impact of an economic disturbance is of sufficient magnitude to have repercussions throughout most of the economy, general equilibrium analysis provides the more relevant answers regarding its ultimate effects. First comes the big splash from the disturbance—partial equilibrium analysis handles this. But waves and then ripples are set up from it, affecting one another and affecting the area of the splash. The ripples run farther and farther out, becoming smaller and smaller until eventually they dwindle away. The tools of general equilibrium are required for analysis of the entire series of readjustments.

Suppose that the higher-order repercussions from the increase in demand for steel are to be examined. The first-order, or partial, equilibrium effects are higher prices, greater outputs with given facilities, larger profits, and higher payments to the owners of resources used in making steel. These effects generate additional disturbances. Higher incomes for the resource owners increase demand for other products, setting off disturbances and adjustments in other industries. Demands also increase for steel substitutes, generating another series of disturbances and adjustments. Productive capacity will be diverted from other activities toward the making of steel. Eventually effects will be felt over the entire economy. If the full impact of such a disturbance is to be determined, general equilibrium analysis must provide the tools to do so.

Since general equilibrium analysis covers the interrelationships among all parts of the economy, it necessarily becomes exceedingly complex. There are two principal variants of it. In the first one, following Léon Walras, most economists find it convenient to discuss general equilibrium in mathematical terms. The interdependence of economic units is shown through a system of simultaneous equations relating the many economic variables to one another. Solving the system of equations establishes those values of the variables that are consistent with general equilibrium for the economic system. The Walrasian version of general equilibrium provides the essential theoretical apparatus for understanding the interrelationships of the various sectors of the economy.

The second variant of general equilibrium analysis is Wassily W. Leontief's input-output analysis.[1] The input-output approach is an empirical descendant of the abstract Walrasian approach. It divides the economy into a number of sectors or industries, including households and the government as "industries" of final demand. Each industry is viewed as selling its output to others; these outputs become inputs for the purchasing industries. Likewise, each industry is viewed as a purchaser of the outputs of other industries. Thus the interdependence of each industry on the others is established. Statistical data gathered around the basic framework of the system provide an informative and useful picture of the interindustry flows of goods, services, and resources. The input-output approach has been used extensively by municipalities, states, and regions for economic development purposes.

The attainment of general equilibrium in an economic system does not imply that Pareto optimality is also attained. A price system tends to move the economy toward general equilibrium. However, unless pure competition exists in both product and resource markets, and unless there are no externalities occurring, Pareto optimality will not follow.

THE CONDITIONS OF OPTIMUM WELFARE

Optimum welfare conditions in an economy are usually grouped into three sets. The first consists of the conditions leading to maximum consumer welfare when supplies of goods and services are fixed. The second consists of the conditions of maximum efficiency in production, assuming that resource supplies are fixed. In the third, consumer welfare and maximum productive efficiency are brought together to determine conditions under which the outputs of different goods and services are optimal.

Maximum Consumer Welfare: Fixed Supplies

The conditions of maximum consumer welfare with fixed supplies of goods and services per time unit are illustrated in the two-good, two-person model of Figure 18.1. If the distribution of goods X and Y between the two consumers H and J is initially off the contract curve at some point such as D, exchanges can be made that will increase the welfare of either without decreasing that of the other. A movement from distribution D to distribution E increases the welfare of both. Once a contract curve distribution is achieved, any further exchanges can benefit only one consumer at the expense of the other. Any point on the contract curve

---

[1]For an excellent survey and analysis of this approach, see Robert Dorfman, "The Nature and Significance of Input-Output," *Review of Economics and Statistics* 36 (May 1954): 121–133.

**Figure 18.1
Optimum Consumer
Welfare: Fixed
Supplies**

Pareto optimality in the
distribution of fixed
supplies of goods among
consumers requires that
the *MRS* between any
pair of such goods for
one consumer be the
same as that for any
other consumer. These
conditions occur at point
E or at any other point
on the contract curve.

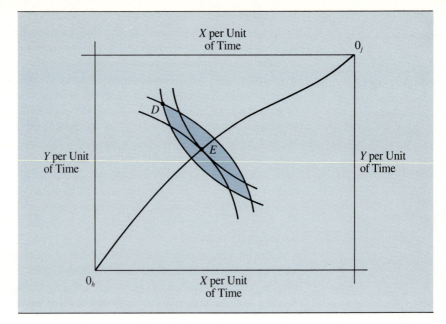

represents a Pareto optimal distribution of *X* and *Y* between the two consumers.
Each such point is defined by the condition that

(18.1)
$$MRS^h_{xy} = MRS^j_{xy}.$$

This condition can be extended to as many goods and services and as many
consumers as there are in the economy.

    Sometimes there are externalities involved in the consumption of a good or
service. An **externality in consumption** occurs if the consumption of a good
by someone else affects the level of satisfaction attained by any given consumer.
Suppose, for example, that *H* and *J* are neighbors, that *H* increases her stereo
capacity, and that *J*, whose musical tastes parallel those of *H*, can now hear
and enjoy the music she plays. *J* receives an external benefit from *H*'s consumption—his set of indifference curves between music and other goods and
services is shifted inward toward the origin of his indifference map. On the
other hand, the externality could have operated in the opposite direction: the
music played by *H* could have annoyed *J*, interfering with his sleep and shifting
his set of indifference curves between music and other goods and services outward from the origin of his indifference map.[2]

    When an externality in consumption occurs, we can no longer be sure that
a point on the contract curve, such as *E* in Figure 18.2, is Pareto optimal.
Suppose that *J*'s satisfaction is enhanced by *H*'s increased purchase of music

**externalities in
consumption**
The effects that con-
sumption of an item by
one consumer may have
on the welfare of others.

_____

[2]The preference function of *J* takes the form $U_j = f(x_j, y_j, x_h)$, in which x_j and y_j represent *J*'s
consumption of two goods, *X* and *Y*, and x_h represents *H*'s consumption of *X*.

**Figure 18.2
Externalities in
Consumption**

External benefits of H's
consumption of music
to J may mean that point
E on the contract curve
is not Pareto optimal.
An increase in H's
consumption of music
to point F along U_h
increases J's satisfaction
level for all combinations
of music and other goods
that he consumes
independently, pulling his
indifference curves
inward toward his origin
so that U_j' is equivalent
to his former U_j. At F
the satisfaction level of J
has increased while that
of H has not decreased.
The combined welfare of
the two is higher.

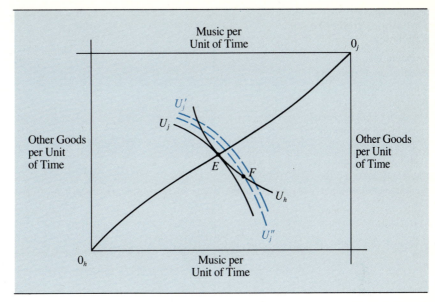

via an expansion of stereo capacity. An exchange of other goods and services
for music that moves the consumers from distribution E to distribution F would
not change H's level of satisfaction. Suppose that the external benefits that J
receives from H's increased consumption of music shift J's indifference curves
toward origin 0_j so that the satisfaction level formerly represented by U_j is now
represented by U_j'. At point F, J will be at a higher level of satisfaction, represented by U_j'', than before; since H's satisfaction has not been lessened, the
welfare of the two consumers combined is greater than it was at point E.

Maximum Efficiency in Production: Given Resource Supplies

We turn now to the production side of the picture, holding resource supplies
constant.

The Conditions of Efficiency: No Externalities   Maximum efficiency in production refers to Pareto optimality in production processes. Given the supplies
of resources available, these must be allocated among the production of goods
and services in such a way that the production of any one good cannot be
increased unless the production of another is decreased.

The conditions of efficiency are illustrated in the two-resource, two-product
model of Figure 18.3. Fixed supplies of resources A and B are used in the
production of products X and Y. Any distribution of resources between the two
products that lies on the contract curve, such as that at E, is more efficient than
is any distribution not on that curve, such as that at N. Given any initial distribution such as N, the output of either product can be increased with no sacrifice
of the other. It is also possible to increase the outputs of both products by
allocating more A and less B to the output of X and less A and more B to the

**Figure 18.3
Optimum Productive
Efficiency**

A Pareto optimal
distribution of resources
among products is
represented by point E, at
which the $MRTS_{ab}$ is the
same in the production
of both products. All
such points of Pareto
optimality trace out the
contract curve.

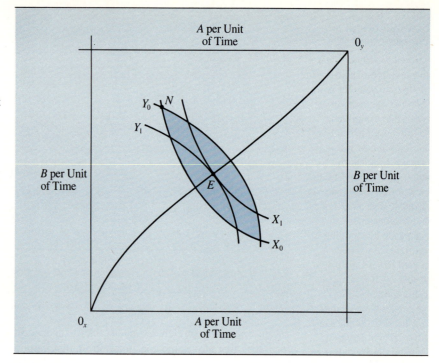

output of Y, thus moving from N to E. With any distribution such as E, neither product's output can be increased unless some of the other is sacrificed. Any point on the contract curve represents a maximum efficiency allocation of resources. The condition that determines any such point is that

$$(18.2) \qquad \text{MRTS}_{ab}^{x} = MRTS_{ab}^{y}.$$

These conditions can be expanded to include as many resources and as many goods and services as exist in the economy.

The infinite number of efficiently produced combinations of X and Y shown by the contract curve of Figure 18.3 are also shown by the transformation curve of Figure 18.4. For every combination of X and Y on the transformation curve, resources are allocated to each product in the optimal combinations. The transformation curve is often appropriately called the production possibilities curve. Its slope at any point measures the rate at which one product must be given up to obtain an additional unit of the other, that is, the MRT_{xy}.

**externalities in
production**
The effects that the production of one product may have on the production possibilities of others.

The Effects of Externalities   If **externalities in production** occur in the production of a good, the contract curve may no longer show the conditions of maximum efficiency. Congested facilities represent a very common type of externality. Suppose, for example, that highways, along with other resources, are used by the producers of wheat and also by the producers of automobiles for getting their commodities to consumers. Initially these two groups of users

**Figure 18.4
A Transformation
Curve**

Transformation curve *AB*
shows all combinations
of two products that can
be produced Pareto
optimally with given
resource supplies and
a constant state of
technology. Data for the
curve would come from a
contract curve like that in
Figure 18.3.

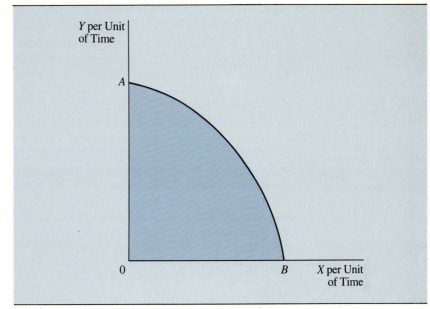

**Figure 18.5
Externalities in
Production**

If there are externalities
in production, a Pareto
optimum distribution of
fixed amounts of
resources among
production facilities may
not occur on the contract
curve. At *E* the *MRTS*
between other resources
and highway facilities is
the same for wheat
producers and automobile
producers. A decrease in
use of highways by
wheat producers that
moves them to *F*
increases the productivity
of automobile producers,
so that isoquant a_1' now
represents the same
number of automobiles as
a_1 did formerly. Thus *F*
shows more autos than *E*
and the same amount of
wheat.

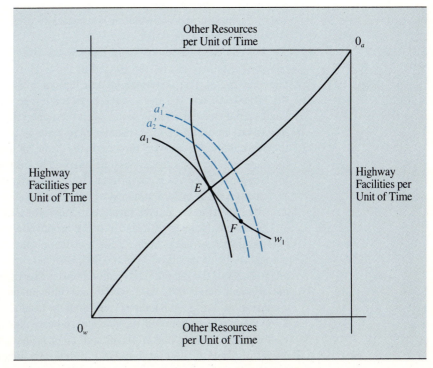

cause the highways to be congested to the extent that transportation delays result. In Figure 18.5, the marginal rate of technical substitution between highway facilities and other resources is the same for producers of wheat and producers of automobiles at point E. But this allocation of resources is not necessarily optimal. If highway congestion exists at E, a reduction in the use of the highways by firms in one industry will increase the productivity of highway facilities for those in the other.

Suppose that wheat producers reduce their use of the highways but maintain their output level at w_1 by increasing their use of alternative forms of noncongested transport, thus moving from point E to point F. This move shifts the set of isoquants of automobile producers toward the 0_a origin, and a_1 units of automobiles is now shown by the dashed line a_1'. At point F automobile production will be at a_2', a higher level than before. At the same time there will have been no change in total wheat production. The efficiency of production has been increased by the resource exchange.

Optimal Outputs of Goods and Services

We have not yet determined which of the combinations of products represented by a transformation curve yield optimal welfare to consumers. If we assume that there are no externalities of production, the transformation curve of Figure 18.6 shows the combinations of X and Y that resources A and B can produce when those resources are used efficiently—that is, when $MRTS_{ab}^x = MRTS_{ab}^y$ for each combination. The slope of the transformation curve at any point, the MRT_{xy}, shows the rate at which it is technically possible to transform Y into X at that combination of goods.

For any combination of X and Y on the transformation curve, an Edgeworth box for consumers can be constructed to show the optimal distributions of supplies making up that combination. For the combination at 0_{j1} in Figure 18.6, the Edgeworth box $0_h y_1 0_{j1} x_1$ is the appropriate one for a two-consumer, two-good model; for the combination at 0_{j2}, the appropriate box is $0_h y_2 0_{j2} x_2$. Note that since the origin 0_h for consumer H remains in a fixed position, H's indifference curves, drawn with respect to the X and Y axes of the transformation diagram, are the same for all possible boxes. The origin of the indifference map for consumer J, however, is different for each different combination of X and Y shown on the transformation curve and for each different box. Consequently J's set of indifference curves must be redrawn for each different box.

If the combination of X and Y being produced were 0_{j1}, would this be the optimal output of each product? Since it lies on the transformation curve, the outputs are being produced with maximum efficiency; moreover, any distribution (such as K) of the output combination between consumers H and J that lies on the contract curve $0_h 0_{j1}$ is a welfare-maximizing distribution of the specific combination. Still, combination 0_{j1} of product outputs, together with distribution K of the products between the two consumers, does not result in maximum welfare. The slope of line $M_1 N_1$ through point K and tangent to the indifference curves of H and J measures the MRS_{xy} for both consumers at point K: it indicates

**Figure 18.6
The Full Conditions
of Maximum Welfare**

Output levels x_1 and y_1 are not the optimal mix for the economy even though produced and distributed efficiently. At K, $MRT_{xy} < MRS_{xy}$ for consumers H and J; consumers are willing to give up more Y to obtain additional units of X than is required in production processes. More X and less Y will be produced until the mix is y_2 and x_2. At distribution L, $MRT_{xy} = MRS_{xy}$ for the consumers.

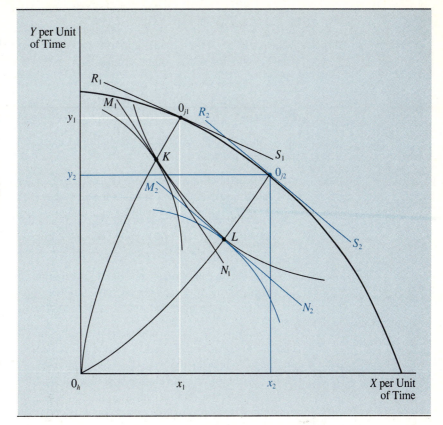

the rate at which *both* consumers would be willing to give up Y for X. The slope of R_1S_1 through point 0_{j1}, tangent to the transformation curve, measures the MRT_{xy} (the rate at which it is technically necessary to give up Y to produce more X). Since $MRS_{xy} > MRT_{xy}$ (that is, consumers are willing to give up more Y to obtain an additional unit of X than is necessary in the production processes), the welfare of both consumers can be increased by increasing the output of X and decreasing that of Y.

The conditions for optimum welfare in terms of the output levels of X and Y and the distribution of that output between consumers H and J are that

(18.3) $$MRS_{xy} = MRT_{xy}.$$

Consider combination 0_{j2} and distribution L. The lines M_2N_2 and R_2S_2 are parallel, indicating that $MRS_{xy} = MRT_{xy}$; therefore, this is an optimum welfare output combination and distribution. A small movement away from L or away from 0_{j2} will decrease the welfare of at least one of the consumers.

The optimum welfare combination of outputs and distribution of product among consumers is not a unique one, however. There may be an infinite number of output combination–product distribution possibilities at which

$MRS_{xy} = MRT_{xy}$. For output combination 0_{j1}, even though at distribution K the $MRS_{xy} \neq MRT_{xy}$, there may be other distributions on contract curve $0_h 0_{j1}$ at which $MRS_{xy} = MRT_{xy}$, although it is not certain that there are. The same thing can be said for other output combinations represented by the transformation curve.

Summary of Optimum Welfare Conditions

In summary, then, for Pareto optimality to exist in an economic system three conditions must be met:

1. The distribution of product outputs must be such that the marginal rate of substitution of any one product for any other is the same for all consumers.

2. The allocation of resources must be such that the marginal rate of technical substitution of any one resource for any other is the same in the production of all commodities for which those resources can be used.

3. The outputs of product and their distribution among consumers must be such that the marginal rate of substitution of any one product for any other is equal to the marginal rate of transformation of the products.

The conditions of Pareto optimality leave us uninformed about which of the optimal distributions of product among consumers is the "optimum" optimum and about which of the optimal combinations of product output is the "optimum" optimum. We can eliminate those distributions of any output combination at which marginal rates of substitution are not equal to the corresponding marginal rates of transformation. After these deletions, however, we may still have a great many alternative possibilities.

PRIVATE ENTERPRISE AND GENERAL EQUILIBRIUM

Will a private enterprise economic system guided and directed by the price mechanism move toward optimum welfare positions as it moves toward general equilibrium positions? The optimum welfare conditions of the preceding subsection apply to any kind of economic system—socialist, private enterprise, or other. To evaluate the performance of a private enterprise system, then, it is necessary to examine the conditions of the equilibrium toward which it moves in order to determine whether these coincide with, or at least approach, the conditions of optimum welfare. Toward this end we draw on, summarize, and extend the principles developed throughout the book.

Consumer Equilibrium: Fixed Supplies

Consider first the problem of consumers' choice. Assume that the supplies of goods and services are fixed—they automatically come into being on the first of each month. The distribution among consumers may be any one, but it will not vary from one month to another. Consumers' preference patterns are fixed; a monetary system exists; and the price pattern is initially random. Each good or service is in the hands of many individuals, with the result that pure competition will exist in the event that exchange occurs. What happens at this point if individuals are free to buy and sell, that is, to exchange? Each consumer will seek to maximize satisfaction.

If for two goods—X and Y, priced initially at p_x and p_y—a consumer finds that $MRS_{xy} \neq p_x/p_y$, that individual will want to engage in exchange. Any consumer for whom $MRS_{xy} > p_x/p_y$ will want to sell Y and buy X in order to move to higher indifference curves; any consumer for whom $MRS_{xy} < p_x/p_y$ will want to sell X and purchase Y in order to move to higher indifference curves.

At the initial price pattern the supplies of some items are likely to be exhausted before all consumers get as much as they desire. The prices of these items will rise, reducing the quantities that consumers want relative to the quantities of other goods. Prices will move to those levels at which consumers are just willing to ration themselves to the entire quantities available per month.

The supplies of other goods may be overabundant at their initial price levels. To reduce the quantities that they have on hand, those who hold surpluses will lower the asking prices. Prices will fall to the levels at which consumers are just willing to take the entire quantities available per month.

General equilibrium exists when goods and services are so priced that each consumer gets the quantity of each that he or she desires relative to the quantities of others and when there is neither a shortage nor a surplus of any item. Any one consumer, H, takes a combination of X and Y such that $MRS_{xy}^h = p_x/p_y$. Any other consumer, J, also takes a combination at which $MRS_{xy}^j = p_x/p_y$. Since p_x/p_y is the same for all consumers, it follows that

(18.1)
$$MRS_{xy}^h = MRS_{xy}^j.$$

All consumers are on the contract curve. Thus under conditions of pure competition and in the absence of externalities, the conditions of general equilibrium with fixed supplies coincide with the conditions of optimum welfare with fixed supplies.

Producer Equilibrium: Given Resource Supplies

We turn now to the operation of the price mechanism in organizing production. To facilitate the discussion, several assumptions will be useful. We shall assume that resource supplies are fixed quantities per month and that their initial prices are random. The range of production techniques is given. We shall start by considering the organization of production in terms of the purely competitive model. Then we shall modify the analysis to take monopoly and monopsony into account.

Pure Competition Suppose that the fixed supplies consumers receive are being produced by firms operating in purely competitive industries and that these firms seek to maximize their profits. Confronted with an initial set of resource prices, each firm attempts to acquire those quantities of different resources at which the marginal revenue product of each resource is equal to its marginal resource cost.

If at the initial set of resource prices firms find that they are not able to obtain enough of some resources to bring their marginal revenue products into line with their respective marginal resource costs, shortages will occur. The prices of these resources will rise, inducing firms to attempt to substitute other resources for them. Prices will reach equilibrium levels when each firm is just able to obtain the quantities that it desires.

Suppose there are other resources that will not be fully employed when at the initial prices every firm takes the quantities at which their marginal revenue products equal their marginal resource costs. Surpluses of these resources will cause those who own them to cut the prices at which they are offered to induce firms to substitute them for now relatively more expensive resources. The prices will be in equilibrium when firms are just willing to absorb the entire quantities placed on the market.

General equilibrium exists when each resource is priced so that neither a surplus nor a shortage exists and when each firm is taking that quantity of each resource at which its marginal revenue product is equal to its marginal resource cost. These conditions, together with pure competition in both resource and product markets, lead to important additional consequences, as we describe next.

Since pure competition exists, the value of marginal product of each resource will be equal to the resource price. For any given resource—say, A—$MRP_a = MRC_a$ means also that $VMP_a = p_a$, because for any product—say, X—that A assists in producing, $MR_x = p_x$, and for any firm purchasing A, $MRC_a = p_a$.

When firms using several common resources to produce several products employ those resources in profit-maximizing quantities, they will also be employing them efficiently from a Pareto optimal point of view. Suppose that two resources, A and B, are employed by firms producing X and Y. Any firm in industry X employs those quantities of the resources at which

$$MPP_{ax} \times p_x = MRC_a = p_a \quad \text{and} \quad MPP_{bx} \times p_x = MRC_b = p_b.$$

$$\text{Thus} \quad \frac{MPP_{ax}}{p_a} = \frac{1}{p_x} \quad \text{and} \quad \frac{MPP_{bx}}{p_b} = \frac{1}{p_x}; \quad \text{therefore,}$$

$$\frac{MPP_{ax}}{p_a} = \frac{MPP_{bx}}{p_b} \quad \text{and} \quad \frac{MPP_{ax}}{MPP_{bx}} = \frac{p_a}{p_b}, \quad \text{or} \quad MRTS_{ab}^x = \frac{p_a}{p_b}.$$

Similarly we can show that $MRTS_{ab}^y = \dfrac{p_a}{p_b}$. Therefore,

(18.2)
$$MRTS_{ab}^x = MRTS_{ab}^y,$$

which is the condition for an efficient allocation of any two resources between any two products.

Monopoly and Monopsony Monopoly in the sale of products will not deter the price system from allocating resources among different products so that they are used efficiently in the production of each, but some degree of monopsony will act as a deterrent. If monopoly exists in the sale of products X and Y but the firms in both industries purchase resources A and B competitively, we can show that when A and B are purchased in each industry in a manner such that the marginal revenue products of the resources equal their respective resource prices, then $MRTS^x_{ab} = MRTS^y_{ab}$. However, if some degree of monopsony exists in the purchase of A and B, then

$$MPP_{ax} \times MR_x = MRC_{ax} \text{ and } MPP_{bx} \times MR_x = MRC_{bx}.$$

$$\text{Therefore, } \frac{MPP_{ax}}{MRC_{ax}} = \frac{MPP_{bx}}{MRC_{bx}} \quad \text{and} \quad \frac{MPP_{ax}}{MPP_{bx}} = \frac{MRC_{ax}}{MRC_{bx}}, \text{ or}$$

$$MRTS^x_{ab} = \frac{MRC_{ax}}{MRC_{bx}}. \quad \text{Similarly we can show that} \quad MRTS^y_{ab} = \frac{MRC_{ay}}{MRC_{by}}.$$

The firm producing X must pay the same price for resource A as the firm producing Y.[3] But if the elasticity of the supply of A to the firm making X differs from that of A to the firm making Y, at whatever the supply price of A to both firms may be, then $MRC_{ax} \neq MRC_{ay}$; similarly, under the same set of circumstances $MRC_{bx} \neq MRC_{by}$. Consequently it is not necessary that

(18.2)
$$MRTS^x_{ab} = MRTS^y_{ab},$$

and the price system will not necessarily bring about optimum efficiency in the use of the resources in the two industries.

Product Output Levels: Given Resource Supplies

In this subsection we shall continue to trace the implications of the general equilibrium results brought about by the price mechanism. Equilibrium exists when (1) price levels of goods and services are such that there are no shortages and no surpluses, (2) price levels of resources are such that there are no shortages and no surpluses, and (3) firms purchase those quantities of different resources at which their marginal revenue products equal their respective marginal resource costs. Again we shall consider purely competitive markets first and then turn to the effects of monopoly and monopsony.

---

[3]Rather than assume pure monopsony, in which resource A would be specialized to one firm only, we assume a degree of monopsony in which units of the resource are mobile among a few firms, any one of which buys a sufficient proportion of the total available supply to have an effect on the resource price.

Pure Competition   Under conditions of pure competition in both product and resource markets, and in the absence of externalities, the allocation of resources and the output levels of product determined by the price system will maximize welfare.

Consider first the allocation of resources between any two products, X and Y. When firms of industry X are using two resources, A and B, and are maximizing profits, then for each firm

$$\frac{MPP_{ax}}{p_a} = \frac{MPP_{bx}}{p_b} = \frac{1}{MC_x} = \frac{1}{p_x}, \quad \text{or} \quad MC_x = p_x.$$

Similarly, for firms in industry Y,

$$\frac{MPP_{ay}}{p_a} = \frac{MPP_{by}}{p_b} = \frac{1}{MC_y} = \frac{1}{p_y}, \quad \text{or} \quad MC_y = p_y.$$

At whatever combination of X and Y is being produced, the MRT_{xy} is the measure of the amount of Y that must be given up by the economic system to produce an additional unit of X; MRT_{xy} can be expressed as $\Delta y / \Delta x$.

Since resources are used efficiently in the production of both X and Y, the cost of giving up Δy of Y must equal the cost of adding Δx of X to the economy's output;[4] that is,

$$\Delta y \times MC_y = \Delta x \times MC_x, \quad \text{and} \quad \frac{\Delta y}{\Delta x} = \frac{MC_x}{MC_y}.$$

Since the price system leads to a product output combination at which

$$MC_x = p_x \text{ and } MC_y = p_y, \quad \text{then} \quad MRT_{xy} = \frac{\Delta y}{\Delta x} = \frac{MC_x}{MC_y} = \frac{p_x}{p_y}.$$

We can now put the pieces together. The price system induces consumers to establish a price ratio for the supplies of any two goods, X and Y, such that for each consumer

$$MRS_{xy} = \frac{p_x}{p_y}.$$

These prices in turn bring about an allocation of resources between the two goods such that

$$MC_x = p_x \text{ and } MC_y = p_y, \text{ or}$$

$$\frac{MC_x}{MC_y} = \frac{p_x}{p_y}.$$

---

[4]This relationship must obtain since the identical quantities of resources released in giving up Δy of Y are used to produce Δx of X.

The ratio MC_x/MC_y in turn is the measure of the MRT_{xy}; thus the price system leads to general equilibrium outputs of X and Y such that

(18.3)
$$MRS_{xy} = MRT_{xy}.$$

This condition for general equilibrium is also the condition for a set of optimum outputs of X and Y.

An output combination on the transformation curve such that $MRS_{xy} \neq MRT_{xy}$ simply means that $MC_x \neq p_x$ and/or $MC_y \neq p_y$. For example, if $MRS_{xy} > MRT_{xy}$, as is the case at point K in Figure 18.6, it follows that $MC_x < p_x$ and $MC_y > p_y$. The price system will bring about an expansion in the output of X and a reduction in the output of Y. These changes will decrease MRS_{xy}, causing p_x to drop and p_y to rise. At the same time they will cause MRT_{xy} to rise, increasing MC_x and decreasing MC_y until $MC_x = p_x$, $MC_y = p_y$, and $MRS_{xy} = p_x/p_y = MC_x/MC_y = MRT_{xy}$.

Monopoly   The sale of a product under conditions of monopoly will prevent the attainment of optimal outputs by way of the price mechanism. Suppose that product X is sold monopolistically and product Y is sold competitively. The price system will lead to a set of outputs such that for each consumer

$$MRS_{xy} = \frac{p_x}{p_y}.$$

But profit maximization will induce the monopolist to produce the output at which $MC_x = MR_x < p_x$. Purely competitive producers of Y produce outputs at which $MC_y = p_y$. Thus

(18.4)
$$MRT_{xy} = \frac{MC_x}{MC_y} = \frac{MR_x}{p_y} < \frac{p_x}{p_y} = MRS_{xy}.$$

The output level of X is too small and the output level of Y too large for optimum welfare.

SUMMARY

In this chapter we summarized the conditions that must be met for an economic system to achieve maximum welfare in the sense of a Pareto optimum. Then we summarized the operation of the price mechanism in a private enterprise type of economic system, examining it to see if its results are Pareto optimal. The price system will lead to Pareto optimality if all markets are purely competitive and if no externalities occur in consumption or production. Where selling markets are monopolized, outputs will be short of the optimal quantities. Monopsony in resource purchases has a further adverse effect, in that it leads to inefficiency in the use of resources by the purchasers.

APPLICATIONS

THE WELFARE CORE OF THE APPLICATIONS

What do the applications that we have used throughout the book have to tell us about the welfare of the economy's population? Suppose we look at a number of them in terms of the conditions necessary for optimum welfare and in terms of general equilibrium in a private enterprise economy.

Consider first the notion of optimum welfare for consumers. When consumers are on their contract curves, the marginal rate of substitution between any pair of goods and services should be the same for each and every one. Reaching back to prohibitions of soft drinks containing certain artificial sweeteners, it is immediately apparent that some knowledgeable consumers are willing to bear the risks of drinking them while others are not. For the former, the marginal rate of substitution of sugared drinks for diet drinks exceeds that of the latter, and optimum welfare distributions of the two kinds of drinks do not occur. The same principle exists, although to a lesser degree, in the jitney versus trolley application. Restrictions on the operations of jitneys brought about shortages of jitney service that affected different consumers to different degrees. The result was differences in marginal rates of substitution between jitney service and trolley service as among different consumers and failure of the economy to provide welfare levels that were optimal. Restrictions on eyeglass advertising create the same results. Consumers in those states restricting advertising pay higher prices than those in states that do not. Consequently the former would be expected to have higher marginal rates of substitution of other goods for eyeglasses. Both sets of consumers are prevented from moving to contract curve combinations of eyeglasses and other goods and services. Price discrimination among medical labs, hospitals, and physicians reinforces the point. Different consumers face different prices for the services provided, bringing about suboptimal welfare distributions of these and other goods and services among consumers.

Second, consider the efficient allocation of resources among their different uses. The welfare goal is an allocation of resources among alternative uses such that the marginal rate of technical substitution between any pair of resources is the same in each and every use. Resource combinations should be contract curve combinations. Units of any one resource should be allocated among alternative uses in such a way that the marginal revenue products are the same in all cases. Several of the applications illustrate instances in which markets are not used to allocate resources among different uses, are prevented to some extent from doing so, or are subjected to various kinds of distortions as they go about their allocatory business.

The allocation of airport landing slots appears to have been much improved through purchase and sale over what occurred from committee deliberations. The arbitrary committee allocations paid scant attention to marginal revenue products of the slots for the different airlines. Consequently marginal rates of technical substitution of other resources for landing slots were higher for some airlines than for others, and contract curve combinations could not be achieved. Sale of slots through competitive bidding moves toward the equating of a slot price with its marginal revenue product and toward uniformity of slot prices among airlines. The result is movement toward contract curves.

Minimum wage laws and Davis-Bacon Act wage rates distort wage rates for workers within homogeneous labor classifications. The former primarily affect unskilled labor, limiting employment levels in covered employments. Those workers unable to find jobs in covered employments are forced into lower-paying uncovered employment or into unemployment. The obvious result is differences in wage rates and differences in marginal revenue products for the same kind of labor in the different uses. The Edgeworth box way of showing these differences is through off-the-contract-curve combinations of labor and other resources in which the marginal rate of technical substitution between the labor and other resources differs for different producers. Since the Davis-Bacon Act generates wage differentials for the same kind of labor in different uses, its effects on efficiency in production and welfare are essentially the same as those of the minimum wage.

The baseball application provides a wonderful illustration of the effects of market structure on the allocation of a resource. With the reserve clause, clubs were able to exert monopsonistic power over players, holding their salary rates well below marginal revenue products. Differing degrees of monopsony assure differences in salary rates paid for comparable players, and these in turn assure differences in marginal revenue products. Thus baseball fans plugged along at suboptimal levels of welfare! The elimination of the reserve clause, and the consequent opening up of bidding for players, moves players from lower to higher marginal revenue product uses and brings about higher levels of national income.

Third, an optimal product mix for the economy requires that for all consumers the marginal rate of substitution between any pair of goods and services be the same; that for all products the marginal rate of technical substitution between any pair of resource inputs be the same and that the product mix be such that the marginal rate of transformation between any pair of products be the same as the marginal rate of substitution. All the applications address these conditions to some extent.

The OPEC cartel application illustrates one kind of departure from an optimum product mix. Through collusion and supply restriction, the cartel was able to extract monopoly prices for crude oil substantially exceeding marginal costs of production. Consumers tend to adjust purchases of oil so that marginal rates of substitution are equal to price ratios. But marginal rates of transformation tend to be equated to marginal cost ratios. The marginal rates of substitution of other products for oil products would thus exceed the marginal rates of transformation of other products for oil, indicating that from a welfare point of view oil was underproduced relative to other products.

Similar results flow from attempts to raise agricultural prices through marketing orders or other cartelizing arrangements. Owing to higher-than-competitive commodity prices, too much is produced and too little is consumed. Moreover, because of an attempt at third-degree price discrimination, different consumers pay different prices. Welfare distributions among consumers of these and other goods are suboptimal.

As for agricultural policies that support commodity prices directly, production incentives as well as the price signals received by consumers are distorted. Storage and loan programs result in surpluses, a clear indication of discrepancies between marginal rates of transformation of other products for agricultural products at support prices and marginal rates of substitution of other products for agricultural products at the prices that would prevail in the absence of support prices. Direct subsidies bring about differences between product prices and marginal costs at the support price levels, even though the markets are cleared at those prices. Since marginal rates of transformation depend upon marginal cost ratios and marginal rates of substitution depend upon price ratios, the two will not be equal. Agricultural products will be overproduced relative to other products.

The applications illustrate that economic problems are frequently not solved by government actions—in fact, in many cases such actions augment the problem. Policies may be enacted with the best of intentions, but—as welfare and general equilibrium analyses indicate—everything depends on everything else, and such policies may have unintended and undesirable results.

Suggested Readings

For a more advanced treatment of the necessary conditions for Pareto optimality, see

Bator, Francis M. "The Simple Analytics of Welfare Maximization," *American Economic Review* 47 (March 1957): 22–59. Reprinted in *Readings in Microeconomics,* 2d ed., edited by William Breit and Harold M. Hochman. New York: Holt, Rinehart and Winston, 1971.

An excellent discussion of the assumptions and implications of both Pareto optimality and general equilibrium theory is

Vickrey, William S. *Microstatics,* Chap. 5. New York: Harcourt, Brace & World, 1964.

The essential role of prices in coordinating myriad separate resource activities in a dispersed economy where each transactor has only partial knowledge is explained by

Hayek, F. A. "The Use of Knowledge in Society." *American Economic Review* 35 (September 1945): 519–530.

Problems and Questions for Discussion

1. It is frequently asserted that the market system underproduces medical services in relation to other goods and services. Usually two sets of causal factors are cited: (1) externalities in the consumption of medical services where, for example, preventing one person from acquiring a communicable disease reduces the likelihood that others will acquire the disease; and (2) blocked entry into medical service professions.
   a. With "Medical Services" on the horizontal axis and "Other Goods and Services" on the vertical axis, diagram and explain each causal factor.
   b. Cite any evidence of which you are aware that supports or refutes the validity of each causal factor.

2. You are asked to render a reasoned opinion with regard to whether or not the government should subsidize housing. What will you use as analytical foundations for your opinions? List these and explain each.

3. Suppose that $MRS_{xy} > MRT_{xy}$ in a market economy. Is it possible that general equilibrium exists? Explain.

4. If a market economy in which $MRS_{xy} > MRT_{xy}$ is one of pure competition with no externalities, what can we expect to occur? Explain in detail, and illustrate with a diagram.

5. Can you provide a justification solely on economic grounds for
   a. A progressive income tax?
   b. Laws against gambling?
   c. State subsidization of education?

6. On January 1, 1984, American Telephone and Telegraph Co. dismembered itself to end a seven-year antitrust proceeding. AT&T's 22 local phone companies were divested and recombined into seven regional systems. AT&T was left with its long-distance services, Western Electric (its enormous manufacturer of telephone equipment), the Bell Labs (its renowned research and development arm), and its domestic and international market-

ing divisions. At various times the following issues have been raised by economists or antitrust lawyers as economic efficiency grounds for separating Bell's unregulated businesses (such as Western Electric) from its local phone companies, whose "natural monopoly" prices and services have been regulated by state public utility commissions. Assess each of the following assertions with respect to its implications for Pareto optimality, assuming each assertion is true. Use diagrams wherever possible.

a.   Public utility commissions typically allow phone companies to earn profits as a target percentage of the value of plant and equipment they have invested. Labor resources they hire are not taken into account.

b.   AT&T required the local phone companies to buy all of their equipment for telephone offices and customer home phones from Western Electric at prices set by AT&T. These costs were covered in the monthly rates set by public utility commissions.

c.   AT&T charged lower rates for long-distance calls to match their long-distance competitors and made up for these revenue losses by charging higher rates for local calls.

d.   Until the early 1980s, Bell System phone companies required their customers to rent Western Electric telephone instruments rather than allowing them to purchase cheaper ones from competitors.

7. The City of Palo Alto, Calif., requires large home builders to sell 10 percent of their new units below cost to moderate-income families that otherwise would not be able to afford them. Prices are set by a public housing agency that also approves both the initial buyer and subsequent buyers to prevent large resale profits. Apparently this program is being adopted in other communities. (G. Christian Hill, "Cut-Rate-Homes Plan Spreads in California, Benefiting Middle Class," *The Wall Street Journal,* January 20, 1980.) Is Palo Alto's policy in keeping with movement of the economy toward Pareto optimality? Explain.

8. Not-for-profit organizations, regulated monopolies, and governmental agencies often have rules or policies against nepotism. Assume that the relative who is hired is paid more than another individual of equal productivity or gets the same wage as another individual who is more productive. Explain which of the conditions for optimal welfare is violated by nepotism and why these organizations have adopted rules against it.

9. Some communities price electricity, water, and other utilities to residences at a flat monthly fee regardless of how far from the sources of origination the homes are built and regardless of the cost of providing them with service. Explain which condition(s) for optimal welfare this practice violates.

10. An Eastern European country in the early 1980s controlled the price of bread at a level about equal to the price of food with the same nutrition content for such animals as pigs. Explain how this pricing policy would

affect the allocation of bread and which condition of optimal welfare it would violate.

* **11.** Review the text and applications on property rights in Chapter 2 and explain which of the conditions for optimal welfare are violated by each of the following variations of property rights and why:

   a. Rights of finders to drug-related cash found in an airport parking lot, described on pp. 28–29.

   b. Rights to solar access that were described on pp. 31–35.

   c. Rights to high seas fish and whales that can be established only by capture, described on pp. 29–31.

* **12.** Review the application materials in Chapter 1, where health care was made available at zero money price to high government officials, and in Chapter 2, where candidates for organ transplants were not permitted to bid for the scarce supply of organs with cash payments. Explain which condition(s) of optimal welfare were violated in each case.

_____

*Denotes application-oriented problem.

SOLUTIONS TO ODD-NUMBERED PROBLEMS _____

Chapter 1

1. **a.** Per-capita income would decline.
   b. Consumers must buy cars other than those that were cheapest or those they would have preferred. More resources are allocated to domestic car production and fewer to other things. Per-capita income falls.
   c. Lower energy costs reduce the production costs of all other goods using energy. More goods can be produced with a given stock of resources. Per-capita income rises.
   d. Per-capita incomes rise in the receiving country and fall in the donor country.

3. All but (c) are matters of personal taste, which price theory does not attempt to explain. A ''bandwagon'' effect of maintaining front yards may occur if each homeowner realizes that the value of his property is affected by the appearance of his neighbor's front yard and vice versa. A neighborhood with uniformly well-maintained yards will have higher home values than a neighborhood with identical homes but unkempt yards.

5. We would expect to find more positive content among the statements of entrepreneurs and science experts unless they were commenting on matters of politics or current public policy. Editorial writers, government officials, and politicians tend more often to make ''ought'' statements.

Chapter 2

1. Absent subsidies, we would expect both agriculture and industry to use relatively little machinery. Labor is abundant relative to capital, so capital would be economized on. Technology would be labor-intensive.

3. Profits play a beneficial role. They indicate to entrepreneurs which goods and services consumers want most, and therefore how consumers want scarce productive resources allocated. This is how the price system accomplishes society's goal of allocating resources to their most productive uses.

5. **a.** The accident rate does not appear to us to be random, but determining this would require a statistical study.
   b. We doubt it. What theory would account for it?
   c. In 1979, California taxpayers paid up to $220 per month on two-year leases for each legislator. This included insurance for collisions, fire, theft, and other damage and covered a $50 deductible for each accident. A $50 deductible for each accident was also paid by the state. Such subsidies would reduce incentives for legislators to protect their cars from accidents.

7. The $6,000, like the $6 million, was abandoned in the course of a crime, so the facts of each case are similar. We suspect the anomaly stems from the different amounts involved.

9. **a.** No. An estate owner can collect the fees for shooting grouse that he has raised and protected. If the breeding season is poor, the owner can raise the shooting fee or cancel the season to preserve his income. Property rights allow poachers to be prosecuted, so profit-making, environment-saving efforts are worthwhile.
   b. Whales migrate enormous distances through unowned oceans that would be very expensive to police against poaching even if they were owned. Lakes are subject to domestic police controls. Nations are sovereign. Any nation attempting to exclude whalers of another from the communal "high seas" is taking a risk. So many nations hunt whales that an agreement to limit killing is expensive to reach and enforce. Thus, overhunting of whales is relatively expensive to prevent.

11. A profit-making kidney transplantation service would have strong incentives to give priority to the highest bidders. This could also occur in not-for-profit hospitals in exchange for big donations for financial support. Where kidneys are allocated on the basis of nonpecuniary factors, physicians may feel more sympathy for other physicians or their families.

Chapter 3

1. **a.** A change in preferences reduces demand for beef relative to chicken.
   b. Cheaper chicken reduces the demand for beef.
   c. Lower costs make beef cheaper and quantity demanded greater; this is a movement down the demand curve, not a shift in the curve.
   d. Bankruptcies do not affect demand.
   e. Demand is lowered.
   f. Demand may increase if consumers find them appealing.

3. **a.** It changes the position of the supply curve; the curve shifts down and to the right as in Figure 3.8 if production costs fall.
   b. It raises costs, shifting supply up and to the left.
   c. It shifts supply up and to the left.

5. **a.** See Figure 3.6 and the accompanying text.
   b. Supply would decline, the price would rise and the quantity exchanged would fall. See Figure 3.8.
   c. The purpose of a boycott is to reduce demand, such as the shift from DD to D_1D_1 in Figure 3.7. The problem facing boycotters is preventing purchases by nonboycotters.
   d. The same as in part (b); demand does not change.

7. Since the initial price is zero, Equation 3.3 cannot be used because it would require dividing by zero. Too many variables are changing to attribute all of the enrollment decline to the $50 fee. The $20 drop charge increases the risk of registering for classes, and the early starting date may not have been anticipated by all students. Each would reduce quantity demanded.

9. We predict it would have been different. To maximize profits, Sears would probably have priced tickets as it prices tools: charging more for better implements, but without tying the purchase of cheap tools to the purchase of premium tools in "package deals." Charging market-clearing prices for the best tickets would have made scalping less likely, so Sears would not have limited the number of tickets each customer bought. Ticket sales would have been more convenient, because Sears stores are more numerous than the locations the committee chose, and consumers could probably have paid for them on charge accounts. Consumers would pay more if they knew with certainty the quality of the seat they were getting, so Sears could have made profits by responding to this demand, too.

Chapter 4

1. Fertilizer and farm equipment producers favor government programs that cause more wheat to be grown, not less, so they would favor (a). They disliked PIK (b), under which the reduction in acres planted set a record in 1983. Acreage was cut over one-third—more than twice the number of acres anticipated when PIK was adopted.

3. Sellers who made enforceable contracts for future gas supplies before the ceiling was imposed are helped. So are buyers who are able to get gas at the ceiling price. Sellers who can sell only at the ceiling price are hurt. So are potential buyers who cannot get gas at the ceiling price.
   We would not advocate a price ceiling because it results in inequities among buyers and sellers and restricts production.

5. **a.** **i.** Adverse effects. Some jurors may be willing to serve at low pay or without pay but others view such service as a "tax."

    ii. Service is more expensive for higher-wage than for lower-wage persons. Women, on the average, earn lower wages and thus would probably be more willing to serve. In the 1950s women, on the average, earned even less relative to men and their costs of serving would have been correspondingly less.

    iii. Higher-income persons would be less willing to serve since doing so is more expensive for them.

    iv. To the extent that higher-income persons are successful in avoiding service, juries will be composed of relatively more people whose time is less valuable; for example, the retired, the unemployed, and lower-skilled or unskilled workers.

  b. Since most jurors are paid less than their values on their regular jobs, judges and attorneys have weaker incentives to economize on their time. Excessive numbers of jurors are called per case and are idle too much of the time. Pricing jurors at their real values would result in fewer jurors used and more efficient use.

  c. Perhaps some firms are more cognizant of the effects of good employee morale on productivity than others. An alternative hypothesis is that it is more expensive for some firms than others to make irregular book-keeping entries for wages and fringe benefits for the irregular amounts of jury time spent.

7. a. Supply shifts to the left and shortages worsen.

  b. People who cannot get apartments cause increases in demand in nearby cities. Rents rise in cities without controls; shortages worsen in those with controls.

  c. He represented San Diego, which had no controls.

  d. The city adopted procedures to delay owners from idling buildings for 60 days and to require them to compensate tenants for relocation costs depending on the size of the apartment lost, the age and disability of the tenant, and the number of children.

9. Measurement of precise effects is difficult, but we would expect decriminalization to have increased demand, increased supply, decreased price, and increased the number of abortions. Comparison shopping to determine quality is less expensive in a legal market, and since supplies are now legal, they would be furnished by physicians who would have avoided the illegal market.

11. a. Your choice.

  b. Seniors may oppose it because they usually get favored treatment under nonprice registration schemes. The Chicago system reveals the intensity of preferences for instructors, so faculty opinion may be divided. Registrars may find the present system a bother, but they justify larger year-around staffs.

  c. We would expect it to be less common at big public universities, where student fees cover a smaller fraction of instructional costs.

Chapter 5

1. a. The consumer is indifferent among the combinations defining one curve.

   b. Any combination on the higher curve is preferred to any combination on the lower curve.

   c. If pork is measured along the horizontal axis, then the new indifference curves are flatter. The consumer is willing to give up less beef at each quantity of pork than before to add another unit of pork.

3. a. Plot food per week along the vertical axis and garbage along the horizontal. The consumer gains satisfaction with combinations of the two that lie up (more food) and to the left (less garbage). The indifference curves are concave to the northwest.

   b. Higher curves indicating higher levels of satisfaction lie to the northwest, rather than to the northeast as is the usual case.

5. a. The preference map becomes flatter in the neighborhood of relevant points on the budget line. More alternative sources of satisfaction are available today than several decades ago—such as luxurious homes and cars—to compete with children.

   b. The budget line becomes steeper by rotating around its intersection with the vertical axis, as in Figure 5.6. Educating children increases the cost of raising them, for example, and reduces the number demanded. Even for public higher education, more education usually means that the student must postpone full-time employment. Also, women obtained more education and higher-paying jobs in the 1970s and 1980s. Higher wages raised the opportunity cost of allocating their time to raising children.

7. Plot dollars worth of gasoline per unit of time along the horizontal axis and income per unit of time along the vertical. The budget line has a slope of -1. The friend appears to maximize satisfaction where the budget line's midpoint is tangent to an indifference curve. The friend can afford more gasoline in the sense that an additional $5 in income could be spent on gasoline. We suspect the friend means that this combination of money and gasoline maximizes satisfaction.

9. The analysis parallels the fringe benefit case of Figure 5.12.

   a. In panel (a) of the following diagram the "no food stamps" budget line is AB, on which combination R is purchased. With food stamps, let the recipient be restricted to an expenditure on food stamps equal to the value AC of other goods. With food stamps, a sacrifice of AC in nonfood items allows a maximum extra purchase of food items equal to DL. The slope of budget line segment AL is p_{fs}/p_n, where p_{fs} is the effective price per unit of food when food stamps are used. The slope of segment LG is p_f/p_n because the market price of food in grocery stores has not changed. With food stamps, combination E is purchased, indicating that the consumer does not purchase the maximum allotment of food stamps.

b. If resale of food purchased with food stamps is possible, the budget line becomes *HLG* and the consumer achieves a higher level of satisfaction at *T*. This may be the de facto result if the prohibition on resale is expensive to enforce.

c. In panels (b) and (c), the recipient's preference map shows a stronger preference for food relative to nonfood items. In each case the combination of food and nonfood items purchased is not affected by removing the prohibition on resale. A consumer with the preference map in panel (b) would maximize satisfaction on U_3 at *E* (which is equivalent to *T*). A consumer with the preference map drawn in panel (c) would maximize satisfaction at *L*, taking the full allotment of food stamps.

(a)

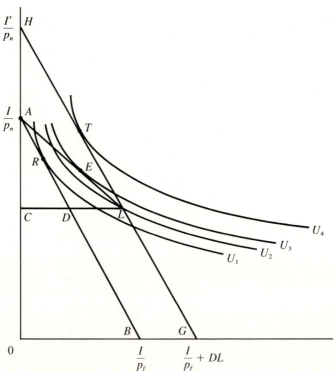

(b)

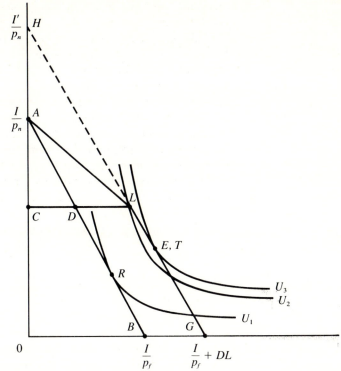

(c)

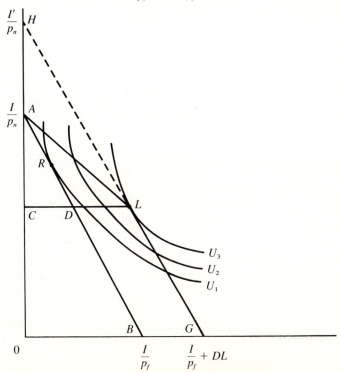

Chapter 6

1. Her *average* must be 1.0. She cannot spend more than 100 percent of the increase in her income on all goods combined.

3. **a.** Assuming children are superior ''goods,'' the simple answer is that (i), (ii), and (iii) reduce the opportunity cost of working mothers, change the budget line's slope to reflect lower prices for children, and cause movement outward along a price consumption curve. The birthrate increases. The degree depends on elasticity. A more complex answer recognizes that when both spouses work, family income increases, and therefore the number of children demanded may increase. For (iv) and (v), the budget line shifts out parallel to itself, so more children are ''purchased.''

   b. We agree that economic factors are not the only forces at work, but attempting to make predictions about fertility without taking them into account would be worse. Analysis requires theory, so ask the critics what their theory is. For evidence, we would look at fertility rates across countries with different pronatalist policies and tax schemes.

5. With concave indifference curves, the budget line touches the highest possible indifference curve on either the X or Y axis, depending on the budget line's slope. An exception occurs if the slope of the budget line equals that of an imaginary line connecting the X and Y intercepts of a concave indifference curve. This yields a solution on either axis.

7. In the following diagram, EF represents the initial budget line where the consumer maximizes satisfaction at A. Product X is an inferior good. As the price of X declines to p_{x2}, the consumer maximizes satisfaction at B, and the quantity of X rises from x_1 to x_3 in spite of an income effect in the opposite direction from x_2 to x_3. The consumer buys more X as its price declines, so the demand curve will be downward sloping. Thus, the consumer will capture consumer's surplus as price falls.

9. Draw an Edgeworth box diagram with A's origin in the southwest corner and B's in the northeast. If A is endowed with more of both gasoline and other goods per period than B, then the point of initial distribution analogous to F in Figure 6.14 will lie closer to B's origin. Label this point R. One indifference curve of each passes through R, defining a lens-shaped area in which both can improve satisfaction. The p_g and p_o that ultimately occur depend on their bargaining strengths but must result in a budget line at which $MRS^A_{go} = MRS^B_{go} = p_g/p_o$.

11. Some shoppers are willing to pay higher prices for brand names that they believe signal higher-quality goods. If cheaper goods without the brand name were known to be just as good, they would not do so. Other shoppers may buy the brand name for the ''snob appeal'' it provides.

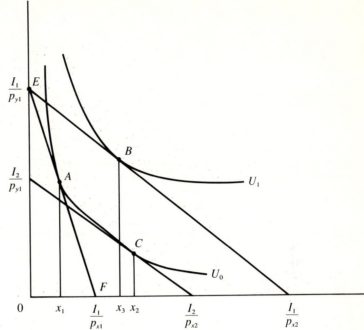

Chapter 7

1. a. He should buy 7 units of food and 9 of clothing, at which
$\dfrac{MU_f}{p_f} = \dfrac{MU_c}{p_c}$ and at which precisely $50 per day at the given prices is spent.

b. Spending $1 less on food costs half of the 7th pound of food for a marginal utility of -10. Spending a dollar more on clothing adds one-quarter of the 10th yard of cloth for a marginal utility of $+7.5$. The change is -2.5.

c. A dollar used to buy one-quarter of the 10th unit of clothing adds 7.5, as does using it to buy one-half of the eighth unit of food. Jones would be indifferent.

d. Since the ratio between the prices of clothing and food is now 4:3, the ratio of marginal utilities should be as close as possible to 4:3. Suppose the consumer reduces the purchase of food to 5 pounds, continuing to take 9 yards of clothing. At this combination $MU_f/p_f = MU_c/p_c$, but the expenditure level at $51 is too high. From which should a $1 purchase be withdrawn? It makes no difference. The reduction in total utility in either case will be 10 utils.

3. No. In the table for Problem 1, would Tom Jones have a higher total utility if he spent $40 to buy 10 yards of cloth or if he spent the $40 to buy 9 yards of cloth and 2 pounds of food?

5. a. It is based on the marginal utility collectors get from scarcity of the 1913 nickels.
   b. Total utility of five 1913 nickels to a person is undoubtedly lower than that of millions of currently circulating nickels.
   c. Owing to its relative scarcity, the marginal utility of a 1913 nickel is much higher than that of a currently circulating nickel.

7. The price of diamonds would fall. The paradox would seem less paradoxical as diamonds became less scarce.

9. It appears that the finches are acting as if they were maximizing their utilities as indicated by Equation 7.7.

Chapter 8

1. This situation is described in the text accompanying Figure 13.6. If rivals will not follow a firm that increases price above a certain level and will always follow its price cuts below that level, then the demand curve is bifurcated with a highly elastic segment above the given price and a less elastic segment below it. This is called the "kinked" demand curve, and the kink occurs at the price which, according to the theory, no firm has an incentive to change.

   We are certain that this situation does not apply to all oligopolists and doubt that it faces many. Assuming that rivals will be willing to follow the leader's price hikes and will refuse to follow its price cuts is just as realistic as assuming the other way around. Oligopoly situations vary so much in practice that we do not see any way to generalize.

3. The implication is that demand curves for such firms are vertical. Perhaps this applies in extreme circumstances to the minimum amount of water necessary for survival, certain medicines, and Shakespeare's King Richard III, who offered his "kingdom for a horse." The higher a good's price, the less is sold; at a sufficiently high price for most goods, none are sold. The idea that any large firm can charge any price it wants and sell enough to maximize its profits is nonsense.

5. It was probably monopolistic, or at least oligopolistic. The cost to consumers of shopping in other cities was relatively high prior to the introduction of the automobile. Mail-order catalogs, therefore, were a boon since they increased the competition.

7. Issues the ratio overlooks include the relative sizes of the four largest firms, whether membership among the four largest changes over time, the characteristics of the smaller firms, whether entry conditions are relatively in-

expensive, whether the market for the good in question is primarily local or national, and whether the ratio's magnitude changes over time.

9. Each of the industries will have nationwide concentration ratios that are lower than local or regional ratios and therefore understate true concentration. Cement, refined oil, bottled soft drinks, and perishable farm products have higher local than nationwide concentration. They must locate close to major markets because their shipment costs are high relative to their unit value. Nationwide airline concentration ratios understate regional concentration since some airlines do not operate everywhere. The same applies to railroading.

11. The word processor has reduced the expenditure of time involved in writing books. We expect that it has led more authors to submit manuscripts to publishers and has led publishers to publish more books. The result is more competition.

Chapter 9

1. **a.** AP_l at 7 = 800/7 or 114 and 2/7 spools; AP_m at 7 = 600/7 or 85 and 5/7 spools.
   b. MPP_l at 7 = 60 spools; MPP_m at 7 = 14 spools.
   c. The gain in spools if no machinery were given up would be 55. Giving up three machines reduces TP by 14 + 16 + 25 = 55 spools. No more machinery can be given up *without loss of product,* since giving up another machine at this point reduces TP by 45 spools.
   d. Choose L and M such that $MPP_l/p_l = MPP_m/p_m$ and $l \cdot p_l + m \cdot p_m = \$5,100$. This occurs at $l = 7$ and $m = 9$.

3. Expansion path GFH in Figure 9.6 shows cost minimization for each rate of output. F is the least-cost combination of A and B for producing x_3, and x_3 is the maximum output obtainable with F or any combination of resources costing T_1. For example, x_4 cannot be achieved with T_1, and x_2 is feasible but less than x_3.

5. **a.** In panel (a) of the following diagram, A represents $0m_1$ of transit and $0h_1$ of highways per unit of time that this city can purchase with specific grants for each. A block grant of T_1 at prevailing prices for highways and transit allows it to purchase any combination along line BC, but note that A with the higher individual grant total lies outside BC. It achieves more transportation, x_2, at D, owing to the block grant's greater flexibility than with individual grants.
   b. This city faces different isoquants. It optimizes at D' on x_1' with the block grant rather than at A on x_2' with individual grants. Even with the block grant's flexibility, it cannot compensate for the lower block grant total.

    c.   Cities getting greater improvements in transportation as a result of block grants would prefer this form of subsidy, while those getting fewer improvements from block grants would prefer to retain individual grants. These values are translated into lobbying expenditures so that Congress "feels" the consequences of its decisions. Lots of lobbying on both sides makes the proposal controversial.

(a)

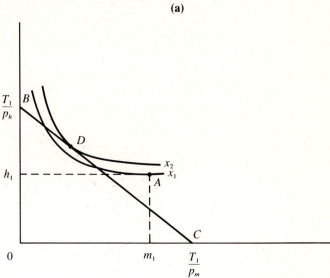

Mass Transit Rides
per Unit of Time

(b)

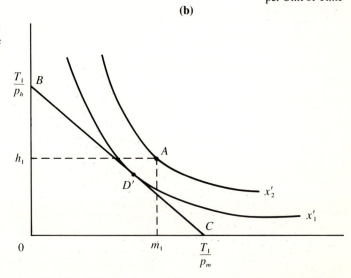

Mass Transit Rides
per Unit of Time

7. Draw a diagram like that below, with 0_a as American's origin and 0_p as Pan Am's, and view the isoquants as isorevenue lines. Plot DC-10 hours on the horizontal axes and 747 hours on the vertical axes. Starting at an initial distribution of equipment such as F, the airlines ended their exchanges at the box's lower right-hand corner.

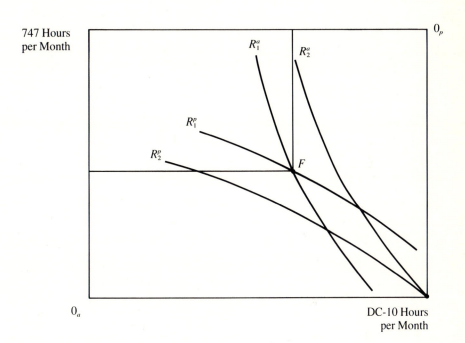

9. a. Keeping its price relatively high.
  b. It seems logical to us.
  c. It depends on the shape of the isoquants (they are linear if the two sweeteners are perfect substitutes) and on the slope of the isocost line (their relative prices).

11. In the following diagram, AB represents the initial isocost for a polluting firm.
  a. The lump-sum fine reduces the total outlay to $T_1 - F$, and the new isocost is CD. (The isocost's slope does not change because the fine is not imposed on a per-unit basis according to the number of polluting inputs used.) For the given outlay T_1, the cost-minimizing resource combination moves from R to S and the rate of output declines from X_2 to X_1.

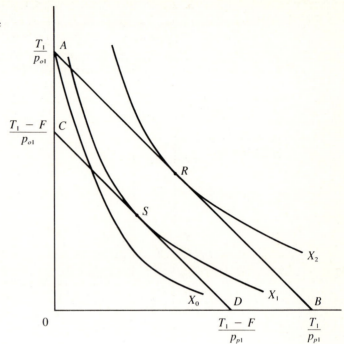

All Other Inputs
per Unit of Time

b. Prohibiting the use of polluting resources leads to the use of A units of the nonpolluting resources with a cost outlay of T_1 dollars. Output will be smaller at X_0.

Chapter 10

1. a. At state universities tax dollars rather than tuition tend to pay the costs of maintenance and operation. Students and their families who pay less in taxes to support state universities than they would have to pay to attend comparable private schools clearly gain. Those who pay more in such taxes than they would have to pay in private school tuitions just as clearly lose.

   b. Given equal output qualities, the costs to the society in terms of resources used should be about the same. It is often argued that private universities have greater incentives to control costs; that is, to be efficient. If this is so the private university would be less expensive to the society. Further, government subsidization of educational costs at state universities may lead to overinvestment in educational facilities, with too many of the economy's resources drawn into them and too few used elsewhere in the economy.

3. a. It lowers the cost of taking out loans to finance trades.
   b. Short-run marginal costs rise with the rate of output.

5. a. In the following diagram, using the same basic approach as in Figure 10.6, the output rate of meat rises from X_1 to X_2 for the same total outlay T. The firm moves from a corner solution at A to a combination of infected and uninfected inputs at B. Alternatively, C shows how X_1 can be produced at lower total outlay T'. Long-run total cost shifts from LTC to LTC', showing either that X_1 can be made more cheaply or that X_2 can be produced with T. The per-unit cost curves would shift accordingly.

(a)

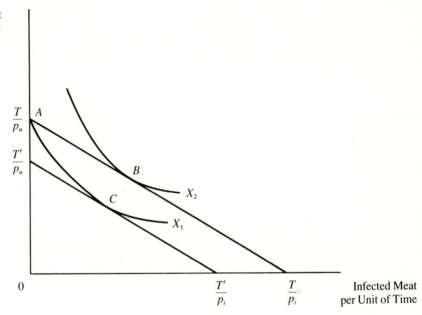

(b)

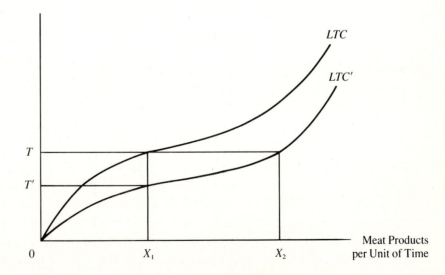

b. In the following diagram, the price of down relative to other resources rises from p_{d1} to P_{d2}. The isocost rotates from AB to AC. The firm initially produces X_1 of parkas with cost T using combination R on AB. After the price change it can produce X_2 on AC with combination S and cost T, or some amount like X_1 on DE at M with T'. Long-run total cost shifts up from LTC to LTC', and the per-unit cost curves would shift accordingly.

(a)

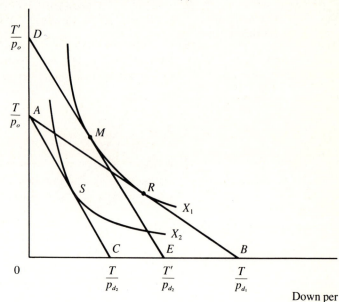

(b)

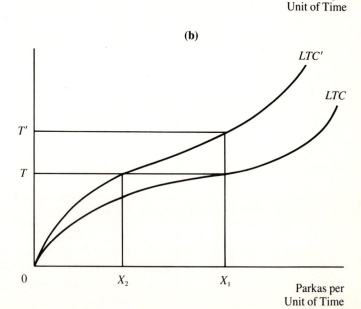

7. **a.** The adjustment lowers long-run total and per-unit cost curves. Trace out the steps as we did in the answer to Problem 5. First make the necessary changes in the isoquant-isocost diagram, and then adjust the cost curves accordingly.

   b. The EPA fine raises long-run total and per-unit cost curves, although not by as much as a prohibition of polluting inputs. Follow the same steps as in part (a).

9. It should assign students so that the *marginal* costs of student occupancy in each dormitory are equal. Review the text accompanying Figure 10.14.

11. The U-shaped curve for the Heileman plant would be tangent to the LAC_{1977} curve at a low output rate and high average cost. The U-shaped curve for the microbrewery would be even more so.

Chapter 11

1. Probably not. The market demand for cars was increased by the decline in the price of a complementary product (financing). Thus, dealers expected sales to increase without discounting the "sticker price."

3. Marginal revenue is the rate of change, or the slope, of the total revenue curve. Marginal cost is the rate of change, or the slope, of the total cost curve. The maximum vertical distance between these two curves—the total profit—is greatest at the output level at which their slopes are the same. See Figure 11.3 and the accompanying text.

5. Figure 11.5 can illustrate each case depending upon the position of $dd = MR$ relative to AVC. In (a), $dd = MR$ lies entirely below AVC. In (b), $d_0 d_0 = MR_0$ is tangent to AVC at output rate x_1. In (c), $d_1 d_1 = MR_1$ is above AVC and close to SAC at output rate x_1.

7. Mexico's producer's surplus is $28.24 per barrel and Saudi Arabia's is $31.50. Unlike Figure 11.6(b), we have assumed that each MC curve is horizontal at different levels. If it were upward sloping, as in Figure 11.6(b), then producer's surplus per barrel would fall as output rates grow.

9. Work with Figure 11.10, assuming that demand decreases rather than increases, as explained in the text accompanying the figure. The new long-run equilibrium will have fewer firms, a smaller total market supply, and, after the decline in demand, a market price that is higher in the long run than in the short run.

11. **a.** In the following diagram, S_C is the supply of liquor in California from California-based distributors, and S_T is the total supply in California including the supplies from Oklahoma. The supply from Oklahoma at each price is the horizontal distance between the two curves. Market price declines from p_1 to p_2 and total output increases from x_1 to x_2.

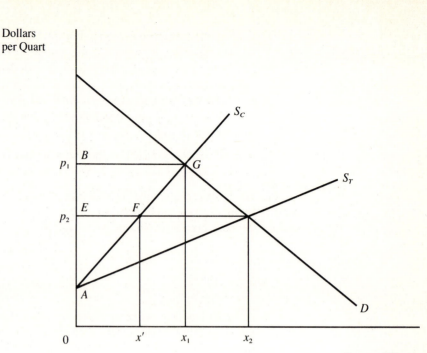

Dollars
per Quart

Quarts of Liquor
per Unit of Time

b. Producer's surplus for the California suppliers is *ABG* before and *AEF*
after the Oklahoma connection.

Chapter 12

1. Successful artists often buy back favorite works, sometimes to ensure their
proper exhibition as well as for monopolistic pricing purposes. Rembrandt
did not have sufficient resources to buy back the major part of the copies,
thus remaining copies in the hands of art dealers and the public were in
competition with those he was able to accumulate to sell for himself. He
was unable to "corner" the market and extract monopoly prices for his
copies. For the record, his unsuccessful attempt at monopolization was a
minor factor in his ultimate insolvency.

3. Selling market structures do not affect the transformation curve. If both
markets were competitive we could draw a line with slope p_x/p_y tangent to
the transformation curve. The point of tangency shows the product mix,
since at that point $MC_x/MC_y = MR_x/MR_y = p_x/p_y$. Further, $MC_x = MR_x$
$= p_x$ and $MC_y = MR_y = p_y$.
    If X were monopolized we could draw a new line with slope MR_x/p_y
tangent to the transformation curve. Since $MR_x < p_x$, it has a lesser slope

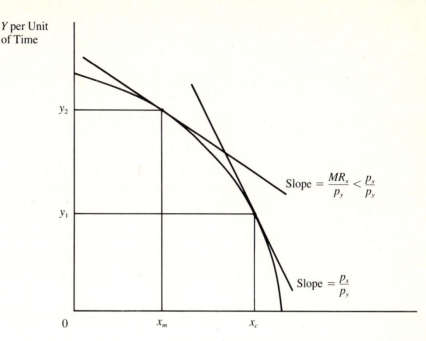

and is tangent farther to the left than in the competitive case, indicating that less of X and more of Y would be produced and sold.

5. Only under first- or second-degree price discrimination. The monopolist will never operate in the inelastic area if the same price must be charged for all units sold.

7. **a.** It would be expensive to prevent resale.
   b. Get the government to prevent resale.

9. **a.** The quantity discounts are offered to any traveler who flies the requisite mileage, so discrimination is second degree.
   b. A market developed as holders of coupons sold them to brokers, who advertised in major newspapers and resold them at premiums of 40 to 100 percent. (Walt Bogdanich, "Buying Cut Rate Airline Tickets May Give You a Good Bargain for Your Travel Dollar," *The Wall Street Journal,* November 28, 1984.) The individual account ensures that the person who flies enough to receive quantity discounts gets them.

11. **a.** Equalization would eliminate the price discrimination among insurance-covered patients.
   b. Per-patient payments would discourage discrimination but would also discourage physicians from accepting high-risk patients.

Chapter 13

1. **a.** It enables them to act as a cartel, charging a monopoly price for labor and securing monopoly profits for the group as a whole.

   b. Each individual firm's demand curve is more elastic at each price than is the market demand curve. See Figure 13.3 and the accompanying text.

   c. It may stimulate new entry, eroding the monopoly profits and inhibiting freedom of pricing actions by the colluding group of firms.

3. Embargoes are difficult to enforce when they involve multiple sovereign countries with divergent interests. The United States sought to cartelize and reduce world grain sales to the USSR. Canada, Argentina, and the United States itself, however, appear to have found the profit incentive for breaking away from the agreement too strong to resist. Apparently there was no effective policing of the embargo agreement.

5. The usual explanation among economists is high financial and product differentiation entry barriers. Automobile production and sales require huge amounts of investment. Consumers hold strong brand loyalties. High profits, however, eventually attracted European and Japanese producers into the market.

7. **a.** It appears to be second-degree price discrimination: discounts applied to additional purchases by big customers. See the text accompanying Figure 13.3.

   b. The restrictions on resale may have been effective for a time, but substantial discounts by the largest seller are bound to be detected and matched by others. This fits with OPEC's experience.

9. Saudi Arabia would have had to hold price low for a longer period. Oil-exporting countries would be foolish to panic just because price was very low for a short while. Only the perception that a low price would persist for a long time would cause higher-cost wells to be closed.

11. The administration's proposal to eliminate ''closed shop'' arrangements for hops and spearmint—that is, quota limits on output that are freely exchangeable among producers—is likely to increase the welfare losses for these crops that agricultural marketing orders create. When quotas or allotments are freely exchangeable, growers have incentives to equalize marginal costs and thereby minimize the total cost of producing a given output. Eliminating exchangeable quotas eliminates this incentive and thus raises welfare losses. As for California-Arizona citrus, welfare losses would decline, other things being equal, if the prorate scheme were replaced with producer allotments. Welfare losses would be eliminated if marketing orders were abolished.

13. Each new gasoline station must offer some advantage of service or location that others lack, or else it would not be built (or, if built, will not survive

in the long run). Persons who say that we don't ''need'' more stations are probably talking about the stations that are not convenient to them.

Chapter 14

1. When one resource is held fixed and the firm is operating in Stage II for the variable resource, the marginal physical product of the variable resource will decline as more units of it are used. In Equation 14.3, if MRC_a is held constant, $1/MC_x$ declines as MPP_a declines. This is the same as saying that MC_x rises as MPP_a declines.

3. **a.** If A in Equation 14.3 is steel, MRC_a falls and MPP_a/MRC_a rises. The firm is thus induced to increase its use of steel. Resources complementary to steel become more productive and those competitive to steel become less productive, therefore GM will increase its use of the former and decrease its use of the latter until it is again using a least-cost combination. The firm's MC_x curve will shift downward.

   b. No. Buying steel from at least two suppliers reduces the risks to GM of strikes, bankruptcies, or other adversities that could affect its steel suppliers.

5. Figure 14.2 shows the MRP_a curve for a resource, in this case the labor of a graduate. Let M be manufactured products and S be services. $MRP_a^m = MPP_a^m \times MR_m$ and $MRP_a^s = MPP_a^s \times MR_s$. Over time the relative decrease in demand for manufactured products and the relative increase in demand for services caused MR_s to shift upward relative to MR_m, increasing MRP_a^s relative to MRP_a^m, and resulting in relatively higher salaries in the services sector.

7. The backward-bending supply-of-labor curve in Figure 14.5 applies only to *an individual* for changes in the *wage rate*. The market supply curve, which is constructed by horizontally summing the hours each individual works at various wage rates, is likely to be forward-rising since the wage rate at which an individual's curve may bend back (such as w_2 in Figure 14.5) probably differs among individuals, and higher wage rates may attract more workers into the market.

   Unique features of Sweden's social and economic system make the problem complex. Sweden has mandatory five-week vacations and optional nine-month maternity (or paternity) leave, time off for study and political activity, and early retirement at age 65 on 75 percent of salary. These policies encourage people not to work, as do income tax rates that *average* 60 percent. Detailed research is required to separate the effect of higher wage rates on leisure-work choices from the other forces at work.

9. The bidding system may lower the prices that GM pays, but monopsony is unlikely. General Motors probably purchases too small a percentage of all steel produced, and steel manufacturers are probably too well informed about alternatives.

11. Anything that encourages the movement of resources from lower- to higher-paying employments will help. This includes governmental retraining and information-dissemination programs, plus the classified job advertisements in newspapers of other cities and regions that are available in local public libraries. It also includes elimination of entry barriers to higher-paying employments.

13. Economic profit is equal to price minus average cost multiplied by the number of units sold. It is competed away in the long run by market entry. Economic rent is price minus average variable cost multiplied by the number of units sold. It is the return to immobile resource units or what is left after variable or mobile resources are paid competitive returns. In the case of two parcels of land, one of which is more productive, rent on the superior parcel rises relative to that of the inferior parcel so that marginal returns per dollar's worth of each are the same.

Chapter 15

1. The marginal revenue product curves and the demand curve for workers would shift farther to the left, causing still lower wage rates and less labor employed.

3. **a.** In the diagram for Nottingham, demand for labor falls, lowering the wage rate and employment. In the diagram for a part of England where machinery is not destroyed, demand for textile workers increases, raising the wage rate and employment.
   b. i. Demand increases.
   ii. Demand decreases.
   iii. Demand increases.

5. It would not appear to be in the interests of Persian Gulf nations to block shipment of their oil. Controlling the strait will not augment their present monopoly power over oil.

7. **a.** Opposed. Faculty at California institutions lose, especially those most in demand. Favored. Faculty outside California gain.
   b. It is monopsonistic collusion by employers.
   c. It would reduce wage rates because bidding for faculty would decline.
   d. Often these agreements are proposed by those with the most to lose from wage competition. Schools wanting to improve and willing to pay for better faculty would lose, and those simply wanting to avoid paying more to keep their faculty would gain.

9. **a.** In the following diagram the union puts a floor of w_2 on wage rates, reducing the employment level from L_1 to L_2. However, at the higher wage rate, L_3 workers desire employment, so unemployment of L_1L_3 is generated.

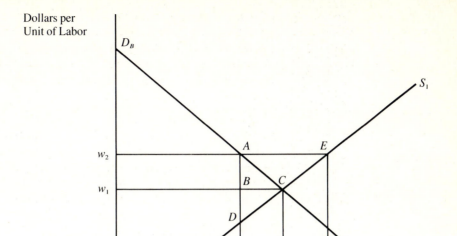

b. The wage bill changes from $0w_1CL_1$ to $0w_2AL_2$. It may be either higher or lower depending on whether demand is inelastic or elastic.

11. Figure 15.3 shows that importers also gain from quotas. Crandall estimates that the average price of a Japanese car was $2,500 higher than otherwise in 1985, and that Japanese producers captured an extra $5 billion per year from American consumers.

Chapter 16

1. a. Differentiate between a unionized and a nonunionized market. Raising the wage rate in the union market initially causes unemployment in that market since fewer workers will be hired. If workers are mobile, the unemployed will migrate to the nonunion market, increasing the supply and causing wage rates to fall in that market.

   b. If coal is sold competitively, national income declines as workers are frozen out of the union market and move to the nonunion market. Their marginal revenue product and value of marginal product in the non-union market are lower than in the union market that they leave.

3. a. Draw a diagram showing that the demand for labor increases in Newcity and decreases in Oldtown. In the absence of a union, the wage rate rises in Newcity and falls in Oldtown, encouraging migration from the latter to the former.

   b. Unemployment occurs in Oldtown at the union rate. Wage incentives to migrate do not occur. However, comparative job opportunities may induce migration.

5. a. Loans per unit of time are measured along the horizontal axis, and the price per unit of time (the interest rate) along the vertical axis. Draw separate diagrams for Arkansas and a neighboring state, such as Texas. A shortage occurs in Arkansas at the controlled price, causing borrowers to go to Texas. The demand for loans in Texas increases and the interest rate rises.

   b. Draw separate diagrams for the legal and illegal markets in Arkansas. A shortage occurs in the legal market, causing demand in the illegal market to be greater and the interest rate higher than otherwise. Loan sharks benefit from Arkansas's policy.

   c. On the Texas side, and they do.

7. a. U.S. supply is decreased and the U.S. equilibrium price would be higher. World market supplies are increased (since the quotas divert supplies from the United States to the world market), causing prices to be lower on the world market than they would be otherwise.

   b. Fructose and sugar are substitutes, so the quota program increases the demand for fructose, aspartame, and others.

   c. They favor quotas.

   d. They oppose. (From *The Wall Street Journal* by Kathleen A. Hughes: "Sugar Refiners Ask to Import Product in Excess of Quotas," February 6, 1985; "Sugar Industry Predicts a Shortage in U.S. if Government Doesn't Raise Import Quota," March 12, 1984.)

9. a. In the following diagrams, the wage rates are initially at market-clearing levels, although w_r is higher than w_u on the assumption that Canadian physicians have the same preference for "the bright lights" as their U.S. counterparts. L_{u1} and L_{r1} are the corresponding labor employed.

   b. Capping the wage rate at w_u for each market generates a shortage of $L_{r2}L_{r3}$ in the rural market.

   c. The four-year rural service requirement for urban practice or further training can be interpreted as a tax on the supply of urban labor. S_u shifts to S_u' and urban labor declines to L_u'. S_r shifts to S_r'. As drawn, an even greater tax on urban supply would be required to eliminate the rural shortage.

11. a., b., and **c.** should yield the same final allocations (or misallocations), although (a) and (c) would result in windfall gains and losses to particular airlines.

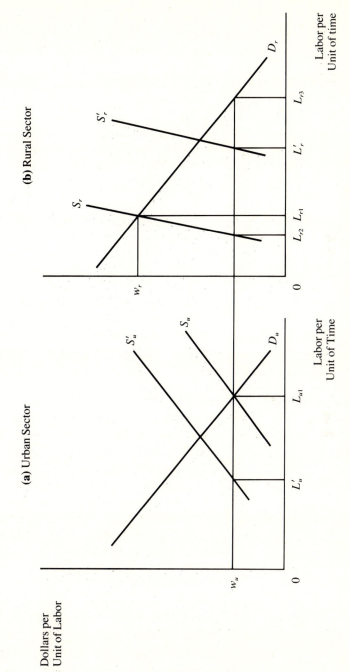

(a) Urban Sector

(b) Rural Sector

Effects of Wage and Supply Restrictions on Canadian Physicians

13. In Figure 16.6, $d_u d_u$ would not shift as far to the right, and unions will find it more difficult to maintain w_2. The supply curve in the nonunion sector, $S_n S_n$, will not shift as far to the left, and the nonunion wage rate will not increase as much.

Chapter 17

1. a. Not much. Monopoly appears to be more a problem relating to efficiency in the economy's operation—that is, to the size of national income—than to the distribution of that income.

 b. Not much. Monopsony appears to be relatively rare in the U.S. economy.

 c. and d. These are the crucial factors.

3. a. It reduced the incomes of players relative to club owners. Player wages rose sharply once the monopsony ended.

 b. Players lose relative to some sports enthusiasts, some student spectators, and academic programs. Gains consist of relatively low ticket prices and relatively high athletic event receipts for colleges and universities, which are not-for-profit organizations. The degree to which players lose depends on their next-best alternatives outside athletics. The losses are probably greatest for players from low-income families.

5. a. The efficiency of consumption will probably be less than is possible with free market prices. The government is unlikely to select prices at which MRS_{xy} is the same for all consumers, since there will be shortages of the price-controlled goods. Efficiency in consumption is more likely to be achieved if money income is redistributed from the rich to the poor and if prices are free to move to market-clearing levels.

 b. Efficiency in production, defined as equal $MRTS_{ab}$ in the production of every product, depends on the freedom of resource prices to move. If these are not controlled, resources may be allocated efficiently in a technical sense.

 c. The product mix will be skewed in favor of items that are not price controlled. The price controls lead to smaller outputs of the price-controlled items, inducing resources to be transferred to the production of goods that are not price controlled.

7. a. and c. The minimum wage has negative effects.

 b. Productivity of employed workers is increased because of the smaller ratio of labor to capital.

9. a. It would probably decrease because of an increase in marginal students who would not have chosen to enroll otherwise.

 b. and c. Covered employment would decline and uncovered employment would rise.

Chapter 18

1. **a.** An externality in consumption is illustrated in Figure 18.2. Assume that better preventive health care makes H no worse off and reduces the likelihood that J gets sick. Both are better off at F than on the contract curve at E. Restriction of entry into medical service professions generates a monopoly gain for suppliers. It is shown in Figure 18.6 with Edgeworth box $0_h y_1 0_{j1} x_1$, where X represents the quantity of medical services supplied. The price of X exceeds its marginal revenue and its marginal cost (in terms of Y).

   b. Licensing restrictions on medical service suppliers that are common in the American economy were discussed in Chapter 12. Subsidized mosquito abatement, vaccination against poliomyelitis and other diseases, and public health services that trace disease carriers are evidence that is consistent with the externality argument as it applies to communicable diseases.

3. Equation 18.3 is a condition of optimum welfare or Pareto optimality. General equilibrium defines the final resting point of an economy after all the adjustments, interrelationships, and interdependencies from some shock or change have occurred throughout the economic system. Whether this series of adjustments has been completed is independent of whether Pareto optimality has been attained.

5. **a.**, **b.**, and **c.** No.

7. No. The welfare condition of equality (18.1) is not met when different consumers pay different prices for identical houses. That of equality (18.3) is not met when the prices of some houses do not cover marginal costs.

9. It violates 18.3 because the ratio of the electricity prices paid by nearby consumers to those paid by distant consumers does not equal the ratio of their marginal costs. Thus, more people than otherwise will live farther from origination sources.

11. Producers use resources differently when resource rights are either nonexclusive or nontransferable (or are transferable only at an excessive cost in relation to their value). Nonprivate resource rights in each case violate 18.2:

    a. Individuals will not locate lost goods if they may not keep at least a significant portion of what they find. Weakening rights of finders alters the allocation of labor relative to capital in finding versus other productive activities.

    b. Effects of new buildings and tree plantings on solar access of neighboring landowners will more often be taken into account if solar rights are inexpensively exchangeable. Legislatures can reduce transaction costs by defining rights unambiguously.

    c. Absence of ownership rights to uncaught high-seas fish and whales prevents them from being priced to reflect the future consequences of capturing too many prematurely.

GLOSSARY

alternative cost principle The principle stating that the underlying basis of cost—the cost of producing a unit of any good or service—is the value of the resources needed to produce that good or service in their best alternative use.

barriers to entry, artificial Restraints on entry into a market imposed by either firms already in the market or government policies, or by a combination of both.

barriers to entry, natural Costs of entry into a market caused by technology that makes the minimum efficient size of a single firm large relative to the size of the market.

budget line or constraint All combinations of goods and services available to the consumer when all of the consumer's income (purchasing power) is being utilized, given that income and the prices of the goods and services.

capital The nonhuman ingredients that contribute to the production of goods and services, including land, raw and semifinished materials, tools, buildings, machinery, and inventories.

cartel An organization of firms in a market in which certain management decisions and functions that would otherwise be performed independently by individual firms are transferred to a collusive group representing them.

cartel, centralized A cartel in which the central association or group makes decisions regarding pricing, outputs, sales, and distribution of profits.

cartel, market-sharing A cartel in which the market shares of the member firms are determined mutually.

competition, monopolistic *See* Monopolistic competition.

competition, nonprice *See* Nonprice competition.

competition, perfect Pure competition plus the additional condition of perfect knowledge of the economy on the part of buyers and sellers that enables them to make instantaneous adjustments to disturbances.

competition, pure A market situation in which (1) individual buyers or sellers of an item are too small relative to the market as a whole to be able to influence its price, (2) units of the item are homogeneous, (3) the price of the item is free to move up or down, and (4) units of the item can be sold by any potential seller to any potential buyer.

competitive goods *See* Substitute goods.

complementary goods Goods related in such a way that an increase in the consumption of one, holding the consumer's satisfaction level and the quantity consumed of the other constant, increases the marginal rate of substitution of the other for money.

constant cost industry An industry in which the entry of new firms causes no changes in resource prices or the cost curves of individual firms already in the market.

constant returns to scale *See* Production function homogeneous of degree one.

consumer's surplus The amount that a person would be willing to pay for any given quantity of an item purchased minus the amount the market requires the person to pay.

contract curve A curve generated in an Edgeworth box showing Pareto optimal distributions of products (resources) between two consumers (producers).

cross elasticity of demand The responsiveness of the quantity taken of one item to a small change in the price of another. The elasticity coefficient or measure is computed as the percentage change in the quantity of one divided by the percentage change in the price of the other.

deadweight loss The total net loss to society in terms of reduced consumers' surplus and producers' surplus owing to monopolization of the market. It differs from wealth transfers because it is a pure loss, caused by the smaller output, that benefits no one.

decreasing cost industry An industry in which the entry of new firms causes resource prices to fall, which in turn causes the cost curves of existing firms to shift downward.

demand The various quantities per unit of time of an item that a buyer (buyers) is (are) willing to buy at all alternative prices, other things being equal; represented in table form as a demand schedule or graphically as a demand curve.

demand curve, constant money income A demand curve in which the consumer's money income is held constant regardless of the price level. Along this curve real income rises (falls) with price decreases (increases), reflecting both the substitution and income effects of the price changes.

demand curve, constant real income A demand curve in which the consumer's real income is held constant based on an initial price level. Along this curve money income rises (falls) as price rises (falls) to keep the initial real income level unchanged, reflecting only the substitution effects of the price changes.

demand curve faced by a firm A curve that shows the quantities of a good or service that a single firm can sell per unit of time at alternative prices, other things being equal.

demand curve, individual consumer A curve that shows the quantities of a good or service that a consumer will take per unit of time at alternative prices, other things being equal.

demand curve, market A curve that shows the quantities of a good or service that all consumers together will take per unit of time at alternative prices, other things being equal; it is the horizontal summation of the individual consumer demand curves for that item.

diminishing returns, law of The principle stating that if the input of one resource is increased by equal increments per unit of time while the quantities of other inputs are held constant, there will be some point beyond which the marginal physical product of the variable resource will decrease.

diseconomies, external Forces outside the activities of any single firm that cause resource prices to rise and cost curves of the firm to shift upward as new firms enter the market.

diseconomies of size The forces causing a firm's long-run average costs to increase as its output level and size of plant are expanded. These are usually thought to be the increasing difficulties of coordinating and controlling the firm's activities for larger sizes and outputs.

distribution, personal income How the income generated in an economy per time period (for example, one year) is shared among individuals and/or households.

economic activity The interaction among economic units involved in the production, exchange, and consumption of goods and services.

economic system The institutional framework within which a society carries on its economic activities.

economies, external Forces outside the activities of any single firm causing resource prices to fall and cost curves of the firm to shift downward as new firms enter the market.

economies of size The forces causing a firm's long-run average costs to decrease as its output level and size of plant are increased. These are usually thought to be (1) increasing possibilities of division and specialization of labor and (2) greater possibilities of using more efficient technology.

Edgeworth box An analytical device in which the indifference maps (isoquant maps) of the two consumers (producers) are placed over each other, but with one turned 180 degrees from the other. The axes form a box the sides of which measure the total quantities of two products (resources) available to the two consumers (producers).

efficiency, economic The ratio of the value of outputs obtained from an economic process to the value of inputs necessary to produce them. The higher the value of output per dollar's worth of resource input, the greater the efficiency of the process.

efficient distribution of resources A distribution of resources among products or uses such that the marginal rate of technical substitution between any two resources is the same for each product or use.

elastic demand A situation in which the absolute value of the price elasticity coefficient is greater than one.

elasticity of demand, arc The coefficient of price elasticity measured between two distinct points on a demand curve.

elasticity of demand, cross *See* Cross elasticity of demand.

elasticity of demand, income The responsiveness of quantity taken of a good or service to small changes in income, other things being equal. The elasticity coefficient or measure is computed as the percentage change in quantity divided by the percentage change in income when the change in income is small.

elasticity of demand, point The coefficient of price elasticity measured at a single point on a demand curve.

elasticity of demand, price The responsiveness of the quantity taken of an item to a small change in its price, given the demand curve. The elasticity coefficient or measure is computed as the percentage change in quantity divided by the percentage change in price.

Engel curve A curve showing the various quantities of a good or service that a consumer (consumers) will take at all possible income levels, other things being equal.

equilibrium A state of rest from which there is either no incentive or no opportunity to move.

equilibrium, general Simultaneous equilibrium of all individual economic units and subsections of the economy.

equilibrium, partial Equilibrium of an individual economic unit and/or subsection of the economy with respect to given data or conditions external to that unit or subsection. Changes in those data or conditions will change the equilibrium position of the unit or subsection.

equilibrium price *See* Price, equilibrium.

excise tax *See* Tax, excise.

expansion path A curve showing the least-cost (maximum output) combinations of resources for all possible output levels (cost outlay levels) of a firm.

explicit costs of production The costs of resources hired or purchased by a firm to use in the process of production.

exploitation, monopolistic The difference between what a unit of a resource is worth to a firm and what it is worth to consumers because of monopoly in product sales; that is, for resource A it is measured by $VMP_a - MRP_a$.

exploitation, monopsonistic The difference between what a unit of a resource is worth to a firm and what it is paid because of monopsony in the purchase of the resource; that is, for resource A it is measured by $MRP_a - p_a$.

externalities in consumption The effects that the consumption of an item by one consumer may have on the welfare of others. Externalities may be positive as, for example, when flowers purchased by one person are enjoyed by others as well. They may also be negative as, for example, when one student in a class eats garlic, making the classroom unpleasant for others.

externalities in production The effects that the production of one product may have on the production possibilities of others. They may be positive, as would be the case if an orchard of fruit trees were grown near a bee farm where honey was produced. They may be negative, as would be the case if one producer polluted water that another producer then had to clean before using.

firms Single proprietorships, partnerships, and corporations engaged in the buying and hiring of resources and in the production and sale of consumer goods and services or of higher-order capital resources.

fixed costs The costs of the fixed resources used by a firm in the short run.

fixed resources Those resources used by a firm whose quantity it cannot change in the short run.

hypotheses Tentative statements of cause-and-effect relationships among variables.

implicit costs of production The costs of self-owned, self-employed resources used by a firm in the process of production.

income consumption curve A curve showing the various combinations of goods and services that a consumer will take at all possible income levels, given the prices of the goods and services.

income distribution, functional The distribution of income by kinds or classes of resources.

income distribution, personal The distribution of income among households of the economy.

income effect of a price change That part of a change in quantity taken of a good or service in response to a price change resulting solely from the change in the real income of the consumer occasioned by the price change.

increasing cost industry An industry in which the entry of new firms causes resource prices to rise, which in turn causes the cost curves of existing firms to shift upward.

indifference curve or schedule A curve or schedule showing the different combinations of two items among which a consumer is indifferent.

indifference map A family of indifference curves showing the complete set of a consumer's tastes and preferences—the individual's preference rankings of different combinations and sets of combinations—for two items.

inelastic demand A situation in which the absolute value of the price elasticity coefficient is less than one.

inferior goods Goods whose consumption decreases as a consumer's (consumers') income(s) increase(s).

isocost curve A curve showing all combinations of two resources that a firm can purchase for a given cost outlay, given the prices of the resources.

isoquant curve A curve showing the combinations of resources required by a firm to produce a given level of product output.

isoquant map The family of isoquant curves of a firm describing the resource combinations required to produce all possible levels of output.

kinked demand curve The demand curve that a firm faces if other firms in the market follow price decreases but not price increases. It has a "kink" or corner in it at the initial price.

labor The capacity for human effort (of both mind and muscle) available for use in producing goods and services, ranging from unskilled, undifferentiated to highly skilled, specialized labor power.

Laspeyres price index An index that measures the relative change in the cost of purchasing a year 0 bundle of goods between year 0 and year 1; provides the maximum estimate of the cost-of-living increase during that time period.

least-cost resource combination A combination of resources for a firm at which the marginal rate of technical substitution between the resources is equal to the ratio of the resource prices ($MRTS_{ab} = p_a/p_b$). It is also a combination at which the marginal physical product per dollar's worth of one resource is equal to the marginal physical product per dollar's worth of every other resource; that is, where

$$\frac{MPP_a}{MRC_a} = \frac{MPP_b}{MRC_b}.$$

living standard The level of well-being or welfare that an economic system provides for the members of a society, usually measured by per capita income.

long run A planning period long enough for the firm to be able to vary the quantities of all the resources it uses.

Lorenz curve A device used to measure the extent of inequality in the distribution of income among households.

losses The difference between a firm's total costs and its total receipts when total receipts are less than total costs, including as costs the alternative costs of all resources used.

macroeconomics The economics of the economy as a whole—the forces causing recession, depression, and inflation together with the forces resulting in economic growth.

marginal cost The change in a firm's total costs per unit change in its output level.

marginal physical product of a resource The change in total output of a firm resulting from a one-unit change in the employment level of the resource, holding the quantities of other resources constant.

marginal productivity theory The theory stating that in a private enterprise economy resource units are paid prices equal to either their values of marginal products or their marginal revenue products. Thus income is distributed among households according to the relative contributions that the resources they own make to the production processes.

marginal rate of substitution The amount of one good or service that a consumer is just willing to give up to obtain an additional unit of another, measured for any combination of goods and services by the slope of the indifference curve through the point representing that combination.

marginal rate of technical substitution The amount of one resource that a firm is just able to give up in return for an additional unit of another resource with no loss in output. For any given resource combination, it is measured by the slope of the isoquant through the point representing that combination.

marginal rate of transformation The quantity of one product that must be given up in order to produce an additional unit of another. For any given combination of products on a transformation curve, it is measured by the slope of the curve.

marginal resource cost The change in a firm's total costs resulting from a one-unit change per unit of time in the purchase of a resource.

marginal revenue The change in a firm's total revenue per unit change in its sales level.

marginal revenue product The value to a firm of the change in output when the firm changes the level of employment of a resource by one unit. For resource A used in producing product X, it is computed as follows:

$$MRP_a = MPP_a \times MR_x.$$

marginal utility The change in the total utility to a consumer that results from a one-unit change in the consumption level of an item.

measurement, cardinal A measurement indicating rankings among items in objectively measurable unit gradations, as for weights and lengths in physical science. For utility, it indicates intensity as well as order of preferences.

measurement, ordinal A measurement indicating rankings among items without constancy or regularity in unit gradations. For utility, it indicates only order and not intensity of preferences.

microeconomics The economics of interacting subunits of the economic system, such as individual consumers and groups of consumers, resource owners, firms, industries, individual government agencies, and the like.

mobility The capability of a seller to sell to any of various alternative buyers or of a buyer to buy from any of various alternative sellers.

monopolistic competition A market situation in which there are many sellers with no one of them important enough to be able to influence any other seller and with each seller's product differentiated from those of the others.

monopoly, natural A form of monopoly that occurs when technology makes the minimum efficient size of a single plant so large relative to market size that it would not be profitable for additional firms to enter the market. Economies of size occur through all profitable output levels.

monopoly, pure A market situation in which a single seller sells a product for which there are no good substitutes.

monopoly rent A greater-than-competitive rate of return to producers caused by artificial protections from new entry contrived by the state or by existing producers.

monopsony A market situation in which there is a single buyer of an item for which there are no good substitutes.

most efficient rate of output The output level at which a firm's short-run average costs are minimum; the most efficient of all possible short-run output levels given the firm's size of plant.

most efficient size of plant That size of plant for which the firm's short-run average cost curve forms the minimum point of its long-run average cost curve; the most efficient of all possible plant sizes for a firm.

nonprice competition Activities by a firm intended to enlarge its market share without cutting the price of the product. The major forms are advertising and variation in the product design and quality.

normative economics The study of the way that economic relationships ought to be. Value judgments play an integral part in the ranking of possible objectives and the choices to be made among them.

oligopoly A market situation in which the number of sellers is small enough for the activities of one to affect the others and for the activities of any or all of the others to affect the first.

oligopoly, differentiated An oligopolistic market situation in which the sellers sell differentiated products.

oligopoly, pure An oligopolistic market situation in which the sellers sell homogeneous or identical products.

opportunity cost principle _See_ Alternative cost principle.

Paasche price index An index that measures the relative change in the cost of purchasing a year 1 bundle of goods between year 0 and year 1; provides the minimum estimate of the cost-of-living increase during that time period.

Pareto optimum A situation in which no event can increase the well-being of one person without decreasing the well-being of another.

plant, size of _See_ Most efficient size of plant.

positive economics The study of the cause-and-effect relationships that exist in economics; no value judgments are involved.

premises The bedrock starting points for the construction of a theory, consisting of propositions or conditions that are taken as given or as being so without further investigation.

price ceiling An administered level above which the price of an item is not allowed to rise.

price consumption curve A curve showing the various combinations of goods or services that a consumer will take at all possible prices of one given the price of the others and the consumer's income.

price discrimination, first-degree A monopolistic practice in which the seller is able to sell each successive unit of product at the maximum price that any buyer is willing to pay, thus capturing the entire consumers' surplus.

price discrimination, second-degree A monopolistic practice in which the seller is able to sell blocks of output, charging the maximum possible price for each block and selling additional blocks at successively lower prices.

price discrimination, third-degree A monopolistic practice in which the seller charges different prices in different markets for a product not accounted for by variations in production or selling costs but based primarily on differences in demand elasticities and prevention of resale among the markets.

price, equilibrium That price at which the quantity per unit of time that buyers want to buy is just equal to the quantity that sellers want to sell. It generates neither a surplus nor a shortage, and there is no incentive for buyers or sellers to change it; if attained, it will be maintained.

price floor An administered level below which the price of an item is not allowed to fall.

price leadership A loose form of collusive arrangement in which one firm is identified as the price setter or leader whose prices are followed by the other firms.

price war A situation in which rival firms drive prices down through attempts to undercut one another's prices.

principles Statements of cause-and-effect relationships that have undergone and survived thorough testing.

private enterprise system An economic system characterized by private property rights, voluntary private production, and exchange of goods and services and of resources.

producers' surplus The difference between the total amount producers receive for any given quantity of product and the minimum amount they would have been willing to accept for that quantity. It is measured diagrammatically by the area above the supply (marginal cost) curve but below the price at which that quantity is sold.

product differentiation A situation in which sellers sell essentially the same product but each seller's product has, at least in the minds of the consumers, certain characteristics that distinguish it from the products of other sellers.

production function The technical physical relationship between the quantities of a firm's resource inputs and the quantities of its output of goods or services per unit of time.

production function homogeneous of degree one A production function with characteristics such that an increase of a given proportion in all resource inputs will increase output in the same proportion.

profits The difference between a firm's total receipts and its total costs when total receipts exceed total costs, including as costs the alternative costs of all resources used.

property rights The rights and duties of ownership that are established by our legislatures and courts.

rent, economic The residual left for the fixed resources of a firm after the variable resources have been paid amounts equal to their alternative costs.

rent, monopoly A greater-than-competitive rate of return to producers caused by artificial protections from new entry contrived by existing producers or by the state.

resources The means or ingredients available for the production of goods and services that are used to satisfy human wants. They consist of labor resources and capital resources.

shortage A situation, caused by a price below the equilibrium level, in which buyers want to buy larger quantities than sellers are willing to sell.

short run A planning period so short that the firm is unable to vary the quantities of some of the resources that it uses; usually thought of as the time horizon during which the firm cannot change its size of plant.

shutdown price The price below which the firm would cease to produce in the short run.

socialistic system An economic system characterized by governmental ownership or control of resources and of goods and services. Production is carried on by the government, which also specifies

the terms or conditions under which exchange may take place.

substitute goods Goods related in such a way that an increase in the consumption of one, holding the consumer's satisfaction level and quantity consumed of the other constant, decreases the marginal rate of substitution of the other for money.

substitution effect of a price change That part of a change in quantity taken of a good or service in response to a price change that results solely from the change in its price. The effects of the price change on the real income of the consumer, and the subsequent effect of the real income change on the quantity taken, have been eliminated.

sunk costs Historical expenditures that are irrelevant for current or future decisions about what to exchange or produce.

superior goods Goods whose consumption increases as consumers' incomes increase, individually or in the aggregate.

supply The various quantities per unit of time of an item that a seller (sellers) is (are) willing to sell at all alternative prices, other things being equal; represented in table form as a supply schedule or graphically as a supply curve.

supply curve, short-run firm A curve showing the different quantities per unit of time of a good or service that the firm will place on the market at all possible prices. It is that part of the firm's short-run marginal cost curve that lies above its average variable cost curve.

supply curve, short-run market A curve showing the different quantities per unit of time of a good that all firms together will place on the market in the short run at various possible prices.

surplus A situation, caused by a price being above the equilibrium level, in which sellers want to sell larger quantities than buyers want to buy.

tax, excise A per unit tax on an item. It may be a specific tax based on the physical unit of the item or an *ad valorem* tax based on its price.

tax incidence The distribution of a tax among economic units.

technology The state of the arts available for combining and transforming resources into goods and services.

theory A set of related principles providing insight into the operation of some phenomenon.

transformation curve A curve showing the maximum production possibilities for two products given the resources available to produce them.

unitary elasticity of demand A situation in which the absolute value of the price elasticity coefficient is equal to one.

utility The satisfaction that a consumer obtains from the goods and services that are consumed.

utility, total The entire amounts of satisfaction a consumer obtains from consuming an item at different possible rates.

value of marginal product The market value of the change in output when a firm changes the employment level of a resource by one unit. For resource A used in producing product X, it is computed as follows:

$$VMP_a = MPP_a \times p_x.$$

variable costs The costs of the variable resources used by a firm in either the short run or the long run.

variable resources Those resources used by a firm that it can change in quantity in either the short run or the long run.

very short run A time period with respect to a given good or service so short that the quantity of it placed on the market cannot be changed.

wants The varied and insatiable desires of human beings that provide the driving force of economic activity.

welfare The level of economic well-being or satisfaction attained by individuals and groups of individuals in a society.

NAME INDEX

SUBJECT INDEX